Annotated Edition

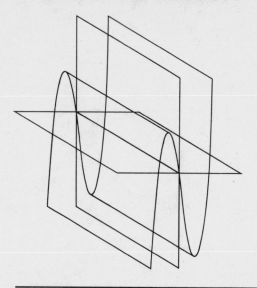

Algebra / Book 1
modern edition

Welchons / Krickenberger / Pearson

Teaching suggestions by Rachel P. Keniston

Ginn and Company
A Xerox Education Company

To the Teacher

We hope this Annotated Edition of *Algebra*, *Book One*, *Modern Edition* will make your teaching of algebra easier by providing

1. The answer to each exercise beside or near the exercise
2. On-the-spot suggestions for teaching the various topics
3. Suggestions for time schedules, use and procurement of teaching aids, and so on.

Relax, and enjoy the text. In keeping with recent recommendations of groups interested in the improvement of mathematics learning, this edition of *Algebra*, *Book One* differs from earlier versions in several important respects.

     1. It does more to show the structure of algebra.

     2. It utilizes the concepts and language of sets.

     3. It treats inequalities along with equations and introduces the concept of compound sentence.

     4. It refines the concepts of relation and function.

     5. It emphasizes the correspondence between the real numbers and points on a line, and between ordered pairs of real numbers and the points of a plane, then uses these concepts to clarify such concepts as relation and function.

     6. It includes selected answers to odd-numbered exercises.

While the book moves in the direction of the so-called modern mathematics, no teacher (no matter how traditional) need feel uncomfortable in using the new text. Each new topic is explained so carefully and introduced so naturally that, except for a few changes in vocabulary (for example, *variable* in the place of *literal number*) and slightly different approaches to such topics as graphing and function, the teacher will, from the beginning, feel quite at home with the new material. The important thing is to lean back and enjoy the new presentation. When a new word or a new concept is introduced, accept it as it is presented. Rest assured that the pieces soon fall into place just as they did in older texts. The new topics will give you some of the feel of the new mathematics yet will not make you uncomfortable if you have not studied modern algebra.

Encourage your students to read the text for themselves. The book is addressed to them. The language is simple and easily understood. Each new concept is carefully explained and illustrated. With your encouragement and guidance students should accept a share of the responsibility for their own learning.

Of course, you will want to show them *how* to read mathematics and you will want to prepare them for each assignment by telling them *what* to study—the important points to hold in mind, the questions to be answered, the learnings to be acquired, and so on—and as a follow-up you will want to provide a discussion period and an opportunity to use the newly acquired learning.

Encourage the abler students to try some of the more difficult exercises. To provide for individual differences we have presented three levels of work. The topics and exercises marked A are for all students; those marked B offer additional work for students with more interest and ambition; while those marked C are a challenge to the best students.

The book contains far more exercises than any one student can be expected to do. You may like to choose part of a group of exercises for class drill and part for homework. For slow students you may want to choose easy exercises, and for good ones, the more difficult exercises. You will need to adjust the amount of drill to the needs of your class and not be misled by the generous supply of exercises into spending too much time on a particular topic. At the beginning of each chapter you will find a suggested number of days to spend on the chapter. Certainly the suggested time need not be adhered to rigidly; it is merely to help you plan. Under the minimum schedule a class should be able to cover Chapters 1–16 in a school year of approximately 140 days, and under the maximum schedule a class should be able to complete the book in a school year of 180 days.

Insist upon a job well done. This is an age that demands good workmanship and constant checking of results. No satellite is considered ready for launching until every instrument, every bolt, every electrical connection has been checked again and again. No jet plane leaves the ground if there is any doubt about its safety. No great industrial or governmental project is placed in the hands of a careless workman. If students are to succeed in a world like this they must

IV

begin now to value thoroughness and carefulness. Insist upon careful preparation of each day's assignment. Insist that each exercise be checked and rechecked. Pupils learn more from short assignments that are well done than from long ones that are carelessly done.

Teach for understanding, not mere skill, in carrying out a given process. The fact that a pupil can glibly give the products for a hundred exercises of the type $x^2 \cdot x^3 = x^5$ does not mean that he knows why adding the exponents gives the correct result. It doesn't even mean that he knows that he is performing a multiplication. It doesn't guarantee that he will be able to use the process in future problem situations.

Do your best to interest your pupils in learning algebra. As a teacher you become a salesman of ideas, and like any salesman, whether he sells ideas, or automobiles, or cereal, you must convince your customer that he needs your product. This is not easy in today's competitive world.

Make your teaching colorful, and appealing, and fascinating. Make full use of the between-chapter articles. These pages were not introduced just to entertain pupils. They can become a powerful aid in keeping your pupils interested and busy at learning algebra. All of us manage to learn those things which seem important to us. Your pupils will throw themselves into the study of algebra in proportion to the value they see in it for themselves. Prepare bulletin-board displays. Prepare exhibits. Make full use of films and film strips. Organize a mathematics club. In short, do anything that will help you to sell your product, algebra.

NOTES

NOTES

NOTES

SUGGESTED TIME SCHEDULE

	Minimum Course 140 days	Maximum Course 180 days
Chapter 1	10 days	10 days
Chapter 2	9 days	9 days
Chapter 3	9 days	9 days
Chapter 4	10 days	10 days
Chapter 5	4 days	5 days
Chapter 6	9 days	10 days
Chapter 7	9 days	10 days
Chapter 8	10 days	11 days
Chapter 9	9 days	9 days
Chapter 10	7 days	7 days
Chapter 11	7 days	8 days
Chapter 12	13 days	13 days
Chapter 13	4 days	5 days
Chapter 14	13 days	15 days
Chapter 15	9 days	11 days
Chapter 16	8 days	12 days
Chapter 17		10 days
Chapter 18		7 days
Chapter 19		9 days
	Total . . .140 days	Total . . .180 days

Answers to Achievement Tests

Chapter 1.   Test A

1. Finite
2. Yes
3. $\{6, 11, 16, 21\}$
4. 12
5. 7
6. $\{1, 9, 25, 49\}$
7. ny (cents)
8. 26
9. 4
10. 16
11. $6\,x^3$
12. yx

13. $y + (x + 2)$
14. $3 \times (6 \times 3);\ (3 \times 6) \times 8$
15. Four

16. 0 1 2 3 4 5 6 7 8 9 10 (points at 5, 6, 7, 8)

17. 0 1 2 3 4 5 6 7 8 9 10 (open point at 4)

18. 6
19. $3\,b + 10\,c$
20. $7\,x^2 + x$

Chapter 1.   Test B

1. Finite
2. A unit set
3. $\{9, 18, 27, 36, 45\}$
4. $2\,a^2 + 2\,ab$
5. $(x + 7)4$
6. $4\,a + (3\,b + 2\,a)$
7. $\{14, 24, 34, 44\}$

8. $\{0, 1, 4, 9\}$
9. 25.12
10. 648
11. $\dfrac{pc}{12}$ (cents)
12. $\frac{1}{2}$
13. $\frac{2}{9}$

14. parentheses
15. 0
16. 525
17. $3\,xy + 2\,y^2$
18. $4(m + 2\,n)$
19. $3\,x^2 + 11\,xy + 9\,y^2$
20. 15

Chapter 2.   Test A

1. a, c, d, e
2. $\{3\}$
3. $\{m \mid m < 2\}$
4. Subtraction

5. Division axiom
6. Subtraction axiom
7. $x = 8$
8. $x = 14$

9. $x = 6$
10. $x = 3\frac{1}{3}$
11. $x = 18$
12. $x = 700$

13. $x > 1$

14. $x < 3$

15. $x > 10$

16. ⊕ number line: 0 1 2 3 4 5 6 7 8 9 10

17. ● number line: 0 1 2 3 4 5 6 7 8 9 10

18. 12

19. 45

20. 18° and 72°

Chapter 2. Test B

1. equation

2. sum

3. supplementary

4. c, d

5. $y = 33$

6. $y = 0$

7. $x = 250$

8. $y = 0.7$

9. $x = 21$

10. $x = 0.44$

11. $x > 14$

12. $x < 17$

13. $x > 4$

14. $x < \frac{3}{2}$

15. ● number line: 0 1 2 3 4 5 6 7 8 9 10

16. ⊕ number line: 0 1 2 3 4 5 6 7 8 9 10

17. 18 in., 36 in., 54 in.

18. Bill, $88.; Joe, $110.

19. 13 years old

20. 96° and 84°

Chapter 3. Test A

1. True   **2.** True   **3.** False   **4.** False   **5.** False

6. $c = 2\,\pi r$ **7.** $A = bh$ or $A = lw$ **8.** $A = \frac{1}{2}\,bh$

9. Pi equals the circumference of a circle divided by its diameter.

10. The length of a rectangular solid equals the volume divided by the product of the width and height.

11. The perimeter (of a square) equals 4 times one of its sides.

12. $p = 5\,s$ **13.** $a + b = 5$ **14.**

p	1	3	6	12	120
v	60	20	10	5	$\frac{1}{2}$

15. $25.20

16. 80 mi.

17. 176 sq. ft.

18. F is increased.

19. 132.66, or 133

20. $A = 4\,r^2 + \frac{1}{2}\,\pi r^2$

Chapter 3. Test B

1. 2.   **2.** E is increased.   **3.** $W = 110.$ **4.** $F = \frac{9}{5}\,C + 32.$

5.

y	1	3	4	5	6	10	100
x	2	8	11	14	17	29	299

6. The volume is multiplied by 8.

7. $S = 4\,a + 4\,b + 4\,c$

8. 51.84 sq. in.

9. V is doubled.

10. 84.78 cu. ft.

11. 1695.6 sq. ft.

12. 128,614.4 gal.

13. h increases.

14. $A = 4\,x^2 - \pi x^2$

15. $F = 212$

16. $C = 93\frac{1}{3}$

17. K.E. is doubled.

18. $A = 330$ sq. in.

19. $A = \dfrac{a + b + c + d}{4}$

20. $I = .242^+$

Chapter 4. Test A

1. -3
2. The plus sign
3. Less
4. 1
5. -15
6. -6
7. $7x$
8. 4
9. -17
10. $-7x$
11. $4y$
12. -56
13. 18
14. $-6x^2$
15. 0
16. 9
17. $-4y$
18. $-5x^2$
19. $2x-7y$
20. $4a-2b$
21. $-11x+18$
22. $9a+c-4$
23. 30
24. -19
25. -13

Chapter 4. Test B

1. -7
2. -3
3. $-21x^3$
4. -5
5. $-5x^2+2x$
6. $-2a$
7. 2
8. -16
9. -4
10. $\dfrac{c^2}{2}$
11. $\dfrac{5}{x}$
12. $-3c$
13. -14
14. 2
15. -6
16. -12
17. 0
18. 0
19. 1
20. $3n$
21. 24
22. $-\dfrac{5}{x}$
23. $-\dfrac{2x^2y}{5}$
24. -20
25. -10

Chapter 5. Test A

1. $x=-5$
2. $x=5$
3. $x=-\frac{1}{3}$
4. $x=-1.25$
5. $y=1$
6. $y=-2\frac{1}{2}$
7. $p=-1$
8. $y=2$
9. $x>2$
10. $x>-5$
11. $y<6$
12. a, d, f
13.
14.
15. $l=18$
16.

x	4	1	20	-10	-2
y	5	20	1	-2	-10

17. $4m$ hours
18. 11 and 23
19. 15 and 35
20. 125, 126, 127

Chapter 5. Test B

1. $c=-4\frac{3}{4}$
2. $x=-3.7$
3. $y=100$
4. $x=-\frac{1}{2}$
5. $y=-\frac{3}{2}$
6. $y=12$
7. $p=15$
8. $h=5$
9. $x<-5$
10. $x<-4$
11. $x<-3$
12. $x>5$
13. $x<-2$
14. $x<-4$
15.
16.
17.
18. $y=2x+6$
19. -18 and -20
20. 13 and 30

Chapter 6. Test A

1. -3

2. $11\,c$

3. $-15\,a^4$

4. $2\,x^2-1$

5. $-2\,c^2$

6. $-125\,m^3$

7. $-a$

8. $3\,x^3-9\,x^2-3\,x$

9. $5\,a^2-5\,a$

10. $-7\,y^2-6\,y-7$

11. $3\,x^2-18\,x+9$

12. $-6\,m^3+24\,m^2-3\,m$

13. $-2\,x^2-3\,x+1$

14. 12

15. $4\,x+7$

16. $11\,m-18$

17. $2-5\,y$

18. $4\,a-4\,b$

19. $6\,x^2-2\,x$

20. $3\,n-2$

Chapter 6. Test B

1. x^5

2. $4\,x^2$

3. $-64\,a^6$

4. $2\,x^3-2\,x^2+6\,x$

5. $9\,c$

6. $-y+1$

7. $2\,y^4-y^2$

8. x^7-x^4

9. $4\,p+6$

10. $\frac{1}{6}\,a+\frac{1}{6}\,b+\frac{4}{3}\,c$

11. $x^3+2\,x^2+6\,x-7$

12. $-4.6\,x^2-2\,x-11$

13. $4\,x^3y^2-12\,x^2y^2-20\,xy^3$

14. $14\,x-2$

15. $10\,x^2-2\,x$

16. $-2\,x^2-4\,x-3$

17. $x^3-2\,x^2-5$

18. $-4\,x^2+3\,x$

19. $-2\,c-5\,d$

20. $+(2\,a-b)-(4\,c-d)$

Chapter 7. Test A

1. $x=5$

2. $x=-2$

3. $p=-\frac{1}{3}$

4. $p=3$

5. $x=1$

6. $y=3\frac{3}{5}$

7. $x=-\frac{5}{6}$

8. $x=0$

9. Conditional

10. Identical

11. Conditional

12. Identical

13. $7=5+2,$ $7-5=2,$ and $7-2=5$

14. $20-n$

15. $25\,x+5\,y$

16. No

17. 35 and 43

18. 33 and 39

19. 14 dimes and 17 nickels

20. 36 lb. and 48 lb.

Chapter 7. Test B

1. $x=6$

2. $y=-3$

3. $h=2$

4. $x=2\frac{5}{6}$

5. $x=-8.6$

6. $x=3\frac{3}{4}$

7. $p=\frac{1}{6}$

8. $x=2$

9. Identical equation.   10. $2(x-1)+4(1-x)-(x+3)=5$. Does $2(-2-1)+4(1+2)-(-2+3)=5$? Yes.   11. No.

12. Yes.   13. 17.   14. 5 tons and 11 tons.   15. 29 ft. and 50 ft.   16. 36 and 60.   17. 65 quarters, 135 nickels, and 155 dimes.   18. Frank, 22 years; his sister, 6 years.

19. 5 ft.   20. 47°, 60°, and 73°.

Chapter 8. Test A

1. divided
2. ratios
3. means
4. margin
5. proportion or fraction
6. $x = 56$
7. $y = 70$
8. $x = 6$
9. $x = 2\frac{2}{3}$
10. $x = 8$
11. $x = 9$
12. $y = -12$
13. $y = -4$
14. 196
15. 126
16. 35 and 21
17. 15 years of age
18. $\frac{19}{24}$
19. \$6500 at 3%; \$3500 at 4%
20. $x = 3a$

Chapter 8.   Test B

1. extremes
2. C
3. par
4. principal
5. selling
6. $x = 6$
7. $y = 1\frac{1}{8}$
8. $y = 21$
9. $x = -\frac{1}{3}$
10. $x = 6$
11. $x = -\frac{7}{12}$
12. $y = -1\frac{3}{11}$
13. $x = 2$
14. $r = .04$, or 4%
15. $n = 2$
16. 45 in., 60 in.
17. 8 months
18. Jane, 11 years; mother, 33 years
19. Bill, \$14.75; Ralph, \$16.75
20. 16 nickels and 5 quarters

Chapter 9.   Test A

1. $3x^3 - 12x^2 - 9x$
2. $3a^2 + 2a - 1$
3. $4x^2 - 9$
4. $a^2 - 2ab + b^2$
5. $3a^2 + 25ab + 28b^2$
6. $x^3 - 8x^2 + 19x - 20$
7. $6x - 1$
8. $h + r$
9. $2x - 3$
10. $5x + 2$
11. $2a - b$
12. $4a^2 - 2a + 1$
13. $(x^2 - 2x)$ miles
14. $y = -1$
15. $x = 4$
16. $x = -3\frac{1}{2}$
17. $y = -2$
18. $4\frac{1}{2}$ hours
19. $72\frac{8}{11}$ bu. corn; $127\frac{3}{11}$ bu. oats
20. $2\frac{2}{9}$ days

Chapter 9. Test B

1. $x^3 - x^2y$

2. $-6\,m^3 + 10\,m^2n$

3. $a^4 - b^4$

4. $x^3 - y^3$

5. $2\,x^3 - 5\,x^2 + x + 2$

6. $a^3 - 3\,a^2b + 3\,ab^2 - b^3$

7. $x - y$

8. $r + h$

9. $a^2 - 2\,a + 4$

10. $m^2 - mn + n^2$

11. $x^2 - 4\,x + 3$

12. $7\,x - 11$

13. $20\,x^2 + 2\,x - 5$

14. $(x - 2)$ m.p.h.

15. $y = -2$

16. $x = 5$

17. $x = -26$

18. 30 lb.

19. $2\frac{1}{4}$ hours

20. 8 mi.

Chapter 10. Test on Graphs

1. origin   2. 2; 4   3. second   4.

6. $y = x$

x	0	1	2	3
y	0	2	4	6

5.

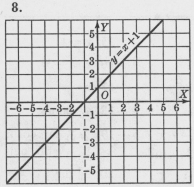

7.

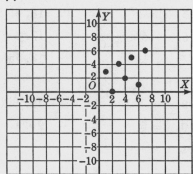

8.

9. b, c

XIV

10.

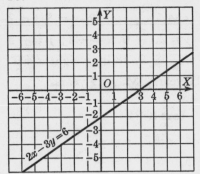

11.

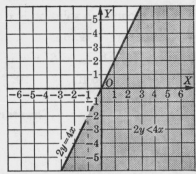

The graph is the shaded area, not including the line $2y = 4x$.

12.

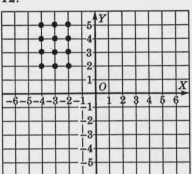

13.

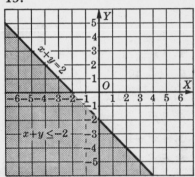

The graph is the shaded area plus the line $x + y = 2$.

14.

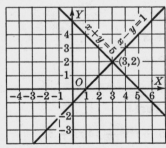

The graph of the compound sentence is the point (3, 2).

15.

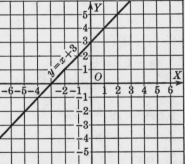

16. Because its graph is a straight line.

Chapter 11. Test A

1. The common solution is $x = 2, y = 4$. **2.** $x = 3, y = 2$.
3. Consistent. **4.** no. **5.** $x = 7; y = 2$. **6.** $x = -1; y = -3$.
7. $x = 4; y = 1$. **8.** $x = 1; y = 3$. **9.** 18 lb. weight is 4 ft.;
12 lb. weight is 6 ft. **10.** Jim, 11 years; Mary, 9 years.

Chapter 11. Test B

1. $x = -3; y = -1$ **4.** $x = 2; y = -3$
2. coincide   **5.** $x = 1; y = -3$
3. $x = 4; y = -1$ **6.** $x = 3500; y = 2500$
7. 20 lb. of 60-cent candy; 20 lb. of 90-cent candy.
8. $7500 at 4%; $1500 at 5%.

Chapter 12. Test A

1. $3x - 21$ **14.** $(y + 4)(y - 4)$
2. $r^2 - 49$ **15.** $(y + 1)(y + 3)$
3. $4x^2 + 11x - 3$ **16.** $5(x + y)(x - y)$
4. $9p^2$ **17.** $(m + 3n)(m - 3n)$
5. $4x^2 - 12x + 9$ **18.** $(x + 4)(2x - 3)$
6. $6x^2 - 29xy + 9y^2$ **19.** $2x(x - 5)(x - 4)$
7. $9a^2$ **20.** $c(c^2 + c + 1)$
8. 16 **21.** $m^2n^2(m - n)$
9. $16x^6$ **22.** $(3k + 1)(k - 1)$
10. $\frac{1}{25}m^4n^2$ **23.** 7
11. $7(x - y)$ **24.** x
12. $(y + 2)(y + 4)$ **25.** $c + d$
13. $(x - 8)(x + 6)$

Chapter 12. Test B

1. $m^3n - m^2n^2 + mn^3$ **6.** $8r^2s^2 + 14rs + 3$
2. $9x^2 - 30x + 25$ **7.** Prime
3. $16x^4 - 25y^4$ **8.** Not prime
4. $21x^2 + 22xy - 8y^2$ **9.** Prime
5. $x^2 - \frac{2}{3}x + \frac{1}{9}$ **10.** $3x$

11. $m - 1$

12. $c + \frac{1}{2}$

13. $(p - 1)(p + 1)$

14. $3x^2(x + 3)(x - 3)$

15. $(a - 10)(a + 8)$

16. $2(4x - 1)(3x + 2)$

17. $2\pi r(r + h)$

18. $2(1 - 7k)(3 + 2k)$

19. $(x^2 + y^2)(x + y)(x - y)$

20. $(xy - 5)(xy - 2)$

21. $a(a + 1)(a - 1)$

22. $(x + 2)(x - 2)(x - 1)(x + 1)$

23. $ab^2(a - 3)(a + 2)$

24. $(1 - 4mn)(1 + 2mn)$

25. $x - 2$

Chapter 13. Test A

1. $x = \pm 2$

2. $x = 0, 2\frac{1}{2}$

3. $x = 1, -6$

4. $x = \pm 6$

5. $x = 1\frac{1}{2}, 1\frac{2}{3}$

6. $x = \dfrac{2}{a}$

7. $x = m + n$

8. $x = a - 2$

9. $F = \frac{9}{5}C + 32$

10. $h = \dfrac{2A}{b + b'}$

11. $n = 5, -2$

12. $y = 4, 7$

13. 7 and 2

14. 9 and 12

Chapter 13. Test B

1. $x = \pm a$

2. $x = c, 4c$

3. $x = \pm 6c$

4. $x = b - c$

5. $x = 0, h$

6. $x = 4a, \frac{5}{3}a$

7. $x = 8, 3\frac{1}{3}$

8. $x = t, 8t, -5t$

9. 85

10. 18 ft. by 12 ft.

Chapter 14. Test A

1. $\dfrac{4x}{5}$

2. $\frac{4}{7}$

3. $\dfrac{x - y}{x + y}$

4. $\frac{2}{25}$

5. x

6. $\dfrac{abc}{4}$

7. $\dfrac{3(m + 1)}{n(m + 2)}$

8. $\dfrac{4(x + 3)}{x(x - 1)}$

9. $\dfrac{2(3x + 2)}{3(x + 4)}$

10. x

11. $\dfrac{2x}{5}$

12. $\dfrac{a + c}{b}$

13. $\dfrac{11x - y}{12}$

14. $\dfrac{7c + 22}{18}$

15. $\dfrac{11x}{(x - 5)(x + 6)}$

16. $\frac{3}{8}$

17. 0.18

18. $3x^2 - 2x + \frac{1}{2}$

19. $\dfrac{a + b}{b}$

20. No. Division by zero is not possible.

1. $\dfrac{a^2}{3\,b^3}$

2. $\dfrac{4\,y}{5\,x - 8\,y}$

3. $\dfrac{2 - y}{2\,y - 3}$, or $-\dfrac{y - 2}{2\,y - 3}$

4. $b - 2 + \dfrac{1}{2\,b^2}$

5. $2\,x + 5 + \dfrac{2}{3\,x - 2}$

6. $k^2 + k + 1 + \dfrac{2}{k - 1}$

7. $\dfrac{h^2 - h + 1}{h}$

8. $\dfrac{2\,a^2 - b^2}{a + b}$

9. $2(x - 1)$

10. $\dfrac{x^2}{2(2\,x - 1)}$

11. $\dfrac{a}{2\,b}$

12. $\dfrac{2(a - 3)}{(2\,a - 1)(3\,a + 4)}$

13. $\dfrac{3(x - 1)(x^2 + 1)}{4(4\,x - 3)}$

14. $\frac{7}{8}$

15. 1.625

16. -6

17. $x^2 - y^2$

18. $\dfrac{2\,y + 6}{(y + 2)(y - 3)}$

19. $\dfrac{2\,b^2}{a^2 - b^2}$

20. $\dfrac{2\,x^2 - 50}{x - 5}$, or $2(x + 5)$ where $x \neq 5$

Chapter 15. Test A

1. $\dfrac{4}{x} + \dfrac{3}{x} = 5$

2. $x = 1\frac{2}{3}$

3. $y = \frac{1}{7}$

4. $x = 2$

5. $y = 4$

6. $x = 4\frac{2}{3}$

7. $y = -\frac{1}{3}$

8. $g = \dfrac{t + Mf}{M}$

9. 50 m.p.h.

10. $\frac{7}{10}$

Chapter 15. Test B

1. $y = 6.$ 2. $x = 4, -9.$ 3. $y = 5.$ 4. $x = 4, y = 2.$

5. $m = 3\,a - 3.$ 6. $w = \dfrac{s}{n + 1}.$ 7. 3 hours and 6 hours.

8. Plane, 120 m.p.h.; Wind, 30 m.p.h.   9. $\frac{3}{4}$ and $\frac{5}{8}$.   10. 8 and 6; -6 and -8.

Chapter 16. Test A

1. a. $25\,m^2$ b. $36\,x^6$ c. $\dfrac{1}{9\,x^2}$ 2. a. 8   b. -9 c. $5\,a$

3. ± 83

4. 6.5

5. a. $3\sqrt{2}$ **b.** $5\sqrt{2}$

6. a. 10   **b.** $3\sqrt{7}$

7. a. $\frac{1}{2}\sqrt{2}$ **b.** $\frac{1}{5}\sqrt{10}$

8. a. $\sqrt{30}$ **b.** 4

9. $3\sqrt{3} - 2\sqrt{5}$

10. $2 + \sqrt{2}$

Chapter 16.   Test B

1. ± 97.3

2. 11.4

3. 16.4

4. a. $9\sqrt{2}$ **b.** $x^2\sqrt{x}$

5. a. $\frac{1}{4}\sqrt{2}$ **b.** $\frac{1}{b}\sqrt{ab}$

6. a. $\frac{1}{m^2}\sqrt{m}$ **b.** $\frac{2}{mn}\sqrt{mn}$

7. a. 0   **b.** $2\sqrt{2} + \sqrt{3}$

8. a. 12   **b.** $20\sqrt{6}$

9. a. $\sqrt{2}$ **b.** $\frac{3\sqrt{5}}{10}$

10. 9

Chapter 17.   Test A

1. $x = \pm 6$

2. $x = \pm 2$

3. $x = 6, -2$

4. $x = 9, 1$

5. $x = 4, -\frac{3}{2}$

6. $x = \dfrac{-1 \pm \sqrt{21}}{5}$

7. $x = 8, 4\frac{3}{5}$

8. 72 feet

9. $8\sqrt{2}$ feet

10. $5, -9$

Chapter 17.   Test B

1. $x = \pm 6\sqrt{c}$

3. $x = \pm \sqrt{a}$

3. $x = \pm \sqrt{a - b}$

4. $t = \pm \frac{1}{2}\sqrt{10}$

5. $x = \frac{3}{2}(1 \pm \sqrt{5})$

6. $x = \dfrac{5 \pm \sqrt{17}}{2}$

7. $x = 3, 3$

8. $6\sqrt{3}$

9. $r = \pm \dfrac{1}{\pi h}\sqrt{\pi h V}$

10. 80 persons

Chapter 18.   Test A

1. $x = 12$

2. $x = \pm 9$

3. $x = \dfrac{mn}{p}$

4. Direct

5. 12 in.

6. b and c

7. $\frac{1}{6}$

8. a. Directly
b. Inversely
c. Directly

9. y is divided by 5.

10. 25 ft.

11. 12 in. and 18 in.

Chapter 18.   Test B

1. $x = \pm 3\sqrt{2}$.   **2.** $x = 11$.   **3.** Inversely.   **4.** Inversely.

5. c and d.   **6.** 891.   **7.** \$2.38.   **8. a.** A.   **b.** 4 and π.

9. Directly. Directly as the square of r.   **10.** Neither inversely

nor directly.   **11. a.** Inversely.   **b.** $xy = 6$.

Chapter 19.   Test A

1. a. 0.05
   b. 1.75
   c. 3.18
2. a. 5380
   b. 7420
   c. 1.79

3. 4.46

4. a. 0.6
   b. 0.8

5. a. 0.6
   b. 1.3

6. $x = 3.5268$, or 4.
7. $y = 6.6636$, or 7.
8. $z = 6.4967$, or 6.
9. 57.36 ft., or 57 ft.
10. 31° (to nearest degree)

Cumulative Test 1 (Chapters 1-7)

1.

2. No
3. $-6\,a^3b^4c$
4. $5\,x^3y^3$
5. 105
6. $x = -3$
7. $4\,a - 4\,b$

8. $2\,x^2 - 2\,x - 1$
9. $3\,x^2 - 2\,x = 4$
10. $-2\,a^4 + 6\,a^3 - 2\,a^2$
11. $3\,x^2 - 12\,x$
12. -13
13. $V = 2\,a^3 + 6\,a^2$

14. $x = -9$
15. $h = \frac{1}{10}$
16. Yes
17. $x > 5$.
18. 11 nickels and 8 dimes
19. Father, 27 years; son, 5 years
20. 16 lb. and 24 lb.

Cumulative Test 2 (Chapters 1-8)

1. $-12\,x^4$
2. x^6
3. $-125\,b^3$
4. $2\,m - 3\,n$
5. $-2\,k^4 + 3\,k^3 - 5\,k^2$
6. x^0, or 1
7. True
8. -39
9. $y = 36$
10. $s = -1$
11. Yes

12. The distributive property
13. {4, 5, 6}
14.

x	0	6	8	4
y	3	0	-1	1

15. 17 girls and 14 boys
16. $A = \pi r^2 - 2\,r^2$, or $A = r^2(\pi - 2)$
17. 9 dimes, 12 quarters, and 11 nickels
18. $x = 12$
19. $x = 7$
20. $65

Cumulative Test 3 (Chapters 1-9)

1. $x > -3$
2. $-12\,c^5$

3. $3\,x$
4. $2(x + 4\,y)$

5. $x = -1$

6. $x = -\frac{1}{7}$

7.

8. -116

9. $s = 552.5$

10. $6x^2 + 7x - 20$

11. $2x - 3$

12. $x + y = 12$

13. $V = 280$

14. $-\dfrac{4a}{b^2}$

15. 48

16.

x	-4	8	-13	-28
y	0	4	-3	-8

17. $x = 1$

18. $x = 3$

19. $c^2 - 6c$

20. Conditional

21. $A = ab + \dfrac{\pi b^2}{4}$

22. Bill, 16 years; his sister, 4 years.

23. 14 2-cent stamps

24. $3600 at 2% and $1400 at 3%

25. $285

Cumulative Test 4 (Chapters 1-12)

1. $(x + 9)(x - 8)$

2. $7a(a - 2b)$

3. $(5x + 7)(5x - 7)$

4. $-2ab - 2b^2$

5. $x = -4$

6. $x = 11$

7. $x > -2\frac{2}{3}$

8. $y = 7$

9. $-30x^4$

10. $x - 4$

11. $x = 3, y = 0$

12. $x = 12, y = -3$

13. $l = \dfrac{s - 2w}{2}$

14.

15. The graph passes through (5, 0) and (0, 4).

16. $x = \dfrac{a + b}{3}$

17. 9; x^3

18. $x^3 - y^3$

19. $C = 25$

20. 18 and 10.

The graph is the shaded area, not including the line $3x + 4y = 12$.

Cumulative Test 5 (Chapters 10-18)

1. a. $y(y-6)$
   b. $(3m-5)(2m-3)$

2. $\dfrac{a+b}{b}$

3. The graph passes through $(-6, 0)$ and $(0, -2)$.

4. a. $2\sqrt{2}$ **b.** $\frac{1}{5}\sqrt{15}$

5. $x = 7, -6$

6. $9x^2 - 6x + 1$

7.

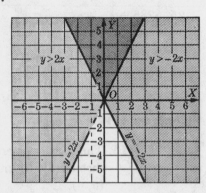

The graph of the truth set is the darkest shaded area between the lines $y = 2x$ and $y = -2x$.

8. $x = -1\frac{1}{2}$

9. $x = 2;\ y = -3$

10.

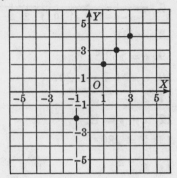

Yes, it represents a function.

11. $x = -1\frac{1}{5}$

12. $y = n - m$

13. $x = 7, -2$

14. $x = 13, -9$

15. $\dfrac{b^2 - a^2}{ab}$

16. $\dfrac{b(a-5b)}{6(a-2b)}$

17. $x = 6, 1$

18. a. Directly
   b. Decreases by 5

19. 30 in.

20. $f(x) = 7$

Cumulative Test 6 (Chapters 11-19)

1. straight line

2. ratios

3. sine

4. factors

5. positive, or principal

6. second

7. radicand

8. directly

9. $3a(a-6)$

10. $(a+5)(a-5)$

11. $(x-12)(x+1)$

12. $a^2(a-2)(a+2)$

13. $x(x-1)^2$

14. $(x^2-5)(x+1)(x-1)$

15. $x = 7, -8$

16. $x = 1\frac{1}{2}$

17. $x = 3, y = 2$

18. $x = -4$

19. $\dfrac{a}{a+4}$

20. $\dfrac{b^2-a^2}{ab}$

21. $\dfrac{a}{a+b}$

22. $3\sqrt{3}$ in.

23. 13 ft.

24. $3\sqrt{2}$

25. $10\sqrt{3}$

26. $\frac{1}{3}\sqrt{6}$

27. 18 quarters, 10 dimes

28. Inversely

29. $5\sqrt{2}$

30. 92

31. 1.8807

32. 9.39 in., or 9 in.

33. 17.658 in., or 18 in.

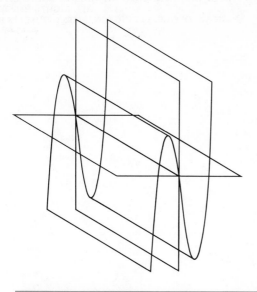

Algebra / Book 1
modern edition

Welchons / Krickenberger / Pearson

Ginn and Company
A Xerox Education Company

This presentation of Algebra, Book One, uses modern concepts within the framework of a traditional algebra course. The text should prove satisfying to those schools and teachers who want their students to have a working knowledge of modern algebra but not at the expense of competence in using algebra.

Definitions and procedures have been updated to bring them in line with the latest mathematical thinking but the text retains its basic structure of step-by-step explanations and examples, an abundance and variety of exercises, and frequent reviews. The text is addressed to the student in simple, easily-understood language. Informal explanations take the place of formal proofs. Modern symbolism is used when it can be truly helpful but is not allowed to become a fetish. Ample opportunities for practice help to clarify understanding and fix ideas. Selected answers are included for chapters 1–19 to reinforce students as they study independently.

This is a text for all algebra classes. The language is simple enough to be understood by less able as well as average and above average students. There is a variety of problems of all degrees of difficulty. These and special topics scattered throughout the text are designed to appeal to a diversity of interests.

Development

Topics are arranged in a spiral so that a pupil meets each topic again and again in new settings and thus gradually deepens and extends his understanding of it.

Meanings are developed before rules are given or principles stated. Carefully prepared questions and problems lead pupils to form their own conclusions and generalizations and often to formulate their own procedures. Once developed, rules and principles are made to stand out on the page in such a way as to emphasize their importance and make them readily available for reference.

Simplicity

The book is written for the pupil and to the pupil who is beginning the study of algebra. The language is direct, concise, and simple. New words are defined, illustrated, and reviewed frequently.

Motivation

Problems relating to science, commerce, and everyday activities make algebra a living subject. The illustrated articles which point out the need in various professions and occupations for men and women trained in mathematics serve to create in some pupils a desire to continue its study.

Visual Aids

A variety of visual helps are employed. Among these may be noted the use of color for emphasis and attractiveness; stimulating photographs; and the many diagrams in both text and exercise material.

Problem-Solving

The technique of problem-solving as presented in this book has been used by the authors and has proved most effective. The drawings which picture some of the problem situations will be helpful to many students.

Practice Material

In order that all pupils may acquire mastery of manipulation and understanding of subject matter, an abundance of practice material has been included. The amount of practice needed by any pupil or class depends upon the pupil's learning ability and preparation. It is assumed that the teacher will adjust the amount of practice to the needs of the class, and not be misled by a generous supply of exercises into spending too much time on any particular topic.

Individual Differences

To aid the teacher in caring for individual differences among pupils, three levels of work are given. The topics and exercises marked A are for all pupils. The B topics and exercises offer additional work for students with more interest and ambition. The C work is a challenge to exceptional students.

Minimum and Maximum Courses

The amount of subject matter covered during a school year depends upon the pupil's ability in mathematics and his mathematical preparation. As a guide in determining the progress of a class the following courses are suggested:

A Minimum Course. First semester: Chapters 1–8, A topics and exercises. Second semester: Chapters 9–15, A topics and exercises.

A Maximum Course. First semester: Chapters 1–10, A topics and exercises and selected B and C topics and exercises. Second semester: Chapters 11–19, A topics and exercises and selected B and C topics and exercises.

Reviews

Constant repetition is a necessary procedure in teaching mathematics. Each of the first eighteen chapters concludes with a chapter review and most of them contain a cumulative review. Preceding each Chapter Review is a summary of the desired learnings in that chapter together with page references to the topics. Chapter 20 is a review by topics.

Tests

The testing material includes four tests in arithmetic, nineteen chapter tests—most of them with A and B sections, and six cumulative tests. The cumulative tests in Chapters 7, 8, and 9 are based upon the subject matter preceding them, and the cumulative tests in Chapters 18 and 19 are based upon the work of the second half year.

These tests may be used in various ways—as diagnostic, practice, or mastery tests. If they are used as practice tests, the teacher may use them as guides in preparing the mastery tests. A separate book of tests is also available.

The Authors

CONTENTS

ALGEBRA, BOOK ONE

YOU ARE NEEDED

Never before in history have men made as many scientific and technological discoveries as are being made today. You who are still in school are the ones who will be needed to carry on this work and to make still other discoveries. Many avenues are open to you. For example—

Engineers are needed who will originate an entirely new mode of travel—one that will eliminate the traffic jams, the inconvenience, and the dangers of today's travel.

Wonderful work is being done by **communications engineers**; would you like a part in it?

You may be interested in **weather control**, or in new ways of providing **heat and light** for our houses. Perhaps the field of **architecture** will appeal to you; you may want to develop a new and superior kind of house.

Medical research workers are needed. You may want to try to find a way to prevent one of the diseases that are still resisting attempts to control them.

Our exploding population requires **agricultural experts** who will find new ways to enrich the soil and to improve crops.

The **space age** will open up entirely new fields of work. Perhaps you hope some day to develop the resources of the moon or to man a space station.

The possibilities ahead of you stagger the imagination.

Giannini Controls Corporation

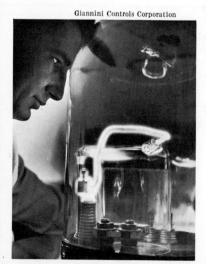

Bell Telephone Laboratories

WILL YOU BE READY?

But to succeed, your plans must be matched by great determination. You must have the will power to choose the high school subjects that will help you the most—mathematics, science, English, social studies, and others. They will not be the snap courses and probably not the most popular courses in your school, but that will not stop you if you are in earnest about succeeding.

Your determination must be great enough to make you study each subject thoroughly, even beyond the daily assignments. Other pupils may be satisfied with a quick "once through" look at the lessons, but not you. And you will want a college education—a very thorough college education. Plan now to be ready for the work you will choose to do.

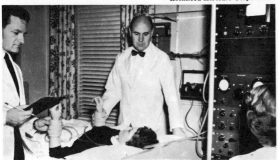

An understanding of the concept of sets is valuable for unification and clarification of many topics of mathematics. This text treats sets informally with a minimum of symbolism, yet adequately for students who have had no previous experience with the terminology.

1

Representing Numbers and Number Relations

Suggested Time Schedule
10 days

In this chapter you will study some characteristics of our number system and consider ways to represent numbers and number relations.

REPRESENTING NUMBERS AND NUMBER RELATIONS

Sets of Numbers [A]

All your life you have used the word "set." You have talked of sets of tools, sets of tires, sets of dishes, and sets of many other things. You will not be surprised, therefore, to find that the word "set" is useful in mathematics, too. As you can probably guess, most of the sets that we consider in algebra are sets of numbers. A set of numbers is a well-defined collection of numbers. By "well-defined" we mean that we know which numbers belong to the set and which do not.

To indicate that we are thinking of a set of numbers we may list the numbers that form the set. Thus we may speak of *the set of numbers 1, 2, 3, 4, 5.* To write "the set of numbers 1, 2, 3, 4, 5" we sometimes use the abbreviation

$$\{1, 2, 3, 4, 5\}.$$

In this expression the braces { } symbolize the words, "the set." By using the braces we indicate that we are considering a collection of numbers rather than the numbers individually. By listing the numbers that compose the set we make clear which numbers belong to the set and which do not.

We may also indicate a set by describing it. Since the numbers 1, 2, 3, and so on are used in counting, we may describe $\{1, 2, 3, 4, 5\}$ as *the set of counting numbers from 1 to 5, inclusive,* or *the set of counting numbers* ①above *less than six.*

The numbers that make up a set are said to be members or elements of the set. Thus, for $\{1, 2, 3, 4, 5\}$, 1 is a member and 2 is a member. Is 7 a member? Is 4 a member?

Since we do not use zero in counting, zero is not a member of any set of counting numbers. It is, however, a member of $\{0, 1, 2, 3, \text{and so on}\}$. This is the set of whole numbers.

[A]

EXERCISES

In each of the exercises below we have given a description of a set. Indicate each set by listing its members between braces. $\{1,2,3,4,5,6,7,8,9,10\}$

1. The set of whole numbers from 1 to 10, inclusive.

2. The set of even counting numbers less than 9. $\{2, 4, 6, 8\}$

3. The set of odd whole numbers between 20 and 26. $\{21, 23, 25\}$

4. A set of proper fractions with the denominator 4. $\{\frac{1}{4}, \frac{2}{4}, \frac{3}{4}\}$

Remind students that a *proper fraction* is one whose value is less than 1.

3

ALGEBRA, BOOK ONE

⟶ ① foot of page

5. The set of fractions that can be formed with the numbers 1, 2, and 3. $\left\{\frac{1}{1}, \frac{1}{2}, \frac{1}{3}, \frac{2}{1}, \frac{2}{2}, \frac{2}{3}, \frac{3}{1}, \frac{3}{2}, \frac{3}{3}\right\}$

6. The set of two-digit numbers whose tens digit is three times its units digit. $\{31, 62, 93\}$

7. The set of two-digit numbers whose units digit is twice its tens digit. $\{12, 24, 36, 48\}$

The Number of Members in a Set [A]

If the number of members in a set can be counted, we say that the set is a <u>finite set.</u> Thus {3, 5, 7, 9} is a finite set because it contains just four members.

If a finite set contains only one member, we say that it is a <u>unit set,</u> and if it contains no members, we say that it is an <u>empty set</u> or <u>null set.</u> Thus the set of whole numbers greater than 5 and less than 7 is the unit set {6} and the set of all whole numbers greater than 8 and less than 9 is an empty set or null set. The symbol for "empty set" is ϕ; we do not use braces with ϕ. The set {0} is a unit set rather than an empty set because it contains the one member, 0.

If the number of members in a set cannot be counted, we say that the set is an <u>infinite set.</u> Thus the set of all counting numbers is an infinite set because there is no largest counting number. If you are in doubt about this, think of the largest counting number that you can imagine. Is this the largest counting number? Of course it isn't, because, as soon as you have thought of the number, you can add 1 to it and get a larger counting number, then you can add 1 to this number and get a still larger counting number, and so on, and on, and on. You can never reach a largest counting number.

Since we cannot list all the members of an infinite set, we sometimes list three or four members and follow them by three dots. Thus, $\cdots$, the three dots meaning *and so on.* For example, to indicate the set of all counting numbers we may write {1, 2, 3, 4, $\cdots$ }. We read this expression as, "the set 1, 2, 3, 4, and so on."

When a finite set has so many members that it is inconvenient to list all of them we may use three dots to mean, *and so on to.* Thus to indicate the set of all <u>counting numbers</u> less than 100 we may write {1, 2, 3, 4, $\cdots$, 99}. We read this expression as, "the set 1, 2, 3, 4, and so on, to and including 99."

① Ex. 5. Encourage students to use a system for answering questions of this type. Here, point out that they may first use 1 for denominator, combining all possible numerators with it. Then 2 for denominator, etc.

4

REPRESENTING NUMBERS AND NUMBER RELATIONS

[A]

1. Indicate which of the following sets are finite and which **EXERCISES** are infinite:

a. The set of counting numbers less than 50. *Finite*

b. The set of even counting numbers. *Infinite*

c. The set of fractions between 0 and 1. *Infinite*

d. The set of counting numbers less than 100 that are divisible by 3. *Finite*

e. The set of fractions between $\frac{1}{3}$ and $\frac{1}{2}$. *Infinite*

2. Indicate each of the sets described below by listing its members between braces. (In case you find an empty set, do not use braces.)   See ①, top of page.

a. The set of counting numbers. $\{1, 2, 3, 4, \cdots\}$

b. The set of odd counting numbers. $\{1, 3, 5, 7, \cdots\}$

c. The set of counting numbers greater than 10. $\{11, 12, 13, \cdots\}$

d. The set of whole numbers greater than 20 and less than 21. ϕ

e. The set of whole numbers that multiplied by 3 give 12. $\{4\}$

f. The set of fractions with the denominator 2. $\{\frac{0}{2}, \frac{1}{2}, \frac{2}{2}, \frac{3}{2}, \cdots\}$

Naming a Set [A]

We name a set with a capital letter. Thus we may give the name A to $\{5, 10, 15, 20\}$ and write, $A = \{5, 10, 15, 20\}$. We read the sentence as, "A is the set 5, 10, 15, 20."

In this text we assign names to the <u>natural</u> (counting) <u>numbers</u> and whole numbers as follows:

$$N = \{1, 2, 3, \cdots\} \qquad W = \{0, 1, 2, 3, \cdots\}$$

Subsets [A]

Let us now consider

$$C = \{1, 2, 3, 4, 5, 6, 7, 8, 9, 10\} \quad \text{and} \quad D = \{2, 4, 6, 8, 10\}.$$

Do you see that every member of set D is also a member of set C? Since this is true we say that set D is a subset of set C. In general, we say: When every member of a set B is a member of a set A, then set B is a <u>subset</u> of set A. As a matter of convenience we consider the null set a subset of every set. A set may be a subset of itself. ② below

② Emphasize the last sentence since it may seem strange that an entire set can be called a subset of itself. The teacher may introduce the term "proper subset" if desired.

5

ALGEBRA, BOOK ONE

① above.

[A]

1. Given $A = \{1, 2, 3, 4, 5, 6, 7, 8, 9, 10\}$, write those of its subsets described below.

a. The subset of even numbers in A. $\{2, 4, 6, 8, 10\}$

b. The subset of members of A that are greater than 6. $\{7, 8, 9, 10\}$

c. The subset of members of A that are less than 7. $\{1, 2, 3, 4, 5, 6\}$

d. The subset of members of A that are less than 1. ϕ

e. The subset of members of A that are greater than 0. $\{1, 2, 3, 4, 5, 6, 7, 8, 9, 10\}$

f. The subset of members of A that are divisible by 4. $\{4, 8\}$

g. The subset of members of A that are greater than 3 and less than 8. $\{4, 5, 6, 7\}$

2. Given $N = \{1, 2, 3, 4, 5, \cdots\}$, write the following:

a. The subset of members of N that are greater than 25. $\{26, 27, 28, \ldots\}$

b. The subset of even numbers in N. $\{2, 4, 6, \ldots\}$

c. The subset of members of N that can be substituted for a in the following sentence to make it state a truth: $a + 9 = 11$. $\{2\}$

Whole Numbers and the Number Line [A]

It is useful to associate numbers with the points of a line. For example, to associate the whole numbers with the points of a line, we proceed as follows.

We draw part of a horizontal line. Arrowheads show that the line extends without end in each of its directions. On the line we select a starting point O and another point A to its right. ② below

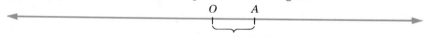

Unit of measurement

The distance from O to A (OA) is our unit of measurement. Using this same distance, we locate and name other successive points to the right of A in the line as shown.

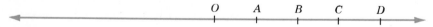

Since OA is the unit distance, we say that the distance is 1 and assign 1 to point A. The distance AB is also 1, the distance BC is 1, and so on. Thus distance OB is $1 + 1$ or 2, so 2 is assigned to B. Distance OC is $1 + 1 + 1$ or 3, and 3 is assigned to point C.

② Emphasize that, since A can be any point to the right of O in the line, the unit distance can vary.

6

Consequently, by assigning the numbers 1, 2, 3, $\cdots$ to the points A, B, C, $\cdots$ as shown, we indicate the distances of the points from O.

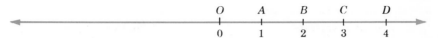

For example, 4 indicates that point D is 4 units of distance from O. Since the distance from point O to itself is zero, we assign the number 0 to point O.

This process has paired each of the whole numbers 0, 1, 2, 3, $\cdots$ with exactly one of the points O, A, B, $\cdots$ in the line. It has also paired each of the points O, A, B, $\cdots$ with exactly one of the whole numbers. This pairing is called a one-to-one correspondence between the whole numbers and the points O, A, B, $\cdots$. We may say that we have mapped the whole numbers onto the set of points O, A, B, $\cdots$.

Each point is the graph of the whole number with which it is paired and the number is the coordinate of the point. Thus point C is the graph of 3, and 3 is the coordinate of point C. The complete set of points, with coordinates 0, 1, 2, 3, $\cdots$, is the graph of the set of whole numbers. The line with this pairing of its points and numbers, is called a number line. The arrangement is a coordinate system for the line. Point O is said to be the origin of the coordinate system.

For any whole number you choose, you can add 1 to find its successor. For example, the successor of 5 is 6, and 110 is the successor of 109.

For any two numbers of the number line as developed here, the greater number is shown to the right. That is, 4 is to the right of 3, and 89 is to the right of 76.

The Integers [A]

In the number line of the preceding section, we now locate points A' (read A *prime*), B', C', $\cdots$ to the left of point O. The distance between A' and O is 1, but instead of assigning A' the coordinate 1, as we did for A, we assign it the coordinate -1 (read *negative 1*). This indicates that although both A' and A are 1 unit distance from O, they are on opposite sides of O. Similarly, we assign B', C', $\cdots$ the coordinates shown. ⌐See below

Insist that students use the correct nomenclature. This includes "Negative one" for -1, "Negative two" for -2, and so on.

7

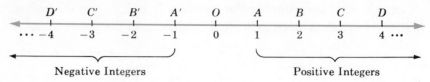

We now have a new set of numbers $\{\cdots, -2, -1, 0, 1, 2, \cdots\}$ known as the set of integers. We assign this set the name I. The numbers $\cdots, -3, -2,$ and -1 are called negative integers and the natural numbers $1, 2, 3, \cdots$ are called positive integers. Zero is neither positive nor negative. The negative integers are opposites of the positive integers and the positive integers are opposites of the negative integers. Zero is its own opposite. Notice that -1 is greater than -3, 0 is greater than -2, and so on.

The Rational Numbers [A]

Between any two successive integers, there are infinitely many numbers that are not integers. For example, between the integers 1 and 2, we can find such non-integer numbers as $\frac{4}{3}$, $\frac{6}{5}$ and $\sqrt{2}$.

The numbers $\frac{4}{3}$ and $\frac{6}{5}$ are rational numbers. A rational number is a number that can be expressed by a fraction whose numerator and denominator are integers and whose denominator is not zero. Not only are there infinitely many rational numbers between any two successive integers, the integers themselves are rational numbers. For example, since $2 = \frac{2}{1} = \frac{4}{2} = \frac{6}{3} = \cdots$, the integer 2 is a rational number. The graph of the set of rational numbers would consist of the points of the graph of the preceding section with infinitely many points between. Strange as it may seem, however, these points would not completely fill the line as we shall soon see.

The Irrational and the Real Numbers [A]

In the preceding section, we mentioned the non-integer number $\sqrt{2}$ that is not a rational number. $\sqrt{2}$ is an irrational number. That is, $\sqrt{2}$ cannot be expressed by a fraction whose numerator and denominator are integers. There are infinitely many such numbers.

The set composed of the rational and the irrational numbers is the set of real numbers. The graph of the set of real numbers completely fills the number line. Each real number corresponds to exactly one point of a line and each point of the line corresponds to exactly one real number.

See below

Be prepared for the inquiring student who says "What are numbers that are not real?" At this point your explanation must be very simple, but even if students do not completely understand your answer about imaginary numbers, it would be best to briefly mention and illustrate them.

Graphing a Set of Numbers [A]

To graph {1, 3, 5, 7}, we draw a number line and on it make dots for the points corresponding to the numbers 1, 3, 5, and 7. The set of black dots in the figure below is the graph of the set.

If we want to graph the set of all real numbers from 1 to 7, inclusive, we recall a statement that we made earlier—that when the complete set of real numbers is considered, there is a number to correspond to each point of the number line. Consequently, to graph the set of all real numbers from 1 to 7, inclusive, we make a solid black rule between, and including, the points for 1 and 7 on the number line.

To graph the set of all real numbers between 1 and 7, but not including 1 and 7, we draw circles around the points for 1 and 7 to show that the graphs of these points are excluded. The graph is shown below.

Sometimes a graph extends without end. But we cannot draw all of such a graph, so we extend the graph as far as convenient and make an arrowhead on the number line. This indicates that the graph continues without end in that direction. Thus, to graph the set of all natural numbers greater than 2, we make dots at the points representing 3, 4, 5, and so on, as far to the right as it is convenient to go. This is shown in graph **A** below. To graph the set of all real numbers less than 2, we draw a circle around the point for 2, then make a black rule as far to the left of the circle as convenient. This is shown in graph **B** below.

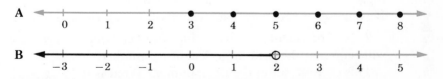

[A]

EXERCISES

1. Graph each of the following sets of numbers.

a. $\{1, 2, 3, 4, 5, 6, 7, 8\}$ **d.** $\{\frac{1}{3}, \frac{2}{3}, \frac{3}{3}, \frac{4}{3}, \frac{5}{3}, \frac{6}{3}, \frac{7}{3}\}$

b. $\{2, 4, 6, 8, 10\}$ **e.** $\{0, 3, 6, 9, 12\}$

c. $\{\frac{1}{2}, 1, \frac{3}{2}, 2, \frac{5}{2}, 3\}$ **f.** $\{1, 2, 3, 4, \cdots\}$

2. Graph the set of all

a. Natural numbers from 1 to 10, inclusive.

b. Natural numbers from 1 to 10, but not including the numbers 1 and 10.

c. Natural numbers greater than 1 and less than 7.

d. Real numbers greater than 1 and less than 7.

e. Real numbers greater than 1.

f. Real numbers greater than or equal to 0.

Variables [A]

A <u>numeral</u> is a symbol for a specific number. For example, the numeral 3 represents the number three.

In algebra it is often convenient to use a symbol for any number in a set of numbers. Thus, in the statement "x represents any whole number," we know that x can represent 0, 1, 2, or any other number in $\{0, 1, 2, 3, \cdots\}$. In this case we say that x is a <u>variable</u> and that $\{0, 1, 2, 3, \cdots\}$ is the <u>domain of the variable</u>. If c is a variable having the domain, $\{1, 3, 5\}$, then $2 + c$ can be replaced by $2 + 1, 2 + 3$, or $2 + 5$. If p is a variable having the domain $\{10, 20\}$, then $3\,p$ (meaning $3 \times p$) can be replaced by 3×10 or 3×20.

EXERCISES

[A]

1. If c represents the number of cents that a notebook costs, then $2\,c$ represents the number of cents that two notebooks cost. If notebooks at your school bookstore cost 10¢, 15¢, and 30¢, what will be the domain of c at your bookstore? If c represents 10¢, how many cents will be represented by $2\,c$? If c represents 30¢, how many cents will be represented by $2\,c$? $\{10, 15, 30\}; 20¢; 60¢.$

2. If n represents any counting number, what expression will represent the next larger counting number? $n+1$

This exercise states the domain of n. What is it? $\{1, 2, 3, \cdots\}$

10

3. If n represents any real number, what expression will represent the quotient when n is divided by 5? $n/5$

4. Choose a variable to represent the number of years in Kay's age. Using the variable, write the expression that will represent her age 5 years from now. Write the expression that will represent her age 8 years ago. We cannot advance from one birthday to the next without passing through all the fractional parts of a year; what do you think will be the domain of the variable that you have chosen, provided Kay lives to be exactly 75 years old? *$n+5$; $n-8$; the set of all real numbers from 0 to 75, incl.*

5. Susan has 20 more stamps than Janice. What variable would you choose to represent the number of stamps that Janice has? Using this variable, write an expression that will represent the number of stamps that Susan has. What is the smallest number of stamps that Janice may have? Is there a largest number that Janice may have? Assuming that Janice has only whole stamps in her collection, state the domain of the variable that you have chosen. *n; $n+20$; 0; no; $\{0,1,2,3,\ldots\}$*

Algebraic Expressions Containing Variables [A]

An <u>algebraic expression</u> is a numeral, a variable, or an arrangement of numerals, variables, and symbols of operation, such that, by replacing the variable of this expression by a member of the domain of the variable, we can name a specific number. Let c have the domain $\{1, 2, 3\}$. When 1, 2, and 3, in turn, replace c in $4 + c$, then $4 + c$ may be replaced by 5, 6, or 7.

c	$4 + c$
1	$4 + 1 = 5$
2	$4 + 2 = 6$
3	$4 + 3 = 7$

Of course, we need not always find the whole set determined by the variable. Thus, if we are interested only in the number represented by $4 + c$ when $c = 3$, we find only that number.

For the remainder of our work in this text, we shall use the word *expression* when we wish to refer to *algebraic expression*.

[A] **EXERCISES**

1. What will be the set determined by the phrase $4 + c$ if the variable c has the domain $\{5, 10, 15, 20\}$? *$\{9, 14, 19, 24\}$*

It is important for each student to develop a meaningful mathematical vocabulary. You can help by insisting upon correct usage of words.

ALGEBRA, BOOK ONE

2. If m has the domain $\{2, 4, 6, 8\}$, what set will be determined by $m - 2$? $\{0, 2, 4, 6\}$

3. If y is a variable having the domain $\{\frac{1}{5}, \frac{1}{4}, \frac{1}{3}, \frac{1}{2}\}$, what set will be determined by the phrase $6\,y$? $\{\frac{6}{5}, \frac{6}{4}, \frac{6}{3}, \frac{6}{2}\}$

4. If the domain of the variable n is the set of all natural numbers, what is the set determined by $4\,n$? $\{4, 8, 12, \cdots\}$

Review the vocabulary of numbers.

5. If a is a variable having the domain $\{1, 2, 3, 4, \cdots, 100\}$, what set will be determined by the phrase $a \div 5$? $\{\frac{1}{5}, \frac{2}{5}, \frac{3}{5}, \frac{4}{5}, \ldots, 20\}$

6. If t is a variable having the domain $\{1, 2, 3, 4\}$, find sets determined by the phrases

    a. 1 less than t $\{0, 1, 2, 3\}$
    b. 3 more than t $\{4, 5, 6, 7\}$
    c. t increased by 5 $\{6, 7, 8, 9\}$
    d. t divided by 2 $\{\frac{1}{2}, 1, \frac{3}{2}, 2\}$
    e. 2 divided by t $\{2, 1, \frac{2}{3}, \frac{1}{2}\}$
    f. the product of 6 and t $\{6, 12, 18, 24\}$

For each of the variables in Exercises 7–10 we have chosen one number from the domain of the variable. Find the numbers represented by the various expressions in each exercise when the variable represents the number selected.

7. If $a = 6$, $b = 2$, and $x = 4$, find the number represented by   See ①, top of page.

  a. $a + b$ 8   **c.** $4 - b$ 2   **e.** $a - x$ 2   **g.** $10 \div b$ 5
  b. $b + x$ 6   **d.** $5\,a$ 30   **f.** $6\,b$ 12   **h.** $\frac{1}{3}\,a$ 2

8. What is the number represented by $7\,x$ if $x = 6$? if $x = 10$? if $x = \frac{1}{2}$? if $x = 3\frac{1}{7}$? if $x = .2$? $42; 70; 3\frac{1}{2}; 22; 1.4$

9. If $m = 8$, $r = 3$, $k = \frac{1}{2}$, $e = .4$, find the number represented by   See ②, foot of page.

  a. $m - r$ 5   **c.** $m + r + k$ $11\frac{1}{2}$ **e.** $m - k$ $7\frac{1}{2}$ **g.** $\dfrac{m}{k}$ 16

  b. $r + k$ $3\frac{1}{2}$ **d.** $4 - r$ 1   **f.** $\frac{1}{2}\,r$ $1\frac{1}{2}$ **h.** $r - e$ 2.6

10. If $a = 0$, $b = 2$, $c = 3$, find the number represented by

  a. $4\,a$ 0   **c.** $b + c$ 5   **e.** $c - b$ 1   **g.** $a \div b$ 0

  b. $c - a$ 3   **d.** $3 \div c$ 1   **f.** $\dfrac{12}{c}$ 4   **h.** $10 - a$ 10

② Challenge thinking by saying "If $m = 8$ and $r = 10$, what meaning could you assign to exercise 9a?" Some will anticipate that the field of numbers to which they are accustomed must be enlarged to care for this contingency.

REPRESENTING NUMBERS AND NUMBER RELATIONS

Indicating Multiplication [A]

You have observed that in indicating a product containing a variable we frequently omit the multiplication symbol. For example, to write *7 times a* we may write *7 a*. Why can we not omit the multiplication symbol in a product that does not contain a variable,—for example, in the product 4 times 5?

When we want to use a multiplication symbol, but prefer not to use the usual ×, we may use a dot or parentheses. Thus, to write 2 × 3, we may write 2 · 3 or 2(3). In using the dot we must be careful to raise it above the line of writing so that it does not appear to be a decimal point. When we use the symbol × we must be careful to make it look different from the letter *x*.

[A]   **EXERCISES**

Write each of the following products in two other ways:

1. 4 × 5   **3.** 8 × *r*   **5.** *x* · *y*   **7.** 3(6)   **9.** *r* · *s*

2. *a* · *b*   **4.** 3 *h*   **6.** 4 *m*   **8.** 9 × *p*   **10.** 5(*a*)

answers above

Factors [A]   (See foot of page.)

When two or more numbers are multiplied, the numbers are factors of the product. Thus, since 3 × 5 = 15, 3 and 5 are factors of 15. Likewise, since 2 × 7½ = 15, we may say that 2 and 7½ are factors of 15. However, for the present we shall consider only factors that are whole numbers.

Coefficient [A]

Any factor, or factors, of a product is the coefficient of the remaining factor or factors. In the product 3 × 5 the number 3 is the coefficient of 5, and the number 5 is the coefficient of 3. In the product 4 *ab*, the number 4 is the coefficient of *ab*, 4 *b* is the coefficient of *a*, 4 *a* is the coefficient of *b*, and *ab* is the coefficient of 4.

If a variable has no coefficient written before it, the coefficient 1 is understood. Thus *x* means 1 *x*, *y* means 1 *y*, and *mn* means 1 *mn*.

[A]   **ORAL EXERCISES**

1. Name the factors of 6; of 10; of 21; of *bc*; of *abc*; of 8 *hk*.

2. In 4 *abc* what is the coefficient of *abc*? of *bc*? of 4 *a*? 4, 4a, bc

3. In the expression 4 *a* + 5 *b* + *c* what is the coefficient of *a*? of *b*? of *c*? 4; 5; 1.

You should frequently refer to and review the meaning of factors and coefficients.

13

ALGEBRA, BOOK ONE

The Meaning of Exponents [A]

The short way of writing $a \times a$ or aa is a^2. The small 2 written to the right of and a little above the a in the expression a^2 is called an exponent. An exponent tells how many times a number is used as a factor. The expression a^2 is read "a to the second power" or "a square." a^3 means $a \times a \times a$ and is read "a to the third power" or "a cube." Notice that a^3 means that three a's are to be multiplied together. If a figure or letter has no exponent written to the upper right of it, the exponent 1 is understood. Thus x means x^1 and 6 means 6^1.

In a product such as ay^3 the exponent 3 applies only to the letter or figure which it follows; that is, only the y is to be cubed. Thus ay^3 means $ayyy$.

$x \cdot x; 5 \times 5; 5 \cdot 25; m \times m; x \cdot x \cdot x; b \times b \times b \times b; c \times c \times c \times c \times c;$ [A]

ORAL EXERCISES

1. What is the meaning of x^2? of 5^2? of m^2? of x^3? of b^4? of c^5? of 8^3? of 6^4? $8 \times 8 \times 8$, or 512; $6 \times 6 \times 6 \times 6$, or 1296.

2. In the expression $4y^3$, which is to be cubed, the y or the $4y$? The y

3. What is the coefficient of x in the expression $4ax$? What is the exponent of x in this expression? $4a$; 1.

4. Tell how the following can be written using exponents:

a. xxx x^3 c. mm m^2 e. $2kk$ $2k^2$ g. $4xx$ $4x^2$

b. aa a^2 d. rrr r^3 f. $cccc$ c^4 h. $3xxx$ $3x^3$

5. What do the following expressions mean? $3 \times y \times y \times y \times y$

a. c^2 $c \times c$ c. p^4 $p \times p \times p \times p$ e. m^2n $m \times m \times n$ g. $3y^4$

b. m^3 $m \times m \times m$ d. k^5 $k \times k \times k \times k \times k$ f. m^2n^2 $m \times m \times n \times n$ h. $7 \cdot 10^3$ or 7000 $7 \times 10 \times 10 \times 10$

6. If the variable x has the domain $\{\frac{1}{2}, 1, \frac{3}{2}, 2, \frac{5}{2}, 3\}$, find the sets indicated by (answers below)

a. x^2 b. x^3 c. $3x^2$ d. $\frac{1}{2}x^2$ e. $4x^3$

⌐→ See second paragraph, top of page.

Order of Operations [A]

To this point we have considered expressions that involve only one of the operations: addition, subtraction, multiplication, and division. But, of course, two or more of these operations may be involved in the same expression. For example, the expression $8 + 6 \div 2$ involves both addition and division. This expression designates a

6. a. $\{\frac{1}{4}, 1, \frac{9}{4}, 4, \frac{25}{4}, 9\}$.   b. $\{\frac{1}{8}, 1, \frac{27}{8}, 8, \frac{125}{8}, 27\}$.

14   c. $\{\frac{3}{4}, 3, \frac{27}{4}, 12, \frac{75}{4}, 27\}$.   d. $\{\frac{1}{8}, \frac{1}{2}, \frac{9}{8}, 2, \frac{25}{8}, \frac{9}{2}\}$.

e. $\{\frac{1}{2}, 4, \frac{27}{2}, 32, \frac{125}{2}, 108\}$

REPRESENTING NUMBERS AND NUMBER RELATIONS

number. The question is: which number? If we do the division first, we have $8 + 6 \div 2 = 8 + 3 = 11$. If we do the addition first, we have $8 + 6 \div 2 = 14 \div 2 = 7$. Unless we decide upon an order in which operations are to be performed, we shall never be sure which number is represented by such an expression. Mathematicians agree on the following:

In a series of operations

1. First perform the multiplications and divisions in the order given.

2. Then perform the additions and subtractions in the order given.

Having accepted this agreement, we are forced to conclude that the expression $8 + 6 \div 2$ represents the number 11.

Symbols of Grouping [A]

When we want to emphasize that a particular operation is to be ① performed first, even contrary to the usual order of operations, we use parentheses ( ), brackets [ ], or bars _____ much as we use punctuation marks. For example, when we write $\dfrac{2+19}{3}$ we indicate that we want the number represented by $2 + 19$ to be divided by 3. Thus we indicate that we want to break away from the usual procedure of performing divisions before additions. Since $2 + 19 = 21$, the expression $\dfrac{2+19}{3}$ really represents $\dfrac{21}{3}$ or 7.

In the expression $\dfrac{18}{7+2}$ the bar appears above $7 + 2$ to indicate that 18 is to be divided by the number represented by $7 + 2$. Thus $\dfrac{18}{7+2} = \dfrac{18}{9} = 2$.

When we write $4(2 + 3)$ we indicate that the sum $(2 + 3)$ is to be found first, and then this sum is to be multiplied by 4. Thus $4(2+3) = 4(5) = 20$. In this case, unlike those above, we obtain the same ② result if we reverse the order of operations. Nothing is wrong. It happens to be true that reversing the order of operations sometimes changes the result and sometimes does not. We shall consider this matter more carefully on page 19.

② Later, you may refer to this discussion when students make the error: $4(2 + a) = 8 + a$.

15

ALGEBRA, BOOK ONE = 3 + 3   This is preferable to a continued one-line solu-
= 6   tion. The replacements are more easily traced.

Brackets are usually reserved for use in complicated expressions involving two or more sets of parentheses. For example, $9 - [(6 + 1) - (8 - 3)]$ means that we are first to find the one number represented by $[(6 + 1) - (8 - 3)]$, then subtract this number from 9. Since $(6 + 1) - (8 - 3) = 7 - 5 = 2$, we see that we are to subtract 2 from 9. Thus the expression $9 - [(6 + 1) - (8 - 3)] = 9 - 2 = 7$.

EXERCISES

[A]

Find the numbers represented by each of the following expressions.   (See ①, top of page.)

1. $4 \times 3 + 1$ *13*

2. $3 + 6 \div 2$ *6*

3. $10 \div 5 + 4$ *6*

4. $4 \div 4 + 4$ *5*

5. $5 - 2 \times 2$ *1*

6. $9 + 5 \div 2$ *11½*

7. $100 - (5 \times 12)$ *40*

8. $80 \div (12 + 4)$ *5*

9. $8 \div 2 + 6 \times 2$ *16*

10. $\dfrac{8 + 7 - 5}{3}$ *3⅓*

11. $\dfrac{40 - 10}{9 + 6}$ *2*

12. $(4 + 5) + (3 + 2)$ *14*

13. $(6 + 7) - (1 + 4)$ *8*

14. $4(6 + 2)$ *32*

15. $3(18 - 2)$ *48*

16. $(6 + 2) \div 4$ *2*

17. $(7 + 8 + 10) \div 5$ *5*

18. $12 + 2(3 + 4)$ *26*

19. $30 - 2(11 - 7)$ *22*

20. $8 - [(2 + 3) - (4 + 1)]$

8

The Closure Properties [A]

Suppose that our number system consisted of only {1, 2, 3}. In this case could you find the number represented by $1 + 3$? You could not because {1, 2, 3} does not contain 4. Could you find $1 + 2$? $2 + 3$? Could you find 2(3)? 1(2)? 3(1)? When we consider the set of all real numbers, however, addition and multiplication are always possible. To express this fact we choose two variables a and b to represent any two real numbers and write:

When a and b are real numbers, $a + b$ is a real number.

When a and b are real numbers, ab is a real number.

We call the first of these properties the closure property of addition and the second the closure property of multiplication. The word "closure" indicates that we may figuratively close the door on the set of numbers being considered—in other words we need not go outside the set to find the sum or product.

16   Have the class make up other illustrations of the closure property. For example, "Is the set of natural numbers closed under subtraction? under division? Why or why not?"

REPRESENTING NUMBERS AND NUMBER RELATIONS

The Addition and Multiplication Properties of Zero and One [A]

You know that $1 + 0 = 1$, $2 + 0 = 2$, and $100 + 0 = 100$. Since the sum of zero and any number is the number, we say:

If a is a real number, $a + 0 = a$.

We call this property the addition property of zero. Since adding zero to any number leaves the number identically as it was, we sometimes speak of zero as the identity element for addition.

You know that $1(0) = 0$, $2(0) = 0$, and so on, for the product of any number and zero. We call this property the multiplication property of zero. To express this property in symbols we write:

If a is a real number, $a(0) = 0$.

You know that $2(1) = 2$, $3(1) = 3$, and so on, for the product of any number and 1. We call this property the multiplication property of 1. To express the property in symbols we write:

If a is a real number, $a(1) = a$.

Since multiplying a number by 1 leaves the number identically as it was, we say that 1 is the identity element for multiplication.

Some Properties of Addition and Multiplication [A]

You know that $3 + 4 = 4 + 3$, $5 + 9 = 9 + 5$, $6 + \frac{1}{2} = \frac{1}{2} + 6$, and so on, for any two of the numbers that you have studied thus far. We sometimes state this characteristic of addition by saying:

The order in which two numbers are added does not affect the sum.

We say that this characteristic of addition is a property of addition. We call this particular property the commutative property of addition. The word commute means to interchange. Why do you think the word commutative is used for this property?

Actually, the commutative property of addition (and the other properties that you will study in this chapter) are properties for not only the real numbers that you have studied, but for all real numbers. If we choose two variables a and b to represent any two members of the set of all real numbers, we may state the commutative property of addition in symbols as follows:

If a and b are real numbers, $a + b = b + a$.

The properties here discussed are a very important part of the structure of mathematics. It is essential not to consider them a "topic" of Chapter 1, but to tie to them every possible subsequent process.

ALGEBRA, BOOK ONE

Since $2 \times 3 = 3 \times 2$, $\frac{1}{4} \times \frac{4}{5} = \frac{4}{5} \times \frac{1}{4}$, and so on, for any two of the real numbers, we may choose two variables a and b to represent any two members of the set of real numbers, and then state:

If a and b are any two real numbers, $ab = ba$.

We call this property the commutative property of multiplication. Try stating this property in words.

If you are given the exercise $2 + 4 + 7$, you may think, $(2 + 4) + 7 = 6 + 7 = 13$, or you may think, $2 + (4 + 7) = 2 + 11 = 13$. Since the sum is 13 in both cases, we agree that $(2 + 4) + 7 = 2 + (4 + 7)$. Since similar statements can be made for any three real numbers that are to be added, we may let a, b, and c represent any three real numbers, and state:

If a, b, and c are real numbers, $(a + b) + c = a + (b + c)$.

We call this property the associative property of addition. Why do you think this property is said to be associative?

Since $(3 \times 2) \times 7 = 3 \times (2 \times 7)$, $(\frac{1}{2} \times 2) \times \frac{1}{4} = \frac{1}{2} \times (2 \times \frac{1}{4})$, and so on, for any three real numbers, we may choose three variables a, b, and c to represent any three real numbers and write:

If a, b, and c are real numbers, $(ab)c = a(bc)$.

We call this property of multiplication the associative property of multiplication.

EXERCISES

See ① below. [A]

1. Use the commutative property of addition to complete each of the following statements:

a. $3 + 2 = ? + ?$ $2+3$
b. $\frac{1}{2} + \frac{1}{3} = ? + ?$ $\frac{1}{3}+\frac{1}{2}$
c. $4 + 0 = ? + ?$ $0+4$
d. $x + y = ? + ?$ $y+x$
e. $4a + 6 = ? + ?$ $6+4a$
f. $(a + 3) + (c + 5) = ? + ?$ $(c+5)+(a+3)$

2. Use the commutative property of multiplication to express each of the following multiplications in another form:

a. $3 \times 9 = ?$ 9×3
b. $4(\frac{1}{2}) = ?$ $(\frac{1}{2})(4)$
c. $ab = ?$ ba
d. $2a^2 \cdot a = ?$ $a(2a^2)$
e. $(a + 3)2 = ?$ $2(a+3)$
f. $(2 + 1)(3 + 5) = ?$ $(3+5)(2+1)$

3. Use the associative law of addition to find each of the following sums in two ways:

a. $2 + 7 + 1$ 10
b. $9 + 8 + 2$ 19
c. $\frac{1}{3} + \frac{1}{2} + \frac{1}{4}$ $\frac{13}{12}$
d. $7 + \frac{1}{3} + \frac{2}{3}$ 8

18 ① These are good exercises for class discussion. Encourage students to make up other illustrations.

4. Use the associative law of multiplication to find each product in two ways:

a. $2 \times 5 \times 7$ **b.** $4 \times 3 \times 6$ **c.** $5 \times \frac{1}{5} \times 3$ **d.** $\frac{1}{4} \times \frac{1}{3} \times \frac{1}{2}$

[handwritten: 70 above a, 72 above b, 3 above c, 24 above d]

An eighth property of addition and multiplication combines these operations. Let us consider the expression $4(2 + 3)$. If we follow the usual order of first finding the number enclosed by the parentheses, we have $4(5)$, a product which we know is 20. If, however, we find $4(2) + 4(3)$, we obtain $8 + 12$, a sum which is 20. Thus we see that $4(2 + 3) = 4(2) + 4(3)$. In the expression on the left we consider $(2 + 3)$ as a single number which is to be multiplied by 4. In the expression on the right we consider 2 and 3 as a pair of numbers each to be multiplied by 4 and the products added. On the right we distribute the multiplication throughout the addition. Hence we call this property the distributive property of multiplication over addition, or simply the distributive property.

Since the distributive property holds for the addition and multiplication of any three real numbers, we may choose three variables a, b, and c, then write:

If a, b, and c are real numbers, $a(b + c) = ab + ac$.

We may also write the distributive property in the form $(b + c)a = ba + ca$. To see how this is possible, let us recall that

By the distributive property as first stated,

$$a(b + c) = ab + ac$$

By the commutative property, $a(b + c) = (b + c)a$, $ab = ba$, and $ac = ca$. Therefore we may write

$$(b + c)a = ba + ca$$

You may assume that the distributive property holds for subtraction. Thus, if a, b, and c are any real numbers,

$$a(b - c) = ab - ac.$$

[A]   **EXERCISES**

1. Write each of the following indicated products as an indicated sum. *Example:* $2(r + t) = 2r + 2t$.

a. $3(1 + 2)$ *[handwritten: 3+6]*   **d.** $a(4 + a)$ *[handwritten: 4a+a²]*   **g.** $(6 + y)y$ *[handwritten: 6y+y²]*

b. $4(3 + s)$ *[handwritten: 12+4s]*   **e.** $(x + 2)x$ *[handwritten: x²+2x]*   **h.** $4xy(x + y)$ *[handwritten: 4x²y+4xy²]*

c. $\frac{1}{2}(8 + 6)$ *[handwritten: 4+3]*   **f.** $x^2(3x + x)$ *[handwritten: 3x³+x³]*   **i.** $5mn(m + 3)$ *[handwritten: 5m²n+15mn]*

① Note that a thorough understanding of the distributive law unifies the inverse processes of multiplying and factoring. When students reach Chapter 12— Special Products and Factoring, they will already know much about it and proceed to study this important chapter more meaningfully.

19

① Note the careful use of the word *numeral* rather than *number*. Remind students that a numeral is a name for a number, not the number itself. Some modern programs are very insistent on this distinction.

ALGEBRA, BOOK ONE

2. Write each of the following indicated sums as an indicated product. *Example:* $2\,a + 2\,b = 2(a + b)$.

a. $3(2) + 3(5)$ $3(2+5)$ **d.** $\frac{1}{3}(6) + \frac{1}{3}(9)$ $\frac{1}{3}(6+9)$ **g.** $ar + as$ $a(r+s)$

b. $2(7) + 2(9)$ $2(7+9)$ **e.** $3\,a + 3(4)$ $3(a+4)$ **h.** $x + bx$ $x(1+b)$

c. $2\,a + 3\,a$ $a(2+3)$ **f.** $2\,x + 2\,y$ $2(x+y)$ **i.** $2\,m + m^2$ $m(2+m)$

3. When Jim was given the exercise $25(6) + 25(4)$, he rewrote the exercise as $25(6 + 4)$. Will the rewriting cause Jim to get the wrong answer? No Why? *Distr. prop.*

4. State the property illustrated by each of the following:

a. $(9 + 4) + 1 = 9 + (4 + 1)$ *Assoc. Prop. of Addition*

b. $3(5) = (5)3$ *Comm. Prop. of Mult.*

c. $(2 \times 5) \times 7 = 2 \times (5 \times 7)$ *Assoc. Prop. of Mult.*

d. $2(3 + 4) = 2(3) + 2(4)$ *Distr. Prop.*

e. $9 + a = a + 9$ *Comm. Prop. of Addition*

f. $(a + b)c = c(a + b)$ *Comm. Prop. of Mult.*

g. $(2+3)+(6+1)=(6+1)+(2+3)$ *Comm. Prop. of Addition*

h. $(5 + 1)(3 + 7) = (3 + 7)(5 + 1)$ *Comm. Prop. of Mult.*

i. $a(6 + 3) = (6 + 3)a$ *Comm. Prop. of Mult.*

j. $2(9) + 2(8) = 2(9 + 8)$ *Distr. Prop.*

5. Replace each ? by a numeral to make the statement true.

a. $6(2 + 3) = 6(?) + 6(?)$ (2, 3)

b. $(4 + 2) + 1 = ? + (2 + 1)$ (4)

c. $?(5) + ?(2) = 4(5 + 2)$ (4, 4)

d. $(6 + 8)? = 2\,(?) + 2\,(?)$ (2, 6, 8)

Subtraction and Division of Real Numbers [A]

We have said much about addition and multiplication but have hardly mentioned subtraction and division. This is because we define subtraction in terms of addition, and division in terms of multiplication. We say that $a - b = d$ means $a = b + d$ and $a \div b = q$ means $a = b \times q$.

Terms of a Polynomial [A]

A monomial is a number, a variable, or a product of a number and one or more variables. For example, 7, 5 a, and xyz are monomials. Note that xyz is the product of the number 1 and the variables x, y, and z. (See **Coefficient**, page 13.) The sum of two monomials is a binomial: For example, $2 + 3\,ab$. The sum of three monomials is a trinomial: For example, $4\,x^2 + 3\,x + 7$. All monomials, binomials, trinomials, and sums of four or more monomials are polynomials. Exponents in a monomial must be nonnegative integers.

Each monomial in a polynomial is a term of the polynomial. Thus, the polynomial $7\,a + b$ has the two terms $7\,a$ and b.

20

It is important to distinguish between terms and factors. Fuzzy thinking on this distinction leads to grave errors later. Ask many questions such as, "In the expressions $3ab$ and $3a + b$ is $3a$ a term or a factor? Why?"

Note how the explanation of combining like terms by the commutative and distributive properties puts these principles to work and helps students see why they could not possibly say that $4x + 5y = 9xy$. Certainly it would be a waste of time to have all exercises completely written out step by

REPRESENTING NUMBERS AND NUMBER RELATIONS   (cont. below)

Like Terms[A]

Terms that contain the same variables to the same powers are called <u>like terms</u>. Thus, in the polynomial $2 x^2 + 3 x^2 + 7 x$, $2 x^2$ and $3 x^2$ are like terms. $7 x$ is unlike $2 x^2$ or $3 x^2$.

Like terms may be combined. For example, to find $2 x^2 + 3 x^2$, we use the distributive property to write $2 x^2 + 3 x^2 = (2 + 3)x^2 = 5 x^2$. Similarly, to find $7 a - 4 a$, we write $7 a - 4 a = (7 - 4)a = 3 a$.

When three or more terms are to be combined we use the associative property of addition. Thus $7 m + 4 m + m = (7 m + 4 m) + m$. By the distributive property, $7 m + 4 m = (7 + 4)m = 11 m$. Hence $(7 m + 4 m) + m = 11 m + m = (11 + 1)m = 12 m$.

By combining like terms we may simplify polynomials. For example, to simplify $4 r + 3 s + 7 r + 2 s + 6$, we may use the commutative property of addition to write $4 r + 3 s + 7 r + 2 s + 6 = 4 r + 7 r + 3 s + 2 s + 6$. Now applying the distributive property we have $4 r + 7 r + 3 s + 2 s + 6 = (4 + 7) r + (3 + 2) s + 6 = 11 r + 5 s + 6$.

When you are combining like terms, you probably will not write all the steps as we have been describing them, but you should be able to write them when called upon to do so.

[A]   **EXERCISES**

Simplify by combining like terms:

1. $4 h + 5 h$ *9h*
2. $2 f + 3 f$ *5f*
3. $9 k - 2 k$ *7k*
4. $6 m - 2 m$ *4m*
5. $5 c - c$ *4c*
6. $4 g + 5 g - 6 g$ *3g*
7. $3 xy + 6 x^2 + 10 x^2$ *3xy+16x²*
8. $x^2 + 7 x^2 + 10$ *8x²+10*

9. $3 b + 5 p + 6 b$ *9b+5p*
10. $a + b + c - b$ *a+c*
11. $2 a + 5 b - 2 a + 5 b$ *10b*
12. $4 x^3 + 5 x^2 - 2 x^2 + x^2$ *4x³+4x²*
13. $10 + m - 6 + m$ *4+2m*
14. $5 a^2 + a + 1 - a$ *5a²+1*
15. $x^2 + 3 x^2 - 4 x^2$ *0*
16. $x^2 + 16 x + x^2 - 10 x$ *2x²+6x*

[B]

Simplify:

17. $12 x^2 + 3 xy + 7 y^2 - 3 y^2 + x^2$ *13x²+3xy+4y²*
18. $1.2 x + 5.6 x + 13.2 x - 4.5 x$ *15.5X*
19. $\frac{1}{2} x + \frac{1}{3} y - \frac{1}{3} x + \frac{5}{6} y$ *⅙x+⁷⁄₆y*
20. $\frac{2}{5} x + \frac{1}{15} y - \frac{1}{10} x + \frac{7}{15} y + .8 x$ *¹¹⁄₁₀x+⁸⁄₁₅y*
21. $40 a^3 + 6 a^2 - 25 a^3 + 10 - 4 a^2$ *15a³+2a²+10*
22. $1.3 a - .3 a - .7 a + a + 6 a$ *7.3a*

ALGEBRA, BOOK ONE

Evaluating an Algebraic Expression [A]

The number which an expression represents is its value. What is the value of the expression $a + b$ if $a = 4$ and $b = 3$? We call the process of finding the value of an expression <u>evaluation</u>. The following examples show you how to evaluate some expressions a little more difficult than any you have been studying.

Example 1. Find the value of $3 x^2 y$ if $x = 5$ and $y = 2$.

Solution. $3 x^2 y = 3(5)^2(2) = 3(25)(2) = 150$

Example 2. Find the value of $26 - y^2$ if $y = 3$.

Solution. $26 - y^2 = 26 - 3^2 = 26 - 9 = 17$

①

Example 3. Evaluate $4 x^3 - 2 xy$ if $x = 3$ and $y = 5$.

Solution.
$$4 x^3 - 2 xy$$
$$= 4(3)^3 - 2(3)(5)$$
$$= 108 - 30 = 78$$

Observe that we find products and quotients before we find sums and differences, unless there are bars, parentheses, or brackets to indicate a different order.

Example 4. Find the value of $\dfrac{x^2 - x + 5}{2}$ when $x = 3$.

Solution. In this example the numerator, $x^2 - x + 5$, is to be divided by 2.

②

Then $\quad \dfrac{x^2 - x + 5}{2} = \dfrac{9 - 3 + 5}{2} = \dfrac{11}{2} = 5\frac{1}{2}$

EXERCISES

[A]

If $x = 4$ and $y = 5$, find the value of

1. $\frac{1}{4} x^2$ 4

4. $x^2 y$ 80

7. $2 x^2 - y^2$ 7

2. $10 y^2$ 250

5. $5 x^2 y$ 400

8. $y^2 + 10$ 35

3. $6 y^2$ 150

6. xy^2 100

9. $30 - x^2$ 14

If $a = 3$, $b = 2$, and $c = 4$, evaluate

10. $2 b^2 + 10$ 18

13. $a^2 + b^2 + c^2$ 29

16. $3 bc - 24$ 0

11. $(ab)^2$ 36

14. $29 - abc$ 5

17. $3 b^2 + 5 a$ 27

12. $a^3 - b^2$ 23

15. $c^2 - ab$ 10

18. $2 c^2 - cb$ 24

22 ① Other values could be assigned the variables as a way of relating this lesson to that of page 11.

② Remind students that the bar is a symbol of grouping. Review pages 14–15 before assigning these exercises.

① You will find Exs. 28 and 29 excellent review of common and decimal fractions.

REPRESENTING NUMBERS AND NUMBER RELATIONS

If $x = 6$, $y = 3$, and $h = 2$, find the value of

19. $\dfrac{2x^2 + xy}{3}$ *30*   **22.** $\dfrac{x}{y} + \dfrac{10}{h}$ *7*   **25.** $\dfrac{2xy}{h} + (hy)$ *24*

20. $\dfrac{x^2 - hy}{9}$ *$3\frac{1}{3}$*   **23.** $\dfrac{h^2 + y^2}{x}$ *$2\frac{1}{6}$*   **26.** $\dfrac{2x^2}{3} + \dfrac{4y}{3}$ *28*

21. $h(2x - y)$ *18*   **24.** $3x^2y - 5h^3$ *284*   **27.** $\dfrac{1}{x} + \dfrac{1}{y} - \dfrac{1}{2h}$ *$\frac{1}{4}$*

28. Solve exercises 19–27 by letting $x = \frac{1}{2}$, $y = \frac{1}{3}$, and $h = \frac{1}{4}$.

29. Solve exercises 19–27 by letting $x = .5$, $y = .2$, and $h = .1$.

[A]

ORAL EXERCISES

1. If n stands for a certain number, how many n's will stand for a number 3 times as large? *3*

2. If x represents the number of years in Henry's age and Frank is twice as old as Henry, how can you represent Frank's age in terms of x? *$2x$*

3. The length of a rectangle is four times its width. If w stands for its width, how can you represent its length in terms of w? *$4w$*

4. If x stands for the number of years in Amy's age, what will stand for the number of years in her age 5 years from now? for the number of years in her age 8 years ago? *$x+5$* *$x-8$*

5. Janice has 6 times as many stamps as Eunice. Let x stand for the number of stamps that Eunice has. What will stand for the number of stamps that Janice has? *$6x$*

6. Charles is 6 years older than Henry. If x stands for the number of years in Henry's age, how can you represent Charles's age? *$x+6$*

7. The difference of two numbers is 7. If y represents the smaller, how can you represent the larger? *$y+7$*

8. The difference of two numbers is 4. If the larger is s, what is the smaller? *$s-4$*

9. A boy has 5 times as many nickels as dimes.

Let $x =$ the number of dimes the boy has.
Then $\_\_?\_$ *$5x$* $=$ the number of nickels the boy has.

28. $\frac{2}{9}$
.1
$\frac{1}{54}$
$\frac{1}{6}$
$41\frac{1}{2}$
$\frac{25}{72}$
$\frac{11}{64}$
① *$1\frac{5}{12}$*
↑ *$\frac{11}{18}$*

29. *0.2*
$0.02\frac{5}{9}$
0.08
102.5
0.1
0.145
2.02
$0.4\frac{1}{3}$
2

23

① Train your class to use chapter summaries as a study guide for self-analysis of their knowledge. These summaries can be used throughout the year when more extensive reviews are required. Chapter 1 has laid an important foundation for the vocabulary and structure of algebra. If your class is still uncertain about parts of this work, do not hurry on until difficulties are cleared up.

ALGEBRA, BOOK ONE

Checking Your Understanding of Chapter 1

If you expect to do well in algebra, it is important that you understand each step before you attempt the next one. Before you start Chapter 2, you should be sure that you know:

These pages will help you review.

9. How to spell and use the following words correctly:

24

REPRESENTING NUMBERS AND NUMBER RELATIONS

[A]

CHAPTER REVIEW

$\{1, 2, 3, 4, \dots, 9\}$

1. Write the set of all counting numbers less than 10.

2. Write the subset of all even numbers in $\{1, 2, 3, 4, 5\}$. $\{2, 4\}$

3. Make a graph of the set of all natural numbers less than 4.

4. Make a graph of the set of all real numbers greater than 5.

5. Make a graph of the set of all real numbers between 1 and 8, inclusive.

6. If c is a variable representing the value in cents of the different U. S. coins minted today, what is the domain of c? $\{1, 5, 10, 25, 50\}$

7. If n represents a counting number, what will represent the next larger counting number? $n+1$

8. If the variable t has the domain 1, $\frac{1}{2}$, 2, $\frac{3}{2}$, write the sets determined by: $\{1, 2, \frac{1}{2}, \frac{2}{3}\}$

a. $t + 2$ **b.** $4t$ **c.** t^2 **d.** $\dfrac{1}{t}$

$\{3, 2\frac{1}{2}, 4, 3\frac{1}{2}\}$ $\{4, 2, 8, 6\}$ $\{1, \frac{1}{4}, 4, \frac{9}{4}\}$

9. What is the name of the 2 in the expression $5\ x^2$? *Exponent*

10. Name the factors of 10; of 15; of ab. $5, 2; 5, 3; a, b.$

11. In the expression $3\ ab$. what is the coefficient of b? $3a$ of ab? 3

12. Find the numbers represented by:

a. $3(5) + 2$ 17 **c.** $\dfrac{14}{2 + 5}$ 2 **e.** $\dfrac{4 + 11}{3}$ 5

b. $4(3)^2 + 6(4)$ 60 **d.** $3(18 - 2)$ 48 **f.** $(6 + 3)2$ 18

13. Find: $(\frac{1}{2})(\frac{2}{3})(\frac{975}{7})(0)$. 0

14. Name the property of addition or multiplication illustrated by each of the expressions below.

a. $a + 2 = 2 + a$ *Comm. Prop. of Add.*
e. $\frac{5}{2}(\frac{2}{2}) = \frac{5}{2}$ *Mult. Prop. of 1*

b. $(a + 2) + 3 = a + (2 + 3)$ *Assoc. Prop. of Add.*
f. $4\ a + 5\ a = (4 + 5)a$ *Distr. Prop.*

c. $4(x + 1) = 4\ x + 4$ *Distr. Prop.*
g. $3(6 + m) = (6 + m)3$ *Comm. Prop. of Mult.*

d. $4(0) = 0$ *Mult. Prop. of Zero*
h. $4(3\ a) = (4 \cdot 3)a$ *Ass. Prop. of Mult.*

25

① Do not use the printed text tests as class examinations. Students soon catch on and do these exercises ahead of time. They are excellent as review assignments or for classroom practice.

In constructing your own examinations, sample the entire chapter, testing for understanding of **ALGEBRA, BOOK ONE** principles. Do not construct a test which is purely manipulative. Insist that all work be shown on test paper.

15. Simplify by combining like terms:

a. $4 x^2 + 8 x^2$ $12x^2$

c. $2 x^3 + 6 x^2 + 7 x^2 + x^3$ $3x^3 + 13x^2$

b. $5 x + 3 y + 7 x$ $12x + 3y$

d. $2 a + 3 b + c + 5 a$ $7a + 3b + c$

16. If $x = 6$ and $y = 4$, find the value of

a. x^2 36 **d.** $4 y^2$ 64 **g.** y^3 64 **j.** $x^2 - y^2$ 20

b. $3 x^2$ 108 **e.** x^3 216 **h.** $2 y^3$ 128 **k.** $xy - 4$ 20

c. y^2 16 **f.** $4 x^3$ 864 **i.** $2 x - 3 y$ 0 **l.** $y^2 - x$ 10

17. Write the following, using the symbols of algebra:

a. The sum of a and b $a + b$ **d.** The product of c and 6 $6c$

b. The square of a a^2 **e.** 10 less than h $h - 10$

c. Twice the square of a $2a^2$ **f.** a divided by m $\frac{a}{m}$

18. If $x = 5$ and $y = 3$, find the value of

a. $\dfrac{8 + xy}{10}$ $2\frac{3}{10}$ **b.** $\dfrac{x^2 y - xy^2}{6}$ 5 **c.** $\dfrac{2 x^3 - 33}{7}$ 31

19. If $a = 7$, $b = 1$, and $c = 2$, find the value of

a. $c + (a + b)$ 10 **c.** $2 b(a - b)$ 12 **e.** $(2 a + b) \div c$ $7\frac{1}{2}$

b. $a + (b + c)$ 10 **d.** $10 - (a - b)$ 4 **f.** $32 \div (9 b + 7)$ 2

CHAPTER TEST

1. Write the set of all counting numbers less than 5. $\{1, 2, 3, 4\}$

2. Write the subset of even numbers in $\{1, 2, 3, 4, 5\}$ $\{2, 4\}$

3. Name the factors of rs. r, s

4. In $4 y + 2$ what is the coefficient of y? 4

5. Write $7\ aaa$ using an exponent. $7a^3$

6. Find the value of $6 a^2$ if $a = 3$. 54

7. Combine like terms: $x^2 + 4 x + 2 x^2 + 3 x$. $3x^2 + 7x$

8. Evaluate $x^2 + y^2 - 10$ when $x = 6$ and $y = 3$. 35

9. Find the number expressed by $4 + [(5 + 3) - 2]$. 10

10. Graph the set of real numbers greater than 2.

11. Graph the set of all counting numbers less than 5.

12. Evaluate $3(x - 2)$ when $x = 9$. 21

13. If $x = 5$ and $y = 2$, find the value of $\dfrac{4 + xy}{7}$. 2

14. What property of addition is illustrated by
$$(a + b) + c = a + (b + c)?\ associative$$

Hold students to good presentation by reducing the grade when necessary. (Separate test pamphlets may be purchased from the publisher.)

By now you should have given at least three short class tests (unannounced) and one main examination (announced) on the chapter.

This test was prepared to help you recall some words whose meaning you should know in this course.

On your paper write one word or number, and only one, for each blank to make each of the following statements true:

1. The __?__ of 5 and 6 is 11. **3.** The __?__ of 4 and 9 is 36.

2. The __?__ of 40 and 4 is 10. **4.** The __?__ of 8 and 6 is 2.

Exercises 5–14 refer to the problems below.

361	123	425	67
144	962	13	72)4824
217	728	1275	432
	1813	425	504
		5525	504

5. The dividend is __?__. **10.** The subtrahend is __?__.

6. The multiplier is __?__. **11.** The difference is __?__.

7. 361 is the __?__. **12.** The divisor is __?__.

8. The multiplicand is __?__. **13.** 1813 is the __?__.

9. 123, 962, and 728 are __?__. **14.** The quotient is __?__.

15. 5% means 5 __?__.

16. Interest is money paid for the use of __?__.

17. 0.7 is a __?__ fraction.

18. The denominator of $\frac{3}{4}$ is __?__.

19. A numeral is a symbol for a __?__.

20. In the fraction $\frac{3}{4}$, 3 is the __?__.

● Check your answers with those below. If you do not make 100% on the test, try the test each week until you make a perfect score.

Answers

1. sum
2. quotient
3. product
4. difference
5. 4824
6. 13
7. minuend
8. 425
9. addends
10. 144
11. 217
12. 72
13. sum
14. 67
15. hundredths
16. money
17. decimal
18. 4
19. number
20. numerator

Friend Doug;

Is it ever cold up here —30° below yesterday! But man, it's a great life. You feel a sense of excitement and urgency. I even feel important — as if I'm doing something for the human race. I know that sounds corny, but that's it

And you'll never believe this! I've decided to go back to school next fall. At last I see the importance of an education. The idea of designing a new oil rig or figuring how and where to drill to get the most oil for the fewest dollars really grabs me. Even though I'm only a glorified "water boy" now, it won't always be that way.

I'll see you next fall if I don't freeze before then.

As always,

Pete

ARCTIC OCEAN

North Slope

Prudhoe Bay

U.S.S.R.

TRANS-ALASKA

ALASKA

Fairbanks

CANADA

PIPELINE

Valdez

BERING SEA

Gulf of Alaska

0   200   400

Scale in Miles

2

Sentences

Suggested Time Schedule
9 days

In this chapter you will learn how to express number relations with sentences.

SENTENCES

Equations and Inequalities [A]

You know that the numeral 3 represents the number three. More-over, you know that the expressions $2 + 1$, $12 - 9$, $15 \div 5$, $1 + 1 + 1$, $14 - (3 + 8)$, and so on, also represent the number three.

Two expressions that represent the same number are said to be equal and two expressions that represent different numbers are said to be unequal. We use the symbol "$=$" to mean "is" or "is equal to," and the symbol "$\neq$" to mean "is not" or "is not equal to."

Thus $12 - 9 = 15 \div 5$ because both $12 - 9$ and $15 \div 5$ represent the same number.

Likewise, $12 - 9 \neq 4$ because $12 - 9$ and 4 designate different numbers.

A sentence stating that two expressions represent the same number is called an <u>equation</u> and a sentence stating that two expressions repre-sent different numbers is called an <u>inequality</u>.

Even though such a sentence as $2 + 1 = 4$ makes a false statement, it is called an equation because it states that the two expressions $2 + 1$ and 4 represent the same number. Likewise, even though such a sentence as $3 + 1 \neq 4$ makes a false statement, it is called an in-equality because it states that the two expressions $3 + 1$ and 4 repre-sent different numbers.

The two expressions in an equation or inequality are called <u>mem-bers</u> of the equation or inequality. Thus $2 + 5$ and 7 are members of the equation $2 + 5 = 7$.

[A]

EXERCISES

Study each of the following sentences; then state
(a) whether the sentence is an equation or an inequality, and
(b) whether the sentence makes a true statement or a false statement.

1. $4 + 3 = 2 + 5$ *Equ., T*

2. $6 + 1 = 4 + 9$ *Equ., F*

3. $2 + 8 \neq 6 + 1$ *Inequ., T*

4. $9 + 4 \neq 10 + 2$ *Inequ., T*

5. $3^2 = 6$ *Equ., F*

6. $2 + 1.4 = 1.2 + 2.5$ *Equ., F*

7. $8(4) \neq 7 + 25$ *Inequ., F*

8. $2(\frac{1}{2}) = 1 + 0$ *Equ., T*

9. $6(5) = 5(6)$ *Equ., T*

10. $7(4 + 2) = 7(4) + 7(2)$ *Eq., T*

11. $5(\frac{3}{7}) = \frac{21}{35}$ *Equ., F*

12. $(4 \times 2) \times 3 = 4 \times (2 \times 3)$ *Equ., T*

It is suggested that pages 31–33 be assigned for independent study following the test day on Chapter 1. The first three sets can be written assignment. Dis-cuss fully the following day. In general, the teacher must plan an assignment following a test day or he will find himself about 15 lessons lacking by the end of the year.

31

Order Relations [A]

If two numbers are unequal, one must be greater than the other. We use the symbol ">" to mean "is greater than," and the symbol "<" to mean "is less than." Thus, to write "4 is greater than 2," we may write "4 > 2," and to write "2 is less than 4," we may write "2 < 4." Do you agree that if 4 > 2, then 2 < 4? It is easy to keep from confusing the symbols if you remember that the small part of the symbol points to the smaller number.

To write "is not greater than," we may use the symbol " $\not>$ " and to write "is not less than," we may use the symbol " $\not<$."

[A]

EXERCISES

State which of the following sentences are true:

1. $2 + 5 > 5 + 2$ F
2. $3 + 1 < 9$ T
3. $6 + 0 < 4(\frac{1}{2})$ F
4. $5^2 > 5(2)$ T
5. $9(0) < 1 + 1$ T

6. $3 + a \not< a + 3$ T
7. $4^2 < 5^2$ T
8. $(3 \cdot 2) \cdot \frac{1}{2} > 3 \cdot (2 \cdot \frac{1}{2})$ F
9. $8(\frac{1}{4}) \not> 2$ T
10. $3(3) > 3 + 3$ T

Open Sentences [A]

Consider the following sentences.

1. $1 + 2 = 3$
2. $2 > 7$
3. $x + 3 = 5$
4. $2(y + 4) = 2y + 8$

Because the first sentence provides true information, it is said to be a <u>true sentence</u>. Because the second sentence provides false information, it is said to be a <u>false sentence.</u> The third sentence provides information, but we cannot decide if the information is true or false. We must know the number represented by the variable x. For example, when $x = 2$, then $2 + 3 = 5$ is true; but when any other number is used for x, the resulting sentence is false. In the fourth sentence, any replacement for y results in a true sentence. Notice that the sentence illustrates the distributive property of multiplication over addition. Any sentence which contains one or more variables is an <u>open sentence.</u> The sentences $x + 3 = 5$ and $2(y + 4) = 2y + 8$ are said to be open sentences.

32   ① The descriptive name "open sentence" is well-established in elementary mathematics. Use it frequently. In fact make every new word an integral part of the classroom discussion until it becomes familiar to the students.

[A]

EXERCISES

For each of the following open sentences possible values of the variables are given at the right. Indicate whether the sentence does or does not state a truth when the variables have the given values.

1. $x + 7 = 11$; $x = 4$ T
2. $y + 9 = 5$; $y = 2$ F
3. $m + 7 \neq 7$; $m = 0$ F
4. $6a = 12$; $a = 2$ T
5. $a^2 = 6$; $a = 3$ F

6. $\frac{1}{3}b > 5$; $b = 15$ F
7. $3 + a = a + 3$; $a = 729\frac{1}{5}$ T
8. $x + y = 8$; $x = 2, y = 6$ T
9. $2a + 3b = 20$; $a = 2, b = 5$ F
10. $m^2 + n^2 = 2$; $m = 0, n = 1$ F

Solution Sets[A]

Let us consider the sentence $x + 1 > 4$ and let us suppose that the variable x in the sentence represents any member of the domain $\{0, 2, 4, 6, 8\}$. By replacing the x in the sentence by each of the numbers 0, 2, 4, 6, and 8, in turn, we have

$0 + 1 > 4$, a false statement
$2 + 1 > 4$, a false statement

$4 + 1 > 4$, a true statement
$6 + 1 > 4$, a true statement
$8 + 1 > 4$, a true statement

Now we see that the sentence $x + 1 > 4$ divides the domain of x into two subsets, $\{0, 2\}$ and $\{4, 6, 8\}$, such that each member of the first set makes the sentence state a falsehood and each member of the second set makes it state a truth. We say that the set that makes the sentence state a truth is the <u>truth set</u> or <u>solution set</u> for the sentence. Thus, for the domain $\{0, 2, 4, 6, 8\}$ the sentence $x + 1 > 4$ has the truth set $\{4, 6, 8\}$. We say that the members of the truth set are <u>solutions</u> or <u>roots</u> of the equation or inequality. 4, 6, and 8 are roots of the inequality $x + 1 > 4$ when the domain of x is $\{0, 2, 4, 6, 8\}$.

Members are ringed

[A]

EXERCISES

Find the truth sets for each of the sentences below when the variable has the domain shown at the right:

1. $x + 2 = 4$; $\{0, 1, 2, 3, 4\}$
2. $y > 6$; $\{5, 10, 15, 20\}$
3. $2x + 1 = 11$; $\{1, 3, 5, 7, 9\}$
4. $m + 1 < 5$; $\{1, 2, 3, 4, 5\}$

5. $2 + m = m + 2$; $\{0, 1, 2, 3\}$
6. $2m + 1 = 6$; $\{\frac{1}{2}, \frac{3}{2}, \frac{5}{2}, \frac{7}{2}\}$
7. $x^2 = 9$; $\{1, 3, 5, 7\}$
8. $x^2 > 6$; $\{1, 2, 3, 4, 5\}$

② These exercises could be part of the second assignment in the chapter. In good classes, challenge by asking "What set *fails* to be the truth set for each of these sentences? Into what two subsets is the original domain divided?" Thus you reemphasize the vocabulary of sets.

33

ALGEBRA, BOOK ONE

None for domain given.

9. $4(x+2)=20$; $\{0, \frac{1}{4}, \frac{1}{2}, \frac{3}{4}, 1\}$ 11. $x(x+2) = 3x$; $\{0, 1, 2\}$

10. $x + \dfrac{1}{x} = 2$; $\left\{\dfrac{1}{2}, 1, \dfrac{3}{2}\right\}$ 12. $\frac{3}{4}x + \frac{3}{2}x = \frac{9}{2}$; $\{0, 1, 2\}$

Using the Subtraction Axiom to Solve Equations [A]

The method of the preceding section is satisfactory for finding the truth set of a sentence when the domain of the variable has only a few members. Suppose, however, that the domain is an infinite set. In this case could you possibly test every member of the domain to determine whether it belongs to the truth set? Since you cannot, you know that we need another method for finding truth sets—a method that will be satisfactory for all domains, large and small. Certain properties of the equality of numbers can help us to find such a method for equations. Later you will study the properties helpful in finding truth sets of inequalities.

One of the properties for equalities is illustrated by the familiar fact that whenever 1 is subtracted from 6 the difference is 5. You know that this is true regardless of the expression that represents 6. Thus, since $6 = 2 + 4$, you know that $6 - 1 = 2 + 4 - 1$. And, since you know that $9 + 3 = 10 + 2$, you know that $9 + 3 - 2 = 10 + 2 - 2$. Since similar statements can be made for any two real numbers (even those you have not yet studied) we say:

If a and b are two expressions for the same real number (that is, if $a = b$) and if c is a real number, then $a - c = b - c$.

We call this property of equality the <u>subtraction axiom</u>.

The subtraction axiom can help us to find the truth set for the equation

$$x + 2 = 7 \tag{1}$$

when the domain of x is the set of all real numbers.

By use of the subtraction axiom we subtract 2 from both $x + 2$ and 7, as shown below:

$$x + 2 - 2 = 7 - 2 \tag{2}$$

Since $2 - 2 = 0$, and since $7 - 2 = 5$, we have

$$x + 0 = 5 \tag{3}$$

By the addition property of zero, $x + 0 = x$. Consequently,

$$x = 5 \tag{4}$$

34

One way to present these pages would be to have the section read aloud by members of the class, stopping for discussion when needed. Then the teacher could dictate a few exercises like those on page 36 to check understanding. Put an exercise on the board, have students solve it, then discuss. Do not let a few always give the answer before the majority of the class have solved the problem. This allows many of your class to drift through algebra without any independent thinking. See also note on p. 38.

① If a student questions the emphasis on "if" in direction 1, you might state that it is possible to write algebraic sentences for which no truth set can be found. For example, restricting the domain to natural numbers, there is no truth set for $x + 14 = 8$.

SENTENCES

Since the properties we have used are true for all real numbers, we know that any member of the truth set of (1) is also a member of the truth sets of sentences (2), (3), and (4). We can see that 5 is the only number for which (4) is true. Thus we know that if $x + 2 = 7$ has a truth set, 5 is its only member. We must now decide *whether* $x + 2 = 7$ has a truth set. To determine this we replace x by 5 in $x + 2 = 7$ and observe whether the resulting statement is true. Since $5 + 2 = 7$ is a true statement, we know that the truth set for $x + 2 = 7$ is $\{5\}$.

When a truth set has only one member we usually omit the braces and say that the number is the solution or root of the equation. Thus 5 is the solution of the equation $x + 2 = 7$.

It is important for you to observe that in showing that 5 is a solution of the equation we showed that:

1. If $x + 2 = 7$ has a truth set, the truth set is $\{5\}$. See ① above.
2. If x in the equation is replaced by 5, $5 + 2 = 7$ is a true statement.

When finding truth sets, we always carry out these two steps. In the second step we test whether or not the *possible* solutions are *actual* solutions. In this text we shall refer to this testing or checking of an actual solution as a proof. Actually both steps are parts of a formal proof. The process of finding the truth set of an equation is called solving the equation or finding the solution of the equation.

It has taken many words to explain how to find the roots of the equation $x + 2 = 7$, but in actual practice we may write;

	$x + 2 = 7$
S_2	$x + 2 - 2 = 7 - 2$
Simplifying both members	$x = 5$

Note. S_2 means, "subtract 2 from each member of the equation."

PROOF. Does $5 + 2 = 7$? Yes.

Therefore 5 is the root.

In the example above we subtracted 2 because we wanted to eliminate 2 in the expression $x + 2$ to obtain a sentence beginning, " $x = $." Since subtraction is the inverse or opposite of addition, subtracting 2 undoes (nullifies) the addition of 2 and gives us x alone in the left member. What number would we have subtracted had the equation been $x + 7 = 9$? Did you answer 7? You should have, because then we have $x + 7 - 7 = 9 - 7$, which simplified becomes $x = 2$.

35

ALGEBRA, BOOK ONE

[A]

Solve the equations below, assuming in each case that the domain of the variable is the set of all real numbers.

1. $x + 6 = 10$ *4*   5. $h + 3.6 = 9.1$ *5.5*   9. $x + 53 = 125$ *72*

2. $x + \frac{2}{5} = \frac{8}{15}$ *$\frac{2}{15}$*   6. $p + 5.4 = 90.7$ *85.3*   10. $x + 14 = 14$ *0*

3. $y + \frac{4}{3} = 18$ *$16\frac{2}{3}$*   7. $x + 120 = 280$ *160*   11. $17 = x + 16$ *1*

4. $y + \frac{3}{4} = \frac{4}{5}$ *$\frac{1}{20}$*   8. $x + 175 = 500$ *325*   12. $25 = x + 22$ *3*

Using the Addition Axiom to Solve Equations [A]

You discovered long ago that whenever 5 is added to 4, the sum is 9. This is true regardless of the expression that represents 4. Thus, since $4 = 3 + 1$, $4 + 5 = 3 + 1 + 5$. And, since $7 = 9 - 2$, then $7 + 3 = 9 - 2 + 3$. Since similar statements can be made for all real numbers (even those you have not yet studied), we say

> If *a* and *b* are two expressions for the same real number (that is, if $a = b$) and if *c* is a real number, then $a + c = b + c$.

We call this property of equality the <u>addition axiom</u>.

The addition axiom can help us to solve the equation

$$x - 8 = 13 \tag{1}$$

in which the domain of *x* is the set of all real numbers.

By use of the addition axiom, if we add 8 to $x - 8$ and to 13, we have

$$x - 8 + 8 = 13 + 8 \tag{2}$$

Since $-8 + 8 = 0$ and since $13 + 8 = 21$, we have

$$x + 0 = 21 \tag{3}$$

By the addition property of zero, $x + 0 = x$. Consequently,

$$x = 21 \tag{4}$$

Since 21 is the only number that will make (4) true, we know that *if* (1) has a truth set, 21 will be its only member. To determine *whether* (1) has a truth set, we ask ourselves,

Does $21 - 8 = 13$?

Since the answer to the question is, "Yes," we know that 21 is the root of the equation $x - 8 = 13$.

① You might encourage self-reliance by having students read this section independently. Follow up by discussion and examples.

In actual practice we write the steps of this explanation as follows:

$$x - 8 = 13$$

A_8 $x - 8 + 8 = 13 + 8$

Simplifying both members $x = 21$

PROOF. Does $(21) - 8 = 13$? Yes.

Therefore 21 is the root.

Note. A_8 means, "Add 8 to both members of the equation."

[A]

EXERCISES

Solve the following equations, assuming that the domain of each variable is the set of all real numbers.

1. $x - 5 = 8$ *13*

2. $h - 1 = 5$ *6*

3. $7 = x - 3$ *10*

4. $0 = x - 1$ *1*

5. $e - 10 = 3.6$ *13.6*

6. $b - .5 = .9$ *1.4*

7. $n - 3.2 = 5$ *8.2*

8. $\frac{3}{4} = x - \frac{1}{4}$ *1*

Using the Division Axiom to Solve Equations [A]

You know that each time 12 is divided by 2 the quotient is 6. This is true regardless of the expressions that represent 12. Thus, since $12 = 8 + 4$, it is true that $\frac{12}{2} = \frac{8 + 4}{2}$. Since similar statements can be made for any two real numbers, with the exception that the divisor cannot be zero, we may state:

If a and b are two expressions for the same real number (that is, if $a = b$) and if c is any real number, with the exception of zero, then $\frac{a}{c} = \frac{b}{c}$.

We call this property of equality the <u>division axiom</u>.

We may use the division axiom to solve the equation

$$2y = 18$$

in which the domain of y is the set of all real numbers. We write:

$$2y = 18$$

D_2 $\frac{2y}{2} = \frac{18}{2}$

Simplifying $y = 9$

PROOF. Does $2(9) = 18$? Yes.

Therefore 9 is the root.

Note. D_2 means, "Divide each member of the equation by 2."

ALGEBRA, BOOK ONE

We divided by 2 because we observed that in the expression $2y$ the 2 and the y are combined by multiplication. Since division is the inverse of multiplication, we know that dividing by 2 will "undo" the multiplication by 2 and give us a sentence beginning, "$y = \quad$."

[A]

EXERCISES

Solve the equations below. In each case assume that the domain of the variable is the set of all real numbers.

1. $3x = 12$ 4

2. $9x = 72$ 8

3. $6y = 48$ 8

4. $5y = 42$ $8\frac{2}{5}$

5. $3y = 0$ 0

6. $.2x = 64$ 320

7. $\frac{1}{4}h = 21$ 84

8. $15y = 120$ 8

9. $38 = 2y$ 19

10. $76 = 19y$ 4

11. $\frac{1}{2}h = \frac{3}{4}$ $\frac{3}{2}$

12. $.04m = 12$ 300

Using the Multiplication Axiom to Solve Equations [A]

Whenever 8 is multiplied by 6 the product is 48. This holds true regardless of the expressions that represent 8. Thus, since $8 = 5 + 3$, we know that $6(8) = 6(5 + 3)$. Since similar statements can be made for the product of any two real numbers, we may state:

If a and b are two expressions for the same real number (that is, if $a = b$) and if c is any real number, then $ac = bc$.

We call this property of equality the multiplication axiom.

We may use the multiplication axiom to solve the equation $\frac{x}{6} = 7$ in which the domain of x is the set of all real numbers. We write

$$\frac{x}{6} = 7$$

M_6
$$6\left(\frac{x}{6}\right) = 6(7)$$

Note. M_6 means, "Multiply both members by 6."

Simplifying $x = 42$

PROOF. Does $\frac{(42)}{6} = 7$? Yes. Therefore 42 is the root.

In the example above we multiplied by 6 because we observed that in the expression $\frac{x}{6}$ the x is divided by 6. Since multiplication is the inverse of division, we know that multiplying by 6 will undo the division by 6 and give us an equation beginning, "$x = \quad$."

38

① Explain that $\frac{x}{6}$ and $\frac{1}{6}x$ are expressions for equal numbers, and that if either is multiplied by 6 the result is x. Also point out that these exercises could be done by the division axiom as were some on page 38.

SENTENCES

①

[A]

EXERCISES

Solve each of the equations below, assuming that the domain of each variable is the set of all real numbers.

1. $\frac{x}{3} = 8$ 24   **3.** $\frac{y}{7} = 10$ 70   **5.** $\frac{p}{2} = 45$ 90   **7.** $\frac{x}{2} = \frac{1}{4}$ $\frac{1}{2}$

2. $\frac{x}{4} = 9$ 36   **4.** $\frac{x}{8} = 4$ 32   **6.** $\frac{h}{8+2} = 5.5$ 55   **8.** $\frac{y}{9} = \frac{1}{3}$ 3

Selecting the Procedure for Solving an Equation [A]

Since two numbers can be combined only by addition, subtraction, multiplication, or division there are only four fundamental forms for equations. They are illustrated by the equations below.

$$x + 2 = 7 \qquad x - 5 = 8 \qquad 3x = 21 \qquad \frac{x}{2} = 5$$

More complicated equations are merely combinations of these forms. Your ability to solve these simple equations will be the foundation of your ability to solve more complicated equations. For your convenience the four procedures are reviewed below. Observe that we always undo the existing process by using the inverse process.

Since x and 2 are combined by addition, we subtract 2.	$x + 2 = 7$ $x + 2 - 2 = 7 - 2$ $x = 5$	Since 5 is subtracted from x, we add 5. $x - 5 = 8$ $x - 5 + 5 = 8 + 5$ $x = 13$ ②
Since 3 and x are combined by multiplication, we divide by 3.	$3x = 21$ $\frac{3x}{3} = \frac{21}{3}$ $x = 7$	Since x is divided by 2, we multiply by 2. $\frac{x}{2} = 5$ $2\left(\frac{x}{2}\right) = 2(5)$ $x = 10$

[A]

EXERCISES

Solve the equations below, assuming that the domain of each variable is the set of all real numbers. ③ below.

1. $x - 5 = 5$ 10   **6.** $h + 3 = 15$ 12   **12.** $.03m = 15$ 500

2. $5x = 45$ 9   **7.** $10 + x = 14$ 4   **13.** $8x = 0$ 0

3. $x + 6 = 8$ 2   **8.** $m - 7 = 18$ 25

4. $\frac{x}{3} = 1$ 3   **9.** $y + 10 = 21$ 11   **14.** $\frac{m}{7} = 1.1$ 7.7

5. $\frac{1}{4}x = 2$ 8   **10.** $x + (4 + 7) = 11$ 0   **15.** $30 = 6m$ 5

11. $r - \frac{1}{2} = \frac{3}{4}$ $\frac{5}{4}$ **16.** $p - 1.4 = 8$ 9.4

② Most students are ready now to omit writing the first step in the solution.
③ Allow flexibility of methods. If students have used different methods, praise them.

39

10.0 **17.** $x - 4.7 = 5.3$ **20.** $m+2(6+5)=89$ **22.** $4+m=18$ *14*

1.3 **18.** $8y = 10.4$ **21.** $a + \dfrac{3+5}{16} = 1\frac{1}{2}$ **23.** $2(6+8)+8=6x$ *6*

23 **19.** $t+4=3(4+5)$ **24.** $18 = \frac{1}{2}p$ *36*

Equations in Which Terms May Be Combined[A]

Complicated equations can often be changed into simpler ones by combining like terms.

Example. Solve the equation $5x - 2x = 18 - 3$ in which the domain is the set of all real numbers.

Solving the equation. $5x - 2x = 18 - 3$

$C.T.$ $\qquad\qquad\qquad\qquad 3x = 15$ $\qquad$ $C.T.$ means, "Combine like terms."

D_3 $\qquad\qquad\qquad\qquad x = 5$ $\qquad$ bine like terms."

PROOF. Does $5(5) - 2(5) = 18 - 3$? Yes.

Therefore 5 is the root of the equation.

[A]

EXERCISES

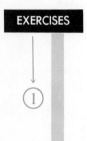

Solve the equations below, assuming that the domain of each variable is the set of all real numbers.

1. $2x + 3x = 15$ *3* **6.** $a + 2a - a = 1$ $\frac{1}{2}$

2. $5x + x = 24$ *4* **7.** $r + 7r - 5r = 45$ *15*

3. $3x + 4x = 35 - 7$ *4* **8.** $3x + 7x + 4x = 70$ *5*

4. $5x + 3x - 2x = 60 + 6$ *11* **9.** $.5m + .5m = 1$ *1*

5. $\frac{1}{2}m - \frac{1}{3}m = 12$ *72* **10.** $.08a + .04a + .03a = 3$ *20*

Using More than One Axiom[A]

Sometimes two or more of the fundamental processes may be involved in an equation. For example, in the equation $4x + 5 = 37$, the variable x is combined with 4 by multiplication, and the product is combined with 5 by addition. In such cases we undo the processes one at a time to get an equation beginning, "$x = \quad$."

Example 1. To solve the equation $4x + 5 = 37$ we might first undo the multiplication by dividing by 4. However, this leads to the hard-to-manage fractions $\dfrac{4x + 5}{4} = \dfrac{37}{4}$.

40

While we could eventually find the solution by this method we see that we can get a simpler equation by first undoing the addition by subtracting 5. We proceed as shown below.

$$4\,x + 5 = 37$$

S_5 $\qquad\qquad 4\,x + 5 - 5 = 37 - 5$

Simplifying $\qquad\qquad\quad 4\,x = 32$

D_4 $\qquad\qquad\qquad\quad x = 8$

PROOF. Does $4(8) + 5 = 37$? Yes.

Therefore the root is 8.

If terms may be combined, it is usually wise to do the combining before applying the axioms, as shown in the example below.

Example 2. Solve: $4\,x + 5\,x + 1 = 26 + 2$

C.T. $\qquad\qquad\qquad 9\,x + 1 = 28$

S_1 $\qquad\qquad\qquad 9\,x + 1 - 1 = 28 - 1$

Simplifying $\qquad\qquad\quad 9\,x = 27$

D_9 $\qquad\qquad\qquad\quad x = 3$

PROOF. Does $4(3) + 5(3) + 1 = 26 + 2$? Yes.

Therefore 3 is the solution.

[A]

EXERCISES

Solve the following equations in which the domain of each variable is the set of all real numbers.

3   **1.** $x + 4\,x = 15$ **11.** $10 = 2\,x + 1$ $4\frac{1}{2}$ **22.** $7\,y - y = 36 + 12$ 8

4   **2.** $4\,x + x = 20$ **12.** $6\,c + 7 = 10$ $\frac{1}{2}$ **23.** $8\,m - m = 84$ 12 ①

6   **3.** $4\,x - 5 = 19$ **13.** $3\,y - 10 = 11$ 7 **24.** $7\,x = 0$ O

5   **4.** $2\,x - 1 = 9$ **14.** $4\,p - 10 = 2$ 3 **25.** $7\,y = 1$ $\frac{1}{7}$

3   **5.** $3\,x + 1 = 10$ **15.** $18 = 9\,m$ $\qquad 2$ **26.** $\frac{2}{3}\,x = 12$ 18

12   **6.** $\dfrac{3\,x}{4} = 9$ **16.** $8 + 2 = y + 4\,y$ 2 **27.** $4\,c - 1 = 13$ $3\frac{1}{2}$

               17. $x + .3 = .7$ 0.4 **28.** $1.25\,x = 8$ 6.4

90   **7.** $1.06\,c = 95.4$ **18.** $c + 1.4 = 6.5$ 5.1 **29.** $2\,m - 15 = 20$ $17\frac{1}{2}$

4   **8.** $3\,y - 7 = 5$ **19.** $0.03\,y = 36$ 1200 **30.** $\frac{1}{3}\,x - 7 = 0$ 21

4   **9.** $5\,c - 1 = 19$ **20.** $.06\,p = 24$ 400 **31.** $4 + 7\,x = 11$ 1

$4\frac{1}{2}$ **10.** $4\,h + 3 = 21$ **21.** $3\,x + 4\,x = 35 + 7$ 6 **32.** $21 + 5\,k = 41$ 4

① Assign about half this set for one lesson. Require proofs. You might save the rest to be done a few at a time in conjunction with the word problem sets that follow. (Lock-step assignment)

Encourage discussion of different approaches. For example, in Ex. 45, "Multiply by 4 and divide by 3, or divide by 3 and multiply by 4, or multiply by 4/3, or divide by 3/4."

ALGEBRA, BOOK ONE

33. $6x + 3 = 19 - 1$ $2\frac{1}{2}$
34. $5m - m + 1 = 10$ $2\frac{1}{4}$
35. $8x = 10 + 5 - 1$ $1\frac{3}{4}$
36. $7m - m - 4 = 8$ 2
37. $4x + 3x = 100 + 5$ 15
38. $x + 2x + 3x = 144$ 24
39. $3y + 5 = 5$ 0
40. $42x - 26 = 100$ 3
41. $15k - 15 = 0$ 1

42. $20 = 10x$ 2
43. $27 + x = 40$ 13
44. $\frac{1}{6}y = 23$ 138
45. $\frac{3}{4}h = 9$ 12
46. $\frac{2}{3}c = \frac{1}{6}$ $\frac{1}{4}$
47. $\frac{7}{8}x = 0$ 0
48. $x + \frac{1}{3}x = 8$ 6
49. $x - .5x = 1.5$ 3
50. $5 = 2c - 3.2$ 4.1

[B]

51. $1.2x + 3.4 = 4.6$ 1
52. $3.1y + 14 = 76$ 20
53. $75y + 136 = 361$ 3
54. $.4m + .1m = 35$ 70
55. $52k + 78 = 390$ 6

56. $9d + 29 = 32$ $\frac{1}{3}$
57. $.24x + .16x = 8.6 - 3.8$ 12
58. $7.2y - 5 = 9.4$ 2
59. $2.28 = 3.14r - 4$ 2
60. $1.5a + 2.5a = 1 - .92$ 0.02

Algebraic Representation [A]

When we solve a problem by algebra, we must do two things,— *first*, we must form an equation (or equations) expressing the number relations of the problem, and *second*, we must solve the equation. The exercises below will give you practice in forming equations.

EXERCISES

Express the following number relations, using algebraic symbols. In exercises 1–20, let x represent the unknown number.

1. Five times a number is 80. $5x = 80$
2. Eight times a number is 48. $8x = 48$
3. A number increased by 5 equals 34. $x + 5 = 34$
4. A number decreased by 13 equals 20. $x - 13 = 20$
5. The product of a number and 5 is 45. $5x = 45$
6. Twice a number, increased by four times the number, equals 66. $2x + 4x = 66$
7. Five times a number, decreased by the number, equals 60. $5x - x = 60$

The successful teaching of verbal problems taxes any teacher's ingenuity. One must try many approaches and devices to reach all students. The greatest challenge is to disperse the *fear* which many students seem to have. In these introductory exercises, show how the sentence stated in words can be abbreviated to an algebraic sentence simply by substituting proper letter symbols and numerals for words. Try writing a sentence on the board in one horizontal line. Below it, rewrite with proper algebraic symbols. This is a *translation* device and is often effective in analysis of verbal problems.

42

8. A number less 6 equals 25. $x - 6 = 25$

9. 6 is 10 less than twice a number. $6 = 2x - 10$

10. When a number is increased by 8, the sum is 34. $x + 8 = 34$

11. The difference between a number and 7 is 13. $x - 7 = 13$

①

12. Eight times a number, diminished by 5, equals 35. $8x - 5 = 35$

13. Nine times a number is as much more than 5 as 42 is more than 20. $9x - 5 = 42 - 20$

14. One seventh of a number is 11. $\frac{1}{7}x = 11$

15. Two thirds of a number is 8. $\frac{2}{3}x = 8$

16. 3% of a number is 18. ($3\% = \frac{3}{100}$ and "of" here means "times.") $\frac{3}{100}x = 18$

$.07x + .04x = 88$

17. 7% of a number plus 4% of the number equals 88.

$5x - 2x = 39$

18. Five times a number minus twice the number equals 39.

19. If 76 is subtracted from seven times a number, the remainder is 92.

$$\text{Let } x = \text{the number}$$
$$7x - 76 = \text{the remainder}$$
$$7x - 76 = \underline{\quad ? \quad} 92$$

②

Complete the last statement to form an equation.

20. One number is four times another and the sum of the numbers is 70.

$$\text{Let } x = \text{the smaller number}$$
4 $\text{Then } ?\,x = \text{the larger number}$
4 $x + ?\,x = 70$

Copy and complete the statements by filling in the blank spaces.

Solving Problems by Algebra[A]

Some of the problems which you will soon be asked to solve by algebra are very easy and you may wish to solve them by arithmetic. However, you are asked to solve them by algebra so that you may learn the algebraic method. You can learn the algebraic method more easily if you begin with easy problems.

Now read the following directions for solving problems by algebra. Then study the solutions of the examples which follow. Notice that there are five steps in any solution.

① In Ex. 11 ask, "How would you indicate the difference between 7 and a number?" $(7 - x)$

② You may find that some students who are not really *thinking* will be willing to write $76 - 7x$.

43

① These directions will be more meaningful to the student as he starts learning the method by doing assigned problems. They should be used as a working guide, frequently read and studied until a procedure of problem solution becomes second nature to the student.

ALGEBRA, BOOK ONE ①

Directions for Solving Problems

1. Read the problem
and determine what number (or numbers) you are asked to find.

2. Represent the unknown number (or numbers) algebraically.
    a. If you are asked to find only one number,
    let some letter equal it (represent it).
    b. If you are asked to find more than one number,
    let some letter equal one of them;
    then represent each of the other numbers
    in terms of this letter.
    c. When possible, make a drawing
    to show steps a and b above
    and the number relations of the problem.

3. From the conditions of the problem
find two expressions or quantities that are equal.
Then connect these two equal expressions by an equals sign,
forming an equation.

4. Solve this equation for the variable.
If you are asked to find more than one number,
do this from step 2b above.

5. Prove by seeing that your answer (or answers)
satisfies all the conditions of the problem.

②If you expect to do well in algebra, be careful not to omit any of the five steps outlined above. When you prepare solutions carefully you force yourself to think carefully.

Example 1. A number increased by six times itself equals 98. What is the number?

Solution. Let $x =$ the number

6 times the number $= 6\,x$

From the problem we get $x + 6\,x = 98$

$$7\,x = 98$$

$D_7 \qquad\qquad x = 14$, the number

PROOF. Does 14 increased by 6 times $14 = 98$? Yes.

Example 2. Dick's father is three times as old as Dick, and the sum of their ages is 48 years. How old is each?
We shall solve this problem in two ways.

44

② Emphasize this paragraph. On ensuing pages, help students by having them refer back to discover their errors of procedure instead of just *telling* them the answers to their questions. It is essential that they become self-reliant.

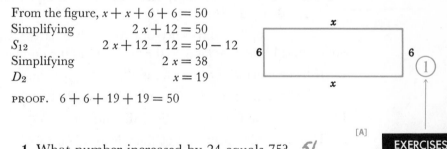

① Do not assign too many problems at one time. You might make an assignment of some of these and some from page 41. Then some of these problems could be worked by the class as a group where you can constructively guide their method of solving. On some, use the *translation* method described on page 42. For some, invent simple visual aids or board diagrams.

SENTENCES

Solution 1	Solution 2
Let $d =$ the number of years in Dick's age	Let $f =$ the number of years in Dick's father's age
Then $3d =$ the number of years in his father's age	Then $\frac{1}{3}f =$ the number of years in Dick's age
Then	Then
$d + 3d = 48$	$f + \frac{1}{3}f = 48$
$4d = 48$	$\frac{4}{3}f = 48$
$D_4 \quad d = 12$, Dick's age	$D_{\frac{4}{3}} \quad f = 36$, father's age
$3d = 36$, his father's age	$\frac{1}{3}f = 12$, Dick's age

PROOF. 36 is 3 times 12. The sum of 36 and 12 is 48.

Which of these two solutions do you think is the easier? Why?

Always prove that your answers to verbal problems are correct by showing that they agree with the data given in the problem.

Example 3. Joe had 50 feet of fence to enclose a garden. He wished to have the garden in the shape of a rectangle with each end 6 feet wide. How long should the garden be?

Solution. Let $x =$ the number of feet in the length of the garden.

From the figure, $x + x + 6 + 6 = 50$
Simplifying $\quad 2x + 12 = 50$
$S_{12} \quad 2x + 12 - 12 = 50 - 12$
Simplifying $\quad 2x = 38$
$D_2 \quad x = 19$

PROOF. $6 + 6 + 19 + 19 = 50$

[A]

EXERCISES

1. What number increased by 24 equals 75? *51*

2. What number increased by 43 equals 97? *54*

3. What number decreased by 31 equals 96? *127*

4. Eight times a certain number is 408. What is the number? *51*

5. Paul said, "I am thinking of a number. If I multiply it by 11, I get 1353 as the product. What is the number?" *123*

45

6. A certain number increased by 5 times itself equals 42. Find the number. *7*

7. One number is 5 times as large as another, and their sum is 54. What are the numbers? (Why will you choose to let *x* represent the smaller number?) *9, 45*

8. One number is 8 times as large as another, and their difference is 56. Find the numbers. (8 *x* − *x* = 56) *8, 64*

9. The difference between a number and 18 is 35. Find the number. *53*

10. Five times a number, plus 4, equals 34. What is the number? *6*

11. The sum of three times a number and four times the number is 98. Find the number. *14*

12. If 8 less than twice a number is 48, what is the number? *28*

13. If five times a number, less 6, equals 19, what is the number? *5*

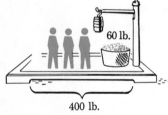

60 lb.

400 lb.

14. Mark said, "If I multiply my weight in pounds by 4 and add 60 pounds, I get 400 pounds." What was his weight? *85 lb.*

15. How old is Elaine if you get 100 years when you multiply her age in years by 6 and then add 16 years? *14*

16. The difference of two numbers is 165 and one of them is 12 times as large as the other. Find the numbers. *15, 180*

17. If three fourths of a number is 27, what is the number? *36*

18. 3% of a number is 18. What is the number? (.03 *x* = 18) *600*

19. 4% of a number is 280. Find the number. *7000*

20. Tim and Jan spent 4% of their income on furniture. If they spent $405, what is their income? *$10,125*

21. The ABC Corporation has invested money at 7% a year to provide two $2100 scholarships per year for children of their employees. How much is invested? *$30,000*

22. A president of a bank receives 8 times as much salary as one of the messenger boys. If the sum of their annual salaries is $18,000, what is the annual salary of each? *messenger $2000; president $16,000*

SENTENCES

23. Separate 276 into two parts so that one part will be twice the other. *92, 184*

24. Apportion $3450 among three people so that the second person will receive twice as much as the first and the third will receive three times as much as the first.

Let $x =$ the number of dollars the first will receive
Then $2x =$ the number of dollars the second will receive
and $3x =$ the number of dollars the third will receive
Complete the solution. *$575, $1150, $1725.*

25. Separate 1000 into three parts so that one part will be three times as large as another and the third part will be as large as the sum of the other two. *125, 375, 500*

26. Two boys mowed a lawn and one did twice as much work as the other. How should they divide the $3.60 which they received for their work? *$1.20, $2.40*

27. Flo and Bernice cared for a neighbor's children and were paid $3.85 for their time. How should they divide the money if Flo spent 2 hours and Bernice spent $1\frac{1}{2}$ hours? $(x + \frac{3}{4}x = ?)$ *Flo, $2.20; Bernice, $1.65*

28. John said, "I am thinking of a number. If I multiply it by 3 and subtract 5 from the result, I get 40." Of what number was he thinking? *15*

29. The rectangle shown is twice as long as it is wide, and its perimeter (the sum of the lengths of its four sides) is 60 feet. Find its dimensions. *10' × 20'*

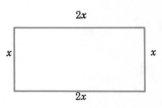

30. A rectangle is 5 times as long as it is wide. If its perimeter is 120 inches, what are its width and length? (Why should you make a drawing whenever it is possible to do so?) *10 in., 50 in.*

31. Patricia lives east of McKinley High School and Jane lives west of the school. Patricia lives five times as far from the school as does Jane. How far is each from the school if their homes are 18 blocks apart? *Jane, 3 blocks; Patricia, 15*

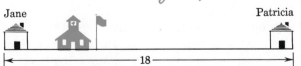

Try to insert some fun or drama in teaching word problems. If you once let your class dread lessons on word problems, you will be sorely tried to overcome this.

47

32. A board 24 feet long is to be cut into three pieces so that the longest piece will be 3 times as long as each of the other two. How long will each piece be? *4.8′, 4.8′, 14.4′*

33. Bill is $\frac{1}{4}$ as old as his father and the sum of their ages is 55 years. How old is each? (Let $x =$ the number of years in Bill's age. Then $4x =$ the number of years in the father's age.) *Bill, 11; father, 44.*

34. Last summer Jane won 6 more tennis games than Sue, and Sue won 3 more than Mary. If the girls won a total of 27 games, how many were won by each girl? (Hint. Use x to represent the number of games Mary won.) *Jan 14, Sue 8, Mary 5*

35. The quotient of two numbers is 6 and their sum is 196. Find the numbers. (Let $x =$ the smaller number.) *28, 168*

[B]

36. A new apartment complex has $2\frac{1}{2}$ times as many apartments with two bedrooms as with three, and $1\frac{1}{2}$ times as many apartments with one bedroom as with three. If the complex contains 250 apartments, how many of each type are there? *75 - 1 bedrooms, 125 - 2 bedrooms, 50 - 3 bedrooms*

37. A mixture contains 1 part of glycerine, 1 part of turpentine, and 4 parts of water. How many ounces of each must be used to make 16 ounces of the mixture? *Glycerine 2⅔ oz., Turpentine 2⅔ oz., Water 10⅔ oz.*

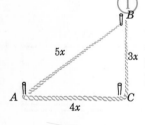

38. If you stretch a rope around three stakes driven into the ground at points A, B, and C, you form a triangle. If $AC = 4x$, $BC = 3x$, and $AB = 5x$, then $\angle C$ is a right angle. How long should each of these sides be to form the right triangle if the rope is 60 feet long? *AC, 20′; BC, 15′; AB, 25′*

39. Fred said, "How long was that fish, Dick?"

Dick said, "The length of the fish equals 12 inches plus the length of the head, and the length of the head is one fifth the length of the fish."

How long was the fish? *15 inches*

Angles[A]

Have you ever stopped to think about the importance of angles? Angles enter our everyday thinking because the shapes of objects depend not only on their dimensions but also upon the sizes of the angles

48 ① Enlarge on this exercise which uses the famous 3-4-5 right triangle relationship. Make some visual aid, like a loop of a string knotted to make 12 equal sections. Perhaps some student whose father is a carpenter might comment on the use of this triangle.

Simple geometric principles are introduced here both to enlarge the field from which simple word problems may be drawn and to conform to the modern trend that favors a spiral development of informal geometry before the demonstrative course which traditionally follows algebra.

SENTENCES

they contain. Notice, for example, the buildings you pass on your way to school. You will see that the roofs and the walls meet to form angles of different sizes.

A ray is part of a line extending infinitely far in one direction from a point. An angle (∠) is a figure formed by two rays drawn from the same point. The rays are the sides of the angle and their point of meeting is the vertex of the angle. In Fig. 1, point *B* is the vertex and rays *BA* and *BC* are the sides. The size of the angle depends upon the amount of opening between the sides and not their length. Angle *y* (∠ *y*) shown in Fig. 2 is larger than angle *m* (∠ *m*) in Fig. 1.

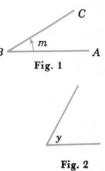

Fig. 1

Fig. 2

There are three common ways of naming an angle:

1. By a small letter or figure written within the angle, as ∠ *m* (Fig.1).
2. By the capital letter at its vertex, as ∠ *B*.
3. By three capital letters, the middle letter being the vertex letter, as ∠ *ABC*.

Kinds of Angles [A]

When two straight lines intersect (cut each other), four angles are formed. If these four angles are equal, each angle is a right angle and contains 90°. When one line forms a right angle with another line, the lines are perpendicular to each other. In the figure, the lines *AD* and *CE* intersect in the point *B* and are perpendicular to each other. Each of the four angles at *B* is a right angle.

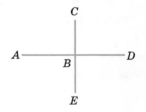

An angle less than a right angle is an acute angle.

If the two sides of an angle extend in opposite directions forming a straight line, the angle is a straight angle.

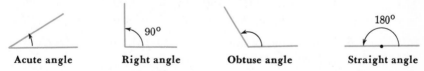

| Acute angle | Right angle | Obtuse angle | Straight angle |

An angle greater than a right angle (90°) and less than a straight angle (180°) is an obtuse angle.

Strips of colored cardboard can be joined by eyelets to make effective visual aids illustrating these concepts of angles and perpendicular lines. Join so that the models may be easily moved to show the effect of change.

49

ALGEBRA, BOOK ONE

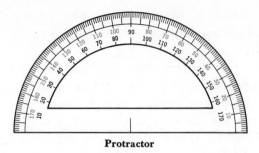

Protractor

① A protractor is an instrument for measuring angles. You probably already know how to measure angles with this instrument.

Complementary Angles [A]

② Two angles are complementary when their sum is 90°. Thus an angle of 50° and one of 40° are complementary; and an angle of 80° and one of 10° are complementary. Each is the complement of the other.

Supplementary Angles [A]

Two angles are supplementary when their sum is 180°. For example, two right angles are supplementary; and an angle of 150° and one of 30° are supplementary. Each is the supplement of the other.

[A]

EXERCISES

1. Using a protractor, draw an angle of 30°.

2. Using a protractor, draw ∠ RST = 110°.

3. At 3 o'clock is the angle made by the hands of a clock an acute angle, a right angle, or an obtuse angle?

4. How large is the angle made by the hands of a clock at 2 o'clock? Which kind of angle is it? *60°, acute angle.*

5. Which kind of angle is made by the hands of a clock at 5 o'clock? *Obtuse*

6. Measure angles 4, 5, 6, and 7 in Fig. 1 on page 51. Which angles are equal? *∠4 = ∠6 and ∠5 = ∠7*

② If students confuse these names, you might say, "c comes before s, and 90 comes before 180, so match <u>c</u>omplementary with 90."

SENTENCES

7. Name ∠4 in Fig. 1 using three letters. Name ∡ 5, 6, and 7 using three letters. ∠AOD; ∠AOC, ∠BOC, ∠BOD.

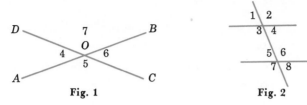

Fig. 1   **Fig. 2**

8. Measure the eight angles in Fig. 2 at the right above.

∠1 = ∠4 ? _ _ = ∠5 ? _ _ = ∠8 ? _ _

∠2 = ∠3 ? _ _ = ∠6 ? _ _ = ∠7 ? _ _

9. Tell which of the pairs of angles, ∠A and ∠B, are complementary and which are supplementary:

a. ∠A = 40° and ∠B = 50° *comp.*
b. ∠A = 80° and ∠B = 100° *supp.*
c. ∠A = 55° and ∠B = 36° *neither*
d. ∠A = 29° and ∠B = 151° *supp.*
e. ∠A = 37° and ∠B = 53° *comp.*
f. ∠A = 10° and ∠B = 80° *comp.*

①

Kinds of Triangles [A]

If a triangle has two equal sides, it is isosceles. If a triangle has its three sides equal, it is equilateral. You can see that an equilateral triangle is isosceles.

Isosceles triangle   **Equilateral triangle**

A right triangle is a triangle that has one right angle.

[A]

1. With your ruler draw three triangles having different shapes. With your protractor measure the angles of each triangle. What is the sum of the angles of each triangle? *180°*

EXERCISES

2. Compare the sums of the angles of the triangles in Exercise 1. Complete this sentence: The sum of the angles of any triangle is _ _ ? _ _ degrees. *180°*

②

② The teacher should have Exs. 1 and 2 done as class work. Then he may state that it can actually be proved that the sum of the angles of any triangle is 180°. This may then be used as a formula for the examples that follow.

This serves as a good example of independent discovery of a fact by inductive means. It also, however, is wise here to discuss that no such piling up of cases constitutes reliable proof.

51

3. One angle of a triangle contains 80° and another angle contains 60°. Find by arithmetic the number of degrees in the third angle. *40°*

4. One angle of a right triangle contains 20°. Find by arithmetic the size of the other acute angle. *70°*

5. How large is the complement of an angle of 60°? of an angle of 10°? of one of 80°? of one of x°? *30°; 80°; 10°; (90−x)°*

6. What is the number of degrees in the supplement of an angle of 70°? of an angle of 100°? of one of 140°? of one of y degrees? *110°; 80°; 40°; (180−y)°*

7. How large is each angle of an equilateral triangle? (The angles are equal to each other.) *60°*

[A]

WRITTEN EXERCISES

Solve the following problems according to the directions given on page 44.

1. Two angles are supplementary and one of them is twice as large as the other. How large is each angle? *60°, 120°*

2. Two angles are complementary and one is 4 times as large as the other. How large is each angle? *18°, 72°*

3. Find the number of degrees in each of two complementary angles if one is 17 times as large as the other. *5°, 85°*

4. One angle of a triangle is twice as large as one of the other angles, and the third angle is equal to the sum of the other two. How large is each angle?

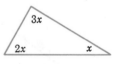

Let $x =$ the number of degrees in the smallest angle *30°*
Then $2x =$ the number of degrees in the second angle *60°*
and $3x =$ the number of degrees in the third angle *90°*

Here the three preliminary statements above and the drawing both express the same facts. Which of the two ways is the shorter? Which is the more helpful in solving the problem? Now complete the solution.

5. Of the three angles of a triangle the largest is five times the smallest, and the remaining angle is three times the smallest. Find the angles. *20°, 100°, 60°*

Always insist on a complete and clear form for presenting verbal problems. Some students like to abbreviate their work by beginning with the equations and not bothering to interpret or prove the answer. Do not accept less than a complete solution.

SENTENCES

6. Find two complementary angles if one of them is one-ninth as large as the other. $9°, 81°$

HINT. $x + \frac{1}{9}x = 90$ or $9x + x = 90$

7. One angle of a triangle contains 54 degrees and the second angle is eight times the third angle. How large are the second and third angles? $14°, 112°$

8. One acute angle of a right triangle contains 18 degrees more than the other acute angle. How many degrees are there in each acute angle? $36°, 54°$

Graphing Solution Sets for Equations [A]   (See ① above.)

In Chapter 1 you studied the graphing of sets of numbers. You are now ready to graph the solution sets of equations. It is true that the solution sets for the equations you have been studying are unit sets, but later you will study equations having truth sets with more than one member.

On the left below we have solved the equation $x + 7 = 9$, and on the right we have graphed the solution set for the equation.

Solving the equation

$$x + 7 = 9$$
S_7 $x + 7 - 7 = 9 - 7$
Simplifying $x = 2$

PROOF.   Does $2 + 7 = 9$?   Yes.
Therefore 2 is the solution.

Graph of the solution set 2

Note. The black dot indicates the graph of 2.

[A]

Solve each of the equations below and make a graph of its solution set.

EXERCISES

1. $x + 2 = 6$ 4

2. $x - 4 = 3$ 7

3. $2r + 3r = 10$ 2

4. $\dfrac{m}{6} = 0$ 0

5. $2y + 1 = 5$ 2

6. $4x - 2x - 3 = 4$ $3\frac{1}{2}$

7. $8x + x = 19$ $2\frac{1}{9}$

8. $y + \frac{1}{3}y = 8$ 6

9. $(x + 4) + 5 = 10$ 1

10. $3 + (x - 2) = 6$ 5

53

ALGEBRA, BOOK ONE

Solving Inequalities with the Addition and Subtraction Axioms [A]

Let us now consider how to solve some inequalities. Since the addition and subtraction axioms that we have been using for equations are true only for equalities, they are not appropriate for inequalities. The axioms for the addition and subtraction of inequalities are stated as follows:

> **Addition Axiom.** If a and b are two real numbers such that $a > b$, and if c is a third real number, $a + c > b + c$.

> **Subtraction Axiom.** If a and b are two real numbers such that $a > b$, and if c is a third real number, $a - c > b - c$.

These axioms may also be stated for "$<$" by replacing each symbol $>$ above with the symbol $<$.

You are already acquainted with these axioms since you have used them throughout most of your life. Thus you know that since $8 > 5$, $8 + 2 > 5 + 2$. Similarly, you know that since $8 > 5$, $8 - 2 > 5 - 2$.

To solve the inequality $x + 2 > 7$ when x is the set of all real numbers, we proceed as follows:

$$x + 2 > 7$$

S_2 $\qquad x + 2 - 2 > 7 - 2$

Simplifying $\qquad x > 5$

Note. S_2 means, "Subtract 2 from each member of the inequality."

PROOF. Does $x + 2 > 7$ state a truth when $x > 5$?

Yes.

Therefore the solution set is the set of all real numbers greater than 5.

Observe that in the example above the solution set is an infinite set. A graph of the solution set helps us to visualize the situation. Why is the circle placed at the point representing 5?

[A]

EXERCISES   Solve each of the inequalities in Exercises 1–6, assuming the domain of each variable is the set of all real numbers. Graph each solution set.

1. $x + 2 > 8$ $\quad x > 6$
2. $x + 1 > 9$ $\quad x > 8$
3. $x - 2 > 2$ $\quad x > 4$
4. $x + 9 > 11$ $\quad x > 2$
5. $x - 8 > 3$ $\quad x > 11$
6. $x + \frac{1}{2} > \frac{3}{4}$ $\quad x > \frac{1}{4}$

54 ① Ask, "Interpret this exercise if $>$ is changed to $<$; to $=$. How does the number line look if all three of these sentences are graphed on it?"

Solve each of the inequalities in Exercises 7–10, assuming that the domain of each variable is the set of the numbers of arithmetic (zero and numbers greater than zero).

7. $x - 8 < 3$ *x < 11* **9.** $x + 1 < 6$ *x < 5*

8. $x - 2 > 5$ *x > 7* **10.** $x - 3 < 7$ *x < 10*

In each of the following exercises form an inequality and solve it to find the answer to the question asked.

Example. In eleven months Mr. Jones earned $9250, but in the next month he earned enough to make his year's income exceed $10,000. What did he earn in the twelfth month?

Solving the problem. Let d = the number of dollars Mr. Jones earned in the twelfth month

Then $9250 + d$ = the number of dollars he earned in twelve months

$$9250 + d > 10,000$$

S_{9250} $\qquad d > 750$

PROOF. Is $9250 + d > 10,000$ true when $d > 750$? Yes.

Therefore Mr. Jones earned more than $750 in the twelfth month.

11. John earned less than half the sum of the amounts earned by his two brothers Bill and Tom. If Bill earned $50.00 and Tom earned $80.00, what do we know about John's earnings? *Less than $ 65.00.*

12. If 12 is added to a number, the sum is more than 15. What can you say about the number? *Greater than 3.*

13. Mrs. Smith wants to add water to two gallons of fruit punch and still have the total amount of the mixture less than 5 gallons. How much water may she add? *Less than 3 gal.*

14. Sue said, "I am determined to spend less than $14.00 when I shop downtown today." If Sue spent $6.98 for a blouse, how much can she spend for a sweater and still meet the requirements she has set for herself? *Less than $ 7.02.*

For added practice, some of the problems on pages 45–48 could be used with "equal" changed to "less than" or "more than."

55

ALGEBRA, BOOK ONE

Checking Your Understanding of Chapter 2

At this time you should determine whether you have mastered Chapter 2. Before you begin the Chapter Review, be sure that you

	PAGE
1. Know what an equation is and what an inequality is.	31
2. Know the meaning of $<$, $>$, $\not<$, and $\not>$.	32
3. Can determine the truth or falsity of an open sentence for any suggested value of the variable.	32
4. Can solve equations by using the addition, subtraction, multiplication, and division axioms.	34
5. Can solve inequalities by the addition and subtraction axioms.	54
6. Can graph solution sets.	53
7. Can use equations and inequalities to solve problems.	43

Review if you need to.

8. Can spell and use the following words correctly:

	PAGE		PAGE
acute	49	inverse	35
angle	49	isosceles	51
axiom	34	obtuse	49
complementary	50	perpendicular	49
equation	31	protractor	50
equilateral	51	solution	33
inequality	31	supplementary	50

CHAPTER REVIEW

[A]

Complete statements 1–5 by supplying the proper words:

1. An equation is a sentence stating that two numbers are __?__ *the same, or equal*

2. An inequality is a sentence stating that two numbers are __?__ *different, or unequal*

3. An equation or inequality containing a variable is an __?__ sentence. *open*

4. Multiplication and division are __?__ operations. *inverse, or opposite*

5. A number that will make an equation state a truth when it replaces the variable of the sentence is called a __?__ of the equation. *truth set, or solution*

6. Find the truth set for $x + 1 > 5$ when x has the domain $\{2, 3, 4, 5, 6\}$. *{5, 6}*

7. Find the truth set for $2x + 3x = 100$ when x has the domain $\{0, 5, 10, 15\}$. *∅*

8. Graph the truth set for $y + 3 > 9$ when the domain of y is the set of all real numbers.

9. Can 2 be a member of the truth set for $3x - 1 = 7$? *No.*

Solve each of the following equations and inequalities when the domain of the variable is the set of all real numbers.

10. $x - 5 = 7$ *12* **14.** $7y = 0$ *0* **18.** $61 = 21 + 5k$ *8*
11. $x + 3 = 12$ *9* **15.** $2y - 5 = 13$ *9* **19.** $108 = 6c + 3c$ *12*
12. $x + 3 > 12$ *x>9* **16.** $\frac{1}{3}m = 15$ *45* **20.** $p + .03p = 12.36$ *12*
13. $4x = 108$ *27* **17.** $p - 1 > 19$ *p>20* **21.** $\frac{2}{3}y = \frac{1}{9}$ *1/6*

22. Write in algebraic language:

a. the sum of a and 9 *a+9*   **c.** 4 greater than c *c+4*
b. the difference of r and s *r-s, or s-r*   **d.** s less than 5 *5-s*

[B]

23. The larger of two numbers is nine times the smaller and their difference is 56. Find the numbers. *7, 63*

24. One of two complementary angles is 5 times as large as the other. How large is each angle? *15°, 75°*

25. Bill chose a number and multiplied it by 9. Then he subtracted 206 from the product, getting 1000 as the remainder. What number did he choose? *134*

26. A rectangle is 7 times as long as it is wide and its perimeter is 104 inches. Find its width and length. *6½ in., 45½ in.*

27. The quotient of two numbers is 8 and their sum is 27. Find the numbers. *3, 24*

28. The perimeter of a triangle is 18 inches. The second side is twice the first side and the third side is 6 inches. Find the lengths of the first side and second side. *4", 8"*

57

29. Each of two angles of a triangle is half as large as the third angle. How large is each angle? *90°, 45°, 45°*

30. A rectangular field is enclosed by a fence $\frac{3}{8}$ of a mile in length. If the length of the field is 5 times its width, how wide is the field? (1 mi. = 5280 ft.) *165 ft.*

CHAPTER TEST

1. Can 4 be a member of the truth set for $5x - 7 = 13$? *yes*

2. Can 2 be a member of the truth set for $4x > 8$? *no*

3. Find the truth set for $a+3=3+a$ when $a=\{1, 2, 3, 4, 5\}$. *{1,2,3,4,5}*

Solve, assuming that the domain of each variable is the set of all real numbers.

4. $5x = 20$ *4* **8.** $3x + 2x = 105$ *21* **12.** $3p + 5 = 17$ *4*

5. $x + 6 = 7$ *1* **9.** $x + 4 > 11$ *x > 7* **13.** $19 = 8y - 5$ *3*

6. $y - 4 = 7$ *11* **10.** $x - 2 < 1$ *x < 3* **14.** $\frac{x}{10} = \frac{1}{5}$ *2*

7. $\frac{3}{4}y = 12$ *16* **11.** $.04h = 36$ *900* **15.** $1.4y - .6y = 1.4$ *1.75*

16. Graph the truth set for $x + 9 > 11$ when x is the set of all real numbers.

17. Graph the truth set for $6y = 0$ when y is the set of all real numbers.

18. Four less than five times a number is 61. What is the number? *13*

19. One of two complementary angles is 8 times as large as the other. How many degrees are there in each angle? *10°, 80°*

20. If Bill earned more than $300 in four months, what do you know about his average earnings per week?

21. A rectangle is 3 times as long as it is wide and its perimeter is 20 inches. What are its length and width? *7½ in., 2½ in.*

20. For 1 mo. = 4 wk., more than $18.75 weekly; for 1 mo. = $\frac{52}{12}$, or 4⅓ wk., more than $17.31 weekly.

ARITHMETIC
TEST 2

This test was made to test your memory on words and facts taken from arithmetic.

On your paper write one word or number, and only one, for each blank to make each statement true.

1. A triangle has __?__ sides.

2. There are __?__ inches in a foot.

3. There are __?__ square inches in one square foot.

4. There are __?__ feet in one mile.

5. The sum of the sides of a polygon is called the __?__ of the polygon.

6. There are __?__ inches in one yard.

7. There are __?__ ounces in one pound.

8. There are two __?__ in one quart.

9. A __?__ angle contains 90 degrees.

10. __?__ is money paid for the use of money.

11. A diameter of a circle is __?__ times as long as the radius.

12. A __?__ is a written order to a bank to pay money.

13. The amount is the __?__ of the principal and interest.

14. The dividend equals the product of the divisor and the quotient plus the __?__.

15. The hypotenuse is a side of a __?__ triangle.

16. A triangle with three sides the same length is __?__.

17. There are __?__ hours in one day.

18. There are four quarts in one __?__.

19. The denominator of a fraction cannot be __?__.

20. A protractor is an instrument used to measure __?__.

●Check your answers with those below. If you do not make 100% on the test, try again in a few days.

5. perimeter	**10.** interest	**15.** right	**20.** angles
4. 5280	**9.** right	**14.** remainder	**19.** zero
3. 144	**8.** pints	**13.** sum	**18.** gallon
2. 12	**7.** 16	**12.** check	**17.** 24
1. 3	**6.** 36	**11.** two	**16.** equilateral

●**Answers**

3

Formulas

Suggested Time Schedule
9 days

In this chapter you will see how mathematics can save your time. ▶

FORMULAS

You are now going to study about formulas—what they are, how you use them, and how you can make them. First you will want to know what a formula is. The following paragraphs will help you to understand that.

What a Formula Is[A]

John Smith and his friend Bill Jones have jobs mowing lawns. Before they began their new work, the boys discussed the matter of how much to charge their customers. John has decided upon a fixed rate of $2 an hour, but Bill has decided to accept whatever his employers give him. The boys are wondering which plan is the better.

John knows that the amount he earns will depend upon the number of hours he works. He knows that if he works 2 hours he will earn 2×2, or 4 dollars. He knows that if he works 3 hours he will earn 3×2, or 6 dollars. He sees that his earnings will fit into a fixed pattern, or model, which can be represented by the equation

$$d = n \times 2 \quad \text{or} \quad d = 2n$$

where n represents any number of hours worked, and d the number of dollars earned in that number of hours.

We call such an equation a formula. A formula is simply an equation which expresses a rule in concise form. John's formula says: To find the number of dollars earned, multiply 2 and the number of hours worked. How much will John earn this fall if he works for 20 hours? for 40 hours? Did you answer $40 and $80? You should have. ①

If John had decided to charge $1.50 an hour, what formula would have represented his earnings for n hours? What would his earnings have been after he had worked 5 hours at this rate? Write a formula showing his earnings for n hours at $1.75 an hour.

Bill's earnings do not fit into a fixed pattern. They vary from job to job. Last Thursday afternoon Mrs. Brown gave him $1.75 for an hour's work. On Saturday the Blacks gave him $6 for 3 hours' work. Yesterday he spent 4 hours working for the family across the street and was paid $5.

There is no formula for Bill's total earnings. Not even Bill himself can tell beforehand how much he will have earned after he has worked 10 hours, or 40 hours, or 100 hours.

① All formulas are equations, but not all equations are called formulas.

When Bob Foster applied for a job as salesman in Kerr's appliance store, Mr. Kerr said, "We pay our salesmen according to a formula. For a young man of your experience the formula is:

$$w = 125 + .05 \ s.$$

The s represents the number of dollars worth of goods you sell during the week and the w represents your wages for the week. The formula means that we shall pay you a basic wage of $125 per week and then add 5% of the selling price of the goods you sell. For example, if you sell $200 worth of goods during one week, we shall pay you $125 + 5% of $200. That would be $125 + $10, or $135."

How much will Bob earn during a week in which he sells $100 worth of merchandise? How much will he make during a week in which he sells $300 worth? $400? Answers: $130, $140, $145.

The instructions accompanying a set of tests given the freshman class of Center High School say, "The score will be found by the formula $S = R - 2 \ W$." That is a compact, easily understood way of saying, "To find a pupil's score, count the number of his correct answers and from that number subtract two times the number of his incorrect answers."

If, on the test, Arthur answered 130 questions correctly and 20 incorrectly, what was his score? Answer: 90.

If Betsy answered 120 correctly and 30 incorrectly, what was her score? Answer: 60.

How Formulas Are Used [A]

Formulas are not the uninteresting statements which many people think they are. It is only when we do not understand what they say, and how they help us, that they seem dull. In reality, formulas are full of excitement and adventure.

① Formulas have helped mankind to understand, and become masters of, the forces of nature. Consider electricity. For two or three thousand years men have known of the existence of electricity. They could see its effects in lightning and in the action of magnets. However, it has been only within recent years that people have discovered that electricity behaves according to such fixed patterns that the patterns can be written as formulas.

① Elaborate on the variety and value of formulas. You might ask volunteers to contact men engaged in professions and industries and from them gather a collection of formulas needed in their work.

FORMULAS

① After men found the formulas, they could begin to control electricity and make it do useful work. Only when there is sudden loss of power in our community do we realize how dependent we are on electricity.

Consider atomic energy. We are only now learning to make it work for us. Albert Einstein, in 1905, and then only twenty-six years of age, discovered the formula

$$E = mc^2.$$

②

According to this formula, the amount of energy (E) stored in any material equals the product of the mass (m) of the material in grams and the square of the speed of light (c) in centimeters per second. Light travels 30,000,000,000 centimeters per second. Try squaring this number. Do you see that a tremendous amount of energy is released when material is changed into energy? That is what happens when the atoms in

Albert Einstein

wood, or coal, or uranium, or other materials are smashed. We call the result atomic energy.

The value of formulas is not confined to science. Business men, machinists, and carpenters have special ones which help them in their work. Almost every trade or profession uses them. The following example shows how easy it is to solve a problem when the right formula is known.

Example. An iron ball is dropped from a balloon and reaches the earth in 12 seconds. How high is the balloon?

③ **Solution.** The formula is $s = 16\,t^2$, where s represents the number of feet the object falls and t represents the number of seconds the object is falling.

First write the formula: $s = 16\,t^2$
Substitute the value of t: $s = 16 \times 12^2$
Perform the multiplication: $s = 2304$
The height of the balloon is 2304 feet.

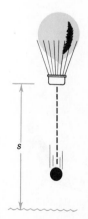

s

(If you study physics later on, you will learn why $s = 16\,t^2$ is the correct formula to use in such problems.)

ALGEBRA, BOOK ONE

Directions for Solving Problems by Formulas

1. Write the proper formula.
2. Replace the known letters of the formula by their values.
3. Perform the indicated operations,
   thus finding the value of the unknown letter.

①

EXERCISES

②

③

[A]

1. Use the formula $s = 16\, t^2$ to find the number of feet of space through which a parachutist will fall before his parachute starts to open if he pulls the rip cord 4 seconds after he jumps. 256.

2. The formula $r = 32\, t$ gives the rate (r) in feet per second at which an object is falling after t seconds. How fast will the parachutist in Exercise 1 be falling after 2 seconds? after 3? when he pulls the rip cord? 64 ft./sec.; 96 ft./sec.; 128 ft./sec.

3. Did you ever punch holes in a can and then fill the can with water? If you have, you may have noticed that the water spurts out of the lower holes with much more force than it does from the upper holes. That is because water pressure follows the pattern $p = .433\, h$ where p is the pressure in pounds per square inch on the bottom of a tank filled to a height of h feet with water. What would be the pressure at the bottom of a tank filled to a height of 10 feet with water? 4.33 lb./sq. in.

4. In Exercise 3, how much pressure would there be on one square inch of the surface of the tank halfway (5 feet) down?

2.165 lb./sq. in.

5. How much pressure would there be on each square inch of a fish swimming 20 feet under the surface of a lake?

8.660 lb./sq. in.

6. Bill has a job which requires that he sometimes move heavy barrels from the ground to a platform 3 feet above. He knows that if he rolls the barrels up an incline to the platform, it will take less force than it would to lift them. He knows that the formula

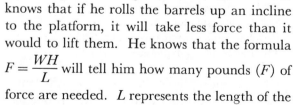

$F = \dfrac{WH}{L}$ will tell him how many pounds (F) of

force are needed. L represents the length of the

① Use a vertical form, thus: $i = prt$
$$= (350)(.04)(3)$$
$$i = \$42.00$$
Suggest that students do details of computation at
one side of the main body of the work.

FORMULAS

incline in feet, H the height in feet of the platform, and W the weight of the barrel in pounds. How many pounds of force will it take to roll a 300-pound barrel up an incline 10 feet long to a platform 3 feet high? *90*

7. A designer of machinery wants to know how many pounds of force will be needed to roll a 500-pound cylinder of metal up an incline 20 feet long to a platform 5 feet high. What is the answer? *125*

8. One formula helpful to all of us is the simple interest formula $i = prt$. In it, i represents the interest in dollars, p the principal in dollars, r the rate per cent, and t the time in years. Find the simple interest on $350 for 3 years at 4%. *$42*

9. What is the simple interest on $420 for 2 years at $4\frac{1}{2}$%? *$37.80*

10. What is the simple interest on $1500 for $3\frac{1}{2}$ years at $4\frac{1}{2}$%? *$236.25*

11. Find the simple interest on $5400 at 5% for 2 years 6 months. *$675*

12. $A = p + i$ is the formula for finding the amount (A) when the principal (p) and the interest (i) are known. Find the amount when the principal is $400 and the interest is $23. *$423*

13. $A = p + prt$ is the formula for finding the amount when the principal, time, and rate are known. For what does prt stand? What is the value for A when $p = \$325$, $r = 4\%$, and $t = 3$ years? *$364* *simple interest*

14. $d = rt$ is the formula for the distance (d) an object will go in t units of time, when it moves r units of distance in each unit of time. If the rate is expressed in miles per hour, the time must be expressed in hours, and the distance in miles. How far will an automobile travel in 5 hours at the rate of 40 miles per hour? *200 mi.*

15. Ed is traveling by bus. How far will he go in 26 hours at the rate of 55 miles per hour? *1430 mi.*

16. How far can Bill run in 10 seconds at the rate of 28 feet per second? *280 ft.*

17. How far will Mary go in 3 minutes on her bicycle if she travels at the rate of 32 feet per second? *5760 ft.*

① Show how these formulas are derived from $d = rt$ by use of the division axiom.
② Exs. 21 and 22 lead informally to the study of variation. Some teachers may find it helpful to read pages 489–494 as background.

ALGEBRA, BOOK ONE

① **18.** The formula $r = \dfrac{d}{t}$ gives the rate when the distance and time are known. What is the average rate in miles per hour of an airplane that travels 550 miles in $2\frac{1}{2}$ hours? *210 m.p.h.*

① **19.** The formula $t = \dfrac{d}{r}$ gives the time when the distance and rate are known. How many hours will it take an airplane to travel 855 miles at the average rate of 190 miles per hour? *$4\frac{1}{2}$*

20. $F = \dfrac{wa}{g}$ is a formula for finding the force (F) necessary to make an object weighing w pounds move faster by a certain amount (a). Find the number of pounds of force necessary to accelerate (speed up) an automobile 8 feet in one second if the automobile weighs 2700 pounds. Let $g = 32$. It represents the force of gravity. *675*

② **21.** Using the formula $s = 16\,t^2$ which was given in the Example of page 63, copy and complete the following table. (Do not write in your book.) When $t = 0$, $s = 16 \times 0^2 = 0$; when $t = \frac{1}{2}$, $s = 16 \times (\frac{1}{2})^2 = 4$, etc.

t (in seconds)	0	$\frac{1}{2}$	1	2	3	4	5	6	8	16
s (in feet)	0	4	?	?	?	?	?	?	?	?

16   64   144   256   400   576   1024   4096

Study the completed table and answer the following questions:

a. Does the distance increase or decrease as the time increases? *Increases*

b. When the time has doubled, how has the distance changed? *It has been multiplied by 4.*

c. If s and t^2 increase together, they are said to vary directly. Does s vary directly as the square of the time? *Yes*

② **22.** $p = \dfrac{100}{v}$ is a formula stating how the pressure and volume of a given amount of air change when the air is confined in a vessel such as a bicycle pump. Copy and complete the following table based on this formula:

v (in cu. ft.)	1	2	4	8	20	25	50	100	500
p (in pounds)	100	50	25	12.5	5	24	2	1	0.22

Study the completed table and answer the following questions:

a. As v increases, how does p change? *Decreases*

b. Is p doubled when v is doubled? *no*

c. If p and v increase together, they vary directly. If p increases when v decreases, they vary inversely. How do p and v vary? *inversely*

23. A formula for finding the normal weight of an adult who is at least 5 feet in height is $W = \dfrac{11(h - 40)}{2}$. W represents the normal weight in pounds and h represents the number of inches in the person's height. For example, if a man is 62 inches tall, we have $W = \dfrac{11(62 - 40)}{2}$. Then, $W = \dfrac{11 \times 22}{2}$ and $W = \frac{242}{2}$ or 121. The man's normal weight is 121 pounds. Copy the following form and complete the table:

Height	Actual Weight	Normal Weight	Pounds Underweight	Pounds Overweight
63 in.	130 lb.	126.5 lb.	? —	? 3.5
70 in.	160 lb.	165 lb.	? 5	? —
72 in.	176 lb.	176? lb.	? 0	? 0

[B]

24. On his way to school Bill passed a corner where the police were investigating an accident. He heard them tell the driver that the marks made by his skidding car showed that he had been going faster than the 30 miles per hour he claimed. Bill wondered how the police knew that, so at school he asked his science teacher, Mr. Smith.

Mr. Smith explained that the faster a car goes, the farther it travels before it can be stopped. He explained that for average road conditions, and for cars with average brakes, the formula $d = .07\, v^2$ represents the stopping distance (d) after the brakes are applied. In the formula, v represents the ve-

Dwell on Exs. 24 and 25 as an aid to impress students with the importance of safe driving. Encourage them to bring in statistics from other sources. Cooperation with social study teachers is indicated here.

① Let the student use squared paper. A stamp for making squared sections on paper might be an advantageous implement for the teacher to acquire. (Edmund Scientific Company, Barrington, New Jersey)

ALGEBRA, BOOK ONE

locity (speed) of the car. He showed Bill how the police might have found the stopping distance of a car going 30 miles per hour by substituting 30 for v in the formula, thus

$$d = .07(30)^2$$
$$d = .07(900)$$
$$d = 63$$

He explained that had the police measured the skid tracks and found them to be more than 63 feet, they would have known that the car was traveling more than 30 miles per hour.

Mr. Smith showed Bill how to make a table like the one at the left below to show the stopping distances of cars at various speeds. Bill then made a chart to show the information he had just assembled. Copy and complete both the table and the chart. (Do not write in your book.) See ① above.

v	d
10	?7
20	?28
30	63
40	?112
50	?175
60	?252

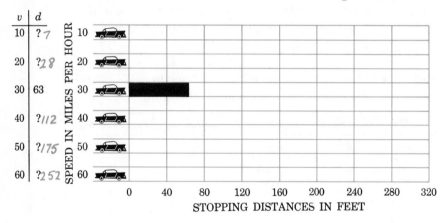

SPEED IN MILES PER HOUR

STOPPING DISTANCES IN FEET

25. The speed limit in a state is 55 miles per hour. How far back from a railroad crossing should a highway warning sign be placed in order to give drivers going 55 miles per hour a chance to stop before driving onto the tracks? *more than 211.75 ft.*

26. A formula for finding the horsepower of an automobile engine is $p = \dfrac{d^2 n}{2.5}$ where d is the diameter of each cylinder in inches and n is the number of cylinders. What is the horsepower of an 8-cylinder engine when each cylinder has a diameter of 3 inches? *28.8*

Have students look up "Horsepower" and "Foot-pound" in the dictionary.

68

27. Industrial engineers are constantly seeking light materials which have great strength. The relative heaviness of a substance is usually given as specific gravity. To find specific gravity, the formula $S = \dfrac{W}{W - w}$ may be used. In it, S represents the specific gravity, W the weight of a body in air, and w its weight in water. Find the specific gravity of a piece of aluminum which weighs 54 ounces in air and 34 ounces in water. 2.7

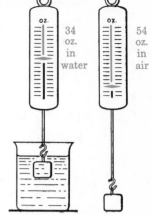

28. Find the specific gravity of a piece of iron which weighs 3.9 pounds in air and 3.4 pounds in water. 7.8

29. $W = Fs$ is a formula for finding the work done (in foot-pounds) when the force F (in pounds) and the distance s (in feet) are known. How much work does a horse do in pulling a wagon with a force of 320 pounds a distance of 2 miles? 3,379,200 ft.-lb.

30. Electric current is measured in amperes (I). The pressure for making electricity flow is measured in volts (E). Materials offer resistance to the flow of electricity. Resistance is measured in ohms (R). The formula which gives the relationship of the three is $I = \dfrac{E}{R}$. Find the number of amperes of current needed to operate a light bulb if the bulb's resistance is 55 ohms and the voltage is 110. 2

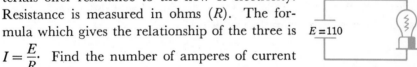

$E = 110$ 55 ohms resistance

31. In the formula $P = \dfrac{N + 2}{r}$, find P when $N = 23$ and $r = 6.25$. 4

32. $I = \dfrac{N - 2}{P}$. Find I when $N = 46$ and $P = 6$. $7\frac{1}{3}$

33. $W = \dfrac{E^2}{R}$. Find W when $E = 110$ and $R = 880$. $13\frac{3}{4}$

34. $F = \dfrac{Wv^2}{32\,r}$. Find F when $W = 80$, $v = 96$, and $r = 1200$. $19\frac{1}{5}$

35. $W = (T - t)V$. Find W when $V = 800$, $T = 300$, and $t = 140$. Notice that $(T - t)$ is multiplied by V. 128,000

69

Formulas Used in Geometry [A]

Formulas to be understood and remembered are those for:
1. Perimeter and area of a rectangle, a parallelogram, and a triangle.
2. Circumference and area of a circle.
3. Volume of a rectangular solid.

Perimeter of a Polygon [A]

Each figure shown below is called a <u>polygon</u>. All sides of a polygon are line segments. Using some unit of length measurement, such as 1 foot, 1 inch, or 1 millimeter, you can assign a number to each side. This number is sometimes called a measure, and may be shown by a variable. If the same measure is shown for two or more sides, the sides are said to be equal. Calculations for geometric figures are done with these numbers. When you are directed, for example, to add the sides of a polygon, you calculate with their assigned numbers, and then give the answer in terms of a unit of measurement.

The formula given below for each figure shows how to find the perimeter of the figure. The <u>perimeter</u> of a polygon is the sum of the lengths of its sides. Briefly, then, to find each perimeter, add the sides. Check each formula and its polygon to see if the formula given is the shortest way to indicate the perimeter.

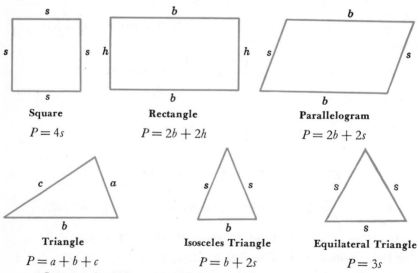

Square	Rectangle	Parallelogram
$P = 4s$	$P = 2b + 2h$	$P = 2b + 2s$

Triangle	Isosceles Triangle	Equilateral Triangle
$P = a + b + c$	$P = b + 2s$	$P = 3s$

Everyone should have a knowledge of the simple formulas for mensuration of these basic geometric figures. Also, this practical geometry will save time in the course in demonstrative geometry. Inexpensive and appropriate models should supplement the text. The teacher will find many suggestions for making these in the 18th Yearbook of the National Council of Teachers of Mathematics and various issues of The Mathematics Teacher. (See bibliography for other references.)

FORMULAS ↑ ①

Area of a Rectangle [A]

The rectangle *ABCD* encloses three rows of small squares, each row containing seven of these squares, called *square units*. In all, there are 3 × 7, or 21 squares. We say that the area of *ABCD* is 21. If each of these small squares is one inch on a side, its area is one square inch and the area of *ABCD* is 21 square inches. If each of these small squares is a foot on a side, its area is one square

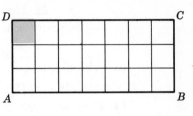

foot, and the area of *ABCD* is 21 square feet. In general, the area of any figure is the number of square units it contains.

From the above discussion you can see that the area of a rectangle is found by multiplying its length by its width. The length and width are often called the base and height. The formula for the area of a rectangle is $A = bh$, or $A = lw$.

Example. Find the area of a sidewalk 4 feet wide and 40 feet long.

Solution. $A = lw$
                     $A = 40 \times 4$
                     $A = 160.$
                     The area is 160 square feet.

[A]

EXERCISES

Find the areas of the rectangles whose bases and heights are:

1. $b = 10$ in., $h = 8$ in. *80 sq. in.* **4.** $b = 10\frac{2}{3}$ ft., $h = 6\frac{1}{3}$ ft. *67⅗ sq. ft.*

2. $b = 32$ in., $h = 15$ in. *480 sq. in.* **5.** $b = 23.1$ in., $h = 14.4$ in. *332.64 sq. in.*

3. $b = 6\frac{1}{2}$ ft., $h = 7\frac{1}{4}$ ft. *47⅛ sq. ft.* **6.** $b = 10.4$ ft., $h = 7.7$ ft. *80.08 sq. ft.*

7. Find the number of square yards in the floor of a room 13 feet wide and 21 feet long. *30⅓*

8. A dining room is 12 feet long, $10\frac{1}{2}$ feet wide, and 9 feet high. Find the number of square feet in the surface of the four walls. *405*

9. Find the perimeter of a city lot 42.5 feet wide and 134.5 feet long. *354.0 ft.*

10. How many square feet are there in a sidewalk 45 feet long and 54 inches wide? *202.5*

② Use the graph chart on the board and color in squares to help make vivid the concept of area. Also, a large rectangle may be drawn and adhesive squares fitted over it.

71

③ Students should be encouraged to draw diagrams for verbal problems. These should be neat. Elaborate on these text exercises by using illustrations from your classroom.

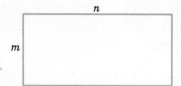

n

m

11. Write a formula for the perimeter of this rectangle, letting *P* stand for the perimeter. What is the area of the rectangle? *P = 2m + 2n; A = mn*

12. How many inches equal one foot? *12*How many square inches are there in one square foot?
144
[B]

13. A rectangle with equal sides is a square. Write a formula for the area of a square whose sides are each equal to *s*. *A = s²*

14. Find the area and the perimeter of a square 11.2 feet on a side. *A = 125.44 sq. ft.; P = 44.8 ft.*

15. In the diagram below at the left, what is the area of the larger square? of the smaller square? Write a formula for the area *A* of the colored part of the figure. *b²; a²; A = b² - a²*

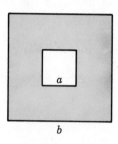

a

b

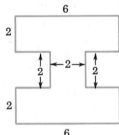

6

2

2 ←2→ 2

2

6

16. Find the perimeter and area of a square if each of its sides is 14¾ inches long. *P = 59 in.; A = 217 9/16 sq. in.*

17. If the numbers shown on the diagram at the right above stand for inches, find the area and the perimeter of the figure.
A = 28 sq. in.; P = 32 in.

Area of a Parallelogram [A]

As was shown on page 70, the figure *ABCD* is a <u>parallelogram</u>. Do you recognize that a rectangle is a parallelogram whose angles are right angles? If the right triangle *BEC* is cut off one end of the parallelogram and placed on the other end, the rectangle *BEFA* is formed. This rectangle and the parallelogram have the same base and altitude. Then the area of the parallelogram is found by multiplying its base by its height. The formula for the area of a parallelogram is <u>*A = bh*</u>.

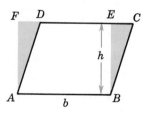

F   D   E   C

h

A   b   B

Use cardboard or plastic models to illustrate the relationship explained above. A set to illustrate area of a parallelogram, a triangle, and a trapezoid could be made and placed on a vertical stand as a permanent display. This would serve to keep these important relationships before all classes.

FORMULAS

[A]
EXERCISES

Find the areas of the parallelograms whose dimensions are as follows:

1. $b = 10$ in., $h = 11$ in. *110 sq. in.* **4.** $b = 7.5$, $h = 2.5$ *18.75*

2. $b = 14$ ft., $h = 17.2$ ft. *240.8 sq. ft.* **5.** $b = 7\frac{1}{2}$, $h = \frac{3}{5}$ *4½*

3. $b = 3\frac{1}{3}$ in., $h = 2\frac{2}{5}$ in. *8 sq. in.* **6.** $b = 12.25$, $h = 4.50$ *55.125*

7. Find the perimeter of a parallelogram if one side is 32.3 and another side is 17.9. (The opposite sides of a parallelogram are equal.) *100.4*

8. Letting A stand for the area and P for the perimeter of this parallelogram, write formulas for its area and perimeter. Is the area of the parallelogram less than, equal to, or greater than mn? *$A = mh$; $P = 2m + 2n$; less*

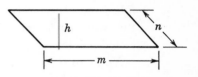

Area of a Triangle [A]

The $\triangle ABC$ is half the $\square ABDC$ and has the same base and height. Since the area of the parallelogram equals bh, the area of the triangle is $\frac{1}{2} bh$. Therefore the formula for the area of the triangle is $A = \frac{1}{2} bh$.

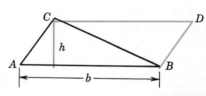

[A]
EXERCISES

Using the formula $A = \frac{1}{2} bh$, find the areas of the triangles whose bases and heights are

1. $b = 12$, $h = 9$ *54*   **4.** $b = 132$, $h = 17.7$ *1168.2*

2. $b = 30$, $h = 20$ *300*   **5.** $b = 112.5$, $h = 37.6$ *2115.00*

3. $b = 14.2$, $h = 17.4$ *123.54*   **6.** $b = 10\frac{1}{2}$, $h = 6\frac{2}{3}$ *35*

7. Find the area of a triangle whose base is x and whose altitude (height) is 8. *4x*

[C]
8. Find the cost of the paint for putting one coat on this garage at $2.75 a hundred square feet. (In figuring the cost add 40 square feet for painting under the eaves, and make no deductions for windows.) *$20.63*

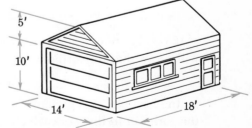

① Here is the chance to check on the efficiency of computational skills. Insist on students using short cuts and mental computations wherever possible.

ALGEBRA, BOOK ONE

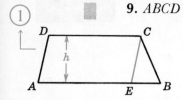

① *9. ABCD* is a trapezoid. It has two parallel sides, *AB* and *DC*, and two sides that are not parallel, *AD* and *BC*. By drawing *CE* parallel to *DA* the trapezoid can be divided into a parallelogram and a triangle. Find the area of *ABCD* if *AB* = 16 inches, *DC* = 12 inches, and *h* = 6 inches. *84 sq. in.*

Circumference of a Circle [A] Emphasize the circle formulas.

The three most common geometric figures are the rectangle, triangle, and circle. Of the three, the circle is perhaps the most beautiful. Study the figure below and see if you remember the meaning of the words *circle, diameter, radius,* and *center.* The length of the circle is called its <u>circumference</u>.

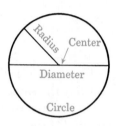

You can perform a simple experiment to determine the relation between the circumference of a circle and the diameter. Obtain three or four circular objects and measure their circumferences and diameters with a tape measure. Then divide the circumference of each object by its diameter. Find the average of these quotients. If you are very careful in making your measurements, you will find that the circumference is about $3\frac{1}{7}$ times the length of the diameter. It is impossible to find the exact value of the fraction $\dfrac{\text{circumference}}{\text{diameter}}$ or $\dfrac{c}{d}$. It is customary to represent the quotient $\dfrac{c}{d}$ by the Greek letter π, pronounced *pī.*

Then $\dfrac{c}{d} = \pi$ and $c = \pi d.$

Since $d = 2r$, we also have $c = 2\pi r.$ For ordinary computations we use $3\frac{1}{7}$ or 3.14 for the value of π. Where greater accuracy is desired, we use 3.1416 for the value of π.

Area of a Circle [A] To help students remember the formula, inscribe a circle in a square. The area of the circle is about ¾ that of the square, or approximately $3r^2$. This reminds us of $3.14r^2$.

If you continue the study of mathematics through geometry, you will prove that the formula for finding the area of a circle is

$$A = \pi r^2.$$

In the formula, *A* represents the area and *r* the radius. You will use this formula in the work which follows.

Page 15, Ex. 8
a. The diameter of a circle equals 2 times the radius.
b. The radius of a circle equals ½ the diameter.
c. The circumference of a circle equals π times the diameter.
d. The circumference of a circle equals 2π times the radius.

To ward off a future question "Is πr^2 or πd the formula for the area of a circle," show now, and later repeat, that a formula for the area of any plane figure must involve the product of two variables, while a perimeter must always consist of terms of the first degree.

FORMULAS

Example. Find the area of a circle whose diameter is 14, using $\pi = 3\frac{1}{7}$.

Solution. $A = \pi r^2$ and $r = 7$
$$A = \tfrac{22}{7} \times 49$$
$$A = 154$$

Using the formulas $A = \pi r^2$ and $c = \pi d$ $(\pi = 3\frac{1}{7})$, find the areas and the circumferences of the circles whose radii are

1. 7 in. *154 sq. in* **2.** 16 ft. *804$\frac{4}{7}$ sq. ft* **3.** 5$\frac{1}{4}$ in. *86$\frac{5}{8}$ sq. in* **4.** 3.5 ft. *38.50 sq. ft;*
44 in.   *100$\frac{4}{7}$ ft.*   *33 in.*   *22 ft.*

5. Using $\pi = 3.14$, copy and complete the following table in which r is the radius of a circle and c and A are the respective circumferences and areas.

C=6.28, 12.56, 18.84, 25.12, 34.54, 50.24, 62.80, 125.60, 188.40, 3.14, 10.47

r	1	2	3	4	5.5	8	10	20	30	$\frac{1}{2}$	$1\frac{2}{3}$
c	?	?	?	?	?	?	?	?	?	?	?
A	?	?	?	?	?	?	?	?	?	?	?

A=3.14, 12.56, 28.26, 50.24, 94.985, 200.96, 314.00, 1256.00, 2826.00, 0.785, 8.72
6. If d in the formula $c = 3\frac{1}{7}d$ is doubled, how is c affected? *doubled*

7. If r in the formula $A = \pi r^2$ is doubled, how does A change? *A becomes 4 times as great*

8. The following formulas apply to circles. Express each as a rule.

a. $d = 2r$ **c.** $c = \pi d$ **e.** $d = \frac{c}{\pi}$ **g.** $A = \frac{1}{4}\pi d^2$

b. $r = \frac{1}{2}d$ **d.** $c = 2\pi r$ **f.** $A = \pi r^2$ **h.** $r = \dfrac{c}{2\pi}$

Show how most of the formulas above are derived from the basic ones by applying axioms.   *For Exs. 9-12, π=3.14 was used.* [B]
9. Find the length of fringe needed to go around the edge of a circular table cover 27 inches in diameter. *2$\frac{4}{2}$ yd.*

10. Find the diameter in feet of a circular half-mile race track. $\left(d = \frac{c}{\pi}\right)$ *840.8*

11. How many revolutions will a 28-inch bicycle wheel make in going a mile? *721*

12. A round table top is 54 inches in diameter. What are the area and circumference of the top? *15.90 sq. ft.; 14.13 ft.*

8 c. The diameter of a circle equals the circumference divided by π.
f. The area of a circle equals π times the square of the radius.
g. The area of a circle equals $\frac{1}{4}\pi$ times the square of the diameter.
h. The radius of a circle equals the circumference divided by 2π.

ALGEBRA, BOOK ONE

Volume of a Rectangular Solid [A]

This figure is called a <u>rectangular solid</u>. It is 5 units long, 4 units wide, and 3 units high. The colored block is called a <u>cube</u>. The length, width, and height of a cube are all equal. This rectangular solid consists of three layers. Each of these three layers contains 20 equal cubes, one for each square unit in the top surface. Since the whole solid contains 60 of these equal cubes, we say that the volume of the solid is 60. If

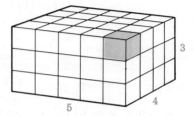

each edge of the small cube is one inch long, the volume of the cube is one cubic inch and the volume of the solid is 60 cubic inches. If each edge of the small cubes is a foot in length, the volume of the cube is one cubic foot and the volume of the solid is 60 cubic feet.

In general, the volume of any rectangular solid is found by multiplying the length by the width by the height. The formula for finding the volume of a rectangular solid is <u>$V = lwh$</u>.

[A]

EXERCISES

Find the value of the missing variable in the formula $V = lwh$ for each of these exercises:

1. $l = 8$, $w = 10$, $h = 16$ *1280* **3.** $l = 16.4$, $w = 8.6$, $h = 6.4$ *902.66*

2. $l = 10.2$, $w = 9$, $h = 6$ *550.8* **4.** $l = 20\frac{1}{2}$, $w = 10\frac{3}{4}$, $h = 8$ *1763*

5. How many cubic inches are there in a box 18 inches by 20 inches by 24 inches? *8640*

6. Find the number of cubic feet of air in a room 18 feet by 14 feet by $9\frac{1}{2}$ feet high. *2394*

7. How many square feet of surface are there in the ceiling and walls of the room of Exercise 6? *860*

8. Show that the volume of a cube with edge e is e^3. Write a formula for the volume of a cube with edge x. *$V = x^3$*

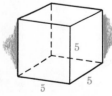

9. Each edge of this cube is 5 inches long. What is the area of each of its six faces? What is the area of all six faces? What is the volume of the cube? *25 sq. in.; 150 sq. in.; 125 cu. in.*

10. Write a formula for finding the area of all six faces of a cube, letting the length of an edge equal e. *$A = 6e^2$*

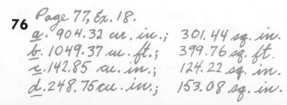

Page 77, Ex. 18.
a. 904.32 cu. in.; 301.44 sq. in.
b. 1049.37 cu. ft.; 399.76 sq. ft.
c. 142.85 cu. in.; 124.22 sq. in.
d. 248.75 cu. in.; 153.08 sq. in.

The combination of algebra, arithmetic, and geometry helps break down artificial barriers among subjects which are often taught for themselves alone. Be sure to have models of these common solids. There is no need to buy them, since they can be easily made from wood, cardboard, plaster, etc. Use bulletin board displays and film strips to develop an appreciation of the form and use of these solids.

FORMULAS

[B]

11. How many bushels of wheat are needed to fill a granary/$79\frac{1}{5}$ 4 feet by 8 feet by 7 feet? (1 bu. = $1\frac{1}{4}$ cu. ft., approximately.)

12. Find the volume of the lower rectangular solid in this figure. Find the volume of the upper solid. Write a formula for the volume of the combined solids. ha^2; bm^2; $V = ha^2 + bm^2$

13. Compare the volumes of two cubes whose edges are 3 feet and 6 feet respectively. *2d is 8 times as large as 1st.*

14. Compare the total surfaces of two cubes whose edges are 2 feet and 3 feet respectively. *2d is 2¼ times that of 1st.*

15. The ordinary vegetable can is an example of a right circular cylinder. Its volume is given by the formula $V = \pi r^2 h$, where r is the radius of the base and h is the height. Find the volume of a right circular cylinder if the radius of the base is 10 inches and the height is 16 inches. *5024 cu. in.*

16. $S = 2\pi rh$ is the formula for finding the area of the curved surface of a right circular cylinder. The area of the curved surface is called the lateral area. Find the lateral area of a tin can if the radius of the base is 2 inches and the height is 4 inches. *50.24 sq. in.*

17. The total area of a right circular cylinder is found by adding the areas of the two ends to the lateral area. Find the total area of a drum 16 inches in diameter and 18 inches high. *1306.24 sq. in.*

18. Find the volume and lateral area of the following right circular cylinders, when (*See foot of p. 76*)

a. $r = 6$ in., $h = 8$ in.   c. $r = 2.3$ in., $h = 8.6$ in.
b. $r = 5\frac{1}{4}$ ft., $h = 12\frac{1}{8}$ ft.   d. $r = 3.25$ in., $h = 7.5$ in.

19. The volume of a sphere is given by the formula $V = \frac{4}{3}\pi r^3$. The area of the surface is found by the formula $S = 4\pi r^2$. What are the volume and area of a spherical tank if its diameter is 20 feet? *4186.67 cu. ft.; 1256 sq. ft.*

20. Find the volume and area of a ball 4 inches in diameter. *33.49 cu. in.; 50.24 sq. in.*

21. Find the volumes and areas of the spheres with radii

a. 6 in.   c. $3\frac{1}{2}$ in.   e. $6\frac{1}{3}$ ft.   g. 16.4 ft.
b. 20 in.   d. $4\frac{1}{4}$ in.   f. 5.25 in.   h. 10.5 ft.

22. How many gallons of oil can be stored in a spherical tank having a radius of 15 feet? (1 gallon = 231 cubic inches.)

21. a. 904.32 cu. in.; 452.16 sq. in.   e. 1063.57 cu. ft.; 503.80 sq. ft.
b. 33,493.33 cu. in.; 5024 sq. in.   f. 605.82 cu. in.; 346.18 sq. in.
c. 179.50 cu. in.; 153.86 sq. in.   g. 18,467.15 cu. ft.; 3378.14 sq. ft.
d. 321.39 cu. in.; 226.86 sq. in.   h. 4846.59 cu. ft.; 1384.74 sq. ft.

ALGEBRA, BOOK ONE

Making Formulas from Rules [A]

In making formulas you should remember that a formula contains ①
two equal expressions connected by an equals sign. For example,
$A = bh$ is a formula, but bh is not a formula.

[A]

ORAL EXERCISES

1. The difference between the selling price (S) and cost (C) of an article is called the margin (M). Which of the following formulas express this fact? *a, f, i*

ⓐ $S = C + M$	**d.** $M = C + S$	**g.** $C = M + S$
b. $S = CM$	**e.** $M = S \div C$	**h.** $C = M - S$
c. $S = M - C$	ⓕ $M = S - C$	ⓘ $C = S - M$

2. The margin is often called the markup. It is really the gross profit. The actual profit or gain (G) is what is left when the expenses (E) are taken out of the margin (M). Which of the following formulas express this fact? *c, d, h*

a. $G = M + E$	ⓓ $M = G + E$	**g.** $E = G - M$
b. $G = E - M$	**e.** $M = G \div E$	ⓗ $E = M - G$
ⓒ $G = M - E$	**f.** $M = G - E$	**i.** $E = M + G$

[A]

EXERCISES

Write formulas for these rules, using the letters suggested:

1. The selling price (s) is found by adding the cost (c), the desired profit or gain (g), and the expenses (e). $s = c + g + e$

2. The number of gallons (g) in a container is found by dividing the number of cubic inches (V) in it by 231. $g = \frac{V}{231}$

3. The reading on a Fahrenheit thermometer (F) is found by taking $\frac{9}{5}$ of the reading on the centigrade thermometer (C) and adding 32 to the result. $F = \frac{9}{5}C + 32$

4. The perimeter (P) of a square is equal to 4 times one of its sides (s). $P = 4s$

5. The average (a) of two numbers (x and y) is equal to the sum of the numbers divided by 2. $a = \frac{x+y}{2}$

6. The volume (V) of a circular cone is equal to the product of one third of the base (b) and the altitude (h). $V = \frac{1}{3}bh$

7. The perimeter (P) of a rectangle is equal to the sum of twice the width (w) and twice the length (l). $P = 2w + 2l$

② Ask students to suggest situations illustrating these formulas. Show how one formula applies to many situations.

③ This practice furnishes another aspect of translating from verbal symbols to mathematical ones. Spend enough time on this set to be sure each formula is thoroughly understood.

The fact in Ex. 8 may seem unbelievable to students. Although the proof is beyond them now, they could draw and measure illustrations. If they do so, have them also check whether x + y = m + n.

FORMULAS

8. In the circle shown, the product of the two line segments m and n is equal to the product of the two line segments x and y. $mn = xy$

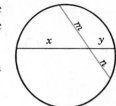

9. The perimeter (P) of a triangle is equal to the sum of the three sides (a, b, and c). $P = a + b + c$

10. The distance (d) passed over by any moving object is equal to the product of the rate (r) and time (t). $d = rt$

11. The sum of the interior angles (A, B, and C) of a triangle is 180°. $A + B + C = 180°$

12. The number of seats (n) in a room is equal to the number of rows (r) multiplied by the number of seats in a row (s). $n = rs$

[B]

Write formulas for the following rules or expressions, using suitable letters to represent each of the numbers.

13. The side opposite a 30° angle in a right triangle is equal to one half the hypotenuse (c). $a = \frac{1}{2}c$

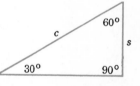

14. The reading on the centigrade thermometer can be found by subtracting 32 from the reading on the Fahrenheit thermometer and taking $\frac{5}{9}$ of the result. $C = \frac{5}{9}(F - 32)$

15. The fare charged by a bus company is 15 cents for the first mile and 5 cents for each additional mile. Let n represent the number of additional miles. $F = 15 + 5n$

16. The square of the hypotenuse of a right triangle is equal to the sum of the squares of the other two sides. $c^2 = a^2 + b^2$

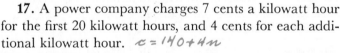

17. A power company charges 7 cents a kilowatt hour for the first 20 kilowatt hours, and 4 cents for each additional kilowatt hour. $c = 140 + 4n$

18. What formula will express the total cost (c) of n articles at b cents each? $c = bn$

19. Write a formula for changing the number of feet into the number of inches. $i = 12f$

20. The distance away, in miles, of a lightning flash is found by dividing the number of seconds between the flash and its accompanying thunderclap by 5. $d = \frac{n}{5}$

① Time permitting, produce models for Exs. 13, 14, 16. Remember, formula work can be dull and routine if not taught with imagination.

79

ALGEBRA, BOOK ONE

21. The temperature in degrees Fahrenheit can be told by counting the number of chirps made by a cricket in 15 seconds and adding 37. $F = n + 37$

Making Formulas from Tables [A]

① In making formulas from tables, we first study how the corresponding numbers change and then write a formula expressing this relation.

Example 1. Write a formula expressing the relation between x and y in this table:

x	1	2	3	4	5	6	7	8	9
y	6	7	8	9	10	11	12	13	14

Solution. From a study of the corresponding values of x and y we see that y is always 5 more than x. Then the formula is $y = x + 5$.

Example 2. Write a formula expressing the relation between a and b in this table:

a	1	2	3	4	5	6	7	8
b	4	7	10	13	16	19	22	25

Solution. From a careful study of this table we see that b is always 1 more than 3 times a. Then the formula is $b = 3a + 1$.

[A]

EXERCISES

In each exercise write the formula that expresses the relation between the numbers, and then complete the table.

1.

Number of gallons of gasoline (n)		1	2	3	4	5	6	7
Cost in cents (c)	$C = 56n$	56	112	168	224	280?	336?	392?

2.

Interest in dollars (i)		1	2	3	4	5	6	7
Total amount in dollars (A)		46	47	48	49	50?	51?	52?

$A = i + 45$

3.

x	1	2	3	4	5	6	7	8	9
y	3	5	7	9	11?	13?	15?	17?	19?

$y = 2x + 1$

80

① You can base some review on Ex. 1. For example, ask "Using the formula $p = 4x + 12$, find the perimeter when the variable has the domain $\{1, 2, 3, 4, 5\}$. When x is doubled, is the perimeter doubled?"

FORMULAS

4.

x	1	2	3	4	5	6	7	8	9
y	1	3	5	7	? *9*	? *11*	? *13*	? *15*	? *17*

y = 2x - 1

Simplifying Formulas [A]

To be most useful a formula should be written in its simplest form.

Example 1. Write a formula for the perimeter of this rectangle.

Solution. Since the perimeter of the rectangle is equal to the sum of the four sides, we have $P = m + m + m + 2 + m + 2$. Simplifying the formula, $P = 4m + 4$.

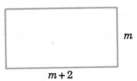

m

m + 2

[A]

1. Each side of this square is $x + 3$. Write the formula for its perimeter in the simplest form. *P = 4x + 12*

x + 3

s   *s + 1*

s + 3

2. Write the formula for the perimeter of this triangle in its simplest form. *P = 3s + 4*

3. Write the formula for the perimeter of a rectangle if the width is x and the length $x + 4$. *P = 4x + 8*

4. The sides of a triangle are b, $b - 1$, and $b + 3$. Write the formula for its perimeter. *P = 3b + 2*

5. Two squares have sides of $x + 2$ and x respectively. Write a formula giving the sum of their perimeters. *P = 8x + 8*

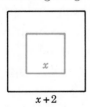

x

x + 2

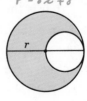

r

6. Write a formula giving the area of the colored part of the larger circle. $A = \frac{3}{4} \pi r^2$

81

Use pages 82 and 83 as suggested at the end of previous chapters.

ALGEBRA, BOOK ONE

Before you leave this chapter be sure that you

PAGE

1. Know what a formula is   61
2. Know how to use formulas in solving
problems   62
3. Know how to make formulas from rules   78
4. Know how to make formulas from tables   80
5. Know how to simplify formulas   81
6. Remember the formulas for
   the circumference of a circle   74
   the area of a circle   74
   the perimeter of a rectangle, a paral-
     lelogram, and a triangle   70
   the area of a rectangle   71
   the area of a parallelogram   72
   the area of a triangle   73
   the volume of a rectangular solid   76

These pages will help you review.

7. Know the meanings of the following words and can spell
them correctly:

	PAGE		PAGE
formula	61	diameter	74
polygon	70	radius	74
perimeter	70	rectangular solid	76
area	71	cube	76
circumference	74	volume	76

CHAPTER REVIEW

1. What is a formula? *a rule written in mathematical symbols.*

2. What is the formula for finding simple interest? $i = prt$

3. Name the three steps used in solving a problem by a formula. *See p. 64*

4. $A = p + prt$. Find A when $p = \$350$, $r = 4\%$, and the time is 4 years 3 months. *$409.50*

5. The formula for finding the distance d when the rate r and the time t are known is $d = rt$. Write the formula for finding d when $r = 30$. Write the formula for finding d when $t = 5$.
$d = 30t$ *$d = 5r$*

82

6. $s = \frac{1}{2}gt^2$. Find s when $g = 32.16$ and $t = 3$. *144.72*

7. Find the number of acres in a farm 180 rods long and 80 rods wide. (160 square rods = 1 acre.) *90*

8. Write a formula for finding the area of a circle. $A = \pi r^2$

9. Write a formula for finding the volume of a rectangular solid. $V = lwh$

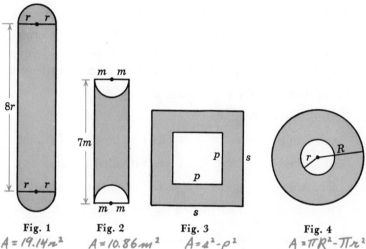

Fig. 1	Fig. 2	Fig. 3	Fig. 4
$A = 19.14 r^2$	$A = 10.86 m^2$	$A = s^2 - p^2$	$A = \pi R^2 - \pi r^2$

10. Write a formula for the colored area of each of the four figures above.

11. A bicycle wheel is 28 inches in diameter. What is its circumference? *87.92 in.*

12. A schoolroom is 30 feet long, 24 feet wide, and 12 feet high. If 30 people are in the room, find the average number of cubic feet of air for each person. *288*

13. Write a formula for finding the cost of n articles at p cents each. $c = np$

14. Write a formula for finding the average of the three numbers x, y, and z. $a = \dfrac{x+y+z}{3}$

15. Write a formula expressing the relation of x and y in the table below. Then complete the table.

$x = y+2$	9	14	17	20	*22*	*27*	*32*	*42*	*52*	*102*	*202*
$y = x-2$	7	12	15	18	20	25	30	40	50	100	200

ALGEBRA, BOOK ONE

[A]

GENERAL REVIEW

Complete the following statements by supplying the proper words:

1. The __?__ of 6 and 2 is 8. *sum*

2. The __?__ of 9 and 3 is 6. *difference*

3. When 10 is divided by 5, the __?__ is 2. *quotient*

4. The __?__ of 7 and 3 is 21. *product*

5. If x represents the number of feet in the length of a room, how many x will represent the number of inches in its length? How many x will represent the number of yards in its length? *$12x; \frac{1}{3}x$*

6. Simplify $p = l + l + w + w$. *$p = 2l + 2w$*

7. Indicate by symbols:

a. x added to y. *$x + y$*

d. The product of m and n. *mn*

b. c diminished by 4. *$c - 4$*

e. a divided by c. *a/c*

c. y increased by 2. *$y + 2$*

f. The sum of $4a$ and $3b$. *$4a + 3b$*

g. The sum of k and 6, divided by the product of 3 and k. *$\frac{k+6}{3k}$*

8. Indicate "h multiplied by five" three different ways. *$h \times 5, h \cdot 5, 5h$*

9. What is the coefficient of y in the expression $3y^2 + 2y - 1$? *2*

10. What is the second term in the expression $4a - 2b + 3c$? *$-2b$*

11. Why do we use parentheses in algebra? *To indicate that the expression in parentheses is to be treated as 1 number.*

Solve:

12. $2x + 3 = 19$ *8* 13. $4x - 1 = 11$ *3* 14. $\frac{3}{4}x = 72$ *96*

15. If $x = 3$, find the value of x^2; of $2x^2$; of x^3. *9; 18; 27*

16. Simplify $9 + 6 \div 3$. *11*

17. Simplify $\frac{1}{2}x - \frac{1}{3}x + x$. *$\frac{7}{6}x$*

18. Simplify $(9 + 6) \div 5$. *3*

19. Find the value of $\dfrac{2a - b}{4}$ if $a = 8$ and $b = 4$. *3*

20. Solve $c + 3c = 12$. *3*

21. Solve $.04y = 56$. *1400*

84

22. Write formulas for finding

a. The area of a rectangle. $A = bh$

b. The area of a triangle. $A = \frac{1}{2}bh$

c. The area of a circle. $A = \pi r^2$

d. The volume of a rectangular solid. $V = lwh$

23. Find the area of a square having a side m. m^2

24. If a man earns $8 a day, write a formula expressing his wages (w) for n days. $w = 8n$

25. The sum of two numbers is 144 and one of them is 5 times as large as the other. How large is each number? $24; 120$

26. Separate 90 into two parts such that one of them will be one fourth as large as the other. $18; 72$

27. The perimeter of a triangle is 210 inches. Find the lengths of its sides if the third side is one and one half times as long as each of the others. $60 in., 60 in., 90 in.$

28. $F = \frac{9}{5}C + 32$. Find F when $C = 80$. 176

29. $C = \frac{5}{9}(F - 32)$. Find C when $F = 98$. $36\frac{2}{3}$

[Test A]

CHAPTER TESTS

Write formulas for

1. The simple interest i. $i = prt$

2. The circumference c of a circle whose diameter is d. $c = \pi d$

3. The area A of a circle whose radius is r. $A = \pi r^2$

4. The area of the colored portion of this rectangle. $A = bh - 4x^2$

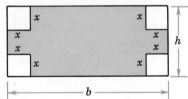

State in words:

5. $r = \frac{1}{2}d$ **6.** $d = \frac{c}{\pi}$ **7.** $i = 12f$ **8.** $V = lwh$

9. $x = 2y - 3$. What is the value of x when $y = 5$? 7

10. $F = \frac{wa}{g}$. Find F when $w = 100$, $a = 8$, and $g = 32$. 25

5. The radius of a circle is equal to $\frac{1}{2}$ the diameter.
6. The diameter of a circle is equal to the circumference divided by π.
7. The number of inches in a distance is equal to 12 times the number of feet in the distance.
8. The volume of a rectangular solid equals the product of the length, the width, and the height.

85

The following sentences are based upon the formulas $p = 4s$ and $A = s^2$. Copy and complete each sentence.

11. The value of p depends upon the value of __?__. *s*

12. If s increases, p __?__. *increase*

13. If s is multiplied by 3, then p is multiplied by __?__. *3*

14. If s is decreased, A is __?__. *decreased*

15. If s is multiplied by 3, then A is multiplied by __?__. *9*.

[Test B]

1. $F = \frac{9}{5} C + 32$. Find F when $C = 40$. *104*

2. $C = \frac{5}{9}(F - 32)$. Find C if $F = 72$. *$22\frac{2}{9}$*

3. $p = 2a + 2b$. What change, if any, is made in p when b is decreased as much as a is increased? *No change*

4. Copy and complete the table for $p = 2n + 7$.

p	? *9*	? *11*	? *13*	? *17*	? *21*	? *25*
n	1	2	3	5	7	9

5. $V = lwh$. Complete: If l and w are doubled and h is trebled, then V is multiplied by __?__. *12*

6. When a bomb is dropped from a plane a mile high, its approximate distance d in feet from the ground after t seconds is given by the formula $d = 5280 - 16t^2$. Find how high the bomb is when t is 4. *5024 ft.*

7. Write a formula for the area of the figure at the left below, consisting of adjoining squares having sides e. *$A = 5e^2$*

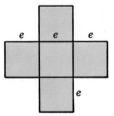

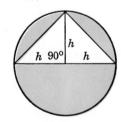

8. Write a formula for the area of the colored portion of the circle in the figure at the right above. *$A = \pi h^2 - h^2$*

86

This test was made to test your skill in the fundamentals of arithmetic. See how well you can do these problems.

1. Add 1728 and 846.

2. From 896 subtract 129.

3. Multiply 147 by 64.

4. Divide 13,056 by 32.

5. Add $\frac{2}{3}$ and $\frac{5}{6}$.

6. From $\frac{7}{8}$ take $\frac{1}{2}$.

7. $\frac{3}{4} \times \frac{6}{7} = ?$

8. $\frac{5}{16} \div \frac{3}{4} = ?$

9. $1.4 + 5.6 = ?$

10. $7.18 - 1.91 = ?$

11. $75 \div 2.5 = ?$

12. $4.7 \times 3.1 = ?$

13. Find 3% of 75.

14. 4 is what % of 40?

15. 6% of what number is 30?

16. Reduce $\frac{14}{21}$ to lowest terms.

17. Change 6% to a decimal.

18. Change $\frac{3}{4}$ to a per cent.

19. Change $\frac{7}{8}$ to a decimal.

20. Change 18% to a common fraction.

●Check your answers with those below.

● **Answers**

5. $1\frac{1}{2}$	**10.** 5.27	**15.** 500	**20.** $\frac{18}{100}$
4. 408	**9.** 7.0	**14.** 10%	**19.** .875
3. 9408	**8.** $\frac{5}{12}$	**13.** 2.25	**18.** 75%
2. 767	**7.** $\frac{6}{14}$	**12.** 14.57	**17.** .06
1. 2574	**6.** $\frac{3}{8}$	**11.** 30	**16.** $\frac{2}{3}$

HISTORICAL NOTE. About 300 B.C., Diophantus of Alexandria simplified problem-solving by allowing a letter to represent the unknown number. The idea of letting a letter stand for a number did not appeal to the thinkers of that time; it was a new and strange idea. The first mathematician to develop the algebraic method in problem-solving was François Viète (1540–1603). This French mathematician is sometimes called "the Father of Algebra."

Carew-Monkmeyer

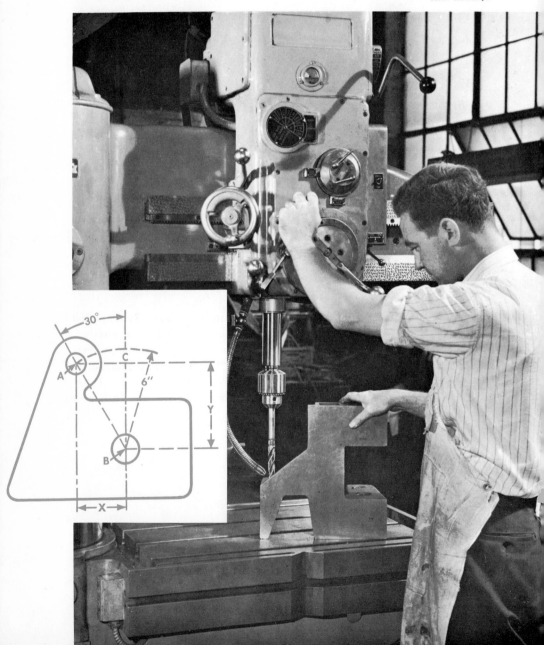

Some machine operators do not use much mathematics in their work. However, a good machinist not only knows how to operate his or her machine, but understands the principles by which the machine operates. A good machine operator knows how to read a handbook, understands graphs and diagrams, can use formulas, and do simple calculations. When given a job, a good machinist can make the necessary calculations, can set his or her machine, and can work without the foreman's assistance.

Some young people learn the machinist trade in vocational or trade schools. Others learn the trade by becoming apprentices to an experienced machinist. In hiring apprentices, however, an experienced machinist is likely to give preference to a young person who has completed high school and who has taken some vocational training.

A good machinist finds knowledge of algebra, geometry, and even some trigonometry helpful. Even though these subjects are not actually used in a particular job, an understanding of them helps the machinist to read about developments in the field. Machinists today cannot afford to allow their methods or products to become outdated.

Often experienced machinists become tool and die makers or set up their own machine shops. Many experiment on their own and invent machines or parts that are patented by the United States Government. Some, like Henry Ford, succeed in building machines that change the whole course of history.

4

Positive
and Negative Numbers

Suggested Time Schedule
10 days

*You will discover in this chapter
that there are numbers smaller than zero
and you will learn how to use them.*

For the first lesson after the examination on Chapter 3, assign pages 91–93. The next day in class discuss this. Explain that when people found there could be numbers less than zero, they had to have a way of symbolizing them in writing. Emphasize that zero is neither positive nor negative. The concept of *direction* shown by positive and negative numbers is important. The first exercises on page 92 help us to see how such numbers can be used to express direction.

Signed Numbers [A]

This chapter will clarify what we did in Chapter 1 when we started to construct the number line. First we located points A, B, C, $\cdots$ equally-spaced to the right of point O in the line. Then we assigned to these points the whole numbers 0, 1, 2, $\cdots$.

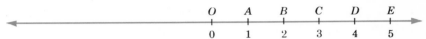

Next we repeated this process for points A', B', C', $\cdots$ in the line and equally-spaced to the left of point O. Since A' is one unit of distance from O (like A), we assigned it the number 1. However we preceded the numeral 1 with the negative symbol, $-$, to indicate that A' and A are on opposite sides of O. We read -1 as *negative one*. Since B' is two units of distance from O, we assigned it the number -2, and so on. We say that -1 and 1 are opposites, or inverses, and -2 and 2 are opposites, or inverses, and so on. Zero is its own inverse. We say that the set of numbers $\cdots$, -3, -2, -1, 0, 1, 2, 3, $\cdots$ is the set of *integers*. We apply the name *negative integers* to the numbers in $\{\cdots, -3, -2, -1\}$ and the name *positive integers* to the numbers in $\{1, 2, 3, \cdots\}$. The number 0 is neither positive nor negative.

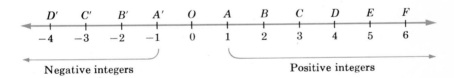

Between any two integers, there are infinitely many non-integer numbers. We cannot list or picture them all in the number line, but we have shown a few sample *rational numbers* in the following drawing.

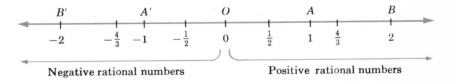

We have said that any number that can be expressed by a fraction whose numerator is an integer and whose denominator is a non-zero integer is a rational number. Clearly, then, since every integer

91

can be expressed by such a fraction, every integer is a rational number. For example, since three may be represented by $\frac{3}{1}, \frac{6}{2}, \frac{9}{3}$ and so on, then three is a rational number.

As in the case of the integers, we can speak of the positive rational numbers, zero, and the negative rational numbers. To this point we have worked entirely with the set of non-negative rational numbers, that is, with zero and the positive rational numbers. In this chapter we shall develop rules for working with any of the rational numbers. We sometimes refer to the positive and negative numbers more briefly as <u>signed numbers</u>.

The following exercises will help you to recognize some of the situations in which both negative and non-negative numbers are used.

[A]

EXERCISES

1. If + 6 stands for a gain of $6, what number will stand for a loss of $3? *−3*

2. If going east 4 miles is represented by + 4 miles, what does − 3 miles represent? *Going west 3 miles*

3. If − 3 feet means 3 feet below sea level, how can you represent 7 feet above sea level? *+ 7 feet*

4. If we let + 80° stand for 80° east longitude, what does − 60° stand for? *60° west longitude*

5. If we let − 80° stand for 80° west longitude, what does + 60° stand for? *60° east longitude*

6. If positive numbers are used for distances to the right of zero, what will negative numbers stand for? *Distance to left of zero.*

7. If + 8 inches means 8 inches above average, what does − 6 inches mean? *6 in. below average*

8. If 10 stories above the ground level are represented by + 10 stories, how would you represent 2 stories below ground level? *− 2 stories*

9. If A.D. 1870 is represented by + 1870, what does − 46 mean? *46 B.C.*

10. What does "6 in the hole" mean when you are keeping score in a game? Would you use + 6 or − 6 to stand for "6 in the hole"? *6 less than zero; −6*

92

POSITIVE AND NEGATIVE NUMBERS

Addition Using the Number Line [A]

We now develop procedures for adding positive numbers, negative numbers, and zero using the number line.

We observe once more that in the number line -1 and 1 are coordinates of points on opposite sides of point O. So are -2 and 2, and every other similar pair of positive and negative numbers. Thus, it seems natural to think of any movement to the right along the line from O as a move in the positive direction and any move to the left from O as a move in the negative direction. In fact, it seems reasonable to consider any move to the right along the line as positive, and any move to the left along the line as negative regardless of the starting point. Let us consider some examples.

Example 1. Find the number represented by $2 + 3$.

Solution. We use the number line as follows:

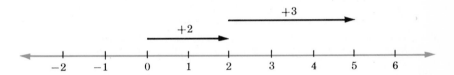

Since 2 is positive, we move 2 units to the right from O. Since 3 is positive, we now move 3 units to the right from 2. This brings us to the point whose coordinate is 5. Thus,

$$(+2) + (+3) = 5.$$

Example 2. Find the sum: $(-1) + (-2)$.

Solution. We use the number line as follows:

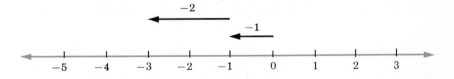

Since -1 is a negative number, we move 1 unit to the left from O. Since -2 is also negative, we move 2 more units to the left from -1. This brings us to the point whose coordinate is -3. Thus,

$$(-1) + (-2) = -3.$$

93

ALGEBRA, BOOK ONE

Example 3. Use the number line to find $3 + (- 4)$.

Solution. We use the number line as follows:

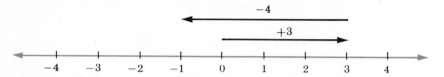

3 can be represented as a move of 3 units to the right from 0. Now $- 4$ can be represented by a move of 4 units to the left from 3. This brings us to the point whose coordinate is $- 1$.

$$3 + (- 4) = - 1$$

Example 4. Find the number represented by $(- 5) + 2$.

Solution. We use the number line as follows:

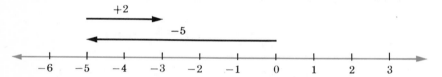

The number $- 5$ can be represented by a move to the left from 0 through a distance of 5 units. Since 2 is positive, we now move 2 units to the right to the point whose coordinate is $- 3$.

$$(- 5) + 2 = - 3$$

Example 5. Find the number represented by $3 + (- 3)$.

Solution. We use the number line shown in Example 4. Since 3 is a positive number, we move to the right three units. Since $- 3$ is negative we now move back to the left from 3 a distance of 3 units. This brings us to the point whose coordinate is 0.

$$3 + (- 3) = 0$$

Example 6. Find $(- 4) + 0$.

Solution. Use the number line shown in Example 4. We represent $- 4$ by a move to the left from 0 for a distance of 4 units. This brings us to the point having coordinate $- 4$. Since 0 is neither positive nor negative, we cannot represent 0 by a move either to the left or the right.

$$(- 4) + 0 = - 4$$

"Count five spaces to the left" means "subtract 5 from 4." If you casually mention this now, you lay the foundation of the operations taught in this chapter. You might discuss other exercises in the same way.

Additive Inverse and Identity Element for Addition[A]

In Example 5 of the preceding section, we found that $3 + (- 3) = 0$. We say that 3 and $- 3$ are <u>additive inverses</u> of each other. In general, if the sum of two numbers is zero, each number is the additive inverse of the other.

In Example 6 of the preceding section, we found that $(- 4) + 0 = - 4$. We say that zero is the <u>identity element for addition.</u> When zero is added to any number, the sum is the number.

Absolute Value[A]

Adding numbers by reference to the number line is not always practical. So, now we shall consider a more efficient procedure which makes use of the idea of <u>absolute value.</u>

If a point B' of the number line has the coordinate $- 2$ and point B has the coordinate 2, then B' and B are each 2 units from point O. In other words, B' and B are equidistant from O regardless of the fact that one has a negative coordinate and the other has a positive coordinate. We say that 2 is the absolute value of both $- 2$ and 2. To represent the words "the absolute value of," we use the symbol $|\ \ |$. Thus, we may write

$$|- 2| = 2 \quad \text{and} \quad |2| = 2.$$

In general, if x is zero or any positive number, then $|x| = x$ and if x is any negative number, then $|x| = - x$.

Consider the following examples.

$$|- 4| = 4, \qquad |4| = 4, \qquad |- 5| = 5, \qquad |5| = 5, \qquad |0| = 0$$

Be sure you understand that if x is a negative number, then its opposite is a positive number. For example, if $x = - 5$, then its opposite is $- (- 5)$. But we know that the opposite of $- 5$ is the positive number 5. Thus $-(- 5) = 5$. When x is a negative number, then $- x$ is a positive number.

Rules for Adding Signed Numbers[A]

On page 96 we state addition rules based upon the idea of absolute value. Study these rules carefully. Try to see how each is a restatement of procedures used in adding by use of the number line. Rule 1 restates the situations of Examples 1 and 2 of page 93. Rule 2 restates the situations of Examples 3 and 4 of page 94.

The concept "When x is a negative number, $|x| = -x$" is difficult for many students. You may need to provide extra help.

1. a. 8   b. -4   c. +2   d. -11   e. -9   f. 14
2. a. -7   b. 1   c. -16   d. +2   e. 0   f. +6
3. a. -a   b. 10b   c. -4c   d. +4x   e. y   f. -16m
4. a -3x²   b. 0   c. -9   d. 3a   e. -k   f. 8m

[A]

5 a. -9xy
b. 4x²
c. -5w
d. 2p
e. 0
f. 9H

ORAL EXERCISES

Think of positive numbers as gains and of negative numbers as losses and add (or combine) the following:

	a	b	c	d	e	f
1.	5	− 8	− 3	− 4	− 3	8
	3	+4	+5	− 7	− 6	6
2.	− 8	+6	− 9	− 4	− 3	− 2
	+1	− 5	− 7	6	+3	+8
3.	− 5 a	7 b	− 7 c	7 x	− 5 y	− 7 m
	+4 a	3 b	+3 c	− 3 x	6 y	− 9 m
4.	5 x²	− 2 r	− 9	2 s	2 k	10 m
	− 8 x²	+2 r	0	s	− 3 k	− 2 m
5.	− 3 xy	5 x²	− 16 w	− 11 p	− 10 st	14 H
	− 6 xy	− x²	11 w	13 p	+ 10 st	− 5 H

7   6. $(10) + (-3)$ 11. $+8 + (6)$ 16. $(-1) + (-1)$
5   7. $(-2) + (+7)$ 12. $(-9) + (-11)$ 17. $(-18) + (-10)$
0   8. $(-5) + (+5)$ 13. $(+3) + (-4)$ 18. $(-\frac{1}{2}) + (-\frac{1}{4})$
17   9. $(-3) + (20)$ 14. $-9 + (+9)$ 19. $(-\frac{2}{3}) + (\frac{5}{6})$
-8   10. $(-3) + (-5)$ 15. $(-5) + (-25)$ 20. $(-.4) + (-.6)$

11. +14
12. -20
13. -1
14. 0
15. -30
16. -2
17. -28
18. -¾
19. ⅙
20. -1.0

Rules for Adding Signed Numbers

1. To add two numbers with like signs,
   use the same sign
   and find the sum of their absolute values.

2. To add two numbers with opposite signs,
   use the sign of the number having the greater absolute value
   and find the difference of their absolute values.

[A]

ORAL DRILL IN ADDITION

To acquire speed and accuracy in the addition (or combining) of positive and negative numbers, practice daily the following exercises:

	a	b	c	d	e	f	g	h
1.	2	− 3	− 2	− 3	4	− 4	− 4	− 4
	3	− 2	3	+3	− 3	− 3	3	+4
	5	-5	1	0	1	- 7	-1	0

96

Page 97, ex. 2. 13 -2 -1 9 -9 3 -8
3. 14 -8 16 0 10 2 -5
4. 0 -10 -17 4 -4 6 9
5. 20 -8 -8 18 -2 -18 -10

Ans. 2-5 at foot of page 96

	a	b	c	d	e	f	g
2.	7	− 7	− 7	6	− 6	− 3	− 2
	6	5	6	3	− 3	6	− 6
3.	6	− 5	7	− 6	4	8	− 9
	8	− 3	9	+ 6	6	− 6	4
4.	5	− 5	− 8	− 5	− 10	11	10
	− 5	− 5	− 9	9	6	− 5	− 1
5.	14	− 14	6	10	− 10	− 10	1
	6	6	− 14	8	8	− 8	− 11
6.	4	− 4	7	− 7	7	− 5	− 7
	7	− 7	3	− 3	5	− 7	− 1
7.	− 3	− 10	21	− 10	− 2	8	− 16
	− 6	− 11	− 5	14	− 13	− 20	+ 16
8.	− 1	14	2	− 8	− 8	40	− 40
	− 12	− 14	− 13	− 8	+ 8	− 1	− 1
9.	$\frac{1}{4}$	$\frac{2}{3}$	$-\frac{1}{2}$	$\frac{2}{5}$	8	$-\frac{3}{5}$	$-\frac{7}{8}$
	$\frac{3}{4}$	$-\frac{1}{3}$	$-\frac{1}{4}$	$-\frac{7}{5}$	$-4\frac{1}{2}$	$+\frac{3}{5}$	$-\frac{1}{8}$
10.	4.0	− 3.0	− 5.0	.00	− 4.3	− 6.3	4.1
	− 1.5	4.7	− 1.0	− .25	− 2.7	− 2.7	− 9.1

See foot of page.

Adding Several Signed Numbers [A]

The addition rules that you have been studying were designed to make negative numbers have the same addition and multiplication properties as the positive numbers. To add the signed numbers 4, − 3, and − 7, we use the associative property of addition as shown in either of the two illustrations below, or if we prefer, we use the commutative property to rearrange the numbers before we use the associative property. Emphasize the names and use of these properties. In applying them, the arrangement and grouping should be done mentally.

$$4 + (− 3) + (−7) = 4 + [(− 3) + (− 7)] = 4 + (− 10) = − 6$$
$$4 + (− 3) + (− 7) = [4 + (− 3)] + (− 7) = 1 + (− 7) \ = − 6$$

To add more than three numbers we add three of them as indicated above, then add the sum to another of the numbers, and so on, until every number has been used once.

8.   −13   0   −11   −16   0   39   −41
9.   1   1/3   −3/4   −1   3½   0   −1
10.   2.5   1.7   −6.0   −.25   −7.0   −9.0   −5.0

[A]

EXERCISES

Find the sum in each exercise.

1.	2.	3.	4.	5.	6.	7.
5	6	− 9	4	− 10	7	− 4
− 3	− 7	+ 9	− 6	6	− 2	− 3
− 4	− 8	7	7	+ 10	+ 5	− 2
-2	-9	7	5	6	10	-9

8. The numbers below are arranged in 5 rows and 8 columns. Add the numbers in each row and in each column. Add the row sums and the column sums to check your work.

	f	g	h	i	j	k	l	m	Sums
a	4	5	− 3	− 2	7	1	6	− 8	? 10
b	− 2	− 3	− 4	− 5	− 2	− 1	− 8	− 7	? -32
c	6	− 4	5	3	2	− 7	− 3	− 2	? 0
d	− 5	3	− 6	9	4	2	3	− 12	? -2
e	− 2	− 3	2	4	− 4	7	− 6	5	? 3
Sums	? 1	? -2	? -6	? 9	? 7	? 2	? -8	? -24	? -21

How to Indicate the Sum of Signed Numbers [A]

We have used the + and − symbols in two ways. When the symbols are used for addition and subtraction, respectively, we refer to them as signs of operation. We read them as "plus" and "minus." When we use them to indicate that a number is positive or negative, we refer to them as signs of opposition. We read them as "positive" and "negative." For variables, we read − as "the inverse of."

In writing additions horizontally, we usually omit the signs of operation and the parentheses. We use only the signs of opposition. When a sign of opposition is the first sign in a number expression, we usually omit it if it is +.

①
    Instead of writing (+ 7) + (+ 3), we write 7 + 3.
    Instead of writing (+ 6) + (− 2), we write 6 − 2.
    Instead of writing (− 3) + (− 4), we write − 3 − 4.
    Instead of writing (− 5) + (+ 3), we write − 5 + 3.

① The meaning of sign notation often causes confusion. You will need to go back to this section. Be sure students understand that unless parentheses are used the signs are signs of *opposition*.

Emphasize and illustrate this.

POSITIVE AND NEGATIVE NUMBERS

You will notice that when the addition $(+6) + (-2)$ is written $6 - 2$ it looks like an ordinary subtraction problem from arithmetic. However, since the result is $+4$ regardless of which interpretation is used, no difficulties can arise. You will soon recognize (if you do not already) that adding a negative number is equivalent to subtracting a positive number. Just remember the following:

> To show that two or more numbers are to be added,
> write the numbers one after the other with their signs of opposition
> but without the signs of operation.

[A]

EXERCISES

Using positive and negative numbers, rewrite the following and then combine the terms.

1. Earning $7 and earning $6. $7 + $6 = $13

2. Losing $6 and gaining $5. $-$6 + $5 = -$1$

3. Going up 30 feet and then going down 50 feet. $30 - 50 = -20$ (ft.)

4. Gaining 10 cents and then losing 4 cents. $10¢ - 4¢ = +6¢$

5. Going 6 steps backward and then going 10 steps forward. $-6 + 10 = +4$ (steps)

6. Gaining 4 pounds, losing 6 pounds, and losing 2 pounds. $4 - 6 - 2 = -4$ lb.

7. Making a profit of $80, a loss of $60, and a profit of $20. $80 - $60 + $20 = +$40

8. A rise of 8°, a drop of 12°, and a rise of 2°. $8° - 12° + 2° = -2°$

Remembering that $4 - 6 + 3$ is the same as $+4$ added to -6 added to $+3$, combine the following:

9. $4 - 6 + 3$ *1*

10. $8 - 5 - 10$ *-7*

11. $7 - 9 + 6$ *+4*

12. $4 - 2 - 2$ *0*

13. $9 + 6 - 4$ *11*

14. $3 - 8 - 5$ *-10*

15. $-7 - 5 + 1$ *-11*

16. $-8 + 5 - 3$ *-6*

17. $-2 - 6 - 7$ *-15*

18. $7 + 2 + 1$ *10*

19. $\frac{1}{2} + \frac{1}{3} + \frac{1}{6}$ *1*

20. $.4 + .3 - .2$ *0.5*

21. What is the absolute value of -8? of $+6$? of 10? of -9? *8; 6; 10; 9*

22. Which is greater: -3 or -5? $+9$ or -7? 0 or -4? 7 or -7? *-3; +9; 0; 7*

99

Simplifying Polynomials [A]

On page 21 you simplified polynomials by adding and subtracting positive numbers. You will now learn how to simplify polynomials such as $- 4x + y - x - 3y$. In simplifying this polynomial, it is necessary to combine negative numbers. Remember that x has the same meaning as $1x$ or $+1x$ and $-x$ has the same meaning as $-1x$. In this instance you would combine $-4x$ and $-x$ to get $-5x$, and $-3y$ and y to get $-2y$. The result is $-5x - 2y$.

Example 1. Simplify $5b - 6b$.

Solution. By the distributive property
$$5b - 6b = (5 - 6)b.$$
Since $(5 - 6) = -1$,
Then $\quad 5b - 6b = -1b$, or $-b$.

Example 2. Simplify $3a + 4a - 5a - 6a$.

Solution. By the distributive property
$$3a + 4a - 5a - 6a = (3 + 4 - 5 - 6)a$$
$$(3 + 4 - 5 - 6) = -4.$$
Then $\quad 3a + 4a - 5a - 6a = -4a$.

[A]

EXERCISES

Simplify by combining like terms: See ① below

1. $3x - 4x - x$ $-2x$

2. $a - 4a + 2a$ $-a$

3. $4b - 6b + 3b$ b

4. $m + m - m$ m

5. $10r + 6r - 13r$ $3r$

6. $-4x - 3x - 5x$ $-12x$

7. $5A - 2A + 3A$ $6A$

8. $7h - 9h - h$ $-3h$

9. $6x - 4x + 9x$ $11x$

10. $r - 4r - 6r$ $-9r$

11. $3a^2 - 6a^2 - 2a^2$ $-5a^2$

12. $2.5x + .5x - 6x$ $-3x$

13. $3.1y + 2.4y - 8y$ $-2.5y$

14. $3m^3 - 8m^3 - m^3$ $-6m^3$

15. $5bc - 8bc - bc$ $-4bc$

16. $-xy - xy - xy$ $-3xy$

17. $\frac{1}{2}x + \frac{5}{6}x - x$ $\frac{1}{3}x$

18. $\frac{1}{3}a - \frac{5}{6}a + \frac{1}{12}a$ $-\frac{5}{12}a$

19. $-\frac{1}{2}b - \frac{1}{4}b - \frac{1}{3}b$ $-\frac{13}{12}b$

20. $\frac{1}{2}x + \frac{3}{4}x - \frac{1}{3}x$ $\frac{11}{12}x$

Example 3. Simplify $4a + 3b + 5a - 8b$.

Solution. $4a$ and $5a$ are like terms and their sum is $9a$.
$3b$ and $-8b$ are like terms and their sum is $-5b$. Then
$$4a + 3b + 5a - 8b = 9a - 5b$$

① Remind students of the commutative and associative principles underlying these solutions. These exercises extend addition through a spiral development. It is now time to test for a thorough understanding and speed in addition.

[A]

Simplify:

1. $3a + 4b - a - 6b$ $2a-2b$ **4.** $5ab + 6 + 8ab - 10$ $13ab-4$

2. $-5x - 7y - 8x$ $-13x-7y$ **5.** $-6x + 9 - 3x - 8$ $1-9x$

3. $x + y - x + 6y$ $7y$ **6.** $a + c + 7a - 4$ $8a+c-4$

7. $m^2 + 2mn + n^2 - m^2 + 2mn + n^2$ $4mn+2n^2$

8. $a^2 - 4ab - b^2 + 4ab + a^2 - b^2$ $2a^2-2b^2$

Indicate the sum of

9. a and $-b$ $a-b$

14. x^2, $-2x$, and -1 x^2-2x-1

10. -3 and $+3$ $-3+3$

15. $4a$, $-b$, and $5c$ $4a-b+5c$

11. $2x^2$ and $5x$ $2x^2+5x$

16. $-3r$, $2s$, and $-5t$ $-3r+2s-5t$

12. s and $-s^2$ $s-s^2$

17. $2x^3$, $-5x^2$, and $-4x$ $2x^3-5x^2-4x$

13. x^2 and y^2 x^2+y^2

18. $-a$, b, and c. $-a+b+c$

Indicate the sum and simplify:

19. 4, 5, and -3 6

22. $2x$, $3y$, and $-4x$ $3y-2x$

20. $2m$, 7, and $-5m$ $7-3m$

23. $-x^2$, $3x$, and $+x^2$ $3x$

21. $4a$, $-2a$, and h $2a+h$

24. $2a$, $-b$, $-2a$, and b 0

Multiplication of Signed Numbers [A]   See ①, foot of page.

In algebra there are four types of products. These are a positive number times a positive number, a positive number times a negative number, a negative number times a positive number, and a negative number times a negative number.

Type I. *A Positive Number Times a Positive Number.* This is the type you learned in arithmetic.

If a man saves $5 a week, he will be $20 wealthier 4 weeks from now. The solution may be written

$$(+4) \times (+\$5) = +\$20$$

Type II. *A Positive Number Times a Negative Number.* If a man loses $5 a week, he will be $20 poorer in 4 weeks.

If saving $5 is represented by $+\$5$, then losing $5 should be represented by $-\$5$; and if $20 richer is represented by $+\$20$, then $20 poorer should be represented by $-\$20$.

Then $(+4) \times (-\$5) = -\$20.$

① One simple way of explaining signs in multiplication is presented here. There are other ways, of course, and you may prefer to use another illustration. Later when students study the axiomatic structure of algebra, they will have a means of deductive proof of these rules. But at the beginning, an explanation seems preferable to involved proofs.

Type III. *A Negative Number Times a Positive Number.* If a man has been saving $5 a week, 4 weeks ago he was $20 poorer than he is now.

If future time is represented by a positive number, then past time should be represented by a negative number.

Then $(-4) \times (+\$5) = -\$20$

Type IV. *A Negative Number Times a Negative Number.* If a man has been losing $5 a week, 4 weeks ago he was $20 richer than he is now. Then $(-4) \times (-\$5) = +\$20$.

The examples above illustrate the following:

Signs in Multiplication

The product of two numbers with *like* signs is positive.
The product of two numbers with *unlike* signs is negative.

EXERCISES

[A]

Multiply, using the statements just above:

	a	b	c	d	e	f	g	h
1.	3	2	−6	−4	−5	+5	−2	7
	5	−7	+3	−3	+1	−1	−2	3
2.	−8	7	−6	−7	−8	−3	+3	−10
	−4	−9	−6	+1	1	−3	+3	−1
3.	−4	−5	−5	6	−5	−9	−9	−9
	−5	4	−10	−2	7	9	1	−1
4.	$\frac{1}{2}$	$-\frac{1}{4}$	8	−9	$-\frac{1}{5}$	$\frac{2}{7}$	$-\frac{1}{2}$	$-\frac{3}{7}$
	$\frac{1}{3}$	$-\frac{1}{3}$	$-\frac{1}{4}$	$\frac{1}{3}$	$-\frac{1}{5}$	$-\frac{3}{7}$	$-\frac{2}{4}$	−1

5. 3(−5) *−15*   **10.** $\frac{1}{2}$ of (−4) *−2*   **15.** −2(−8) *16*

6. −6(4) *−24*   **11.** $\frac{1}{3} \times (6)$ *2*   **16.** .3 × −.4 *−0.12*

7. 9(−1) *−9*   **12.** −12($\frac{1}{4}$) *−3*   **17.** .01 × (100) *1*

8. (−2)(10) *−20*   **13.** 25(−$\frac{1}{5}$) *−5*   **18.** −2(.05) *−0.1*

9. 8(−10) *−80*   **14.** ($\frac{1}{2}$)(−$\frac{1}{3}$) *−$\frac{1}{6}$*   **19.** −4(25) *−100*

102

1. 15	−14	−18	12	−5	−5	4	21
2. 32	−63	36	−7	−8	9	9	10
3. 20	−20	50	−12	−35	−81	−9	9
4. $\frac{1}{6}$	$\frac{1}{12}$	−2	−3	$\frac{1}{25}$	−$\frac{6}{49}$	$\frac{1}{4}$	$\frac{3}{7}$

20. (1) $8, -5, -3, -7, -4, 4, -4, 10.$ (3) $-9, -1, -15, 4, 2, 0, -8, -10.$
(2) $-12, -2, -12, -6, -7, -6, 6, 11.$ (4) $\frac{5}{6}, -\frac{7}{12}, 7\frac{3}{4}, -8\frac{2}{3}, -\frac{2}{3}, \frac{1}{7}, -1, -1\frac{3}{7}.$

POSITIVE AND NEGATIVE NUMBERS

20. Add the numbers in each part of exercises 1, 2, 3, and 4.

21. Multiply 7, − 3, 4, and − 6 in turn by 1. $7, -3, 4, -6.$

Complete: When a number is multiplied by 1, the product is the __?__ as the number itself.
same

22. Multiply 7, − 3, 4, and − 6 in turn by − 1. $-7, +3, -4, +6$

Complete: A number can be multiplied by − 1 by __?__ its sign.
changing

23. The expression − 4 x means that the number x is to be multiplied by − 4. What is the value of − 4 x when $x = 3$? -12 when $x = -3$? $+12$

24. Find the values of the following expressions when $a = 4$, $b = -5$, and $c = -6$.

a. $4 b$ -20 **d.** $-4 b$ 20 **g.** ab -20 **j.** $\frac{1}{2} a$ 2

b. $-3 a$ -12 **e.** $-3 c$ 18 **h.** ac -24 **k.** $-\frac{1}{5} b$ 1

c. $4 a$ 16 **f.** $6 b$ -30 **i.** bc 30 **l.** $.3 c$ -1.8

How to Find the Product of Three or More Numbers [A]

To multiply three numbers we use the associative property of multiplication as shown in the first two illustrations below. To rearrange the numbers before we multiply, we use the commutative property of multiplication as shown in the third line. For more than three numbers, we multiply the product of three of them by a fourth, and so on, until every number is used once. The product $(-4)(+3)(-5)$ may be found in any of the following ways:

$$(-4)[(+3)(-5)] = -4(-15) = 60$$

$$[(-4)(+3)](-5) = (-12)(-5) = 60$$

$$[(-4)(-5)](+3) = (+20)(+3) = 60$$

When finding the value of an expression such as $-4 x^2$, we first do the multiplication indicated by the exponent.

Example. Find the value of $-7 x^2$ when $x = -3$.

Solution. If $x = -3$, $x^2 = (-3)^2 = (-3)(-3) = 9$
Then $-7 x^2 = -7(9) = -63$

ALGEBRA, BOOK ONE

Multiplication by Zero and One [A]

By the multiplication property of zero, the product of any number and zero is zero. Thus $3(0) = 0$, $0(10) = 0$, $0(-8) = 0$, and $1000(0) = 0$. By the multiplication property of 1, the product of 1 and any number is that number. Thus $3(1) = 3$, $1(-5) = -5$, and $(-9)1 = -9$.

EXERCISES

①

[A]

1. In each of the exercises below replace the variable by a numeral to make the sentence true.

a. $1 + x = 1$ *0*

b. $3y = 3$ *1*

c. $4x = 0$ *0*

d. $0y = 0$ *any numeral*

e. $0 + r = 3$ *3*

f. $\frac{y}{2}(3) = 3$ *2*

g. $8(3 - x) = 0$ *3*

h. $y(4 + 9) = 0$ *0*

i. $5 = 5\left(\frac{z}{6}\right)$ *6*

2. If $a = 1$, $b = 2$, $c = 0$, and $d = -3$, find the value of

a. abc *0*

b. ab^2 *4*

c. $-4ab$ *-8*

d. $-3cd^2$ *0*

e. $-5c^2d$ *0*

f. $abcd$ *0*

g. $ac - a$ *-1*

h. $ad - c^8$ *-3*

3. Explain how the following process for finding $\frac{1}{2} = \frac{?}{6}$ uses the multiplication property of 1: $\frac{1}{2}\left(\frac{3}{3}\right) = \frac{1(3)}{2(3)} = \frac{3}{6}$.

Division of Signed Numbers [A]

You know from your study of arithmetic that if the product of two numbers is divided by either of them, the quotient is the other number. For example, if 15 (the product of 3 and 5) is divided by 3, the quotient is 5. This fact is true for either positive or negative numbers; it is not true for zero, which is neither positive nor negative. Zero separates the positive numbers from the negative. We cannot divide by zero. That is easily seen by trying to divide some number, say 4, by 0. According to the reasoning above there would then have to be a quotient which multiplied by 0 gives 4. There is none, for when a number is multiplied by 0, the product is always 0, never 4.

We can learn the law of signs for division by studying four examples.

1. Since $(+5)(+3) = +15$, then $(+15) \div (+3) = +5$.
2. Since $(-5)(+3) = -15$, then $(-15) \div (+3) = -5$.
3. Since $(+5)(-3) = -15$, then $(-15) \div (-3) = +5$.
4. Since $(-5)(-3) = +15$, then $(+15) \div (-3) = -5$.

104

POSITIVE AND NEGATIVE NUMBERS

The examples just given illustrate the following statements:

Signs in Division

The quotient of two numbers with like signs is positive.
The quotient of two numbers with unlike signs is negative.

[A]

EXERCISES

1. How do the statements above, for division, compare with those for multiplication? *The same law of signs applies in both operations.*

Divide as indicated: *answers 2-6 at foot of page.*

	a	b	c	d	e	f	g
2.	$\frac{-12}{-3}$	$\frac{-10}{5}$	$\frac{-30}{5}$	$\frac{25}{-5}$	$\frac{8}{-1}$	$\frac{-6}{6}$	$\frac{0}{4}$
3.	$\frac{8}{-2}$	$\frac{-15}{5}$	$\frac{14}{-7}$	$\frac{-10}{-2}$	$\frac{12}{-2}$	$\frac{-4}{-4}$	$\frac{-18}{9}$
4.	$\frac{-15}{-1}$	$\frac{20}{-5}$	$\frac{-12}{3}$	$\frac{-8}{-4}$	$\frac{7}{1}$	$\frac{-7}{-1}$	$\frac{0}{3}$
5.	$\frac{2.8}{-7}$	$\frac{-20}{-10}$	$\frac{-.04}{-2}$	$\frac{-3.0}{6}$	$\frac{100}{-10}$	$\frac{-80}{6}$	$\frac{-2.7}{.9}$
6.	$\frac{10}{-.2}$	$\frac{7}{3}$	$\frac{-.4}{2}$	$\frac{6\frac{2}{7}}{3\frac{1}{7}}$	$\frac{-60}{-30}$	$\frac{-99}{33}$	$\frac{80}{-16}$

7. $56 \div (-7)$ *-8*   **11.** $54 \div .06$ *900*   **15.** $(-5\frac{1}{3}) \div (2\frac{2}{9})$ *-2⅖*

8. $-16 \div 8$ *-2*   **12.** $-63 \div 7$ *-9*   **16.** $8.4 \div (-.4)$ *-21*

9. $(-20) \div (-4)$ *5*   **13.** $40 \div 80$ *½*   **17.** $-50 \div 2.5$ *-20*

10. $6\frac{2}{3} \div (-\frac{5}{6})$ *-8*   **14.** $(-7\frac{1}{2}) \div (-\frac{3}{4})$ *10*   **18.** $20 \div (-.05)$ *-400*

19. Find the quotient if the dividend is -8 and the divisor is -1. *8*

20. Find the quotient if the dividend is -27 and the divisor is -3. *9*

21. The product of two numbers is -32. If one of the numbers is -16, what is the other? *2*

22. If the multiplicand is -405 and the product is -2025, what is the multiplier? *5*

2. 4	-2	-6	-5	-8	-1	0
3. -4	-3	-2	5	-6	1	-2
4. 15	-4	-4	2	7	7	0
5. -0.4	2	.02	-0.5	-10	-13⅓	-3
6. -50	2⅓	-0.2	2	2	-3	-5

23. If $a = -12$, find the value of

a. $\frac{a}{4}$ -3 d. $\frac{3a}{2}$ -18 g. $5a$ -60 j. $a^2 \div 6$ 24

b. $\frac{3}{4}a$ -9 e. $-\frac{2}{3}a$ 8 h. $-\frac{3}{2}a$ 18 k. $-a^2$ -144

c. $-\frac{1}{2}a$ 6 f. $-.5a$ 6 i. a^2 144 l. $-a^2 \div 72$ -2

24. Simplify:

a. $\frac{2 \times 3}{2}$ 3 c. $\frac{8 \times -6}{4}$ -12 e. $\frac{9 \times 10}{-5 \times 3}$ -6

b. $\frac{8 \times 9}{6}$ 12 d. $\frac{(-10)(-4)}{8}$ 5 f. $\frac{-4(100)}{50}$ -8

[B]

25. If $x = 4$, $y = -6$, and $z = -8$, find the value of

a. xy -24 c. $\frac{-xy}{-1}$ -24 e. $\frac{xz}{y}$ $5\frac{1}{3}$ g. $\frac{x^2}{y}$ $-2\frac{2}{3}$

b. $\frac{xy}{z}$ 3 d. xz -32 f. $-5xz$ 160 h. $\frac{-yz}{x}$ -12

26. If $a = -6$, $b = 3$, and $c = -2$, find the value of

a. $\frac{a+b}{2}$ $-1\frac{1}{2}$ c. $\frac{b+c}{-1}$ -1 e. $abc \div (-9)$ -4

b. $\frac{a+c}{-4}$ 2 d. $(ab) \div c$ 9 f. $bc \div a$ 1

27. $F = \frac{9}{5}C + 32$. Find the value of F when $C = 10$; when $C = -10$; when $C = -30$. 50; 14; -22

[C]

28. $C_t = \dfrac{1}{\dfrac{1}{C_1} + \dfrac{1}{C_2} + \dfrac{1}{C_3}}$. In this formula C_1, C_2, and C_3 represent different values in the same way that the letters a, b, and c do. Find the value of C_t if $C_1 = 20$, $C_2 = 30$, and $C_3 = 40$. $9\frac{3}{13}$

REVIEW EXERCISES

	a	b	c	d	e	f	g
answers	-1;	2;	1;	8;	-4;	0;	-7A]
1. Add:	-4	5	-7	-2	9	-10	-3
	3	-3	8	10	-13	+10	-4
2. Multiply:	-9	-6	-10	8	-3	.4	-8
	4	-3	10	-5	7	.3	.5
	-36	18	-100	-40	-21	.12	-4

POSITIVE AND NEGATIVE NUMBERS

3. Simplify:

a. $(-4) + (-2)$ _-6_   **d.** $(-12)(-3)$ _36_   **g.** $0 \div 6$ _0_

b. $6 - 8 + 7$ _5_   **e.** $-12 \div 3$ _-4_   **h.** 7×0 _0_

c. $-10 - 11$ _-21_   **f.** $(-10) \div (-10)$ _1_   **i.** $3 \div (-6)$ _-½_

How to Multiply One Monomial by Another [A]

On page 14 it was said that an exponent is a small letter or figure placed above and to the right of a number to show how many times the number is used as a factor. Thus 6^2 is a short way of writing 6×6, m^3 is a short way of writing mmm, and $(2x)^4$ is a short way of writing $(2x)(2x)(2x)(2x)$. We shall now learn how to multiply monomials, for example, $7m$ and $-3m^2$.

Example 1. Multiply $7a$ by 4.

Solution. $7a$ means 7 times a. Then 4 times $7a$ means 4 times 7 times a, or $4 \times 7 \times a$. This answer can be simplified because we can multiply 7 by 4, getting 28. The product of 28 and a can only be indicated, as $28a$.

Then $7a \times 4 = 28a$

Notice that we multiply only one of the two factors of $7a$ by 4.

Example 2. Multiply x^3 by x^2.

Solution. x^3 means xxx and x^2 means xx. Then $x^3 \cdot x^2 = xxx \cdot xx$. The short way of writing $xxxxx$ is x^5.

Then $x^3 \cdot x^2 = x^5$

How is the exponent 5 obtained?

Example 3. Multiply $4x^3$ by $-5x^4$.

Solution. $(4x^3)(-5x^4) = 4x^3(-5)x^4$. Since the multiplications may be performed in any order, this product may be written $4(-5)(x^3x^4)$. Since $4(-5) = -20$, and $x^3x^4 = x^7$, the product is $-20x^7$.

Then $(4x^3)(-5x^4) = -20x^7$

Example 4. Multiply $-6b$ by $+3a$.

Solution. $(-6b)(3a) = -6b \cdot 3a = -6 \cdot 3ab = -18ab$

107

ALGEBRA, BOOK ONE

ORAL EXERCISES

1. Study the examples on page 107 and then tell how to complete the following law of exponents for multiplication:

> The exponent of any letter in a product is found by _adding_ _?_ _ _ the exponent of that letter in the multiplicand to the exponent of that letter in the multiplier.

①
↑

2. The law of exponents for multiplication may be expressed as follows: $a^m \cdot a^n = a^{m+n}$. Explain.

Multiply:

12x **3.** 4 x by 3   -4 by **8.** − 4 y by b   -4xy **13.** 2 xy by − 2

-6m **4.** 3 m by − 2   8cd **9.** − 8 c by − d -12ab **14.** 3 ab by − 4

-20a **5.** − 5 a by 4   4rs **10.** 4 r by s   **15.** − xy by z

30x **6.** − 6 x by − 5 -6hk **11.** 6 h by − k   -xyz / 10bc **16.** − 2 bc by − 5

-12c **7.** − 3 c by 4   -18p **12.** 3 p by − 6   4ghk **17.** 4 hk by g

Example 5. $4\,a \times -5\,a = -20\,a^2$.

EXERCISES

Multiply:

-35x² **1.** $(-7\,x) \cdot (5\,x)$ 6h² **6.** $-2\,h(-3\,h)$ x² **11.** $(.2\,x) \cdot (5\,x)$

12a² **2.** $(3\,a) \cdot 4\,a$ -⅙k² **7.** $-\frac{1}{2}\,k(\frac{1}{3}\,k)$ 13x² **12.** $(1.3\,x) \cdot (10\,x)$

-12m² **3.** $(6\,m) \cdot (-2\,m)$ ⅓c² **8.** $\frac{2}{3}\,c(\frac{1}{2}\,c)$ 0.1p² **13.** $(0.02\,p) \cdot (5\,p)$

20c² **4.** $(-4\,c) \cdot (-5\,c)$ ⅖h² **9.** $-\frac{2}{5}\,h(-\frac{1}{2}\,h)$ 7.2w² **14.** $(1.2\,w) \cdot (6\,w)$

x² **5.** $(-x) \cdot (-x)$ ²⁄₅s² **10.** $\frac{3}{5}\,s(\frac{2}{3}\,s)$ 0.5c² **15.** $(1.5\,c) \cdot (\frac{1}{3}\,c)$

Example 6. $(5\,a^2)(-3\,a^4) = -15\,a^6$.

In multiplying one monomial by another, first determine the sign of the product. Next find the numerical part of it. Then find the product of the variables.

EXERCISES

Find the following products:

-28a³ **1.** $(4\,a^2)(-7\,a)$ -80m **3.** $8(-10\,m)$ x¹⁰ **5.** $x^4 \cdot x^6$

-15x⁷ **2.** $(-5\,x^2)(3\,x^5)$ 6a⁵ **4.** $(3\,a^2)(2\,a^3)$ -30b⁶ **6.** $-6\,b^2 \cdot 5\,b^4$

POSITIVE AND NEGATIVE NUMBERS

7. $(-5 a^2)(-5 b^4)$ $25 a^2 b^4$

8. $(-4 x^3)(5 a^3)$ $-20 a^3 x^3$

9. $6 b^4(-7 b^3)$ $-42 b^7$

10. $-14(2 x)$ $-28 x$

11. $-15 x^3(\frac{2}{3} x)$ $-10 x^4$

12. $(8 m^2)(-4 mn)$ $-32 m^3 n$

13. $(-3 c^2 x)(-3 c^2 d)$ $9 c^4 dx$

14. $(4 h)(5 h^2)$ $20 h^3$

15. $(.2 x^4)(4 x^5)$ $8 x^9$

16. $4^3 \cdot 4^2$ 4^5

17. $10^2 \cdot 10^5$ 10^7

18. $(1\frac{1}{4} m)(4 m^7)$ $5 m^8$

How to Divide One Monomial by Another [A]

Study the three examples below and see if you can learn how to divide monomials without any help from your teacher.

Example 1. $a^7 \div a^2 = ?$

Solution. Since $a^2 \times a^5 = a^7$, then $a^7 \div a^2 = a^5$.

Also,
$$\frac{a^7}{a^2} = \frac{\overset{1 \cdot 1}{\cancel{aa}aaaaa}}{\underset{1 \cdot 1}{\cancel{aa}}} = a^5$$

Which of these two explanations do you prefer?

Example 2. Divide $12 x$ by $-4 x$.

Solution.
$$\frac{12 x}{-4 x} = \frac{\overset{-3 \cdot 1}{\cancel{12} \cancel{x}}}{\underset{1 \cdot 1}{-\cancel{4} \cancel{x}}} = -3$$

Example 3. Divide $-24 a^3$ by $4 a$.

Solution.
$$\frac{-24 a^3}{4 a} = \frac{\overset{-6 \cdot 1}{-\cancel{24} \cancel{a}aa}}{\underset{1 \cdot 1}{\cancel{4} \cancel{a}}} = -6 a^2$$

[A]

1. Study the three examples above and tell how to complete the following rule of exponents for division:

The exponent of any variable in a quotient is found by __?__ *subtracting* the exponent of that variable in the divisor from the exponent of that variable in the dividend.

ALGEBRA, BOOK ONE

2. When x^6 is divided by x^2, is the quotient x^3 or x^4? If you are not sure of your answer, think what the exponents mean, as in Example 1 on page 109. x^4

3. The law of exponents for division may be expressed by $a^m \div a^n = a^{m-n}$. Explain.

4. When x^9 is divided by x^3, how do you find the exponent of x in the quotient? x^6 *by Ex. 3.*

Divide as indicated:

5. $x^3 \div x$ x^2

6. $m^4 \div m$ m^3

7. $a^6 \div a$ a^5

8. $\dfrac{x^7}{x^3}$ x^4

9. $n^5 \div n$ n^4

10. $x^4 \div x^4$ 1

11. $c^5 \div c$ c^4

12. $\dfrac{-m^{10}}{m^5}$ $-m^5$

13. $-x^5 \div x^2$ $-x^3$

14. $5^3 \div 5$ 5^2

15. $10^4 \div 10$ 10^3

16. $\dfrac{-8^4}{-8^4}$ 1

[A]

WRITTEN EXERCISES

Divide:

1. $18\,a^2 \div 6$ $3a^2$

2. $8\,a \div 2$ $4a$

3. $-6\,x \div 3$ $-2x$

4. $20\,m^2 \div (-4)$ $-5m^2$

5. $(4\,ab) \div (-1)$ $-4ab$

6. $3\,x^2 \div (-.3)$ $-10x^2$

7. $-14\,x \div (-7)$ $2x$

8. $-x^7 \div (-x^2)$ x^5

9. $(-4\,x^6) \div (2\,x^3)$ $-2x^3$

10. $16\,a^6 \div (4\,a)$ $4a^5$

11. $(12\,p^3) \div (-6\,p)$ $-2p^2$

12. $(4\,x^2) \div (-4\,x^2)$ -1

13. $(-8\,a^2) \div (-2\,a^2)$ 4

14. $(15\,x^2 y) \div (3\,y)$ $5x^2$

15. $(-3\,m^4) \div (-1)$ $3m^4$

Simplify the following fractions by dividing the numerators by the denominators:

16. $\dfrac{-28\,x}{4}$ $-7x$

17. $\dfrac{16\,m}{8}$ $2m$

18. $\dfrac{-14\,m^3}{-2}$ $7m^3$

19. $\dfrac{-24\,x}{-2\,x}$ 12

20. $\dfrac{16\,m^5}{4\,m}$ $4m^4$

21. $\dfrac{-30\,a}{-15}$ $2a$

22. $\dfrac{8\,y^6}{y^6}$ 8

23. $\dfrac{-2\,ab}{2\,a}$ $-b$

24. $\dfrac{abc}{bc}$ a

110

POSITIVE AND NEGATIVE NUMBERS

Evaluation with Positive and Negative Numbers [A]

Example. If $a = 2$ and $b = -3$, find the value of $\dfrac{2\,ab - 3\,b^2}{ab}$.

Solution. This fraction means that the numerator $2\,ab - 3\,b^2$ is to be divided by the denominator ab. We shall first evaluate the numerator. The value of the term $2\,ab = 2 \times 2 \times -3 = -12$. The value of $-3\,b^2$ is $-3(-3)^2$, which is -3×9, or -27. Then $-12 - 27 = -39$. The value of the denominator $ab = 2(-3) = -6$. Then $(-39) \div (-6) = 6\frac{1}{2}$.

The solution should be written as follows:

① $$\frac{2\,ab - 3\,b^2}{ab}$$
$$= \frac{2(2)(-3) - 3(-3)^2}{2(-3)}$$
$$= \frac{-12 - 27}{-6} = \frac{-39}{-6} = 6\tfrac{1}{2}$$

[A]   **EXERCISES**

If $a = -3$ and $b = -4$, find the value of

1. $a^2 + b^2$ 25

2. $b^2 + 6\,a$ -2

3. $\dfrac{a^3}{b^2} + \dfrac{1}{9}$ $2\frac{27}{144}$

4. $2\,a + b^2$ 10

5. $-3\,b + ab$ 24

6. $\dfrac{a}{b} + \dfrac{b}{a}$ $2\frac{5}{12}$

7. $ab^2 + 4$ -44

8. $ab + 12$ 24

9. $\dfrac{ab + 6}{a^2 + b}$ $3\frac{3}{5}$

10. If $x = -4$, what is the value of $-x$? of $-x^2$? of $-x^3$?
$+4; -16; 64$

11. If $-x = -6$, what is the value of $+x$? of $-3\,x$? of $3\,x$?
$+6; -18; 18$

12. If $a = 0$, what is the value of $2\,a^2 - 3\,a + 4$?
4

13. If $b = -3$, find the value of $b^3 + 3\,b^2$. 0

14. If $x = -4$, find the value of $x^2 + (x^3 - x)$. -44

[C]

15. If $a = 5$ and $b = -2$, find the value of $ab + 3\,a + 4$ 9

16. If $a = 1$ and $b = -3$, find the value of $10 + (ab)^3$. -17

17. Repeat exercises 1–9 inclusive letting $a = \frac{1}{2}$ and $b = \frac{1}{3}$.

18. Repeat exercises 1–9 inclusive letting $a = .3$ and $b = -.1$.

17. (1) $\frac{13}{36}$ (2) $3\frac{4}{9}$ (3) $\frac{89}{72}$ (4) $1\frac{1}{9}$ (5) $-\frac{5}{6}$ (6) $2\frac{1}{6}$ (7) $4\frac{1}{8}$
(8) $12\frac{1}{6}$ (9) $10\frac{4}{7}$

18. (1) 0.1 (2) 1.81 (3) $2\frac{73}{90}$ (4) 0.61 (5) 0.27 (6) $-3\frac{1}{3}$ (7) 4.003
(8) 11.97 (9) -597

111

ALGEBRA, BOOK ONE

Subtraction of Signed Numbers [A]

Subtraction may be thought of as the process of finding what number must be added to a given number to equal another given number. Thus subtracting 2 from 5 is finding what number must be added to 2 so that the sum is 5.

If we wish to subtract 2 from 5 by the use of the vertical scale at the left, we count the number of spaces between the subtrahend + 2 and the minuend + 5. The distance is 3, and since the direction is upward, the difference is + 3.

To subtract − 3 from + 5, we count from − 3 to + 5. The distance is 8 and the direction is upward, so the difference is + 8.

To subtract + 6 from − 2, we count from + 6 to − 2. The distance is 8 and the direction is downward, so the difference is − 8.

To subtract − 3 from − 7, we count from − 3 to − 7. The distance is 4 and the direction is downward, so the difference is − 4.

These examples illustrate the following rule:

To subtract one number from another using the number scale, count the number of spaces from the subtrahend to the minuend, and to this number prefix a positive sign if the counting is upward and a negative sign if the counting is downward.

[A]

EXERCISES

1. In arithmetic can 10 be subtracted from 8? What is the remainder when 10 is subtracted from 8 using the number scale? *No; −2*

2. Using a number scale, subtract:

	a	b	c	d	e
Minuend	4	− 3	5	0	3
Subtrahend	− 3	+ 1	− 6	5	− 7
Remainder	? *7*	? *−4*	? *11*	? *−5*	? *10*

3. Using a number scale, subtract:

	a	b	c	d	e
Minuend	− 2	3	− 6	− 4	− 8
Subtrahend	7	6	7	− 5	− 8
Remainder	? *−9*	? *−3*	? *−13*	? *1*	? *0*

112 ② This informal procedure and the tie-in with the number scale are designed to help the student to form the actual procedure before the formal rule is given. At this point students become confused and you may find it necessary to go over addition and subtraction many times to be sure they really understand what they are doing.

5. (1) Yes. (2) Same numerical values but opposite signs.
(3) Same. (4) Change sign of subtrahend and add.

4. Add the following:

	a	b	c	d	e
Addend	− 2	3	− 6	− 4	− 8
Addend	− 7	− 6	− 7	+ 5	+ 8
Sum	?-9	?-3	?-13	? 1	? 0

5. Compare Exercise 4 with Exercise 3. Are the upper addends of Exercise 4 like the minuends of Exercise 3? How do the lower addends of Exercise 4 compare with the subtrahends of Exercise 3? How do the sums of Exercise 4 compare with the remainders of Exercise 3? How can you change a subtraction problem into an addition problem?

Tell how to complete the following rule:

> To subtract a number, __?__ *add* its opposite.

This rule is often stated as follows:

To subtract one number from another, change the sign of the subtrahend and add the result to the minuend.

Example 1. Subtract − 6 from + 10.

Solution. We change the sign of − 6 and get + 6. Then we add + 6 and + 10, obtaining + 16.

Example 2. − 10 − (− 3).

Solution. This means that − 3 is to be subtracted from − 10, so we change the sign of − 3, getting + 3. Then we combine − 10 and + 3, getting − 7. The solution can be written as follows:

$$- 10 - (- 3)$$
$$= - 10 \quad + 3$$
$$= - 7$$

Example 3. From − 15
take + 9

Solution. When the problem is written in this form, we usually do the work mentally. We think this way: "Change the sign of + 9, getting − 9. Then − 15 and − 9 make − 24."

① Students should now see the meaning of this rule, but do not let them just mechanically accept it without understanding.

113

ALGEBRA, BOOK ONE

Difference, sum, & product listed beside each ex. 1–5, reading down. [A]

EXERCISES

Subtract the lower number from the number above it.

	a *6*	**b** *-3*	**c** *9*	**d** *11*	**e** *-2*	**f** *-45*	**g** *20*
1.	9 *12*	-8 *-13*	7 *5*	5 *-1*	8 *18—20*	5	18 *16*
	3 *27*	-5 *40*	-2 *-14*	-6 *-30*	10 *80*	25 *-500—2*	-2 *-36*
2.	7 *10* *-5*	-8 *-11*	5 *-1* *11*	10 *20* *0*	-8 *-16* *0*	0 *-7* *7*	0 *6* *-6*
	-3 *4* *-21*	-3 *24*	6 *30—10* *-100*	8 *-64*	7 *0*	-6 *0*
3.	-5 *1* *-11*	-6 *-1* *-11*	9 *13* *5*	-4 *-13* *5*	3 *1* *5*	2 *-1* *5*	7 *15* *-1*
	-6 *30*	-5 *30*	-4 *-36*	9 *-36*	2 *6*	3 *6*	-8 *-56*
4.	9 *3* *15*	6 *-3* *15*	-9 *-15* *-3*	6 *15* *-3*	-3 *-1* *-5*	8 *8* *0*	0 *-8* *8*
	6 *54*	9 *54*	6 *-54*	-9 *-54*	-2 *6*	0 *8* *0*	8 *0*
5.	-4 *6* *-14*	-10 *-6* *-14*	-13 *-19* *-7*	15 *23* *7*	-15 *-7* *-23*	15 *7* *23*	-11 *-28* *6*
	-10 *40*	-4 *40*	6 *-78*	-8 *-120*	-8 *120*	8 *120*	17 *-187*

6. In exercises 1–5 above, find the sum in each case.

7. In exercises 1–5, find the product in each case.

Subtract:

8.

$4x$	$6a$	$3c$	$-7a$	$-6x$	$-8m$	$4r$
$3x$ *x*	$4a$ *2a*	$5c$ *-2c*	$9a$ *-16a*	$2x$ *-8x*	$-3m$ *-5m*	$-4r$ *8r*

9.

$4x^2$	$5m^3$	s^2	xy	$-ab$	$-18m$	$5c$
$-3x^2$ *7x²*	m^3 *4m³*	$4s^2$ *5s²*	$-4s^2$	xy *2xy*	$-ab$ *0*	$2m$ *-20m*	$-c$ *6c*

10.

$3ab$	$-5c^2$	$-5h$	$3x^2$	$6y$	$4y$	0
$4ab$ *-ab*	$-7c^2$ *-12c²*	$14h$ *19h*	$2x^2$ *x²*	$5y$ *y*	$5y$ *-y*	rs *-rs*

11.

x	c^2	$\frac{3}{5}x$	$-\frac{2}{3}h$	$2\frac{1}{3}p$	$-7\frac{1}{2}k$	$3\frac{1}{3}y$
$\frac{1}{2}x$	$-\frac{1}{2}c^2$	$\frac{1}{5}x$	$-\frac{5}{6}h$	$4\frac{1}{3}p$	$\frac{1}{2}k$	$4\frac{2}{3}y$

12.

$1.4h$	$5.0c$	$-4w$	$-m$	$-5.6c$	$2k$	$1.5r$
$.4h$	$.4c$	$1.5w$	$.8m$	$-.6c$	$.5k$	$-.5r$
h	*4.6c*	*-5.5w*	*-1.8m*	*-5.0c*	*1.5k*	*2.0r*

Do as indicated by the signs connecting the parentheses:

13. $(4) + (-6)$ *-2*

14. $(4) - (-6)$ *10*

15. $(10) + (8)$ *18*

16. $(10) - (8)$ *2*

17. $(-6) + (8)$ *2*

18. $(-6) - (-8)$ *2*

19. $(-5) + (-7)$ *-12*

20. $(-5) - (-7)$ *2*

21. $(5) + (-3)$ *2*

22. $(5) - (-3)$ *8*

23. $(-7) + (-7)$ *-14*

24. $(-7) - (-7)$ *0*

114 *11. $\frac{1}{2}x, 1\frac{1}{2}c^2, \frac{2}{5}x, \frac{1}{6}h, -2p, -8k, -1\frac{1}{3}y$*

POSITIVE AND NEGATIVE NUMBERS

25. The Battle of Thermopylae was fought in 480 B.C. and Carthage was destroyed in 146 B.C. How many years apart were these two events? *334 yr.*

Reducing Fractions to Lowest Terms [A]

A fraction is in its lowest terms when the numerator and denominator have no common integral divisor except 1. The multiplicative property of 1 is useful in reducing a fraction to its lowest terms. Do you recall that this property states that if a is any real number $a(1) = a$?

Example 1. Reduce $\dfrac{5x}{-15x^2}$ to lowest terms.

Solution. The greatest common divisor of $5x$ and $-15x^2$ is $5x$ or $-5x$.

Then
$$\frac{5x}{-15x^2} = \frac{5x(1)}{5x(-3x)}$$

$$\frac{5x}{-15x^2} = \left(\frac{5x}{5x}\right)\left(\frac{1}{-3x}\right)$$

> Avoid using the word "cancellation." Instead, use the longer but more meaningful phrase "Divide both members of the fraction by . . ."

But $\dfrac{5x}{5x} = 1$. Substituting 1 for $\dfrac{5x}{5x}$ in the statement above,

we have
$$\frac{5x}{-15x^2} = (1)\left(\frac{1}{-3x}\right)$$

Hence
$$\frac{5x}{-15x^2} = \frac{1}{-3x}$$

If we had used $\dfrac{-5x}{-5x}$ as a factor we would have had

$$\frac{5x}{-15x^2} = \frac{-5x(-1)}{-5x(3x)} = \left(\frac{-5x}{-5x}\right)\left(\frac{-1}{3x}\right) = (1)\left(\frac{-1}{3x}\right) = \frac{-1}{3x}.$$

$\dfrac{1}{-3x}$ and $\dfrac{-1}{3x}$ represent the same number. Why?

Reduce to lowest terms when possible:

[A]

ORAL EXERCISES

1. $\dfrac{4}{8}$ *½*   4. $\dfrac{30}{42}$ *5/7*   7. $\dfrac{4a}{5a}$ *4/5*   10. $\dfrac{x^4}{x^2}$ *x²*   13. $\dfrac{-6a^3}{12a}$ *-a²/2*   16. $\dfrac{8a^2}{12a}$ *2a/3*

2. $\dfrac{7}{21}$ *⅓*   5. $\dfrac{25}{63}$ 8. $\dfrac{3x}{5x}$ *3/5*   11. $\dfrac{a}{a^3}$ *1/a²*   14. $\dfrac{a^2b}{ab}$ *a*   17. $\dfrac{x^5}{x^8}$ *1/x³*

3. $\dfrac{8}{20}$ *2/5*   6. $\dfrac{24}{33}$ *8/11*   9. $\dfrac{2x^2}{3x^2}$ *2/3*   12. $\dfrac{x^4}{x^3}$ *x*   15. $\dfrac{xy^2}{x^2y}$ *y/x*   18. $\dfrac{5a^2}{-10a^2}$ *a/-a/2*

Repeating often an important method of procedure in the same concise language is good teaching. You might want to use this sentence as a basic guide for all processes with fractions: "A fraction may be changed in form without change of value if it is multiplied or divided by 1 in the form of m/m for all values of m except 0." When applying this—for example, to changing 3/4 to 6/8, say, "Multiply 3/4 by 1 in the form of 2/2. Change the form but not the value."

Multiplication and Division of Fractions [A]

If $\dfrac{a}{b}$ and $\dfrac{c}{d}$ are fractions, and b and $d \neq 0$, then $\dfrac{a}{b} \times \dfrac{c}{d} = \dfrac{ac}{bd}$. If $\dfrac{ac}{bd}$ is not in its lowest terms, it should then be reduced.

Example 1. Simplify $\tfrac{2}{5} \times \tfrac{5}{6}$.

Solution.

$$\dfrac{\overset{1}{\cancel{2}}}{\underset{1}{\cancel{5}}} \times \dfrac{\overset{1}{\cancel{5}}}{\underset{3}{\cancel{6}}} = \dfrac{1}{3}$$

Example 2. Multiply $\dfrac{a}{b}$ by 6.

Solution.

$$\dfrac{a}{b} \cdot \dfrac{6}{1} = \dfrac{6a}{b}$$

Example 3. Find the product of $\dfrac{3\,x^2}{4}$ and $\dfrac{6}{x}$.

Solution.

$$\dfrac{\overset{3x}{\cancel{3x^2}}}{\underset{2}{\cancel{4}}} \cdot \dfrac{\overset{3}{\cancel{6}}}{\underset{1}{\cancel{x}}} = \dfrac{9\,x}{2}$$

If the product of two numbers is 1, then the two numbers are reciprocals or multiplicative inverses of each other. Thus, 3 and $\tfrac{1}{3}$ are reciprocals of each other. Similarly, $\tfrac{3}{4}$ and $\tfrac{4}{3}$ are reciprocals.

If $\dfrac{a}{b}$ and $\dfrac{c}{d}$ are fractions, and b, c, and $d \neq 0$ then $\dfrac{a}{b} \div \dfrac{c}{d} = \dfrac{a}{b} \times \dfrac{d}{c}$.

In other words, instead of dividing by $\dfrac{c}{d}$, we may multiply by its reciprocal, $\dfrac{d}{c}$.

Example 4. Divide $\dfrac{4\,a^3}{21}$ by $\dfrac{2\,a}{7}$.

Solution. Since the reciprocal of $\dfrac{2\,a}{7}$ is $\dfrac{7}{2\,a}$, we multiply by $\dfrac{7}{2\,a}$.

$$\dfrac{4\,a^3}{21} \div \dfrac{2\,a}{7} = \dfrac{\overset{2a^2}{\cancel{4a^3}}}{\underset{3}{\cancel{21}}} \times \dfrac{\overset{1}{\cancel{7}}}{\underset{1}{\cancel{2a}}} = \dfrac{2\,a^2}{3}$$

A division may be checked by multiplying the divisor by the quotient.

116

POSITIVE AND NEGATIVE NUMBERS

Perform the indicated operations:

[A] **EXERCISES**

1. $\frac{2}{3} \times \frac{6}{7}$ $\frac{4}{7}$

2. $6 \div \frac{1}{3}$ 18

3. $\frac{7\,m}{5} \times 3$ $\frac{21m}{5}$

4. $\frac{a}{b} \times \frac{c}{d}$ $\frac{ac}{bd}$

5. $\frac{-c}{d} \times \frac{3}{4}$ $\frac{-3c}{4d}$

6. $\frac{x}{3} \div \frac{x}{2}$ $\frac{2}{3}$

7. $\frac{m}{n} \times \frac{4}{5}$ $\frac{4m}{5n}$

8. $\frac{c}{5} \div \frac{c}{3}$ $\frac{3}{5}$

9. $10 \div \frac{1}{5}$ 50

10. $b^2 \div \frac{b}{a}$ ab

11. $b^2 \times \frac{b}{a}$ $\frac{b^3}{a}$

12. $\frac{2y}{3} \times \frac{6}{y}$ 4

13. $\frac{4x^2}{1} \cdot \frac{1}{x}$ $4x$

14. $\frac{-ab}{3} \div \frac{b}{4}$ $\frac{-4a}{3}$

15. $15 \div \frac{2}{3}$ $\frac{45}{2}$

16. $\frac{15}{a} \div \frac{2}{3\,a}$ $\frac{45}{2}$

17. $\frac{4\,xy}{1} \div \frac{2\,x^2}{3}$ $\frac{6y}{x}$

18. $6 \div \frac{1}{9}$ 54

19. $\frac{1}{10} \div \frac{a}{50}$ $\frac{5}{a}$

20. $\frac{c}{d} \div \frac{a}{b}$ $\frac{bc}{ad}$

21. $\frac{-8\,a^3}{15\,x} \div \frac{-4\,a}{3\,x}$ $\frac{2a^2}{5}$

Combining Fractions[A]

Fractions which have the same denominator may be added (or subtracted) by placing the sum (or difference) of their numerators over their common denominator.

Example 1. $\frac{2}{3} + \frac{5}{3} = \frac{7}{3}$ **Example 2.** $\frac{a}{b} - \frac{3}{b} = \frac{a-3}{b}$

[A] **EXERCISES**

Combine the fractions as indicated, giving the answers at sight.

1. $\frac{2}{3} + \frac{1}{3}$ 1

2. $\frac{4}{3} - \frac{2}{3}$ $\frac{2}{3}$

3. $\frac{3}{7} + \frac{1}{7}$ $\frac{4}{7}$

4. $\frac{3}{7} - \frac{1}{7}$ $\frac{2}{7}$

5. $\frac{4}{3} + \frac{2}{3}$ 2

6. $\frac{a}{6} + \frac{3\,a}{6}$ $\frac{2a}{3}$

7. $\frac{x}{4} + \frac{3\,x}{4}$ x

8. $\frac{a}{3} + \frac{b}{3}$ $\frac{a+b}{3}$

9. $\frac{a}{c} + \frac{b}{c}$ $\frac{a+b}{c}$

10. $\frac{2}{a} + \frac{3}{a}$ $\frac{5}{a}$

11. $\frac{1}{c} + \frac{1}{c}$ $\frac{2}{c}$

12. $\frac{3}{x} - \frac{4}{x}$ $\frac{-1}{x}$

13. $\frac{4}{xy} - \frac{3}{xy}$ $\frac{1}{xy}$

14. $\frac{-4}{m} - \frac{3}{m}$ $\frac{-7}{m}$

15. $\frac{5\,x}{8} + \frac{3\,x}{8}$ x

117

When fractions which are to be added or subtracted do *not* have the same denominator, they must be changed to equal fractions which do have the same denominator.

Example 3. $\dfrac{2x}{3}+\dfrac{x}{6}=\dfrac{4x}{6}+\dfrac{x}{6}=\dfrac{5x}{6}$. Notice that both terms of the first fraction are multiplied by 2. This multiplies the fraction by 1 and leaves its value unchanged. Why?

[A]

EXERCISES   Combine:

$1\frac{1}{2}$ 1. $\dfrac{2}{3}+\dfrac{5}{6}$

$\dfrac{5x}{4}$ 2. $\dfrac{x}{2}+\dfrac{3x}{4}$

$\dfrac{3c}{8}$ 3. $\dfrac{5c}{8}-\dfrac{c}{4}$

$\dfrac{3m}{10}$ 4. $\dfrac{m}{5}+\dfrac{m}{10}$

$\dfrac{2x}{9}$ 5. $\dfrac{x}{3}-\dfrac{x}{9}$

$-\dfrac{5a}{4}$ 6. $\dfrac{a}{4}-\dfrac{3a}{2}$

$\dfrac{5m}{12}$ 7. $\dfrac{m}{4}+\dfrac{m}{6}$

$-\dfrac{3h}{10}$ 8. $\dfrac{h}{5}-\dfrac{h}{2}$

$-\dfrac{x}{2}$ 9. $\dfrac{x}{10}-\dfrac{3x}{5}$

$-\dfrac{5}{6}$ 10. $-\dfrac{1}{3}-\dfrac{1}{2}$

$\dfrac{7m}{12}$ 11. $\dfrac{m}{3}+\dfrac{m}{4}$

$\dfrac{a}{6}$ 12. $\dfrac{a}{2}-\dfrac{a}{3}$

$\dfrac{-a}{12}$ 13. $\dfrac{a}{4}-\dfrac{a}{3}$

$\dfrac{1}{6c}$ 14. $\dfrac{1}{2c}-\dfrac{1}{3c}$

$\dfrac{-1}{2a}$ 15. $\dfrac{2}{a}-\dfrac{5}{2a}$

Checking Your Understanding of Chapter 4

Unless you have mastered this chapter you will have difficulty with the chapters which follow. Make sure, therefore, that you

1. Can add (p. 96), subtract (p. 112), multiply (p. 101), and divide (p. 104) signed numbers without an error. If you make mistakes or need frequent help from your teacher, you have not mastered these operations.   *The pages in parentheses will help you to review.*

2. Know the meaning of the following expressions and can spell the words in them correctly:

positive numbers (p. 91)   absolute value (p. 95)
negative numbers (p. 91)   signs of operation (p. 98)
signed numbers (p. 92)   signs of opposition (p. 98)

[A]

CHAPTER REVIEW

Complete the following statements:

1. Subtracting $+6$ from a number gives the same result as __?__ __?__ . *adding* -6

2. Subtracting -3 from a number gives the same result as __?__ __?__ . *adding 3*

	a	**b**	**c**	**d**	**e**	**f**	**g**
3. Add:	7	-9	-5	-9	10	12	7
(ans. in right margin)	6	-3	$+6$	8	-6	10	-4

3. *a.* 13
b. -12
c. 1
d. -1
e. 4
f. 22
g. 3

4. From $\rightarrow$	10	6	-8	6	5	3	0
take $\rightarrow$	6	10	4	-4	3	-5	8
	4	*-4*	*-12*	*10*	*2*	*8*	*-8*

	a	**b**	**c**	**d**	**e**	**f**	**g**
5. Add:	$-2x$	$-6x$	x^2	w	T	10	$-18c$
	$4x$	$-3x$	$-x^2$	$-4w$	$-T$	-10	$-6c$
	2x	*-9x*	*0*	*-3w*	*0*	*0*	*-24c*

Simplify the following:

6. $8 - 6 + 3$ *5*

7. $10 - 4 - 12$ *-6*

8. $-4 - 5 - 1$ *-10*

9. $x^2 - 2x + 6 - x^2 - x - 1$ *-3x+5*

10. $2a + 5b - c - a - 7b$ *a-2b-c*

11. $3m^2 - 10m - 1 + 7 - m$ *3m²-11m+6*

12. $(-4)(3)$ *-12*

13. $(-3)9$ *-27*

14. $(-6)(-6)$ *36*

15. $7(-10)$ *-70*

16. $x^2 x^3$ *x⁵*

17. $(-3x)(4x)$ *-12x²*

18. $(5w)(3w)$ *15w²*

19. $x^3 \cdot x^4$ *x⁷*

20. $(-3x)(4x^2)$ *-12x³*

21. $(-4c)(5c)$ *-20c²*

22. $10(-4x)$ *-40x*

23. $4c^2(-3c^3)$ *-12c⁵*

24. $12 \div (-3)$ *-4*

25. $(-18) \div (-9)$ *2*

26. $42 \div 3$ *14*

27. $-30 \div 10$ *-3*

28. $40 \div (-1)$ *-40*

29. $(-x^9) \div (-x)$ *x⁸*

30. $4xy \div 4$ *xy*

31. $(6x^2y) \div (2y)$ *3x²*

32. $(xyz) \div z$ *xy*

33. $(20x^2) \div (5x)$ *4x*

34. $(-18x^3) \div (6x)$ *-3x²*

35. $40x \div (8x)$ *5*

36. $10 + (-4)$ *6*

37. $10 - (-4)$ *14*

38. $2c - 4c$ *-2c*

39. $3h - (-5h)$ *8h*

40. $-5x + (-2x)$ *-7x*

41. $-5x - (-2x)$ *-3x*

42. $-9 - 6$ *-15*

43. $x - 4x$ *-3x*

44. $10 - 18$ *-8*

45. $-3c + 4c$ *c*

46. $0 - (-8)$ *8*

47. $90 + (-90)$ *0*

By this time much of the foundation of algebra has been laid. Now is the time to check on the understanding and usage of the basic procedures. Test, practice in class, and reteach.

ALGEBRA, BOOK ONE

GENERAL REVIEW

1. Write the following using the symbols of algebra:

a. The sum of x and y. $x+y$

b. Twice x, decreased by three times y. $2x-3y$

c. The sum of 4, $-$ 6, and m. $m-2$

d. The square of h, decreased by the cube of m. h^2-m^3

e. The larger of two numbers when the smaller is 10 and the difference between them is d. $10+d$

2. Write the following using exponents:

a. xx x^2 **d.** $hh+h$ h^2+h **g.** $(xx)(xxx)$ x^5

b. xxx x^3 **e.** $xx+xxx$ x^2+x^3 **h.** $2\,yy-yyy$ $2y^2-y^3$

c. mmm m^3 **f.** $2\,cc+3\,ccc$ $2c^2+3c^3$ **i.** $10\times 10\times 10$ 10^3

3. Write a formula for

a. The area of a parallelogram whose base is b and altitude h. $A=bh$

b. The perimeter of a rectangle whose base is b and altitude a. $P=2a+2b$

c. The circumference of a circle whose diameter is d. $c=\pi d$

d. The volume of a rectangular solid whose dimensions are a, b, and c. $V=abc$

4. If $x=2$, $y=-4$, and $z=3$, evaluate:

a. $3x+4z$ 18 **c.** $xy-z$ -11 **e.** $2x^2-10$ -2

b. $xz-4$ 2 **d.** x^3+y^3 -56 **f.** y^2-z^2 7

5. A taxi charges 15 cents a mile plus a flat rate of 35 cents. Write a formula for the cost c (in cents) of riding m miles. $c=35+15m$

6. $c=125+\frac{9}{2}(n-15)$ is a formula for finding the cost (c) in cents of sending a telegram of fifteen or more words between two cities, where n is the number of words.

a. Find the cost of sending 15 words. $\$1.25$

b. Find the cost of sending 20 words. $\$1.48$

c. What is the minimum charge? $\$1.25$

120

7. Write formulas expressing the relation between x and y as shown in the tables. Then copy and complete the tables.

a. *y = 10 - x*

When x =	0	1	2	3	4	5
Then y =	10	9	8	? 7	? 6	? 5

b. *x = y / 5*

When x =	0	1	2	? 3	8	? 20
Then y =	0	5	10	15	? 40	100

y = 5x

8. $F = \frac{9}{5}C + 32$. Find F if $C = 20$; if $C = 100$. *68; 212*

9. $C = \frac{5}{9}(F - 32)$. Find C when $F = 32$; when $F = 212$; when $F = 0$. *0; 100; -17⅗*

10. Write a formula for finding the cost c of n articles at y cents each. *c = ny*

11. Write a formula for the statement, "The amount is found by multiplying the principal, the rate, and the time together and adding this product to the principal." *A = p + prt*

12. What operation cannot always be performed by using positive numbers only, but can always be performed by using both positive and negative numbers? *subtraction*

13. Complete: In the expression $5x^2$, the 5 is called the __?__ of x^2 and the 2 is called the __?__ of x. *coefficient, exponent*

14. Write the formula for the perimeter p of this rectangle. What is the perimeter of this rectangle when $x = 1$? *p = 6x + 6; 12*

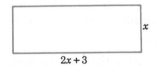

x

$2x + 3$

15. Solve the following equations:

a. $7x + 3x = 30$ *3*

b. $8p + 3p - p = 50$ *5*

c. $7c + c = 82 + 80$ *20¼*

d. $2c - .4c = 18 - 12$ *3.75*

e. $7.2x - 3.5x = 6 + 14$ *5.405⁺*

f. $.04p = 100$ *2500*

16. A rectangular field is enclosed by a fence 3960 rods in length. If the length is 5 times the width, how wide is the field? *330 rd.*

121

17. The sum of three numbers is 1280. The first is 5 times the second and the third is 4 times the second. Find the numbers. *640, 128, 512*

18. Two angles are complementary and one is 5 times the other. Find the angles. *15°, 75°*

19.

When t =	0	1	2	3	4	5	6	7
s =	0	16	64	? *144*	? *256*	? *400*	? *576*	? *784*

When *t* is doubled, how does *s* change? *Multiplied by 4.*
Complete the formula $s = $ __?__ t^2. *s = 16 t²*
Complete the table.

20. Write the formula for the area (*A*) of Fig. 1, which consists of a square and halves of four circles. *A = 4x² + 2π·x²*

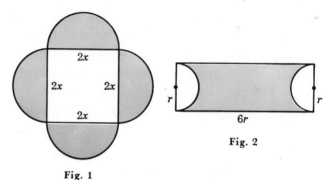

Fig. 1

Fig. 2

21. Write the formula for the area of the shaded surface of Fig. 2. *A = 12 r² - π r²*

22. Dick Smith joined the Ace Club on January 10. On the day he joined the club he paid an initiation fee of 50 cents. The monthly dues of the club are 10 cents and they are payable on the first day of each month.

a. If Dick is in good standing, how much money has he paid to the club by July 4 of the same year? *$1.10*

b. Write a formula for finding the amount of money he has paid to the club at the end of *m* months. *A = 50 + 10 m*

Simplify:

23. $\dfrac{-28\,x^2}{-4\,x}$ *7x* **25.** $\dfrac{6\,x^2}{-2\,x}$ *-3x* **27.** $\dfrac{a}{a^2}$ $\frac{1}{a}$ **29.** $\dfrac{16\,a^2}{24\,a^5}$ $\frac{2}{3a^3}$

24. $\dfrac{8\,y^3}{y^3}$ *8* **26.** $\dfrac{2\,x^3}{5\,x^3}$ $\frac{2}{5}$ **28.** $\dfrac{ab}{a^2b^2}$ $\frac{1}{ab}$ **30.** $\dfrac{17\,xy}{51\,x^2y^2}$ $\frac{1}{3xy}$

Perform the indicated operations:

31. $5 \times \dfrac{a^3}{15}$ $\frac{a^3}{3}$ **33.** $\dfrac{x}{5} \div \dfrac{x}{3}$ $\frac{3}{5}$ **35.** $\dfrac{5}{c} \div \dfrac{3}{c}$ $1\frac{2}{3}$

32. $\dfrac{8}{x^3} \cdot 2\,x$ $\frac{16}{x^2}$ **34.** $10\,a^2 \div \dfrac{2\,a}{7}$ *35a* **36.** $\dfrac{1}{x} \cdot 4\,x^2$ *4x*

[Test A]

CHAPTER TESTS

Find the sum in each of the following:

1.	**2.**	**3.**	**4.**	**5.**
8	-4	-7	$8\,c$	$-4\,a$
-3	-9	$+3$	$-c$	$2\,a$
5	*-13*	*-4*	*7c*	*-2a*

Subtract each lower number from the one above it:

6.	**7.**	**8.**	**9.**	**10.**
-7	-12	$7\,c$	$2\,a$	$9.1\,y$
-10	12	$-2\,c$	$5\,a$	$4.6\,y$
3	*-24*	*9c*	*-3a*	*4.5y*

Multiply:

11.	**12.**	**13.**	**14.**	**15.**
-9	$4\,y$	$-6\,x$	$10\,p$	0
4	-5	$-7\,x$	-7	6
-36	*-20y*	*42x²*	*-70p*	*0*

Find the quotients:

16. $-9 \div 3$ *-3* **17.** $(-6\,x) \div (-2)$ *3x* **18.** $18\,y^3 \div (-9\,y)$ *-2y²*

Simplify by collecting like terms:

19. $5\,x - 6 - 4\,x$ *x-6* **21.** $5\,h - k + 7\,k - 3\,k$ *5h+3k*

20. $4\,a + 6\,a - 12\,a$ *-2a* **22.** $9\,x^2 - 4\,x - 6\,x^2 - 3\,x$ *3x²-7x*

Which of the statements in exercises 23–25 are true?

23. $3\,x$ and 3 are similar terms. *False*

24. $-2\,x$ and $2\,x$ are similar terms. *True*

25. The product of $\dfrac{2\,x}{3}$ and $\dfrac{x}{2}$ is $\dfrac{3\,x}{5}$. *False*

Solve:

26. $9x + 3x = 30$ $2\frac{1}{2}$

27. $y + y = 4$ 2

28. $3a + 5a = 16$ 2

29. $4c + 10c = 7\frac{1}{2}$

30. $1.2x = 6$ 5

31. $\frac{2}{3}k = 12$ 18

If $a = -4$ and $b = 2$, find the value of

32. $7a + 4b$ -20

33. $ab + 5$ -3

[Test B]

Perform the indicated operations:

1. $(+6) - (1.5)$ 4.5

2. $24 \div (-4)$ -6

3. $(-15) + (+17)$ 2

4. $(-10) - (-20)$ 10

5. $x^2 \cdot x^3$ x^5

6. $20a^4 \div (-4a)$ $-5a^3$

7. $(7x^2)(-2x)$ $-14x^3$

8. $x^8 \div x^3$ x^5

9. $(a)(-b)(-c)$ abc

10. $10p + (4p) - (6p)$ $8p$

Simplify by collecting like terms:

11. $5x^2 - 10xy + y^2 - 8xy - x^2 - 9y^2$ $4x^2 - 18xy - 8y^2$

12. $4a - 3b + 4c - 7b - 5c$ $4a - 10b - c$

13. Reduce the fraction $\dfrac{4xy}{2x}$ to lowest terms. $2y$

14. Multiply: $\dfrac{2m^2n}{3x} \times \dfrac{x}{4m^3}$ $\dfrac{n}{6m}$

15. Add: $\dfrac{x}{5} + \dfrac{y}{5}$ $\dfrac{x+y}{5}$

16. Subtract: $\dfrac{5}{m} - \dfrac{3}{2m}$ $\dfrac{7}{2m}$

Solve:

17. $8x + 2x = 15 - 6$ $.9$

18. $2.1c - 1.4c = 2.8$ 4

19. $3b + 4b = 19$ $2\frac{5}{7}$

20. $8p - 4p = -6 + 12$ $1\frac{1}{2}$

21. What is the absolute value of -3? 3

22. What must be added to -9 to give $+4$? 13

23. The sum of two numbers is -11. If one of them is -5, what is the other? -6

24. The product of two numbers is $5x^4$ and one of the numbers is x^3. Find the other number. $5x$

25. The difference between two numbers is $3c$. What is the larger number if the smaller is $-4c$? $-c$

124

This test, like Test 3, is intended to help you maintain your skill in the processes of arithmetic. If you do not make a perfect score, try the test again in a few days.

1. Divide $3\frac{1}{5}$ by $\frac{4}{15}$.

2. Multiply $7\frac{3}{4}$ by $\frac{3}{4}$.

3. $7.5 + 13.24 = ?$

4. $11.92 - 1.07 = ?$

5. Find 100% of $8.

6. Divide 107.164 by 1.46.

7. Find 18% of 35.

8. Change $\frac{15}{25}$ to lowest terms.

9. Change .173 to a per cent.

10. $11.4 \times .003 = ?$

11. $10 - \$1.87 = ?$

12. $9 + \$1.87 + \$0.65 = ?$

13. $7\frac{1}{2} - 5\frac{1}{3} = ?$

14. $\frac{5}{9} = \frac{?}{36}$.

15. $\frac{5}{12} + \frac{7}{36} = ?$

16. Change 1.13 to a per cent.

17. If 8% of a number is 48, what is the number?

18. Change $4\frac{1}{3}$ to an improper fraction.

19. Change 64% to a common fraction.

20. How many thirds are there in $4\frac{1}{3}$?

●Check your answers with those below.

●**Answers.**

1. 12	**6.** 73.4	**11.** $8.13	**16.** 113%
2. $5\frac{13}{16}$ or $\frac{93}{16}$	**7.** 6.3	**12.** $11.52	**17.** 600
3. 20.74	**8.** $\frac{3}{5}$	**13.** $2\frac{1}{6}$	**18.** $\frac{13}{3}$
4. 10.85	**9.** 17.3%	**14.** $\frac{20}{36}$	**19.** $\frac{64}{100}$, or $\frac{16}{25}$
5. $8	**10.** .0342	**15.** $\frac{11}{18}$	**20.** 13

125

Babcock & Wilcox Co.

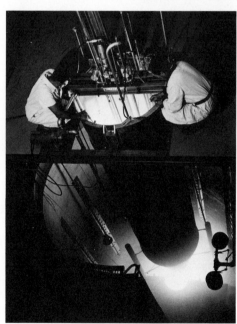

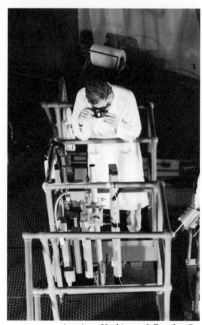

General Dynamics   American Machine and Foundry Co.

By the use of equations scientists are able to think more clearly and express their thoughts more concisely than they otherwise could. As the scientist has learned more about the laws that govern the universe, he has depended more upon mathematics to express these laws. The physicist and the astronomer have used mathematics in their work for centuries. In more recent years mathematics has been applied to various fields. For example, it is now used in the study of economics.

Let us examine a few cases that show how mathematics is associated with scientific research.

Near the close of the sixteenth century Kepler, a German astronomer, after years of observation proclaimed that the planets move around the sun in elliptical paths. Sir Isaac Newton (1642–1727), the great English physicist and mathematician, used mathematics to show that the path of a planet is an ellipse only if the force between the sun and planet varies as the square of the distance between them. Michael Faraday (1791–1867), one of the greatest scientific investigators of the nineteenth century, reasoned that if electricity can produce magnetism, then magnetism should produce electricity. By experimenting he discovered that moving a bar magnet into or out of a coil of wire causes a flow of electricity in the wire of the coil. This is the underlying principle of the electric generator. James Clerk-Maxwell (1831–1879) extended the discovery of Faraday. By the use of mathematics he came to the conclusion that magnetic action travels through space in the form of waves and with the speed of light, and that light waves are magnetic in character. His views were later verified by the experiments of Heinrich Hertz (1857–1894).

Until the early part of the twentieth century matter was thought to be indestructible. Matter was thought to be one thing and energy another. Now we know that matter and energy are different manifestations of the same thing and that either can be changed into the other.

More than forty years ago Albert Einstein (1879–1955), who was one of the greatest mathematical physicists of all time, startled the world by his theory of relativity. By the use of mathematics he came to the conclusion that matter and energy are interchangeable. He gave us the formula $E = mc^2$ for converting mass into energy. In this formula **c** is the speed of light. The formula tells us that the energy of one pound of matter is equivalent to the energy produced by burning $1\frac{1}{2}$ million tons of coal. This formula of Einstein's was a great aid to the scientists who studied atomic energy and succeeded in smashing the atom.

5

More Equations and Problems

Suggested Time Schedule
Minimum   4 days
Maximum   5 days

*You will find in this chapter
how useful negative numbers can be.* ▶

The subject matter of this chapter is not new to the students, as it consists of the solution of equations, formulas, inequalities, and verbal problems. However, the material is treated the second time around in an expanded and deepened development.   Now that the student knows about negative numbers, more varied exercises can be solved.   The teacher is urged to tie each process of this chapter to the student's previous experiences.

MORE EQUATIONS AND PROBLEMS

In this chapter we shall learn more about solving equations. So far in our work we have used only positive numbers in the equations, but from now on both positive and negative numbers will be used. At this time you should review the section about solving equations on page 39.

Equations Having the Variable in One Member [A]

Example 1. Solve $-7x = 28$.

Solution. Solving an equation for x is finding the value of $+1x$. To obtain $+1x$ or x in the left member, we must divide by -7. If we divide the left member of the equation by -7, we must also divide the right member by -7. Dividing both members of the equation by -7, we obtain $x = -4$.

[A]

ORAL
EXERCISES

Solve the following equations mentally, first telling what number you are dividing both members of the equation by, and then stating the value of the variable x.

1. $-5x = 60$ -/2
2. $4x = -20$ -5
3. $-2x = -12$ 6
4. $7x = 21$ 3
5. $3x = -18$ -6

6. $-3x = -18$ 6
7. $-3x = 18$ -6
8. $3x = 18$ 6
9. $4x = 14$ $3\frac{1}{2}$
10. $-11x = 22$ -2

11. $5x = -12.5$ -2.5
12. $-2x = 7$ -$3\frac{1}{2}$
13. $1.5x = 3$ 2
14. $5x = 3$ $\frac{3}{5}$
15. $6x = 2$ $\frac{1}{3}$

Example 2. Solve $-5x + x = 2 - 18$.

Solution. Simplifying each member, we have
$$-4x = -16$$
$$D_{-4} \qquad x = 4$$

① PROOF. Does $\quad -5(4) + 4 = 2 - 18$?
Does $\quad -20 + 4 = 2 - 18$? Yes.

[A]

WRITTEN
EXERCISES

Solve and prove:

1. $-3x = 24$ -8
2. $-x = 10$ -10
   (This means $-1x = 10$.)
3. $-x = -12$ 12
4. $-c = 30$ -30

5. $7x = 35$ 5
6. $-4x = 9$ -$2\frac{1}{4}$
7. $c - 3c = 14$ -7
8. $3x - 7x = -20$ 5
9. $y + 4y = -15$ -3

Since the exercises on the next few pages differ from those in Chapter 2 only in the use of negative numbers, you will not need to assign all of them to your best classes. Try assigning parts of the three sets on pages 129–131 as one lesson. Include those which involve decimals.

129

10. $2 m - 5 m = 42$ _-14_

11. $x - 2 x = 8$ _-8_

12. $- .5 h = - 4$ _8_

13. $16 = x - 5 x$ _-4_

14. $22 = - y - 10 y$ _-2_

15. $.2 c + .3 c = 2$ _4_

16. $- 5 x - x = 60$ _-10_

17. $- 2 y - y = 1$ _-⅓_

Example 3. Solve $3 x - 5 = 7$.

Solution. We wish only terms containing x in the left member. We do not wish $- 5$ in the left member. Since $+ 5$ added to $- 5$ equals 0, we shall add $+ 5$ to the left member, giving $3 x$ as the result. Since we are adding 5 to the left member, we must also add it to the right member. The solution should be written as follows:

$$3 x - 5 = 7$$

A_{+5} $3 x - 5 + 5 = 7 + 5$

Simplifying $3 x = 12$

D_3 $x = 4$

PROOF. Does $3(4) - 5 = 7?$

       Does $12 - 5 = 7?$ Yes.

Example 4. Solve $7 x + 2 = 16$.

Solution. $7 x + 2 = 16$

S_2 $7 x + 2 - 2 = 16 - 2$

Simplifying $7 x = 14$

D_7 $x = 2$

PROOF. Does $7(2) + 2 = 16?$

       Does $14 + 2 = 16?$ Yes.

[A]

EXERCISES   Solve and prove:

_13_ **1.** $x - 5 = 8$ _9_ **4.** $c + 7 = 16$ _-2_ **7.** $h - 3 = - 5$

_4_ **2.** $x + 3 = 7$ _-7_ **5.** $h + 5 = - 2$ _7_ **8.** $3 c - 9 = 12$

_7_ **3.** $c + 1 = 8$ _-6_ **6.** $2 x + 5 = - 7$ _-5_ **9.** $3 m + 5 = - 10$

_-3_ **10.** $5 x - 10 = - 25$ _-2_ **16.** $- 4 m - 13 = - 5$

_7_ **11.** $- 2 x + 1 = - 13$ _-1_ **17.** $x + 1 = 0$

_-5_ **12.** $- 3 c + 8 = 23$ _2½_ **18.** $8 y - 20 = 0$

_-2_ **13.** $+ 9 h + 1 = - 17$ _9_ **19.** $- x + 9 = 0$

_5⅓_ **14.** $- 3 x + 4 = - 12$ _-6_ **20.** $4 r + 24 = 0$

_-4_ **15.** $6 k + 24 = 0$ _0.7_ **21.** $c + 2 = 2.7$

130

22. $-h - 1 = 5$ -6

23. $m + 2.3 = 3$ 0.7

24. $-7x + 11 = -66$ 11

25. $n - 3.2 = 5$ 8.2

26. $7.2x - 5 = 9.4$ 2

27. $2m + 1.75 = 4.45$ 1.35

28. $-7m - 7 = 0$ -1

29. $3.14x + 4 = -2.28$ -2

30. $-6.1p - 11 = 7.3$ -3

Equations Having the Variable in Both Members [A]

We have learned how to solve equations in which all the terms containing the variable are in one member. We shall now learn how to solve equations in which the variable appears in both members.

Example 1. Solve $6x = 2 + 4x$.

Solution. We wish to have all terms containing x in the left member. To undo the addition of $4x$ in the right member, we subtract $4x$ from $2 + 4x$. Then we must subtract $4x$ from the left member. (The same result can be had by adding $-4x$ to each member.)

$$6x = 2 + 4x$$
S_{4x} $\qquad 6x - 4x = 2 + 4x - 4x$
Simplifying $\qquad 2x = 2$
D_2 $\qquad x = 1$

PROOF. Does $\qquad 6(1) = 2 + 4(1)$?
Does $\qquad 6 = 2 + 4$? Yes.

Example 2. Solve $-7y = 24 - y$

Solution. To eliminate $-y$ in the right member, we add y.
$$-7y = 24 - y$$
A_y $\qquad -7y + y = 24 - y + y$
Simplifying $\qquad -6y = 24$
D_{-6} $\qquad y = -4$

PROOF. Does $\qquad -7(-4) = 24 - (-4)$?
Does $\qquad 28 = 24 + 4$? Yes.

[A]

EXERCISES

1. $3x = x + 4$ 2

2. $6m = m + 20$ 4

3. $3x = 10 - 2x$ 2

4. $-5c = 12 + c$ -2

5. $-6c = 30 - 4c$ -15

6. $2p - 9 = 12$ $10\frac{1}{2}$

7. $5h + 13 = -27$ -8

8. $4s = -25 - 6s$ $-2\frac{1}{2}$

9. $2x = -7x + 18$ 2

10. $3r = 5r - 8$ 4

11. $y = 12 + 4y$ −4

12. $10p = 4p - 54$ −9

13. $5x = 2 + x$ $\frac{1}{2}$

14. $15 + 5y = 23y$ $\frac{5}{6}$

15. $9 = 2x - 5$ 7

16. $0 = 6 - 2x$ 3

17. Explain why subtracting a positive number from each member of an equation is sometimes described as "Using the addition axiom."

①

Equations Containing Fractions [A]

Equations which contain fractions are usually more easily solved by changing them into equations which do not contain fractions. An equation containing fractions can be changed into another equation free from fractions by multiplying each member by a number that is exactly divisible by each denominator. The smallest number that is exactly divisible by each denominator is called the lowest common denominator (abbreviated L.C.D.).

Example. Solve $\frac{1}{3}x = \frac{1}{5}$.

Solution. The L.C.D. is 15.

$$\frac{1}{3}x = \frac{1}{5}$$

M_{15} $$15\left(\frac{1}{3}x\right) = 15\left(\frac{1}{5}\right)$$

$$5x = 3$$

D_5 $$x = \frac{3}{5}$$

PROOF. Does $\frac{1}{3}\left(\frac{3}{5}\right) = \frac{1}{5}$? Yes.

[A]

EXERCISES Solve and prove the following equations, using the multiplication axiom:

②

15 **1.** $\frac{x}{5} = 3$	135 **7.** $\frac{x}{3} = 45$	12 **13.** $\frac{y}{4} = 3$
18 **2.** $\frac{1}{3}m = 6$	$-\frac{1}{3}$ **8.** $-\frac{1}{2}x = \frac{1}{6}$	6 **14.** $\frac{1}{6}n = 1$
49 **3.** $\frac{2}{7}x = 14$	−49 **9.** $\frac{3}{7}m = -21$	0 **15.** $\frac{1}{3}x = 0$
2 **4.** $\frac{c}{8} = \frac{1}{4}$	$\frac{2}{3}$ **10.** $\frac{s}{10} = \frac{1}{15}$	$1\frac{9}{16}$ **16.** $\frac{4}{5}n = \frac{5}{4}$
35 **5.** $.2x = 7$	200 **11.** $.03k = 6$	$-3\frac{3}{4}$ **17.** $\frac{1}{2}c = -\frac{15}{8}$
7 **6.** $.3x = 2.1$	210 **12.** $.06k = 12.6$	30.6 **18.** $.2r = 6.12$

① Emphasize Ex. 17.
② Do part of these orally, and combine the rest with part of page 133 for a written lesson. Discuss the alternate method of solution, using the *division* axiom.

① By this time, all your students should be able to solve equations neatly, quickly, and accurately. The teacher is urged *not* to use the term "transposition." This is a mechanical and meaningless process. If, however, the student *notices* a "short cut" because he observes that if a term disappears from one member of the equation it appears in the other with sign changed, he has based this conclusion on an inductive process and should be allowed to use his "rule."

MORE EQUATIONS AND PROBLEMS

Additional Practice in Equation Solving [A]

① The exercises of this section will give you additional practice in equation solving.

[A]

EXERCISES

Solve and prove:

1. $x + 7 = 15$ 8
2. $x - 6 = 0$ 6
3. $3m - 5 = 16$ 7
4. $2x = 20 - 8x$ 2
5. $3c = 7 - 4c$ 1
6. $3m - 8 = 37$ 15
7. $5r = 9r - 20$ 5
8. $5x - 7x - 10 = 0$ -5
9. $16 = 10 - 3x$ -2
10. $7m = 3m - 20$ -5

11. $6x - 15 = 84 - 3x$ 11
12. $6x + 15 = 40 + 2x$ $6\frac{1}{4}$
13. $8 - 5y = y - 4$ 2
14. $7c + 28 = 5c + 6$ -11
15. $9k + 2 = 8 + 5k$ $1\frac{1}{2}$
16. $2x + 15 - 10 = -3x$ -1
17. $10h - 2 = -7 + 5h$ -1
18. $0 = 8x - 24$ 3
19. $8y - 2 - 5y - 8 = 0$ $3\frac{1}{3}$
20. $14 = 6x - 2 + 2x$ 2

21. $5x - 3x + 18 = 36 - 4x$ 3
22. $9y - 13 + 6y - 7 = 2y$ $1\frac{7}{13}$
23. $5m + 10 - m = 12 - m + 3$ 1
24. $5r + 12 - 3r = -2r - 13 - r$ -5
25. $8x + 15 - 6x - 6 = 45$ 18
26. $10y + 13y - 5y - 6 = 7y + 6 + 12y - 5$ -7

Solving Problems by Formulas [A]

The formula $A = bh$ can be used to find the area (A), base (b), or height (h) of a rectangle or parallelogram when 2 of the 3 variables are known.

Example. The area of a wall is 210 square feet and the base is 12 feet. What is the height?

Solution. $A = bh$. Substituting 210 for A and 12 for b, we have,

$$210 = 12h$$
$$12h = 210$$
D_{12} $h = 17.5$ ↓ ②

PROOF.   Does $210 = 12(17.5)$? Yes.

133

② In practice, students should proceed to $h = 17.5$ without writing down the step $12h = 210$. The variable in an equation does not need to be in the *left* member of the equation.

Insist on students continuing to write the solutions in good form. This set affords good practice in arithmetic.

ALGEBRA, BOOK ONE

To Solve a Problem by a Formula:

1. Write the formula.
2. Substitute the values for the known variables.
3. Solve the resulting equation for the remaining variable.

EXERCISES

Using the formula $A = lw$ or $lw = A$, find the value of l when

1. $A = 320$, $w = 16$ 20
2. $A = 576$, $w = 24$ 24
3. $A = 324$, $w = 12$ 27
4. $A = 242.54$, $w = 13.4$ 18.1
5. $A = 453.75$, $w = 12.5$ 36.3
6. $A = 42.78$, $w = 4.6$ 9.3

Using the same formula, find w when

7. $A = 136$, $l = 8$ 17
8. $A = 225$, $l = 15$ 15
9. $A = 70.98$, $l = 15.1$ 4.7
10. $A = 19.44$, $l = 5.4$ 3.6

Using the formula $A = \frac{1}{2} bh$, find the value of the variable:

11. $b = 8$, $h = 22$ 88
12. $A = 324$, $b = 36$ 18
13. $h = 14$, $A = 182$ 26
14. $A = 750$, $h = 6$ 250
15. $A = 1008$, $h = 56$ 36
16. $b = 3\frac{1}{3}$, $A = 11\frac{1}{4}$ $6\frac{3}{4}$

Using the formula $V = lwh$, find the value of the variable:

17. $l = 18$, $w = 8$, $h = 6$ 864
18. $V = 60$, $l = 15$, $w = 4$ 1
19. $V = 567$, $h = 7$, $w = 9$ 9
20. $V = 175$, $l = 5$, $h = 7$ 5
21. $V = 147.56$, $w = 7$, $h = 3.4$ 6.2
22. $l = 10\frac{1}{2}$, $w = 2\frac{1}{4}$, $h = 3\frac{1}{2}$ $82\frac{11}{16}$

Using the formula $i = prt$, find the value of the variable:

23. $p = \$500$, $r = 6\%$, $t = 3$ yr. $\$90$
24. $i = \$150$, $r = 4\%$, $t = 5$ yr. $\$750$
25. $i = \$63.75$, $r = 2\frac{1}{2}\%$, $t = 6$ yr. $\$425$
26. $p = 452$, $r = 4\frac{1}{2}\%$, $i = \$50.85$ $2\frac{1}{2}$ (yr.)
27. $i = \$150$, $p = \$600$, $t = 5$ yr. 5%

Solve each of the following formulas and equations:

28. $2x + 3y = 13$ when $x = 2$. 3
29. $3y = 13 - 2x$ when $x = 6$. $\frac{1}{3}$

134

30. $3x - y = 7$ when $x = 5$. $y = 8$
31. $2x - 3y = 12$ when $x = 0$. $y = -4$
32. $4x - 5y = 4$ when $x = -4$. $y = -4$
33. $V = abc$ when $V = 2730$, $a = 13$, and $b = 14$. $c = 15$
34. $A = p + prt$ when $p = 150$, $r = 4\%$, and $t = 3\frac{1}{2}$. $A = 171$

[B]

Solve:

35. $T = t + 273$ when $t = -80$. 193
36. $F = \frac{9}{5}C + 32$ when $C = -10$. 14
37. $F = \frac{9}{5}C + 32$ when $F = 72$. $22\frac{2}{9}$
38. $A = \dfrac{h(b + b')}{2}$ if $b = 8$, $b' = 18$, and $h = 14$. 182

39. $V = \pi r^2 h$ is a formula for finding the volume of a cylinder. Evaluate the formula when $r = 6$, $h = 14$, and $\pi = 3\frac{1}{7}$.

40. $K = \frac{1}{2}mv^2$ is a formula used in physics. Evaluate it ^{1584} when $K = 306.3125$ and $v = 6.5$. 14.5

[C]

41. Solve $C = \frac{5}{9}(F - 32)$ for F when $C = 100$. 212
42. Solve $C = \frac{5}{9}(F - 32)$ for F when $C = -273$. -459.4
43. Evaluate $V = \frac{4}{3}\pi r^3$ when $r = 2$ and $\pi = 3.14$. $33.49\frac{1}{3}$
44. In the formula $A = p + prt$, A is the amount, p is the principal, r is the rate, and t is the time. Find the value of p when $A = \$306.25$, $r = 5\%$, and $t = 4\frac{1}{2}$ years. $\$250$

Making Tables from Equations [A]

See ① below.

We shall now continue making tables from equations, as you did in Chapter 3.

Copy and complete the following tables:

[A]   **EXERCISES**

1. $x = 3y$

x	? 0	? 3	? 6	? 9	? 12	? -3	? -6	? -9	? -12
y	0	1	2	3	4	−1	−2	−3	−4

a. As the values of y increase, what can you say about the values of x? *They increase*
b. How does x change when the values of y decrease?
Decreases

① This section affords the opportunity of teaching dependence—a very important concept in mathematics. In better classes, try having the questions answered before completing the table. Remember, the table here is a crutch to aid students in observing the relationships between the variables.

2. $x + y = 10$

x	?10	?8	?6	?4	0	2	4	6
y	0	2	4	6	?10	?8	?6	?4

Do x and y increase together? *No.*

3. $x - 2y = 10$

x	?2	?6	?10	?14	?18	?22	?26	?30
y	−4	−2	0	2	4	6	8	10

When y increases, does x increase or decrease? *Increases.*

4. $xy = 16$

x	16	8	4	2	1	$\frac{1}{2}$	$\frac{1}{4}$	$\frac{1}{8}$
y	?1	?2	?4	?8	?16	?32	?64	?128

When x decreases, how does y change? *Increases* .

5. When two numbers, x and y, change together and their quotient $\left(\dfrac{x}{y}\right)$ always remains the same, the two numbers *vary directly*; when two numbers change together and their product (xy) always remains the same, the numbers *vary inversely*.

a. How do x and y vary in the equation $x = 3y$? *Directly.*

b. How do m and n vary in the equation $mn = 16$? *Inversely.*

c. How do x and y vary in the equation $x - 2y = 0$? *Directly.*

Making Equations from Tables [B]

In the last set of exercises you made tables which contained sets of values satisfying equations. We shall now reverse the process and make the equations whose solutions are given in the tables.

Example. Write the equation which expresses the relation between x and y as shown in the following table:

x	1	3	5	7	9	11	13	15
y	0	1	2	3	4	5	6	7

Solution. By inspection, $x = 1$ when $y = 0$. This fact tells us that x equals 1, plus some term containing y. From the table

136

① Suggested additional questions: Ex. 2: "When x is increased by 4, how does y change? Does x increase as fast as y decreases? If you know the value of x, how can you find the value of y?" For more practice, use similar equations, such as $m + n = 15$ and pose the same questions.

Ex. 3: "When y is increased by 2, how does x change? When y is increased by 3, how does x change?"

② Emphasize the vocabulary in Ex. 5.

MORE EQUATIONS AND PROBLEMS

we know that x is increased by 2 when y is increased by 1. In other words, x increases twice as fast as y. From these two facts the equation $x = 1 + 2y$ is suggested. Then we check the equation $x = 1 + 2y$ with each set of values of x and y given in the table. On doing so we find that $x = 1 + 2y$ is the required equation.

[B]

Write equations which express the relation between the variables in the following tables, and complete the tables.

EXERCISES

1.   *(handwritten: $y = 2x$)*

y	0	2	4	6	8	10	12	14
x	0	1	2	3	4	?5	?6	?7

2.   *(handwritten: $x = 3y$)*

y	0	1	2	3	4	5	6	?7
x	0	3	6	9	12	15	?18	21

3.   *(handwritten: $m = n+7$)*

m	7	8	9	10	11	?12	17	21
n	0	1	2	3	4	5	?10	?14

4.   *(handwritten: $a + b = 10$)*

a	10	9	8	7	6	5	?3	?-2
b	0	1	2	3	4	5	7	12

SUGGESTIONS. What is the value of a when $b = 0$? Does a increase or decrease when b increases? Does a decrease as fast as b increases?

5.   *(handwritten: $x + 3y = 18$)*

x	18	15	12	9.	6	?3	?0	?-3
y	0	1	2	3	4	5	6	7

6.   *(handwritten: $pv = 36$)*

p	144	72	36	18	12	9	?6	?4
v	$\frac{1}{4}$	$\frac{1}{2}$	1	2	3	4	6	9

SUGGESTION. What is the product of p and v?

7.   *(handwritten: $s = 4t^2$)*

s	0	4	16	36	64	100	?44	?96
t	0	1	2	3	4	5	6	7

SUGGESTIONS. Note that when either s or t is zero, the other is zero also. As t is increased by one, is s increased by the same amount each time? Divide the different values of s by their greatest com-

137

mon divisor. What relation do these quotients bear to the corresponding values of *t*?

[C]

8.

n	3	5	10	11	20	25	30	35
m	15	21	36	39	66	? 81	? 96	? 111

SUGGESTIONS. Observe that as *n* changes from 3 to 5, *m* changes from 15 to 21; that is, an increase of 2 in the value of *n* causes an increase of 6 in the value of *m*. Again, observe that as *n* changes from 5 to 10, *m* changes from 21 to 36; that is, an increase of 5 in the value of *n* causes an increase of 15 in the value of *m*. In both cases *m* seems to increase 3 times as fast as *n*. If this is true, then a decrease of 3 in the value of *n* will cause a decrease of 9 in the value of *m*; that is, if *n* decreases from 3 to 0, *m* decreases from 15 to 6. Therefore the formula is $m = 6 + 3n$. Check this formula with the other sets of values and, if true, complete the table.

9.

d	3	5	8	9	10	12	20	24
c	14	22	34	38	? 42	? 56	? 82	? 98

$c = 4d + 2$

10. Some pupils using a protractor measured the angles of polygons having 3, 4, 5, 6, and 7 sides. Then they made the following table:

Number of sides (n)	3	4	5	6	7
Sum of the angles (S)	180°	360°	540°	720°	900°

Write the formula for finding the sum of the angles of any polygon in terms of the number of sides. $S = 180(n - 2)$

Solving Inequalities with the Multiplication and Division Axioms [A]

In Chapter 2 we considered inequalities that can be solved by the addition and subtraction axioms for inequalities. Let us now consider inequalities that require multiplication and division axioms. First we must consider the axioms themselves.

If we multiply each member of the statement $8 > 3$ by 2, we obtain the statement $2(8) > 2(3)$. However, if we multiply both members by -2 we have the statement $(-2)(8) < (-2)(3)$. Thus we see that multiplying both members of $8 > 3$ by 2 preserves the order of the inequality, but multiplying both members by -2 reverses the order (causes $>$ to become $<$). Since .similar statements can be made for all real numbers, we have:

If a, b, and c are real numbers and if $a > b$,
$ac > bc$ if c is positive, and $ac < bc$ if c is negative.

We call this property the multiplication axiom for inequalities. The corresponding division axiom for inequalities follows:

If a, b, and c are real numbers and if $a > b$,
$\dfrac{a}{c} > \dfrac{b}{c}$ if c is positive, and $\dfrac{a}{c} < \dfrac{b}{c}$ if c is negative.

Both the multiplication axiom and the division axiom may be stated with each $<$ replaced by $>$ and each $>$ replaced by $<$.

Example. Find the truth set for $-2x + 3 < 9$.

Solution. $-2x + 3 < 9$
S_3 $-2x + 3 - 3 < 9 - 3$
Simplifying $-2x < 6$
D_{-2} $x > -3$

PROOF. Is $-2x + 3 < 9$ when $x > -3$? Yes.

Therefore the truth set is the set of all real numbers greater than -3.

① ↓

[A]

EXERCISES

Find the truth sets for each of the following inequalities.

1. $8x > 16$ $x > 2$

2. $\dfrac{x}{4} > 5$ $x > 20$

3. $-5y > 10$ $y < -2$

4. $\dfrac{-z}{2} < 8$ $z > -16$

5. $-3x + 2 > -10$ $x < 4$

6. $y + 1 < 7 - \dfrac{y}{2}$ $y < 4$

7. $4 - 2m < -m - 5$ $m > 9$

8. $2x + x < -1 + x$ $x < -\dfrac{1}{2}$

Compound Sentences [A]

Such a sentence as "$x = 2$ and $x > 6$" is called a compound sentence because it is compounded from the simple sentence "$x = 2$" and the simple sentence "$x > 6$." A compound sentence in which two simple sentences (clauses) are connected by *and* is true if and only if both clauses are true. If $x = 2$, then x cannot be greater than 6.

① Note how the skills of solving inequalities are combined with those used for equations. This is a commendable modern trend in elementary algebra. Class discussion should be held to tie in this work with equations. Ask, "What are the truth sets for $-2x + 3 > 9$; $-2x + 3 < 9$; and $-2x + 3 = 9$? Let's graph these on the number line. What do you notice about the graphs?"

Consequently, we know that the sentence "$x = 2$ and $x > 6$" makes a false statement. On the other hand, the compound sentence "$x = 2$ and $x < 6$" makes a true statement.

In other compound sentences two clauses may be connected by *or*. In mathematics we consider that a compound sentence containing the connective *or* is true if either of its clauses is true or if both are true; otherwise we consider the sentence false. In the sentence "$2 < 1$ or $9 > 7$," the clause $2 < 1$ is not true, but since the clause "$9 > 7$" is true, we consider the sentence true.

EXERCISES [A]

Which of the compound sentences below are true?

1. $2 = 1 + 1$ and $8 = 4(2)$ T
2. $3 = 1 + 2$ or $9 + 5 = 13$ T
3. $4 > 1$ and $5 \neq 7$ T
4. $-2 < 0$ or $2 > 0$ T
5. $8 > -8$ and $-2 > 2$ F
6. $7 = -2 + 9$ or $-4 < 5$ T

Graphs of Compound Sentences [A]

Since a compound sentence with the connective *and* is true only if both clauses are true, the graph of the sentence will consist of only those points appearing on the graphs of both clauses. Thus the graph of the sentence "$x > -2$ and $x < 4$" will consist of only those points *common* to the graph of the clause "$x > -2$" and the graph of the clause "$x < 4$." Let us examine these two graphs.

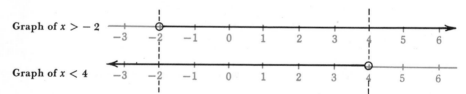

Graph of $x > -2$

Graph of $x < 4$

As we study these graphs we see that the only points for which $x > -2$, and at the same time $x < 4$, are the points between -2 and 4 on the number line. Thus the graph of "$x > -2$ and $x < 4$" is the graph shown below.

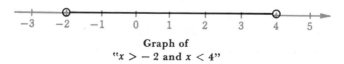

Graph of
"$x > -2$ and $x < 4$"

140

MORE EQUATIONS AND PROBLEMS ①

Since a compound sentence with two clauses connected by *or* is true if either or both of its clauses are true, its graph will consist of all the points on the graphs of both of its clauses. Thus the graph of "$x > -3$ or $x = -3$" will consist of all the points on the graph of $x > -3$ and on the graph of $x = -3$. The graph of each of the clauses and of the complete sentence are shown below.

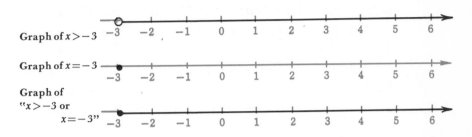

Graph of $x > -3$

Graph of $x = -3$

Graph of "$x > -3$ or $x = -3$"

[A]

EXERCISES

Graph each of the compound sentences below.

1. $x > -3$ and $x < 4$
2. $x > 2$ or $x = 2$
3. $m < 5$ or $m > 5$
4. $y = 4$ or $y < 4$
5. $x = 2$ or $x = -2$
6. $y > 7$ and $y < 7$
7. $x + 5 < 9$ and $x + 1 > -3$
8. $x + 6 > 7$ or $x = 1$

Algebraic Representation [A]

You know that in order to solve problems algebraically it is necessary to express number relations by the use of symbols. Here is some further practice of this sort.

[A]

EXERCISES

1. The sum of two numbers is 10. If x represents one of them, represent the other in terms of x. $10 - x$

2. n stands for a certain number.
Represent: (a) the number 5 times as large; $5n$
(b) the number 5 larger than n; $n + 5$
(c) the number 4 less than n; $n - 4$
(d) the number two-thirds as large as n. $\frac{2}{3}n$

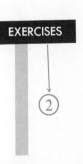
②

② Try doing these exercises in class. But make sure that all are thinking—not just waiting for some classmate to answer the teacher's questions. One way to avoid inattention is to ask the question first, wait while students think, and then call on an individual. Often saying the name first releases others for daydreaming. Since many of these phrases will reappear in the verbal problems following, you may need to refer to this set again.

141

3. Indicate: the sum of 4 and 6; the sum of x and y; the sum of r and $-s$. $4+6; x+y; r-s$

4. The difference of two numbers is 3. If x stands for the larger, what will represent the smaller? If x stands for the smaller, what will represent the larger? $x-3; x+3$

5. What is the cost of x ounces of syrup at 9 cents an ounce? of 2 x ounces of candied fruit at 23 cents an ounce? $9x¢; 46x¢$

6. How many cents are there in 3 dimes? in x dimes? in 2 x dimes? $30; 10x; 20x$

7. How many inches are there in 5 feet? in y feet? in 3 c feet? $60; 12y; 36c$

8. How many ounces are there in 4 pounds? in x pounds? in 5 p pounds? $64; 16x; 8p$

9. How many oranges at 15 cents each can be bought for 60 cents? for 30 x cents? for 90 y cents? for 15 xy cents? $4; 2x; 6y; xy$

10. The product of two numbers is 8 x and one of them is 4. What is the other number? $2x$

11. An integer is a number such as 3, 9, 10, -4 or -68. If x represents one integer, what will represent the next larger integer? $x+1$

12. The quotient of two numbers is 3 c and the divisor is 4 c. What is the dividend? $12c^2$

13. The difference of two numbers is 6 and the smaller is 3 x. What is the larger? $3x+6$

14. Find 6% of 1020; 4% of 80; 100% of 32; 200% of 35; 4% of x; 10% of y. $61.2; 3.2; 32; 70; 0.04x; 0.10y$

15. Find x% of 80; y% of 25; r% of s; p% of m. $0.8x; 0.25y; 0.01rs; 0.01pm$

16. A rope is x yards long. If 6 yards are cut off, how many yards are left? $x-6$

17. What is the perimeter of a rectangle x feet wide and 2 x feet long? What is the area of the rectangle? $6x ft.; 2x^2 sq. ft.$

18. What is the area of a rectangle 6 a^2 feet long and 3 a feet wide? What is its perimeter? $18a^3 sq. ft.; (12a^2+6a) ft.$

19. The length of a rectangle is 6 feet more than its width. If x represents the width, express the length in terms of x. $(x+6) ft.$

MORE EQUATIONS AND PROBLEMS

20. A train travels 60 miles an hour. How far will it travel in 3 hours? in 4 hours? in x hours? in y^2 hours? *180 mi.; 240 mi.; 60x mi.; 60y² mi.*

21. If an automobile travels 50 miles an hour, how long will it take to go 150 miles? $833\frac{1}{3}$ miles? $\frac{5}{3}x$ miles? 200 x miles? *3 hr.   16²/3 hr.   x/30 hr.   4x hr.*

22. Find the cost of 72 cookies at 60 cents a dozen; of x cookies at y cents a dozen; of 12 b cookies at 48 cents a dozen. *$3.60   xy/12¢,   48b¢*

23. How many pints are there in 8 quarts? in 12 quarts? in k quarts? in 2 c quarts? *16; 24; 2k; 4c*

24. If n stands for one side of an equilateral triangle, what will represent its perimeter? *3n*

25. If 2 numbers are in the ratio of 2 : 3 and 2 x represents the smaller number, then 3 x represents the larger. If two numbers are in the ratio of 3 : 5 and 3 x stands for the smaller number, what will represent the larger? *5x*

26. A boy is x years old. How old will he be in 6 years? in 10 years? in y years? *(x+6) yr.; (x+10) yr.; (x+y) yr.*

27. A girl is y years old. How old was she 5 years ago? 8 years ago? x years ago? *(y-5) yr; (y-8) yr; (y-x) yr.*

28. Letting x stand for the unknown number, write in algebraic language

a. A number increased by 7 equals 28. *x+7=28*

b. Twice a number plus the number equals 81.

c. One third of a number, less 8, equals 13. *⅓x - 8 = 13*

d. Seven times a number equals the number increased by 30. *7x = x + 30*

Problems

Before you attempt to solve any of these problems, you should review the directions for solving problems on page 44.

[A]

EXERCISES

1. The sum of a certain number and 21 is 84. Find the number. *63*

2. A certain number is equal to 25 diminished by 13. What is the number? *12*

3. 42 is equal to a number increased by 54. What is the number? *=12*

ALGEBRA, BOOK ONE

4. The sum of a number and $- 5$ is 4. Find the number.

5. Four times a certain number is equal to 96 increased by the number. Find the number. *9* *32*

6. If 15 is subtracted from 4 times a certain number, the remainder is 17. Find the number. *8*

7. If 6 is subtracted from a certain number, the difference is 36. What is the number? *42*

8. If 20 is added to 3 times a certain number, the sum is 101. Find the number. *27*

9. The sum of two numbers is 60 and one is 3 times the other. Find the numbers. *15, 45*

10. The sum of two numbers is 63 and one of them is 27 larger than the other. Find the numbers. *18, 45*

Let $n =$ the smaller number
Then $n + 27 =$ the larger number
and $n + n + 27 =$ _ _?_ _. Complete the equation and solve.

11. The sum of two numbers is 44 and one of the numbers is 18 larger than the other. What are the numbers? *13, 31*

12. Four times a certain number, decreased by 5, equals 25 decreased by 6 times the number. Find the number. *3*

13. A man paid $4045 for two used cars, paying $255 more for one than the other. What was the cost of each?

$1895, $2150

$$x + 255 \quad + \quad x \quad = 4045$$

14. One number is 3 more than twice the other. What are the numbers if their sum is 18? *5, 13*

15. A man uses 360 feet of fencing to enclose a rectangular lot whose length is 20 feet more than 3 times the width. What are the dimensions of the lot? *40 ft. × 140 ft.*

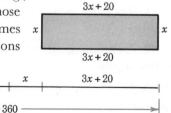

16. The number of boys in an algebra class is one less than 3 times the number of girls. If there are 39 pupils in the class, how many of them are girls? *10*

[B]

17. The sum of two consecutive integers is 37. What are the numbers? *18, 19*

SUGGESTION. 1, 2, 3, 4, 5 etc., are integers.
Let x = the smaller number
Then $x + 1$ = the larger number

18. The sum of three consecutive integers is 117. What are the numbers? *38, 39, 40*

19. The sum of three consecutive integers is − 345. What are the integers? *−114, −115, −116*

20. The sum of three consecutive integers is 21 more than the smallest integer. Find the three integers. *9, 10, 11*

21. The sum of two consecutive odd integers is 92. What are they? *45, 47*

SUGGESTION. The odd integers are 1, 3, 5, 7, etc.
Let x = the smaller integer
Then $x + 2$ = the larger integer

22. Find three consecutive odd integers whose sum is 51. *15, 17, 19*

23. The sum of three consecutive even integers is 60. Find the integers. *18, 20, 22*

24. The sum of three consecutive even integers is 50 more than the smallest one. Find the integers. *22, 24, 26*

(1)

Percentage Problems [A]

A per cent of a given number is called the percentage. The number of which the per cent is taken is the base. The per cent is the rate. The expression "per cent" (abbreviated %) means hundredths. Thus 6% means .06 or $\frac{6}{100}$. When solving percentage problems you should always keep in mind that a common way of expressing a fraction whose denominator is 100 is as a number of per cent.

Percentage problems are of three kinds, and most people who try to do them by arithmetic become confused and do not know what operations are to be performed with the numbers. With the use of algebra the three kinds of percentage problems are easy.

① Your students may need help here, since weaker ones often see the "2" and think that "x + 2" must therefore be even. You might ask such questions as "Start with any odd number. Add 1. Is the result even or odd? Add 2. Answer the same question." Or, "Could x + 5, x + 7, x + 9 represent three consecutive odd or three consecutive even integers? If so, under what circumstances?"

145

Some teachers prefer to solve all percentage problems by applying the formula $p = br$. This text treats percentage like any other verbal problem which states a sentence in *word* symbols that can be translated into *mathematical* symbols. If you have been accustomed to the strict formula method, try this alternate way to see if you like it.

ALGEBRA, BOOK ONE

The Three Kinds of Percentage Problems

1. Finding a per cent of a number
   Example: What is 3% of 120?
2. Finding what per cent one number is of another.
   Example: 26 is what per cent of 65?
3. Finding a number when a per cent of it is known
   Example: 169 is 65% of what number?

We shall now solve each of the above examples.

Example 1. What is 3% of 120?

Solution. In this problem the word "what" means "What number" and the word "of" means "times."

Let $x =$ the required number

Then $x = .03 \times 120$

$x = 3.6$, the number

This type of a percentage problem is usually solved by arithmetic.

Example 2. 26 is what per cent of 65?

Solution. The words "what per cent" mean "what number of per cent."

Let $x =$ the required number of per cent

Then $26 = \dfrac{x}{100} \times 65$

Interchanging the members of the equation, we have $\dfrac{65\,x}{100} = 26$.

M_{100} $65\,x = 2600$

D_{65} $x = 40$, the number of per cent

PROOF. 40% of 65 $= .40 \times 65 = 26$.

Example 3. 169 is 65% of what number?

Solution. Let $x =$ the required number

Then $169 = .65\,x$

M_{100} $16900 = 65\,x$

$65\,x = 16900$

$x = 260$, the number

PROOF. $.65 \times 260 = 169$.

It should not be necessary to do all these routine exercises in your better classes. Instead, sample the first section and proceed to parts B and C on pp. 148 and 149.

MORE EQUATIONS AND PROBLEMS

1. Find the following numbers:

a. 4% of $180 *$7.20* **d.** 40% of 75 *30* **g.** 500% of 1 *5*

b. 3% of $250 *$7.50* **e.** 300% of 18 *54* **h.** 18% of 18 *3.24*

c. 7% of $900 *$63* **f.** 200% of 70 *140* **i.** 25% of 100 *25*

2. Find the following per cents or rates:

a. 8 is what % of 16? *50%*   **e.** What % of 60 is 48? *80%*

b. 24 is what % of 40? *60%*   **f.** What % of 100 is 33? *33%*

c. 18 is what % of 72? *25%*   **g.** What % of 250 is 50? *20%*

d. 72 is what % of 18? *400%*   **h.** What % of 6 is 4800?

80,000%

3. Find the following:

a. 15 is 40% of what number? *37.5*

b. 40% of a certain number is 28. What is the number? *70*

c. 84 is 400% of what number? *21*

d. 8% of a number is 1640. Find the number. *20,500*

e. 11 is 11% of what number? *100*

4. Find $3\frac{1}{2}\%$ of 720. $(3\frac{1}{2}\% = .035 = \frac{7}{200}.)$ *25.2*

5. Find $37\frac{1}{2}\%$ of 124. *46.5*

SUGGESTION. Write $37\frac{1}{2}\%$ as $\dfrac{37\frac{1}{2}}{100}$ and reduce to $\frac{3}{8}$.

6. What is $12\frac{1}{2}\%$ of 96? *12*

7. Find $8\frac{1}{3}\%$ of 48. *4*

8. What is $a\%$ of b? *$\frac{ab}{100}$*

9. What per cent of 90 is 20? *$22\frac{2}{9}\%$*

10. $292.50 is what % of $900? *32.5%*

11. 32% of a number is 9.6. What is the number? *30*

12. A baseball team won 14 games and lost 6. What per cent of its games did it win? *70%*

13. 18 pupils in a class of 24 made a mark of B or better in an algebra test. What per cent of the pupils made a mark of less than B? *25%*

147

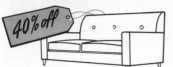

14. A store had a 40% discount sale. What was the former price of a small couch which sold at the sale for $117? *$195*

15. 15% of a man's monthly income is spent for rent. Find his income each month if his rent is $135 a month. *$900*

[B]

16. What is $\frac{1}{2}$% of 250? *1.25*

SUGGESTION. $\frac{1}{2}\% = \frac{\frac{1}{2}}{100} = \frac{1}{200}$. Also, $\frac{1}{2}\% = .005$.

17. Find $\frac{1}{8}$% of 96. *0.12*

18. What is .1% of 2000? *2*

19. A man received $18 interest on an investment of $400. What rate did he receive? *4.5%*

20. A suit of clothing that was marked to sell for $60 was sold for $52. The actual selling price was what per cent of the marked price? *$86\frac{2}{3}$%*

21. A chair was marked to sell for $55. If a discount of $10 was allowed for cash, the cash discount was what per cent of the marked price? *$18\frac{2}{11}$%*

22. A farmer took clover seed containing 1.5% plantain seed to be "cleaned," or have the plaintain seed removed. If 9.6 pounds of plantain seed were removed, how much seed did the farmer have originally? *640 lb.*

[C]

Example. 10% of a number increased by 24% of the same number equals 142.8. What is the number?

Solution. Let $\qquad x =$ the number

Then $\qquad .10\,x + .24\,x = 142.8$

$\qquad\qquad\qquad .34\,x = 142.8$

$M_{100} \qquad\qquad\quad 34\,x = 14280$

$D_{34} \qquad\qquad\qquad x = 420$

$\qquad$ The number is 420.

PROOF. 10% of 420 is 42.

$\qquad$ 24% of 420 is .24 × 420, or 100.8.

$\qquad$ 42 + 100.8 = 142.8.

148

23. 8% of a number plus 12% of the number is 62. Find the number. *310*

24. 14% of a number plus 12% of the number, less 8% of the number, is 380. Find the number. *2111⅑*

25. A number decreased by 10% of itself equals 405. What is the number? *450*

26. A merchant sold goods for $2592 and made a gain of 8% of the cost. What was the cost of the goods? *$2400*

27. How cheaply can a grocer afford to sell bleach that costs 12 cents a quart if he must make a profit of 20% based on the selling price? *15¢ a quart*

28. A baseball team with a standing of .816 has won 84 games. How many games has it lost? *19*

29. An air conditioner sold for $105.30 after discounts of 10% and 10% were given. What was the original price? *$130*

SUGGESTION. If p represents the marked price, the first discount is .10 p and the second discount is .09 p. Why?

30. A radio was sold for $69.50 after discounts of 10% and 5% were allowed. What was the marked price of the radio? *$81.29*

You have now completed Chapter 5. Before you attempt the Chapter Review, be sure that you

	PAGE	
1. Can solve equations	39	Review
2. Can use formulas to solve problems	133	if you
3. Can make tables from equations	135	need to.
4. Can solve inequalities	54	
5. Can graph compound sentences	140	

6. Know how to solve percentage problems by algebra   145

7. Know how to spell and use the following words correctly in sentences:

	PAGE		PAGE
rate	145	percentage	145
per cent	145		

33. a. The percentage is equal to the base times the rate.
b. The interest is equal to the product of the principal, the rate, and the time
ALGEBRA, BOOK ONE

[A]

CHAPTER
REVIEW

See
①
next
page.

Solve the following equations:

1. $2x - 1 = 15$ *8*

2. $3x + 12 = -9$ *-7*

3. $-3x - 5 = 9x -$ $-\frac{5}{12}$

4. $3.14c = 9.42$ *3*

5. $\frac{1}{3}n = 5$ *15*

6. $y - 48 = 2.6y$ *-30*

7. $-x + 1 = x - 5$ *3*

8. $5c - 6 = c + 2$ *2*

9. $3h - 1 = 5h + 7$ *-4*

10. $3p - 10 = 7p - 150$ *35*

11. $\frac{5}{6}y - 1 = 9$ *12*

12. $x - 8 = -6 - 2x + 1$ *1*

13. If $x - 2y = 7$, find y when $x = 3$.   *-2*

14. If $2x - y = 5$, find y when $x = 0$.   *-5*

15. If $7x + 2y = 11$, find y when $x = -1$.   *9*

16. If $5x + 3y = 12$, find y when $x = -3$.   *9*

Write, using algebraic language:

17. The sum of x and -6.   *x - 6*

18. 10 subtracted from y.   *y - 10*

19. a increased by twice b.   *a + 2b*

20. The product of m and n.   *mn*

21. 4 less than c.   *c - 4*

22. 2 less x.   *2 - x*

Let x stand for the numbers in exercises 23–26.

23. Twice a number plus three times the number equals 30.   *2x + 3x = 30*

24. A number decreased by 8 equals 22.   *x - 8 = 22*

25. 8 increased by twice a number equals 40.   *8 + 2x = 40*

26. One fourth of a number is 16.   *$\frac{1}{4}x = 16$*

27. How many cents are there in 2 quarters? in y quarters? in $4x$ quarters?   *50; 25y; 100x*

28. What is the cost of $4x$ books at $2x$ cents each?   *$8x^2$ cents*

29. How many feet are there in $24x$ inches? in $6c$ inches?   *2x; $\frac{c}{2}$*

30. If b bananas cost c cents, what is the cost of n bananas?   *$\frac{nc}{b}$ cents*

31. Separate 106 into 2 parts so that one part will be 16 more than the other.   *45, 61*

32. Separate 64 into 2 parts such that one part will be $\frac{7}{9}$ of the other.   *28, 36*

33. Write the rules expressed by the following formulas:

a. $P = br$ c. $V = lwh$ e. $A = \frac{1}{2}bh$

b. $i = prt$ d. $A = bh$ f. $C = 2\pi r$

c. The volume of a rectangular solid is equal to the product of the length the width, and the height.

d. The area of a parallelogram is equal to the product of the base and the altitude.

e. The area of a triangle is equal to ½ the product of the base and altitude.

f. The circumference of a circle is equal to the product of 2, π, and the radius.

MORE EQUATIONS AND PROBLEMS

34. 15 is what per cent of 75? *20%*

35. 32 is 8% of what number? *400*

36. How much money must be invested at 4% to earn $100 a year? *$2500*

37. $V = lwh$. Find w, when $V = 1080$, $l = 12$, $h = 9$. *10*

38. $i = prt$. Find p, when $i = 43.20$, $r = .04$, $t = 3$. *360*

39. $A = \frac{1}{2} bh$. Find h when $A = 38$ and $b = 10$. *7.6*

40. $C = 2 \pi r$. Find r when $C = 18.84$ and $\pi = 3.14$. *3*

41. $x - 2y = 2$. Copy and complete the table by inserting values of y.

x	− 4	− 2	0	2	4	6	8
y	? *-3*	? *-2*	? *-1*	? *0*	? *1*	? *2*	? *3*

[A]

On your paper write one word, number, or letter, and only one, for each blank to make the following nine statements true:

1. In algebra figures and __?__ are used to represent numbers. *letters*

2. xy means x __?__ y. *times*

3. The figure 3 in the expression $4 x^3$ is called an __?__ *exponent*

4. The sign = means __?__. *equal (or equals)*

5. The __?__ sign is omitted in the expression ab. *times*

6. There are three __?__ in the expression $2 x^2 - 5 x + 1$. *terms*

7. The coefficient of y is __?__ *1 (understood)*

8. $2 m$ is a short way of writing $m +$ __?__. *m*

9. The coefficient of b^3 in the expression $7 b^3$ is __?__. *7*

10. Simplify:

a. $5 - 4 - 1$ *0* **d.** $10 + (-4)$ *6* **g.** $0 - (-9)$ *9*

b. $6 - (-3)$ *9* **e.** $(3 m)(-n)$ *-3mn* **h.** xxx *x^3*

c. $-6 \cdot 10$ *-60* **f.** $-3x + 4x$ *x* **i.** $x + x + x$ *3x*

② Use this review according to the needs of the class. In some, it could be omitted for the present and used later as written or class review of miscellaneous topics.

151

12. a. The number increased by 2.   *b. Twice the number.*
c. The square of the number.   *d. One third of the number.*

11. In the expression $x^3 + 4x - 2x^3 + 8$, x^3 and 8 are --?-- terms. *unlike*

12. If n stands for a certain number, tell what each of the following expressions means:

a. $n + 2$ **b.** $2n$ **c.** n^2 **d.** $\dfrac{n}{3}$

see foot of page

13. In what operation in algebra do we change signs of terms?

14. Why should one make a sketch when it is possible to do so in solving a verbal problem?

15. If $2y - x = 5$, find y when $x = -7$. *-1*

If $x = 2$ and $y = -3$, find the values of:

16. $3xy$ *-18*   **19.** x^2 *4*   **22.** $(xy)^2$ *36*

17. $-xy$ *+6*   **20.** $2y^3$ *-54*   **23.** $xy - 10$ *-16*

18. $10 + y$ *7*   **21.** $-y^3$ *+27*   **24.** $10 - xy$ *16*

25. Divide:

a	b	c	d	e	f
$\dfrac{x^2}{x}$ *x*	$\dfrac{y^3}{y}$ *y²*	$\dfrac{4xy}{y}$ *4x*	$\dfrac{8c}{-4}$ *-2c*	$\dfrac{ab}{-a}$ *-b*	$\dfrac{-9k}{k}$ *-9*

26. Give an example of each of the following:

a. Monomial. *-3ab²*   **d.** Binomial with like terms. *3x - 7x*

b. Binomial. *3x²+7*   **e.** Binomial with unlike terms. *3y -7x*

c. Trinomial. *2x³+7x-1*   **f.** Monomial with exponent 4. *-3x⁴*

27. Find the area of a triangle whose base is 10.3 and whose altitude is 5.2. *26.78*

28. Find the radius of a circular 1-mile race track. (Use $\pi = 3.14$.) *840.76 ft.*

29. Find the missing values of x and y which satisfy the equation $3x - y = 6$.

x	*? 2*	*? 1⅔*	*? 3*	-3	-1	0	*? 1*	*? -2*
y	0	-1	3	*? -15*	*? -9*	*? -6*	-3	-12

30. The sum of two numbers is 119 and their difference is 9. Find the numbers. *55, 64*

152

13. An subtraction
14. Relationships are better understood when sketch is drawn.

31. A farmer divided his farm of 257 acres among his three sons so that the eldest received 13 more acres than the youngest, and the third son received 6 acres less than the eldest. How many acres did each son receive? *Youngest, 79A.; eldest, 92A.; third, 86A.*

32. If a sum of money is increased by $21, the result is the same as when 5 times the sum is subtracted from $177. What is the original sum of money? *$26*

33. What principal will produce $4320 interest in 3 years, at 6% per year? *$24,000*

[B]

34. Combine:

$$x^3 - 3\,x^2y - 2\,x^2y + 3\,xy^2 - 5\,y^3 - 4\,xy^2 + 5\,x^2y - 6\,y^3 - 7\,x^3.$$
$-6x^3 - xy^2 - 11y^3$

Find the numerical value of each expression when $a = \frac{3}{4}$, $b = \frac{1}{2}$, $c = \frac{2}{3}$, and $x = 3$.

35. $\dfrac{a - b}{a + b} + \dfrac{a + b}{a - b}$ *$5\frac{1}{5}$*

37. $\left(\dfrac{1}{b} - \dfrac{1}{a}\right)\left(\dfrac{1}{c} + \dfrac{1}{x}\right)$ *$\frac{11}{9}$*

36. $\dfrac{12\,a - 10\,b + 12\,c}{4\,a - 8\,b + 6\,c}$ *4*

38. $\dfrac{abc}{x} - c^3$ *$\frac{-23}{108}$*

39. $F = .004\,Av^2$ is a formula for finding the force of a wind that blows against any flat surface. F is the number of pounds in the force, A is the number of square feet in the surface, and v is the velocity of the wind in miles an hour.

If a wind blows at 40 miles an hour directly against a flat sail with an area of 120 square feet, what is the force of the wind against the sail? *768 lb.*

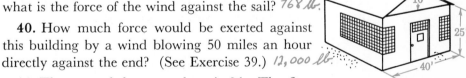

40. How much force would be exerted against this building by a wind blowing 50 miles an hour directly against the end? (See Exercise 39.) *12,000 lb.*

41. The sum of three numbers is 96. The first is $\frac{1}{5}$ of the second and $\frac{1}{2}$ of the third. What are the numbers? *12, 60, 24*

42. Distribute $174 among three people so that the first may receive 5 times as much as the second, and $42 more than the third. *1st, $98.18; 2d, $19.64; 3d, $56.18*

43. Divide 155 marbles among three boys so that one will receive 5 times as many as the second, and $\frac{1}{5}$ as many as the third. *1st, 25; 2d, 5; 3d, 125*

153

[Test A]

Part I. Equations and Inequalities (60%)

Solve:

1. $-7c > 21$ $c < -3$
2. $4y = 12$ 3
3. $0.5c = -15$ -30
4. $7y - 3 = -17$ -2
5. $6x + 5 = 23$ 3
6. $8y - 8 = 0$ 1
7. $4y < 2 + 2y$ $y < 1$
8. $9x + 28 = 7x + 16$ -6
9. $0.03h = 0.12$ 4
10. $3x + 4 < x - 10$ $x < -7$

11. Show that 3 is a root of $7x - 5 = x + 13$.

12. Graph $x > 8$ or $x = 8$. $x > 8$ or $x = 8$ 2

13. $A = lw$. Find l when $A = 144$ and $w = 9$. 16

14. $i = prt$. Find i if $p = \$600$, $r = 4\%$, and $t = 2\frac{1}{2}$ years. $\$60$

15. Copy and complete the following table for $x = 4y - 2$:

x	? -2	? 2	? 6	? 10	? -6	? -10
y	0	1	2	3	-1	-2

Part II. Problems (40%)

1. The sum of two numbers is 18 and one of them is x. What is the other one? $18 - x$

2. Find $x\%$ of $\$150$. $1.5x$ dollars

3. The difference between two numbers is 5. If x represents the smaller number, what will represent the larger? $5 + x$

4. A number increased by 32 equals 75. Find the number. 43

5. If 7 is subtracted from twice a certain number, the remainder is 23. Find the number. 15

6. Find 4% of $\$270$. $\$10.80$

7. The attendance on Friday at Ewing High School was 782. What was the per cent attendance that day if the enrollment was 850? 92%

8. June made 80% on a spelling test when she spelled 32 words correctly. How many words were there on the test? 40

Part I. Equations and Inequalities (60%)

Solve:

1. $7c + 7 > -35$ $c > -6$

2. $-8c = 32$ -4

3. $0.4x = -15$ -37.5

4. $-2x + 6 < 0$ $x > 3$

5. $7y - 9 = y + 7$ $2\frac{2}{3}$

6. $11x - 5 = x - 32$ -2.7

7. $0 = 8x + 40$ -5

8. $10 = 6x - 4 + 2x$ $1\frac{3}{4}$

9. $-7p = -2p - 20$ 4

10. $\dfrac{x}{5} + \dfrac{x}{3} > -64$ $x > -120$

11. $7c - 4d = 15$. Find d if $c = 3$. $1\frac{1}{2}$

12. $i = prt$. Find r if $p = \$350$, $i = \$31.50$, and $t = 2$ years. $4\frac{1}{2}\%$

13. $T = t + 273$. Find T when $t = -100$. 173

14. Show that -2 is not a root of the equation $4x + 5 = x + 1$.

15. Graph $x > -3$ and $x < 5$. -12

Part II. Problems (40%)

1. The sum of two numbers is 26 and one of them is n. What is the other? $26 - n$

2. The larger of two numbers is 13. Find the smaller if their difference is d. $13 - d$

3. There are 30 boys and girls in Miss Kendrick's algebra class and there are two-thirds as many boys as girls. How many girls are there in the class? 18

4. The sum of three consecutive integers is 135. Find them. $44, 45, 46$

5. A student spends $90 a month for rent, which is 12% of her monthly income. What is her income per month? $\$750$

6. Dale wishes to make a picture frame using 65 inches of picture moulding. In order that the frame may have the right shape, the width of the frame will be 0.62 of the length. How long shall each of the four sides of the frame be?   2 sides 20.1 in. each, 2 sides 12.4 in. each

.62 l

l

7. An article priced at $18 is sold at a discount of 20%. Find the selling price after the discount is allowed. $\$14.40$

Photos: *Better Living* (Du Pont)

It is common today for some young people to say "I am going to be an engineer" without really knowing the requirements of that profession. This article might make them think constructively about engineering as a career. Acquaint less able but ambitious students with the opportunities offered as *engineering aides*. Above all, let your girls know that there are possible positions for them also.

WHAT DOES IT MEAN TO BE AN ENGINEER?

There was a time when being an engineer meant designing, constructing, and using engines. Today, however, an engineer is one who makes practical applications of such sciences as physics, chemistry, and biology.

Electrical engineers. In electrical engineering there are engineers who plan plants for generating electricity, others who plan ways to transmit the electricity generated, and others who design instruments and appliances that use the electricity transmitted. Electronic engineers design radar, radio, and television systems, and the equipment used in the systems. Other electronic engineers develop high speed computors.

Chemical engineers. Chemical engineers develop new chemical products and new uses for those already developed. Some chemical engineers work at processing foods, some at producing new medicines, some at producing new detergents, some at developing new plastics, some at developing new paints, and so on, and on, and on. The list has no limits.

Mining and Metallurgical engineers. Mining and metallurgical engineers solve the problems of locating and extracting mineral deposits, of refining the ore extracted, and of manufacturing products that use the minerals.

Mechanical engineers. Mechanical engineers design and produce machinery, tools, refrigerators, heating systems, automobiles, trains, planes, and so on.

We do not have nearly enough engineers. Consequently, this field, with its many branches, offers great opportunities. Both men and women are urgently needed. If you enjoy studying books and magazines on scientific subjects, try to keep pace with the new developments in science, and are a leader in your science and mathematics courses, you should consider whether you would like to be an engineer. Meanwhile, take all the science and mathematics you can.

6

Operations with Polynomials

Suggested Time Schedule
Minimum   9 days
Maximum   10 days

*A chapter in which you learn
to manage expressions
having more than one term.*

In this chapter the four fundamental operations introduced in chapters 1 and 4 are applied to more complicated algebraic expressions. In order to continue with algebra, the student must be able to work such exercises correctly and quickly. Throughout the chapter, have your students get the correct answers the *first time*. Frown on the habit of doing the work on scrap paper and then copying it for the written assignment. Try some suitable motto such as "Goals: neatness, accuracy, speed." Find some way to hold students to high standards of competency. Give frequent short tests (unannounced) made up of miscellaneous exercises.

Adding Polynomials [A]

In this chapter you will learn how to add and subtract polynomials and how to multiply and divide them by monomials.

Polynomials may be added by writing them one after another and then combining like terms; but an easier method of adding is to write them so that like terms are in columns, and then add the columns. We shall use the latter method.

Example 1. Add $2a + 6b + 3$, $4a + b - 5$, and $a - 8b + 4$.

Solution.

$$
\begin{array}{r}
2a + 6b + 3 \\
4a + b - 5 \\
\underline{a - 8b + 4} \\
7a - b + 2
\end{array}
$$

Additions may be checked by adding the columns in the reverse order. For example, if the columns are first added from top to bottom, the solutions may be checked by adding the columns from bottom to top.

A more common method of checking additions is through substitution, as shown below. In this check a has been given the value 2 and b the value 3, though any numbers could have been used.

Solution   **Check**

$$
\begin{array}{l}
2a + 6b + 3 = 2 \cdot 2 + 6 \cdot 3 + 3 = 4 + 18 + 3 = 25 \\
4a + b - 5 = 4 \cdot 2 + 3 - 5 = 8 + 3 - 5 = 6 \\
\underline{a - 8b + 4 = 2 - 8 \cdot 3 + 4 = 2 - 24 + 4 = -18} \\
7a - b + 2 = 7 \cdot 2 - 3 + 2 = 14 - 3 + 2 = 13
\end{array}
$$

For $a = 2$ and $b = 3$, the values of the three polynomials of the example are 25, 6, and -18 respectively, and the value of their sum $(7a - b + 2)$ is 13. Since the sum of 25, 6, and -18 is 13, we know that the solution checks.

While any numbers could have represented a and b in the check, most mathematicians hesitate to use 0 or 1. A mistake could be overlooked when 0 is substituted, since 0 times any number is 0. When $a = 1$, an expression such as $3a$ has the same value as 3, and an expression such as a^2 has the same value as a^3 or a^4. It is easy, therefore, to overlook errors when 1 is substituted.

The fact that a solution checks is not a conclusive proof that the solution is correct, as you can see from the following incorrect addition

①While this method of checking is good to emphasize meanings, it would take too long to check all addition exercises in this fashion. Do not get behind in your schedule because of checking.

159

ALGEBRA, BOOK ONE

that checks for $x = 5$ and $y = 3$. The method does, however, provide some assurance that there are no errors.

Check

$$x + 3y = \ 5 + 9 = 14$$
$$2x - \ \ y = 10 - 3 = \ 7$$
$$6x - 3y = 30 - 9 = 21$$

21

Example 2. Find the sum of $3x^3 - 2y^3$, $x^2y + 2xy^2 + y^3$, and $-4x^3 - 7x^2y + 5xy^2 - 6y^3$. Check by letting $x = 2$ and $y = 3$.

①

Solution	Check

$$3x^3 + 0 \quad +0 \quad -2y^3 = \quad 24 + \ 0 + \quad 0 - \ 54 = -\ 30$$
$$x^2y + 2xy^2 + \ y^3 = \quad 0 + 12 + \ 36 + \ 27 = \quad 75$$
$$-4x^3 - 7x^2y + 5xy^2 - 6y^3 = -32 - 84 + \ 90 - 162 = -188$$
$$-\ x^3 - 6x^2y + 7xy^2 - 7y^3 = -\ 8 - 72 + 126 - 189 = -143$$

-143

You can save time and have a more orderly solution if you arrange the polynomials in descending (or ascending) powers of one of the letters. In the Solution of Example 2 the terms are arranged in descending powers of x. Notice that the first column contains the third power of x, the second column contains the second power of x, the third column contains the first power of x, and the fourth column contains no x factor. It so happens that the polynomials were arranged in ascending powers of y. Can you give a reason why the zeros were written in the first polynomial?

The solutions of these two examples illustrate the rule below.

> To add two or more polynomials,
> write them with like terms in the same column and add the columns.

EXERCISES

[A]

Add the following polynomials, checking as many solutions as your teacher indicates. *(ans. 1-3 at foot of page)*

1. 6 ft. + 7 in.
  3 ft. + 5 in.

2. 3 lb. + 7 oz.
  7 lb. − 4 oz.

3. $3x + 2y - z$
  $5x - 4y$

4. $-2a + 4b - 6c$
  $3a - 9b + 5c$
  $a - 5b - c$

5. $4c + 5b - \quad a$
  $-3c - 5b + 7a$
  $c \qquad + 6a$

6. $2m + \ 6$
  $-m + 10$
  $m + 16$

160 1. 10 ft.   2. 10 lb. + 3 oz.   3. 8x − 2y − z

7. $-2k^2 - 11k - 5$ 8. $-x^2 - x - 4$ 9. $-9a - 13b$

OPERATIONS WITH POLYNOMIALS

(7.) $-3k^2 + 4k - 9$ **(8.)** $x^2 - 4x + 3$ **(9.)** $2a - 3b + 7c$
$ 2k^2 - 5k + 3$ $ -3x^2 + 5x - 2$ $ -4a - 9b - 8c$
$ -k^2 - 10k + 1$ $ \underline{x^2 - 2x - 5}$ $ \underline{-7a - b + c}$

10. $-m - n + p$ **11.** $x^2 - xy + y^2$
$ m - n - p$ $ -3x^2 - 7xy - 4y^2$
$ \underline{m + 2n - p}$ *m − p* $ \underline{2x^2 - 3xy - 8y^2}$ *−11xy − 11y²*

12. $3m^2 - m - 6$ **13.** $4ax - 3ab - 6$
$ m^2 - 4$ $ -2ax - 5ab - 10$
$ \underline{4m - 1}$ *4m²+3m − 11* $ \underline{ax + 8ab - 1}$ *3ax −17*

14. $x^4 - ax^3$ **15.** $x^3 - 3x^2 - 2$
$ -2ax^3 - bx^2$ $ -4x^3 - x^2 + 1$
$ \underline{ax^3 + 4bx^2}$ $ \underline{x^3 - 10}$
$x^4 - 2ax^3 + 3bx^2$ $-2x^3 - 4x^2 - 11$

Add:

16. $2x + 4y - 12$, $8x - 5y - 2$, and $-9x - 8y - 1$ *x −9y −15*

17. $7a - 9b + c$, $-5a + c$, and $3a + 8b - 2c$ *5a −b*

18. $-5x^2 - 3x + 2$, $-3x^2 + 6$, and $-4x^2 - 7x$ *−12x² −10x + 8*

19. $x - y - z$, $2x - 3y - 7z$, and $2z - 5x + y$ *−2x −3y −6z*

20. $x^2 - 6 + 7x$, $7x - 4 + x^2$, and $2x^2 - x - 1$ *4x²+13x −11*

21. $a^2 - b^2 + ab$, $b^2 - a^2 - ab$, and $4ab + b^2$ *4ab +b²*

22. $3xy - 7z$, $5xy - 4z$, $-7xy + z$; and $-xy - 10z$ *−20z*

23. $5a + b + 4c$, $-3a - 6b$, and $4b - 6c + 5a$ *7a −b −2c*

24. $2x^2 - 3xy + y^2$, $-8xy - 9y^2 - x^2$, and $-3x^2$ *−2x²−11xy−12y²*

25. The length of a rectangle is $3a + 1$ and the width is $a - 6$. Find its perimeter.   *8a − 10*

26. The width of a rectangle is $x - 4$ and its length is $x^2 - x$. Find its perimeter.   *2x² −8*

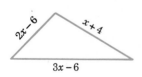
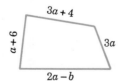
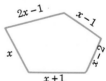

27. Find the perimeter of the triangle above.   *6x −8*

28. Find the perimeter of the quadrilateral (4 sides).   *9a +10 −b*

29. Find the perimeter of the pentagon (5 sides).   *6x −3*

33. $-15x^3 + 2x^2 - 3x$
34. $x^4 + x^2y^2 + y^4$
35. $\frac{5}{6}x - \frac{1}{2}y + \frac{3}{5}z$
36. $\frac{5}{6}a - \frac{1}{8}b - c$

[B]

Add:

30. $13x + 4y - 12$, $18x - 5y - 2$, and $-9x - 8y - 4$

31. $4x^4 - 7x^3 + 6x^2 - x + 1$ and $-x^4 + x^3 - 5x^2 + 6x - 9$

32. $2a + 3b - 4c + 8d - 1$ and $-6a - 5b - 9d + 5$

33. $-8x^3 + 5x^2 - 9x - 15$ and $-7x^3 + 5 + 6x - 3x^2 + 10$

34. $x^4 - x^3y + x^2y^2$, $x^3y - x^2y^2 + xy^3$, and $x^2y^2 - xy^3 + y^4$

35. $\frac{1}{3}x + \frac{1}{4}y - \frac{1}{5}z$ and $\frac{1}{2}x - \frac{3}{4}y + \frac{4}{5}z$

36. $\frac{1}{2}a + \frac{1}{3}b - \frac{1}{4}c$ and $\frac{1}{3}a - \frac{1}{2}b - \frac{3}{4}c$

37. $\frac{2}{3}a^2 - \frac{1}{4}a - 3$, $\frac{1}{2}a^2 - a + \frac{2}{3}$, and $\frac{3}{4}a - \frac{1}{6}a^2$

see foot of page

38. $2.3x^2 - 3.2x - 4$, $x^2 + .7$, and $4.1x - 5.6 - 4.7x^2$

39. $.3x + .2y - .6z$ and $.3x - 1.4y + 15.6z$

40. $3.15x - 1.60y + .70z$ and $1.25x - 3.40y - 1.00z$

41. $(x^2 - 2xy + y^2) + (3x^2 - 8xy - y^2)$ $4x^2 - 10xy$

42. $(a - b + c) + (2a + b - 3c) + (a + b - c)$ $4a + b - 3c$

43. Find the sum of the lengths of the 12 edges of this rectangular solid. $8a + 8b - 4c$

44. Find the sum of the lengths of the 12 edges of this rectangular solid when $a = 3$, $b = 2$, and $c = 1$.

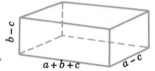

36

45. Find the volume of this solid when $a = 3$, $b = 2$, and $c = 1$. *12*

REVIEW EXERCISES

[A]

Simplify:

1. $9x - 3x + 5x$ *11x*

2. $7m - 9m - m$ *-3m*

3. $-4 - 6 + 1$ *-9*

4. $4xy - 8xy + 6xy$ *2xy*

5. $3m - 4m - m$ *-2m*

6. $2a^2 + 3a^2 - 5a^2$ *0*

7. $\frac{1}{2}x - \frac{1}{3}x + \frac{1}{4}x$ *$\frac{5}{12}x$*

8. $-4.3y - 2.7y$ *-7.0y*

9. $\frac{1}{3}c - \frac{1}{6}c - \frac{5}{6}c$ *$-\frac{2}{3}c$*

10. $h - \frac{1}{2}h - \frac{1}{3}h$ *$\frac{1}{6}h$*

11. $x^2 - 4xy + y^2 - 2x^2 - y^2 - 10xy$ *$-x^2 - 14xy$*

12. $abc - c^2 - 6abc - 10c^2$ *$-5abc - 11c^2$*

162

37. $a^2 - \frac{1}{2}a - \frac{7}{3}$
38. $-1.4x + 0.9x - 8.9$

39. $0.6x - 1.2y + 15z$
40. $4.40x - 5.00y - 0.30z$

OPERATIONS WITH POLYNOMIALS

Subtract: (*Ans. 13, 14 above*)

	a	b	c	d	e	f	g
13.	-8	10	-6	-1	14	15	$+10$
	$+3$	-2	-5	-7	10	20	-10

	a	b	c	d	e	f	g
14.	$7h$	$10c$	$-4x$	$3b$	0	c	$-9m$
	$-h$	$3c$	$5x$	$-5b$	$7x$	$-5c$	m

	a	b	c	d	e	f	g
15.	x	$3y$	$.1x$	$.55p$	$-4.1y$	$2.3h$	$-c$
	$\frac{1}{2}x$	$.5y$	$.4x$	$-.15p$	$1.1y$	$2.1h$	$.01c$
	$\frac{1}{2}x$	$2.5y$	$-.3x$	$.70p$	$-5.2y$	$0.2h$	$-1.01c$

Multiply:

	a	b	c	d	e	f	g
16.	4	-9	-20	25	-14	-3	0
	2	2	-4	-1	2	9	7

	a	b	c	d	e	f	g
17.	x^2	x	x^3	x^4	a^2	y^6	m^4
	x^2	x	x	x	a^7	y	m^3

	a	b	c	d	e	f	g
18.	$2x$	$3a$	$5c$	$10h$	a^2b	$3ac^2$	$-4b$
	5	-4	c	$2h$	a	$4c$	$3c$
	$10x$	$-12a$	$5c^2$	$20h^2$	a^3b	$12ac^3$	$-12bc$

Divide:

	a	b	c	d	e	f
19.	$-2)\overline{10}$ -5	$-4)\overline{-20}$ 5	$6)\overline{-18}$ -3	$7)\overline{-14}$ -2	$-3)\overline{-30}$ 10	$-7)\overline{42}$ -6

20.	$\dfrac{x^5}{x}$ x^4	$\dfrac{x^7}{x^2}$ x^5	$\dfrac{-6a}{2}$ $-3a$	$\dfrac{-20c}{c}$ -20	$\dfrac{12y}{-3y}$ -4	$\dfrac{8m^5}{2m}$ $4m^4$

Subtracting Polynomials [A]

The method of subtracting one polynomial from another will be illustrated by the solution of two examples. At this time review the rule for subtracting one number from another on page 112.

Example 1. Subtract $x^2 - 4x + 3$ from $4x^2 + 2x + 1$, and check by letting $x = 2$.

Solution	Check

$$4x^2 + 2x + 1 = 16 + 4 + 1 = 21$$
$$\underline{x^2 - 4x + 3 = 4 - 8 + 3 = -1} \Big]= 22$$
$$3x^2 + 6x - 2 = 12 + 12 - 2 = 22$$

163

1. $2x + 7$
2. $2b$

3. $2x + 4y + 4z$
4. $a - 2b - 2c$

5. $-3z - 5z + 2t$
6. $-2xy + 6y^2$

7. $a - 8b + 6$
8. $90 + 2x$
9. $-3x^2 - 2x - 3$

ALGEBRA, BOOK ONE

Example 2. From $x^3 + 4x$ take $5x^3 + x^2 - 5x + 7$, and check by letting $x = 2$.

Solution	Check

$$\begin{array}{ll} x^3 + 0 + 4x + 0 = & 8 + 0 + 8 + 0 = \quad 16 \\ 5x^3 + x^2 - 5x + 7 = & 40 + 4 - 10 + 7 = \quad 41 \\ \hline -4x^3 - x^2 + 9x - 7 = -32 - 4 + 18 - 7 = -25 \end{array} \Big] = -25$$

The solution of a subtraction problem may also be checked by adding the difference to the subtrahend. This sum should equal the minuend.

①

[A]

EXERCISES

Subtract and check: (ans. 1-9 at top of page)

1. $3x + 6$
  $\underline{x - 1}$

2. $a + b + c$
  $\underline{a - b + c}$

3. $4x - 3y + \quad z$
  $\underline{2x - 7y - 3z}$

4. $2a - 3b + 4c$
  $\underline{a - \quad b + 6c}$

5. $2r - 4s + t$
  $\underline{5r + \quad s - t}$

6. $x^2 - xy + 2y^2$
  $\underline{x^2 + xy - 4y^2}$

7. $2a - \quad b$
  $\underline{a + 7b - 6}$

8. $100 - 4x$
  $\underline{10 - 6x}$

9. $\quad x^2 - 3x$
  $\underline{4x^2 - \quad x + 3}$

10. Take $x - 1$ from 20. $-x + 21$

11. Subtract $2k + 3m - 6n$ from $4k + 6$.
  $2k - 3m + 6n + 6$

12. Subtract $-4a + 5b - 6$ from 0.
  $4a - 5b + 6$

13. From $a - b + c$ take $2a - 5b - 3c$.
  $-a + 4b + 4c$

14. The minuend is $2a + 5b + 4c$ and the subtrahend is $7a - b + 6c$. Find the difference. $-5a + 6b - 2c$

15. $a + 2b - 3c$ is how much greater than $-a - b - 5c$?
  $2a + 3b + 2c$

16. Take $2x^3 - 4x^2 + 6x - 7$ from $x^3 - 3x^2 + 4x - 5$.
  $-x^3 + x^2 - 2x + 2$

17. From 0 subtract $y - x$. $-y + x$

18. $x^2 - 6x + 7$ is how much larger than $x^2 + 6x - 7$?
  $-12x + 14$

19. How much greater than $2a - b$ is $a + 3b + 2$?
  $-a + 4b + 2$

20. How much less than $x - 4y + 3z$ is $3x - 6y - z$?
  $-2x + 2y + 4z$

21. The perimeter of a triangle is $7x - 10$. One of the sides is $x - 6$ and another is $2x + 1$. Find the third side. $4x - 5$

22. From the sum of $a + 2b - 1$ and $3a - b + 6$ subtract $7a - 2b - 10$. $-3a + 3b + 15$

① The method of checking by addition of subtrahend to remainder is rapid and emphasizes that subtraction and addition are inverse processes. Use it for most exercises.

② In Exs. 10–32, the subtraction has been indicated in many ways. Students often have trouble deciding which shall be the subtrahend. It helps them to make up similar arithmetic problems. For example, illustrate Ex. 15 by saying, "12 is how much greater than 7?" After the answer 5 is given, say, "Would you represent this as $12 - 7 = 5$ or as $7 - 12 = 5$?"

23. Subtract $\frac{3}{4} a - \frac{1}{4} b + \frac{1}{5} c$ from $\frac{1}{2} a - \frac{1}{3} b + \frac{2}{5} c$. $-\frac{1}{4}a - \frac{1}{12}b + \frac{1}{5}c$

24. The perimeter of a rectangle is $10 x - 80$. If one side is $2 x - 7$, find the sum of the remaining sides. $8x - 73$

[B]

25. Subtract $5 a^2 - 3 a + 6$ from $7 a^2$. $2a^2 + 3a - 6$

26. Take $2 x^3 - 3 x^2y + 7 xy^2$ from $x^3 - 2 x^2y - y^3$. $-x^3 + x^2y - 7xy^2 - y^3$

27. By how much does $2 a - b$ exceed $4 a + b - c$? $-2a - 2b + c$

28. Take $x^2 - 3 xy + 21$ from the sum of $x^3 - 21$ and $2 x^2 - 4 xy$. $x^3 + x^2 - xy - 42$

29. From $\frac{1}{10} a - \frac{1}{5} b - \frac{1}{2} c$ take $\frac{2}{5} a + \frac{1}{4} b - \frac{1}{3} c$. $-\frac{3}{10}a - \frac{9}{20}b - \frac{1}{6}c$

30. Take $.2 m + .35 n + p$ from $.3 m - .45 n - p$. $0.1m - 0.80n - 2p$

31. From $16 a^3 - 7$ take $3 a^3 + 2 a^2 - 5 a + 4$. $13a^3 - 2a^2 + 5a - 11$

32. From $\frac{1}{5} a - \frac{1}{3} b + \frac{1}{6} c$ take $\frac{2}{15} a - \frac{1}{5} b - \frac{1}{8} c$. $\frac{1}{15}a - \frac{2}{15}b + \frac{7}{24}c$

33. The length of a rectangle is $x^2 - 4 x + 9$ and the length exceeds the width by $7 x - 2$. Write a formula for the perimeter of the rectangle. $P = 4x^2 - 30x + 40$

34. The side of a square is $2 x$. The width of a rectangle is $3 x - 1$ and its length is $x^2 + 2 x + 1$. How much larger than the perimeter of the square is the perimeter of the rectangle? $2x^2 + 2x$

Multiplying Monomials [A]

As a preparation for the problems which you will soon be asked to solve, you need to be able to multiply one monomial by another with speed and accuracy: It is for this reason that the following review is given.

[A]

Multiply:

1. $3 x$ by 6 $18x$

2. $10 x^2$ by 4 $40x^2$

3. $8 m$ by $- 1$ $-8m$

4. $- 12 y^2$ by 6 $-72y^2$

5. $- 8 m$ by $- 1$ $8m$

6. $4 r$ by r $4r^2$

7. x by x x^2

8. abc by d $abcd$

9. xy by $- 4$ $-4xy$

10. $- a$ by a $-a^2$

11. πr by r πr^2

12. $2 xy$ by $- 2$ $-4xy$

13. $- 4 x^3$ by 9 $-36x^3$

14. x^2y by y^3 x^2y^4

15. 2π by r $2\pi r$

16. $4 x$ by $3 x$ $12x^2$

17. $- 4 a$ by $5 a$ $-20a^2$

18. $- 7 h$ by $- 4 h$ $28h^2$

19. h by $- h$ $-h^2$

20. $- x^2$ by x^2 $-x^4$

21. $4 x$ by $\frac{1}{2} x$ $2x^2$

ORAL REVIEW EXERCISES

① As you do these exercises in class, review the basic commutative and associative principles. Try for speed. You might say, "Write the answers to the first five exercises." Say "stop" before all have finished. Then do the next five, etc.

22. 0.06 mw
23. 4x²y²
24. -12a²bc
25. 8p²
26. -0.01n²
27. 1/10 y³
28. 2w²
29. -18a³y³

22. .2 m by .3   **25.** $(\frac{4}{7}p)(14\,p)$ **28.** $(-.4\,w)(-5\,w)$

23. $(4\,xy)(xy)$ **26.** $(.1\,r)(-.1\,r)$ **29.** $(6\,a^2y)(-3\,ay^2)$

24. $(-3\,ab)(4\,ac)$ **27.** $(\frac{1}{2}y)(\frac{1}{5}y^2)$ **30.** $(ch)(c^2h)$ *c³h²*

31. $(4\,ab)(2\,ac)(-3\,bc)(-2)$ *48a²b²c²*

32. $(-2\,a^2y)(-2\,ay^2)(-3\,b^2z)(-3\,bz^2)$ *36a³b³y³z³*

Powers of Monomials [A]

You are again reminded that when you are working with exponents you should always keep in mind what the exponents mean. For example, x^2 means $(x)(x)$; m^4 means $(m)(m)(m)(m)$; and $(2\,ab^2)^3$ means $(2\,ab^2)(2\,ab^2)(2\,ab^2)$.

Study the following solutions:

Example 1. Find the square of x^3.

Solution. $(x^3)^2 = (x^3)(x^3) = x^6$

Example 2. Simplify $(x^7)^2$.

Solution. $(x^7)^2 = (x^7)(x^7) = x^{14}$

Example 3. Find the indicated power in $(-5\,x^4)^3$.

Solution. $(-5\,x^4)^3 = (-5\,x^4)(-5\,x^4)(-5\,x^4) = -125\,x^{12}$

After you have had sufficient practice, you will be able to omit the parts of the solutions printed in color.

[A]

EXERCISES

Find the indicated powers:

1. $(x^2)^2$ *x⁴*   **6.** $(x^2)^3$ *x⁶*   **11.** $(-3\,a)^2$ *9a²*

2. $(x^3)^2$ *x⁶*   **7.** $(x^3)^3$ *x⁹*   **12.** $(4\,x^3)^2$ *16x⁶*→

3. $(a^4)^2$ *a⁸*   **8.** $(a^4)^3$ *a¹²*   **13.** $(-5\,a^3)^2$ *25a⁶* ① below

4. $(b^5)^2$ *b¹⁰*   **9.** $(x^5)^3$ *x¹⁵*   **14.** $(-6\,x)^3$ *-216x³*

5. $(c^6)^2$ *c¹²*   **10.** $(m^6)^3$ *m¹⁸*   **15.** $(xy)^2$ *x²y²*

16. Choose some small negative number. Find the 1st, 2d, 3d, 4th, 5th, 6th, 7th, and 8th powers of it. What is the sign of each odd power? What is the sign of each even power? What sign has any power of a positive number? *neg.; pos.; pos.*
Take advantage of this chance to let students discover a procedure inductively.

166 ① Students often confuse such exercises as $(x^2)^3$ and $x^2 \cdot x^3$ in spite of careful explanation as above. When errors are made, ask students to restudy the *Examples.* (Such confusion may crop up many weeks from now. Any process in algebra needs constant practice.) Do not let them use the short cut of multiplying the exponents until you are sure they are ready for it. Try to get them to form inductively the principle $(x^m)^n = x^{mn}$.

Simplify:

17. x^2x^3 x^5 **20.** $(a^4)^3$ a^{12} **23.** $(\frac{1}{2}x)^2$ $\frac{1}{4}x^2$ **26.** $(2x)^3$ $8x^3$

18. $(x^2)^3$ x^6 **21.** a^2a^5 a^7 **24.** $(.5c)^2$ $0.25c^2$ **27.** $(-m^2n)^3$ $-m^6n^3$

19. a^4a^3 a^7 **22.** $(a^5)^2$ a^{10} **25.** $(a^2b^3)^2$ a^4b^6 **28.** $(-4c^2)^3$ $-64c^6$

29. $(2a)(3a)(4)$ $24a^2$

30. $(-3)(4x)(-a)$ $12ax$

31. $(5c)(-c)(b)$ $-5bc^2$

32. $-8(ax)(x)$ $-8ax^2$

33. $(-4)(-3)(cd)$ $12cd$

34. $+a+a+a+a$ $4a$

35. $a\cdot a\cdot a\cdot a$ a^4

36. $aaa+aaa$ $2a^3$

Multiplying a Polynomial by a Monomial [A]

In the following illustration, 8 has been multiplied by 3 in two ways. On the left, 8 has been written as $6 + 2$, and both terms of the binomial have been multiplied by 3. On the right, the single number 8 has been multiplied by 3. Notice that the products are the same.

$$\begin{array}{cc} 6+2 & 8 \\ \underline{3} & \underline{3} \\ 18+6 = 24 & 24 \end{array}$$

In the next illustration, 234 has been represented as $2h + 3t + 4u$ where $h = 100$, $t = 10$, and $u = 1$.

$$\begin{array}{cc} 2h+3t+4u & 234 \\ \underline{2} & \underline{2} \\ 4h+6t+8u & 468 \end{array}$$

When $h = 100$, $t = 10$, and $u = 1$, $4h + 6t + 8u = 468$.

These multiplications demonstrate the important rule shown below, which follows from the distributive property.

> To multiply a polynomial by a monomial,
> multiply each term of the polynomial by the monomial.

The same rule can be demonstrated by areas, as shown below.

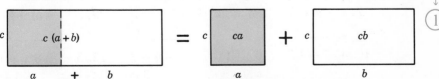

① Emphasize the word each. Review the distributive principle of multiplication over addition. Try to forestall the common error of expanding an expression such as $3(2 + 5a)$ to $6 + 5a$. This error often occurs when students are simplifying equations or fractions.

167

Example 1. Multiply $a - b + 6$ by 4.

Solution 1	Solution 2
$$\begin{array}{r} a - b + 6 \\ 4 \\ \hline 4\,a - 4\,b + 24 \end{array}$$	$4(a - b + 6) = 4\,a - 4\,b + 24$

You should acquire the habit of working from the *left to the right*. Do you know why?

Example 2. $- 2\,x(3\,x^2 - 4\,x + 1) = ?$

Solution 1	Solution 2
$$\begin{array}{r} 3\,x^2 - 4\,x + 1 \\ - 2\,x \\ \hline - 6\,x^3 + 8\,x^2 - 2\,x \end{array}$$	$$\begin{aligned} &- 2\,x(3\,x^2 - 4\,x + 1) \\ &= - 6\,x^3 + 8\,x^2 - 2\,x \end{aligned}$$

We can check multiplications by substitution in the same way that we check additions and subtractions. To check the product obtained for Example 2, we could substitute 2 for x, and write

$$\begin{array}{rl} 3\,x^2 - 4\,x + 1 = & 12 - 8 + 1 = 5 \\ - 2\,x = & -4 = -4 \end{array} \bigg\} - 20$$
$$- 6\,x^3 + 8\,x^2 - 2\,x = -48 + 32 - 4 = -20$$

After you have learned to divide a polynomial by a monomial, you can easily check multiplications like those just described by dividing the product by the multiplier to see if it produces the multiplicand.

EXERCISES

Multiply: *(ans. 1–9 at foot of page)* [A]

1. $a + 5$
   $\underline{4}$

2. $a^2 - 6$
   $\underline{4}$

3. $- 3\,b + c$
   $\underline{- 6}$

4. $- 3\,x + 4\,y$
   $\underline{- 10}$

5. $4\,x^2 - 5\,y$
   $\underline{+ a}$

6. $m + n - p$
   $\underline{- c}$

7. $a - b + 5\,c$
   $\underline{- 3}$

8. $x^2 - 4\,x + 3$
   $\underline{+ x}$

9. $c^2 - 4\,cd + 3$
   $\underline{- 4}$

10. $4\,a^2 + 7\,a - 10$
    $\underline{2\,a}$
    $8a^3 + 14a^2 - 20a$

11. $7\,m^2 - m + 3$
    $\underline{3\,m}$
    $21m^3 - 3m^2 + 9m$

12. $3\,x^2 - 8\,x + 1$
    $\underline{4\,x^2}$
    $12x^4 - 32x^3 + 4x^2$

168

1. $4a + 20$
2. $4a^2 - 24$
3. $18b - 6c$
4. $30x - 40y$
5. $4ax^2 - 5ay$
6. $-mc - nc + pc$
7. $-3a + 3b - 15c$
8. $x^3 - 4x^2 + 3x$
9. $-4c^2 + 16cd - 12$

Have you tried the lock-step type of assignment, suggested earlier? That is, when possible, save exercises from long sets so that you can advance and review at the same time. This avoids boring, routine work. It also unifies the procedures and makes the subject unfold logically and continuously.

OPERATIONS WITH POLYNOMIALS

13. $3 x(2 x^2 - 3 x - 1)$ $6x^3 - 9x^2 - 3x$

14. $a(a^2 - a + 3)$ $a^3 - a^2 + 3a$

15. $- 5(6 a + b - 7)$ $-30a - 5b + 35$

16. $\pi r(r + l)$ $\pi r^2 + \pi r l$

17. $- 7(- c^2 + 2 c + 3)$ $7c^2 - 14c - 21$

18. $x(x^2 - 4 x + 5)$ $x^3 - 4x^2 + 5x$

19. $2 x(x^2 + x + 1)$ $2x^3 + 2x^2 + 2x$

20. $x(x^2 - xy + y^2)$ $x^3 - x^2 y + xy^2$

21. $- 1(x^2 + 3 x + 6)$ $-x^2 - 3x - 6$

22. $- 1(a + b - c)$ $-a - b + c$

23. Find the area of a rectangle if its base is $4 a - 6$ and its altitude is $2 a$. $8a^2 - 12a$

24. Copy and complete this table of areas of rectangles:

Base	$x + 6$	$m - 6$	$8 x - 3 y$	$a^2 - 3 a + 4$
Altitude	x	$2 m$	$4 xy$	$+ 5 a$
Area	? $x^2 + 6x$	? $2m^2 - 12m$	? $32xy - 12y^2$	? $5a^3 - 15a^2 + 20a$

25. Find the cost of $7 c - d$ articles at $+ 2 c$ cents each. $(14c^2 - 2cd)$¢

26. Find the interest on x dollars, for y years, at p per cent.
$\left(p \text{ per cent means } \dfrac{p}{100}.\right)$ $\dfrac{pxy}{100}$ dollars

27. Find the area of a triangle whose base is $x + 8$ and altitude $2 x$. $x^2 + 8x$

[B]

Multiply:

28. $- 2 ab^2(2 a^2 - 7 ab - ab^2)$ $-4a^3 b^2 + 14a^2 b^3 + 2a^2 b^4$

29. $5 cd(c^2d - cd^2 + 3 cd)$ $5c^3 d^2 - 5c^2 d^3 + 15c^2 d^2$

30. $\frac{3}{4}(12 a^2 - 16 a + 8)$ $9a^2 - 12a + 6$

31. $(7 x^2 - 4 xy + 16 y^2)4 y$ $28x^2 y - 16xy^2 + 64y^3$

32. $(- 2 x^2 - x + 3)(- 1)$ $2x^2 + x - 3$

33. $- 5 w(- 1 + w + 3 w^2)$ $5w - 5w^2 - 15w^3$

34. $12(\frac{2}{3} a - \frac{1}{6} b - \frac{1}{12} c)$ $8a - 2b - c$

35. Show that $A = p(1 + rt)$ is the same as $A = p + prt$.

36. Change the formula $T = 2 \pi r(r + l)$ so that it has no parentheses. $T = 2\pi r^2 + 2\pi r l$

37. Remove the parentheses in the formula $A = \pi(R^2 - r^2)$. What does each term in the new formula represent? $A = \pi R^2 - \pi r^2$. Each term in right member represents the area of a circle, and A represents the difference between the areas of the two circles.

169

ALGEBRA, BOOK ONE

Equations Containing Fractions [A]

When an equation contains either common or decimal fractions, the solution can often be simplified by first multiplying both members of the equation by the lowest common denominator.

Example. Solve $\frac{2}{3}x - 5 = \frac{3}{4}x - \frac{9}{2}$.

Solution.	$\frac{2}{3}x - 5 = \frac{3}{4}x - \frac{9}{2}$
M_{12}	$8x - 60 = 9x - 54$
$S_{9x};\ A_{60}$	$8x - 9x = 60 - 54$
Simplifying	$-x = 6$
D_{-1}	$x = -6$

PROOF. Does $\frac{2}{3}(-6) - 5 = \frac{3}{4}(-6) - \frac{9}{2}$?

Does $-4 - 5 = -\frac{9}{2} - \frac{9}{2}$? Yes.

[A]

EXERCISES

1. $\frac{2}{3}x - 2 = 10$ /8
2. $\frac{3}{5}y - 1 = \frac{3}{4}$ $2\frac{11}{12}$
3. $\frac{4x}{3} - 1 = \frac{1}{6}$ $\frac{7}{8}$
4. $\frac{7a}{8} + 1 = \frac{1}{2}$ $-\frac{4}{7}$
5. $.4x + 5 = 9$ /0
6. $p + .05p = 31.5$ 30
7. $8.2r + 6 = 3.4r + 3.6$ $-.5$
8. $.09c + 11 = 10.8$ $-2\frac{2}{9}$

9. $\frac{3}{5}x + 3 = \frac{2}{5}x + 5$ /0
10. $9 + \frac{1}{10}x = \frac{1}{5}x - 6$ /50
11. $\frac{y}{3} + \frac{y}{2} = 10$ /2
12. $\frac{m}{5} + \frac{m}{3} = 24$ 45
13. $.4x + .5x - 3.2 = 0$ $3\frac{5}{9}$
14. $.03x - 2.8 + .04x = 0$ 40
15. $1.8y = 7.5 - 2.17y$ /.89
16. $4.3m - .68 - .9m = 0$ 0.2

Dividing a Polynomial by a Monomial [A]

When a polynomial is multiplied by a monomial, each of its terms is multiplied by the monomial. Since division is the inverse of multiplication, in dividing a polynomial by a monomial, *each term* of the dividend must be divided by the monomial.

Compare the multiplication and division below.

2 hr. + 3 min. + 5 sec.	2 hr. + 3 min. + 5 sec.
4	4)8 hr. + 12 min. + 20 sec.
8 hr. + 12 min. + 20 sec.	

What is the multiplicand? the multiplier? the product? the dividend? the quotient?

Remember that the quotient has the same number of terms as the dividend.

170

Notice how the rule below is applied in the three examples which follow. This rule follows from the distributive property.

> **To divide a polynomial by a monomial, divide each term of the polynomial by the monomial.**

Example 1. $\dfrac{60 + 42 - 30}{2} = 30 + 21 - 15$

Example 2. $\dfrac{15\,x^3 - 40\,x^2 - 15}{-5} = -3\,x^3 + 8\,x^2 + 3$

Example 3. $(12\,x^3 - 8\,x^2 + 4\,x) \div (4\,x) = 3\,x^2 - 2\,x + 1$

CHECK. $4\,x(3\,x^2 - 2\,x + 1) = 12\,x^3 - 8\,x^2 + 4\,x$

Do not make the error of omitting the $+1$ in the quotient. Omitting the $+1$ in the quotient changes the value of the answer.

[A]

EXERCISES ①

1. Explain why the quotient of $\dfrac{8\,x^2 y}{2\,xy}$ is written $4\,x$ and not $4\,x\,1$. *When 1 is a factor, its omission does not change the value of the answer.*

2. Explain why the quotient of $\dfrac{8\,x^2 + 4\,x}{4\,x}$ is written $2\,x + 1$ and not $2\,x$. *$4x \div 4x = 1$. Here 1 is a term, and its omission would change the value of the answer.*

Find the quotients:

3. $(4\,x - 8) \div 2$ *$2x - 4$*

4. $(10\,x^2 - 15) \div 5$ *$2x^2 - 3$*

5. $(18\,r + 6\,s) \div 6$ *$3r + s$*

6. $(x^2 + x) \div x$ *$x + 1$*

7. $(20\,m^2 - 12) \div (-4)$ *$-5m^2 + 3$*

8. $(x^3 - x^2) \div x^2$ *$x - 1$*

9. $(ab - ac) \div a$ *$b - c$*

10. $(\pi R - \pi r) \div \pi$ *$R - r$*

11. $(an - am) \div a$ *$n - m$*

12. $(x^4 - x^3) \div x^2$ *$x^2 - x$*

13. $(24\,a^3 + 6\,a^2) \div 3$ *$8a^3 + 2a^2$*

14. $(14\,m^2 - 21\,m) \div (-7)$ *$-2m^2 + 3m$*

15. $\dfrac{7\,c^3 - 14\,c^2 - c}{-c}$ *$-7c^2 + 14c + 1$*

16. $\dfrac{-4\,a^3 + 16\,a^2 - 10\,a}{-2}$ *$2a^3 - 8a^2 + 5a$*

17. $\dfrac{24\,m^3 - 16\,m^2 - 8\,m}{8}$ *$3m^3 - 2m^2 - m$*

18. $\dfrac{8\,x^5 - 10\,x^4 + x^3}{x^3}$ *$8x^2 - 10x + 1$*

19. $\dfrac{a^{10} - a^9 + a^7}{a^3}$ *$a^7 - a^6 + a^4$*

20. $\dfrac{8\,a^3 - 4\,a^2 + 4\,a}{-4\,a}$ *$-2a^2 + a - 1$*

21. $(ax^2 - ax) \div (ax)$ *$x - 1$*

① The check should be done mentally, but make sure that the students do not neglect this checking procedure. Besides, checking will help them avoid the common error of omitting the ''1'' in the quotient of exercises such as 6 and 8. You might bring out in a discussion that the divisor and the quotient are factors of the dividend.

22. $(14\,a - 7\,a^2) \div (7\,a)$ _2-a_   **27.** $(\pi r_1{}^2 - \pi r_2{}^2) \div \pi$ _$r_1^2-r_2^2$_

23. $(18\,x^2 - 6\,x) \div (-6\,x)$ _-3x+1_   **28.** $(r^6 - r) \div r$ _r^5-1_

24. $(b^3 - 8\,b^2) \div b^2$ _b-8_   **29.** $(vt - \frac{1}{2}\,gt^2) \div t$ _$v-\frac{1}{2}gt$_

25. $(-3\,x^2 - 6\,x) \div (2\,x)$ _$-\frac{3}{2}x-3$_ **30.** $(180\,n - 360) \div 180$ _n-2_

26. $(\pi r^2 - \pi rh) \div (\pi r)$ _r-h_

31. How many feet are there in $(24\,x - 36\,y)$ inches? _2x-3y_

32. At $2\,y$ cents each how many pencils can be bought for $(8\,y^2 + 6\,y)$ cents? _4y+3_

33. How long will it take to travel am^2 miles if you travel at the rate of m miles a day? _am days_

34. If you save c cents a day, how many days are needed to save $(bc + c)$ cents? _b+1_

Divide:

35. $(16\,x^4 - 20\,x^3 + 8\,x^2 + 4\,x) \div (4\,x)$ _$4x^3-5x^2+2x+1$_

36. $(27\,a^3 - 24\,a^2 - 15\,a + 9) \div (-9)$ _$-3a^3+\frac{8}{3}a^2+\frac{5}{3}a-1$_

37. $(x - x^2 + 2\,x^3 - 3\,x^4 + x^5) \div (-1)$ _$-x+x^2-2x^3+3x^4-x^5$_

38. $(x^3 - 6\,x^2 - 7\,x + 6) \div (-1)$ _$-x^3+6x^2+7x-6$_

39. $(4\,x^5 - 32\,x^4 + 8\,x^3 - 4\,x^2) \div (-4\,x^2)$ _$-x^3+8x^2-2x+1$_

40. $(8\,x^2y^3 + 4\,x^3y^4 - 2\,xy^3) \div (2\,xy^3)$ _$4x+2x^2y-1$_

41. $(4.2\,ab^2 - .49\,a^2b) \div (.07\,ab)$ _60b-7a_

42. $(\frac{3}{4}\,m^2n^2 + \frac{5}{16}\,mn^3) \div (\frac{1}{4}\,mn)$ _$3mn+\frac{5}{4}n^2$_

Simplifying Expressions Containing Parentheses [A]

You have learned that parentheses are used to show that all terms or factors within them are to be treated as a whole. For example, $4(2\,a - b)$ means that $2\,a - b$ is to be multiplied by 4, and $-x(x + 2)$ means that $x + 2$ is to be multiplied by $-x$.

Example 1. Remove parentheses in the expression

$$4\,x^2(x^2 - 3\,x + 2).$$

Solution. $4\,x^2(x^2 - 3\,x + 2) = 4\,x^4 - 12\,x^3 + 8\,x^2$

① This is merely another illustration of the distributive law, but you may need to point this out to the students. Again, point out that $4x^2$ and $x^2 - 3x + 2$ are factors of the product, and that this multiplication is the inverse process of division, which was the topic in the preceding lesson.

172

OPERATIONS WITH POLYNOMIALS

Find the indicated products:

1. $4(2x - 5)$ $8x-20$ **9.** $- 3(1 - x)$ $-3+3x$ **17.** $8(\tfrac{1}{2}a + \tfrac{1}{4}b)$ $4a+2b$

2. $3(a - b)$ $3a-3b$ **10.** $- 7(5 - 2c)$ $-35+14c$ **18.** $6(.2x + y)$ $1.2x+6y$

3. $- 2(c - m)$ $-2c+2m$ **11.** $4(m - 7)$ $4m-28$ **19.** $20(\tfrac{1}{5}x - 3)$ $4x-60$

4. $- 5(x - 1)$ $-5x+5$ **12.** $- 8(c^2 - 5)$ $-8c^2+40$ **20.** $- a^2(a - 5)$ $-a^3+5a^2$

5. $6(- 2 + x)$ $-12+6x$ **13.** $4(a^2 - x^2)$ $4a^2-4x^2$ **21.** $.2(5x - 10)$ $x-2$

6. $x(x - 1)$ x^2-x **14.** $\pi(R + r)$ $\pi R+\pi r$ **22.** $- .4(25c + 1)$ $-10c-.4$

7. $x^2(x - 1)$ x^3-x^2 **15.** $p(1 + rt)$ $p+prt$ **23.** $18(\tfrac{1}{2}x - \tfrac{1}{3}y)$ $9x-6y$

8. $- 4(a + b)$ $-4a-4b$ **16.** $x^2(x + 4)$ x^3+4x^2 **24.** $\tfrac{1}{2}x(4x - 6y)$ $2x^2-3xy$

Example 2. Simplify $- 4(a + b) - 3a$.

Solution. There are two terms in this expression. The first term is $- 4(a + b)$ and the second is $- 3a$.

Then
$$- 4(a + b) - 3a$$
$$= - 4a - 4b - 3a$$
$$= - 7a - 4b$$

Example 3. Remove parentheses and simplify $4 - 5(c - 4)$.

Solution.
$$4 - 5(c - 4)$$
$$= 4 - 5c + 20$$
$$= 24 - 5c$$

Remove parentheses and simplify:

1. $4(2p - 3) - 4$ $8p-16$ **6.** $2 + 7(a - 5)$ $7a-33$

2. $2(m - 5) + 7$ $2m-3$ **7.** $3c - 5(2c - 4)$ $20-7c$

3. $- 3(2x - 1) - 4$ $-6x-1$ **8.** $5c - 4(c + 1)$ $c-4$

4. $- 7(x - 4) - x$ $28-8x$ **9.** $7y - 4(y + 5)$ $3y-20$

5. $8(2 - y) - 4y$ $16-12y$ **10.** $8 - 3(- 3y + 1)$ $9y+5$

Example 4. Simplify $2(4x - 3) - 4(x - 5)$.

Solution. This expression means that $4x - 3$ is to be multiplied by 2; that $x - 5$ is to be multiplied by $- 4$; and that the two products are to be combined.

Then
$$2(4x - 3) - 4(x - 5)$$
$$= 8x - 6 - 4x + 20$$
$$= 4x + 14$$

173

[A]

Simplify:

1. $4(2\,x - 1) + 3(x + 1)$ //x-/

2. $7(2\,c + 1) - 5(3\,c + 1)$ 2-c

3. $1(x + 3) - 2(2\,x - 5)$ /3-3x

4. $a(a + 1) - a(3\,a - 1)$ 2a-2a²

5. $4(3\,c + 2) + 5(c - 1)$ /7c +3

6. $3(m - n) - 4(n - m)$ 7m-7n

7. $-1(a + b) + 1(a - b)$ -2b

8. $5(3 + h) - 6(h - 2)$ 27-h

9. $b(b - a) + a(b - 1)$ b²-a

10. $c(c - 5) - 5(c^2 + 2\,c)$ -4c²-15c

11. $x(x - 4) + x(2 - x)$ -2x

12. $h(2\,h - 3) - 3(h^2 + 1)$ -h²-3h-3

13. $p^2(1 - p) + p(p^2 + 1)$ p²+p

14. $\pi r^2(h - r) - \pi r^3$ πr²h-2πr³

Example 5. Simplify $(a + 5) + (3\,a - 6)$.

Solution 1	Solution 2
The expression means that $3\,a - 6$ is to be added to $a + 5$, as shown below. $$\begin{array}{r} a + 5 \\ 3\,a - 6 \\ \hline 4\,a - 1 \end{array}$$	Since the expressions in the parentheses are to be added, we write the polynomials one after the other without changing their signs: $$\begin{aligned} (a + 5) &+ (3\,a - 6) \\ &= a + 5 + 3\,a - 6 \\ &= 4\,a - 1 \end{aligned}$$

①

Solution 3. Since a number is not changed when it is multiplied by 1, we may proceed as in Example 4.

$$\begin{aligned} (a + 5) &+ (3\,a - 6) \\ &= 1(a + 5) + 1(3\,a - 6) \\ &= a + 5 + 3\,a - 6 \\ &= 4\,a - 1 \end{aligned}$$

Example 6. Simplify $(y - 5) - (3\,y - 4)$.

Solution 1	Solution 2
The expression means that $3\,y - 4$ is to be subtracted from $y - 5$. In this solution the signs of the subtrahend are changed mentally before adding. $$\begin{array}{r} y - 5 \\ 3\,y - 4 \\ \hline -2\,y - 1 \end{array}$$	Since $3\,y - 4$ is the quantity that is to be subtracted, $3\,y$ is changed to $-3\,y$, and -4 is changed to $+4$. $$(y - 5) - (3\,y\ \ - 4)$$ $$\downarrow\qquad\downarrow$$ $$\begin{aligned} &= y - 5 \quad -3\,y + 4 \\ &= -2\,y - 1 \end{aligned}$$

① While solution 1 is correct and probably faster, the second solution will be used more frequently in solution of equations and operations with fractions.

Solution 3. Placing 1 before the parentheses does not change the value of the expression.

$$(y - 5) - (3y - 4)$$
$$= 1(y - 5) - 1(3y - 4)$$
$$= y - 5 - 3y + 4$$
$$= -2y - 1$$

Removing Parentheses

Rule 1. Parentheses preceded by a plus sign may be removed without changing the signs of the terms within.
Parentheses preceded by a minus sign may be removed if the signs of the terms within are changed.

Another way of putting it is as follows:

Rule 2. If parentheses are preceded by a plus sign or a minus sign, write the monomial 1 before the parentheses and multiply as indicated.

[A]

EXERCISES

Simplify, following the method of either Rule 1 or Rule 2 above:

1. $x - (x - 1)$ /   **7.** $x^2 - (x^2 - 6)$ 6 **13.** $4 - (x - 2)$ $6 - x$

2. $c + (2c + 1)$ $3c+1$ **8.** $2b + (-b + 1)$ $b+1$ **14.** $2x - (8 - x)$ $3x - 8$

3. $5a + (4 - a)$ $4a+4$ **9.** $-c - (c + 3)$ $-2c - 3$ **15.** $6t - (32 + 3)$ $6t - 35$

4. $3x - (2 - 4x)$ $7x - 2$ **10.** $5y - (2y - 1)$ $3y+1$ **16.** $3p + (-p - 4)$ $2p - 4$

5. $10 - (5 + y)$ $5 - y$ **11.** $10 - (8 - m)$ $2 + m$ **17.** $5h + (2h - 1)$ $7h - 1$

6. $8 + (4 + y)$ $12 + y$ **12.** $8 + (5 + b)$ $13 + b$ **18.** $R - (4r + 2)$ $R - 4r + 2$

Remove parentheses and combine like terms:

19. $3x - (4 - 2x) + 5$ $5x + 1$ **25.** $2(x - 1) - (3x + 4)$ $-x - 6$

20. $3c - 5(c - 1) + 6$ $11 - 2c$ **26.** $(5c + 2)3 - 10$ $15c - 4$

21. $(x + 6) - (x - 4)$ 10 **27.** $x(x + 1) - (x^2 - 5x)$ $6x$

22. $(4m - 3) - 5(m + 1)$ $-m - 8$ **28.** $4(m - 3) - 5(2m + 3)$ $-6m - 27$

23. $2x - y - (x + y)$ $x - 2y$ **29.** $a^2 + b^2 + a(a + b)$ $2a^2 + ab + b^2$

24. $x - (x - y) + 2y$ $3y$ **30.** $a^2 + a(a + b)$ $2a^2 + ab$

① You may need to discuss these rules in detail. In using Rule 1, you are really considering the sign before the parentheses as a sign of operation. In using Rule 2, you are employing the distributive law of multiplication, considering the sign as a sign of opposition.

[B]

Simplify:

31. $(2 a + 3 b) + (a - 5 b) - 2(2 a - 7 b)$ *12b-a*

32. $x(x - 5) - 3 x(x + 4) - (x^2 - 7 x + 1)$
-3x²-10x-1

33. $ab(a^2 - ab + b^2) - 3 a(a^2b + ab^2)$ *-2a³b-4a²b²+ab³*

34. $m^2(m - 1) - m(m^2 + 2 m - 4)$ *4mw-3mw²*

35. $4 p - (2 p^2 + 3 p + 6) + (- 4 p^2 + 5 p)$ *-6p²+6p-6*

Enclosing Terms in Parentheses[B]

It is sometimes convenient or necessary to enclose two or more terms of a polynomial in parentheses.

When terms are removed from parentheses preceded by a plus sign, the signs of the terms are not changed. Therefore when this operation is reversed, that is, when terms are placed within parentheses preceded by a plus sign, the signs of the terms are not changed.

When terms are removed from parentheses preceded by a minus sign, the signs of the terms are changed. Therefore when terms are enclosed in parentheses preceded by a minus sign, the signs of the terms must be changed.

Example 1. Enclose the last three terms of the polynomial $4 x^3 - 2 x^2 - 5 x + 3$ in parentheses preceded by a plus sign.

Solution. $4 x^3 - 2 x^2 - 5 x + 3$
$= 4 x^3 + (- 2 x^2 - 5 x + 3)$

Example 2. Enclose the last two terms of $2 a + 3 b + 4 c - d$ in parentheses preceded by a minus sign.

Solution. $2 a + 3 b + 4 c - d$
$= 2 a + 3 b - (- 4 c + d)$

EXERCISES

[B]

Enclose the first three terms of each polynomial in parentheses preceded by a plus sign, and the last three terms in parentheses preceded by a minus sign.

1. $m^2 - 2 mn + 3 - 4 y^2 - 3 y + 2$ *(m²-2mn+3)-(4y²+3y-2)*

2. $c^2 - 3 c + 1 - 7 d^2 - 8 d + 9$ *(c²-3c+1)-(7d²+8d-9)*

3. $- 4 x^2 - 3 x - 1 + h^2 + 5 h - 8$ *(-4x²-3x-1)-(-h²-5h+8)*

① These exercises have been marked B since the procedure is not needed in elementary work. However, they do illustrate nicely the process inverse to that of page 175.

OPERATIONS WITH POLYNOMIALS

Enclose the terms containing powers of x in parentheses preceded by a plus sign, and the terms containing powers of y in parentheses preceded by a minus sign.

4. $2x^2 - y^2 - 3y + 4x - 5cx + 2y^2 - by$

$(2x^2 + 4x - 5cx) - (by + 3y - y^2)$

5. $2x - 3y + bx + cy + 3x^2 - 8y^2$

$(3x^2 + bx + 2x) - (8y^2 - cy + 3y)$

6. $x^2 + y^2 + 3x - 5y + cx^3 - dy^3$

$(cx^3 + x^2 + 3x) - (dy^3 - y^2 + 5y)$

If you expect to be able to use polynomials in the work which follows, you should make sure now that you know how to

1. Add polynomials, whether they are written in columns or horizontally (p. 159). Be sure you know how to check your additions (p. 159). This includes knowing the shortcomings of 0 and 1 as numbers to use in your checking (p. 159). It also includes knowing that a check by substitution does not necessarily prove that your work is correct (p. 159).

The pages in parentheses will help you to review.

2. Subtract polynomials, whether they are written in columns or horizontally (p. 163). Be sure you know how to check your subtraction work (p. 163).

3. Multiply polynomials by monomials (p. 167). Be sure you can check your multiplications (p. 168).

4. Divide polynomials by monomials (p. 170). Be sure you can check your divisions (p. 171).

You should also make sure that you know how to

5. Solve equations containing fractions (p. 170).

6. Simplify expressions containing parentheses (p. 172).

7. Enclose terms in parentheses (p. 176).

8. Spell and use correctly the following words:

addend	divisor	multiplicand	subtrahend
difference	minuend	product	sum
dividend	multiplier	quotient	

If you are in doubt about one of the words, use a dictionary.

[A]

Add:

1. $5x + 7y - 8z$
$3x + y - 4z$
8x + 8y - 12z

2. $60 - 7x$
$4x - y$
60 - 3x - y

3. $3x^2 - 2x + 7$
$-x^2 + 2x - 5$
2x² + 2

4. $3c + 5d + 3$
$11c + d - 9$
14c + 6d - 6

5. $x^2 - 7xy + y^2$
$-6x^2 - 8xy - 9y^2$
-5x² -15xy - 8y²

6. $2x^4 - x^3 + x^2$
$+5x^4 + 4x^3 - x^2$
7x⁴ + 3x³

Subtract:

7. $a - b + c$
$2a - b - c$
-a + 2c

8. $4a - 3b + 6$
$a - 4b - 1$
3a + b + 7

9. $x^2 - 20$
$x^3 + x^2$
-x³ - 20

10. 40
$2x - 5$
-2x + 45

11. $3a - 2b + 7c$
$-5a + b - c$
8a - 3b + 8c

12. $x^3 - 1$
$x^2 + x$
x³ - x² - x - 1

Multiply:

13. $x^2 - 4x + 3$
-4
-4x² + 16x - 12

14. $2m^2 - m + 2$
3
6m² - 3m + 6

15. $a + b + c$
$-a$
-a² - ab - ac

16. $2x^2 - 5x + 3$
-4
-8x² + 20x - 12

17. $m^2 - 4m + n^2$
mn
m³n - 4m²n + mn³

18. $x^2 - 4xy + y^2$
$-3xy$
-3x³y + 12x²y² - 3xy³

Divide:

19. $\dfrac{4a - 8b + 12c}{3}$
4/3 a - 8/3 b + 4c

20. $\dfrac{5x^3 - 20x^2 - 5}{-5}$
-x³ + 4x² + 1

21. $\dfrac{x^3 - 4x^2 + x}{x}$
x² - 4x + 1

22. $\dfrac{3x^3 - 6x^2 - 18x}{-3x}$
-x² + 2x + 6

23. $-7 \overline{\smash{\big)}\,21x^2 - 14x}$
-3x² + 2x

24. $5c \overline{\smash{\big)}\,10abc - 5c^3}$
2ab - c²

25. $(18 c^3 - 12 c^2 + 9 c) \div (-3 c) = ?$ $-6c^2 + 4c - 3$

26. Find the total area of the cube shown here. $54a^2$

27. Find the volume of the cube. $27a^3$

28. $(-3 x)^4 = ?$ $81x^4$

29. $(-4 x^2)(-x)(-6 x^4) = ?$ $-24x^7$

State the products:

$3a$

30. $a^2b^3 \cdot a^3b$ a^5b^4 **32.** $(-ab)(-ab)$ a^2b^2 **34.** $m \times n$ mn

31. $m^2n \cdot mn^4$ m^3n^5 **33.** $(-x^3y^2)(x^2y)$ $-x^5y^3$ **35.** $7 ab \times 0$ 0

State the quotients:

36. $(8 x^4) \div (-4 x)$ $-2x^3$ **38.** $(14 t^3) \div (-7 t^3)$ -2

37. $(30 ab^3) \div (-15 a)$ $-2b^3$ **39.** $(-12 mn) \div (-6 m)$ $2n$

40. $(x^3 - 4 x^2 + 5 x - 8) \div (-1)$ $-x^3 + 4x^2 - 5x + 8$

41. $(4 x^5 + 16 x^4 - 20 x^3 + 8 x^2 - 4 x) \div (4 x)$
$x^4 + 4x^3 - 5x^2 + 2x - 1$ [B]

Simplify by removing parentheses and combining like terms:

42. $2 a - 3(a + b)$ $-a - 3b$ **44.** $2 x(x^2 - 4) - x^2(1 - 3 x)$
$5x^3 - x^2 - 8x$

43. $(a - b + c)4 - 6$ $4a - 4b + 4c - 6$ **45.** $-3(3 x + 1) - 4(2 x - 3)$
$9 - 17x$

Enclose the first two terms of each polynomial in parentheses preceded by a plus sign and the last two terms in parentheses preceded by a minus sign:

46. $4 c + 1 - 3 c^2 - 1$
$(4c + 1) - (3c^2 + 1)$

48. $x^2 - 6 x - y^2 - 9$
$(x^2 - 6x) - (y^2 + 9)$

47. $a + b - c + d$ $(a + b) - (c - d)$ **49.** $a^2 - b^2 - c^2 + d^2$
$(a^2 - b^2) - (c^2 - d^2)$ [C]

Simplify:

50. $2(x - 4) - 3(2 x - 6) - (4 x - 28)$ $38 - 8x$

51. $2 c(c^2 - 3 c + 1) - 3 c(c^2 + c - 2)$ $8c - 9c^2 - c^3$

Enclose the last four terms in parentheses preceded by a minus sign:

52. $a^2 - 2 ab + b^2 - 2 bc + c^2 - 9$
$a^2 - 2ab - (-b^2 + 2bc - c^2 + 9)$

53. $x^2 - a^2 - 4 ab - 4 b^2 + 16$
$x^2 - (a^2 + 4ab + 4b^2 - 16)$

179

[A]

GENERAL
REVIEW

1. The area of a rectangle is $4a - 8$ and its base is 4. Find its height. $a-2$

Solve:

2. $5x + 4 - 12 = 32$ 8

5. $x + .06x = 424$ 400

3. $3y + 5y - 7 = 4y$ $1\frac{3}{4}$

6. $c - .1c = 81$ 90

4. $3x + 14 = 11x - 2$ 2

7. $\frac{3}{4}y = \frac{2}{3}$ $\frac{8}{9}$

8. Find by substitution which of the numbers 2, -2, 3, and -3 are roots of the equation $x^2 - x = 6$. $-2,3$

9. This triangular pennant is cut from a rectangular-shaped piece of felt. What fraction of the felt is wasted? $\frac{1}{2}$

10. What must be added to $2a - 4b$ to make the expression equal to zero? $-2a + 4b$

11. $2x - 3y = 12$. What is the value of x when $y = 4$? when $y = -4$? when $y = 0$? $12; 0; 6$

12. Subtract $+99$ from -99. -198

13. $i = prt$. Find p when $i = \$33.75$, $r = 6\%$, and $t = 2\frac{1}{2}$ years. $\$225$

14. Simplify $(2x - 4) - 10 + (3x + 6)$. $5x - 8$

[B]

15. Simplify $(4x - 3xy) + 5y^2 - 2(x^2 - xy - y^2)$. $2x^2 + 4x - xy + 7y^2$

16. Simplify $x(xy^2 - y) - 6 - 4(x^2y^2 + 3)$. $-3x^2y^2 - xy - 18$

Enclose the last two terms in parentheses preceded by a minus sign:

17. $x^2 - 4x + 3$ $x^2 - (4x - 3)$

19. $p^2 - 3p + 2$ $p^2 - (3p - 2)$

18. $c^2 + 5c - 3$ $c^2 - (-5c + 3)$

20. $8x^2 + 9x - 4$ $8x^2 - (-9x + 4)$

21. Find three consecutive integers whose sum is 1353. $450, 451, 452$

[Test A]

CHAPTER
TESTS

Simplify:

1. $7c + (-3c)$ $4c$

4. $(-3x^2)^2$ $9x^4$

7. $\frac{12x - 4}{4}$ $3x - 1$

2. $2x - (-4x)$ $6x$

5. $-7p - 4p$ $-11p$

8. $\frac{4y^2 - y}{-1}$ $-4y^2 + y$

3. $-x^3 \div x^2$ $-x$

6. $-19 - (+19)$ -38

180

9. Add $3a^2 - 4 + 5a$ and $6a - a^2 - 10$. $2a^2 + 11a - 14$

10. Subtract $7x^2 - 9x + 7$ from $4x - x^2 + 6$. $-8x^2 + 13x - 1$

11. Multiply $2m^2 - 6m + 3$ by $-3m$. $-6m^3 + 18m^2 - 9m$

12. Divide $9x^3 - 6x^2 + 15$ by 3. $3x^3 - 2x^2 + 5$

Remove parentheses and combine like terms:

13. $a - (a - b)$ b

15. $2(x - 1) - 3(x + 4)$ $-x - 14$

14. $2c + (d - 3 \cdot c)$ $-c + d$

16. $5(y - 1) + 2(2y - 3)$ $9y - 11$

17. Find the cost of $2n$ articles at $(n + 1)$ cents each. $(2n^2 + 2n)$ ¢

18. Find the perimeter of the triangle at the right. $3s + 14$

19. The area of a rectangle is $2x^2 - 4x$ and the altitude is $2x$. Find the base. $x - 2$

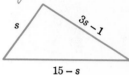

s $3s - 1$ $15 - s$

20. In a schoolroom there are n rows and $n + 2$ pupils in each row. How many pupils are there in the n rows? $(n^2 + 2n)$

[Test B]

Simplify:

1. $6c + (-3c)$ $3c$

2. $(8xy)(6y^2)$ $48xy^3$

3. $(-2x)^3$ $-8x^3$

4. $xy(x - y)$ $x^2y - xy^2$

5. $\dfrac{12xy - x^2}{x}$ $12y - x$

6. $-2a^2(a - ab)$ $-2a^3 + 2a^3b$

7. $(c^2 - 8c) \div c$ $c - 8$

8. $\frac{1}{2}x(x^2 - 6x + 10)$ $\frac{1}{2}x^3 - 3x^2 + 5x$

9. $7h - (-5h)$ $12h$

10. $20 - (-20)$ 40

11. Add: $2a^2 - a + 6$; $a - 9$; and $5a - 10a^2$. $-8a^2 + 5a - 3$

12. From $a^3 - 1$ subtract $2a^2 - 5a - 1$. $a^3 - 2a^2 + 5a$

13. Multiply $x^2 - 2xy - y^2$ by $2xy$. $2x^3y - 4x^2y^2 - 2xy^3$

14. Find the area of a rectangle if its base is $m^2 - m - 1$ and its altitude is $2m$. $2m^3 - 2m^2 - 2m$

15. Find the area of the base of this rectangular solid. $2ab + 4b^2$

16. Find the area of each end of the solid. $6ab$

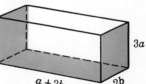

$a + 2b$ $2b$ $3a$

17. From the sum of $x^2 - x + 3$ and $2x^2 - 4x - 7$ subtract $4x^2 - 7x - 1$. $-x^2 + 2x - 3$

Remove parentheses and simplify:

18. $5(c - 3) - (c + 2)$ $4c - 17$

19. $p - (p + 3) - 3(2p + 1)$ $-6p - 6$

20. Insert the first two terms of $a - b + 3c - 5d$ in parentheses preceded by a plus sign and insert the last two terms in parentheses preceded by a minus sign. $(a - b) - (-3c + 5d)$

181

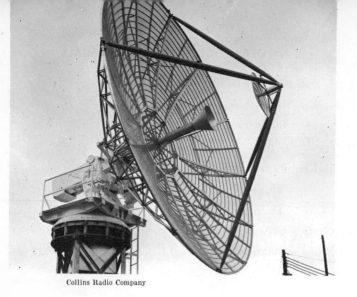

Collins Radio Company

Radar

Without mathematics radar would never have been possible, for radar is the product of electronic engineering. Radar's greatest development occurred during World War II when it was used to locate enemy planes and ships. Its development was so rapid that before the war ended enemy ships could be sighted by radar though not visible to the eye. Radar is now used in many fields.

The word *radar* is derived from the words *RAdio Detecting And Ranging*. The word *ranging* means to find the distance to an object. A radar set can be used to find the direction and distance of an object, and can almost immediately show a flat picture of the area around an object.

Radar uses the echo of radio waves to locate objects. You know what an echo is. You can see a light-wave echo when you see your face in the mirror. You may be able to hear a sound-wave echo by going outdoors and shouting the word "Hello" through a megaphone in the direction of a cliff or other obstruction about a quarter of a mile away. When the sound waves strike the cliff, they bounce back in different directions. Some of the  waves will return to you and if they are sufficiently strong and numerous, you will hear the word "Hello" repeated. The repeated word is a sound echo.

By placing the megaphone to your ear, you can collect more sound waves and so hear a louder echo. Even though you were blindfolded

Although the word *radar* is familiar to everyone, some of the information in this article, such as the meaning of radar itself, will be new and interesting to most.

you could find the direction of the cliff by noting the direction from which you hear the loudest echo. You can find the approximate distance to the cliff by counting the number of seconds for the sound to go to and return from the cliff. For example, if you hear the echo 4 seconds after the shout, you know that it took the sound 2 seconds to go to the cliff and 2 seconds to return. Since sound travels in air about 1100 feet per second, the cliff is 2200 feet away (approximately).

In a similar way radar uses radio waves to locate objects. Radio waves travel 186,000 miles per second. Since they travel so fast, the *microsecond* (one-millionth of a second) is used as the unit of time.

A radar set consists of five parts,—the electronic timer, the transmitter, the receiver, the cathode-ray tube or visual indicator, and the antenna (shown in the photograph).

The transmitter sends out through the antenna regular short pulses which consist of electrically controlled electromagnetic waves a few inches long and which are focused in narrow beams. When these beams strike an object, some are reflected back to the receiver and affect the flow of electrons in the cath-

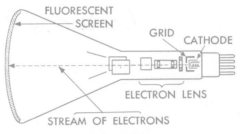

Cathode-Ray Tube

ode-ray tube. The initial and echo pulses are shown on the picture tube.

Three methods are used to show the results on the picture-tube screen. In the range-indicator method the picture consists of a white line, called the time base line, with range marks and pips (peaks) on it, the first pip indicating the start of the pulse and the other pips the echo pulses. The range marks give the scale.

In the plan-position indicator the picture shows the territory around the set. Its time base line starts at the center of the picture and sweeps to the outer edge. The echo impulses appear on the screen as bright spots. As the antenna rotates and scans the ter-

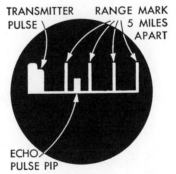

Range Indicator

ritory around the set, the time base line rotates to make the picture.

By a third method it is possible to show a map-like outline of the topographical features of a small area. This method has important uses in air navigation.

7

Equations
Containing Parentheses

Suggested Time Schedule
Minimum   9 days
Maximum   10 days

In this chapter you will take another step
toward mastery of algebra—
learning to handle parentheses
in equations.

In this chapter there are no wholly new processes. The student will use the techniques of simplifying expressions containing parentheses, which he studied in the preceding chapter, in the solution of equations. The greater part of the chapter is devoted to deepening his knowledge of solving word problems. Often you will find a large number of your students both fear and dislike word problems. Too often some will say "I never could do word problems," thus indicating a defeatist attitude right from the start. You will need to use patience and ingenuity. But do not give up, for this is the heart of algebra. Many problems the student will be asked to solve are not of importance in themselves, but the experience of analyzing the verbal sentences and translating to mathematical equations is very valuable.

Removing Parentheses in Equations [A]

In solving equations containing parentheses, we first remove the parentheses.

Example 1. Solve and prove: $(6x - 5) - (6 - x) = 3$.

Solution. Here $6 - x$ is to be subtracted from $6x - 5$. The minuend is $6x - 5$ and the subtrahend is $6 - x$. We can write the equation without the parentheses if we change the signs of the subtrahend. Our work should appear as follows:

$$(6x - 5) - (6 - x) = 3$$

Removing parentheses	$6x - 5 - 6 + x = 3$
Simplifying	$7x - 11 = 3$
A_{11}	$7x = 3 + 11$
	$7x = 14$
	$x = 2$

PROOF. Does $(12 - 5) - (6 - 2) = 3$?
Does $7 - 4 = 3$? Yes.

Example 2. Solve $3(x - 5) - 4(2x - 4) = -2x + 22$.

Solution. In this equation $(x - 5)$ is to be multiplied by $+3$ and $(2x - 4)$ is to be multiplied by -4. The work appears as follows:

A common error is not to obtain the $+16$, especially if the parenthesis groups more than two terms.

	$3(x - 5) - 4(2x - 4) = -2x + 22$
Multiplying	$3x - 15 - 8x + 16 = -2x + 22$
Simplifying	$-5x + 1 = -2x + 22$
$A_{2x}; S_1$	$-5x + 2x = 22 - 1$
	$-3x = 21$
D_{-3}	$x = -7$

PROOF. Does $3(-7 - 5) - 4(-14 - 4) = 14 + 22$?
Does $3(-12) - 4(-18) = 14 + 22$?
Does $-36 + 72 = 36$? Yes.

[A]

EXERCISES

Solve, and prove as directed by your teacher:

1. $3(x + 6) = 21$ *1*
2. $5(x - 1) = 6(x - 3)$ *13*
3. $6x - (3x - 4) = 14$ *3⅓*
4. $2x - (13 - 2x) = 61$ *18½*
5. $15 + 6x = 7(x - 2)$ *29*
6. $5(x + 4) - 4(x + 3) = 0$ *-8*
7. $3x - 8 = 3(7 - x)$ *4⅚*
8. $3 - (x + 29) = 12x$ *-2*
9. $3c - 4(c + 2) = 5$ *-13*
10. $(3x + 3) = (x + 4)$ *½*
11. $3y - (y + 4) = 0$ *2*
12. $4(x - 3) - 6(x + 1) = 0$ *-9*

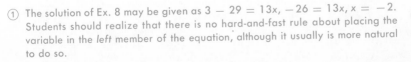

① The solution of Ex. 8 may be given as $3 - 29 = 13x$, $-26 = 13x$, $x = -2$. Students should realize that there is no hard-and-fast rule about placing the variable in the *left* member of the equation, although it usually is more natural to do so.

185

ALGEBRA, BOOK ONE

3   **13.** $9x - (3x - 18) = 36$ $\frac{1}{7}$ **22.** $5(2 - 3x) = 15 - (x + 7)$

$\frac{5}{6}$ **14.** $8x - (2x + 5) = 0$ 4 **23.** $5 + (6m + 3) = 8m$

$1\frac{1}{2}$ **15.** $9x - (5x - 2) = 8$ $5\frac{1}{2}$ **24.** $7(x - 5) = 10 - (x + 1)$

$1\frac{1}{3}$ **16.** $2p - (4 - p) = 0$ $\frac{1}{2}$ **25.** $9x = 2x + 6 - (4 - 3x)$

7 **17.** $-(5y + 4) = -6y + 3$ **26.** $(r - 9) - (r + 6) = 4r$

0 **18.** $13x - (3 + 12x) = -3$ **27.** $5c - (3c + 2) = 15$

-1 **19.** $9r = 5 - (10 - 4r)$ **28.** $40 = 16 - 4(9 - 3k)$

0 **20.** $10s + 3 + (-6s - 3) = 0$ **29.** $5x + 2(4x - 5) = 30$

$-8\frac{1}{2}$ **21.** $5(2p + 3) = 2(4p - 1)$ **30.** $6x - (x - 7) = (x + 15)$

[B]

Solve:

31. $20h - (5h + 9) + (7 - 9h) = (12h - 5)\frac{1}{2}$

32. $7(5y - 1) - 18y = 12y - (3 - y)$ 1

33. $\frac{1}{3}(6x - 9) = \frac{1}{2}(8x - 4)$ $-\frac{1}{2}$

34. $(.6y + .08) - 1.2y = -.8y - .22$ $-1\frac{1}{2}$

35. $(4x - 13) + (17 - 2x) - 3(x - 7) = 3(x - 5)$ 10

36. $2(x + 1) - (x + 5) - (x - 4) - (3x - 4) = 0$ $1\frac{2}{3}$

37. $6(x - 2) - 2(x - 5) - 2(x + 6) = 0$ 7

38. $3(5 - n) - 4(2n - 7) = -11 - (10 + 3n)$ 8

39. $5y - 4(y - 6) - 2(y + 6) + 12 = 0$ 24

40. $3x - .2(x - 30) = x + .3(8x - 30)$ 25

41. $24x^2 + 147 = 27 - 16x - 4x(1 - 6x)$ -6

42. $5(m - 3) + 21(m - 2) = 11 - 4(17 - m)$ 0

43. $x + 6.25 - 3(4x - 1) = 8(x + .25) - 3(x + .25)$ $\frac{1}{2}$

44. $190 - 21(y + 3) = 196 - 15(2y - 5)$ 16

45. $2x - 5(.8x - 1.8) + 5(x + 4) = 41$ 4

Conditional and Identical Equations [A]

The equation $3(x + 2) = 3x + 6$ is true for all values of x, since $3(x + 2)$ and $3x + 6$ are always equal. An equation like this is called an <u>identical equation</u> or an <u>identity</u>.

The equation $3x + 2 = 14$ is true when $x = 4$, and only when $x = 4$. No other value of x will satisfy the equation. In other words, the con-

① You may prefer to do only a few of these for one lesson, proceed to the foot

of the page, and then weave in the remainder of the exercises on equations with the word problems from pages 188 to 202. Thus techniques of equation solving are maintained, the student sees the chapter as a whole, and the sections of word problems seem less burdensome.

Emphasize the vocabulary. Students work so often with equations having one solution that an identity does not seem to them to be an equation at all. Remind them that an expression such as the
illustration of the distributive law is really an identity: $3(x - 5) = 3x - 15$.
EQUATIONS CONTAINING PARENTHESES

dition for $3x + 2$ to equal 14 is that x shall equal 4. An equation such
as $3x + 2 = 14$ is called a <u>conditional equation</u>. Can you give a reason
for its name? Thus we see that every number is a member of the
truth set for an identity, but only certain numbers are members of
the truth set for a conditional equation.

If the two members of an equation can be changed into the same
form, the equation is an identity, or, if an equation is an application
of one of the properties of addition or multiplication, it is an identity.

Example. Is the equation $3(x + 5) + 4 = 3x + 19$ conditional or identical?

Solution. $3(x + 5) + 4 = 3x + 19$
Removing parentheses $3x + 15 + 4 = 3x + 19$
Collecting like terms $3x + 19 = 3x + 19$
The equation is an identity since both members are the same.

[A]   **EXERCISES**

Tell which of the following statements are identities and
which conditional equations:

1. $4x - 12 = 0$ *Cond.*
2. $3x + 2 = 14$ *Cond.*
3. $2(x - 4) = 2x - 8$ *Iden.*
4. $3(m - 9) = 4m + 25$ *Cond.*
5. $4(x - 1) = 10x + 11$ *Cond.*

6. $3x - 5 = x - 5 + 2x$ *Iden.*
7. $2(c - 5) - c = c - 6$ *Neither*
8. $7m - 4 = 4(2m - 1) - m$ *Iden.*
9. $5(x + 1) - 4x = x - 5$ *Neither*
10. $3(x + 1) = 3(x - 1) + 6$ *Iden.*

Using Parentheses with Algebraic Expressions [A]

In arithmetic all our expressions for numbers can be written as monomials. For example, 5, $2\frac{3}{4}$, and 356 are all monomials. In algebra
we cannot write all our numbers or expressions as monomials. For
example, $4x$, $7y - 14$, and $c^2 + 6c - 4$ are all in their simplest forms,
but only the first expression is a monomial. When we wish to indicate
that we are to multiply or divide or subtract an expression such as
$7x - 14$, it is necessary to enclose it in parentheses.

For example $2(7y - 14) = 14y - 28$
But $2 \times 7y - 14 = 14y - 14$
Also $(7y - 14) \div 7 = y - 2$
But $7y - 14 \div 7 = 7y - 2$

187

ALGEBRA, BOOK ONE

Example. Write the product of 6 and the sum of $2x$ and y in algebraic symbols.

Solution. Since the sum of $2x$ and y is to be multiplied by 6, we must write the $2x + y$ in parentheses. Then our expression becomes

$$6(2x + y)$$

[A]

EXERCISES

Express the following, using algebraic symbols:

1. The sum of x and 3; the sum of $2x$ and -3; the sum of $4m$ and $m + 4$. $x+3; 2x-3; 5m-4$

2. The product of x and y; the product of 4 and $3x - 1$; the product of -6 and $y + 5$; the product of $2x$ and $x + 8$. $xy; 4(3x-1); -6(y+5); 2x(x+8)$

3. The square of a; twice the square of a; the cube of b; the square of $3c - 1$. $a^2; 2a^2; b^3; (3c-1)^2$

4. If a truck can haul a load of 4 tons each trip, how many tons can it haul in 2 trips? in 6 trips? in x trips? in $(x + 6)$ trips? $8; 24; 4x; 4(x+6)$

5. In 8 trips how many tons can a 2-ton truck haul? In x trips how many tons can a y-ton truck haul? In $(y + 3)$ trips how many tons can a 7-ton truck haul? $16; xy; 7(y+3)$

6. What is the value of 4 pints of milk at 10 cents a pint? at c cents a pint? at $(c + 1)$ cents a pint? $40¢; 4c¢; 4(c+1)¢$

7. The product of two numbers is $8x^2 + 4$, and one of them is 4. What is the other number? $2x^2+1$

Letting x stand for the number, write the following, using algebraic symbols:

8. The sum of four times a certain number and 3 is 35.

9. Four times the sum of a certain number and 3 is 35. $4x+3=35$

10. Four times the sum of 12 and a certain number is 60. $4(x+3)=35$

11. 9 is as much more than a certain number as 4 times the number is more than 1. $4(x+12)=60$ $9-x = 4x-1$

12. If to a certain number 3 is added and the sum is multiplied by 5, the result is 20. $5(x+3)=20$

13. If 6 is subtracted from a certain number and the remainder is multiplied by 8, the result is 16. $8(x-6)=16$

188

EQUATIONS CONTAINING PARENTHESES

14. If a certain number is subtracted from 11 and the remainder is multiplied by 4, the result is 24. $4(11-x) = 24$

15. 5 times a number which is 10 larger than x is 20.
$5(x+10) = 20$

16. If a number is decreased by 6 and then multiplied by 5, the result is 2 more than the number. $5(x-6) = x+2$

①

Parentheses in Problem Solving [A]

Before you study the following example, you should review the directions for solving problems on page 44.

Example. One number is 8 less than another. If 3 times the smaller is subtracted from 4 times the larger, the difference is 47. What are the numbers?

Solution. Let $\qquad x =$ the larger number
Then $\qquad x - 8 =$ the smaller number
and $\quad 4x - 3(x - 8) = 47$
$\qquad 4x - 3x + 24 = 47$
$\qquad 4x - 3x = 47 - 24$
$\qquad x = 23$, the larger number
$\qquad x - 8 = 15$, the smaller number

PROOF. 15 is 8 less than 23. Three times the smaller number is 45. Four times the larger number is 92. $92 - 45 = 47$.

[A]

EXERCISES

1. One number is 4 larger than another. If twice the larger is added to the smaller, the sum is 62. What are the numbers? $18, 22$

Let $x =$ the smaller number
$x + 4 =$ the larger number
$2(x+4) + x =$

2. The difference of two numbers is 10. If twice the larger is subtracted from 5 times the smaller, the difference is 25. What are the numbers? $15, 25$

189

3. A certain truck can haul 4 tons of freight at a time, and a larger truck can haul 6 tons at a time. How many trips must each truck make to haul 58 tons if the smaller truck makes 2 more trips than the larger truck? *large, 5; small, 7*

4. The capacity of a certain truck is 3 tons more than the capacity of another. The combined haul of 7 loads of the smaller truck and 5 loads of the larger is 99 tons. What is the capacity of each truck? *7T., 10T.*

5. One transport carried 1600 more soldiers than another. How many soldiers did each transport carry in each trip if in 8 trips of the smaller and 6 trips of the larger 100,600 soldiers were transported? *6500, 8100*

6. One number is 8 less than another. If 3 times the larger is subtracted from 9 times the smaller, the remainder is 18. Find the numbers. *15, 7*

7. The difference of two numbers is 13 and their sum is 61. Find the numbers. *24, 37*

8. A boy is 5 years older than his sister. If 3 times the sister's age is subtracted from twice the boy's age, the remainder is 1. Find their ages. *Sister, 9 yr.; boy, 14 yr.*

[B]

9. A farmer sold two steers for $1564. If they both sold at 92 cents a pound and the difference of their weights was 140 pounds, what was the weight of each steer? *780 lb., 920 lb.*

10. For her breakfasts last week, Sara ate 4 oranges, 3 apples, and 1 banana. Assume that an orange has 6 fewer calories than an apple and 13 fewer calories than a banana, and the total number of calories of this fruit is 879. How many calories are there in an apple, in an orange, and in a banana? *orange 106, apple 112, banana 119*

11. One angle of a triangle is 2 degrees larger than a second and the third angle is 16 degrees less than the sum of the other two. Find the number of degrees in each angle. *50°, 48°, 82°*

Do not assign too many problems per lesson. It is better to give the student time to think and gain confidence. In most classes, have the problems put on the board following the assignment. Discuss as needed. If time, there should be class work on problems where the teacher can guide the procedure by proper questions. The students should be working at their seats, but the teacher should write results of questions on the board as the discussion progresses. Help students without making them too dependent on you.

Exceeds and Excess [A]

The word "exceeds" is often used in place of the words "is greater than." Thus the expression "7 exceeds 5 by 2" is used instead of the expression "7 is greater than 5 by 2." The amount of the exceeding is called the excess. The excess is the difference of the numbers. The number that exceeds is the larger number and the number that is exceeded is the smaller number.

Thus if Lucille's height is 67 inches and Sue's height is 62 inches, Lucille's height exceeds Sue's height by 5 inches.

Some pupils have difficulty in forming equations for problems which contain the words "exceeds" or "excess." It is helpful in such cases to substitute the words "is greater than" for "exceeds," and the words "difference of" for "excess over."

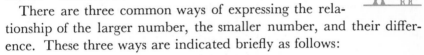

There are three common ways of expressing the relationship of the larger number, the smaller number, and their difference. These three ways are indicated briefly as follows:

1. *Larger − smaller = difference*
2. *Larger = smaller + difference*
3. *Larger − difference = smaller*

[A]

EXERCISES

1. John's age exceeds Frank's by 6 years. Let x = the number of years in Frank's age. Is John's age greater or less than Frank's age? Which of the following expressions will represent John's age? $x - 6$; $6 - x$; $x + 6$. *Greater; $x+6$*

2. Write the equation $x = y + 3$ so that both x and y are in the left member. Write the equation so that only y is in the right member. *$x-y=3$; $x-3=y$*

3. Write the expression "8 exceeds 6 by 2" in equation form three different ways. *$8-6=2$, $8=6+2$, $8-2=6$*

4. A's age exceeds B's age by 4 years. If x stands for B's age, what will represent A's age? *$x+4$*

5. The excess of B's age over A's age is 10 years. If x stands for A's age, what will represent B's age? *$x+10$*

6. Write the expression "b exceeds c by 9" in equation form three different ways. *$b-c=9$, $b=c+9$, $b-9=c$*

Do not neglect this page, since the word "exceeds" is often a real source of trouble. If you are teaching for the first time, you will be surprised how often students will apparently understand this discussion and then in later problems be willing to set up an equation which in effect says "larger + difference = smaller" and then wonder why they get a negative number for an answer! Try drawing a large rectangle and a small one on the board, enclosing the representation of the quantities involved. Then ask, "Can you make these equal by *adding* something to the larger figure?"

191

7. The weight of one stone exceeds three times the weight of another by 7 pounds. If x represents the weight of the smaller stone, what will represent the number of pounds in the weight of the larger? $3x+7$

8. One number exceeds twice another by 4. Express the larger number in terms of m when m stands for the smaller number. $2m+4$

9. The rate of one train exceeds by 18 twice the rate of another. If x is the rate of the slower train in miles per hour, what is the rate of the faster train in miles per hour? $2x+18$

[A]

NUMBER PROBLEMS

Example. The sum of two numbers is 40 and the larger exceeds three times the smaller by 4. What are the numbers?

Solution. Let $\qquad x =$ the smaller number
Then $\qquad 3\,x + 4 =$ the larger number
Then $\qquad x + 3\,x + 4 = 40$
$$x + 3\,x = 40 - 4$$
$$4\,x = 36$$
$$x = 9, \text{ the smaller number}$$
$$3\,x + 4 = 31, \text{ the larger number}$$

PROOF. The sum of 9 and 31 is 40. Also 31 is 4 more than 3 times 9.

1. One number is represented by x and another by $x - 4$. If the sum of the two numbers is 320, find the numbers. *162, 158*

2. Separate 800 into two parts such that one part will exceed the other by 32. *384, 416*

3. The sum of two numbers is 92 and one exceeds the other by 40. What are the numbers? *26, 66*

4. One of two numbers exceeds the other by 10 and their sum is 126. What are the numbers? *58, 68*

5. Separate 147 into two parts such that the larger will exceed three times the smaller by 27. *30, 117*

6. Separate 119 into three parts such that the second will exceed the first by 8 and the third one will exceed twice the second by 3. *23, 31, 65*

7. The sum of two numbers is 42. Find the numbers if the excess of the larger over 3 times the smaller is 2. *10, 32*

192

EQUATIONS CONTAINING PARENTHESES

The Word "Sum" [A]

Let us consider the following problem: "The sum of two numbers is 36. If 3 times the larger is added to 4 times the smaller, the result is 123. What are the numbers?" Suppose we let x represent the smaller number. What will represent the larger number? The answer to this question will be easier after you have done the following exercises.

[A]

1. If the sum of two numbers is 8 and one of them is 3, what is the other? *5*

2. The sum of two numbers is 13 and the smaller is 5. What is the larger? *8*

3. The sum of two numbers is 20 and the larger is 11. What is the smaller? *9*

4. The sum of two numbers is 25. If you know one of the numbers, how can you find the other? In finding the second number, do you subtract the sum of the numbers from the first number, or do you subtract the first number from the sum? *(See top of page)*

5. The sum of two numbers is 20 and x is one of the numbers. Is the other number $x - 20$? Is it $20 - x$? *No; Yes*
Does $x - 20 = 20 - x$? *No*

6. If 15 is the sum of two numbers and one of them is m, what is the other? *15 - m*

7. The perimeter of the rectangle shown is 80. Represent its length in terms of x. *40 - x*

x

8. A radio and a violin cost $200. If the cost of the radio is r dollars, what is the cost of the violin? *$ (200 - r)*

9. If x is one of two complementary angles, what is the other? *90° - x*

10. If one of two supplementary angles is 3 c, what is the other? *180° - 3c*

11. The perimeter of a rectangle is P and the length is l. Represent the width in terms of P and l. *$w = \frac{1}{2} P - l$*

These oral exercises are designed to help the student master the interpretation of problems involving sums. Many seem willing to represent the two parts of 80, for example, by x and x — 80.

12. a. Let x = smaller number; then 35 − x = larger number.
b. Let x = number boy owns; then 50 − x = number girl owns.
c. Let x = number of boys; then 32 − x = number of girls.

12. How would you start the solution of problems beginning as follows?

a. The sum of two numbers is 35.

b. A boy and girl together own 50 rabbits.

c. There are 32 boys and girls in an algebra class.

WRITTEN PROBLEMS	**Example.** The sum of two numbers is 36. If 3 times the larger is added to 4 times the smaller, the result is 123. What are the numbers?

Solution. Let $\quad\quad\quad x =$ the smaller number

Then $\quad\quad 36 - x =$ the larger number

and $\quad\quad 3(36 - x) + 4x = 123$

$$108 - 3x + 4x = 123$$
$$-3x + 4x = -108 + 123$$
$$x = 15, \text{ the smaller number}$$
$$36 - x = 21, \text{ the larger number}$$

[A]

1. The sum of two numbers is 45. If 3 times the larger is increased by 4 times the smaller, the sum is 155. Find the numbers. *20, 25*

2. The sum of two numbers is 47. What are the numbers if twice the larger added to 3 times the smaller makes a sum of 106? *12, 35*

3. The sum of two numbers is 250. If 4 times the smaller is added to the larger, the sum is 592. What are the numbers? *114, 136*

4. The sum of two numbers is 138. If 4 times the smaller is subtracted from 3 times the larger, the remainder is 99. Find the numbers. *45, 93*

5. Separate 1200 into two parts so that one part will be 800 less than 3 times the other. *500, 700*

6. A farmer sold 425 bushels of wheat and oats for $785.87. How many bushels of each did he sell if he received $4.10 a bushel for the wheat and $1.39 a bushel for the oats?
Wheat, 72 bu.; oats, 353 bu.

[B]

7. The second of three numbers exceeds the first by 13, and a third number exceeds the second by 11. What are the numbers if their sum is 91? *18, 31, 42*

Another way to conquer the error mentioned on page 193: Assume the student says in Ex. 1 "x and x − 45 are the parts." Have him check by adding: "Is x + (x − 45) = 45?" No. "Is x + (45 − x) = 45?" Yes. This mental check at the beginning of all such problems will help.

8. The sum of two numbers is 154. If the larger exceeds 4 times the smaller by 44, what are the numbers? *22, 132*

9. The larger of two numbers is 7 more than the smaller, and exceeds twice the smaller by 1. What are the numbers? *6, 13*

10. Separate 62 into two parts such that if the larger is added to 18 and the smaller to 32 the two results will be equal. *24, 38*

11. Separate 140 into two parts such that the sum of the larger and 100 will exceed twice the smaller by 36. *68, 72*

[C]

12. The sum of two numbers is 108. If twice their difference is subtracted from the smaller, the remainder is 9. What are the numbers? *45, 63*

13. Divide 76 into two parts such that if the smaller be taken from 43 and the larger from 61, the remainders are equal. *29, 47*

14. The sum of two numbers is 40. The difference of 5 times the larger and 4 times the smaller exceeds 7 times the smaller by 8. Find the numbers. *12, 28*

15. The sum of two numbers is 156. The excess of 4 times the larger over 4 times the smaller is 75. What are the numbers? $68\frac{5}{8}, 87\frac{3}{8}$

[A]

COIN PROBLEMS (Oral)

1. How many cents are there in 3 nickels? in 4 nickels? in x nickels? in $2x$ nickels? How do you find the number of cents in a given number of nickels? *15; 20; 5x; 10x; multiply the given number of nickels by 5.*

2. How many cents are there in 4 dimes? in 10 dimes? in x dimes? in d dimes? How do you find the number of cents in any number of dimes? *40; 100; 10x; 10d; multiply the given numbers of dimes by 10.*

3. How many cents are there in 3 quarters? in 5 quarters? in x quarters? in $5x$ quarters? How do you find the number of cents in a given number of quarters? *75; 125; 25x; 125x; multiply the given number of quarters by 25.*

4. How many cents are there in $3? in $3.15? in x dollars? in $4y$ dollars? *300; 315; 100x; 400y*

5. How many cents are there in 3 half-dollars? in x half-dollars? *150; 50x*

6. How many cents are there in $(x - 3)$ dimes? *10(x-3)*

7. How many cents are there in $(2x - 4)$ nickels? *5(2x-4)*

8. How many cents are there in $2(x + 3)$ quarters? *50(x+3)*

Help the student to choose the simplest way of representing the conditions of each problem. In Ex. 7, page 194, use "their sum is 91" in forming the equation. Occasionally assign an example to be worked in two ways, and ask which seems the better way for that particular example. Do not discourage, but praise, the student who says "I did that problem another way."

195

9. (1) The number of Harry's nickels. (2) The number of cents in d dimes. (3) The number of cents in (d + 12) nickels.

(4) 10d + 5(d+12), or 270 (5) No (6) No (7) Yes

9. Harry has 12 more nickels than dimes and $2.70 in all. If d = the number of Harry's dimes, what does $d + 12$ represent? What does $10\,d$ represent? What does $5(d + 12)$ represent? How many cents does Harry have? Does $d + d + 12 = 2.70$? Does $d + d + 12 = 270$? Does $10\,d + 5(d + 12) = 270$?

[A]

COIN PROBLEMS

1. A man has 2 more nickels than dimes. He has $1.15 in all. How many coins of each kind has he? 7 nickels, 7 dimes

Let	x = the number of dimes
Then	$x + 2$ = the number of nickels
and	$10\,x + 5(x + 2) = 115$

Why is x multiplied by 10? Why is $x + 2$ multiplied by 5? Why is 1.15 multiplied by 100? Complete the solution.

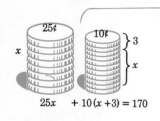

25¢   10¢ } 3
x } x

$25x + 10(x + 3) = 170$

2. A boy has 3 more dimes than quarters. The value of all his dimes and quarters is $1.70. How many coins of each kind has he? 7 dimes, 4 quarters

3. A boy has twice as many nickels as dimes and 5 more half-dollars than nickels. If the total value of the coins is $6.10, how many coins of each kind has he? 3 dimes, 6 nickels, 11 half-dollars

4. A girl has 2 more nickels than dimes, and 3 more quarters than nickels. She has $3.35 in all. How many coins of each kind has she? 7 nickels, 5 dimes, 10 quarters

5. A purse contains 21 coins, consisting of nickels and dimes. Find the number of coins of each kind if their total value is $1.65. 9 nickels, 12 dimes

6. A safe contains 160 coins worth $14.30. The coins are nickels and dimes. Find the number of coins of each kind. 34 nickels, 126 dimes

7. Carla bought 28 postage stamps. Some were ten-cent stamps, and the remainder were twenty-five-cent stamps. The total cost of the stamps was $3.25. How many stamps of each kind did she buy? 25 10-cent stamps, 3 25-cent stamps

8. The initiation fee for joining a travel club is $150 and the annual dues are $72 per family. How many years has a family belonged when it has spent $726 in initiation fees and annual dues? 8 yr.

In spite of the careful introduction on page 195, you may still have some willing to say in Ex. 5, for example, "x + (21 — x) = 1.65." Students seem too willing to "follow a pattern" rather than to *think* about problems.

EQUATIONS CONTAINING PARENTHESES

[B]

9. A sum of money amounting to $10.70 consists of nickels, dimes, and quarters. There are 10 more quarters than nickels, and the number of dimes is 2 less than 3 times the number of nickels. How many coins of each kind are there? *14 nickels, 40 dimes, 24 quarters*

10. Dick gave the grocer $3.60, consisting of half-dollars, dimes, and nickels. If there were 3 times as many nickels as half-dollars and 2 more nickels than dimes, how many coins of each kind were there? *12 nickels, 10 dimes, 4 half-dollars*

[A]

AGE PROBLEMS (Oral)

1. If John is 10 years old now, how old will he be in 6 years? in 7 years? in x years? in $2x$ years? *16 yr.; 17 yr.; $(10 + x)$ yr.; $(10 + 2x)$ yr.*

2. If Emily is x years old now, how old will she be in 4 years? in 7 years? How old was she 3 years ago? 10 years ago? → *2. $(x + 4)$ yr.; $(x + 7)$ yr.; $(x - 3)$ yr.; $(x - 10)$ yr.*

3. A is x years old. Represent B's age if B is 4 times as old as A. How old will A be in 3 years? *$4x$ yr.; $(x + 3)$ yr.*

4. Sarah is m years old. How old is a person 4 times as old? How old is a person 7 years older than Sarah? 6 years younger than Sarah? *$4m$ yr.; $(m + 7)$ yr.; $(m - 6)$ yr.*

5. A is x years old and C is 3 times as old as A. How old was each 8 years ago? *A, $(x - 8)$ yr.; C, $(3x - 8)$ yr.*

6. The difference in the ages of two men is $(m - 4)$ years. If the age of the older is $10 + m$, what is the age of the younger? *14 yr.*

7. John is 9 years old and Patricia is 1 year old. One year from now John's age will be how many times Patricia's age? Compare their ages 3 years from now. Was John's age ever 1000 times Patricia's age? Will her age ever equal his age? *Ans. at foot of page*

[A]

AGE PROBLEMS

Example. A man is 9 times as old as his son. In three years the father will be only 5 times as old as his son. What is the age of each?

Solution. It is usually advisable to make four preliminary statements in the solution of an age problem.

Let x = the number of years in the son's age now

Then $9x$ = the number of years in the father's age now

        $x + 3$ = the number of years in the son's age in 3 years

    $9x + 3$ = the number of years in the father's age in 3 years

(cont. on page 198)

197

7. (1) 5 times   (2) John will be 3 times as old as Patricia.
(3) Yes, when Patricia's age was 2.92 days. (4) No.

① It helps some students to insert here a sentence written in abbreviated words, thus: Father's fut. age is 5 × son's fut. age. Then this can be directly translated into mathematical symbols by substitution from the table. Emphasize that it is helpful to make a declarative sentence in which the verb

ALGEBRA, BOOK ONE   is a form of *to be* (translated by the equal sign).

Many pupils prefer to arrange these statements in box form, as follows:

PERSON	AGE NOW	AGE IN 3 YEARS
son	x	$x + 3$
father	$9x$	$9x + 3$

①

Then

$$9x + 3 = 5(x + 3)$$
$$9x + 3 = 5x + 15$$
$$9x - 5x = -3 + 15$$
$$4x = 12$$
$$x = 3, \text{ the son's age now}$$
$$9x = 27, \text{ the father's age now}$$

1. Henry is 10 years older than James. In 8 years twice Henry's age will equal 3 times James's age. How old is each at present? *J., 12 yr.*
H., 22 yr.

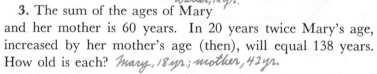

2. Walter is 8 years older than Ray. In 6 years 5 times Walter's age will equal 9 times Ray's age. How old is each at present? *Ray, 4 yr.; Walter, 12 yr.*

3. The sum of the ages of Mary and her mother is 60 years. In 20 years twice Mary's age, increased by her mother's age (then), will equal 138 years. How old is each? *Mary, 18 yr.; mother, 42 yr.*

4. Robert is 14 years old and his father is 38 years old. How many years ago was the father exactly seven times as old as Robert? *10*

5. Two years ago a man was 4 times as old as his son. Three years from now the father will be only three times as old as the son. How old is each at present? *Son, 12 yr.; father, 42 yr.*

SUGGESTION. Let x and $4x$ represent their ages 2 years ago.

6. A man was 30 years of age when his son was born. The father's age now exceeds three times the son's age by 6 years. How old is each at present? *Son, 12 yr.; father, 42 yr.*

7. Frank is 4 times as old as Carl. In 10 years he will be only twice as old as Carl is then. How old is each?
Carl, 5 yr.; Frank, 20 yr.

②

② Another device: Ask the student to guess the ages. In Ex. 7, guess 8 and 32. The ages in 10 years are then 18 and 42. This is wrong. Guess again. Then use x and 4x, and follow the arithmetic pattern used for the guessed numbers. In other words, it is easier for the student to think with definite arithmetic numbers as he analyzes the relationships.

EQUATIONS CONTAINING PARENTHESES

8. Elsie said to the class, "The sum of Mary Jane's age and my age is 29 years. Four times my age 10 years ago exceeded Mary Jane's age 5 years ago by 2 years. How old is each?"

Elsie, 13⅗ yr.; Mary Jane, 15⅘ yr.

Principle of Levers [A]   See ① above.

A <u>lever</u> is a stiff board or bar which is balanced upon a support called the <u>fulcrum</u>. The parts of the lever on either side of the fulcrum are called the lever arms. In the figure, AB is a lever, AC and BC are the lever arms, and C is the fulcrum. When equal weights are placed

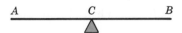

at the ends A and B, the lever will balance when C is the middle of the lever.

Most of you have played on a teeterboard, or seesaw, and know that two people will balance only when the heavier of the two sits nearer the fulcrum. Thus if Frank weighs 100 pounds and John weighs 40 pounds, they will balance on the teeterboard when Frank sits 4 feet from the fulcrum and John sits 10 feet from the fulcrum ($100 \times 4 = 40 \times 10$). It has been found by experiment that a lever (disregarding its weight) will balance when the left weight times its distance from the fulcrum equals the right weight times its distance from the fulcrum. The principle of the lever can be expressed by the formula $\underline{w_1 d_1 = w_2 d_2}$. ($w_1$ is read "w sub one" and w_2 is read "w sub two.") How do you read d_1 and d_2? In the figure below, $w_1 = 100$, $d_1 = 4$, $w_2 = 40$, and $d_2 = 10$.

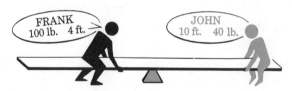

[A]

Disregard the weights of the levers in these problems:

1. Will this lever balance when $w_1 = 4$, $d_1 = 6$, $w_2 = 3$ $d_2 = 8$? *Yes*

ORAL EXERCISES

199

ALGEBRA, BOOK ONE

2. Will the lever balance if $w_1 = 7$, $d_1 = 7$, $w_2 = 8$, and $d_2 = 6$? If they do not balance, which end will rise? *no; w_2*

3. Will the lever balance when $w_1 = 60$, $w_2 = 40$, $d_1 = 5$, and $d_2 = 7\frac{1}{2}$? *Yes*

4. Find w_1 when $w_2 = 100$, $d_2 = 4$, $d_1 = 5$, and w_1 balances w_2. *80*

5. Find d_1 when $w_1 = 50$, $w_2 = 80$, $d_2 = 5$, and w_1 balances w_2. *8*

[A]

LEVER PROBLEMS

Make a sketch for each problem, and solve.

1. Jack sits 6 feet from the fulcrum and balances Carl who sits 8 feet from the fulcrum. If Jack weighs 70 pounds, how much does Carl weigh? *$52\frac{1}{2}$ lb.*

2. Mary, who weighs 135 pounds and sits 4 feet from the fulcrum, balances Imogen, who weighs 67.5 pounds. How far from the fulcrum is Imogen? *8 ft.*

3. A weight of 30 pounds balances a weight of 50 pounds on the other side of the fulcrum. If one weight is 2 feet farther from the fulcrum than the other, where is each weight placed?

4. A weight on the short arm of a lever is 27 pounds heavier than the weight it balances on the other arm. If the arms are 6 feet and 8 feet in length, find each weight. *short, 108 lb.; long, 81 lb.*

5. Two weights whose sum is 128 pounds are placed at the ends of a balanced lever. If one lever arm is 7 feet long and the other is 9 feet long, find the two weights. *72 lb.; 56 lb.*

6. Where is the fulcrum of a lever 93 inches long if a weight of 170 pounds at one end balances a weight of 54 pounds at the other end? *about 22.4 in. from 170 lb. weight*

7. When cutting a branch of a hedge a man applied a force of 40 pounds on the handles A and B of the shears shown here. If AF is 24 inches and the branch is $1\frac{1}{2}$ inches from F, what force was exerted on the limb? *640 lb.*

3. *30 lb., 5 ft. from fulcrum; 50 lb., 3 ft.*

[B]

8. Two girls weighing 80 pounds and 120 pounds respectively wish to sit at the ends of a 10-foot teeterboard and teeter. How far from the larger girl should the fulcrum be placed? *4 ft.*

9. A lever is 30 feet long. How far from each end must a fulcrum be placed so that a $7\frac{1}{2}$-pound weight at one end will balance a 6-pound weight at the other end? *(ans. at top of p.)*

10. A man who can exert a force of 170 pounds on a pinch bar is just able to move a freight car weighing 60,000 pounds. If the pinch bar is 5 feet long and the short end is $1\frac{1}{4}$ inches from the fulcrum, what force is applied to the wheel of the car?

7990 lb.

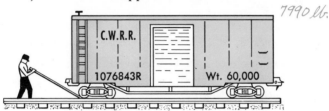

C.W.R.R.

1076843R   Wt. 60,000

11. Betty, Fern, and Bob, weighing 115 pounds, 120 pounds, and 140 pounds respectively, balance on a teeterboard. If Betty sits 6 feet from the fulcrum and Fern sits $4\frac{1}{2}$ feet from the fulcrum on the same side as Betty, how far from the fulcrum must Bob sit to balance the girls? *about 8.79 ft.*

12. A man places one end of a crowbar $5\frac{1}{2}$ feet long under a rock. At $4\frac{1}{2}$ inches from the rock he places a stone to act as a fulcrum. If he uses a force of 160 pounds on the other end of the crowbar, he just raises the rock. What weight of rock has he lifted? *2186⅔ lb.*

[A]

GEOMETRY PROBLEMS

1. The perimeter of a rectangle is 170 feet. If the length exceeds 5 times the width by one foot, what is its area? *994 sq. ft.*

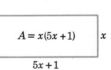

$$A = x(5x + 1) \quad x$$

$$5x + 1$$

2. One angle of a triangle exceeds another by 12° and the third angle exceeds twice the smallest by 48°. How large is each angle? *30°, 42°, 108°*

3. Five times one of two complementary angles equals 4 times the other. How large is each? *40°, 50°*

4. Two angles are supplementary. If 7 times the smaller is subtracted from 3 times the larger, the remainder is 190°. How large is each angle? *35°, 145°*

5. Find the size of the angle whose supplement is 3 times as large as its complement. *45°*

[B]

6. One angle of a triangle is 115° larger than another. The third angle exceeds twice the smallest by 9°. How large is each angle? *14°, 129°, 37°*

7. One angle of a triangle exceeds another by 2°. The sum of these two angles exceeds the third angle by 28°. How large is each angle? *51°, 53°, 76°*

8. How large is a rectangular field whose length exceeds twice the width by 10 rods and whose perimeter is 1 mile? *50 rd. × 110 rd.*

9. One angle of a triangle exceeds another by 23°. Twice the smallest angle exceeds the third angle by 11°. How large is each angle? *42°, 65°, 73°*

10. One angle of a triangle exceeds another by 30° and the third angle exceeds the smallest by 15°. How many degrees are there in each angle? *45°, 75°, 60°*

Checking Your Understanding of Chapter 7

Have you mastered this chapter? Be certain that you

Review if you need to.

7. Know how to spell and use the following words correctly:

The student who can do this lesson confidently has learned the important procedures of the chapter. This is good for an over-all review.

EQUATIONS CONTAINING PARENTHESES

CHAPTER
REVIEW

Solve:

1. $(x + 4) + 2 = 7$ *1*

3. $12 - 9(2 - m) = 30$ *4*

2. $2(6c - 5) - 2 = 36$ *4*

4. $9(1 + 2y) - 8y - 69 = 0$ *6*

5. $4(x - 20) + 2(x + 6) + 83 = 0$ *-2½*

6. $2(5c - 1) - 6 = 3(c - 7) - 14$ *-3 6/7*

7. $13x - (3x + 2) = 12x - (5x - 4)$ *2*

8. $6x + 7(4 + x) - 6(3 - 4x) = 0$ *-10/37*

9. Is $5(x + 2) = 10 + 5x$ a conditional or an identical equation? *Identical*

10. Is $5(x + 2) = 3x - 12$ a conditional or an identical equation? *Conditional*

11. Mary has $3.45 in quarters and dimes. She has 10 more dimes than quarters. How many of each coin has she? *17 dimes, 7 quarters*

12. Find two numbers if their sum is 45 and their difference is 13. *16, 29*

13. A man carries two packages weighing 28 and 42 pounds by fastening them to the ends of a 5-foot pole which he places over his shoulder. At what point does the pole rest on his shoulder when the packages balance? *2 ft. from 42-lb. wt.; 3 ft. from 28-lb. wt.*

14. The capacities of two trucks are 3 tons and 4 tons respectively. If the larger truck makes 3 more trips than the smaller, its total haul is 20 more tons than that of the smaller. How many trips does each truck make? *Smaller, 8; larger, 11*

15. The capacities of two trucks are 3 tons and 5 tons respectively. If the smaller truck makes 18 more trips than the larger, it can deliver 12 more tons of freight than the larger. How many trips does each truck make? *Smaller, 39 larger, 21*

16. A is 11 years old and B is 68 years old. In how many years will B be just 4 times as old as A? *8*

17. Mrs. West is 14 years younger than her aunt. If Mrs. West's age in years is as much below 60 as her aunt's age is over 40, how old is each? *Mrs. West, 43 yr.; aunt, 57 yr.*

18. The perimeter of a rectangle is 256 inches. How long are the sides if the length exceeds the width by 16 inches? *56 in. × 72 in.*

203

ALGEBRA, BOOK ONE

[A]

GENERAL REVIEW

In the following twelve sentences certain words have been omitted. On your paper write the words which best fit the blank spaces:

1. $x = 3$ is a __?__ of the equation $4x = 12$. *solution*

2. Since the equation $4x = 12$ has only one __?__, it is a } an } __?__ equation. *value of x; conditional*

3. $3(x + 1) = 3x + 3$ is called an __?__ equation because it has an infinite number of __?__. *identical; values of x*

4. The __?__ of 8 divided by 2 is 4. *quotient*

5. The __?__ of 8 and 2 is 16. *product*

6. The __?__ of 8 and 2 is 10. *sum*

7. The __?__ of 8 and 2 is 6. *difference*

8. 9 __?__ 7 by 2. *exceeds*

9. The __?__ of 8 over 6 is 2. *excess*

10. To find the number of cents in a given number of dimes, we __?__ the number of dimes by __?__. *multiply; 10*

11. The equation $w_1d_1 = w_2d_2$ expresses the principle of the __?__. *lever*

12. The supplement of an angle of 50° is an angle of __?__ degrees. *130*

13. Indicate the following by algebraic expressions:

a. m increased by twice x. *m + 2x*
b. The square of x decreased by the cube of y. *x² - y³*
c. Four more than twice the number x. *2x + 4*
d. Eight times the sum of x and $3y$. *8(x + 3y)*

If $a = 4$, $b = 5$, $c = -7$, and $d = 0$, find the value of

14. $a^3 - b^3$ *-61*

15. $abd - d$ *0*

16. $c^3 - ab$ *-363*

17. $2ab + d^2$ *40*

18. $bc - a^2$ *-51*

19. $-4b + 5c$ *-55*

20. $\dfrac{3d - 5a}{b - a}$ *-20*

21. $\dfrac{a^3 + b^2 + c}{5c - b - 2}$ *-82/42*

22. If $5x - 3y = 9$, find y when $x = 0$. *-3*

23. A newspaper costs 20 cents a copy. Write a formula for the number of copies that can be bought for x dollars. *n = 5x*

204

24. A basketball team has won 7 of its games and lost 3. If it wins all of its remaining games, it will have won $\frac{5}{6}$ of the games. How many games remain? (Hint. The number of games remaining is the number of games in all minus 10.) *8 games*

25. $C = 2\pi r$. Find C when $\pi = 3.14$ and $r = 16$. *100.48*

26. $A = \pi r^2$. Find A when $\pi = 3.14$ and $r = 12$. *452.16*

27. $C = \frac{5}{9}(F - 32)$. Find C when $F = 77$. *25*

28. A room is 30 feet long, 24 feet wide, and 11 feet high. How many cubic feet are there in the room? If 40 pupils are in the room, how much space is there in it for each pupil?

29. A cylindrical silo 40 feet high has an inside diameter of 8 feet 6 inches. What is its volume? $(V = \pi r^2 h,\ \pi = 3.14.)$ *7920 cu. ft.; 198 cu. ft.*

30. A spherical balloon has a diameter of 27 feet. What is the volume? $(V = \frac{4}{3}\pi r^3,\ \pi = 3.14.)$ *2268.65 cu. ft. 10,300.77 cu. ft.*

31. From $x^2 - 2x + 3$ take $2x^2 + 3x - 2$. *$-x^2 - 5x + 5$*

32. Take $1 - x$ from $3x^2 - 4x$. *$3x^2 - 3x - 1$*

33. From the sum of $2x^2 - 5x - 3$ and $x^3 - x^2 + 4$ take $2x^3 - x^2 + 8$. *$-x^3 + 2x^2 - 5x - 7$*

34. Write $xxxx$ using an exponent. *x^4*

35. Do as indicated:

a. $x^2 x^3$ *x^5*

b. $5a^2(-3b)$ *$-15a^2 b$*

c. $(4x)^3$ *$64x^3$*

d. $x^2(x^2 - 5x)$ *$x^4 - 5x^3$*

e. $7(x^2 + y^2)$ *$7x^2 + 7y^2$*

f. $(3x - 6) \div (-2)$ *$-\frac{1}{2}x + 3$*

g. $(-26x^2 y^3) \div (2x^2 y)$ *$-13y^2$*

h. $(15a^2 - 10a) \div 5a$ *$3a - 2$*

i. $(7x^3 - 14x^2 + 21x) \div (-7)$ *$-x^3 + 2x^2 - 3x$*

j. $(4x^4 - 12x^3 - 20x^2 - 2x) \div (2x)$ *$2x^3 - 6x^2 - 10x - 1$*

36. One number is 7 larger than another. The sum of the numbers is 43. What are they? *18, 25*

37. The sum of three numbers is 63. The second is 8 larger than the third and the first is 5 more than 5 times the third. What are the numbers? *$40\frac{5}{7}, 15\frac{4}{7}, 7\frac{4}{7}$*

38. One number is 3 less than another. Six times the larger decreased by 7 times the smaller is 7. What are the numbers? *11, 14*

205

43. $3a - 1\frac{1}{2}b - 9c$ 44. $-\frac{1}{2}a - \frac{1}{12}b - 4\frac{1}{4}c$

39. If 4 times the complement of a certain angle is subtracted from twice its supplement, the result is 104°. How large is the angle? $52°$

40. Ann is 4 years older than Jane. Eight years ago Ann was twice as old as Jane. How old are the girls?

Jane, 12 yr.; Ann, 16 yr.

[B]

$8a-2$ **41.** Simplify: $2a + [a - 3a] - \{6 - 5a\} - (-4 - 3a)$

42. Simplify:

$9-22x$ $(2x^2 - 3x + 9) - (-5x^2 - 3) + (-7x^2 - 19x - 3)$

see top of page **43.** Simplify: $4(\frac{1}{4}a - \frac{1}{2}b + 3c) - 6(-\frac{1}{3}a - \frac{1}{12}b + 3\frac{1}{2}c)$

44. Simplify: $\frac{1}{3}(3a - 4b - 6c) - \frac{1}{4}(6a - 5b + 9c)$

45. $A = 4\pi r^2$. Find A to the nearest tenth if $\pi = 3.1416$ and $r = 4.63$. 269.4

46. $l = a + (n - 1)d$. Find l if $a = 5$, $d = -2$, and $n = 24$. -41

47. $S = \frac{n}{2}(a + l)$. Find S if $a = 5$, $n = 24$, and $l =$ the value found in Exercise 46. -432

Solve:

48. $x + 1.2x = 560$ 254.54

49. $.2y - 19 = 10 - .3y$ 58

50. $x - 4944.6 + .05x = 0$ $4709.14\cdots$

51. $(2x + 3) - (x - 6) + (3x + 7) = 18$ $\frac{1}{2}$

52. $10x - [.2x - 6] = 8x + [2.4x - 9]$ 25

53. In 7 years William will be 3 times as old as Helen. What are their present ages, if William's age 7 years ago was 6 times Helen's age 8 years ago? *Helen, $18\frac{1}{3}$ yr.; William, 69 yr.*

54. If the supplement of a certain angle is subtracted from 9 times its complement and the remainder is multiplied by 2, the product is 15° less than the angle itself. How many degrees are there in the angle? $75°$

55. There are 3 consecutive integers such that the sum of the first, twice the second, and 3 times the third is 98. What are the integers? (Represent the integers by x, $x + 1$, and $x + 2$.) $15, 16, 17$

206

56. There are 4 consecutive odd integers whose sum exceeds twice the largest by 102. Find the integers. (Represent the integers by x, $x + 2$, $x + 4$, and $x + 6$.) *51, 53, 55, 57*

57. In an election there were 5760 votes cast for Brown, Jones, and Smith. Jones received 5 times as many votes as Brown. If Smith had received 1320 more votes and Jones had received 1460 less votes, Smith would have received twice as many votes as Jones. How many votes did each receive?

Brown, 625; Jones, 3125; Smith, 2010 [Test A]

Part I. Equations

Solve:

1. $3(x + 2) = 15$ *3*

2. $3y - 4(y + 2) = 5$ *-13*

3. $6c + 2(c + 1) = -14$ *-2*

4. $4b - 1 = 2(b + 3)$ *3½*

5. $x - 7 - (x + 2) = 3$ *x-3*

6. $m - 3(m + 1) = -7$ *2*

7. Is $2(x - 1) = 2x - 2$ a conditional or an identical equation? *Identical*

8. Prove that -3 is a root of $2(x - 1) - (x + 1) = -6$.

Part II. Problems

1. One number is 5 less than another. If 4 times the smaller is subtracted from 3 times the larger, the remainder is 17. Find the numbers. *3, -2*

2. Write in three ways in equation form the fact that x exceeds y by 4. *x = y+4, x-y=4, x-4=y*

3. If n stands for the number of degrees in one of two complementary angles, what will represent the number of degrees in the other angle? *90 - n*

4. The sum of two numbers is 15. If 4 times the smaller is added to 3 times the larger, the sum is 49. Find the numbers. *4, 11*

5. A is 3 times as old as B. Five years ago A was 8 times as old as B. How old is each now? *B, 7 yr.; A, 21 yr.*

6. A purse contains 4 more dimes than nickels. Find the number of nickels and the number of dimes if their value is $1.60. *8 nickels, 12 dimes*

207

7. Find the number of degrees in ∠ A and in ∠ B.

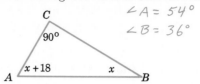

$\angle A = 54°$

$\angle B = 36°$

8. Tom weighs 38 more pounds than Jack. They find that they balance on a teeterboard when Tom's distance from the fulcrum is 6 feet and Jack's distance from the fulcrum is 9 feet. What is the weight of each? *Tom, 114 lb.; Jack, 76 lb.*

[Test B]

Part I. Equations

Solve:

1. $10 - (x - 4) = 1$ *13*

2. $3(c + 2) - c = 4$ *-1*

3. $2(x + 1) - 3(2x + 3) = 3x$ *-1*

4. $4(v + 2) - 6(y + 3) = y - 4$ *-2*

5. $2(c - 3) = 8 - 3(c - 2)$ *4*

6. $4(x + 9) - 18x = 4(1 - 2x) - 5(2 - 3x)$ *2*

7. Complete: An equation that is true for only one value of the letter is called $\left.\begin{array}{l} a \\ an \end{array}\right\}$ __?__ equation. *conditional*

Part II. Problems

1. The sum of two numbers is 13. If s represents the smaller number, represent the larger number in terms of s. *13-s*

2. Jane's age exceeds Betty's by 12 years. Eight years ago Jane was twice as old as Betty. How old is each? *Jane, 32 yr.; Betty, 20 yr.*

3. The value of 40 coins consisting of dimes and quarters is $6.70. Find the number of coins of each kind. *18 quarters, 22 dimes*

4. The length of a tennis court for singles is 3 feet less than 3 times its width. Find the dimensions of the court if its perimeter is 210 feet. *27 ft. × 78 ft.*

5. A teeterboard 20 feet long is balanced at its middle. One child weighs 40 pounds and another weighs 56 pounds. When the children are balanced on the teeterboard, one child is 2 feet nearer the fulcrum than the other. How far is each from the fulcrum? *56 lb., 5 ft.; 40 lb., 7 ft.*

EQUATIONS CONTAINING PARENTHESES

Time, 40 Minutes. 19–20 correct, excellent; 16–18, good; 13–15, fair.

CUMULATIVE TEST (Chapters 1–7)

1. Simplify $8\,b - 5\,b^2 + 2\,b - 3\,b^2 - 10$. $-8b^2 + 10b - 10$

2. Subtract $9\,a - 2\,b + 5\,c$ from $8\,a - b - 2\,c$. $-a + b - 7c$

3. Divide $-8\,x^8 y^4$ by $-4\,x^4 y^2$. $2x^4 y^2$

4. Multiply $-6\,a^6 b^4$ by $2\,a^2 b^4$. $-12a^8 b^8$

5. If $x = -5$ and $y = -5$, find the value of

a. xy^2 -125 **c.** $-x^3$ 125 **e.** $\dfrac{x^2}{xy}$ 1

b. $4\,xy$ 100 **d.** $4\,x - 2\,y$ -10

6. Solve $3\,x - 2 - 4\,x = 0$. -2

7. Add $x^2 - x + 3$, $-3\,x^2 + 6\,x - 5$, and $x^2 + x - 4$. $-x^2 + 6x - 6$

8. Divide $28\,x^7 - 40\,x^5 + 24\,x^3 - 4\,x$ by $-4\,x$. $-7x^6 + 10x^4 - 6x^2 + 1$

9. Multiply: $-3\,y^2(2\,y^3 - 3\,y^2 + 6\,y)$. $-6y^5 + 9y^4 - 18y^3$

10. If $x = -5$ and $y = 10$, find the value of $2\,x^3 - xy - y^2$. -300

11. Find the area of a triangle if its height is 10.6 inches and its base is 6.4 inches. 33.92 sq. in.

12. One morning the temperature was $-14°$ Fahrenheit. What was the temperature centigrade? $C = \frac{5}{9}(F - 32)$. $-25\frac{5}{9}°$, or $-25.6°$

13. Write a formula for the total surface, T, of a rectangular solid a inches long, b inches wide, and c inches high. (See diagram.) $T = 2ab + 2ac + 2bc$

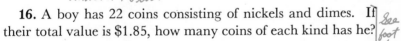

14. $x = 10 - 4\,y$. If y increases, how does x change? Decreases

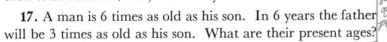

15. The perimeter of a rectangle is 120 inches. Find its width and length if the length is 4 times the width. 12 in. $\times 48$ in.

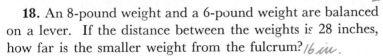

16. A boy has 22 coins consisting of nickels and dimes. If their total value is $1.85, how many coins of each kind has he? See foot of page

17. A man is 6 times as old as his son. In 6 years the father will be 3 times as old as his son. What are their present ages? page

18. An 8-pound weight and a 6-pound weight are balanced on a lever. If the distance between the weights is 28 inches, how far is the smaller weight from the fulcrum? 16 in.

19. If 8% of a man's income is $192, what is his income?

20. Solve: $3(x - 6) - (x - 2) = 0$. 8 4200

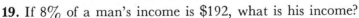

16. 7 nickels, 15 dimes
17. Son, 4 yr.; father, 24 yr.

MATHEMATICS *IN JET ENGINE PRODUCTION*

Courtesy Allison Division, General Motors Corporation

$(x \cdot a)^2 + (\quad) \cdot r2$
$x \cdot y \tan \Theta \quad \tan 30°$
$\quad 1997$

DRAFTING

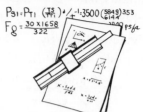

$P_{S1} = P_{T1} \left(\frac{TS}{TT}\right)^{?} + 3500 \left(\frac{5849}{6144}\right) 353$
$Fg = \frac{30 \times 1658}{322} \quad 1949 \, psfa$

ENGINEERING

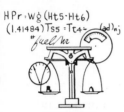

$HPr = W\dot{g}(Ht5 - Ht6)$
$(1.41484) Tss = Tt4 \div (ad)_{nj}$
$\#fuel/hr$

TESTING

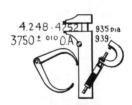

$4.248 - 4.252 \quad 935 \text{ DIA}$
$3750 \pm {}^{010} O.A \quad 939$

INSPECTION

$\cot \tfrac{1}{2}° \text{ or } \cot 10°$
$\tan (90° - 10°) = \tan$
$80° = 5.6717$

TOOL MAKING

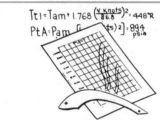

$Tt1 = Tam + 1.768 \left(\frac{V \text{ knots}}{86.8}\right)^2 = 448°R$
$PtA = Pam \, [\quad ts)^2] = .894 \, psia$

PERFORMANCE CALCULATIONS

$Hours \times Rate$ Overtime Prem.
withold $\quad$ VCA = Net Pay

PAY ROLL

18 pcs. $\quad$ r hr.
drill pre

PRODUCTION

$5\tfrac{1}{2}'' O.D \times 3'' I.D \times 2''$
Finish $4\tfrac{1}{2}'' O.D$

MATERIAL CONTROL

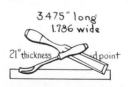

3.475" long
1.786 wide
21° thickness $\quad$ dpoint

PATTERN MAKING

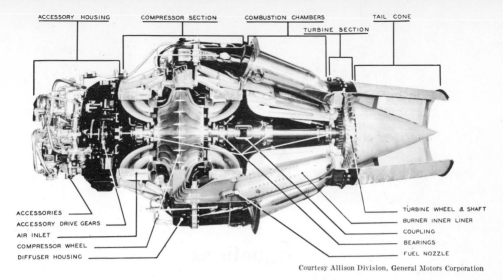

ACCESSORY HOUSING · COMPRESSOR SECTION · COMBUSTION CHAMBERS · TAIL CONE

TURBINE SECTION

ACCESSORIES
ACCESSORY DRIVE GEARS
AIR INLET
COMPRESSOR WHEEL
DIFFUSER HOUSING

TURBINE WHEEL & SHAFT
BURNER INNER LINER
COUPLING
BEARINGS
FUEL NOZZLE

Courtesy Allison Division, General Motors Corporation

HOW A JET ENGINE WORKS

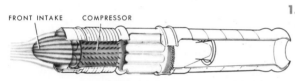

FRONT INTAKE   COMPRESSOR

1. Air (almost three tons per minute) is sucked into the engine through the front intake. A compressor, acting like a large fan, compresses the air to more than five times atmospheric pressure and forces it through ducts to combustion chambers.

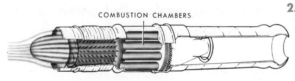

COMBUSTION CHAMBERS

2. In the combustion chambers, fuel is sprayed into the compressed air and ignited. The burning gases expand rapidly and blast their way out the rear of the engine. It is this jet blast that gives the engine and airplane their enormous forward push. This forward push is due to the change in velocity of the vaporized fuel and the air that passes through the engine. The thrust can be measured by applying the formula $F = \dfrac{W_s v^2}{2g}$.

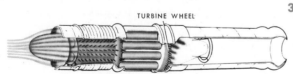

TURBINE WHEEL

3. As the hot gases rush out of the engine, they pass through a fan-like set of blades, the turbine wheel. These blades react like a windmill and turn the main engine shaft. This turning power is transmitted to the compressor, which packs in more fresh air.

Courtesy General Electric Company

8

Equations Containing Fractions

Suggested Time Schedule
Minimum   10 days
Maximum   11 days

In this chapter you will get help in handling equations that contain common fractions or decimal fractions.

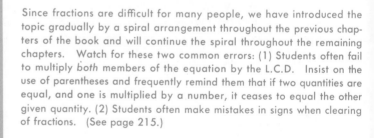

Since fractions are difficult for many people, we have introduced the topic gradually by a spiral arrangement throughout the previous chapters of the book and will continue the spiral throughout the remaining chapters. Watch for these two common errors: (1) Students often fail to multiply *both* members of the equation by the L.C.D. Insist on the use of parentheses and frequently remind them that if two quantities are equal, and one is multiplied by a number, it ceases to equal the other given quantity. (2) Students often make mistakes in signs when clearing of fractions. (See page 215.)

Clearing Equations of Fractions [A]

In this chapter you will make a more thorough study of equations which contain fractions. In most cases equations containing fractions can be solved more easily by changing them into equivalent equations which do not contain fractions. When you change an equation with fractions into one without fractions, you are clearing the equation of fractions. Study the following examples:

Example 1. Solve $\dfrac{x}{3} - \dfrac{x}{5} = 6$.

Solution. The smallest number that can be exactly divided by 3 and 5 is 15. If we multiply each member of the equation by 15, there will be no fractions left in the equation. When the left member of the equation is multiplied by 15, each term of the equation must be multiplied by 15. The solution is set down as follows:

$$\frac{x}{3} - \frac{x}{5} = 6$$

Some teachers prefer this form for Step 1:

$$15\left(\frac{x}{3} - \frac{x}{5}\right) = 15(6).$$

M_{15} $15\left(\dfrac{x}{3}\right) - 15\left(\dfrac{x}{5}\right) = 15(6)$

Then the next step applies the distributive law.

Then $5x - 3x = 90$

$$2x = 90$$

D_2 $x = 45$

PROOF. Does $\dfrac{45}{3} - \dfrac{45}{5} = 6$?

Does $15 - 9 = 6$? Yes.

The parentheses are used to denote multiplication. They make the solutions more easily understood.

Example 2. Solve $\dfrac{1}{3} + \dfrac{5x}{6} = \dfrac{7}{12}$.

Solution. The smallest number which can be exactly divided by the denominators 3, 6, and 12 is 12. It is called the lowest common denominator, abbreviated L.C.D. The solution should be written as follows:

$$\frac{1}{3} + \frac{5x}{6} = \frac{7}{12}$$

M_{12} $12\left(\dfrac{1}{3}\right) + 12\left(\dfrac{5x}{6}\right) = 12\left(\dfrac{7}{12}\right)$

$$4 + 10x = 7$$

$$10x = 7 - 4$$

$$10x = 3$$

D_{10} $x = \dfrac{3}{10}$

ALGEBRA, BOOK ONE

You should now learn the steps in solving simple equations containing fractions and parentheses.

1. If an equation contains one or more fractions, clear it of fractions by multiplying each of its members by the lowest common denominator.
2. Remove parentheses.
3. Simplify each member.
4. Change the equation so that the terms containing the variable are in one member and the other terms are in the other member.
5. Simplify each member.
6. Divide each member by the coefficient of the variable.
7. Prove the solution correct by substituting the root in the original equation.   (See ① above.)

   Note. In some cases it is advisable to remove parentheses in an equation before clearing it of fractions.

[A]

EXERCISES   Solve and prove:

1. $\dfrac{x}{4} = \dfrac{1}{3}$ $1\frac{1}{3}$

2. $\dfrac{3}{4} x = \dfrac{2}{3}$ $\frac{8}{9}$

3. $\dfrac{5\,m}{7} = \dfrac{1}{14}$ $\frac{1}{10}$

4. $3\frac{1}{7} r = 44$ 14

5. $\dfrac{2\,y}{5} - 7 = y - 11\frac{2}{3}$

6. $p - \dfrac{5}{6} p = 3$ 18

7. $\dfrac{k}{3} - \dfrac{k}{4} = 8$ 96

8. $\dfrac{x}{3} + \dfrac{2\,x}{5} = \dfrac{11}{15}$ 1

9. $\dfrac{2\,c}{9} - 4 = \dfrac{c}{6}$ 72

10. $\dfrac{b}{3} + \dfrac{b}{2} = 5$ 6

11. $\dfrac{x}{3} + \dfrac{x}{4} = 1$ $1\frac{5}{7}$

12. $\dfrac{m}{2} + 1 = \dfrac{2\,m}{5}$ -10

13. $\dfrac{5\,x}{18} = \dfrac{x}{6} - 4$ -36

14. $\dfrac{2\,x}{7} - \dfrac{x}{3} = 4$ -84

15. $\dfrac{3\,x}{4} - 2 = \dfrac{x}{5}$ $3\frac{7}{11}$

16. $\dfrac{7\,x}{6} - \dfrac{5}{3} = \dfrac{3\,x}{4}$ 4

17. $\dfrac{3\,h}{4} = \dfrac{2\,h}{5} + \dfrac{7}{20}$ 1

18. $\dfrac{2\,x}{3} + \dfrac{5\,x}{4} = \dfrac{23}{24}$ $\frac{1}{2}$

19. $y = 14 + \dfrac{y}{3} + \dfrac{y}{5}$ 30

20. $\dfrac{2\,c}{.9} - 1 = \dfrac{c}{6}$ 18

21. $\dfrac{3\,c}{7} + \dfrac{5\,c}{3} = 44$ 21

214

EQUATIONS CONTAINING FRACTIONS

Example 3. Solve and prove: $\dfrac{2x}{3} + \dfrac{3}{4}(28 - x) = 20$.

Solution. The L.C.D. is 12.

M_{12} $\qquad \overset{4}{\cancel{12}}\left(\dfrac{2x}{\cancel{3}}\right) + \overset{3}{\cancel{12}}\left(\dfrac{3}{\cancel{4}}\right)(28 - x) = 12(20)$

$$8x + 9(28 - x) = 240$$
$$8x + 252 - 9x = 240$$
$$8x - 9x = 240 - 252$$
$$-x = -12$$
$$x = 12$$

PROOF. Does $\quad \tfrac{2}{3}(12) + \tfrac{3}{4}(28 - 12) = 20?$

Does $\qquad\qquad 8 + 12 = 20?$ Yes.

[A]

EXERCISES

1. $\tfrac{1}{5}(x - 2) = 4$ 22

2. $\dfrac{c+6}{7} = \dfrac{c-3}{8}$ -69

3. $\tfrac{1}{3}(2x - 1) = \tfrac{1}{7}(11 - 8x)$ $1\tfrac{1}{19}$

4. $\dfrac{h+1}{2} = 1 - \dfrac{1-2h}{5}$ 3

5. $\tfrac{1}{4}(3c + 5) - \tfrac{1}{2}(2c + 3) = \tfrac{1}{2}$ -3

6. $\tfrac{2}{3}x + \tfrac{3}{4}(35 - x) = 25$ 15

7. $\tfrac{1}{6}y - \tfrac{1}{8}(20 - y) = 1$ 12

8. $\dfrac{c}{6} - \dfrac{2}{9}(90 - c) = 1$ 54

9. $\tfrac{1}{2}(x - 7) = \tfrac{1}{5}(7 - x)$ 7

10. $\dfrac{x - 4}{5} - \dfrac{3(x - 2)}{10} = 0$ -2

CAUTION. $10 \times 0 = 0$

11. $\dfrac{c-4}{9} - \dfrac{c+2}{6} = \tfrac{1}{3}c$ -2

12. $x - 2 = \dfrac{5x}{3} - \dfrac{2(x-1)}{9}$ -5

13. $\tfrac{1}{2}(y + 1) - \tfrac{1}{3}(y - 1) = \tfrac{7}{3}$ 9

14. $\dfrac{3x - 1}{6} - \dfrac{x - 3}{4} = \dfrac{4}{3}$ 3

15. $12 - \dfrac{2k + 9}{5} = \dfrac{k + 3}{7}$ 18

16. $\dfrac{x + 4}{3} - \dfrac{x + 12}{6} = \dfrac{x - 2}{12}$ 6

17. $2k - \dfrac{11 + k}{2} = \dfrac{19 + k}{3}$ $10\tfrac{1}{7}$

18. $\dfrac{3c - 3}{4} - \dfrac{3}{2} + \dfrac{5c - 7}{4} = 0$ 2

19. $\dfrac{2x + 3}{5} - \dfrac{x - 3}{3} = 2$ 6

20. $\dfrac{10x + 7}{8} = \dfrac{11x + 4}{2} - \dfrac{5x}{4}$ $-\tfrac{3}{8}$

[B]

21. $\dfrac{x - 12}{10} - \dfrac{3(2x + 1)}{3} + \dfrac{3(x - 2)}{2} = 0$ -13

22. $\dfrac{x + 6}{7} - \dfrac{x + 7}{8} + \dfrac{x + 8}{9} = 1$. The L.C.D. $= 7 \times 8 \times 9$. 1

23. $\dfrac{1}{4}x + 20 = \dfrac{x}{8} - \dfrac{5}{6}x + \dfrac{1}{2}x + 7$ $-28\tfrac{4}{11}$

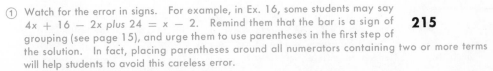

① Watch for the error in signs. For example, in Ex. 16, some students may say $4x + 16 - 2x$ plus $24 = x - 2$. Remind them that the bar is a sign of grouping (see page 15), and urge them to use parentheses in the first step of the solution. In fact, placing parentheses around all numerators containing two or more terms will help students to avoid this careless error.

215

24. $5y + \frac{1}{7}(3y - 4) + \frac{1}{3}(5y + 3) = 43$ 6

25. $\dfrac{x - 10}{5} + \dfrac{x - 8}{6} - \dfrac{x - 5}{10} = \dfrac{x - 11}{3} - \dfrac{5}{2}$ 50

26. $\dfrac{2x - 1}{3} - \dfrac{x + 10}{6} = \dfrac{10 - 3x}{5} - \dfrac{x + 40}{2}$ −10

Equations containing Decimal Fractions [A]

Equations containing decimal fractions are often solved more easily by clearing them of decimals.

A decimal fraction is a fraction whose denominator, being a power of 10, is not written but is indicated by a decimal point. Thus .3 means $\frac{3}{10}$; 1.23 means $1\frac{23}{100}$ or $\frac{123}{100}$; and 4.162 means $4\frac{162}{1000}$ or $\frac{4162}{1000}$. Notice that there are as many digits to the right of the decimal point in the decimal as there are zeros in the denominator of the equal common fraction.

Example 1. Solve $.2x = 50$.

Solution. The L.C.D. is 10.

$$.2x = 50$$
M_{10} $\qquad 2x = 500$
D_2 $\qquad x = 250$

PROOF. Does $.2(250) = 50$?
Does $\qquad 50 = 50$? Yes.

Example 2. Solve $.3(2x - 4) - .025(x - 3) = 3.475$.

Solution. Either the parentheses may be removed and the equation then cleared of decimals, or the equation may be cleared of decimals and the parentheses then removed. This example will be solved by the second method.
The L.C.D. is 1000.

$$.3(2x - 4) - .025(x - 3) = 3.475$$
$M_{1000},\quad 1000(.3)(2x - 4) - 1000(.025)(x - 3) = 1000(3.475)$
$$300(2x - 4) - 25(x - 3) = 3475$$
$$600x - 1200 - 25x + 75 = 3475$$
$$575x - 1125 = 3475$$
$$575x = 4600$$
$$x = 8$$

PROOF. Does $.3(16 - 4) - .025(8 - 3) = 3.475$?
Does $\qquad 3.6 - .125 = 3.475$? Yes.

Show students that it is not necessary to clear of decimals in the way shown. In Example 1, both sides of the equation may be divided by .2; and in Example 2 a partial clearing of fractions by multiplying by 10 may be preferred. Encourage variety of methods.

[A]

Solve and prove:

1. $.3 x = 12$ *40* **6.** $.003 k = 1.5$ *500* **11.** $1.04 y = 52$ *50*

2. $.05 y = 6$ *120* **7.** $2.3 b = 11.5$ *5* **12.** $1.20 p = 9$ *7.5*

3. $.08 p = 16$ *200* **8.** $.004 t = .02$ *5* **13.** $.4 r = 32$ *80*

4. $1.25 h = 12$ *9.6* **9.** $.08 y = 12$ *150* **14.** $.625 h = 10$ *16*

5. $.2 r = 4$ *20* **10.** $.012 m = .06$ *5* **15.** $.375 x = 24$ *64*

20.969+

16. $4 x - 2.3 = 3 x - .5$ *1.8* **21.** $3.47 x - 8 - 1.2 x = 39.6$

17. $7 y - 1.7 = 2 y - 4.2$ *-0.5* **22.** $1.2 y - 17 = 8 + .7 y$ *50*

18. $.4 x + 5 = 9$ *10* **23.** $p + .12 p = 280$ *250*

19. $.09 y - 10.8 = - 11$ $-2\frac{2}{9}$ **24.** $c + .04 c = 228.80$ *220*

20. $5.2 x - .68 = 1.8$ *0.4769+* **25.** $1.3 x + 604 = 2.7 x + 142$ *330*

[B]

In solving some equations it is advisable to remove parentheses before clearing the equation of decimals. Use your own judgment when solving the following equations.

26. $2.17 x + (1.5 x - 3) = 2.14 x + 2.4$ *3.529+*

27. $0.006 x + 0.296 = (0.15 x - 0.07 x)$ *4*

28. $1.25 x - .25(2 x + 1) = 1.25$ *2*

29. $x = 4.25 - .25(2 x - 1)$ *3*

30. $0.25 x = .3125 - 1.25(x + 1)$ *-0.6253*

31. $3(0.4 y + 0.5) + 4(0.5 y - 0.15) = 26$ *7.843+*

32. $0.5(c + 0.2) + 0.07 - (0.3 - c) = 0.02$ *0.1*

Meaning of the Word "of" [A]

Many pupils are unable to solve written problems because they do not *understand* the problems. The failure in understanding a problem is often due to not knowing the meaning of a word. One word which is much used in mathematics and should not be misunderstood is *of*. The word *of* very often means "times" and you should learn when its meaning is "times." For example, "$\frac{1}{3}$ of x" means "$\frac{1}{3}$ times x," and can be written $\frac{1}{3} \times x$, $\frac{1}{3} \cdot x$, $\frac{1}{3} x$, or $\frac{x}{3}$.

217

Similarly, "$\frac{2}{5}$ of c" can be written $\frac{2}{5} \times c$, $\frac{2}{5} \cdot c$, $\frac{2}{5} c$, or $\frac{2c}{5}$. Likewise,

"$\frac{2}{5}$ of the sum of x and 3" can be written $\frac{2}{5}(x+3)$ or $\frac{2(x+3)}{5}$.

The following exercises will assist you in solving some problems that will appear later.

EXERCISES *note: Other forms are acceptable for Ex.1-10.* [A]

Express the following, using algebraic symbols:

$\frac{2}{3}m$ **1.** $\frac{2}{3}$ of m. $a+b$ **6.** The sum of a and b.

$\frac{3}{4}k$ **2.** Three fourths of k. $m-5$ **7.** The sum of m and -5.

$\frac{1}{2}c$ **3.** One half of c. $\frac{1}{2}(x+y)$ **8.** One half the sum of x and y.

$\frac{2}{3}h$ **4.** Two thirds of h. $\frac{4}{5}(2x-3)$ **9.** Four fifths of $(2x-3)$.

$\frac{4}{7}y$ **5.** Four sevenths of y. $p+\frac{2}{3}q$ **10.** The sum of p and $\frac{2}{3}q$.

11. Is $\frac{3}{4}x+5$ the sum of $\frac{3}{4}x$ and 5, or is it $\frac{3}{4}$ the sum of x and 5? *The sum of $\frac{3}{4}x$ and 5*

12. Is $\frac{1}{4}(m+7)$ the sum of $\frac{1}{4}m$ and 7, or is it $\frac{1}{4}$ the sum of m and 7? *$\frac{1}{4}$ the sum of m and 7*

13. What is the difference in meaning between $\frac{2}{5}x+15$ and $\frac{2}{5}(x+15)$? *$\frac{2}{5}x+15$ is the sum of $\frac{2}{5}x$ and 15, while $\frac{2}{5}(x+15)$ is $\frac{2}{5}$ the sum of x and 15.*

Let x stand for the unknown number in exercises 14–17 and express

14. $\frac{5}{7}$ of the sum of a number and -14. *$\frac{5}{7}(x-14)$*

15. The sum of $\frac{5}{7}$ of a certain number and -14. *$\frac{5}{7}x-14$*

16. Six added to $\frac{3}{8}$ of a number. *$\frac{3}{8}x+6$*

17. Four added to one ninth of a certain number. *$\frac{1}{9}x+4$*

18. If x stands for the smaller of two numbers and their sum is 10, what will stand for the other? *$10-x$*

19. The sum of two numbers is 20 and the larger one is y. What is the smaller? What is $\frac{3}{5}$ of the smaller? *$20-y$; $\frac{3}{5}(20-y)$*

20. John is x years old. Frank is 4 years older than John. How old is Frank? What is $\frac{2}{3}$ of John's age? What is $\frac{3}{4}$ of Frank's age? What was John's age 7 years ago? What was $\frac{3}{4}$ of John's age 7 years ago? *$(x+4)$ yr.; $\frac{2}{3}x$; $\frac{3}{4}(x+4)$; $(x-7)$ yr.; $\frac{3}{4}(x-7)$*

This begins another round of word problems, with emphasis on those involving fractions. Point out in this first set that there is more than one way of expressing these phrases. For example, Ex. 2 may be written $\frac{3}{4}k$ or $\frac{3k}{4}$, and Ex. 8 may be written $\frac{1}{2}(x+y)$ or $\frac{x+y}{2}$ or even $.5(x+y)$. Recognizing these equivalent epressions is necessary.

21. The perimeter of a rectangle is 40 feet. What is its length if its width is w? What is $\frac{5}{6}$ of its width? What is $\frac{7}{8}$ of its length? $20-w; \frac{5}{6}w; \frac{7}{8}(20-w)$

22. A board 24 feet long had x feet cut off. What is $\frac{2}{3}$ of the part that is left? $\frac{2}{3}(24-x)$

Form equations, letting x stand for the number:

23. Two thirds of a number is 60. $\frac{2}{3}x = 60$

24. Three fourths of a number is 45. $\frac{3}{4}x = 45$

25. Seven eighths of a number, increased by six, equals 20. $\frac{7}{8}x+6=20$

26. The sum of one seventh of a number and one fourth of the number is 10. $\frac{1}{7}x+\frac{1}{4}x = 10$

27. If $\frac{1}{6}$ of a number is subtracted from $\frac{1}{4}$ of it, the remainder is 1. $\frac{1}{4}x - \frac{1}{6}x = 1$

[A]

PROBLEMS

1. One half of a number is 15. Find the number. 30

2. The difference between one third of a number and one fourth of it is 4. Find the number. 48

3. The width of a rectangle is $\frac{3}{4}$ of its length, and the perimeter is 210 feet. What are the length and width of it? $60 ft. \times 45 ft.$

4. The perimeter of a rectangle is 234 inches and the width is $\frac{4}{5}$ of the length. Find the dimensions of the rectangle. $65 in. \times 52 in.$

5. The sum of two numbers is 60. What are the numbers if the sum of $\frac{3}{5}$ of the smaller and $\frac{2}{7}$ of the larger is 25? $25,35$

Let $\qquad\qquad s =$ the smaller
Then $\qquad\quad 60 - s =$ the larger
$$\frac{3s}{5}+\frac{2}{7}(60-s)=25$$
Complete the solution.

6. The difference of two numbers is 9. If $\frac{2}{3}$ of the larger is added to $\frac{1}{6}$ of the smaller, the sum is 21. What are the numbers? $18,27$

7. One of two complementary angles is $\frac{4}{5}$ as large as the other. How large is each angle? $40°,50°$

8. One of two supplementary angles is one fourth as large as the other. How large is each? $36°, 144°$

Note that these problems cover the same topics as in Chapter 7. Therefore the student should be more independent in his work. Be sure he is checking his solutions correctly. Students have a tendency to substitute an answer in the equation, which is no check for a word problem, of course. Perhaps you will be lucky enough to bring this out dramatically some day when a student says, "But I checked it!" and you point out that he has correctly solved an *incorrect* equation.

219

9. Two angles are supplementary. If $\frac{2}{9}$ of the smaller is added to $\frac{3}{4}$ of the larger, the sum is 116°. How large is each angle? *36°, 144°*

10. If $\frac{1}{6}$ of an angle is subtracted from $\frac{1}{4}$ of its complement, the remainder is 5°. How large is each angle? *42°, 48°*

11. Find the angle such that the sum of one fourth of its complement and one seventh of its supplement is 27°. *54°*

12. A girl, after having spent one fifth of her allowance for candy and one half of what was left for flowers, had 72 cents remaining. How many cents did she have at first? *180*

13. The numerator of a certain fraction is 3 less than the denominator. If 1 is added to the numerator, the value of the fraction becomes $\frac{3}{4}$. Find the fraction. *$\frac{5}{8}$*

SUGGESTION. Let $\quad x =$ the denominator
Then $\qquad x - 3 =$ the numerator
and $\qquad \dfrac{x-3}{x} =$ the fraction

$$\frac{x-2}{x} = \frac{3}{4}$$

The L.C.D. is $4\,x$.

14. John's age now is $\frac{2}{5}$ of what it will be in 15 years. How old is he? *10 yr.*

15. Mary's age now is $\frac{2}{3}$ of what it will be in 6 years. How old is she now? *12 yr.*

16. Dick is one third as old as his father. In 6 years he will be three sevenths as old as his father. How old is Dick now? *12 yr.*

17. A man is 6 years older than his brother. In 8 years the sum of one fifth of his age and one half of his brother's age will be 32 years. How old is each man? *man, 42 yr.; brother, 36 yr.*

18. Separate 100 into two parts such that the sum of one ninth of the smaller part and one fourth of the larger part is 20. *36, 64*

19. A farmer keeps $\frac{1}{20}$ of his wheat for seed, gives $\frac{2}{5}$ of it to his landlord, and sells the remainder. If the amount he sells is 462 bushels, how many bushels are there in his whole crop? *840*

20. The width of a rectangular building is $\frac{5}{7}$ of its length, and its perimeter is 560 feet. Find its dimensions. *$116\frac{2}{3}$ ft. × $163\frac{1}{3}$ ft.*

21. Elsie has 80 cents and Tillie has 60 cents. How many cents must Elsie give Tillie so that she will have $\frac{17}{18}$ as much money as Tillie?/2

22. What number divided by 13 will give 40 for a quotient and 3 for a remainder?523

23. The perimeter of a triangle is 44 inches. One side is $\frac{2}{3}$ of the longest side and the third side is $\frac{3}{7}$ of the longest side. How long is each side?21 in., 14 in., 9 in.

24. A lever is 20 feet long. How far from one end must the fulcrum be placed if a $7\frac{1}{2}$-pound weight at this end is to balance a 5-pound weight at the other end?8 ft.

25. Two boys wish to carry a bag of hickory nuts on a pole 5 feet long. Where shall they place the bag so that the smaller boy may carry $\frac{2}{3}$ as much as the larger boy?2 ft. from larger boy

26. One number is $\frac{3}{5}$ of the other. Find the numbers if their sum is 35 less than 3 times the smaller./75, 105

[B]

27. The difference of two numbers is 12. If one half their sum is subtracted from four fifths of the larger, the remainder is zero. Find the numbers./8, 30

28. Hazel is $\frac{2}{3}$ as old as Elizabeth. In 9 years she will be $\frac{3}{4}$ as old as Elizabeth. How old are they?H., 18 yr.; E., 27 yr.

29. Frank has $20 more than Elmer. After Frank gives Elmer $5 he finds that he has only $\frac{7}{6}$ as much money as Elmer. How much has Frank at first?$75

30. The difference of two numbers exceeds (is more than) the smaller by 4. Find the numbers if the larger exceeds one half their sum by 4. 4, /2

31. A father is 12 times as old as his son. In 6 years the son's age will lack 2 years of being one third of the father's age. How old is the father?24 yr.

32. A man has $4.50, consisting of quarters, nickels, and dimes. There are half as many dimes as quarters, and three times as many nickels as dimes. How many coins of each kind has he? 6 dimes, 12 quarters, 18 nickels

Solving Business Problems by Algebra [A]

As was shown in Chapter 5, many problems which confront a businessman are more easily solved by algebra than by arithmetic. In business the words *overhead* and *margin* are frequently used.

The margin is the sum of the profit and the overhead; and the overhead is the cost of doing business. The overhead includes among other items the cost of the rent, lighting, heating, depreciation, telephone, and insurance.

Then
$$\text{margin} = \text{profit} + \text{overhead}$$
$$\text{cost} + \text{margin} = \text{selling price}$$
$$\text{cost} + \text{profit} + \text{overhead} = \text{selling price}$$

Example 1. A merchant buys a dress wholesale for $31.20 and wishes to sell it so that his profit will be 15% of the selling price. He knows that his overhead is 20% of the selling price. At what price shall he sell the dress?

Solution. He cannot multiply the selling price by 15% to find his profit and by 20% to find his overhead. Why? Let us see how the problem is solved by algebra.

Let $\quad s =$ the number of dollars in the selling price

Then $\quad .15\,s =$ the number of dollars in the profit

and $\quad .20\,s =$ the number of dollars in the overhead

$$31.20 + .15\,s + .20\,s = s$$

$M_{100} \qquad 3120 + 15\,s + 20\,s = 100\,s$

$$15\,s + 20\,s - 100\,s = -3120$$

$$-65\,s = -3120$$

$D_{-65} \qquad\qquad\qquad s = 48$

PROOF. 15% of $48 = $7.20; 20% of $48 = $9.60; $7.20 + $9.60 + $31.20 = $48.00.

Example 2. At a 20% discount sale an article sold for $8.96. What was the selling price before the discount was deducted?

Solution. Let $\quad x =$ the number of dollars in the original selling price

Then $\qquad x - .20\,x = 8.96

$M_{100}, \quad 100\,x - 20\,x = 896$

$$80\,x = 896$$

$$x = 11.20, \text{ the number of dollars in the original price}$$

Point out that some verbal problems are a direct application of basic formulas, as in this case. A direct substitution in the formula usually produces the required equation. Most students will recall their struggles in arithmetic with business problems. They may appreciate a more orderly algebraic system of solution.

[A]

PROBLEMS

1. A dining room suite is purchased by a furniture dealer for $210. At what price must he sell it so that his margin will be 30% of the cost price? *$273*

$$c + .30c = s$$

2. At what price must the merchant (in Problem 1) sell the suite so that his margin will be 30% of the selling price? *$300*

$$c + .30s = s$$

3. At what price must an article be purchased in order that he may sell it for $12 and make a margin of 25% of the selling price? *$9*

4. At what price must an article be purchased so that it may sell for $12, with a margin of 25% of the cost? *$9.60*

5. A retail furniture dealer paid $13.32 for a chair. At what price must he mark its sale ticket if his profit is to be 12% and his overhead is 18%, both based upon the selling price? *$19.03, or $19*

6. The regular price of a television set was $159.95. What was the reduced price of the television set when the store offered a 10% discount on all its stock? *$143.95*

7. At this discount sale a bicycle sold for $36.99. What was the regular price of the bicycle? *$41.10*

8. A grocer wishes to sell goods at 20% more than the cost price. At what price must he buy goods that are to sell at $28.80? *$24*

9. At a 15% discount sale a corn popper sold for $8.67. What was the original price of the popper? *$10.20*

10. After a reduction of 5%, a slightly damaged small car was sold for $2326.55. Find the original price. *$2449*

[B]

11. A man bought a house for $35,000 and sold it for $37,500. His expenses of selling were $150. What was his margin? What was his profit? His profit was what per cent of the cost? What per cent of the selling price was his profit? *$2500, $2350, about 6.71%, about 6.27%*

12. The present population of a certain city is 785,755. In the last decade it increased 10%. What was its population 10 years ago? *714,323*

223

Interest [A]

Interest is money paid for the use of money. The money that is borrowed is the principal. To find the simple interest for any length of time, we multiply the principal by the rate per year, and then multiply this product by the number of years. The formula for simple interest is $i = prt$. This formula contains four letters. When the values of any three of them are known, the value of the fourth one can be found by substituting the values of the known letters in the formula and solving the resulting equation for the fourth letter.

Example 1. Find the simple interest on $400 at 6% for $2\frac{1}{2}$ years.

Solution. 1. Write the formula, $i = prt$
2. Substitute the known values. $i = 400 \times \frac{6}{100} \times \frac{5}{2}$
3. Find the value of i. $i = 60$
The simple interest is $60.

                                  → ② below.

Example 2. At what rate will $1260 produce $382.20 simple interest in 4 years 4 months?

Solution. Write the formula, $i = prt$
Substitute the values of the known letters.

$$382.20 = 1260 \times r \times \frac{13}{3}$$

M_3 $3(382.20) = 3 \times 1260 \times r \times \frac{13}{3}$

$$1146.60 = 16{,}380\,r$$
$$16{,}380\,r = 1146.60$$
$$r = .07. \text{ The rate is } 7\%.$$

[A]

EXERCISES

1. Find i when $p = \$4000$, $r = 5\%$, and $t = 3$ yr. $600
2. Find i when $p = \$350$, $r = 4\frac{1}{2}\%$, and $t = 3$ yr. 3 mo. $51.19
3. Find p when $i = \$300$, $r = 5\%$, and $t = 4$ yr. $1500
4. Find t when $i = \$945$, $p = \$4500$, and $r = 6\%$. $3\frac{1}{2}$ yr.
5. Find r when $p = \$800$, $i = \$110$, and $t = 2$ yr. 6 mo. $5\frac{1}{2}\%$
6. Find p if $t = 3$ yr., $r = 5\%$, and $i = \$825$. $5500
7. Find r when $p = \$260$, $i = \$23.40$, and $t = 2$ yr. $4\frac{1}{2}\%$
8. Find t when $p = \$37,500$, $r = 8\%$, and $i = \$9000$. 3 yr.

① Everyone should know and be able to use these formulas concerning interest on pages 224 and 225. You should show how they are derived.
② You may prefer to represent 6% by .06.

[B]

9. Find i when p = $40, r = 6%, and t = 6 mo. 21 da. * *$1.34*

10. Find i when p = $625, r = $7\frac{1}{2}$%, and t = 3 yr. 4 mo. 24 da. * *$159.38*

11. Find the interest on $375.40 for 1 yr. 8 mo. at 6%. *$37.54*

12. Find the principal if the interest is $19.01, the time is 3 yr. 5 mo., and the rate is 6%. *$92.73*

13. At what rate will $560 produce $106.40 simple interest if the time is 2 yr. 4 mo. 15 da.? *8%*

14. How long will it take $456 to produce $79.04 interest if the rate is 5%? *3 yr. 5 mo. 18 da.*

The Amount [A]

In interest problems the <u>amount</u> means the sum of the principal and interest. There are two formulas used in connection with amounts. One is $A = p + i$ and the other is $A = p + prt$. Each one states that the amount is equal to the principal plus the interest.

Example. If A = $3720, r = 6%, and t = 4 years, find p.

Solution. We are asked to find p, so we shall write the formula with p in the left member. Is this necessary?

$$p + prt = A$$
$$p + \tfrac{6}{100} \times 4 \times p = 3720$$
$$p + \tfrac{24}{100}p = 3720$$

M_{100} $\qquad\qquad 100\,p + 24\,p = 372{,}000$
$$124\,p = 372{,}000$$
$$p = 3000.$$

The principal is $3000.

[A]

Find A, p, r, or t:

[A] **EXERCISES**

1. p = $4000, t = 6 years, and r = 6%. *$5440*

2. p = $750, t = 1 year, and r = $4\frac{1}{2}$%. *$783.75*

3. p = $650, A = $695.50, and t = 1 year. *7%*

4. A = $1234 and p = $1000. Find i. *$234*

5. Find p when A = $1756.50 and i = $324.50. *$1432*

6. Find t when p = $425, r = 5%, and A = $488.75. *3 yr.*

7. Find i when A = $57,120, t = 4 years, and r = 5%. *$9520*

*In figuring time, count 30 days to the month and 12 months to the year.

225

8. Find t when $p = \$375$, $r = 8\%$, and $A = \$465.$ 3 yr.

9. Find t when $A = \$1675$, $p = \$1200$, and $r = 10\%$.

3 yr. 11 mo. 15 da.

10. How long will it take any principal at simple interest to double itself at 6%? 16 yr. 8 mo.

Baseball Problems [A]

Batting averages are usually expressed as decimals. Thus if a player makes 3 hits in 10 times at bat, he is batting .300. The batting average equals the number of hits divided by the number of times at bat.

$$\text{B.A.} = \frac{\text{hits}}{\text{times at bat}}.$$

In a recent year, a star player made 37 hits and had a batting average of .407.

Suppose we wish to find how many times he was at bat.

Let $x = $ the number of his times at bat.

Then
$$\frac{37}{x} = .407$$

M_x
$$x\left(\frac{37}{x}\right) = .407\, x$$
$$37 = .407\, x$$

M_{1000}
$$37000 = 407\, x$$
$$90.9 = x$$

He was at bat 91 times.

EXERCISES

[A]

Find the missing numbers in the following:

	PLAYERS	TIMES AT BAT	HITS	BATTING AVERAGE
.337 **1.**	Musial	593	200	?
159 **2.**	Robinson	484	?	.329
141 **3.**	Kell	460	?	.307
598 **4.**	Rosen	?	201	.336
.300 **5.**	Bell	610	183	?
608 **6.**	Vernon	?	205	.337

226

Investments [A]

One of the most common forms of business organization is the <u>corporation</u>. The capital stock of the corporation is the amount invested in it. This capital stock is divided into shares of equal value, say $100 each. The <u>par value</u> of a share is the value stated in the stock certificate. Not all stock has a par value. The true value of stock is usually not its par value; the prices of stocks vary from day to day. A person owning one or more of these shares is a stockholder. The profits distributed by a corporation to its stockholders are known as <u>dividends</u>.

If a corporation or a government needs to borrow money, it may do so by selling bonds. A <u>bond</u> is a kind of promissory note. Bonds are issued at a face value, or par value, often $1000 each, but the selling price may fluctuate. The rate of interest on a bond is based upon the face value. However, this rate does not always represent the actual yield. For example, a 6% $1000 bond pays interest of $60 per year, but if the bond was bought at 120 (meaning $120 for each $100 of face value), the yield is only 60 ÷ 1200, or 5%.

[A]

EXERCISES

1. Why is it sometimes necessary for a school board to issue and sell school bonds? Who buys these bonds? *To construct school buildings; the people.*

2. A man bought ten $1000 6% bonds at par value. How much did they cost him? What is his annual dividend from them? *$10,000; $600*

3. Frank Robinson bought 60 shares of stock at $90 a share, and receives a yearly dividend of $243 from them. What rate of income does he receive on his investment? If the par value of a share is $100, what rate of dividend is declared? *$4½%; 4 5/20%, or $4.05 a share*

4. Find the cost of 80 municipal $100 bonds that sell at $103½. *$8280*

5. A man invests x dollars in bonds and $800 more than this in stocks. How much does he invest in stocks? *$(x + 800)*

6. What is 4% of $$x$? What is m% of $30? *$0.04x; $0.3m*

7. A man invests $3000 in stocks and bonds. If x dollars of this amount is invested in stocks, how much is invested in bonds? If the stocks pay 6% on the investment and the bonds pay 5% on the investment, how much income does he receive on both investments? *$(3000 − x); $(.01x + 150)*

227

PROBLEMS

Example. Amy Wilson invested $8000, part at 6% per year and the remainder at 5% per year. Her yearly income on the two investments is $460. How much does she have invested at each rate?

Solution. Let x = the number of dollars invested at 6%.
Then $8000 - x$ = the number of dollars invested at 5%.

INVESTMENTS	RATES	INCOMES
x	.06	.06 x
$8000 - x$	.05	.05($8000 - x$)

The sum of the two incomes is $460.

Then $.06x + .05(8000 - x) = 460$

$.06x + 400 - .05x = 460$

S_{400} $.06x - .05x = 460 - 400$

M_{100} $6x - 5x = 46000 - 40000$

$x = 6000$

$8000 - x = 2000$

The boxed outline is optional. Your stronger students will prefer not to use this crutch.

PROOF. Does $6000 + 2000 = 8000$? Yes.
Does 6% of 6000 + 5% of 2000 = 460? Yes.
$6000 is invested at 6% and $2000 is invested at 5%.

x
8%

$x + 500$
5%

1. A farmer invested part of his money at 8% and $500 more than this at 5%. If his income on both investments was $545, how much was invested at each rate? *8%, $4000; 5%, $4500*

2. A nurse invested $11,000, part at 7% and the remainder at 5%. Her yearly income from these investments was $750. How much was invested at 7%? *$10,000*

3. One sum of money was invested at 8% and $1500 more than this sum was invested at 6%. If the total income from the two investments was $1770, how much was invested at each rate? *8%, $12,000; 6%, $13,500*

4. Part of $7000 was invested at 6% and the other part at 4%. If the 4% investment yielded $160 more than the other, what was the amount of each investment? *6%, $1200; 4%, $5800*

5. A man invested some money at 5% and a sum $1300 less at 4%. If the first investment produces $80 more interest per year than the second, how much is invested at each rate? *5%, $2800; 4%, $1500*

228

This may seem like a new type of problem to students. Point out to them that they are using the formula $i = prt$ to obtain a representation of the income, and then that they can form the equation by the familiar translation system. You may need to help them search for the key sentence which becomes the equation. These problems also lend themselves well to the "guess" method of analyzing a problem. (See p. 198.)

6. How can $8000 be invested, part at 4% and the remainder at 6%, so both investments produce the same income? *4%, $4800; 6%, $3200*

7. A man lends some money at 8% and an equal amount at $7\frac{1}{2}\%$. If the income from the $7\frac{1}{2}\%$ loan is $25 less than that from the 8% loan, how much money was loaned at each rate? *$5000*

[B]

8. How can $6000 be divided so that one part can be loaned at 4% and the other part at 7%, making an average of 6% on the $6000? *4%, $2000; 7%, $4000*

$$4\% \, x + 7\% \, ? = 6\% \, (6000)$$

9. A part of $8500 is invested at 6% and the remainder at $5\frac{1}{2}\%$. If the income from the first investment is $222.50 more than that from the second investment, what is the amount invested at each rate? *6%, $6000; $5\frac{1}{2}$%, $2500*

10. How much can one afford to pay for eight $1000 5% bonds in order to yield $4\frac{1}{2}\%$ on his investment? *$8888.88*

11. A man has invested $12,000 at 8%. How much money should he invest at $7\frac{1}{2}\%$, so that the combined interest from the two investments is approximately equal to a single investment at 7.83%? *$6181.82*

Literal Equations [A]

A literal equation is one in which at least one of the known numbers is represented by a variable. From this definition any formula is a literal equation. For example, the formula $i = prt$ is used to find the unknown number i when the known numbers are p, r, and t.

Literal equations are solved like numerical equations.

But conversely, not every literal equation is a formula.

Example 1. Solve for x: $3x = 6c$

Solution. $3x = 6c$

D_3 $x = 2c$

Example 2. Solve for x: $2(x - 3a) = 6b$

Solution. $2(x - 3a) = 6b$

                  $2x - 6a = 6b$

                    $2x = 6b + 6a$

D_2 $x = 3b + 3a$

229

Example 3. Solve for C: $F = \frac{9}{5} C + 32$

Solution.

$$F = \frac{9}{5} C + 32$$

$M_5 \qquad 5(F) = 5(\frac{9}{5} C) + 5(32)$

$$5 F = 9 C + 160$$

$$-9 C = -5 F + 160$$

$D_{-1} \qquad 9 C = 5 F - 160$

$D_9 \qquad C = \dfrac{5 F - 160}{9}, \text{ or } \dfrac{5}{9} (F - 32)$

Notice that the original formula tells how to find F when C is known and that the last formula tells how to find C when F is known. F is the <u>subject</u> of the equation $F = \frac{9}{5} C + 32$ and C is the subject of the equation $C = \frac{5}{9}(F - 32)$.

[A]

ORAL
EXERCISES

Solve for x, explaining each step of the solution:

1. $bx = b$ _1_

2. $x + 5 = a$ _a-5_

3. $x - 5 = a$ _a+5_

4. $x + 3 = b$ _b-3_

5. $3 x = a$ _a/3_

6. $x - b = a$ _a+b_

7. $2 ax = 4 ab$ _2b_

8. $bx = b^3$ _b²_

9. $m - n = x$ _m-n_

10. $x - h = 0$ _h_

11. $\dfrac{x}{4} = p$ _4p_

12. $\dfrac{x}{5} = c$ _5c_

13. $b - a = -x$ _a-b_

14. $dx = c$ _c/d_

15. $mx = m^2 - 2 m$ _m-2_

16. $5 ax = 10 ab$ _2b_

17. $\dfrac{x}{4} = \dfrac{1}{c}$ _4/c_

18. $\frac{1}{2} x = c$ _2c_

19. $\frac{1}{3} x = v$ _3v_

20. $2 x - 5 a = 7 a$ _6a_

21. $3 x - 4 x = a$ _-a_

22. $3 bx = 12 b^2$ _4b_

23. $\frac{1}{4} x - 5 = 0$ _20_

24. $\dfrac{x}{c} = \dfrac{a}{b}$ _ac/b_

25. $\dfrac{x - a}{c} = b$ _a+bc_

[A]

EXERCISES

Solve for x or y:

_a-b_ 1. $b + x = a$

_b-c_ 2. $b - x = c$

_b+h_ 3. $-b + x = h$

_-a-b_ 4. $-b - x = a$

_2a_ 5. $3 x + 2 a = 8 a$

_-5a_ 6. $3 x + 6 a = -9 a$

_25c/3_ 7. $3 y - 9 c = 16 c$

_2b_ 8. $2 y - 3 b = 5 y - 9 b$

_3m/2_ 9. $4 m - 3 y = 5 y - 8 m$

_3/2 a_ 10. $7 x - (3 x - 2 a) = 8 a$

_6k_ 11. $2(x - 3 k) = 6 k$

_6c_ 12. $3(x - 4 c) - 6 c = 0$

_23b/6_ 13. $6(5 b - x) = 7 b$

_7d_ 14. $3 y - 10 d = 4(d - y)$

_3a_ 15. $2(a - y) = 5 y - 19 a$

_a+3b/b_ 16. $b(x - 3) = a$

Teachers often find it helpful to show students that it is permissible to multiply both members of an equation by -1. This device is used when there are many minus signs which make the work awkward. Sometimes we say, "All the signs of an equation may be changed."

EQUATIONS CONTAINING FRACTIONS

17. $5bx - a = b(b + 2x)\frac{a+b^2}{3b}$ 19. $ax - (a - 2) = 2$

18. $a(x + 2 - a) = 1$ $\frac{a^2-2a+1}{a}$ 20. $b(x + b) = b^2 - ab-a$

Solve the following formulas for the letters indicated:

21. $A = lw$ for l; for w.   27. $S = \frac{1}{2}gt^2$ for g. $g=\frac{2S}{t^2}$

22. $d = rt$ for r; for t.   28. $A = p + prt$ for r; for t.

23. $A = \frac{1}{2}lw$ for l; for w.   29. $l = a + d(n - 1)$ for a. $a = l - dn + d$

24. $c = \pi d$ for π; for d.   30. $pv = k$ for p. $p = \frac{k}{v}$

25. $S = 180(n - 2)$ for n.   31. $A = \frac{h}{2}(b + b')$ for b. $b = \frac{2A-hb'}{h}$

26. $V = \frac{1}{3}Bh$ for h.   28. $r = \frac{A-p}{pt}$; $t = \frac{A-p}{pr}$

Ratios [A]

The ratio of one number to another is the *first* number divided by the *second*. Thus the ratio of 4 to 8 is $\frac{4}{8}$, or $4 \div 8$, or $4 : 8$; the ratio of x to y is $x \div y$, or $\frac{x}{y}$, or $x : y$; and the ratio of 7 inches to 9 inches is $\frac{7}{9}$, or $7 \div 9$, or $7 : 9$.

There can be no ratio between two unlike quantities. Thus we cannot find the ratio of 4 pounds to 6 feet. If two quantities of the same kind are expressed in different units of measurement, they must be changed to the same units of measurement before we can find their ratio. For example, to find the ratio of 4 ounces to 3 pounds, we can change 3 pounds to ounces and find the ratio of 4 ounces to 48 ounces, which is $\frac{4}{48}$, or $\frac{1}{12}$.

[A]

ORAL EXERCISES

1. State these ratios in their simplest forms:

a. 4 to $12\frac{1}{3}$

b. 12 to $4\frac{3}{1}$

c. 10 in. to 15 in. $\frac{2}{3}$

d. a^2 to $3 a^2$ $\frac{1}{3}$

e. $3x$ to $8x$ $\frac{3}{8}$

f. 12 in. to 1 ft. $\frac{1}{1}$

g. 40 cents to $\$1\frac{2}{5}$

h. 6 yd. to 4 ft. $\frac{9}{2}$

i. 1 in. to 1 ft. $\frac{1}{12}$

j. 1 in. to 1 yd. $\frac{1}{36}$

k. 75 to 100 $\frac{3}{4}$

l. 2 ft. 3 in. to 1 yd. $\frac{3}{4}$

2. If x and y are in the ratio of 3 to 5, then $\frac{x}{y} = ?$; $x : y = ? : ?$. $3/5$ $3:5$

The subject of ratio and proportion fits nicely with the work in fractions, and is valuable because of its many practical uses.

231

3. Below are two rectangular solids. What is the ratio of their lengths? of their heights? of their widths? of their volumes? $\frac{4}{2}; \frac{3}{4}; \frac{2}{3}; \frac{1}{4}$

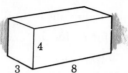

4. Two numbers are in the ratio 2 : 3. They may be represented by 2 x and 3 x, for $\frac{2\,x}{3\,x} = \frac{2}{3}$. Represent two numbers in the ratio of

a. 3 : 8
3x and 8x

b. 4 to 5
4x and 5x

c. 6 to 7
6x and 7x

Proportions [A]

A <u>proportion</u> is an equation whose two members are ratios. Thus $\frac{4}{5} = \frac{12}{15}$, $\frac{x}{3} = \frac{1}{4}$, and 2 : 8 = 6 : x are proportions. If the ratio of two numbers is equal to the ratio of two other numbers, the four numbers are said to be in proportion.

Since the proportion $\frac{a}{b} = \frac{c}{d}$ may be written in the form $a : b = c : d$, it is easy to remember the names of the four parts. The <u>first term</u> is a, the <u>second term</u> is b, the <u>third term</u> is c, and the <u>fourth term</u> is d. Since a and d are at the ends of the proportion, they are called the <u>extremes</u>. The second and third terms are the <u>means</u>, meaning the middle terms.

ORAL EXERCISES

[A]

1. Complete: In the proportion $\frac{x}{4} = \frac{5}{6}$, x is the __?__ *first* term, __?__ *5* is the third term, and __?__ *6* is the fourth term.

2. Complete: The means of the proportion $\frac{x}{4} = \frac{5}{6}$ are __?__ *4* and __?__ *5*, and its extremes are __?__ *x* and __?__ *6*.

3. Complete: In the proportion $\frac{3}{7} = \frac{5}{m}$, the fraction $\frac{3}{7}$ is a __?__. *ratio*

4. Which of the following are proportions? *a , b, e*

(Remember that the two ratios of a proportion are equal.)

a. $\frac{2}{3} = \frac{10}{15}$ **c.** $\frac{10}{15} = \frac{9}{6}$ **e.** $\frac{7}{8} = \frac{21}{24}$

b. $\frac{4}{5} = \frac{8}{10}$ **d.** $\frac{10}{11} = \frac{11}{12}$ **f.** $\frac{3}{4} = \frac{15}{19}$

5. Explain why $x = \frac{2}{3}$ may be written $\frac{x}{1} = \frac{2}{3}$. Change $y = \frac{3}{4}$ into a proportion. *any integer may be considered as having 1 for a denominator.* $\frac{y}{1} = \frac{3}{4}$

6. Is $\frac{x}{7} = \frac{4}{5}$ a proportion for all values of x? *no*

7. Can you write $3x = 7$ in the form of a proportion? $\frac{1}{x} = \frac{3}{7}$

8. Solve the following proportions for x:

a. $\frac{x}{3} = \frac{1}{4}$ *$\frac{3}{4}$*   **c.** $\frac{3x}{7} = \frac{4}{5}$ *($\frac{13}{15}$)*   **e.** $\frac{1}{x} = \frac{2}{8}$ *4*

b. $\frac{x}{4} = \frac{2}{1}$ *8*   **d.** $\frac{5}{6} = \frac{3}{x}$ *$3\frac{3}{5}$*   **f.** $\frac{3}{7} = \frac{x}{14}$ *6*

9. Is $\frac{x}{15} = \frac{12}{15}$ a proportion for one value of x? What is the product of its means? What is the product of its extremes? *yes* *180* *15x*

10. Is $\frac{10}{15} = \frac{12}{18}$ a proportion? Is the product of its means equal to the product of its extremes? *yes ; yes*

[A]

WRITTEN EXERCISES

1. $\frac{a}{b} = \frac{c}{d}$. Clear the equation of fractions by multiplying both members by bd. What is the product of the means? What is the product of the extremes? *ad = bc; bc; ad*

Copy and complete:

> In a proportion the product of the __?__ equals the __?__ of the extremes. *means , product*

2. Using the principle in the rectangle above, tell whether or not the following are proportions:

a. $\frac{1}{3} = \frac{4}{12}$ *yes*   **c.** $7 : 2 = 13 : 4$ *no*   **e.** $\frac{7}{4} = \frac{12}{7}$ *no*

b. $\frac{7}{2} = \frac{2}{7}$ *no*   **d.** $\frac{9}{4} = \frac{7}{3}$ *no*   **f.** $\frac{125}{20} = \frac{25}{4}$ *yes*

① Do not allow the misleading expression "cross multiply."

①

3. Solve the following proportions for y:

24 **a.** $\dfrac{1}{4} = \dfrac{6}{y}$ 10 **c.** $\dfrac{4}{y} = \dfrac{2}{5}$ 12 **e.** $\dfrac{1}{3} = \dfrac{4}{y}$ 3m **g.** $\dfrac{m}{y} = \dfrac{1}{3}$

1 **b.** $\dfrac{y}{8} = \dfrac{3}{24}$ $\frac{1}{2}$ **d.** $\dfrac{3}{y} = \dfrac{6}{1}$ $\frac{ab}{c}$ **f.** $\dfrac{y}{a} = \dfrac{b}{c}$ $\frac{1}{7}$ **h.** $\dfrac{1}{y} = \dfrac{7}{1}$

4. Find two numbers whose sum is 80 and which have the ratio 2 : 3. 32, 48

(Let $2x =$ the smaller number. Then $3x = $ __?__.)

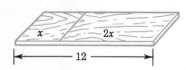

5. A board 12 feet long is to be cut into two parts having the ratio 1 : 2. How long should each part be? 4 ft., 8 ft.

6. If Bill earns \$6.75 in 5 hours, how much will he earn in 11 hours? $\left(\dfrac{6.75}{x} = \dfrac{5}{11}\right)$ \$14.85

7. If 7 yards of muslin cost \$8.75, how many yards can be bought for \$11.25? 9 yd.

8. If 2 inches on a map represent 150 miles, how many inches will represent 500 miles? $6\frac{2}{3}$

9. $\triangle ABC$ is similar to $\triangle A'B'C'$. In similar triangles the corresponding sides are proportional. Then $\dfrac{x}{9} = \dfrac{12}{18}$. Find BC.

6

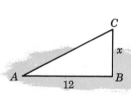
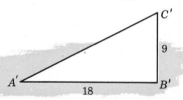

10. A tree casts a shadow of 65 feet when a boy 5 feet 4 inches tall casts a shadow of 7 feet. How high is the tree?

49.523⁺ ft.

EQUATIONS CONTAINING FRACTIONS

Checking Your Understanding of Chapter 8

Before you attempt the Chapter 8 Review, be sure that you have learned:

Review if you need to.

[A]

CHAPTER REVIEW

1. How do we clear an equation of fractions? *Multiply both members of the equation by the L.C.D.*

Solve:

2. $\dfrac{c}{4} - \dfrac{c}{3} = 5$ -60

3. $\dfrac{c}{3} + \dfrac{2c}{4} = 1$ $1\frac{1}{5}$

4. $\dfrac{3p}{5} = 1 + \dfrac{p}{2}$ 10

5. $\dfrac{y+5}{2} - \dfrac{2y+4}{3} = 0$ 7

6. $\dfrac{2k-1}{5} - \dfrac{k+1}{2} = -1$ $\frac{1}{3}$

7. $\dfrac{1}{3}(2m-1) + \dfrac{1}{7}(8m-11) = 0$ $1\frac{1}{19}$

8. $.007\,x = 21$ 3000

9. $c + .18\,c = 35.4$ 30

10. $x = 583 - .06\,x$ 550

11. $.6\,x + 1.1 = .2\,x + 1.9$ 2

12. $.03\,y + .14 = .09\,y + .08$ 1

13. $4.2 = .7\,s - .7$ 7

14. If a tree 75 feet high casts a shadow of 54 feet, how long will the shadow of a 50-foot tree be? $36\,ft.$

15. If a number is increased by 8% of itself, the result is 297. Find the number. 275

235

16. Find the simple interest when the principal is $800, the rate is 3%, and the time is 1 year 2 months. *$28*

17. At a 20% discount sale, a chair was sold for $19.96. What was the original price of the chair? *$24.95*

[B]

18. A furrier buys a coat for $1989. At what price shall he sell it to have a margin of 15% of the selling price? *$2340*

19. Solve for c: $\dfrac{2c-3}{8} - \dfrac{5c+2}{6} = \dfrac{8c-1}{9} - \dfrac{3c+5}{12}$ *$-\frac{13}{88}$*

20. Solve: $.5(x+.2) + .07 - (.3 - x) = .02$

21. Solve: $.25(5 - 2x) - x = -2 - .5(6x - 8)$

22. A woman wishes to invest $15,000, part at 5% and the remainder at 7%, so as to produce an income of $990. How much must she invest at each rate? *7%, $12,000 5%, $3000*

[C]

23. A man marked goods so that he had a margin of 40% of the cost. What per cent of the selling price was his margin? *28.6%*

24. A man buys eggs at x cents apiece and sells them at y cents a dozen. What is his profit? What is his per cent of profit based on the cost? *$(y-12x)$ ¢/doz.; $100\left(\frac{y-12x}{12x}\right)$*

[A]

GENERAL REVIEW

1. Simplify $4x^2 - 6x - 3 - 5x^2$. *$-x^2-6x-3$*

2. From $2a - 5b + 6c$ take $-2a + 3b - c$. *$4a-8b+7c$*

3. Find the products:

a. $x^3 \cdot x^7$ *x^{10}*   c. $x^3(xy)$ *x^4y*   e. $\dfrac{a}{b} \times \dfrac{b}{a^2}$ *$\frac{1}{a}$*   f. $\dfrac{1}{2x} \times \dfrac{8x}{3}$ *$\frac{4}{3}$*

b. $-4c \cdot c^5$ *$-4c^6$*   d. $(-x)(x^2)(x^3)$ *$-x^6$*

4. Find the powers:

a. $(x^2)^2$ *x^4*   b. $(-3)^3$ *-27*   c. $(.1p)^3$ *$0.001p^3$*   d. $(-2a^2)^4$ *$16a^8$*

5. Do as indicated:

a. $8x^2 \div (-4x)$ *$-2x$*   c. $8 \div \frac{1}{2}$ *16*   e. $(-63y^2) \div (-9y^2)$ *7*

b. $4x(x^2 - 5x - 1)$ *$4x^3-20x^2-4x$*   d. $a \div \frac{1}{a}$ *a^2*   f. $(7c - 3d + 4) \div (-1)$ *$-7c+3d-4$*

236

6. Change $\frac{3}{20}$ to a per cent. *15%*

7. 25 is what per cent of 75? *$33\frac{1}{3}$%*

8. If $a = -2$, $b = 1$, and $c = 0$, find the value of $\dfrac{a^3 + 3bc + 1}{a}$. *$3\frac{1}{2}$*

9. What is the name of the value of the unknown in an equation? *Root*

10. By substitution determine which of the numbers $+2$, -2, $+1$, and -1 are roots of the equation $x^2 - x = 2$. *2 and -1*

Solve:

11. $13m + 7 = 49 + 6m$ *6*   **13.** $6(7y + 3) = 60$ *1*

12. $3d + 2 = 9d + 5$ *$-\frac{1}{2}$*   **14.** $3(k + 2) - 5(k + 1) = -11$ *7*

15. A girl has 12 coins consisting of nickels and dimes. If the total value of the coins is $1, how many coins of each kind has she? *4 nickels, 8 dimes*

16. A boy is 10 years old and his sister is 18 years old. How soon will the boy be $\frac{3}{4}$ as old as his sister? *In 14 yr.*

[Test A]

Part I. Equations (50%)

Solve:

1. $\dfrac{x}{3} = 10$ *30*

2. $.04x = 2$ *50*

3. $\dfrac{y}{2} - \dfrac{y}{3} = 4$ *24*

4. $\dfrac{3}{4} = \dfrac{12}{x}$ *16*

5. $x + .04x = 78$ *75*

6. $\dfrac{m}{2} - 2 = \dfrac{2}{3}m - 1$ *-6*

7. $\dfrac{c}{5} + 1 = \dfrac{c}{4} - 1$ *40*

8. $\frac{1}{4}(x - 5) - \frac{1}{3}(2x + 1) = 3$ *-11*

9. $ax - b = 0$ for x. *$\frac{b}{a}$*

10. *Complete:* In a proportion the product of the means equals the product of the __?__. *extremes*

Part II. Problems (50%)

1. Three fifths of a number is 54. Find the number. *90*

2. In a football practice a player lost 7 pounds, which was 4% of his weight. What was his weight just before the practice? *175 lb.*

3. The difference between $\frac{3}{4}$ of a number and $\frac{1}{7}$ of it is 17. Find the number. *28*

4. One number exceeds another by 18. What are the numbers if $\frac{2}{3}$ of the smaller increased by $\frac{1}{9}$ of the larger equals 23? *27, 45*

5. John is one fourth as old as his father, who is 60 years old. How soon will he be one half as old as his father? *30 yr.*

[Test B]

Part I. Equations (40%)

Solve:

1. $.125\,c = 7$ *56*

2. $\dfrac{3\,y}{5} = \dfrac{8}{15}$ *8/9*

3. $x + .08\,x = 59.4$ *55*

4. $\frac{3}{4}y - \frac{2}{3}y = \frac{1}{6}y + 1$ *-12*

5. $\frac{3}{4}p - 2 = \frac{5}{8}p$ *16*

6. $3\,h - 7.5 = 12.5 + 0.5\,h$ *8*

7. $\dfrac{2\,x - 7}{3} - \dfrac{x - 5}{6} = 1$ *5*

8. Solve for y: $cy - 3\,c = 3\,c^2$ *3(c+1)*

9. Solve for n: $l = a + d(n - 1)$ *$\frac{l - a + d}{d}$*

10. Solve: $0.5(y - 1) + 2(3\,y + 4) = 5.875$ *-0.25*

Part II. Problems (60%)

1. The width of a rectangle is $\frac{5}{6}$ of its length. What are the dimensions of the rectangle if its perimeter is 154 inches? *35 in. x 42 in.*

2. One of two complementary angles is $\frac{3}{5}$ as large as the other. How large is each angle? *$33\frac{3}{4}°$, $56\frac{1}{4}°$*

3. Dick has $2.85 consisting of nickels, dimes, and quarters. How many coins of each kind has he if the number of nickels is one third the number of dimes, and the number of quarters is one half the number of nickels? *18 dimes, 6 nickels, 3 quarters*

4. Gordon Heights has a population of 297, which is an increase of 8% over the population 5 years ago. What was the population 5 years ago? *275*

5. Part of $10,000 was invested at 5% and the remainder at 7%. The income on the 5% investment exceeded the income of the 7% investment by $80. How much of the $10,000 was invested at 5%? *$6500*

6. What principal at 6% simple interest will amount to $3360 in 2 years? *$3000*

EQUATIONS CONTAINING FRACTIONS

Time, 40 Minutes

1. $(2 x^2)(- 3 x^4) = ?$ $-6x^6$

2. $x^{12} \div x^2 = ?$ x^{10}

3. $(- 4 m)^3 = ?$ $-64m^3$

4. $(15 c - 25 d) \div 5 = ?$ $3c - 5d$

5. $- c^2(c^2 - c + 1) = ?$ $-c^4 + c^3 - c^2$

6. $(2 x - 5) - (7 - 6 x) = ?$ $8x - 12$

7. Simplify: $7 a - 4 b - b + 6 a$ $13a - 5b$

8. If $x = - 2$ and $y = 4$, find the value of $x^3 - 5 y.$ -28

9. $(8 x^2 y - 4 xy - 32 y^2) \div (- 4 y) = ?$ $-2x^2 + x + 8y$

10. Solve: $\frac{3}{4} x = \frac{2}{5} x - 7$ -20

11. Solve: $3(m - 2) - 7 = 5(2 m + 5) - 3$ -5

12. $ab(a^2 + ab + b^2) = ?$ $a^3 b + a^2 b^2 + ab^3$

13. Write the interest formula. $i = prt$

14. $24(\frac{2}{3} - \frac{3}{4} x + \frac{1}{2} x^2) = ?$ $16 - 18x + 12x^2$

15. Subtract $c^2 - c + 1$ from $3 c + 6.$ $-c^2 + 4c + 5$

16. John is 9 years older than Henry. In 3 years, 7 times John's age will equal 10 times Henry's age. How old is each? *Henry, 18 yr.; John, 27 yr.*

17. Write a formula for the colored area of the square at the right. $A = 4m^2 - \pi m^2$

18. Find the altitude of a triangle whose area is 200 square inches and base 40 inches. *10 in.*

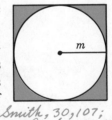

m

19. At an election among three candidates Brown had twice as many votes as Smith and Douglas had 10,319 more votes than Smith. If all three had a total of 130,747 votes, how many did each receive? *Smith, 30,107; Brown, 60,214; Douglas, 40,426*

20. The larger of two numbers is 5 more than 6 times the smaller. Find the numbers if their sum is 75. *10, 65*

21. In a triangle the second angle is 3 times the first and the third is 5 degrees larger than the first. How many degrees are there in each angle? *35°, 105°, 40°*

22. Solve: $2(y - 9) = 7(4 - y) - 6(y + 2)$ $2\frac{4}{15}$

23. Solve: $1.1 x - 8.2 = 4.7 - 1.9 x$ 4.3

24. From the sum of $x - y$ and $2 x - y$ take $7 - 4 x.$ $7x - 2y - 7$

25. Solve for y: $b(b + 2 y) = 5 by + b^2$ 0

239

*The control of the radio telescope
at Jodrell Bank, England.*

(c) Keystone Press Agency Ltd.

Astronomy is the science which makes a study of the heavenly bodies, including our own solar system. The study of astronomy becomes more interesting and fascinating as the student acquires more knowledge of the subject.

Much of the world's progress can be attributed to astronomy. It is through astronomy that we can tell to the minute when an eclipse of the sun or moon will appear. Astronomers prepare star maps and almanacs, which are used in air and sea navigation.

To obtain the correct time, the astronomer determines when a particular star should be directly overhead. Then with a photographic zenith tube he observes when this star is exactly overhead. With this information the correct time can be found to within 0.002 second.

Astronomers have learned much about the stars and planets. They know the sizes and shapes of the planets, how far they are from the sun, what paths they travel in going around the sun, and many other interesting facts.

Astronomers measure the distances to stars in light-years. A light-year is the distance light travels in one year (about six trillion miles). Astronomers know that

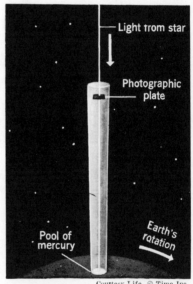

Light from star

Photographic plate

Pool of mercury

Earth's rotation

Mechanics of Zenith Tube

the star nearest us is about $4\frac{1}{4}$ light-years away and that some stars are so far away that their light requires billions of years to reach us.

One does not need very much mathematics to begin the study of astronomy, but to make an intensive study of the subject much mathematics is needed. Besides the mathematics learned in high school, one needs college algebra, trigonometry, analytic geometry, calculus, and mechanics to understand advanced astronomy.

9

Additional Work with Polynomials

Suggested Time Schedule
9 days

In this chapter you will find problems calling for greater skill with polynomials.

ADDITIONAL WORK WITH POLYNOMIALS

Review of Multiplying by Monomials [A]

Be sure that you can manage the review exercises which follow. They will help you in the work of this chapter.

Example 1. $6^3 \cdot 6^2 = 6^5.$

Example 2. $(a^2)^3 = a^2 \cdot a^2 \cdot a^2 = a^6.$

Find the indicated products:

ORAL . EXERCISES

1. $x^2 \cdot x^3$ x^5
2. $a^2 \cdot a$ a^3
3. $m^3 \cdot m$ m^4
4. $c^5 \cdot c^4$ c^9
5. $(-x^2)(-a^4)$ $a^4 x^2$
6. $(-3y)(6y)$ $-18y^2$
7. $(-x^3)(-x^4)$ x^7
8. $a(-a^2)$ $-a^3$

9. $3x^2(-5y)$ $-15x^2y$
10. $(2x)(3x^2)(-x)$ $-6x^4$
11. $-4a^2(2a^2)(5a)$ $-40a^5$
12. $(ab)(bc)c$ ab^2c^2
13. $2(-a)\ 3(-a)$ $6a^2$
14. $(5a^2bc)(3abc^2)$ $15a^3b^2c^3$
15. $4^2 \cdot 4^3$ 4^5
16. $3^2 \cdot 3^2$ 3^4

17. $7^4 \cdot 7$ 7^5
18. $10^6 \cdot 10$ 10^7
19. $10^2 \cdot 10^3$ 10^5
20. $(a^3)^2$ a^6
21. $(x^5)^2$ x^{10}
22. $(-y^5)^2$ y^{10}
23. $(-m^3)^3$ $-m^9$
24. $(c^4)^3$ c^{12}

25. $5(y^2 - 3y + 6)$ $5y^2-15y+30$
26. $-3x(x^2 - 4x + 8)$ $-3x^3+12x^2-24x$
27. $10\left(\dfrac{a^2}{5} + 3a - \dfrac{1}{10}\right)$ $2a^2+30a-1$
28. $5ab(a^2 - ab + b^2)$ $5a^3b-5a^2b^2+5ab^3$
29. $3x^2(3x^2 - 7x - 5)$ $9x^4-21x^3-15x^2$
30. $\frac{1}{2}xy(x^2 - 2xy + 6y^2)$ $\frac{1}{2}x^3y-x^2y^2+3xy^3$

Multiplying a Polynomial by a Polynomial [A]

By the distributive property, $a(b + c) = ab + ac$. In this case we have the product of the monomial a and the binomial $b + c$. In the expression $(r + s)(b + c)$ we have the product of two binomials. However, we know that the expression $r + s$ represents a single number just as a does. In other words, we may use the distributive property just as we did above. Thus we have $(r + s)(b + c) = (r + s)b + (r + s)c$.

Now let us use the distributive property again, and we have $(r + s)b + (r + s)c = rb + sb + rc + sc$. In this last statement we have used the alternate form of the distributive property: $(b + c)a = ba + ca$. Let us now consider the expression $(r + s)(b + c + d)$. Do you agree that we may write $(r + s)(b + c + d) = (r + s)b + (r + s)c + (r + s)d = rb + sb + rc + sc + rd + sd$? Do you agree that we may use the distributive property to find the product of any two polynomials?

① The student may need some guidance in seeing the connection between this general explanation and its application on page 244. It is worthwhile, however, to develop meanings instead of making arbitrary rules for multiplying polynomials.

① Show students that although the product can be obtained without such arrangement, the preliminary steps are so mixed up that it takes longer to do the work and errors may result.

ALGEBRA, BOOK ONE

In multiplying a binomial by a monomial we usually write the product in horizontal form, thus: $3(a + 2) = 3a + 6$. However, in multiplying two polynomials, many people prefer to write the steps of the multiplication in a pattern like that used for long multiplications in arithmetic. For example, to find $(x + 2)(x + 5)$ we may use either of the forms below.

$$(x + 2)(x + 5) = (x + 2)x + (x + 2)5$$
$$= x^2 + 2x + 5x + 10$$
$$= x^2 + 7x + 10$$

$$x + 2$$
$$x + 5$$
$$x^2 + 2x$$
$$5x + 10$$
$$x^2 + 7x + 10$$

It is interesting to notice that the correctness of the procedure just outlined can be shown by areas. If the rectangle shown has its base $x + 5$ and its altitude $x + 2$, its area will be $(x + 5)(x + 2)$. Notice that the area is also $x^2 + 2x + 5x + 10$, or $x^2 + 7x + 10$.

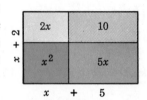

Example 2. Multiply $a + b$ by $c + d$.

Solution.
$$a + b$$
$$c + d$$
$$ac + bc$$
$$+ ad + bd$$
$$ac + bc + ad + bd$$

In this example no terms of the partial products are alike.

Example 3. Multiply $a^2 - 3b^2 + 4ab$ by $2a - b$.

Solution. When possible, both the multiplicand and the multiplier should be arranged according to either the descending or the ascending powers of *one* letter. We have arranged them in descending powers of a. Notice that the term containing the highest power of a is written first, the term containing the next highest power of a is written second, and so on.

CHECK. Let $a = 4$ and $b = 3$.

$$a^2 + 4ab - 3b^2 \qquad = 16 + 48 - 27 \qquad = 37$$
$$2a - b \qquad\qquad = 8 - 3 \qquad\qquad = 5$$
$$2a^3 + 8a^2b - 6ab^2 \qquad\qquad\qquad\qquad\qquad 185$$
$$- a^2b - 4ab^2 + 3b^3$$
$$2a^3 + 7a^2b - 10ab^2 + 3b^3 = 128 + 336 - 360 + 81 = 185$$

244 ②

② Do not require much checking by this method.

ADDITIONAL WORK WITH POLYNOMIALS

In addition to the method of checking just shown, it is possible to check by interchanging the multiplicand and the multiplier before performing the multiplication a second time. Of course, if you are a careful worker, you will usually catch any errors by merely performing the multiplication a second time without interchanging.

> To multiply one polynomial by another,
>> multiply each term of the multiplicand by each term of the multiplier and (if possible) combine the partial products.

[A]

EXERCISES

Multiply:

1. $x + 1$ by $x + 1$ $x^2 + 2x + 1$
2. $x + 3$ by $x + 3$ $x^2 + 6x + 9$
3. $a + 3$ by $a + 2$ $a^2 + 5a + 6$
4. $c + 2$ by $c + 4$ $c^2 + 6c + 8$
5. $g + 6$ by $g + 7$ $g^2 + 13g + 42$
6. $r - 1$ by $r - 2$ $r^2 - 3r + 2$
7. $x - 4$ by $x - 4$ $x^2 - 8x + 16$
8. $c + 5$ by $c - 8$ $c^2 - 3c - 40$
9. $x - 7$ by $x + 7$ $x^2 - 49$
10. $r - 6$ by $r + 6$ $r^2 - 36$

11. $r + s$ by $r + s$ $r^2 + 2rs + s^2$
12. $a + b$ by $a + b$ $a^2 + 2ab + b^2$
13. $a + b$ by $a - b$ $a^2 - b^2$
14. $a - b$ by $a - b$ $a^2 - 2ab + b^2$
15. $x - 3y$ by $2x + y$ $2x^2 - 5xy - 3y^2$
16. $m - 3n$ by $2m - 5n$ $2m^2 - 11mn + 15n^2$
17. $2x - 3y$ by $3x - 2y$ $6x^2 - 13xy + 6y^2$
18. $5m + 3n$ by $m - 5n$ $5m^2 - 22mn - 15n^2$
19. $m - n$ by $x + y$ $mx - nx + my - ny$
20. $x - 3y$ by $5x + 2$ $5x^2 - 15xy + 2x - 6y$

Multiply as indicated:

21. $(x^2 - x + 1)(x + 3)$ $x^3 + 2x^2 - 2x + 3$
22. $(c^2 - 3c + 2)(2c + 3)$ $2c^3 - 3c^2 - 5c + 6$
23. $(3x + 5 - x^2)(x + 3)$ $-x^3 + 14x + 15$
24. $(r + s)(r^2 - rs + s^2)$ $r^3 + s^3$
25. $(-2x + x^2 + 3)(x - 2)$ $x^3 - 4x^2 + 7x - 6$
26. $(2a - 1)(2a^2 + 4a - 1)$ $4a^3 + 6a^2 - 6a + 1$

27. $(a^2 - 6a + 9)(a - 1)$ $a^3 - 7a^2 + 15a - 9$
28. $(2x - 3y)^2$ $4x^2 - 12xy + 9y^2$
  SUGGESTION. $(2x - 3y)^2 =$ $(2x - 3y)(2x - 3y)$
29. $(4a + 1)^2$ $16a^2 + 8a + 1$
30. $(\tfrac{1}{2}a - 3)(\tfrac{1}{2}a + 3)$ $\tfrac{1}{4}a^2 - 9$
31. $(x^2 - 4x + 6)^2$ $x^4 - 8x^3 + 28x^2 - 48x + 36$

Simplify:

32. $2x(x - 3) - 4x(2x - 1)$ $-6x^2 - 2x$
33. $2a(a - 3) - 5a(a - 1)$ $-3a^2 - a$
34. $5a(a + 4) + 2a(a - 5)$ $7a^2 + 10a$
35. $2y(3y - 6) - (2y^2 - 5)$ $4y^2 - 12y + 5$

245

In exercises 36 and 37 copy the drawings and replace each question mark with the area of the small square or rectangle in which it is written.

36.

37.

38. The base of a parallelogram is $x + 2y$ and its altitude is $x - 2y$. What is its area? $x^2 - 4y^2$

39. Find the area of a triangle if the base is $4x - 6$ and the altitude is $2x - 3$. $4x^2 - 12x + 9$

40. Find the area of a square if one side is $2x + 3$. $4x^2 + 12x + 9$

41. Find the cost of $(x + 3)$ articles if each cost $(x - 6)$ cents. $(x^2 - 3x - 18)¢$

42. How far will an automobile go in $(h + 3)$ hours at an average rate of $(m + 1)$ miles an hour? $(hm + 3m + h + 3)$ mi.

[B]

Multiply as indicated: (ans. at foot of pages 246, 247)

43. $(x^2 - y^2)(x^2 + y^2)$

44. $(4x - 6)(\frac{1}{2}x + 1)$

45. $(.4x - 3)(5x + 1)$

46. $(7x^2 - 3xy + y^2)(2x + 3y)$

47. $(x^2 - x + 1)(x^2 + x + 1)$

48. $(2x - 1)(x^3 - x^2 + x - 1)$

49. $(2y^2 + y - 1)(2 - 3y + y^2)$

50. $(x^2 - x + 1)(2 - x + x^2)$

51. $(a + b - c)(a - b + c)$

52. $(x + y + 3)(x + y - 3)$

53. $(3x^2 - 4 - 3x)(2x^2 + 3x)$

54. $(4x^2 - 4x + 3)(2 - x)$

55. $(x + y + z)^2$

56. $(x + y)^3$

57. $(a - b)^3$

58. $(a^2 + b^2)(c + d)$

Example.[B] Simplify $(3x - 1)(5x + 2) - (x + 4)(3x - 2)$.

Solution.

$$
\begin{array}{ll}
3x - 1 & x + 4 \\
5x + 2 & 3x - 2 \\
\hline
15x^2 - 5x & 3x^2 + 12x \\
 + 6x - 2 & - 2x - 8 \\
\hline
15x^2 + x - 2 & 3x^2 + 10x - 8
\end{array}
$$

Then
$$(3x - 1)(5x + 2) - (x + 4)(3x - 2)$$
$$= (15x^2 + x - 2) - (3x^2 + 10x - 8)$$
$$= 15x^2 + x - 2 - 3x^2 - 10x + 8$$
$$= 12x^2 - 9x + 6. \quad Ans.$$

246

43. $x^4 - y^4$
44. $2x^2 + x - 6$
45. $2x^2 - 14.6x - 3$
46. $14x^3 + 15x^2y - 7xy^2 + 3y^3$

47. $x^4 + x^2 + 1$
48. $2x^4 - 3x^3 + 3x^2 - 3x + 1$
49. $2y^4 - 5y^3 + 5y - 2$
50. $x^4 - 2x^3 + 4x^2 - 3x + 2$

ADDITIONAL WORK WITH POLYNOMIALS

When simplifying expressions containing the products of polynomials, always place the products in parentheses, and then simplify the resulting expression.

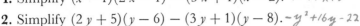

[B]

EXERCISES

1. Simplify $(x - 1)(2x - 1) - (3x + 1)(x - 2)$. $-x^2 + 2x + 3$

2. Simplify $(2y + 5)(y - 6) - (3y + 1)(y - 8)$. $-y^2 + 16y - 22$

3. Simplify $(3c - 1)^2 - (2c + 4)^2$. $5c^2 - 22c - 15$

4. Simplify $(3x + 2)^2 - 3(x + 4)(2x - 3)$. $3x^2 - 3x + 40$

Equations [A]

On page 185 you learned how to solve equations such as Example 1, below.

Example 1. Solve $3 - 2(3x + 2) = 7$.

Solution. The quantity $3x + 2$ is to be multiplied by -2. Then we have

$$3 - 6x - 4 = 7$$
$$-6x = 7 - 3 + 4$$
$$-6x = 8$$
$$x = -1\tfrac{1}{3}$$

There is a slight difference between Example 1 and Example 2.

In Example 1, $3x + 2$ is to be multiplied by 2 and the result is to be subtracted from 3. You were able to do this a short way by multiplying $3x + 2$ by -2 and adding the result to 3.

In Example 2, $(x + 2)$ is to be multiplied by $(x - 5)$ and the result is to be subtracted from 8. Pupils often forget to subtract as indicated. To prevent errors of this kind you should always place the products of the two binomials in parentheses.

Example 2. Solve $8 - (x - 5)(x + 2) = 3 - x^2$.

Solution.
$$8 - (x - 5)(x + 2) = 3 - x^2$$
$$8 - (x^2 - 3x - 10) = 3 - x^2$$
$$8 - x^2 + 3x + 10 = 3 - x^2$$
$$-x^2 + x^2 + 3x = -8 - 10 + 3$$
$$3x = -15$$
$$x = -5$$

$$
\begin{array}{r}
x - 5 \\
x + 2 \\
\hline
x^2 - 5x \\
+2x - 10 \\
\hline
x^2 - 3x - 10
\end{array}
$$

PROOF. Does $8 - (-5 - 5)(-5 + 2) = 3 - (-5)^2$?
Does $8 - (-10)(-3) = 3 - (25)$?
(Page 246) Does $8 - 30 = -22$? Yes.

51. $a^2 - b^2 + 2bc - c^2$
52. $x^2 + 2xy + y^2 - 9$
53. $6x^4 + 3x^3 - 17x^2 - 12x$
54. $-4x^3 + 12x^2 - 11x + 6$

55. $x^2 + 2xy + 2xz + y^2 + 2yz + z^2$
56. $x^3 + 3x^2y + 3xy^2 + y^3$
57. $a^3 - 3a^2b + 3ab^2 - b^3$
58. $a^2c + b^2c + a^2d + b^2d$

247

ALGEBRA, BOOK ONE

EXERCISES

Solve, and prove as directed by your teacher: [A]

1. $9x - (3x - 18) = 36$ 3

2. $-(5x + 4) - 6x = 7$ -1

3. $y + (2y - 1) = 2$ 1

4. $3(2 - y) = 5(3 - y)$ $4\frac{1}{2}$

5. $3c - (c + 2) = 2$ 2

6. $14 = 5x + 3(2 - x)$ 4

7. $3(3x - 1) = 13 + 2(x + 6)$ 4

8. $2(x + 14) = 3 - 7(x - 1)$ -2

9. $2(3x + 1) - 2(15 - 4x) = 0$ 2

10. $2(x - 40) - 3(50 - x) = 20$ 50

11. $x + 5 = 7 - (2x + 1)$ $\frac{1}{3}$

12. $10x - 17 = 2 - (7x - 15)$ 2

13. $(x - 2)(x + 3) = x(x + 4)$ -2

14. $(2x - 1)(2x + 3) = 4x^2 + 9$ 3

15. $(x - 2)(x - 6) - (x - 8)(x - 3) = 0$ 4

CAUTION. Do not forget to place the products in parentheses.

16. $(x - 1)(3x + 4) - (x - 3)(3x + 2) = 0$ $-\frac{1}{4}$

17. $(x - 1)^2 - (x + 1)^2 = 4$ -1

18. $9x(x + 3) - (3x - 1)^2 = 32$ 1

19. $(4x - 1)(x + 1) - (2x - 5)(2x + 4) = 4$ -3

20. $(2x - 1)(3x + 2) = 15 + (3x - 1)(2x + 5)$ -1

21. $(5x + 7)(6x - 2) - 15x(x - 3) = 35 + 15x^2$ $\frac{7}{11}$ [B]

22. $(3x + 5)(4x - 1) - 2(3x - 1)(2x + 3) = 0$ $-\frac{1}{3}$

23. $(3x - 1)(3x + 1) - (3x + 2)^2 = 7$ -1

24. $(x - 3)^2 - (2x - 1)^2 = 3(2 - x^2)$ 1

25. $3(4x - 3)^2 - (x + 6)(x - 5) = 47x^2 - 16$ 1

26. $(4x + 1)(2x - 5) - 2(6x - 1)(6x + 1) + 37 = -64x^2$

27. $4(x - 6)^2 - (x - 1)^2 - 3x(x - 8) = -11$ 7 $1\frac{8}{9}$

28. $(x - 2)(x + 2)(x - 3) = (x - 1)^3 - 1$ 2

29. $(x - 1)(x + 1)(x - 2) = x^3 - 2x^2 - 3$ 5

30. $(x - 3)^3 - (x - 2)^3 = -3x(x - 4) - 19$ 0

Motion Problems [A]

You have already learned that the formula $d = rt$ gives the distance traveled when the rate and time of travel are known. We sometimes call problems about rate, time, and distance *motion problems*.

248

The solution of motion problems must be taught with patience, imagination, and thoroughness since i
seems to be difficult for many students.   See previous suggestions on teaching word problem
(e.g., pp. 188, 189, 190, 195, 199).

ADDITIONAL WORK WITH POLYNOMIALS

[A]

1. How far will a man walk
    a. In 4 hours at the rate of 2 miles an hour? *8 mi*
    b. In 7 hours at the rate of r miles an hour? *7r mi*
    c. In t hours at the rate of r miles an hour? *rt mi.*
    d. In $(x + 3)$ hours at the rate of 5 miles an hour? *5(x+3) mi*
    e. In $(x - 1)$ hours at the rate of x miles an hour? *x(x-1) mi.*

2. How is the formula $r = \dfrac{d}{t}$ obtained from the formula
$d = rt$? How is the rate found when the distance and time are
known? *Divide both members of equation by t; divide the distance by the time.*

3. Find the rate in miles an hour for an airplane to go
    a. 1000 miles in $2\frac{1}{2}$ hours; *400 m.p.h.*
    b. 600 miles in 2 hours; *300 m. p. h.*
    c. 900 miles in 2 hours; *450 m.p.h.*
    d. $(4x + 8)$ miles in 4 hours; *(x+2) m. p. h.*
    e. $(x^2 + 5x)$ miles in x hours. *(x+5) m. p. h.*

4. How is the formula $t = \dfrac{d}{r}$ obtained from the formula
$d = rt$? How is the time found when the distance and rate are
known? *Divide both members of the equation by r; divide the distance by the rate.*

5. How much time is required for an automobile to go
    a. 120 miles at 40 miles an hour? *3 hr.*
    b. $4x$ miles at x miles an hour? *4 hr.*
    c. $(x - 3)$ miles at 8 miles an hour? $\left(\dfrac{x-3}{8}\right)$ *hr.*
    d. $(m^2 + m)$ miles at m miles an hour? *(m+1) hr.*

6. Find the missing numbers in the table below.

	TIME	RATE	DISTANCE			TIME	RATE	DISTANCE
a.	3	? *4*	12		d.	2 t	t − 4	*2t(t−4)*
b.	4	x + 2	*4(x+2)*		e.	? *t*	8	8 t
c.	? *8b*	a	8 ab		f.	*x−4*	x	x² − 4 x

In solving motion problems many people find it helpful to set down
the given information in charts, as shown in the following examples.

249

Example 1. An hour after Bill left on a week-end bicycle trip his family noticed that he had forgotten a package. Tom, an older brother, jumped into his car and started after Bill. If Bill was traveling at the rate of 8 miles per hour, and Tom drove at the rate of 40 miles per hour, how long did it take Tom to catch up with Bill?

Solution.

WHAT THE PROBLEM SOLVER
THINKS

WHAT THE PROBLEM SOLVER
WRITES

1. A sketch will help me to understand the facts given. (Note. The red numbers are written in later.)

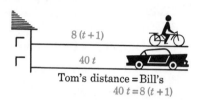

2. Since the problem is about time, rate, and distance, I will make a chart to show information about those things.

Tom's distance = Bill's
$40 t = 8 (t + 1)$

3. Since the problem is about two people, I shall need to record times, rates, and distances for each.

	RATE	×	TIME	=	DISTANCE
Bill	8		$t + 1$		$8(t + 1)$
Tom	40		t		$40 t$

4. Since the rates are given, I can fill in the rates on the chart.

Let $t =$ Tom's time, in hours.

5. The problem asks, "How long did it take Tom to catch up with Bill?" I can let t equal Tom's time. I can put that information in the chart.

Then
$$40 t = 8(t + 1)$$
$$40 t = 8 t + 8$$
$$32 t = 8$$
$$t = \tfrac{1}{4}$$

Tom needed $\tfrac{1}{4}$ hour to catch up with Bill.

6. Bill had been gone an hour when Tom started, so Bill's time will be $t + 1$. I can put that in the chart.

PROOF. Tom went $\tfrac{1}{4}$ hour at 40 m.p.h., or 10 miles.

7. Since rate *times* time *equals* distance, $8(t + 1)$ is Bill's distance and $40 t$ is Tom's.

Bill went $1\tfrac{1}{4}$ hours at 8 m.p.h., or 10 miles.

The distances are equal.

8. Since both started from home and traveled to the same spot, the distances are equal. I can express that as an equation.

This is the type of analysis which needs to be done in class and by the student when doing independent work. Urge that students study it carefully. You might further discuss the box chart as follows: "Note that the formula $d = rt$ must be used *somewhere* in the solution—usually in the preparation of the chart. Then the equation is formed by comparing the expressions in the column last obtained by use of the formula. The information for this comparison is found in the words of the problem." If comparing distances, you might ask, "Are the distances equal? Do you know their sum? their difference? their quotient?"

Example 2. Ann and Sue have agreed to meet and attend a show. Ann has just phoned Sue to say that she is ready to start. Sue is also ready. In how many minutes will the girls meet if they walk toward each other, Sue at the rate of one block per minute, and Ann at the rate of $\frac{3}{4}$ block per minute? Their homes are 14 blocks apart. How far from Ann's home will they meet?

Solution.

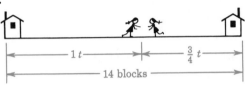

Since the girls started at the same time and walked until they met, they walked the same number of minutes.

	RATE	×	TIME	=	DISTANCE
Sue	1		t		$1 \cdot t$
Ann	$\frac{3}{4}$		t		$\frac{3}{4}t$

Let t = the number of minutes each girl walks.
$$t + \tfrac{3}{4}t = 14$$
$$4t + 3t = 56$$
$$7t = 56$$
$$t = 8$$

The girls will meet 8 minutes after they start.

Since Ann's distance is $\frac{3}{4}t$, she will walk $\frac{3}{4} \cdot 8$, or 6 blocks.

[A]

WRITTEN EXERCISES

1. Al goes 8 miles an hour. Ben goes 20 miles an hour in the opposite direction. How many hours has Ben traveled when they are 180 miles apart? (They travel the same time, t.) $6\frac{3}{7}hr.$

2. Al and Ben, who are 566 miles apart, start in automobiles toward each other. Al drives 45 miles an hour and Ben drives 55 miles an hour. How soon will they meet if Al has an accident and is delayed an hour? $6hr. 7 min., approx.$

3. Al and Ben started from the same place and went in opposite directions, Al traveling 30 miles an hour and Ben 10 miles an hour. If Ben started 3 hours before Al, how long had Al traveled when they were 90 miles apart? $1\frac{1}{2}hr.$

4. A boat started from Chicago toward Muskegon at 10 miles an hour. Two hours later another boat started from Chicago to Muskegon at 14 miles an hour. How long did it take the second boat to overtake the first? $5hr.$

5. Horace started west on road U. S. 50, riding a bicycle at an average rate of 9 miles an hour. Four hours later Charles started after Horace on a motorcycle and overtook him in 2 hours. What was Charles's rate? *27 m. p. h.*

6. Portland, Oregon, and Seattle, Washington, are about 175 miles apart by road. Driver *A* travels at the rate of 45 miles an hour. Driver *B* travels at the rate of 50 miles per hour. Driver *A* leaves Portland for Seattle at 8 o'clock and driver *B* leaves Seattle for Portland at 9 o'clock. When will the drivers pass each other? *10:22 o'clock*

SUGGESTION. Let *t* = the number of hours *B* travels before they meet.

7. A train traveling 50 miles an hour left a station 30 minutes before a second train running 55 miles an hour. How soon did the second train overtake the first? *In 5 hr.*

8. A boat which travels 10 knots (nautical mi./hr.) is followed six hours later by another boat which travels 14 knots. In how many hours will the second boat overtake the first? *15 hr.*

9. Two planes start at the same time from towns 1530 miles apart and meet in $1\frac{1}{2}$ hours. If the rate of one plane is 180 miles an hour less than the rate of the other, what is the rate of each? *420 m. p. h. ; 600 m. p. h.*

[B]

10. Dick can run the 440-yard dash in 55 seconds, and Jack can run it in 88 seconds. How great a handicap must Dick give Jack in order that the boys may finish the race at the same time? *165 yd.*

11. The Indianapolis Speedway is $2\frac{1}{2}$ miles around. How long will it take a driver going 156.25 miles an hour to gain a lap on a driver going 150 miles an hour? *24 min.*

12. Mr. Jackson drove his automobile from his home to Boston at a rate of 40 miles an hour and returned at a rate of 45 miles an hour. Find his time going and returning if the time returning was one hour less than the time going. *9 hr. going ; 8 hr. returning*

13. In 2 hours 42 minutes, how far can a plane go and return if the rate going is 280 miles an hour and the rate returning is 350 miles an hour? *420 mi.*

Watch for original methods. For example, in Ex. 5, someone may assign x to represent the number of miles traveled by each. Point out that this method is permissible, and in fact sometimes preferable, *provided the answer is interpreted so that the question is correctly answered.*

ADDITIONAL WORK WITH POLYNOMIALS

14. A rancher drove to town at 40 miles an hour and returned at 50 miles an hour. What was his time in each direction if his total driving time was 1 hour 21 minutes? *go 45 min.* *return 36 min.* ①

Work Problems [A]

Work problems usually deal with the amount of time needed to do a piece of work.

Example 1. One printing press can print 6000 copies an hour, and another can print 4000 an hour. After the second press has been running 2 hours, the first press is started. How soon after the first press is started will 40,000 copies be finished?

Solution. Let $x =$ the number of hours the first press runs

$x + 2 =$ the number of hours the second press runs

Then $6000 x + 4000(x + 2) = 40,000$

$6000 x + 4000 x + 8000 = 40,000$

$6000 x + 4000 x = 40,000 - 8000$

$10,000 x = 32,000$

$x = 3\frac{1}{5}$, the number of hours that the first press runs

Example 2. Jim can do a piece of work in 3 days, and Harry can do the same work in 2 days. How long will it take them to do the work if they work together?

Solution. In solving a problem like this we first find what part of the work each individual can do in one unit of time.

If Jim can do all the work in 3 days, he can do $\frac{1}{3}$ of the work in one day. If Harry can do all the work in 2 days, he can do $\frac{1}{2}$ of the work in one day.

Let $x =$ the number of days required to do the work when they work together

Then $x\left(\frac{1}{3}\right)$ or $\frac{x}{3} =$ the part of the work that Jim does in x days. Why?   ② below

And $x\left(\frac{1}{2}\right)$ or $\frac{x}{2} =$ the part of the work that Harry does in x days.

Since both together do the whole of the work,

$\frac{x}{3} + \frac{x}{2} = 1$

$2 x + 3 x = 6$

$5 x = 6$

$x = 1\frac{1}{5}$, the number of days required

There is no magic in the number 1. Students should think of it as 3/3, 2/2, 6/6. Extend some of the exercises to read, "How long will it take to do 3/4 of the work?"

ALGEBRA, BOOK ONE

[A]

WORK PROBLEMS

1. Frank can mow a lawn with one lawn mower in 2 hours and Jessie can mow it with another lawn mower in 3 hours. How long will it take them to mow the lawn if they work together? $1\frac{1}{5}$ *hr.*

2. Alan can do a piece of work in 8 days and Bill can do the same work in 10 days. How long will it take them working together to do the work? $4\frac{4}{9}$ *da.*

3. One printing press can print 4000 copies an hour and another press can print 3000 copies an hour. After the first press has been going 3 hours, the second press is started. How soon after the start of the second press will 50,500 copies be printed? $5\frac{1}{2}$ *hr.*

4. John can build a bird house in 24 hours and Wilbur can build one like it in 30 hours. After John has worked 10 hours on the construction of a bird house, Wilbur begins to help him. How many more hours are needed for the boys to complete the house? $7\frac{3}{9}$ *hr.*

5. Mary can grade a set of papers in 45 minutes, Jane can grade the set in 50 minutes, and Frances can grade the set in 40 minutes. How long will it take all three girls working together to do the grading? 14.9 *min.*

6. Frank can dig a trench in 15 hours and his father can dig it in 9 hours. How long will it take Frank and his father working together to dig the trench? $5\frac{5}{8}$ *hr.*

7. Bob can do a task in 10 hours and Roy can do it in 12 hours. After Bob has worked on the job for 3 hours, how many hours are needed for both boys to complete the job? $3\frac{9}{11}$ *hr.*

Mixture Problems [A]

In solving mixture problems you will find it helpful to make sketches and imagine you are actually making the mixtures.

Example 1. A seedsman has clover seed worth $1.60 a pound and timothy seed worth $1.00 a pound. How many pounds of each should he use to make a mixture of 300 pounds worth $1.20 a pound?

254

ADDITIONAL WORK WITH POLYNOMIALS

Solution.

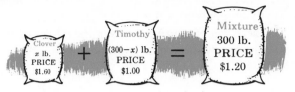

Let x = the number of pounds of clover seed.
Value of clover + value of timothy = value of mixture

$$1.60\,x + 1.00(300 - x) = 1.20(300)$$
$$1.60\,x + 300 - x = 360$$
$$.60\,x = 60$$
$$x = 100, \text{ pounds of clover.}$$
$$300 - x = 200, \text{ pounds of timothy.}$$

[A]

MIXTURE PROBLEMS

1. How many pounds of cashew nuts worth $2.10 a pound must be mixed with 10 pounds of pecans worth $2.25 a pound to make a mixture worth $2.15 a pound? *20 lb.*

2. A dealer in tea has one brand of instant tea worth $5.28 a pound and another worth $6.72 a pound. How many pounds of each kind must he use to make a 60-pound mixture worth $6.08 a pound? *$5.28, 26⅔ lb.; $6.72, 33⅓ lb.*

3. Suppose oats are selling for $1.38 per bushel and wheat for $4.10 per bushel. How many bushels of each should be used in a 100-pound mixture of the two that can be sold for $3.42 per bushel? *Oats-25 bu., Wheat - 75 bu.*

4. One kind of syrup selling for $6.10 per gallon is mixed with corn syrup selling for $2.95 per gallon to make a mixture that can be sold for $3.58 per gallon. How much of each kind of syrup is needed for 50 gallons of the mixture? *$6.10, 10 gal. $2.95, 40 gal.*

5. Some Girl Scouts wish to make a mixture of two kinds of candy which they can sell at 46 cents per pound. They use 12 pounds of candy which they can sell alone for x cents a pound and 18 pounds of candy which they can sell alone for $(x + 20)$ cents per pound. For how much per pound can each of these two kinds of candy be sold? *12 lb., 34¢; 18 lb., 54¢*

6. An order of candy cost $14. It contained one kind of candy worth 60 cents a pound and another worth 50 cents a pound. If there were 5 more pounds of the 60-cent candy than of the 50-cent candy, how many pounds of each kind were in the order? *50¢, 10 lb.; 60¢, 15 lb.*

[B]

7. a. In preparing for a party, a caterer mixed cans of orange juice worth 39 cents per can, pineapple juice worth 47 cents per can, and grapefruit juice worth 57 cents per can to make a fruit drink worth $44\frac{2}{3}$ cents per can. Assume that the cans were of the same size. He used 2 more cans of orange juice than of grapefruit juice and 1 more can of pineapple juice than of grapefruit juice. How many of each did he use? *1 Grapefruit, 2 pineapple, 3 Orange*

b. Suppose the caterer had added 2 cans of ginger ale worth 48 cents per can (of the same size) to the ingredients of the fruit drink in part **a.** What would be the cost per can of the mixture? *45½¢*

c. Assume that the caterer mixed only orange juice and grapefruit juice. The cans of juice were the same size and their prices were the same as in part **a.** He used 46 cans of orange juice and charged $36.75 for the mixture. How many cans of grapefruit juice did he use in the mixture? *33 cans.*

Example 2. A 10% solution of iodine contains 10% iodine and 90% alcohol. How much alcohol must be added to one quart of a 10% solution of iodine to produce a 6% solution of iodine?

Notice that pure alcohol is 100% alcohol and 0% iodine. Notice also that in a 6% solution of iodine, 6% of the solution will be iodine and the remaining 94% alcohol. These facts make it possible to solve the problem in two ways.

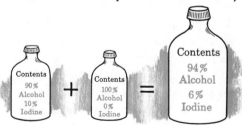

ADDITIONAL WORK WITH POLYNOMIALS

Solution 1 (Based on iodine content)	**Solution 2** (Based on alcohol content)

Let x = quarts of alcohol added

Iodine in 10% solution	+	Iodine in pure alcohol	=	Iodine in mixture

$$.10 \cdot 1 + 0\,x = .06(1 + x)$$
$$.10 = .06 + .06\,x$$
M_{100} $\qquad 10 = 6 + 6\,x$
$$4 = 6\,x$$
$$x = \tfrac{2}{3}, \text{ quarts of}$$
$$\text{alcohol}$$
$$\text{added}$$

Let x = quarts of alcohol added

Alcohol in 10% solution	+	Alcohol in pure alcohol	=	Alcohol in mixture

$$.90 \cdot 1 + 1.00\,x = .94(1 + x)$$
$$.90 + 1.00\,x = .94 + .94\,x.$$
$M_{100}, 90 + 100\,x = 94 + 94\,x$
$$6\,x = 4$$
$$x = \tfrac{2}{3}, \text{ quarts of}$$
$$\text{alcohol}$$
$$\text{added}$$

8. A 3-gallon antifreeze solution of water and alcohol is 20% alcohol. How much alcohol must be added to make the solution 40% alcohol? *1 gal.*

9. In an alloy of copper and zinc there are 75 pounds of copper and 25 pounds of zinc. How many pounds of pure copper must be added to the alloy so that it will be 80% copper? *25*

10. Nickel bronze is an alloy of copper and nickel. How much nickel must be melted with 100 pounds of nickel bronze which is 25% nickel to produce an alloy that is 40% nickel? *25 lb.*

11. Some United States silver coins are $\frac{9}{10}$ pure silver or "$\frac{9}{10}$ fine." How much pure silver must be melted with 200 ounces of silver $\frac{3}{5}$ fine to make it of the standard fineness for coinage? *600 oz.*

12. How much pure gold must be added to 120 ounces of gold 16 carats fine ($\frac{16}{24}$ pure) to make an alloy 22 carats fine? *360 oz.*

13. How many tons of 8% copper ore and of 3% ore should be mixed to make 300 tons of 6% ore? *8%, 180 T.; 3%, 120 T.*

14. How many gallons of cream containing 40% fat must be mixed with 160 gallons of skim milk to make milk containing 8% fat? *40*

[C]

15. A solution of 60 pounds of salt and water is 5% salt. How much water must be evaporated so that the solution will be 10% salt? *30 lb.*

16. An automobile radiator contains 4 gallons of a mixture of water and antifreeze. If the mixture is now 20% antifreeze, how much of the mixture must be drawn off and replaced by pure antifreeze to get a mixture containing 30% antifreeze? *½ gal.*

Review of Dividing by Monomials [A]

In the next article we shall learn how to divide one polynomial by another. The following exercises are intended to give you the necessary preparation for this new work.

[A]

ORAL EXERCISES

Divide as indicated:

1. $x^3 \div x$ *x^2*
2. $6x \div 6$ *x*
3. $-30a \div 6$ *$5a$*
4. $\dfrac{12x^2}{-2x}$ *$-6x$*
5. $-\dfrac{x^7}{x^3}$ *$-x^4$*

6. $(8x^2) \div (8x^2)$ *1*
7. $4xy \div (2y)$ *$2x$*
8. $-x^3y^2 \div (xy^2)$ *$-x^2$*
9. $\dfrac{-18ab}{-9b}$ *$2a$*
10. $\dfrac{x^3y^2z}{xy^2}$ *x^2z*

11. $(x^3y^5) \div (x^2y)$ *xy^4*
12. $(4.5a^2b^4) \div 1.5$ *$3a^2b^4$*
13. $\left(\dfrac{1}{2}x^3y\right) \div (2xy)$ *$\frac{1}{4}x^2$*
14. $(20x^7) \div (-4x)$ *$-5x^6$*
15. $\dfrac{10^3}{10}$ *10^2*

Divide:

16. $4x - 8$ by 4 *$x-2$*
17. $18r + 12s$ by -6 *$-3r-2s$*
18. $8x^2 - x$ by x *$8x-1$*
19. $25ce + 30e$ by $5e$ *$5c+6$*
20. $9cz - 18c^2z$ by cz *$9-18c$*
21. $12x^4 - 18x$ by $-6x$ *$-2x^3+3$*
22. $y^3 + y$ by y *y^2+1*
23. $x^4 - x$ by x *x^3-1*
24. $r^5 + r$ by $-r$ *$-r^4-1$*

25. $8a^2b^2 - 6ab$ by $-2ab$ *$-4ab+3$*
26. $7c^2 - 14c^5$ by $(-7c^2)$ *$-1+2c^3$*
27. $\left(\dfrac{1}{2}x^3 - \dfrac{1}{3}y\right)$ by $\dfrac{1}{6}$ *$3x^3-2y$*
28. $\left(\dfrac{2}{3}c + \dfrac{3}{2}\right)$ by $\dfrac{5}{6}$ *$\frac{4}{5}c+\frac{9}{5}$*
29. $(.5a + .15)$ by $.5$ *$a+0.3$*
30. $(a^2c - ac^2)$ by $(-ac)$ *$-a+c$*
31. $(x^3 - x^2 + x)$ by $.1x$ *$10x^2-10x+10$*
32. $(4x^4 - 2x^2)$ by $(.2x^2)$ *$20x^2-10$*
33. $(a^3b - ab^3)$ by (ab) *a^2-b^2*

Dividing a Polynomial by a Polynomial [A]

The division of one polynomial by another is very similar to long division in arithmetic. As you are learning how to divide by a polynomial, think how you divide by long division in arithmetic. Compare the two divisions on the next page.

258

Example 1.

Divide 695 by 31

$$\begin{array}{r} 2 \\ 31\overline{)695} \end{array}$$

We divide the first digit/term (that is, in arithmetic the first digit and in algebra the first term) of the dividend by the first digit/term of the divisor to find the first digit/term of the quotient.

Divide $x^2 - 8x + 17$ by $x - 3$

$$x - 3\overline{)x^2 - 8x + 17}^{\ \ \ x}$$

$$\begin{array}{r} 2 \\ 31\overline{)695} \\ 62 \\ \hline 75 \end{array}$$

Then we multiply the whole divisor by this digit/term of the quotient and subtract the result from the dividend to obtain a new dividend.

$$\begin{array}{r} x \quad\quad\quad\quad \\ x - 3\overline{)x^2 - 8x + 17} \\ \underline{x^2 - 3x} \\ -5x + 17 \end{array}$$

$$\begin{array}{r} 22 \\ 31\overline{)695} \\ 62 \\ \hline 75 \end{array}$$

Now we divide the first digit/term of the new dividend by the first term of the divisor to obtain the next digit/term of the quotient.

$$\begin{array}{r} x \ - 5 \\ x - 3\overline{)x^2 - 8x + 17} \\ \underline{x^2 - 3x} \\ -5x + 17 \end{array}$$

$$\begin{array}{r} 22 \\ 31\overline{)695} \\ 62 \\ \hline 75 \\ 62 \\ \hline 13 \end{array}$$

We multiply the whole divisor by the last digit/term of the quotient and subtract the result from the new dividend.

$$\begin{array}{r} x \ - 5 \\ x - 3\overline{)x^2 - 8x + 17} \\ \underline{x^2 - 3x} \\ -5x + 17 \\ \underline{-5x + 15} \\ 2 \end{array}$$

$$695 \div 31 = 22 + \tfrac{13}{31}$$

$$(x^2 - 8x + 17) \div (x - 3)$$
$$= x - 5 + \frac{2}{x - 3}$$

CHECK

$$\begin{array}{r} 31 \\ 22 \\ \hline 62 \\ 62 \\ \hline 682 \\ 13 \\ \hline 695 \end{array}$$

To check a division we multiply the quotient by the divisor, then add the remainder to the product. The resulting number should be the dividend.

CHECK

$$\begin{array}{r} x \ - 3 \\ x \ - 5 \\ \hline x^2 - 3x \\ -5x + 15 \\ \hline x^2 - 8x + 15 \\ 2 \\ \hline x^2 - 8x + 17 \end{array}$$

Note the careful development of the analogy between division in arithmetic and in algebra. You might do a second example like this before turning to the rule on page 260, which should be the result of this approach.

To Divide by a Polynomial

1. Arrange the terms of both dividend and divisor
in descending (or ascending) powers of one ietter.
2. Divide the *first term* of the dividend by the *first term* of the divisor
to find the first term of the quotient.
3. Multiply the *whole* divisor by this term of the quotient
and subtract the result from the dividend
to obtain a new dividend.
4. Continue this process
until the first term of the dividend cannot be divided exactly
by the first term of the divisor.

Example 2. Divide $x^3 - 17 xy^2 + 66 y^3 - 5 x^2y$ by $x - 6y$.

Solution.

Arrange both dividend and
divisor in descending powers of x
(pay no attention to y); then
divide according to instructions.

①

$$
\begin{array}{r}
x^2 + xy - 11 y^2 \\
x - 6y \overline{\smash{\big)}\, x^3 - 5 x^2y - 17 xy^2 + 66 y^3} \\
\underline{x^3 - 6 x^2y} \\
x^2y - 17 xy^2 + 66 y^3 \\
\underline{x^2y - 6 xy^2} \\
- 11 xy^2 + 66 y^3 \\
\underline{- 11 xy^2 + 66 y^3} \\
0
\end{array}
$$

CHECK. $(x - 6y)(x^2 + xy - 11 y^2) = x^3 - 5 x^2y - 17 xy^2 + 66 y^3$

Example 3. Divide $a^2 - 25$ by $a - 5$.

Solution.

Since there is no term in a,
$0\, a$ is inserted.

$$
\begin{array}{r}
a + 5 \\
a - 5 \overline{\smash{\big)}\, a^2 + 0\, a - 25} \\
\underline{a^2 - 5 a} \\
5 a - 25 \\
5 a - 25
\end{array}
$$

Checking Division[A]

A division may be checked in three ways:
1. By performing the division again.
2. By substitution.
3. By multiplying the quotient by the divisor and adding the remainder to the product to obtain the dividend.

②

260 ① Emphasize the word *arrange*. Division is the one of the four processes where arrangement is essential, not just preferable.

② Method 3 is the preferable one. But for meaning, you might have the class do an example, and then divide the dividend by the obtained quotient, and come to a conclusion about the result.

ADDITIONAL WORK WITH POLYNOMIALS

[A]

EXERCISES

Divide, and check as directed by your teacher:

1. $x^2 - 6x + 9$ by $x - 3$ *x-3*   11. $2x^2 - 5x + 72$ by $x - 7$ *2x+9+$\frac{135}{x-7}$*

2. $m^2 + 8m + 12$ by $m + 2$ *m+6*   12. $4c^2 - 8c + 3$ by $2c - 3$ *2c-1*

3. $c^2 + 11c + 24$ by $c + 3$ *c+8*   13. $3x^2 + x - 1$ by $x - 2$ *3x+7+$\frac{13}{x-2}$*

4. $x^2 - 7x + 10$ by $x - 5$ *x-2*   14. $8x^2 + 3x + 4$ by $x - 3$ *8x+27+$\frac{85}{x-3}$*

5. $x^2 - 9x + 20$ by $x - 4$ *x-5*   15. $x^2 - 1$ by $x - 1$ *x+1*

6. $y^2 - 9y + 15$ by $y - 2$ *y-7+$\frac{1}{y-2}$*   16. $m^2 - 9$ by $m + 3$ *m-3*

7. $x^2 + 4x - 12$ by $x + 6$ *x-2*   17. $x^2 - 4$ by $x + 2$ *x-2*

8. $y^2 - 2y - 15$ by $y - 5$ *y+3*   18. $x^2 - 16$ by $x - 4$ *x+4*

9. $t^2 - 3t - 28$ by $t - 7$ *x+4*   19. $x^2 - y^2$ by $x - y$ *x+y*

10. $x^2 - x - 42$ by $x + 6$ *x-7*   20. $h^2 - 64y^2$ by $h - 4y$ *h+4y-$\frac{48y^2}{h-4y}$*

21. $12x^2 - 11xy - 36y^2$ by $4x - 9y$ *3x+4y*

22. $m^2 - 3mn - 88n^2$ by $m + 8n$ *m-11n*

23. $x^4 + 6x^2 - 27$ by $x^2 - 3$ *x²+9*

24. $12x^3 - 11x^2 + 8x - 4$ by $3x - 2$ *4x²-x+2*

25. $24x^2 + 15 - 38x$ by $6x - 5$. (Rearrange dividend.) *4x-3*

26. $2y^3 - 6y - 5 - 11y^2$ by $y - 5$ *2y²-y-11-$\frac{60}{y-5}$*

27. $a^3 - 17a - 5a^2 + 66$ by $a - 6$ *a²+a-11*

28. $a^3 - 6a^2 - 8 + 12a$ by $a - 2$ *a²-4a+4*

29. One factor of $x^3 - 5x^2 + 7x - 2$ is $x - 2$. What is the other factor? *x²-3x+1*

[B]

30. $2a^3b - 6a^2b + 18ab$ by $a^2 - 3a + 9$ *2ab*

31. $2x^3 + 11x - 3 - 9x^2$ by $2x - 3$ *x²-3x+1*

32. $4a^4 - 9a^2 - 6a - 1$ by $2a^2 - 1 + 3a$ *2a²-3a+1-$\frac{12a}{2a²+3a-1}$*

33. One factor of $6x^3 - 18x + 12$ is $x - 1$. What is the other factor? *6x²+6x-12*

34. $a^3 - 1$ by $a - 1$ *a²+a+1*   37. $a^3 - 8$ by $a - 2$ *a²+2a+4*
    $a^3 - 1 = a^3 + 0a^2 + 0a - 1$ 38. $x^3 - y^3$ by $x - y$ *x²+xy+y²*

35. $a^3 + 1$ by $a + 1$ *a²-a+1*   39. $x^3 + y^3$ by $x + y$ *x²-xy+y²*

36. $a^3 + 8$ by $a + 2$ *a²-2a+4*   40. $x^3 - 27$ by $x - 3$ *x²+3x+9*

261

48. $2x^2 + x + 3 + \dfrac{16x}{3x^2 - 5x + 7}$ 45. $x^3 - x^2 + x - 1 + \dfrac{2}{x+1}$

$x^4 - 2x^3 + 4x^2 - 8x + 16$

41. $x^3 + 64$ by $x + 4$ $x^2 - 4x + 16$ **44.** $x^5 + 32$ by $x + 2$

42. $27\,x^3 + 8$ by $3\,x + 2$ **45.** $x^4 + 1$ by $x + 1$

$9x^2 - 6x + 4$

43. $x^4 - 1$ by $x - 1$ **46.** $x^5 - 1$ by $x - 1$

$x^3 + x^2 + x + 1$ $x^4 + x^3 + x^2 + x + 1$ [C]

47. $a^4 + a^2b^2 + b^4$ by $a^2 - ab + b^2$ $a^2 + ab + b^2$

48. $-7\,x^3 + 21 + 8\,x + 18\,x^2 + 6\,x^4$ by $3\,x^2 - 5\,x + 7$

49. One factor of $x^5 + 1$ is $x + 1$. What is the other?

$x^4 - x^3 + x^2 - x + 1$

50. $x^6 - y^6$ by $x^4 + x^2y^2 + y^4$ $x^2 - y^2$

51. $a^3 - b^3 + c^3 - 3\,abc$ by $a + b + c$

$a^2 - ab - ac + b^2 - bc + c^2 - \dfrac{2b^3}{a + b + c}$

Checking Your Understanding of Chapter 9

Make sure that you can

1. Multiply polynomials by polynomials (see p. 243). This includes being able to perform the multiplications when the factors are not arranged in the best order (p. 244).

The pages in parentheses will help you to review.

2. Check your multiplications (pp. 244, 245).

3. Solve equations which involve products of polynomials (p. 247).

4. Divide polynomials by polynomials (pp. 258, 259).

This includes being able to divide polynomials in which the terms are not well arranged (p. 260) and those in which some terms are zero (p. 260).

5. Spell and use the following words and expressions:

ascending powers	monomial	polynomial
descending powers	parentheses	partial product

[A]

CHAPTER REVIEW

1. If c is the cost of a dozen oranges, what is the cost of one orange? $\dfrac{c}{12}$

2. What is the cost of x dozen pencils at y cents a dozen? xy ¢

3. Find the cube of $-4\,x$. $-64x^3$

4. Simplify:

a. x^3x^4 x^7 **d.** $(m^3n^2)mn$ m^4n^3 **g.** $a(bc)(ac)$ a^2bc^2

b. x^2yx^3 x^5y **e.** $(xy)^4$ x^4y^4 **h.** $(b + c)b$ $b^2 + bc$

c. $mmmn$ m^4 **f.** $c^2d^3(2\,cd^2)$ $2c^3d^5$ **i.** $2\,x(x - 3)$ $2x^2 - 6x$

5. Divide as indicated:

a. $(16\,c^2) \div (4\,c)$ $4c$

b. $(mn^3) \div (mn)$ n^2

c. $(32\,x^4) \div (8\,x)$ $4x^3$

d. $(-18\,a^2b^3) \div (-6\,ab^2)$ $3ab$

6. Divide, and check by multiplying the quotient by the divisor:

a. $x^2 - 7x + 12$ by $x - 4$ $x-3$

b. $x^3 - x + 6$ by $x + 2$ x^2-2x+3

c. $y^3 - 3y^2 + 3y + 1$ by $y - 1$ $y^2-2y+1+\dfrac{2}{y-1}$

d. $a^2 - b^2$ by $a + b$ $a-b$

e. $x^2 - 9$ by $x - 3$ $x+3$

f. $x^2 + 1$ by $x + 1$ $x-1+\dfrac{2}{x+1}$

7. Solve:

a. $3x - 2(4 - x) = 2(5x + 8)$ $-4\frac{4}{5}$

b. $4(y + 1) - 3(y - 3) = 2(y - 5)$ 23

c. $0.4(2x + 1) - 0.3(5 - x) = 0$ 1

d. $51 - (2x + 6) = 3x - 5(3x - 1)$ -4

e. $(x + 2)^2 - (x - 2)^2 = 16$ 2

f. $18 - (3x + 1)(2x + 4) = 57 - (6x - 1)(x - 4)$ -1

8. Multiply:

a. $(x + 7y)(2x - 3y)$ $2x^2+11xy-21y^2$

b. $(x^2 - 3x + 1)(x + 2)$ x^3-x^2-5x+2

c. $(x^2 - 2xy + y^2)(x - y)$ $x^3-3x^2y+3xy^2-y^3$

d. $(x^3 - 2x^2 + 3x + 1)(x - 2)$ $x^4-4x^3+7x^2-5x-2$

9. Simplify:

a. $3(x - 1) + 2(x - 4)$ $5x-11$

b. $2x(x + 6) - 3x(x - 5)$ $-x^2+27x$

c. $2x(3x + 2) + x(x - 3)$ $7x^2+x$

d. $16 - 2(x + 1) - 2x$ $14-4x$

10. Karl and Ben start at the same point and travel in opposite directions, Karl at the rate of 4 miles an hour, and Ben at the rate of 5 miles an hour. If Karl starts an hour before Ben, how many hours has each been traveling when they are 49 miles apart? $B., 5\,hr.; K., 6\,hr.$

11. One automobile goes 36 miles an hour and another automobile goes 48 miles an hour in the same direction. If they start from the same place at the same time, how many hours have elapsed when they are 36 miles apart? $3\,hr.$

12. Sam can wash and polish the family car in 2 hours. It takes Jack 3 hours to do the same job. How long should it take the boys if they work together? $1\frac{1}{5}\,hr.$

13. Cranberry juice worth 59 cents a quart and apple juice worth 49 cents a quart are used to make a mixture worth 53 cents a quart. How much of each kind of juice is needed for 25 quarts of the mixture? *Cranberry: 10 qt.; Apple Juice: 15 qt.*

[A]

GENERAL REVIEW

1. What is the cost of 7 c books if 2 x books cost 4 cx cents? *14c² ÷*

2. Change the fraction $\frac{2}{5}$ to a per cent. *40%*

3. 80 is what per cent of 20? *400%*

4. Subtract $\frac{1}{2}$ from $\frac{1}{3}$. *–⅙*

5. Simplify $7a - 3b + 4c - 8b - 9a - c$. *–2a–11b+3c*

6. Add $4x^3 - 7x^2y - y^3$, $xy^2 - 2x^2y - 4y^3$, and $x^3 - x^2y + 5xy^2 - 10y^3$. *5x³–10x²y +6xy²–15y³*

7. From the sum of $3x - 10$ and $x^2 + x - 1$ take the sum of $2x + 6$ and $3x^2 - 5x + 4$. *–2x²+7x–21*

8. Divide, and check by multiplying the quotient by the divisor: *c³–2c² + 1*

a. $(4c^3 - 8c^2 + 4) \div 4$ *–a³+2a² – 1.*

b. $(5q^3 - 10a^2 + 5) \div (-5)$ *–x²+x +1*

c. $(x^3 - x^2 - x) \div (-x)$

d. $(12x^3y^2 + 10x^2y^3) \div (2x^2y^2)$ *6x + 5y*   *–5a +6b –7c*

e. $(5a - 6b + 7c) \div (-1)$

f. $(vt - \frac{1}{2}gt^2) \div t$ *v–½gt.*

9. Solve:

a. $4x - 7 - x = -8x$ *7/11*

b. $2(x + 2) = 8$ *2*

c. $(6c + 4) - (3c + 1) = 11$ *2⅔*

d. $4(2x - 9) = 14x - 36$ *0*

e. $x - \dfrac{x + 7}{4} = \dfrac{x - 7}{4}$ *0*

f. $\dfrac{3p - 4}{2} - \dfrac{5p - 2}{14} = 5$ *6*

g. $\dfrac{3m - 1}{4} - \dfrac{4m - 2}{5} = \dfrac{1}{12}$ *7⅓*

10. Solve for x:

a. $3x - 5x = 2a$ *–a*

b. $4x - 5a = 3a$ *2a*

c. $cx - a = b$ *a+b/c*

d. $\dfrac{x}{a} = \dfrac{b}{c}$ *ab/c*

e. $2bx - b^2 = 3b^2$ *2b*

f. $2cx + 3cd = 4cx + 7cd$ *–2d*

g. $5ax - b = 3c - 4ax$ *3c+b/9a*

h. $\dfrac{a}{x} = \dfrac{b}{c}$ *ac/b*

① Remember, constant reviewing is necessary in mathematics or students forget and do not see the over-all development of the subject. Perhaps now is a good time to take a day for review. If so, you might follow up with the cumulative test on page 268.

11. If $x = 3$, $y = -2$, and $z = 0$, find the value of

a. $x^3 + 4y^3$ -5

b. $y - x^2 - 6$ -17

c. $\dfrac{xy + z^2 - 6}{y^2}$ -3

d. $xy + yz + xz$ -6

e. $z^2 + x^3 + y^3$ 19

f. $\dfrac{4x^2 - 5y^2}{6z - 4}$ -4

12. $T = 2\pi r(r + h)$. Find T if $h = 12$, $\pi = 3.14$, and $r = 3$. 282.6

13. $s = vt + \frac{1}{2}gt^2$. Find the value of g if $s = 699.6$, $v = 20$, and $t = 6$. 32.2

14. Where is the fulcrum of a lever 31 inches long if a weight of 54 pounds at one end balances a weight of 70 pounds on the other end? $17\frac{1}{2}$ in. from 54 lb. weight

15. A man weighing 160 pounds wishes to use a piece of timber 12 feet long as a lever to lift 1500 pounds. Where should the fulcrum be placed so that all of his weight is needed to lift the 1500 pounds? (Disregard the weight of the timber.)

13.92 in. from stone

16. Write a formula for the shaded portion of the figure below. Write a formula for the difference between the perimeter of the rectangle and the circumference of the circle by expressing the difference d in terms of w, l, r, and π.

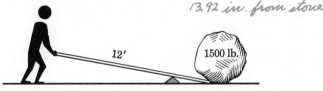

$A = lw - \pi r^2$
$d = 2w + 2l - 2\pi r$

17. How can a $5 bill be changed into quarters, dimes, and nickels, so that there will be the same number of nickels as dimes, and $\frac{2}{5}$ as many quarters as dimes? 20 nickels, 20 dimes, 8 quarters [B]

Find the indicated products:

18. $(4 - 5y^2 - 3y)(3 - 2y)$ $10y^3 - 9y^2 - 17y + 12$

19. $(3x^2 - xy - 5y^2)(x - 2y)$ $3x^3 - 7x^2y - 3xy^2 + 10y^3$

20. $(3\,a^2 - 5 - 3\,a)(2\,a^2 + a - 2)$ $6a^4 - 3a^3 - 19a^2 + a + 10$
21. $(a^3 - 4\,a + a^2 - 2)(2\,a - 1)$ $2a^4 + a^3 - 9a^2 + 2$
22. $(a^2 - 2\,ab + b^2)^2$ $a^4 - 4a^3b + 6a^2b^2 - 4ab^3 + b^4$

Solve:

23. $\dfrac{k-5}{3} + \dfrac{2(7\,k+4)}{8} - \dfrac{10+3\,k}{6} = -8\tfrac{2}{3}$ $\;-4$

24. $\dfrac{x+40}{2} + \dfrac{2\,x-1}{3} - \dfrac{x+10}{6} - \dfrac{10-3\,x}{5} = 0$ $\;-10$

Simplify:

25. $2\,x(x^2 - x + 1) + 3\,x(x^2 + x + 1)$ $5x^3 + x^2 + 5x$
26. $2\,c(c^2 - 3\,c + 4) - c(2\,c^2 - 1)$ $-6c^2 + 9c$
27. $(2\,y - 1)^2 - (y - 3)^2$ $3y^2 + 2y - 8$
28. $(x - y)^2 - (y - z)^2 + (x + z)^2$ $2x^2 - 2xy + 2yz + 2xz$

Divide:

29. $a^4 + a^2 + 1$ by $a^2 + a + 1$ $\;a^2 - a + 1$
30. $a^3 + 64$ by $a + 4$ $\;a^2 - 4a + 16$
31. $4\,a^3 + 15\,a^2b + ab^2 - 6\,b^3$ by $a^2 + 3\,ab - 2\,b^2$ $\;4a + 3b$

32. $s = \dfrac{n}{2}(a + l)$. Find l when $s = 3775$, $n = 50$, and $a = 2$.
$\;149$
33. $A = P(1 + rt)$. Find r when $A = 300$, $P = 200$, $t = 10$.
$\;0.05$
34. The length of a rectangle exceeds its width by 11 feet. If the width is decreased by 1 foot and the length is increased by 4 feet, the area remains unchanged. What are the dimensions of the rectangle? $5ft. \times 16ft.$
35. A vessel contains 4 gallons of a 3% salt solution. How many gallons of water must be added to make it a 2% solution?
$\;2$
[Test A]

CHAPTER TESTS

Part I. Multiplying Polynomials

Multiply: $2a^3 - 12a^2 + 10a$
1. $2\,a(a^2 - 6\,a + 5)$ **6.** $(r - s)^2$ $\;r^2 - 2rs + s^2$
2. $x^2(3\,x - 4)$ $\;3x^3 - 4x^2$ **7.** $(-4\,x + 3)(x + 1)$ $\;-4x^2 - x + 3$
3. $(3\,m - 1)(m + 4)$ **8.** $2\,\pi r(r + h)$ $\;2\pi r^2 + 2\pi rh$
4. $(a - 3)(a + 3)$ $\;a^2 - 9$ **9.** $(m^2 + m + 1)(m - 1)$ $\;m^3 - 1$
5. $(x - 3\,y)(x + 2\,y)$ **10.** $(h^2 - 2\,h + 2)(1 + h)$
$\;x^2 - xy - 6y^2$ $\;h^3 - h^2 + 2$

$\;3. \; 3m^2 + 11m - 4$

Part II. Division of Polynomials

Divide:

1. $(8 x^2 - 6 x) \div 2 x$ *4x-3*
2. $(p + prt) \div p$ *1+rt*
3. $(4 x^2 - 14) \div -2$ *-2x²+7*
4. $(x^2 - 8 x + 7) \div (x - 1)$ *x-7*
5. $(y^2 - 36) \div (y - 6)$ *y+6*

6. $(3 x^2 + 4 x - 15) \div (3 x - 5)$ *x+3*
7. $(x^2 + 5 x + 6) \div (x + 2)$ *x+3*
8. $(c^2 - 4 cy - 32 y^2) \div (c - 8 y)$ *c+4y*
9. $(56 - 15 x + x^2) \div (7 - x)$ *8-x*
10. $(x^3 - 1) \div (x + 1)$ *x²-x+1-$\frac{2}{x+1}$*

Part III. Equations and Problems

1. How far will a plane fly in y hours at an average speed of $(2 y + 10)$ miles an hour? *(2y²+10y) mi.*

2. Find the area of a rectangle if its base is $2 s - 3$ and its altitude is $s + 1$. *2s²-s-3*

3. Solve $2 x + 1 = 16 - 3(2 x - 3)$. *3*

4. Solve $5(2 x + 5) - (4 x - 1) = 44$. *3*

5. Two trains start at the same time from stations 600 miles apart and meet in 5 hours. If the rate of one train is 10 miles an hour faster than that of the other, what is the rate of each? *55 m.p.h., 65 m.p.h.*

6. How many pounds of 90¢ candy must be mixed with 50 pounds of 60¢ candy to make a mixture worth 70 cents a pound? *25*

[Test B]

Part I. Multiplying Polynomials

Multiply:

1. $x^2(x^2 - 3 x - 5)$ *x⁴-3x³-5x²*
2. $m^2(- m + n)$ *-m³+m²n*
3. $(r - 4 s)(r + 4 s)$ *r²-16s²*
4. $(x^2 - y^2)(x^2 + y^2)$ *x⁴-y⁴*

5. $(a + 2)(2 a - a^2 + 5)$ *-a³+9a+10*
6. $(a - \frac{1}{3})(a + \frac{1}{3})$ *a²-$\frac{1}{9}$*
7. $(3 x^2 - 1 + 2 x)(x - 2)$ *3x³-4x²-5x+2*
8. $(x^2 + 2 xy + y^2)(x + y)$ *x³+3x²y+3xy²+y³*

9. Simplify $(x - 2)^2 - (x + 1)(x - 1)$. *-4x+5*
10. Simplify $x(x - y) - y(v - x)$. *x²-y²*

Part II. Division of Polynomials

1. $(a^2 b - ab^2) \div (- ab)$ *-a+b*
2. $(a^2 - 3 ab + b^2) \div (a - b)$
3. $(c^2 + cd + d^2) \div (c + d)$
4. $(x^3 + 1) \div (x + 1)$ *x²-x+1*
5. $(x^3 - y^3) \div (x - y)$ *x²+xy+y²*
6. $(6 x^2 - 11 x - 10) \div (3 x + 2)$ *2x-5*
7. $(2 x^3 - 12 + 11 x^2 + 13 x) \div (x + 4)$ *2x²+3x+1-$\frac{16}{x+4}$*
8. $(a^4 + 3 a - 2) \div (a^2 + a - 1)$ *a²-a+2*

2. a-2b-$\frac{b^2}{a-b}$
3. c+$\frac{d^2}{c+d}$

267

Part III. Equations and Problems

1. Solve $4y - (2y - 3) = 7$ 2

2. Solve $(x - 3)^2 - (x - 2)(x + 3) = 29$ -2

3. Solve $18 - 2y(5 - 7y) = 7y(2y - 1)$ 6

4. The area of a triangle is $c^2 - 2c - 15$ and the base is $c + 3$. Find the altitude. 2c- 10

5. Plane A can make a flight from one airport to another in $3\frac{1}{2}$ hours. Plane B can fly the same distance in 3 hours. Find the rate of each plane if the speed of one is 40 miles an hour more than that of the other. A, 240 m.p.h.; B, 280 m.p.h.

Time, 80 Minutes

Find your grade in per cent by the formula $P = 40 + \frac{3}{2}R$, where R is the number right.

1. Combine: $3a + 2b - 5a + 4c - 4b$ -2a-2b+4c

2. Multiply: $-5a^3b \cdot 3ab^4$ -15a⁴b⁵

3. Divide $-35r^3t^2$ by $-7r^2t^2$. 5r

4. If $r = 3$ and $s = 4$, find the value of $\dfrac{2r^2 + rs}{3}$. 10

5. Solve $12 - a = a - 12$. 12

6. The sum of two numbers is 13; one exceeds twice the other by 1. What are the numbers? 4, 9

7. Add $-5x^3 + 3x^2 + 5$; $-2x^2 - x - 3$; and $-5x^3 + x - 10$. -10x³+x²-8

8. A farmer has 172 rods of fencing. How long will his field be if he makes it 15 rods wide? 71 rods

9. If $S = \frac{1}{2}gt^2$, find S when $g = 32$ and $t = 5$. 400

10. Solve $3(4 - x) - 7(x - 2) = 9x + 7$. 1

11. $a = -\frac{1}{3}b$. As b increases does a increase or decrease? decreases

12. Multiply: $-4a^2(5a)(-2a^3)$ 40a⁶

13. Fifty coins in nickels and dimes amount to $3.50. How many are there of each kind? 30 nickels, 20 dimes

14. Multiply $x^2 - 2xy + y^2$ by $x - y$. x³-3x²y+3xy²-y³

15. Divide $a^3 - 4a^2b + 3ab^2 + 2b^3$ by $a - 2b$. a²-2ab-b²

16. Find the value of $x^2 - 3xy + 4y^2$ when $x = 3, y = -2$. 43

17. Solve $\frac{5}{6} x + 21 = \frac{2}{3} x - 18$. -234

18. A man gave to one son $\frac{1}{3}$ of his money, and to another son $\frac{1}{4}$ of his money. He has $10 left. How much had he at first? $24

19. Write the formula for finding the area of a circle. $A = \pi r^2$

20. Subtract: $-3a + 9b - 6c$
$\underline{2a + 3b - 7c}$
$-5a + 6b + c$

21. $y = 3x + 1$. Find y when $x = -5$. -14

22. 3 is what per cent of 15? 20%

23. Two angles of a triangle are each twice the third angle. How many degrees are there in the third angle? $36°$

24. Solve $-8 + 3(y + 2) - (2y - 7) = 7$. 2

25. How much larger than $8a - 5b$ is $-3a + 5b$? $-11a + 10b$

26. Simplify $4x(2x^2 + 8x - 3) - 5x^2(2x + 3)$. $-2x^3 + 17x^2 - 12x$

27. If $a = 3$, $b = 2$, $c = -4$, find the value of $\dfrac{4a - 10b + 5c}{7b}$. -2

28. Solve $\dfrac{3n}{4} + \dfrac{2n}{5} = \dfrac{5n}{6} + \dfrac{19}{3}$. 20

29. Subtract $x^2 - 3x + 6$ from $x + 6$. $-x^2 + 4x$

30. Simplify $2a(b - 2c) - 2b(a + c) - ac$. $-5ac - 2bc$

31. Is $x = -4$ the solution of $5x + 12 - 3x = 15 - 2x$? no

32. What name is given to the 4 in $3x^4$? $Exponent$

33. Solve $\dfrac{r + 6}{3} - \dfrac{r + 1}{5} = \dfrac{r + 3}{6} + \dfrac{3}{2}$. -6

34. A is 5 times as old as B. In 9 years he will be 3 times as old as B. Find their present ages. $A, 45 \, yr.; \, B, 9 \, yr.$

35. Write a formula for the perimeter p of the larger of the two rectangles illustrated. $p = 10m + 4$

36. Write a formula for the area A of the shaded portion of the figure. $A = 4m^2 + 4m$

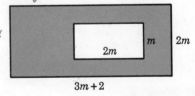

37. Solve $\dfrac{x - 12}{10} = \dfrac{6x + 3}{5} - \dfrac{3x - 6}{2}$. 12

38. Is $(x + 2)^2 = x^2 + 4x + 4$ an identical equation? yes

39. What is the root of the equation $7(x - 2) - 4 = x$? 3

40. Write the formula for the circumference of a circle. $C = 2\pi r,$ $or \ C = \pi d$

Do YOU *WISH TO BECOME AN ARCHITECT?*

If your answer to the question above is "Yes," you should also be able to answer "Yes" to each of the following questions:

1. Do you have artistic ability which can be the basis for design and drawing?

2. Do you enjoy reading scientific literature and do you read it without its being assigned?

3. Do you do superior work in mathematics?

4. Will you be able to secure a broad general education? Will you also be able to acquire the necessary mathematical and engineering qualifications by intensive study at a college or university?

I. M. Pei & Associates

10

Graphs

Suggested Time Schedule
7 days

In this chapter you will study the correspondence between ordered pairs of real numbers and the points of a plane.

You will find this chapter an up-to-date treatment of graphing. First there is a careful explanation of the graphing of relations and functions, leading naturally to the graphing of linear equations. Then this is expanded by the graphing of related inequalities—an excellent new modern trend in elementary work. Those of you who have had experience in teaching first-year algebra will welcome the opportunity of teaching graphing in a way which deepens students' understanding of the topic and makes it much more worthwhile.

①↰ In Chapter 1 we explored ideas about a number line. We said that to each real number there corresponds exactly one point of a line and to each point of the line there corresponds exactly one real number. In this chapter we consider a similar relationship between pairs of real numbers and the points of a plane. You should recall that a plane is a set of points forming an endless flat surface.

Number Pairs and the Points of a Plane [A]

In the figure at the left below, P and Q are two points in a plane and l is a number line in the plane. Since Q is on the number line it represents a real number—in this case the number $\frac{3}{2}$. What can we ② say concerning point P which does not lie on the line? To find the answer to this question we draw a line from P to the number line so

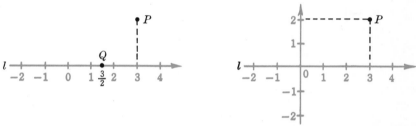

that it is perpendicular to the line, that is, it makes right angles with l. Since our line passes through the point representing 3 we see that P is associated with the number 3. But P is *above* the point representing 3. To determine how far above we need another number line. Accordingly we draw the vertical number line shown in the figure at the right above. It is an exact copy of the original number line. We are careful to make this new line perpendicular to the first. We also make its zero point fall on the zero point of the first and we make the points which represent positive numbers lie above the first line. Now, by drawing a line from P perpendicular to the new line, we see that P is also associated with the number 2. Thus we may think of P as representing the pair of real numbers 3 and 2.

In writing such a number pair we state the number from the horizontal line before we state the number from the vertical line and we enclose the numbers within parentheses. Thus we may say that the point P represents the number pair (3, 2). Since the order in which the members are written has meaning, we say that the pair is an ③ ordered pair.

② Note the meaningful approach to the use of two perpendicular axes. This emphasizes the one-to-one correspondence between number pairs and points. It
might be well to have this section read aloud in class. The illustrations can be
duplicated on the graph chalkboard.
③ Emphasize the name "ordered pair" as you continue through the chapter.

273

① Be sure the student understands the vocabulary in these paragraphs and uses it in doing and discussing the exercises on page 275.

ALGEBRA, BOOK ONE

We have now observed that the point P, which does not fall on the number line, represents a pair of real numbers and that the point Q, which falls on the number line, represents a single real number. However, if we wish to do so, we may consider this single real number as one member of a pair in which the other number is zero. Thus we may think of the point Q as representing the number pair $(\frac{3}{2}, 0)$. By doing this we are able to say that each point in a plane represents a pair of real numbers.

Moreover, each pair of real numbers can be represented by a point in the plane. For example, if we consider the number pair $(4, -1)$, we may locate the point representing 4 on the horizontal number line and the point representing -1 on the vertical number line, then draw lines through these points perpendicular to the number lines. These perpendiculars will intersect in a point K. K represents the number pair $(4, -1)$.

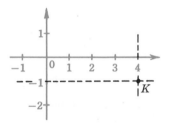

Now we see that each point of the plane may be considered as representing a pair of real numbers and each pair of real numbers may be considered as represented by a point in the plane.

We call the first member of each of these number pairs the abscissa of the point in the plane, the second member the ordinate, and the pair of numbers the coordinates of the point. Thus the point K has the abscissa 4, the ordinate -1, and the coordinates $(4, -1)$.

We call the horizontal number line the x-axis and the vertical number line the y-axis. The plural of *axis* is *axes*. The point where the axes intersect is the origin. We sometimes say that the axes are coordinate axes.

By using coordinate paper we save ourselves the work of drawing perpendiculars and measuring distances. Coordinate paper is paper upon which lines have already been drawn perpendicular to each other and so spaced that they form squares. In the figure shown

② Have the student select coordinate paper with squares about the size of those in the text. Smaller squares are undesirable for this work. Insist on proper labeling of axes and scales. However, just enough numbers may be placed on the axes to indicate the scale used. Otherwise written work is apt to look cluttered.

274

below we have drawn the axes and have located the points A, B, C, D, E, and F on coordinate paper.

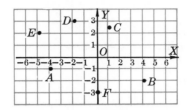

Point A has the abscissa -4, the ordinate -1, and the coordinates $(-4, -1)$. Which point has the coordinates $(4, -2)$? Point C has the abscissa 1, the ordinate $2\frac{1}{2}$, and the coordinates $(1, 2\frac{1}{2})$. What are the coordinates of point D? Which point has the coordinates $(0, -3)$? the coordinates $(-5, 2)$?

1. State the coordinates of each of the points in the figure below.

EXERCISES

A (2,2)
B (0,3)
C (-1,1)
D (-4,0)
E (-2,-3)
F (1,-2)
G (3,-½)

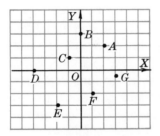

2. On coordinate paper draw a pair of axes; then locate the point representing each of the following number pairs. Name the point with the capital letter that appears beside the number pair.

a. $(0, 0)$; A **c.** $(\frac{7}{2}, 1)$; C **e.** $(-7, -4)$; E
b. $(4, 3)$; B **d.** $(-6, 2)$; D **f.** $(2\frac{1}{2}, 0)$; F

3. On coordinate paper draw a pair of axes; then locate the points represented by the following number pairs:

$(3, -4)$, $(3, -2)$, $(3, 0)$, $(3, 1\frac{1}{2})$, $(3, 6)$.

What seems to be true of all points with the abscissa 3?
They all lie in the vertical line through the point +3 on the horizontal axis.

① These exercises should be assigned for written work. Papers may be exchanged and corrected in class. Two axes can be drawn on the board, and you could then point out the position of the various points as the papers are corrected.

4. On coordinate paper draw a pair of axes; then locate the points having the following coordinates:

$(-5, 2)$,　　　$(-1, 2)$,　　　$(0, 2)$,　　　$(\frac{5}{2}, 2)$,　　　$(3, 2)$.

What seems to be true of all points having the ordinate 2?

5. On coordinate paper draw an x-axis and a y-axis; then locate the point represented by each of the number pairs:

$(0, 0)$,　　　$(1, 1)$,　　　$(2, 2)$,　　　$(3, 3)$.

6. On coordinate paper draw an x-axis and a y-axis and locate the point representing each of the following number pairs: $(-2, -4)$,　　$(-1, -2)$,　　$(1, 2)$,　　$(2, 4)$,　　$(3, 6)$.

Relations [A]

We say that a set of ordered pairs is a <u>relation</u> and that a relation is a set of ordered pairs. Thus $\{(-2, 3), (0, 1), (3, 4)\}$ is a relation. In this case we have *defined* the relation by listing its members between braces.

Instead of listing the members of a relation between braces we sometimes list them in a table. To make a table for the relation $\{(-2, 3), (0, 1), (3, 4)\}$ we choose one variable to represent the first members of the number pairs and a second variable to represent the second members. Since the first members correspond to points on the x-axis, we use the variable x as their representative, and since the second members correspond to points on the y-axis, we choose the variable y as their representative. Using x and y as the variables, we write the number pairs in a table as follows:

x	-2	0	3
y	3	1	4

In this case the table defines the relation.

To graph a relation we graph each of the number pairs that make up the relation. Thus, to graph the relation above, we graph the three number pairs $(-2, 3)$, $(0, 1)$, and $(3, 4)$ on a single pair of axes as shown at the right. The complete graph is the set of three points shown. We say that the graph defines the relation.

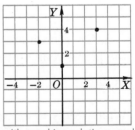

① Observe the use of set notation in connection with graphing relations, and then the use of the table as an alternative method of displaying ordered pairs. The student will probably use the table form for most of his work in graphing.

GRAPHS

We may want to describe a relation by use of words. For example, to describe the relation shown in the graph below (where the band of points extends infinitely far to the right and to the left) we might use the words: the set of number pairs (x, y) in which x is an integer and y is an integer such that $0 < y < 4$. The expression $0 < y < 4$ means that y is greater than 0 but less than 4. (The arrows indicate that the graph continues infinitely.)

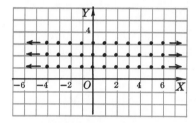

In this case the relation defined by the graph was also defined by the word description, "the set of number pairs (x, y) in which x is an integer and y is an integer such that $0 < y < 4$."

Sometimes (but not always) we can define a relation by an equation or an inequality, as we shall see later in this chapter.

> **Example 1.** Write the set of all ordered pairs that can be formed with the numbers 1, 2, 3; then graph the resulting set.
>
> **Solution.** We can combine 1 with 1, 2, and 3 to form the ordered pairs $(1, 1)$, $(1, 2)$, and $(1, 3)$. We can combine 2 with 1, 2, and 3 to form the ordered pairs $(2, 1)$, $(2, 2)$, and $(2, 3)$. We can combine 3 with 1, 2, and 3 to form the ordered pairs $(3, 1)$, $(3, 2)$, and $(3, 3)$. Thus the set of all ordered pairs that can be formed with 1, 2, and 3 is the set $\{(1, 1), (1, 2), (1, 3), (2, 1), (2, 2), (2, 3), (3, 1), (3, 2), (3, 3)\}$. The graph of the set is shown below.

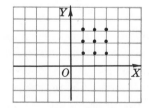

277

Example 2. Graph the set of ordered pairs (x,y) such that x and y are integers, $-4 < x < -1$, and $0 < y < 4$.

Solution. Since x is an integer such that $-4 < x < -1$, x can represent -3, or -2. Since y is an integer such that $0 < y < 4$, y can represent 1, 2, or 3.

We can combine -3 with 1, 2, and 3 to form the ordered pairs $(-3, 1)$, $(-3, 2)$, and $(-3, 3)$. We can combine -2 with 1, 2, and 3 to form the ordered pairs $(-2, 1)$, $(-2, 2)$, and $(-2, 3)$. Thus the relation consists of the ordered pairs $(-3, 1)$, $(-3, 2)$, $(-3, 3)$, $(-2, 1)$, $(-2, 2)$, and $(-2, 3)$. The graph of the set is shown below.

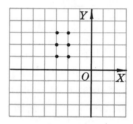

Observe that in Example 1 of the preceding page the relation under consideration was defined by the word description, "the set of ordered pairs that can be formed with the numbers 1, 2, 3." What word description defined the relation in Example 2, above?

[A]

EXERCISES

1. During the first hours of February 1 the temperatures in Clarksville were those shown in the table below. In the table x represents the hours and y the temperatures from 1 A.M. to 8 A.M., inclusive. Graph the relation defined by the table.

x	1	2	3	4	5	6	7	8
y	2°	0°	−1°	−3°	−6°	−7°	−7°	−4°

2. In each of five successive games Joe's scores were those shown in the table at the right. In the table x represents the scores and y the game numbers. Graph the relation defined by the table.

x	3	10	5	11	15
y	1	2	3	4	5

① If you have time, some data of local interest similar to that in exercises 1–3 might be gathered and graphed.

3. The Attendance Department of Springdale High School issued the accompanying report on tardiness to class during one month. The first member of each number pair in the report is the number of a homeroom and the second member is the number of cases of tardiness in that room. Rewrite the set of ordered pairs in a table, with x representing the number of cases of tardiness and y the number of the homeroom. Graph the relation.

Tardiness to class by rooms	
1 _ _3	6 _ _0.
2 _ _0	7 _ _0
3 _ _0	8 _ _3
4 _ _1	9 _ _0
5 _ _2	10 _ _1

4. Express each of the relations below by means of a table and a graph.

   a. $\{(1, 0), (2, -3), (3, -1), (4, 2), (5, 4)\}$

   b. $\{(-4, 6), (-2, 3), (0, 0), (2, 3), (4, 6)\}$

   c. $\{(4, 0), (3, \frac{11}{4}), (0, 4), (-3, \frac{9}{4}), (-4, 0), (-3, -\frac{9}{4}),$
$(0, -4), (3, -\frac{11}{4})\}$

   d. $\{(1, 1), (1, 2), (1, 3), (1, 4), (2, 1), (2, 2), (2, 3), (2, 4)\}$

   e. $\{(1, \frac{1}{2}), (2, 1), (3, \frac{3}{2}), (4, 2)\}$

   f. $\{(-2, 0), (-1, 0), (0, 0), (1, 0), (2, 0), (0, -2),$
$(0, -1), (0, 1), (0, 2)\}$

5. Graph the set of all ordered pairs (x, y) such that x and y are natural numbers, $0 < x < 4$, and $0 < y < 4$.

6. Graph the set of all ordered pairs that fit the description: the set of number pairs (x, y) in which x is an integer such that $-5 < x < -2$ and y is any integer.

7. Make a table to express the relation defined by each of the graphs below.

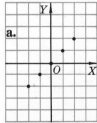

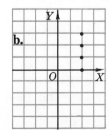

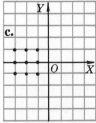

To save paper when you wish to include just one graph on a test, you might wish to purchase a stamp for making small sections of graph paper. See advertisements in The Mathematics Teacher for places to purchase these stamps.

An understanding of functions in mathematics is very important. Here is begun a spiral development of the topic. Be sure to emphasize paragraph four, which covers a point often difficult for
students to understand.

ALGEBRA, BOOK ONE

Functions [A]

When for each x in a relation there is exactly one value, of y we
say that y is a <u>function</u> of x.

Thus, in Fig. 1 below, the relation that is defined by the graph is
not a function because when $x = 1$, y may be either 1 or 3.

The relation defined by the graph shown in Fig. 2 is a function because there is one and only one value of y for each value of x.

The relation defined by the graph shown in Fig. 3 is also a function. Observe that, in this case, when $y = 2$, $x = 1$ or $x = 2$. Although
there are two values of x for a single value of y, this does not prevent
the relation from being a function. It is only when two or more
values of y correspond to a single value of x that a relation is not a
function.

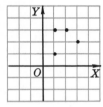

Fig. 1

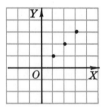

Fig. 2

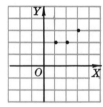

Fig. 3

[A]

EXERCISES

Which of the graphs below represent functions? If a graph
does not represent a function, explain why it doesn't.

1.

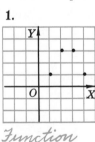

Function

2.

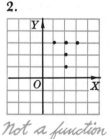

Not a function

3.

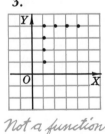

Not a function

Equations having Two Variables [A]

Let us now turn our attention to relations that can be expressed
by equations. First let us consider the relation described in the
paragraph which follows.

280

The Broad Street Bookstore had a sale on books last week. A sign over the books on sale said, "$2.00 each. Sales limited to five per customer."

Below we have made a table in which the variable x represents the number of such books that could be purchased by a customer and y represents the number of dollars that could be spent for books. Since no customer could buy more than five books and since it is unlikely that a customer bought a fractional part of a book, the domain of x consists of the numbers 0, 1, 2, 3, 4, and 5. Each value of x is matched by a single value of y. Thus zero books cost nothing, one book costs $2, two books cost $4, three books cost $6, and so on. Consequently the relation contains only the set of six number pairs

(0, 0)   (1, 2)   (2, 4)   (3, 6)   (4, 8)   (5, 10)

The graph of this relation consists of the six points represented by the black dots in the diagram below.

x	0	1	2	3	4	5
y	0	2	4	6	8	10

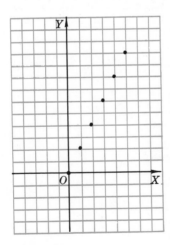

The relation is defined by the equation $y = 2\,x$ in which the domain of x is $\{0, 1, 2, 3, 4, 5\}$ and y is a real number.

Here you find a natural lead to the graphing of $y = 2x$, where the domain of x is infinite. Try to anticipate the conclusions on page 282 by directed class discussion. Ask such questions as "Let us extend the domain of x. Suppose we should use some point between 2 and 3 such as $2\frac{1}{2}$. What is the position of the point?" Such discussion is best if you have a diagram on the board and have individual students locate additional points.

Now let us consider the relation suggested by the paragraph:

> Mary Adams' young brother Tommy likes to multiply. Sometimes he and his father play a game in which Tommy writes twice any number that his father mentions. (Mr. Adams mentions only real numbers.)

If we let x represent any number that Mr. Adams may mention and let y represent the corresponding number that Tommy should write, we have another relation defined by the equation $y = 2x$. This time, however, the domain of x is the set of all real numbers.

Since the domain of x is an infinite set, the relation will consist of an infinite number of ordered pairs. Since we cannot list all these pairs in a table we must be content with listing a few representative ones for study. Let us use the same pairs used for the relation on page 281. (We can do this because both relations are of the form $y = 2x$.)

This time the graph of the six number pairs (the six pairs in Fig. 1, below) form only a part of the complete graph. To find other points that belong to the graph we observe that the six we have located appear to lie in a straight line. This suggests that the others may lie in the same line. (See Fig. 2.) Let us investigate this possibility.

x	0	1	2	3	4	5
y	0	2	4	6	8	10

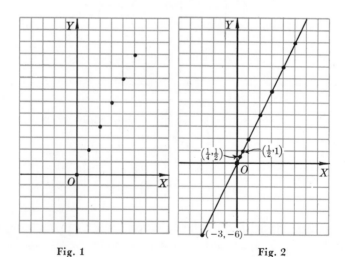

Fig. 1   Fig. 2

 ① If you used the inductive method of approach as suggested on page 281, this section might be read by students silently, and then their questions might be answered in a discussion.

We see that if Mr. Adams mentions the number $\frac{1}{2}$ Tommy should write 1. We graph the pair $(\frac{1}{2}, 1)$ and find that this point appears to lie on the line. The pairs $(\frac{1}{4}, \frac{1}{2})$, $(\frac{1}{10}, \frac{1}{5})$, and so on, also appear to lie on the line.

These facts suggest that if we could graph all the possible number pairs they would form a solid line between the points we have already located.

Moreover, we see that the line can be extended in both directions for it is possible for Mr. Adams to suggest -3, in which case Tommy should write -6 to give the number pair $(-3, -6)$, or Mr. Adams might suggest the number 6 in which case Tommy should write 12 to give the number pair $(6, 12)$, and so on. The pairs $(-3, -6)$ and $(6, 12)$ appear to have graphs on the line.

It appears that if we locate only a few points on the graph, we can draw a straight line between them and thereby graph all the remaining number pairs as far as the size of our paper will allow us to go. In later courses you will be able to prove that this procedure is correct. Moreover, you will be able to prove that all points of the line have coordinates that belong to the relation.

In the remaining pages of this chapter we shall assume that in all equations containing the variables x and y, x and y are any real numbers.

Degree of Equations [A]

Before we continue with the work in graphing, you should learn what is meant by the "degree of an equation." Later in the course you will understand why you need to know this.

The <u>degree of a monomial</u> is the sum of the exponents of its variables. Since, in a polynomial, each monomial is a term, the <u>degree of a term</u> is the sum of the exponents of its variables. Monomials, or terms, such as x, $3y$, and $-4z$ are of the first degree; monomials, or terms, such as x^2, xy, and $-4y^2$ are of the second degree; and monomials, or terms, such as x^3, $-x^2y$, mnp, and y^3 are of the third degree.

The <u>degree of a polynomial</u> or the <u>degree of an equation</u> is the same as that of its highest-degree term. So to find the degree of an equation we clear the equation of fractions, remove parentheses, and find its highest degree term. The degree of this term is the degree of the equation.

Examples.

First-degree equations

$$4x + 8 = 0$$
$$x + 3y = 12$$
$$x - y = 0$$

Second-degree equations

$$x^2 = 36$$
$$xy = 30$$
$$x^2 - 4y = 4$$

$\frac{2}{x} + 3 = 2y$ is a second-degree equation because, when it is cleared of fractions, it becomes $2 + 3x = 2xy$.

[A]

State the degrees of the following equations:

1. $3x = 10$ *First*   **4.** $y - 6 = 4$ *First*

2. $x^2 = 25$ *Second*   **5.** $xy = 36$ *Second*

3. $x - y = 10$ *First*   **6.** $x^2 - x = 6$ *Second*

Graphs of First-Degree Equations [A]

As we have said, if it were possible to plot all the points whose coordinates satisfy a given first-degree equation, they would be in the same straight line. Also, the coordinates of any point of this line would satisfy the given equation. A first-degree equation is called a linear equation since its graph is a straight line. By the graph of an equation, we mean the graph of the set of ordered pairs of numbers which satisfy the equation.

Example. Graph the equation $3x - 4y = 12$.

Solution. Since we know that $3x - 4y = 12$ is a linear equation, we know that its graph is a straight line. Two points are needed to determine a straight line, and a third point is needed to check the graph.

$3x - 4y = 12$

x	0	4	2
y	-3	0	$-1\frac{1}{2}$

$3x - 4y = 12$

x	y
0	-3
4	0
2	$-\frac{3}{2}$

284 To conserve students' time, you may advise them not to draw the outside border on tables. Insist on the inclusion of the points with $x = 0$ and $y = 0$. These have significance in later work and are easy points to find and graph. Some teachers and students prefer horizontal tables, and some vertical tables. We suggest that the student be allowed to choose for himself.

We make a table of values, using either of the forms just given. Let either x or y have any convenient value. Suppose we let $x = 0$. Then $3(0) - 4y = 12$. $0 - 4y = 12$, and $y = -3$. Then $x = 0$, $y = -3$ is one set of values satisfying the equation. Can you give a reason why we let $x = 0$ instead of letting it equal some other number?

Suppose we let $y = 0$. Then the equation becomes $3x - 4(0) = 12$, or $3x - 0 = 12$, and $x = 4$. That is, another set of values is $x = 4$, $y = 0$.

Next we draw the x- and y-axes and plot the points $(0, -3)$ and $(4, 0)$. Then we draw a straight line through these two points.

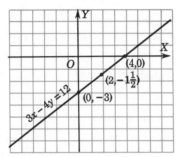

To check the correctness of the graph we let $x = 2$. Then $3(2) - 4y = 12$, $6 - 4y = 12$, $-4y = 6$, and $y = -1\frac{1}{2}$. We plot the point $(2, -1\frac{1}{2})$ and find that it is on the line. This checks our solution.

We could have solved the equation for y, getting $y = \dfrac{3x}{4} - 3$.

Then we could have assigned values to x and have evaluated for y.

[A]

EXERCISES

Draw a graph for each equation:

1. $x = y + 8$ 4. $x + y = 0$ 7. $a + 6b = -4$

2. $y = 4x$ 5. $x = 2y - 6$ 8. $y = 3x - 2$

3. $x - y = 6$ 6. $4x + y = 12$

9. On the same set of axes draw the graphs of:

a. $y = 4x + 2$ c. $y = -2x + 2$

b. $y = 0x + 2$ d. $y = -3x + 2$

Name one property that the four graphs have in common.
They all pass through point (0,2).

① Some teachers may prefer to have students make a table of three values right at the start.

② Instruct students to do some exercises this way and then to decide which method seems preferable to them.

285

10. On the same set of axes draw the graphs of:

a. $y = 3x$ **c.** $y = 3x - 1$

b. $y = 3x + 4$ **d.** $y = 3x - 4$

What common property do the graphs of these equations have? *They are parallel.*

[B]

Draw a graph for each equation:

11. $y = 10x - 4$ **14.** $\frac{2}{3}x - \frac{1}{2}y = 4$

12. $9x + 5y = 40$ **15.** $5x - y = 0$

13. $s = 16t$ **16.** $y + 18 = -3x$

17. Draw a graph showing that a certain number is always 4 more than another. $(y = \underline{?} x + 4)$ *(Graph of $y = 5x$)*

18. Draw a graph showing that one number is 5 times another.

19. Draw the graph of $y = 3$. (Suggestion: $y = 0x + 3$.)

20. $A = 3\frac{1}{7}r^2$ is the formula for the area of a circle. Is this a first-degree equation? The graph of this equation is not a straight line. See if you can draw it. *No, second-degree*

21. A captain of police said, "When traffic is doubled, the accidents are eight times as many." Which of the two formulas, $A = 4t$ or $A = t^3$, expresses this fact? *$A = t^3$*

The Relations of a Linear Equation to Its Graph [C]

When graphing the equations on page 285, did you observe how the line graphs extended in different directions and how they intersected (cut) the axes at different points? Did you know what changes in the equations produced them? Consider the following equation and its graph:

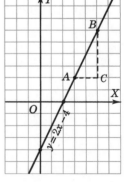

$$2x - y = 4$$
$$-y = -2x + 4$$
$$y = 2x - 4$$

x	0	2	3
y	-4	0	2

Note that we have solved $2x - y = 4$ for y and have found that $y = 2x - 4$. Then,

① This C section is designed for your better students. It presents the important
concept of slope by an inductive method of approach which students will enjoy.

286

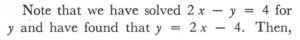

by assigning different values to x, we were able to find the corresponding values for y. Since we assign values to x, we call x the independent variable; and since the value of y depends upon the value of x, we call y the dependent variable. The equation of $y = 2x - 4$ is of the form $y = mx + b$. Do you see that 2 is a special value of m and that -4 is a special value of b? The equation $y = 2x - 4$ is a solution of $2x - y = 4$. It states that y is always 4 less than twice x.

To understand better the changes in the value of y, imagine the graph to be made on the blackboard or hold your book so that its pages are vertical. Do you see that y increases in any movement upward and decreases in any movement downward? Remember that x increases when going from left to right and decreases when going from right to left. Let us choose two convenient points A and B on the graph. The co-ordinates of A are $(3, 2)$ and those of B are $(5, 6)$. When a point moves on the graph from A to B, x increases from 3 to 5 and y increases from 2 to 6. In other words, y has an increase of 4 when x has an increase of 2. This means that y increases twice as fast as x when the point moves from A to B.

Do you know what we mean by the slope of a hill? Do you know that a steep hill has a greater slope than a hill not so steep? When referring to the steepness of a hill we usually use the word *slope*. Do you know how we measure the slope of a hill? The slope of a hill is found by dividing its change in elevation by the corresponding horizontal change.

The slope of a line and the slope of a hill have a like meaning. We define the slope of a line as follows:

The slope of a line equals the change in y divided by the change in x.

From this definition the slope of the line

$$AB = \frac{CB}{AC} = \frac{4}{2} = 2$$

In general, the slope is the ratio of the change of the dependent variable to the change of the independent variable. Since the line does not change in direction this ratio is the same for all parts of the line.

This graph intersects the x-axis where $x = 2$ and the y-axis where $y = -4$. We say that the x-intercept is 2 and the y-intercept is -4.

① Your students should not need help in solving for y, but they should understand that any equation can be put in the form $y = mx + b$. The significance of m and b should be pointed out in the exercises that follow.

ALGEBRA, BOOK ONE

Example. Change the equation $3x + 4y = 12$ to the form $y = mx + b$ and graph it. Find: the values of m and b; an x increase and the corresponding y increase; the slope; and the intercepts.

Solution.

$$3x + 4y = 12$$
$$4y = -3x + 12$$
$$y = -\tfrac{3}{4}x + 3$$

x	0	4	2
y	3	0	1.5

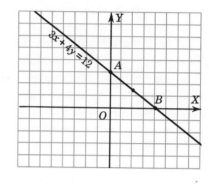

$y = mx + b$
$y = -\tfrac{3}{4}x + 3$
Then $m = -\tfrac{3}{4}$
and $b = 3$

We choose two convenient points $A\,(0, 3)$ and $B\,(4, 0)$. As x increases from 0 to 4, y decreases from 3 to 0. Then an increase of 4 in x causes a decrease of 3 in y. In other words, an increase of 4 in x produces an increase of -3 in y. The slope of the

line $= \dfrac{y\text{-increase}}{x\text{-increase}} = -\dfrac{3}{4}.$ The x-intercept is 4 and the y-intercept is 3.

[C]

EXERCISES

1. Following the method used in the solution above, graph the following equations and make a table for each equation, giving: the values of m and b; the x and y increases; the slopes; and the intercepts.

a. $y = x + 4$ **c.** $y = 8x + 4$ **e.** $y = -2x + 4$

b. $y = 4x + 4$ **d.** $y = 0x + 4$ **f.** $y = -4x + 4$

Study the tables and state what you discover.

2. Treat the following equations as in exercise 1.

a. $y = 2x + 8$ **c.** $y = 2x + 0$ **e.** $y = 2x - 4$

b. $y = 2x + 4$ **d.** $y = 2x - 2$ **f.** $y = 2x - 6$

What do you deduce from the tables?

3. Complete: The graph of $y = mx + b$ crosses the y-axis in the point $y = $ __? and has the slope __?

288

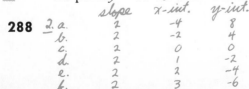

Margin notes (handwritten):

1.
	m	b
a.	1	4
b.	4	4
c.	8	4
d.	0	4
e.	-2	4
f.	-4	4

x-inc. y-inc.
a.	4	4
b.	1	4
c.	0.5	4
d.	1	0
e.	2	-4
f.	1	-4

slope x-int. y-int.
a.	1	-4	4
b.	4	-1	4
c.	8	-0.5	4
d.	0	none	4
e.	-2	2	4
f.	-4	1	4

2.
	m	b
a.	2	8
b.	2	4
c.	2	0
d.	2	-2
e.	2	-4
f.	2	-6

x-inc. y-inc.
a.	4	8
b.	2	4
c.	3	6
d.	1	2
e.	2	4
f.	3	6

2.
	slope	x-int.	y-int.
a.	2	-4	8
b.	2	-2	4
c.	2	0	0
d.	2	1	-2
e.	2	2	-4
f.	2	3	-6

3. b ; m

Your better students will be intrigued by the slope-intercept form of graphing a linear equation.   For Example 2, ask "As x increases one unit, how does y change?   As x increases 6 units, how does y change?"   Other similar questions can be asked until the student becomes aware of the importance of m and no longer needs a table to analyze such connection between **GRAPHS** x and y.   It also helps to draw corresponding triangles which overlap and are similar.

Using the Slope-Intercept Form in Graphing [C]

You have discovered that the graph of $y = mx + b$ has the slope m and intersects the y-axis at $y = b$. When a linear equation is written in the form $y = mx + b$, we know immediately the slope and y-intercept of its graph and can easily draw the graph.

Example 1. Graph $y = 3x + 4$.

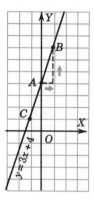

Solution. The slope of the graph is $+3$ and the y-intercept is $+4$. We plot the point A (0, 4), which is the y-intercept. Since the slope is $+3$, an increase of 1 in x produces an increase of 3 in y. As x increases one unit, y increases 3 units. To find a second point B of the graph, start at A and go one unit to the right and 3 units up. The coordinates of B are (1, 7). Then we draw a line through A and B. To check the solution, we let $x = -1$. Then $y = 1$. We plot the point C (-1, 1). It is on the line.

Example 2. Graph $2x + 3y + 6 = 0$.

Solution.
$$2x + 3y + 6 = 0$$
$$3y = -2x - 6$$
$$y = -\tfrac{2}{3}x - 2$$

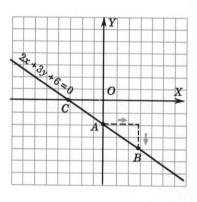

The slope is $-\tfrac{2}{3}$ and the y-intercept is -2. We plot the point A (0, -2). Since the slope is negative, y decreases as x increases. As x increases 3 units, y decreases 2 units. Then we find the point B on the graph by starting at A, going 3 units to the right and then 2 units down. The abscissa of B is 3 more than that of A and the ordinate of B is 2 less than that of A. We draw the straight line through A and B and check the solution with the point C (-3, 0).

[C]

EXERCISES

1. Give the slopes and y-intercepts of the following equations:

a. $y = 4x + 1$ $4, 1$ **c.** $y = \tfrac{2}{5}x$ $\tfrac{2}{5}, 0$ **e.** $y = x + 10$ $1, 10$

b. $y = 2x + 5$ $2, 5$ **d.** $y = \tfrac{3}{4}x - 1$ $\tfrac{3}{4}, -1$ **f.** $y = -\tfrac{1}{2}x + 3$ $-\tfrac{1}{2}, 3$

289

Graph the following equations by using the slopes and the y-intercepts.

2. $y = 3x + 5$ **4.** $2x - 5y = 10$ **6.** $y = x$

3. $y = -x + 1$ **5.** $x + y = 0$ **7.** $2y + 5x = 6$

Graphing Inequalities [A]

Let us now consider the graphing of inequalities. First, let us graph the inequality $y > x$. We begin by considering the graph of the equation $y = x$. This graph is shown by the black line in Fig. 1. P, having the coordinates $(2, 2)$, is a point on the line. Now let us graph the number pair $(2, 3)$. Since the graph, Q, of this number pair has the same abscissa as the point P but a greater ordinate, it must lie directly above P. We see that the graph of any number pair in which the second member is greater than the first member will lie above the line representing $y = x$.

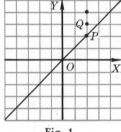

Fig. 1

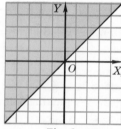

Fig. 2

We can represent all these points by shading the area above the graph of $y = x$. Thus, in Fig. 2 above, the red shaded portion is the graph of the inequality $y > x$. The black line $y = x$ is not part of the graph of $y > x$. By the graph of an inequality, we mean the graph of the relation whose ordered pairs of numbers satisfy the inequality. In this case the relation is not a function.

To graph the inequality $y - 2x < 5$, we first graph the equation $y - 2x = 5$, then shade the area below the line. The graph is shown at the right.

The graph of $y - 2 < 5$ does *not* include the line $y - 2x = 5$.

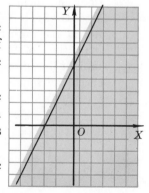

① As you discuss this in class, ask students to locate several more points such that $y > x$. At the same time, you might ask for some y values that are *less* than x. Thus students might conclude by an inductive approach that if the three graphs $y = x$, $y > x$, and $y < x$ are all made on one pair of axes, the entire number plane is covered.

① As you discuss these exercises, expand some of them as indicated in note 1 on page 290.

You may consider an inequality such as $y > 3$ an inequality in one variable and graph it on a number line. The graph of $y > 3$ is the red portion of the number line below.

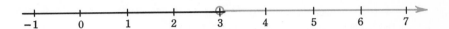

On the other hand, you may consider the inequality $y > 3$ as the sentence $y + 0\,x > 3$. When you take this point of view you will graph the equation $y + 0\,x = 3$, and shade the portion of the plane above the graph. The shaded area in the diagram, excluding the line $y + 0\,x = 3$, is the graph of the inequality.

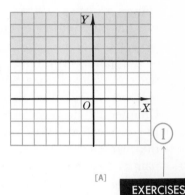

[A]

EXERCISES

Graph each of the inequalities below.

1. $y < x$

2. $y < 2\,x$

3. $y > x + 3$

4. $x + y < 4$

5. $y - 2\,x < 6$

6. $y > 3$

7. $y > \dfrac{x}{2}$

8. $y > \dfrac{x}{2} + 3$

9. $x + y > 0$

10. $2\,x + 3\,y < 6$

Graphing Compound Sentences [B]

To graph the compound sentence $y \geq x$, which means "y is greater than or equal to x," we proceed as we do in graphing the inequality $y > x$, but we make the line part of the graph. Thus the graph of the sentence $y \geq x$ is the line $y = x$ and the shaded portion of the plane shown.

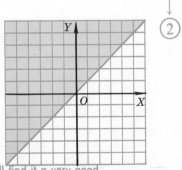

② While this section is not required for all students, you will find it a very good introduction to the solution of simultaneous equations by graphing in Chapter 11. It is suggested that you cover this section in most classes. Emphasize the distinction between compound sentences containing or and those containing and. (For your very best students, show them some of the modern mathematics with the accompanying symbolism if you have such books available.) The sentences with and will be most useful in Chapter 11. At that time, you might point out that the two compound sentences with or correspond to the union of two sets, while those with and correspond to the intersection of two sets.

291

The graph of the compound sentence "$y = x$ or $y = -x$" will consist of the graph of the line "$y = x$" and the graph of the line "$y = -x$." This graph is shown below.

The graph of the compound sentence "$y = x$ and $y = -x$" will consist of only the single point O in which the two lines intersect.

This is because a compound sentence with the connective *and* is true only if both clauses are true. Of all the points on the two lines the only one representing a number pair that will make both clauses true is the point of intersection. Chapter 11 will be devoted to a study of compound sentences with the connective *and*. In Chapter 11, however, we have not written the connective. We have merely written

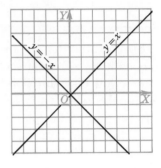

the two clauses as two separate sentences and have referred to the pair as a system of equations or a system of inequalities.

The graph of the compound sentence "$y > x$ or $y > -x$" will consist of the shaded portion of the plane which is the graph of the inequality $y > x$ and the shaded portion of the plane which is the graph of $y > -x$, including the portion which is in both graphs.

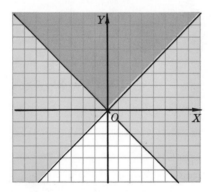

The graph of the compound sentence "$y > x$ and $y > -x$" will consist of only the deeply shaded portion (the overlapping section) of the graph shown. This is because it is only this portion which is common to the two graphs—the graph of $y > x$ and the graph of $y > -x$. This deeply shaded portion contains the points that represent the number pairs that will make either inequality true.

[B]

Graph each of the following compound sentences:

1. $y = 3x$ and $y = -3x$ **6.** $y < x - 3$ and $y < 2 - x$

2. $x + y = 5$ or $y - x = 3$ **7.** $y > x - 3$ or $y < 2 - x$

3. $x + y = 5$ and $y - x = 3$ **8.** $x = 2$ and $y = 4$

4. $y \leq 5x$ **9.** $x + y \leq -4$

5. $x + y = 6$ and $x - y = 0$ **10.** $x + y = 5$ and $y \geq 2$

Checking Your Understanding of Chapter 10

Except for the Review and Tests, you have completed Chapter 10. At this time you should know:

1. How to find a point of the plane cor-responding to a number pair and how to find a number pair corre-sponding to a point of the plane   PAGE   273

Do you need to review?

2. How to express a relation by means of a (an)

    a. List enclosed within braces   276

    b. Table   276

    c. Description   277

    d. Equation or inequality   281

3. How to recognize a function   280

4. How to graph first-degree equations by finding two points of the graph   283

5. How to graph first-degree equations by the slope-intercept method [C]   289

6. How to spell and use the following words:

	PAGE		PAGE
abscissa	274	infinitely	277
axis	274	intercept	287
coordinates	274	ordered	273
define	276	ordinate	274
degree of a polynomial	283	relation	276
function	280	variable	276

293

[A]

1. Express $\{(0, 0), (1, 3), (2, 6), (3, 9)\}$ in a table.

2. Graph the relation of Ex. 1.

3. Express the number pairs in the table below by a graph:

x	− 3	− 2	− 1	0	1	2
y	− 2	− 4	− 3	− 1	− 4	− 3

4. Graph each of the equations below.

a. $x + y = 2$ **e.** $\frac{1}{2} y = 4 + x$

b. $y = 4 x$ **f.** $y = - 2$

c. $2 y = 5$ **g.** $3 x - y = 9$

d. $2 x + y = 3$ **h.** $x - y = 3$

5. Graph each of the inequalities below.

a. $y > 3 x$ **d.** $y - x < 3$

b. $y < x + 1$ **e.** $2 x + y > 1$

c. $y + x > 4$ **f.** $y > 2 x + 2$

6. Graph the compound sentence "$y > 2 x - 1$ and $y > - x + 3$."

7. Which of the graphs below are graphs of functions? $/, 3$

 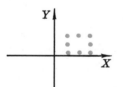 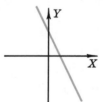 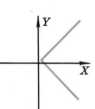

[A]

1. Simplify: $4a - 7b + c - 8a - 4c$ $-4a-7b-3c$

2. If $3x^2 - 4xy + 6y^2$ is the remainder in a subtraction problem and the subtrahend is $-4x^2 - xy + y^2$, find the minuend. $-x^2-5xy+7y^2$

3. Find the indicated powers:

a. $(-5c)^2$ $25c^2$ **c.** $(x^3)^2$ x^6 **e.** $(10^3)^2$ 10^6

b. $(-3ab^2)^2$ $9a^2b^4$ **d.** $(x^5)^2$ x^{10} **f.** $(x^4)^3$ x^{12}

4. Multiply $2x^2 - 3xy - y^2$ by $3x - y$. $6x^3-11x^2y+y^3$

5. Divide $16a^3 - 8a^2 - 12a$ by $-4a$. $-4a^2+2a+3$

6. Divide $2m^3 - 11m^2 + 19m - 11$ by $2m - 5$. $m^2-3m+2, R, -1$

7. If $x = -1$ and $y = 2$, find the value of $4x^2y - (xy)^2$. 4

8. Simplify: $2c - (3c + 1) + c(c - 2)$. c^2-3c-1

9. Remove parentheses in $(2x - 1)(x + 3)$. $2x^2+5x-3$

Solve:

10. $2x - 6 = 10$ 8 **13.** $\frac{4}{9}c = \frac{2}{3}c - 8$ 36

11. $-6 - y = 0$ -6 **14.** $2(p - 3) - 4(2p + 1) = 2$ -2

12. $\frac{7}{8}x = 21$ 24 **15.** $5(x - 4) - 3(2x + 6) + 38 = 0$ 0

16. Two angles of a triangle are equal and the third angle is twice the sum of the other two. How large is each angle? $30°$ $30°$ $120°$

17. Today we use 42.7% less fresh fruit than was used 35 years ago. Today we average 77.7 pounds per person per year. What was the average 35 years ago? $135.6 lb.$

18. Liquid carbon dioxide boils at $-79°$ centigrade. Find its boiling point, Fahrenheit. $(F = \frac{9}{5}C + 32)$ $-110.2°$

19. Bismuth melts at $518°$ Fahrenheit. Find its melting point, centigrade. $C = \frac{5}{9}(F - 32)$ $270°$

20. Graph the equation $2x - y = 12$.

[B]

21. Divide $10a^3b^4 - 12a^2b^3 - 8a^2b^5$ by $2a^2b^3$. $5ab-6-4b^2$

22. $S = \frac{n}{2}(a + l)$ and $l = a + (n - 1)d$. If $a = -10$, $n = 8$, and $d = 3$, find l and then find S. $l=11$ $S=4$

23. Simplify: $(x-1)^2 - (2x-3)(x+4)$ $-x^2-7x+13$

24. Solve: $(x-1)^2 = (x-3)^2$ 2

25. Solve: $(y+5)(2y-1) - y(2y+4) = 0$ 1

26. Solve: $\dfrac{b-1}{2} + \dfrac{b-2}{3} - \dfrac{b-3}{4} = 6$ 11

27. Find three consecutive integers whose sum is 297. $\begin{smallmatrix}98\\99\\100\end{smallmatrix}$

28. Find three consecutive integers whose sum is 282. $93, 94, 95$

29. How can a five-dollar bill be changed into 29 coins consisting of nickels, dimes, quarters, and half-dollars if there are the same number of dimes and nickels, and the number of half dollars is one more than the number of quarters? (Let $x =$ the number of quarters.) *Quarters, 4; half-dollars, 5; nickels, 10; dimes, 10*

7%
$\$2500$
30. A part of $6000 is invested at 7% and the remainder at 6%. If the 6% investment produces $35 more interest than the 7% investment, what is the amount invested at each rate?
6%
$\$3500$

31. $A = p + prt$. If $A = \$376.20$, $t = 1$ year, $p = \$360$, $r = ?$ $4\frac{1}{2}\%$

32. Solve for x: $(ax-1)x + 2 = b + ax^2 - c$ $2-b+c$

33. Solve for y: $y + 2 + 4c = 3y + 2$ $2c$

34. $4a + 4b - 5x - 5y = 4(?) - 5(?).$ $= 4(a+b) - 5(x+y)$

35. Frank is x years old and Chester is 6 years older. In 8 years, twice Chester's age increased by three times Frank's age will equal 97 years. How old is each? $F. 9, C. 15$

36. Find the volume of a cylinder if its height is 18 inches and the radius of its base is 6 inches. ($V = \pi r^2 h$)

2034.72 *cu. in.*

[A]

1. On graph paper draw two perpendicular axes and graph the number pairs below. Name the point with the letter preceding the number pair. $A(2, 3)$; $B(-3, -2)$; $C(4, -5)$; $D(-3, 6)$; and $E(7, 0)$.

2. State the number pairs represented by the graph at the right. *(See foot of page.)*

3. Is the relation expressed by the graph in Ex. 2 a function? Explain. *no.*

4. Graph the relation expressed by the table below: $y = -x$

x	−4	−3	−2	−1	0
y	4	3	2	1	0

5. Express the equation $y = 4$ as an equation with two variables. Graph the equation. $y = 0(x) + 4$

6. Graph the equation $x + y = 3$.

7. Graph the inequality $y > 2x$.

8. Graph the equation $2x - y = 6$.

9. Graph the equation $x - y = 0$.

10. Study the two line graphs at the right and give the values of x and y that satisfy both equations. $x = 2, y = 1$

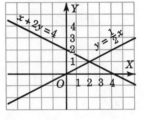

2. $(1, 1)$
   $(2, 1); (2, 2)$
   $(3, 1); (3, 2); (3, 3)$

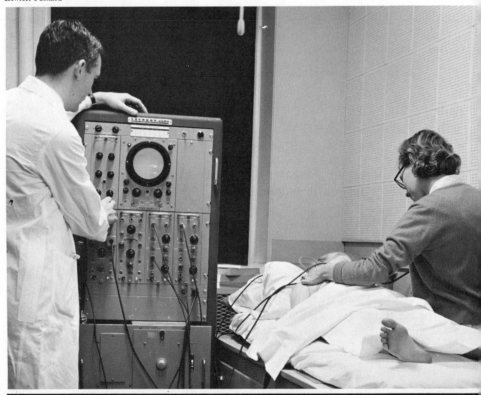

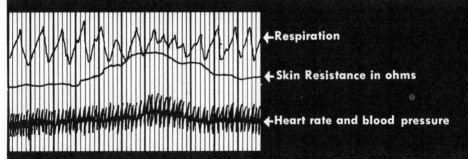

←Respiration

←Skin Resistance in ohms

←Heart rate and blood pressure

GRAPH–MAKING MACHINES

Machines which make graphs are not uncommon today. You can find them in science laboratories, in various industries, and in other fields. For example, in powerhouses you can find instruments that record the voltage and current.

You may have heard of a cardiogram. It is a graph which shows the force and intervals of a person's heartbeats. The machine used in making this graph is a cardiograph.

At the Weather Bureau you will find many graphing instruments in use. The barograph is used to record changes in atmospheric pressure. The thermograph records variations in temperature; the graph it traces is called a thermogram. The instrument which registers earth tremors caused by earthquakes is known as a seismograph and it makes a graph called a seismogram.

The lie detector, or polygraph, is a comparatively new instrument. Such machines are often of great assistance to investigators of crime. When an individual is suspected of withholding the truth, he may be asked to submit to the lie-detector test. While he is being questioned, the polygraph records the changes in his respiration, blood pressure and pulse rate, and skin resistance to electrical current. Typical graphs are shown on the opposite page.

11

Systems of Linear Equations

Suggested Time Schedule
Minimum   7 days
Maximum   8 days

In this chapter you will discover how two equations may be used together in solving a problem.

So far in this course, you have been solving verbal problems by representing the problem situation by an equation involving one unknown. You used a variable to represent the unknown. When there have been two or more unknowns involved, you have expressed these unknowns in terms of the one variable.

Very often a problem involving more than one unknown may be solved more easily by representing each of the unknowns by a separate variable. If a problem has two unknowns, it may be solved by using two variables in two equations. If the problem involves three unknown quantities, it may be solved by using three variables in three equations. In this chapter we shall learn how to solve two equations having two unknowns.

Example. Find two numbers whose sum is 12 and whose difference is 4.

When using two letters, we start the solution as follows:

Let $x =$ the larger number
and let $y =$ the smaller number

> A modern and helpful way to consider a system of equations.

Then $x + y = 12$
and $x - y = 4$

Actually, the two equations may be considered as the two clauses of the compound sentence "$x + y = 12$ and $x - y = 4$." If you have not studied pages 139–141, you may find it helpful to do so now.

Graphs of Pairs of Linear Equations [A]

If the graphs of two linear equations in two unknowns are made on the same set of axes, there are three possibilities, which will now be discussed.

First, the lines intersect.

$$x + y = 12$$

x	0	12	6
y	12	0	6

$$x - y = 4$$

x	0	4	6
y	-4	0	2

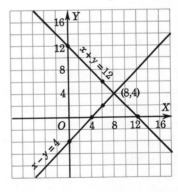

ALGEBRA, BOOK ONE

The graphs of these two equations (page 301) intersect in the point (8, 4). Both equations have the common solution $x = 8$, $y = 4$. Although there is an infinite number of sets of values which satisfy each equation, $x = 8$, $y = 4$ is the only set which satisfies both equations. $x + y = 12$ and $x - y = 4$ are consistent and independent equations. Two equations in two variables which have at least one solution in common are <u>consistent</u>. If consistent linear equations have only one solution in common, they are said to be <u>independent</u>. (Sometimes independent equations having one common solution are called simultaneous. Why do you think they are so called?)

Have you observed that we have solved the example given on the preceding page?

PROOF. If we substitute $x = 8$ and $y = 4$ in $x + y = 12$, we have $8 + 4 = 12$. Substituting $x = 8$ and $y = 4$ in $x - y = 4$, we have $8 - 4 = 4$.

If the solution cannot be proved, there is an error in the work. A mistake may be made either in finding one or more points or in plotting one or more points.

Second, the lines are parallel.

$$x - y = -2$$

x	0	-2
y	2	0

$$x - y = -5$$

x	0	-5
y	5	0

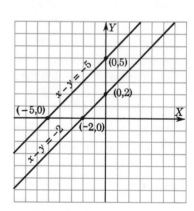

The graphs of these two equations are parallel lines, that is, they never meet. No set of values of x and y which satisfies one equation will satisfy the other equation. In other words, they have no common solution. Two linear equations whose graphs are parallel are said to be <u>inconsistent</u>. You can see why they are so called. For one equation states that the difference of two numbers is -2 and the other equation states that the difference of the two numbers is -5. Two such numbers do not exist.

Use set language (see Chapter 1). When two lines intersect, the two sets of points for the equations have one common point which is a *unit subset*. When the two lines are parallel, the intersection of the two sets is the *null* or *empty* set. When the lines coincide, the two sets are equal.

Third, the lines coincide.

$2x + 3y = 6$

x	0	3
y	2	0

$6x + 9y = 18$

x	-3	6
y	4	-2

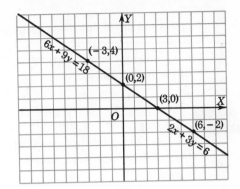

This situation illustrates the third of the possibilities mentioned on page 301.

The graphs of these two equations just given coincide (one fits exactly on the other). Two consistent linear equations whose graphs coincide are called <u>dependent</u> equations, because one is said to depend on the other. The equation $6x + 9y = 18$ may be obtained from the equation $2x + 3y = 6$ by multiplying both members of the latter by 3. How may the equation $2x + 3y = 6$ be obtained from the equation $6x + 9y = 18$?

In graphing sets of linear equations, try to choose values of x that will give whole numbers for y. In finding sets of points, many people prefer first to solve each equation for y. For example, if we solve the equation $2x - y = 5$ for y, we have

$$2x - y = 5$$
$$-y = -2x + 5$$
$$D_{-1} \qquad y = 2x - 5$$

Then if $x = 0, y = -5$, and if $x = 3, y = 1$. These two points, $(0, -5)$ and $(3, 1)$, may be used to draw the graph.

Solving Pairs of Equations by Graphing [A]

From the preceding discussion, we know.

1. If two linear equations have intersecting graphs, they have one common solution.

2. If they have parallel graphs, they have no common solution.

3. If their graphs coincide, they have an infinite number of common solutions, any solution of either of them being a solution of the other.

303

① Encourage students to use the points on the two axes, by assigning 0 in turn to x and y. These points can be found quickly from the original equation. Also, the x and y intercepts have significance later in mathematics.

To solve two linear equations by graphing, graph both equations on the same pair of axes.

The co-ordinates of the intersection point represent the common solution of the two equations.

Consistent and independent: Ex. 1-5, 7, 8, 10, 11, 13, 14, 16-21;
Consistent and dependent: Ex. 6, 12; Inconsistent: Ex. 9 [A]

EXERCISES

Graph each of the following pairs of equations on the same axes. Tell whether each pair is consistent or inconsistent. If a pair is consistent and independent, give its solution, and prove.

x=3, **1.** $x + y = 5$ *x=3,* **5.** $y = 2x - 8$ **9.** $3x - y = 9$
y=2 $x - y = 1$ *y=-2* $y = 4 - 2x$ *none* $6x - 2y = 8$

x=7, **2.** $x - y = 6$ *none* **6.** $3x + 6y = 12$ *x=-4,* **10.** $2x - y = -6$
y=1 $x + y = 8$ $x + 2y = 4$ *y=-2* $x + 3y = -10$

x=2, **3.** $y = x$ *x=4,* **7.** $x + y = 8$ *x=-1,* **11.** $y = -2x$
y=2 $x + y = 4$ *y=4* $x - y = 0$ *y=2* $x + y = 1$

x=2, **4.** $y = 3x$ *x=-* **8.** $3x + 5y = -6$ **12.** $6x + 3y = 12$
y=6 $x + y = 8$ *y=0* $x - 2y = -2$ *none* $4x + 2y = 8$

13. $5x + 4y = 7$ *x=3,*   **14.** $2x - y = 6$ *x=4*
     $6x = 28 + 5y$ *y=-2* $y = 6 - x$ *y=2*

15. Copy and complete each table, based upon the equation above it.

$$2x - y = 5$$

x	−1	? 2½	3	? 4	0	? 2	±2	? −3
y	? −7	0	? 1	3	? −5	−1	? −9	−11

$$x + 3y = 13$$

x	? 1	2	4	5	? 6	0	−2	? −5
y	4	? 3⅔	? 3	? 2⅔	2⅓	? 4⅓	? 5	6

How many solutions have you found for each equation? What is their common solution? *Eight; x=4, y=3*

[B]

Solve by graphing, and prove:

16. $5x - 3y = 1$ *x = 4/17,*   **17.** $4s - 5 = 3t$ *s = -1*
     $3x + 5y = 1$ *y = 1/17* $2s - 1 = t$ *t = -3*
     Or approx. x = ¼, y = 0.

304

Have students use suitable graph paper, preferably not ruled finer than 8 spaces to the inch. In graphing, axes should always be labeled (see p. 301) and the scale on both axes should be the same. A few numerals on the axes are enough to indicate the scale.

Although integral values are convenient, they are not necessary, as students can estimate fractions fairly well.

19. $x = 3\frac{2}{7}$, $y = -7\frac{1}{7}$; Or
$x = 3.3$, $y = -7.1$, approx.

18. $3x - 2y = -5$ $x = -3$,
     $5x + 2y = -19$ $y = -2$

19. $4x + y - 6 = 0$
     $3x - y - 17 = 0$

20. $5x + 3y - 3 = 0$ $x = 3$,
     $7x - 2y - 29 = 0$ $y = -4$

21. $y = 6x + 1$ $x = \frac{1}{2}$,
     $2x = 3y - 11$ $y = 4$

Historical Note. The graphical method of solving sets of equations was discovered by the French mathematician and philosopher, DESCARTES, about 1637. Others had plotted points using positive numbers, but he was the first to plot negative numbers.

Solving Pairs of Equations by Addition or Subtraction [A]

You will now learn another method of solving a pair of linear equations. A pair of linear equations can be solved if they can be combined to form a third equation which has only one unknown.

Example 1. Solve $3x + y = 7$ (1)
                 $x - y = 1$ (2)

Solution. In order to find the common solution for these two equations, it is necessary to derive a third equation, containing only x or y. Since there is the same number of y's in

$$3x + y = 7 \tag{1}$$

and $x - y = 1$ (2)

we may add the left members and make the y's disappear. Since we add the left members, we must add the right members also. Performing these two additions, we get $4x = 8$. We have eliminated y. Dividing by 4, $x = 2$.

If we multiply both members of the first equation by 1 and both members of the second equation by 3, we have the same number of x's in each equation.

We then have $3x + y = 7$
                   $3x - 3y = 3$

If we add these two equations, we obtain $6x - 2y = 10$, which we cannot solve. But if we subtract the lower equation from the one above it, we obtain the equation $4y = 4$. Then $y = 1$.

We can also solve for y by substituting $x = 2$ in *either* of the two equations. If we substitute $x = 2$ in the first equation, we have $3(2) + y = 7$. Solving this equation, we get $y = 1$. The solution of the set of equations

$$3x + y = 7$$
$$x - y = 1$$

is $x = 2$, $y = 1$. Prove by substituting $x = 2$ and $y = 1$ in both equations.

① Ask in what other case this was used. (In clearing equations of fractions.)

ALGEBRA, BOOK ONE

Directions for Solving a Pair of Linear Equations by the Addition-Subtraction Method:

1. If necessary, multiply both members of the equations by such numbers as will make the coefficients of one of the variables numerically equal.

2. Add or subtract the two resulting equations to obtain an equation having only one variable.

3. Solve the equation containing one variable.

4. Solve for the other variable

(a) by substituting the value of the variable found in step 3 in either of the two given equations; or

(b) by using steps 1, 2, and 3.

5. Prove by substituting in each of the given equations.

Example 2. Solve
$$5x + 2y = -5$$
$$-3x + 4y = 29$$

Solution.

To solve for y we must eliminate x. The smallest number that can be exactly divided by 5 and 3 is 15. We must therefore have 15 x in each equation.

$$
\begin{array}{ll}
M_3 & 5x + 2y = -5 \\
M_5 & -3x + 4y = 29 \\
\hline
& 15x + 6y = -15 \\
& -15x + 20y = 145 \\
\hline
\text{Adding,} & 26y = 130 \\
D_{26} & y = 5
\end{array}
$$

To solve for x we must eliminate y. The smallest number that can be exactly divided by 2 and 4 is 4. We must therefore have 4 y in each equation.

$$
\begin{array}{ll}
M_2 & 5x + 2y = -5 \\
M_1 & -3x + 4y = 29 \\
\hline
& 10x + 4y = -10 \\
& -3x + 4y = 29 \\
\hline
\text{Subtracting, } & 13x = -39 \\
D_{13} & x = -3
\end{array}
$$

After the value of y has been found, we can find the value of x by substituting $y = 5$ in the equation $5x + 2y = -5$. We then have $5x + 10 = -5$. Solving this equation, we get $x = -3$, as we found in the right-hand column above.

② In this method you may at first have trouble deciding whether the equations are to be added or subtracted. You should formulate your own rule. In the above solution was $-15x$ added to or subtracted from $+15x$ to make 0? Was $+4y$ added to $+4y$ or subtracted from $+4y$ to make 0?

PROOF. Does $x = -3$ and $y = 5$ satisfy both equations? Yes.

② After the value of one variable has been found, it is usually shorter to use the substitution technique to obtain the other. Ask students why it does not matter which equation is used. Connect this with the intersection set found by graphing.

SYSTEMS OF LINEAR EQUATIONS

When systems of equations are to be solved by the addition-subtraction method, they should be written in the <u>standard form</u> $ax + by = c$.

[A]

Read the equations in exercises 1–18 below and tell what multipliers can be used to eliminate the first variable. Tell what multipliers can be used to eliminate the second variable.

[A]

WRITTEN EXERCISES

Solve and prove: *(ans. to Ex. 1-6 in right margin)*

1. $x + y = 10$
$x - y = 2$

3. $2x - y = 14$
$x - y = 5$

5. $3x - 2y = 25$
$5x - 2y = 39$

2. $x - y = 13$
$x + y = 15$

4. $-2x + 5y = -3$
$2x - y = -1$

6. $a + 2b = 8$
$2a - b = 6$

7. $5m + 3n = -1$ $m = -2,$
$2m + 9n = 23$ $n = 3$

13. $7r - 4s = 56$ $r = 20,$
$3r - 5s = -45$ $s = 21$

8. $3x - y = 10$ $x = 4,$
$4x - 9y = -2$ $y = 2$

14. $6m - 2n = 1$ $m = \frac{1}{2},$
$8m + n = 5$ $n = 1$

9. $5x - 2y = 0$ $x = 2,$
$x - y = -3$ $y = 5$

15. $3x + 2y = 118$ $x = 16,$
$x + 5y = 191$ $y = 35$

10. $3x - 2y = 11$ $x = 5,$
$2x + y = 12$ $y = 2$

16. $-p - 5q = 0$ $p = 10,$
$-3p - 10q = -10$ $q = -2$

11. $3E - 4F = 1$ $E = 11,$
$5E - 4F = 23$ $F = 8$

17. $3x - y = 6$ *no solution*
$y = 3x$

12. $3x + 2y = -9$ $x = -11,$
$5x + 3y = -19$ $y = 12$

18. $\frac{1}{2}x + \frac{1}{3}y = 4$ $x = 6,$
$x - y = 3$ $y = 3$

[B]

Solve and check:

19. $8h - 7k = 0$ $h = -7,$
$7h - 8k = 15$ $k = -8$

21. $8x + 17y = 536$ $x = 50,$
$12x - y = 592$ $y = 8$

20. $9x - 8y = -15$ $x = 25,$
$-10y + 7x = -125$ $y = 30$

22. $7r - 3s = 23$ $r = 2,$
$21r + 4s = 30$ $s = -3$

23. $5y - 3x + 8 = 4y + 2x + 7$ $x = \frac{1}{7},$
$4x - 2y = 3y + 2$ $y = -\frac{2}{7}$

24. Work exercises 2–5 on page 309 by the method above.

25. Do you think the addition-subtraction method is superior to graphing in solving pairs of equations? Why? *more accurate; quicker.*

Answers in right margin:

1. $x = 6,$ $y = 4$

2. $x = 14,$ $y = 1$

3. $x = 9,$ $y = 4$

4. $x = -1,$ $y = -1$

5. $x = 7,$ $y = -2$

6. $a = 4,$ $b = 2$

307

① While all the first-degree equations can be solved by the addition-subtraction method, the substitution method is often preferable and is actually *essential* in advanced work. Therefore, although this section is marked B, it is urged that all your students do part of it.

① ALGEBRA, BOOK ONE

Elimination by Substitution [B]

The method of solving a set of linear equations by the substitution method will be illustrated by two examples.

Example 1. Solve
$$3x - 4y = 5 \qquad (1)$$
$$x + 7y = 10 \qquad (2)$$

Solution. Solving equation (2) for x, we get
$$x = 10 - 7y \qquad (3)$$

Why did we solve for x instead of y?

Substituting this value of x in equation (1), we get
$$3(10 - 7y) - 4y = 5$$
$$30 - 21y - 4y = 5$$
$$-21y - 4y = 5 - 30$$
$$-25y = -25$$
$$y = 1$$

Substituting $y = 1$ in equation (3), we get
$$x = 10 - 7$$
$$x = 3$$

The solution of these equations, then, is $x = 3$, $y = 1$.

② Point out that $y = 1$ could be substituted in equations (1) and (2) to obtain $x = 3$. Ask why equation (3) is preferable.

PROOF. Does $3(3) - 4(1) = 5$? $\quad\mid\quad$ Does $3 + 7(1) = 10$?

Does $\quad 9 - 4 = 5$? Yes. $\mid$ Does $\quad 3 + 7 = 10$? Yes.

Example 2. Solve
$$5x + 3y = -5 \qquad (1)$$
$$4x - 5y = 33 \qquad (2)$$

Solution. From (1) $\qquad\qquad 5x = -3y - 5 \qquad (3)$

$D_5 \qquad\qquad\qquad\qquad\qquad x = \dfrac{-3y - 5}{5} \qquad (4)$

Substituting this value of x in equation (2), we obtain
$$4\left(\frac{-3y - 5}{5}\right) - 5y = 33$$

$M_5 \qquad 5(4)\left(\dfrac{-3y - 5}{5}\right) - 5(5y) = 5(33)$

$$-12y - 20 - 25y = 165$$
$$-12y - 25y = 165 + 20$$
$$-37y = 185$$

$D_{-37} \qquad\qquad\qquad\qquad\qquad y = -5$ ③

Substituting in (4) $\qquad\qquad x = \dfrac{-3(-5) - 5}{5}$

$$x = 2$$

The proof is left to the pupil.

308

③ Lead the student to discover that his work is most easily done if he can avoid the use of an awkward fraction. Help him to discover the best variable to solve for in the first step to accomplish this purpose. You might do this by re-solving Example 1, choosing equation (1) and solving for y.

As a class exercise you might have some of the exercises solved by the addition-subtraction method.

SYSTEMS OF LINEAR EQUATIONS

Either of the given equations can be solved for x or for y in terms of the other variable. Then this value of the variable is substituted in the other equation. Often in sets of linear equations one equation is already solved for one variable. In that case it is easier to solve the set by the substitution method than by the addition-subtraction method.

[B]

EXERCISES

1. Read Exercises 2–17 below, and tell in which exercises one equation is already solved for one variable.

Solve by the substitution method: *Ex. 2, 3, 4, 5, 7, 11*

2. $3x - y = 14$ $x = 5,$
$\quad x = 5y$ $y = 1$

3. $y = x + 2$ $x = -1,$
$\quad x + 2y = 1$ $y = 1$

4. $3x - 2y = 1$ $x = -1,$
$\quad x = y + 1$ $y = -2$

5. $a = 2b$ $a = 6,\ b = 3$
$\quad 4a - 3b = 15$

6. $x + y = 1$ $x = 0, y = 1$
$\quad 3x + 4y = 4$

7. $1 - y = x$ $x = -4,$
$\quad 5y - x = 29$ $y = 5$

8. $5x + y = 15$ $x = 4\frac{3}{8},$
$\quad x - 3y = 25$ $y = -6\frac{7}{8}$

9. $5x = 1 - 2y$ $x = 1,$
$\quad 11x + 5y = 1$ $y = -2$

10. $y + 3p = 10$ $p = 4,$
$\quad 4y + 5p = 12$ $y = -2$

11. $m = 9n$ $m = 3, n = \frac{1}{3}$
$\quad 13m - 12n = 35$

12. $2x = 5y$ $x = 1\frac{1}{2}, y = \frac{3}{5}$
$\quad 10x - 15y - 6 = 0$

13. $8B + A = -46$ $A = -6, B = -5$
$\quad 13A + B = -83$

14. $2p - 3q = 3$ $p = 1, q = -\frac{1}{3}$
$\quad 6p - 3q = 7$

15. $3y - 2x = 16$ $x = -5, y = 2$
$\quad 3x + 7y + 1 = 0$

16. $7x + 8y = 36$ $x = -4, y = 8$
$\quad 11x + 5y = -4$

17. $5x + 2y = 7$ $x = 3, y = -4$
$\quad 3x - 4y = 25$

[C]

Solve by any method:

18. $3x + y + 11y = 99$ $x = 5, y = 7$
$\quad 5 - 15x + 21y - 7 = 70$

19. $3(2x + y) - (x + 30) = 0$ $x = 3, y = 5$
$\quad 4y - (x + 17) = 0$

20. $2x - y + 21x = 7(2y - 6)$ $x = 6, y = 12$
$\quad 6(y + 3) + 5(y - x) = 30(2x - 8)$

Sets of Equations Containing Fractions and Parentheses [A]

Sets of equations which contain fractions and parentheses should be simplified and reduced to the standard form $ax + by = c$. Then either the addition-subtraction method or the substitution method can be used to complete the solution.

309

Example. Solve

$$\frac{5x}{6} = 7 - \frac{y}{4} \qquad (1)$$

$$\frac{2x}{3} + 1 = 4 + \frac{y}{8} \qquad (2)$$

Solution. Multiplying both members of (1) by 12, we get

$$10x = 84 - 3y$$
$$10x + 3y = 84 \qquad (3)$$

Multiplying both members of (2) by 24, we get

$$16x + 24 = 96 + 3y$$
$$16x - 3y = 96 - 24$$

or $\qquad\qquad 16x - 3y = 72 \qquad (4)$

The two equations are now in standard form:

$$10x + 3y = 84 \qquad (3)$$
$$16x - 3y = 72 \qquad (4)$$

Adding $\qquad\qquad 26x \quad\;\; = 156$

D_{26} $\qquad\qquad\qquad x = 6$

Substituting $x = 6$ in equation (3), we obtain

Warn that substitution in the derived equations will not prove the correctness of the solution for the original.

$$60 + 3y = 84$$
$$3y = 84 - 60$$
$$3y = 24$$
$$y = 8$$

Then we must substitute $x = 6$ and $y = 8$ in the (original) equations (1) and (2) in order to prove our solution correct. Substituting in equations (3) and (4) would not be a proof. Why?

[A]

EXERCISES

Solve:

1. $x + \dfrac{3y}{4} = 2$ $\qquad x = \frac{1}{2},$

$\quad 2x + \dfrac{5y}{4} = \dfrac{7}{2}$ $\qquad y = 2$

2. $2x + 3(x + y) = 15$ $\qquad x = 2,$
$\quad 2x - 3y = -1$ $\qquad y = 1\frac{2}{3}$

3. $2x = 8(y + 1)$ $\qquad x = 8,$
$\quad 3(x - 3y) = 15$ $\qquad y = 1$

4. $x + y = 2000$ $\qquad x = 1500,$
$\quad .04x + .05y = 85$ $\quad y = 500$

5. $\dfrac{5x}{2} - 5y = 20$ $\qquad x = -1\frac{3}{5},$
$\quad x = \frac{1}{3}y$ $\qquad y = -4\frac{4}{5}$

6. $\dfrac{x}{3} - \dfrac{y}{2} = -\dfrac{8}{3}$ $\qquad x = 1,$

$\quad \dfrac{x}{7} - \dfrac{y}{3} = -\dfrac{39}{21}$ $\qquad y = 6$

7. $x - 2 = 3(x + y)$ $\qquad x = 5,$
$\quad x + 6 = 3x + y$ $\qquad y = -4$

8. $x + y = 4$ $\qquad x = -1\frac{2}{9}, y = 5\frac{2}{9}$
$\quad 2(x + y) + 3(3x + 5) = 12$

9. $\frac{1}{2}(x + y) - \frac{1}{3}(y + 5) = 3$
$\quad 2x - 3y = 4$ $\qquad x = 8, y = 4$

10. $x + y = 5000$ $\qquad x = 1800,$
$\quad \dfrac{4x}{100} + \dfrac{6y}{100} = 264$ $\quad y = 3200$

Although the students know how to solve equations now, they will make many careless errors in these complicated problems—often because of confused arrangement of their work. Urge them not to crowd their work, to group companion equations with brackets, and to use other devices to keep the process clear. Do not let them write the final answer separated as if $x = $ ___ and $y = $ ___ were two answers.

[B]

Solve:

11. $\dfrac{7a}{4} + \dfrac{5b}{3} + 3 = 0$

$\dfrac{a}{2} - \dfrac{b}{3} = 4$ $a = 4, b = -6$

12. $x - 4y = 10$ $x = 20, y = 2\frac{1}{2}$

$\dfrac{x+y}{5} - \dfrac{x-y}{7} = 2$

13. $2(5x - y) + 3(y - 2) = 0$

$5(3x + 1) = 2y$ $x = \frac{1}{5}, y = 4$

14. $x - y + 2 = 5(3x + y)$ $x = \frac{2}{5}$,

$3x - y = 9(1 - 2x)$ $y = -\frac{2}{5}$

15. $4(x+y) + 5(x + 1) = -16$

$3(3x - 2y) - (2x - 3y) = 2$

$x = -1, y = -3$

16. $\dfrac{5x}{6} + \dfrac{7y - x}{5} = 16$ $x = 33\frac{7}{8}$,

$5y + \dfrac{2x - 3y}{3} = 7$ $y = -3\frac{43}{48}$

17. $x + y = 8000$ $x = 3000, y = 5000$

$.04x + .06y = .0525(x+y)$

18. $12(x - y) + 11y = 14$ $x = \frac{5}{6}$,

$18x + 5(y + 1) = 0$ $y = -4$

19. $a - b = \frac{1}{7}(a + b)$ $a = 1$,

$2(a + 2b) = 5$ $b = \frac{3}{4}$

20. $(9a + 5b) + 7(1 - 2b) = 0$

$3b - 2(b + 1) = 1 + 4a$ $a = \dfrac{-20}{27}, b = \dfrac{1}{27}$

Solving Problems by Systems of Equations [A]

Some problems are solved more easily by using one variable and one equation; others are solved more easily by using two variables and two equations. We shall solve the following example two ways.

Example. The difference of two numbers is 18. The sum of twice the larger and three times the smaller is 151. Find the numbers.

Solution with One Variable	Solution with Two Variables
Let $\quad s = $ the smaller no.	Let $\quad s = $ the smaller no.
Then $\quad s + 18 = $ the larger no.	and $\quad l = $ the larger no.
$2(s + 18) + 3s = 151$	$l - s = 18$
$2s + 36 + 3s = 151$	$2l + 3s = 151$
$2s + 3s = 151 - 36$	$M_2\begin{vmatrix} l - \quad s = 18 \end{vmatrix}$
$5s = 115$	$M_1\begin{vmatrix} 2l + 3s = 151 \end{vmatrix}$
$s = 23$, the smaller	$2l - 2s = \quad 36$
$s + 18 = 41$, the larger	$2l + 3s = \quad 151$
	$-5s = -115$
	$s = 23$, the smaller
	$l - 23 = 18$
	$l = 41$, the larger
PROOF. $41 - 23 = 18$	PROOF. $41 - 23 = 18$
$2(41) + 3(23) = 151$	$2(41) + 3(23) = 151$

Most students will appreciate this method of problem solving. It often seems the easier way. Point out that "$s + 18 = $ larger" in Solution 1 corresponds to $l - s = 18$ in Solution 2.

311

ALGEBRA, BOOK ONE

To Solve a Problem with Two Variables:

1. Let one variable represent one unknown quantity
and another variable represent the other.
2. Form two equations
from the conditions of the problem or from facts you know.
3. Solve the two equations and prove,
using all the numerical relations of the problem.

[A]

PROBLEMS

1. Find two numbers if their sum is 33 and their difference is 9. *21, 12*

2. The sum of two numbers is 84 and the larger exceeds the smaller by 22. What are the numbers? *53, 31*

x	y

3. The difference of two numbers is 3. If twice the larger is subtracted from three times the smaller, the remainder is 9. Find the numbers. *18, 15*

4. Find two numbers such that four times the smaller plus five times the larger equals 73; and three times the smaller decreased by twice the larger equals 3. *9, 7*

5. One of two complementary angles is 4 times as large as the other. How many degrees are there in each angle? *18°, 72°*

6. Two angles are complementary. Find the number of degrees in each angle if twice the smaller exceeds the larger by 8°. $32\frac{2}{3}°, 57\frac{1}{3}°$

7. The difference of two supplementary angles is 44°. Find the angles. *112°, 68°*

8. Two angles are supplementary. Find the number of degrees in each angle if 5 times one angle equals 4 times the other. *100°, 80°*

9. The perimeter of a rectangle is 848 inches and the length exceeds the width by 200 inches. Find the dimensions of the rectangle. *112 in. × 312 in.*

10. A woman wishes to invest $20,000 in bonds and in some stocks so as to receive an annual income of $1330. How should she distribute the investments if the bonds pay 7% and the stocks pay 6%? *bonds, $13,000 ; stocks, $7000*

312

11. A man wishes to invest $15,000, part at 6% and the remainder at 8% so as to have an income of $980. How much must he invest at each rate? *6%, $11,000 ; 8%, $4000*

12. If 4 oranges and 6 grapefruit cost $2.62, and 7 oranges and 5 grapefruit cost $2.66, what is the cost of each? *oranges, 13¢ Grapefruit, 35¢*

13. The sum of the ages of a father and son is 44 years. Four years ago the father was 8 times as old as the son. What are their present ages? *Father, 36 yr.; son, 8 yr.*

14. A father is three times as old as his daughter. Ten years ago the father was seven times as old as his daughter. How old is each at present? *Father, 45 yr.; daughter, 15 yr.*

15. Find the capacity of two trucks if 6 trips of the smaller and 4 trips of the larger make a total haul of 39 tons, and 6 trips of the larger and 4 trips of the smaller make a total haul of 41 tons. *$3\frac{1}{2}$ T., $4\frac{1}{2}$ T.*

16. A weight of 16 pounds on one end of a lever balances a weight of 10 pounds on the other end. If the weights are 12 feet apart, how far is each from the fulcrum? *16 lb., 4.62 ft.; 10 lb., 7.38 ft.*

17. If Charles were two years older, he would be half as old as Fred is now. If Fred were six years older, he would be three times as old as Charles is now. How old is each? *Charles, 10 yr.; Fred, 24 yr.*
[B]

18. The length of a rectangular flower bed is to be 50% greater than the width, and its perimeter must be 30 feet. How long and how wide must the bed be? *9 ft. x 6 ft.*

19. In a right triangle one angle contains 90°. Find the number of degrees in each of the other angles if the larger angle lacks 7° of being one half the other's supplement. *76°, 14°*

20. Two weights balance on a lever when one is 5 feet from the fulcrum and the other is 6 feet from the fulcrum. If 8 pounds are added to each weight, they balance when they are respectively 7 feet and 8 feet from the fulcrum. Find the number of pounds in each weight. *24 lb., 20 lb.*

21. A butcher sold 4 pounds of round steak and 3 pounds of rib steak for $13.70. If he had sold 3 pounds of round steak and 4 pounds of rib steak, he would have received $14.65. What was the selling price per pound of each kind of steak? *round, $1.55 ; rib, $2.50*

313

22. When Greg rides his bike for 2 hours, he goes 15 miles farther than when he hikes for 3 hours. When he hikes for 2 hours, he goes one-sixth as far as when he rides his bike for 3 hours. What is his speed while riding? Hiking? *riding, 12 m.p.h.; hiking, 3 m.p.h.*

23. Mr. Baxter mixed 90-cent candy and 75-cent candy. How many pounds of 90-cent candy must he add to 20 pounds of 75-cent candy to make a mixture of 85-cent candy?

24. Phil is twice as old as Tom was when Phil was as old as Tom is now. If the sum of their present ages is 28 years, how old is each now? *Phil, 16 yr. old; Tom, 12 yr. old*

Checking Your Understanding of Chapter 11

You now have almost completed Chapter 11. Before you study the Chapter Review, be sure that you know:

	PAGE
1. The difference between consistent dependent equations and consistent independent equations	302 303
2. The difference between consistent and inconsistent equations	302
3. How to solve a pair of equations by graphing and by the addition-subtraction method	303 305
4. How to use two letters to solve problems	311
5. How to spell and use each of the following words correctly:	

Review if you need to

	PAGE		PAGE
abscissa	274	linear equations	284
dependent equations	303	origin	274
eliminate	305	simultaneous	302
inconsistent	302	substitution	308

[A]

CHAPTER REVIEW

Solve graphically:

1. $x + y = 6$ $x = 4,$
$2x - y = 6$ $y = 2$

2. $x + 5y = 7$ $x = 1.3,$
$2y - x = 1$ $y = 1.1,$ *approx.*

Solve algebraically:

3. $2x - y = 2$ $x = 2,$
$7x - y = 12$ $y = 2$

4. $4x + 3 = y$ $x = -\frac{3}{5},$
$x + y = 0$ $y = \frac{3}{5}$

5. $a - 4b = -4$ $a = 4,$
$a - 3b = -2$ $b = 2$

6. $2r + 3s = 13$ $r = 1\frac{1}{4}$
$4r + 3s = 15$ $s = 3\frac{2}{3}$

314

As you review, you might tell students that three equations in three variables can be solved by expansion of the addition-subtraction method. Some of your better students who do not need the review might try to do some of these by themselves (see any second-year book for exercises). Mention that there are other methods (determinants) and also that the computing machines have made possible the solution of a great number of equations with an equal number of variables.

SYSTEMS OF LINEAR EQUATIONS

Tell whether the following equations are dependent, independent, or inconsistent:

7. $2x - y = 15$ *Dependent*
$6x - 3y = 45$

9. $4x - y = 8$ *Inconsistent*
$4x - y = 21$

8. $2x - 7y = 11$ *Consistent,*
$5x - y = 11$ *Independent*

10. $3a + 2b = 2$ *Consistent,*
$a - 3b = 19$ *Independent*

Solve:

11. $y + 1 = 4 - 2(x - 2)$
$x - y = 7x - 3y - 16$
$x = 3, \quad y = 1$

12. $\dfrac{x}{3} + \dfrac{y}{4} = 4$ $\quad x = 6, \quad y = 8$
$\dfrac{x}{6} - \dfrac{y}{2} = -3$

13. Find two numbers if their sum is 36 and their difference is 6. *15, 21*

14. How many degrees are there in each of two complementary angles if their difference is 10°? *50°, 40°*

15. Two boys balance on the ends of a seesaw 12 feet long. One boy weighs 60 pounds and the other boy 40 pounds. How far does each boy sit from the fulcrum? *4.8 ft., 7.2 ft.*

16. The perimeter of a rectangle is 54 feet. The length exceeds the width by 5 feet. Find the length and the width of the rectangle. *16 ft. × 11 ft.*

[A]

GENERAL
REVIEW

1. Subtract $3x^2 + 11$ from $7x^2 - 3x + 2$. $4x^2 - 3x - 9$

2. Add $3a^2 + 7a - 4$, $11a + 7$, and $2a^2 - 12a$. $5a^2 + 6a + 3$

Multiply as indicated:

3. $x(x^5)$ x^6

5. $3x^2(3xy)$ $9x^3y$

7. $2n(n)(-2)$ $-4n^2$

4. $3a^2(5a^3)$ $15a^5$

6. $-2b(-3b)$ $6b^2$

8. $2n(n-2)$ $2n^2 - 4n$

9. $(x - 3y)(2x + 5y)$

12. $(x^2 - 3x + 1)(x + 2)$

10. $(3n^2 + 4)(3n^2 - 4)$

13. $(a - b)(a + b)$

11. $-3x^2(x^4 - 5x^3 + 6x^2)$

14. $5a(a^2 - a + 1)$

Divide as indicated:

15. $(-15x^2y) \div (-3y)$ $5x^2$

18. $(10a^2b + 5ab^2) \div (5ab)$ $2a + b$

16. $(18a^2b^2c) \div (3a^2b^2)$ $6c$

19. $(3xy - 21x^2y^2) \div (3xy)$ $1 - 7xy$

17. $\dfrac{x^3 + 3x^2 - 6x}{x}$ $x^2 + 3x - 6$

20. $\dfrac{2a^2b - 4ab + 8ab^2}{2ab}$ $a - 2 + 4b$

→ 9. $2x^2 - xy - 15y^2$
10. $9n^4 - 16$
11. $-3x^6 + 15x^5 - 18x^4$

→ 12. $x^3 - x^2 - 5x + 2$
13. $a^2 - b^2$
14. $5a^3 - 5a^2 + 5a$

315

21. Find $(x^2 - 7x + 12) \div (x - 3)$. $x-4$

22. Find $(10 x^3 - 11 x^2 - 4x - 3) \div (2x - 3)$.
$5x^2+2x+1$

Find the value of each of the following expressions when $x = 2$, $y = -3$, and $z = 0$:

23. x^2yz 0 **25.** $x^2y - z$ -12 **27.** $x^2 + y^2 + z^2$ 13

24. xy^3 -54 **26.** $xy^2 + 6z$ 18 **28.** $x^3 - y^3 - z^3$ 35

29. What per cent of 60 is 6? 10% **30.** What per cent of 6 is 60? 1000%

[B]

Solve the following sets of equations:

31. $5 - 2(x + y) = 3$ $x=4,$ **32.** $x + y = 6000$

$x + 2(x - y) = 18$ $y=-3$ $.06x + .03y = .04(x + y)$
$x=2000, y=4000$

Solve:

33. $\dfrac{6y - 5}{8} - \dfrac{4y - 1}{3} = \dfrac{1}{3} - y$ $1\frac{1}{2}$ **34.** $y - \dfrac{3y + 4}{6} = \dfrac{1}{2}$ $2\frac{1}{3}$

35. $y - 1 = \dfrac{5y + 1}{4} - \dfrac{4y + 6}{9}$ 3

Simplify:
$7x^2+14x$ $3a^2+b^2+3c^2$
36. $3x(x - 2) + 4x(x + 5)$ **38.** $3(a^2 + b^2 + c^2) - 2b^2$ $5x^2-x$

37. $2y^2 + 3y(y - 1) - 6y$ **39.** $2x(x + y) - 3x(x - y)$
$5y^2-9y$
40. Multiply $(a^2 + 2ab + b^2)(a - b)$ $a^3+a^2b-ab^2-b^3$

41. Divide $x^8 - y^8$ by $x^2 - y^2$. $x^6+x^4y^2+x^2y^4+y^6$

42. John can do a certain piece of work in 12 days and Ben in 15 days. After John has worked alone for 5 days he hires Ben to help him finish. How many days does Ben work? $3\frac{8}{9}$

43. What principal will amount to \$55,000 in 5 years at $7\frac{1}{2}\%$? $(A = p + prt)$ $\$40,000$

44. At the beginning of a school year a mother made the following agreement with her daughter Mary. Each month that Mary's algebra grade was 90 or above Mary was to receive a quarter. Each month that her grade was below 90 she was to give her mother a dime. At the end of the school year (10 months) Mary had \$1.45. How many months did Mary fail to receive a grade of 90 or above? 3

[Test A]

1. Graph the equation $x + y = -6$.

2. Solve graphically: $2x - y = 4$
$$x + 2y = 7 \quad x=3, y=2$$

Solve the following sets of equations by the addition-subtraction method:

3. $x + y = 8$ $x=5,$
   $x - y = 2$ $y=3$

4. $2x - y = 14$ $x=6,$
   $3x + y = 16$ $y=-2$

5. $.5x - .3y = 1.7$ $x=4,$
   $.4x - .1y = 1.5$ $y=1$

6. $8x - 3y = 2$ $x=1,$
   $3x - 5y = -7$ $y=2$

Are these equations dependent or independent?

7. $3x - y = 16$ *Independent*
   $2x + 7y = 26$

8. $x + 3y = 5$ *Dependent*
   $4x + 12y = 20$

9. Find two numbers if their sum is 30 and five times the larger number decreased by three times the smaller number is 54. $12, 18$

10. If 4 grapefruit and 2 pineapples cost $2.40, and 5 grapefruit and 3 pineapples cost $3.30, what is the cost of one pineapple? $60\cancel{c}$

[Test B]

1. Solve graphically: $3x + 2y = 14$
$$y = \tfrac{1}{2}x \quad x = 3\tfrac{1}{2}, y = 1\tfrac{3}{4}$$

Solve by the substitution method:

2. $9x - 2y = 31$ $x = 1\tfrac{26}{31},$
   $3y = -2x$ $y = -1\tfrac{7}{31}$

3. $x + 5y = 23$ $x = -2,$
   $3x - y = -11$ $y = 5$

Solve by any method:

4. $.07x + .5y = 1.06$ $x = 8,$
   $.2x - .07y = 1.53$ $y = 1$

5. $2(x - y) + 11 = 5x$ $x = 5$
   $3x - 2(x + y) = 2x - 1$ $y = -2$

6. A butcher makes 100 pounds of a mixture of hamburger and soy protein that sells for $1.04 per pound. If hamburger sells for $1.20 and soy protein for 40 cents a pound, how many pounds of each are used in the mixture? *hamburg, 80 lb. soy protein 20 lb.*

7. Two weights balance on a lever when one is 4 feet from the fulcrum and the other is 5 feet from the fulcrum. If 10 pounds are added to each weight, they balance when they are respectively 6 feet and 7 feet from the fulcrum. How many pounds are there in each weight? $25, 20$

THIS SCIENTIFIC AGE

At the beginning of this century no one could envision the scope and depth of the progress that would be made in science and technology in the years ahead. At this time the automobile industry was in its infancy, the steam turbine was beginning to replace the large reciprocating engine, the Wright Brothers were trying to fly a biplane, wireless telegraphy was being developed, the farmers were using horses instead of tractors, and teenagers patronized the nickelodeons.

Although the first thirty years of the twentieth century saw great progress in research and discovery, this progress was small compared to that which was to follow in the next thirty years. Since 1930 there has been a greater advance in science and technology than in all previous existence. Volumes would be needed to name and describe the achievements of scientists during this period. Let us consider a few of them.

Before 1932 it was thought that the proton was the only constituent of the nucleus of the atom. In 1932 James Chadwick discovered the neutron of the nucleus. This discovery was very important, as the neutron became a powerful weapon in smashing the atom.

By using atom smashers, such as the cyclotron and betatron, and devices such as the cloud chamber and bubble chamber, scientists have been able to obtain a better picture of the atom. For example, since 1936 the known number of particles of the nucleus has increased from six to thirty-six. The information gained by the study of the atom and the use of the Einstein theory of relativity made possible the fission and fusion of atoms.

During the past few years technology has used larger telescopes, made observation rockets, introduced large radar equipment, and developed spectroscopic analysis. As a result, scientists have gained much knowledge of the atmosphere and outer space. For example, it is now known that the universe is at least billions of light years in extent. Space exploration will add to man's knowledge.

Technology has not neglected the home and farm during these years. It is responsible for the improved radio, the television, household appliances, tractors, trucks, and so on.

We may ask ourselves if there are any fields in pure science and technology that are not completely explored. The answer is "yes." Science and technology, like mathematics, have no boundaries. The fields of knowledge are infinite, both in depth and extent.

NASA

12

Special Products and Factoring

Suggested Time Schedule
13 days

*In this chapter you learn
to multiply binomials mentally
and mentally tear products apart.*

Factoring is an important topic. This chapter deals with the elementary basic types. An abundance of practice is given, designed to help the student learn to factor quickly and accurately. Not all these exercises can be done by all the students, for there would not be time. Also, it is desirable that much of the material should be used as oral class work, thus forcing students to think quickly. Following this chapter, factoring will be used considerably in Chapters 13 and 14. There, students will be able to clinch their knowledge in a spiral development.

Although there are many "types" taught, try to make students see the over-all picture by frequently showing how the distributive law of multiplication is applied.

SPECIAL PRODUCTS AND FACTORING

Products and Factors [A]

When two or more numbers are multiplied together, they are called the factors of the result, and the result is called their product. Since $3 \times 7 = 21$, the number 21 is the product of 3 and 7, and the numbers 3 and 7 are the factors of 21. Likewise, since $x(x + 3) = x^2 + 3x$, the expression $x^2 + 3x$ is the product of x and $x + 3$, and the numbers x and $x + 3$ are the factors of $x^2 + 3x$.

Factoring [A]

You recognize the example $x(x + 3) = x^2 + 3x$ above as an application of the distributive property $a(b + c) = ab + ac$. You know that $a(b + c)$ and $ab + ac$ are two expressions for the same number. Since $a(b + c)$ expresses that number as a product, we say that it is the factored form of the number $ab + ac$. One factor of $ab + ac$ is a and the other is $b + c$. We call the process of finding the factors, the process of factoring.

[A]

EXERCISES

Express each of the following sums in its factored form and each factored form as a sum.

1. $3(a + 2)$ $3a + 6$
2. $y(y + 3)$ $y^2 + 3y$
3. $a(b - 4)$ $ab - 4a$
4. $r(r + s)$ $r^2 + rs$
5. $ab(c + 2)$ $abc + 2ab$

6. $3x + 3y$ $3(x + y)$
7. $4a - 4b$ $4(a - b)$
8. $x^2 + 2x$ $x(x + 2)$
9. $2a + 6$ $2(a + 3)$
10. $4x^2 + 4x$ $4x(x + 1)$

Multiplying and Dividing by Monomials [A]

Since $3(2) = 6$, then $6 \div 2 = 3$ and $6 \div 3 = 2$. This example illustrates the fact that if a number is divided by one of its factors, the quotient is the other factor. In order to factor well you should be able, not only to multiply well, but also to divide well. The following exercises will give you practice in multiplying and dividing.

[A]

ORAL
EXERCISES

Multiply:

1. $3(x + y)$ $3x + 3y$
2. $2m(m^2 + 4)$ $2m^3 + 8m$
3. $x^2(x - 1)$ $x^3 - x^2$

4. $7x(x^2 - 2x + 3)$ $7x^3 - 14x^2 + 21x$
5. $-4a(a^2 - 2ab + b^2)$ $-4a^3 + 8a^2b - 4ab^2$
6. $xy(x^2 - 2xy + y^2)$ $x^3y - 2x^2y^2 + xy^3$

321

8. $-2x^7 + 2x^5 + 2x^3$
9. $-x^3 + x^4y + x^3y^2$
10. $-3c^5 + 12c^4 - 3c^3$

14. $x^5y^3 - x^4y^4 - x^4y^3z$
15. $-5a^5 + 30a^4 - 35a^3$
16. $-2x^{13} + 20x^{11} + 4x^{10}$

ALGEBRA, BOOK ONE

$3x^4y - 8x^3y^2 - x^2y^3$

7. $x^2y(3x^2 - 8xy - y^2)$

8. $-2x^3(x^4 - x^2 - 1)$

9. $-x^3(1 - xy - y^2)$

10. $-3c^3(c^2 - 4c + 1)$

11. $2\pi r(r + h) = 2\pi r^2 + 2\pi rh$

12. $a(x - y + z)$ $ax - ay + az$

$a^4b^2 + a^2b^4 + a^2b^2$

13. $a^2b^2(a^2 + b^2 + 1)$

14. $x^4y^3(x - y - z)$

15. $-5a^3(a^2 - 6a + 7)$

16. $-2x^{10}(x^3 - 10x - 2)$

17. $\pi(R^2 - r^2) = \pi R^2 - \pi r^2$

18. $\pi h(r^2 + R^2 + rR)$
$\pi hr^2 + \pi hR^2 + \pi hrR$

Divide:

19. $(5m - 10) \div 5$ $\quad m - 2$

20. $(7x - 14y) \div 7$ $\quad x - 2y$

21. $(20a^3 - 15a) \div a$ $\quad 20a^2 - 15$

22. $(20a^3 - 15a) \div (5a)$ $\quad 4a^2 - 3$

23. $(mc - md) \div m$ $\quad c - d$

$6x - 9y$
24. $(12x^2 - 18xy) \div (2x)$

25. $(8x^2 - 12x + 4) \div 4$ $\quad 2x^2 - 3x + 1$

26. $(P + Prt) \div P$ $\quad 1 + rt$

27. $(\pi R^2 + \pi r^2) \div \pi$ $\quad R^2 + r^2$

28. $(\frac{1}{3}\pi r^2h + \frac{1}{3}\pi R^2h) \div (\frac{1}{3}\pi h)$
$r^2 + R^2$

Name the missing factors:

$3 - 2b^3$
29. $15b^2 - 10b^5 = 5b^2(\ ? \ )$ 31. $my + ny = ?(m + n)$ y

$2y - x^2$
30. $8xy - 4x^3 = 4x(\ ? \ )$ 32. $m^4 - 5m^3 - m^2 = m^2(\ ? \ )$
$m^2 - 5m - 1$

33. $ab + bc + b = b(\ ? \ )$ $a + c + 1$

34. $6x^3 - 4x^2 - 2x = ?(3x^2 - 2x - 1)$
$2x$

Factoring a Polynomial Which Has a Monomial Factor [A]

When you factor a number, you not only find the quotient but you also find the divisor. So in factoring you first find a divisor and then find the quotient. The divisor and quotient are the factors of the number. Let us look at some examples.

Example 1. Factor $4x - 12$.

Solution. Each term of $4x - 12$ is exactly divisible by 2 and by 4. Then either 2 or 4 may be used as a divisor of $4x - 12$. In factoring polynomials it is customary to use the *largest monomial divisor* as one of the factors. So 4 is one factor of $4x - 12$. Since $(4x - 12) \div 4 = x - 3$, the other factor is $x - 3$. Although 4 is not a prime factor (one that cannot be factored), we do not separate it into its factors 2×2. The solution is set down as follows: $4x - 12 = 4(x - 3)$.

To check the solution, multiply $x - 3$ by 4.

Example 2. Factor $5 x^4 - 15 x^3 - 20 x^2$.

Solution. Note that 5 is the largest numerical factor that will exactly divide 5, -15, and -20; and that x^2 is the highest power of x that will exactly divide x^4, x^3, and x^2. Then $5 x^2$ is the largest monomial factor. In factoring, find both numerical and literal parts of the monomial divisor. The solution is set down as $5 x^4 - 15 x^3 - 20 x^2 = 5 x^2(x^2 - 3 x - 4)$.

① If a polynomial cannot be factored, it is prime.

[A]
EXERCISES

Factor when possible:

1. $3 n + 3$ $3(n+1)$ **6.** $2 a + 6$ $2(a+3)$ **11.** $c^2 - c$ $c(c-1)$

2. $4 a - 8$ $4(a-2)$ **7.** $3 ab + 3 ac$ $3a(b+c)$ **12.** $bc - b$ $b(c-1)$

3. $5 x - 25$ $5(x-5)$ **8.** $15 x - 20$ $5(3x-4)$ **13.** $ax + a$ $a(x+1)$

4. $ax + ay$ $a(x+y)$ **9.** $5 x - 11 y$ Prime   **14.** $y^3 - y$ $y(y^2-1)$

5. $6 x - 6 y$ $6(x-y)$ **10.** $a^2 + 4 a$ $a(a+4)$ **15.** $\pi R - \pi r$ $\pi(R-r)$

16. $m^2x + m^2y$ $m^2(x+y)$ **25.** $5 a - 7 b + c$ Prime

17. $20 c - 30 d$ $10(2c-3d)$ **26.** $x^3y^3 + x^2y^2 + xy$ $xy(x^2y^2+xy+1)$

18. $9 - 27 x$ $9(1-3x)$ **27.** $x^3 - x^2 - 42 x$ $x(x^2-x-42)$

19. $7 xy - 14 y$ $7y(x-2)$ **28.** $a^4 + 7 a^3 + 12 a^2$ $a^2(a^2+7a+12)$

20. $10 - 3 c$ Prime   **29.** $5 k^3 + 5 k^2 - 60 k$ $5k(k^2+k-12)$

21. $P + Prt$ $P(1+rt)$ **30.** $7 p^5 + 70 p^2 - 112 p$ $7p(p^4+10p-16)$

22. $h^2 - 9 h$ $h(h-9)$ **31.** $22 m^2 - 33 m + 66$ $11(2m^2-3m+6)$

23. $5 x^2 - 5 x - 10$ $5(x^2-x-2)$ **32.** $3 a^2b^2 - 6 a^2b + 9 ab$ $3ab(ab-2a+3)$

24. $6 x^2 + 48 x + 72$ $6(x^2+8x+12)$ **33.** $\frac{1}{2} x + \frac{1}{2} y - \frac{1}{2} z$ $\frac{1}{2}(x+y-z)$

[B]

34. $180 n - 360$ $180(n-2)$ **40.** $42 x^2y^3 - 35 x^3y^4 - 14 x^5y^6$ $7x^2y^3(6-5xy-2x^3y^3)$

35. $\pi r^2 + \pi rl$ $\pi r(r+l)$ **41.** $3 y^5 - 6 y^4z - 9 y^5z$ $3y^4(y-2z-3yz)$

36. $2 \pi r^2 + 2 \pi rh$ $2\pi r(r+h)$ **42.** $x^4 - x^3 + x^2 - x$ $x(x^3-x^2+x-1)$

37. $x^2y^3 - x^4y^5$ $x^2y^3(1-x^2y^2)$ **43.** $abcx - ab^2cx + b^2x$ $bx(ac-abc+b)$

38. $1.5 a^2 + 2.5 b^2$ $0.5(3a^2+5b^2)$ **44.** $27 a^2b^3 - 18 a^3b^2 + 9 a^2b^3$ $18a^2b^2(2b-a)$

39. $\frac{1}{8} tx - \frac{3}{8} ty$ $\frac{1}{8}t(x-3y)$ **45.** $24 a^7b^2 + 40 a^{10}b^5 - 48 a^{12}$ $8a^7(3b^2+5a^3b^5-6a^5)$

323

① Explain that while there are other possible factors, such as $5(x^4 - 3x^3 - 4x^2)$, polynomial factors should be prime. Similarly, $4a - 8$ could be factored as $8(\frac{1}{2}a - 1)$, but this would not normally be considered a good form.

ALGEBRA, BOOK ONE

46. The area of a rectangle is $4\,ax + 4\,bx$. What are the sides of the rectangle if they are factors of the area? $4x, a+b$

47. What is the area of the larger circle shown here? of the smaller circle? Show that the area of the circular ring may be expressed by $A = \pi R^2 - \pi r^2$. Show that the formula $A = \pi(R + r)(R - r)$ will give the area of the ring. $\pi R^2; \pi r^2$

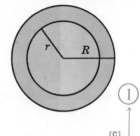

[C]

48. Show that $T = 2(lw + lh + wh)$ is a formula for finding the total area of the rectangular solid in Fig. 1.

49. $S = \frac{1}{2}\,na + \frac{1}{2}\,nl$. Change this formula by factoring its right member. $S = \frac{1}{2}n\,(a+l)$

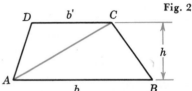

Fig. 1

Fig. 2

50. The figure $ABCD$ in Fig. 2 is a trapezoid having a height h and bases b and b'.

a. Write a formula for the area of $\triangle\ ABC$ $A = \frac{1}{2}\,bh$

b. Write a formula for the area of $\triangle\ ADC$ $A = \frac{1}{2}\,b'h$

c. Write a formula for the area of $ABCD$ $A = \frac{1}{2}bh + \frac{1}{2}b'h$

d. Rewrite the formula for the area of $ABCD$ again, having the right member of the formula factored $A = \frac{1}{2}h\,(b+b')$

Squaring Monomials [A]

In finding certain kinds of products (called *special products*), it is necessary to square monomials quickly. Squaring a monomial is using it twice as a factor, or multiplying it by itself.

Example 1. Square $4\,x^3y$.

Solution. $(4\,x^3y)^2 = 4\,x^3y \cdot 4\,x^3y = 16\,x^6y^2$

Can you give the answer by thinking "4 squared is 16, x^3 squared is x^6, and y squared is y^2"?

324 Facility in working with squares and square roots is desirable. It is suggested that students learn the squares of the integers from 1 to 25.

Example 2. $(-6 a^3 b^4)^2 = ?$

Solution. The even powers of negative numbers are positive; 6 squared is 36, a^3 squared is a^6, and b^4 squared is b^8.

Then $$(-6 a^3 b^4)^2 = 36 a^6 b^8$$

ORAL EXERCISES

Square as indicated:

[A]

1. 3^2 9
2. $(-4)^2$ 16
3. -4^2 -16
4. $(-1)^2$ 1
5. $(8 m)^2$ $64m^2$

6. $(7 a^2)^2$ $49a^4$
7. $(-2 r^2 s)^2$ $4r^4 s^2$
8. $(5 s^2 t^4)^2$ $25 s^4 t^8$
9. $(\frac{1}{2} gt)^2$ $\frac{1}{4} g^2 t^2$
10. $(-ab^2 c^3)^2$ $a^2 b^4 c^6$

11. $(.4 \bar{x}^2)^2$ $0.16 x^4$
12. $(\frac{1}{3} abc^3)^2$ $\frac{1}{9} a^2 b^2 c^6$
13. $(1.2 c^7)^2$ $1.44 c^{14}$
14. $(20 x^5)^2$ $400 x^{10}$
15. $(.01 a^{10})^2$ $0.0001 a^{20}$

Finding the Square Roots of Monomials [A]

When a number has two equal factors, either of the factors is called the square root of that number. Since $16 = 4 \times 4$, the number 4 is a square root of 16. Since 5 squared is 25, the 5 is a square root of 25. Since the square of $a^3 b^2$ is $a^6 b^4$, then $a^3 b^2$ is a square root of $a^6 b^4$.

We know that $(-4)^2 = (-4)(-4) = 16$. Then -4 is also a square root of 16. Likewise -5 is a square root of 25 and $-a^3 b^2$ is a square root of $a^6 b^4$. These three cases illustrate the fact that any number (except zero) has two square roots which are equal numerically but opposite in sign. In this chapter we shall consider only the positive, or plus, square roots.

The sign $\sqrt{}$, which indicates that the positive square root is to be taken, is called the radical sign. It is usually combined with the bar, or vinculum, which is written above the number. Thus $\sqrt{9}$ means "the positive square root of 9," which is $+3$. Likewise, $\sqrt{x^6} = x^3$, $\sqrt{4 y^6} = 2 y^3$; and $\sqrt{25 m^{10}} = 5 m^5$.* REMEMBER: If no sign is written before the radical, the plus sign is understood.

Example 1. $\sqrt{25 p^8} = 5 p^4$.   CHECK. $(5 p^4)^2 = 25 p^8$

Example 2. $\sqrt{x^4 y^{12}} = x^2 y^6$.   CHECK. $(x^2 y^6)^2 = x^4 y^{12}$

Example 3. $\sqrt{\dfrac{25 k^6}{36}} = \dfrac{5 k^3}{6}.$ CHECK. $\left(\dfrac{5 k^3}{6}\right)^2 = \dfrac{25 k^6}{36}$

*In this text it will be assumed that any number shown below a radical sign is positive. For example, in $\sqrt{x}$, we assume that x is a positive number.

↓

We make this assumption because only real numbers are considered in this text.

[A]

1. Show that x^7 is a square root of x^{14}. Show that $-x^7$ is a square root of x^{14}.

2. Find the positive square roots of

a. 16 *4*	**d.** 36 *6*	**g.** 49 *7*	**j.** 324 *18*
b. 1 *1*	**e.** 81 *9*	**h.** 9 *3*	**k.** 289 *17*
c. 64 *8*	**f.** 25 *5*	**i.** 225 *15*	**l.** 400 *20*

3. Which of the following are perfect squares (numbers whose exact square roots can be taken)? What are the positive square roots of these perfect squares? Check your answers.

$8p^3$ **a.** 64 p^6 **c.** 125 x^4 **e.** 4 x^5 $\frac{1}{2}x^5$ **g.** $\frac{1}{4} x^{10}$

b. ab^2 **d.** $-9 x^{10}$ $4a$ **f.** 16 a^2 $9c^3$ **h.** 81 c^6

Find the following indicated roots:

7 **4.** $\sqrt{49}$ $15 a^4$ **9.** $\sqrt{225\ a^8}$ 0.2 **14.** $\sqrt{.04}$

hk^2 **5.** $\sqrt{h^2k^4}$ ac^2 **10.** $\sqrt{a^2c^4}$ 1.5 **15.** $\sqrt{2.25}$

$7p^3$ **6.** $\sqrt{49\ p^6}$ $3mx^3$ **11.** $\sqrt{9\ m^2x^6}$ $10a^5$ **16.** $\sqrt{100\ a^{10}}$

$11p$ **7.** $\sqrt{121\ p^2}$ $a+b$ **12.** $\sqrt{(a+b)^2}$ $5ab^2c^3$ **17.** $\sqrt{25\ a^2b^4c^6}$

$12a^2$ **8.** $\sqrt{144\ a^4}$ $x-y$ **13.** $\sqrt{(x-y)^2}$ $\frac{7a}{8b}$ **18.** $\sqrt{\dfrac{49\ a^2}{64\ b^2}}$

19. Think of some number and square it. Take the square root of the result. What is your answer? *your original number*

Find the value of

20. $\sqrt{a} + \sqrt{b}$ if $a = 16$ and $b = 25$. *9*

21. $\sqrt{c} - \sqrt{d}$ if $c = 64$ and $d = 81$. *-1*

22. $\sqrt{2x} + \sqrt{5y}$ if $x = 50$ and $y = 45$. *25*

23. $\sqrt{c^2 - a^2}$ if $c = 17$ and $a = 15$. *8*

24. $\sqrt{c^2} - \sqrt{a^2}$ if $c = 17$ and $a = 15$. *2*

25. $\sqrt{(c+b)(c-b)}$ if $c = 5$ and $b = 4$. *3*

26. $\sqrt{b^2 - 4\ ac}$, if $a = 1$, $b = -5$, and $c = 6$. *1*

How to Find the Product of Two Binomials Mentally[A]

In Chapter 9 you learned that one polynomial is multiplied by another by multiplying *each* term of the multiplicand by *each* term

326

SPECIAL PRODUCTS AND FACTORING

of the multiplier and then combining the like terms of the products. Let us see how we can shorten the process of multiplying when both multiplicand and multiplier are certain binomials. Suppose we are to multiply $3x - 4$ by $2x + 5$.

The Long Method	The Short Method

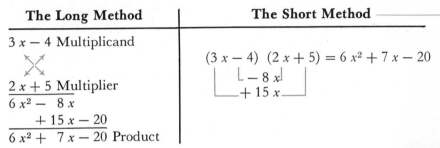

$3x - 4$ Multiplicand

$2x + 5$ Multiplier

$6x^2 - 8x$

$ 15x - 20$

$6x^2 + 7x - 20$ Product

$$(3x - 4)(2x + 5) = 6x^2 + 7x - 20$$
$$-8x$$
$$+15x$$

[A]

ORAL EXERCISES

Refer to the examples above in answering the following questions:

1. How many times is $6x^2$ written in the long method? in the short method? How many times is -20 written in each method? *2; 1; long, 2; short, 1.*

2. What is the first term of $3x - 4$? of $2x + 5$? of $6x^2 + 7x - 20$? How is the first term of the product obtained? *3x; 2x; 6x² multiply 1st terms of factors.*

3. What is the last term of $3x - 4$? of $2x + 5$? of $6x^2 + 7x - 20$? How is the last term of the product found? *-4; 5; -20; multiply last terms of factors.*

4. Why do you think $-8x$ and $+15x$ are called cross products? *From their position in the long method*

5. Study the two methods and tell how the middle term $+7x$ is found in each method. *add the two cross products.*

The three steps in the short, or inspection, method just studied are given below.

1. The first term of the product
is the product of the first terms of the binomials.

2. The middle term of the product
is the sum of the cross products.

3. The last term of the product
is the product of the last terms of the binomials.

② Some teachers, hunting for a device to help the weak student, call this the FOIL system of multiplying, where the letters of FOIL stand for the order of the terms multiplied—first, outer, inner, last. We do not necessarily advise this, but you may wish to mention it provided understanding has first been developed.

327

ALGEBRA, BOOK ONE

Example 1. Find by inspection the product $(2x-3)(4x+7)$.

Solution. $(2x-3)(4x+7)$. The first terms of the binomials are $2x$ and $4x$. Their product is $8x^2$, which is the first term of the answer. The last terms of the binomials are -3 and $+7$. Their product is -21, which is the last term of the answer. Then $(2x-3)(4x+7) = 8x^2 \cdots -21$. We shall now find the middle term. After you have learned the short method, you will find the middle term before the third. One cross product is $-12x$ and the other is $+14x$. Their sum is $+2x$, which is the middle term of the answer. Now we can write the solution:
$$(2x-3)(4x+7) = 8x^2 + 2x - 21.$$

Example 2. By inspection find the product $(3a+1)(a-2)$.

Solution. 1. The first term of the answer $= (3a)(a) = 3a^2$.
 2. $(3a)(-2) = -6a$ and $(+1)(a) = a$. Adding, $-6a + a = -5a$.
 3. The last term of the answer $= (+1)(-2) = -2$.
The written work is $(3a+1)(a-2) = 3a^2 - 5a - 2$.

[A]

ORAL EXERCISES

What are the missing terms in the following statements?

1. $(x+1)(x+2) = x^2 + 3x + (\ ?\ )$ *2*
2. $(a-3)(2a+1) = (\ ?\ ) - 5a - 3$ *2a²*
3. $(m+3)(4m+1) = 4m^2 + (\ ?\ ) + 3$ *13m*
4. $(2x+4)(x-1) = 2x^2 + (\ ?\ ) - 4$ *2x*
5. $(3k-1)(2k+3) = (\ ?\ ) + 7k - (\ ?\ )$ *6k²,3*
6. $(7c-1)(c+1) = 7c^2\ \ ?\ \ -1$ *+6c*

7. What is the first term in the answer of each of the first twenty exercises in the following set?

8. What is the middle term in the answer of each of these exercises?

9. What is the last term in the answer of each of these exercises?

[A]

EXERCISES

Find the following products mentally and check each solution by using the long method of multiplying:

1. $(a+1)(a+2)$ *a²+3a+2*   4. $(m-1)(m-1)$ *m²-2m+1*
2. $(c+2)(c+3)$ *c²+5c+6*   5. $(c+3)(c-4)$ *c²-c-12*
3. $(c+3)(c+4)$ *c²+7c+12*   6. $(a-2)(a-2)$ *a²-4a+4*

328

You might treat long sets in this chapter as follows, if you wish. Do the even-numbered exercises as class work orally, and assign the odd ones for written work. Watch that no one reverts to the long method of multiplying. Have students write the full problem, thus: $(2x - 1)(x + 1) = 2x^2 + x - 1$. Then the reverse process of factoring will be automatic.

7. $(a-2)(a+2)$ a^2-4

8. $(x+5)(x+8)$ $x^2+13x+40$

9. $(1+x)(1+2x)$ $1+3x+2x^2$

10. $(k+3)(k+7)$ $k^2+10k+21$

11. $(2-x)(7+x)$ $14-5x-x^2$

12. $(m-7)(m-7)$ $m^2-14m+49$

13. $(x+2)(x-5)$ $x^2-3x-10$

14. $(y-6)(-y+3)$ $-y^2+9y-18$

15. $(a-20)(a-1)$ $a^2-21a+20$

16. $(x+4)(x-15)$ $x^2-11x-60$

17. $(y+10)(y-8)$ $y^2+2y-80$

18. $(7c-1)(2c+3)$ $14c^2+19c-3$

19. $(7c-1)(7c+5)$ $49c^2+28c-5$

20. $(3p-1)(2p+3)$ $6p^2+7p-3$

Find the following products mentally:

21. $(4c+1)(5c-4)$ $20c^2-11c-4$

22. $(5+a)(6-a)$ $30+a-a^2$

23. $(x^2-3)(x^2-4)$ x^4-7x^2+12

24. $(a+b)^2=(a+b)(a+b)$
$=?$ $a^2+2ab+b^2$

25. $(x+2y)^2$ $x^2+4xy+4y^2$

26. $(x-y)^2$ $x^2-2xy+y^2$

27. $(2-3y)(3-4y)$ $6-17y+12y^2$

28. $(x^2-3y)(x^2+4y)$ $x^4+x^2y-12y^2$

29. $(a^2-4)(3a^2-1)$ $3a^4-13a^2+4$

30. $(10a-1)(9a-2)$ $90a^2-29a+2$

31. $(a^2-1)(a^2-4)$ a^4-5a^2+4

32. $(x^2-1)(x^2-9)$ x^4-10x^2+9

33. $(11x+1)(x-2)$ $11x^2-21x-2$

34. $(xy+3)^2$ $x^2y^2+6xy+9$

35. $(m+8n)(m-8n)$ m^2-64n^2

36. $(2y-5)(2y+5)$ $4y^2-25$

37. $(xy-12)(xy+1)$ $x^2y^2-11xy-12$

38. $(x-1)(-x-1)$ $-x^2+1$

39. $(3a-4b)(3a+4b)$ $9a^2-16b^2$

40. $(x^3+1)(x^3-2)$ x^6-x^3-2

41. $(x^2+y^2)(x^2+2y^2)$ $x^4+3x^2y^2+2y^4$

42. $(c^2-3)(3c^2-7)$ $3c^4-16c^2+21$

43. $(x+0.3)(x+0.4)$ $x^2+0.7x+0.12$

44. $(a-\frac{1}{2})(a-\frac{1}{3})$ $a^2-\frac{5}{6}a+\frac{1}{6}$

45. $(b-\frac{1}{4})(b+\frac{1}{3})$ $b^2+\frac{1}{12}b-\frac{1}{12}$

[B]

Multiply:

46. $(4n-7p)(6n+8p)$

47. $(x^2y-3)(x^2y-4)$

48. $(7-3y)(4-y)$

49. $(\frac{1}{2}x-p)(\frac{1}{3}x+p)$

50. $(9a-\frac{1}{2}b)(9a+\frac{1}{2}b)$

51. $(6c+ab)(\frac{1}{5}c+\frac{1}{2}ab)$

52. $(\frac{3}{4}x+8y)(\frac{1}{3}x-8y)$

53. $(\frac{1}{8}x+\frac{2}{5})(5x-8)$

54. $(\frac{1}{2}x-\frac{1}{3}y)(3x-4y)$

55. $(x+0.1)(x+0.1)$ $x^2+0.2x+0.01$

56. $(2c+0.3)(2c-0.3)$ $4c^2-0.09$

57. $(x+\frac{1}{2})(x+\frac{1}{4})$ $x^2+\frac{3}{4}x+\frac{1}{8}$

58. $(x-\frac{1}{2}y)(x-\frac{1}{2}y)$ $x^2-xy+\frac{1}{4}y^2$

59. $(x-4c)(\frac{1}{4}x-c)$ $\frac{1}{4}x^2-2cx+4c^2$

60. $(a^3-\frac{1}{5})(a^3+\frac{1}{5})$ $a^6-\frac{1}{25}$

61. $(x+\frac{2}{3}y)(x-\frac{1}{3}y)$ $x^2+\frac{1}{3}xy-\frac{2}{9}y^2$

62. $(m-0.4n)(m-0.1n)$ $m^2-0.5mn+0.04n^2$

63. $(c^2-0.3b)(c^2-0.8b)$ $c^4-1.1bc^2+0.24b^2$

46. $24n^2-10np-56p^2$
47. $x^4y^2-7x^2y+12$
48. $28-19y+3y^2$
49. $\frac{1}{6}x^2+\frac{1}{6}px-p^2$

50. $81a^2-\frac{1}{4}b^2$
51. $\frac{6}{5}c^2+\frac{16}{5}abc+\frac{1}{2}a^2b^2$
52. $\frac{1}{4}x^2-\frac{10}{3}xy-64y^2$

53. $\frac{5}{8}x^2+x-3\frac{1}{5}$
54. $\frac{3}{2}x^2-3xy+\frac{4}{3}y^2$

329

64. Find the area of a rectangle whose base is $3c - 4$ and altitude $c - 6$. $3c^2 - 22c + 24$

65. Find the area of a ~~triangle if its base~~ is $2c + 6$ and its altitude is $c - 1$. $c^2 + 2c - 3$

How to Factor a Trinomial of Form $ax^2 + bx + c$ [A]

When two binomials are multiplied together, their product is a binomial, a trinomial, or a four-term polynomial. For example,

$(x + 2)(x - 2) = x^2 - 4$, a binomial
$(x + 2)(x - 3) = x^2 - x - 6$, a trinomial
$(x + a)(x + b) = x^2 + ax + bx + ab$, a polynomial of 4 terms

When the product of two binomials is a trinomial, it is of the form $ax^2 + bx + c$. When such a trinomial is the product of two binomials, these binomials can be found by reversing the method used in finding their product. You will now learn how to factor such a trinomial. No general rule can be given for factoring trinomials of this kind, so you should study the solutions of the examples very carefully.

Example 1. Factor $x^2 + 6x + 8$.

Solution. To factor this trinomial we must find two binomials whose product is $x^2 + 6x + 8$. We know at once that the first terms of the two binomials are x and x. So we can write

$$x^2 + 6x + 8 = (x \quad)(x \quad),$$

leaving space for the signs and last terms in the parentheses.

Since there are no minus signs in the trinomial, there are no minus signs in the factors. Now we can write this much of the solution:

$$x^2 + 6x + 8 = (x + \quad)(x + \quad)$$

The last terms of the binomials are either 8 and 1, or 4 and 2. Why? (We are not considering fractions.) Let us try 8 and 1 as the last terms. Then does $x^2 + 6x + 8 = (x + 1)(x + 8)$? We know that the answer is "no" because $(x + 1)(x + 8) = x^2 + 9x + 8$. Now let us try 2 and 4 for the last terms. Does $x^2 + 6x + 8 = (x + 2)(x + 4)$? The answer is "yes." The solution is set down as

$$x^2 + 6x + 8 = (x + 2)(x + 4)$$

[A]

Factor each of the following trinomials by the method shown in Example 1 on the opposite page.

1. $a^2 + 6a + 8$ $(a+2)(a+4)$

2. $c^2 + 5c + 4$ $(c+4)(c+1)$

3. $m^2 + 3m + 2$ $(m+1)(m+2)$

4. $x^2 + 3x + 2$ $(x+1)(x+2)$

5. $a^2 + 2a + 1$ $(a+1)(a+1)$

6. $y^2 + 4y + 3$ $(y+1)(y+3)$

7. $y^2 + 9y + 8$ $(y+1)(y+8)$

8. $y^2 + 7y + 10$ $(y+5)(y+2)$

9. $x^2 + 11x + 24$ $(x+3)(x+8)$

10. $b^2 + 9b + 14$ $(b+7)(b+2)$

11. $x^2 + 7x + 6$ $(x+6)(x+1)$

12. $h^2 + 7h + 12$ $(h+4)(h+3)$

13. $k^2 + 8k + 15$ $(k+5)(k+3)$

14. $m^2 + 8m + 12$ $(m+6)(m+2)$

Example 2. Factor $x^2 - 2x - 15$.

Solution. The first terms of the two binomial factors are x and x. Then we have

$$x^2 - 2x - 15 = (x \quad)(x \quad)$$

The -15 tells us that one of the last terms of the factors is plus and one is minus. Why? Then we have

$$x^2 - 2x - 15 = (x + \quad)(x - \quad)$$

The last terms of the factors may be $+15$ and -1, -15 and $+1$, -5 and $+3$, or $+5$ and -3. Let us try $+5$ and -3.

Does $\qquad x^2 - 2x - 15 = (x + 5)(x - 3)$?

No, because $\quad (x + 5)(x - 3) = x^2 + 2x - 15$

The sign of the middle term is wrong. In such a case we try changing the middle signs of the factors. Let us do this. Does

$$x^2 - 2x - 15 = (x - 5)(x + 3)?$$

Yes.

Note. It so happened in Example 2 that we made a good guess in choosing the numbers 5 and 3. If these had not been the correct numbers, we should have had to try $+15$ and -1, or -15 and $+1$. This method of factoring is called the *"guess" method* or the *"try" method*. Which name do you prefer?

[A]

Factor:

1. $c^2 - c - 2$ $(c-2)(c+1)$

2. $m^2 + m - 30$ $(m+6)(m-5)$

3. $m^2 - m - 30$ $(m-6)(m+5)$

4. $c^2 - c - 20$ $(c-5)(c+4)$

5. $c^2 + c - 20$ $(c+5)(c-4)$

6. $a^2 + a - 12$ $(a+4)(a-3)$

7. $a^2 + a - 42$ $(a+7)(a-6)$

8. $x^2 - 2x - 3$ $(x-3)(x+1)$

Students will soon learn the most reasonable combinations to try first. For example, in Ex. 7, possible factors of 42 are 1×42, 2×21, 3×14, 6×7. The sensible one to try first is 6×7 since the difference is 1 and the coefficient of a is 1. You will observe many hints of this sort applying to different situations as you proceed. This speeds up the work.

9. $x^2 + 2x - 3$ $(x-1)(x+3)$ **12.** $x^2 - 5x - 14$ $(x-7)(x+2)$

10. $m^2 - 2m - 63$ $(m-9)(m+7)$ **13.** $y^2 - 6y - 40$ $(y-10)(y+4)$

11. $x^2 - 7x - 18$ $(x-9)(x+2)$ **14.** $p^2 + 3p - 4$ $(p+4)(p-1)$

Example 3. Factor $x^2 - 9x + 18$.

Solution. The first terms of the two factors are x and x. Then

$$x^2 - 9x + 18 = (x \quad)(x \quad)$$

The $+18$ tells us that the signs of the last terms of the factors are alike. Why? Since the sign before $9x$ is minus, the signs of the last terms of the factors are minus. Then

$$x^2 - 9x + 18 = (x- \quad)(x- \quad)$$

For the last terms of the factors we may try -3 and -6, or -2 and -9, or -1 and -18. Let us try -2 and -9.

Does $x^2 - 9x + 18 = (x-9)(x-2)$?

The answer is "no." Now let us try -3 and -6. Does

$$x^2 - 9x + 18 = (x-3)(x-6)?$$

The answer is "yes." Then

$$x^2 - 9x + 18 = (x-3)(x-6)$$

[A]

EXERCISES

Factor:

1. $x^2 - 5x + 4$ $(x-4)(x-1)$ **5.** $x^2 - 11x + 18$ $(x-2)(x-9)$

2. $x^2 - 8x + 15$ $(x-5)(x-3)$ **6.** $y^2 - 6y + 8$ $(y-4)(y-2)$

3. $x^2 - 4x + 3$ $(x-3)(x-1)$ **7.** $a^2 - 9a + 20$ $(a-5)(a-4)$

4. $c^2 - 7c + 12$ $(c-4)(c-3)$ **8.** $a^2 - 10a + 24$ $(a-4)(a-6)$

Example 4. Factor $8x^2 - 22x + 15$.

Solution. In factoring a trinomial such as $x^2 - 2x - 24$ we do not need to guess what the first terms are. We know immediately that they are x and x. But in this example we are forced to guess both the first terms and last terms of the factors. The first terms of the factors are either x and $8x$ or $2x$ and $4x$. The plus sign before the 15 tells us that the signs of the last terms of the factors are alike and the minus sign before the $22x$ tells us that they are minus. The last terms of the factors are -1 and -15, or -3 and -5. The eight possible solutions are:

1. $(x \cdot 1)(8x - 15)$ 5. $(2x - 1)(4x - 15)$
2. $(x - 15)(8x - 1)$ 6. $(2x - 15)(4x - 1)$
3. $(x - 3)(8x - 5)$ 7. $(2x - 3)(4x - 5)$
4. $(x - 5)(8x - 3)$ 8. $(2x - 5)(4x - 3)$

332 Show the student that if the original polynomial has no common factor, none of the binomials do. This fact avoids wasting time trying such combinations as $2x^2 - 9x + 4 \overset{?}{=} (2x - 2)(x - 2)$. Also urge the student to consider mentally the original signs as an aid to selecting correct factors quickly. Refer students to the inverse process of multiplication which they have just studied.

Any one of these eight combinations will give $8x^2$ as the first term of the product and $+15$ as the last term of the product. Only one of the combinations will give $-22x$ as the middle term of the product. By trial we find that combination 7 is the correct one, for the cross products are $-10x$ and $-12x$ and their sum is $-22x$.

Then $\qquad 8x^2 - 22x + 15 = (2x-3)(4x-5)$.

When factoring trinomials of this kind, it is sometimes necessary to make several guesses. If you do not guess right the first time, keep on trying other combinations until you find the correct one. After you factor many trinomials, you will be able to factor with fewer trials. Keep in mind that the sign of the third term of the trinomial tells whether the signs of the last terms of the factors are like or unlike. If a trinomial cannot be factored, it is prime.

[A]

EXERCISES

Factor when possible:

1. $3x^2 - 14x - 5 = (3x + ?)(x\ ?\ ?)$ $(3x+1)(x-5)$
2. $6x^2 - 13x - 5 = (?-5)(?+1)$ $(2x-5)(3x+1)$
3. $6x^2 + x - 5 = (6x - ?)(x\ ?\ ?)$ $(6x-5)(x+1)$
4. $5x^2 - 17x + 14 = (5x - 7)(\ ?\ )$ $(5x-7)(x-2)$
5. $9x^2 + 3x - 2 = (3x + ?)(3x - ?)$ $(3x+2)(3x-1)$
6. $5y^2 + 17y + 14$ $(5y+7)(y+2)$
7. $x^2 + 3x - 28$ $(x+7)(x-4)$
8. $x^2 + 4x - 12$ $(x+6)(x-2)$
9. $15x^2 + 22x + 8$ $(3x+2)(5x+4)$
10. $x^2 - 4x + 4$ $(x-2)^2$
11. $9x^2 - 6x + 1$ $(3x-1)^2$
12. $2m^2 - m - 3$ $(2m-3)(m+1)$
13. $3c^2 - 2c - 5$ $(3c-5)(c+1)$
14. $2m^2 + 3$ Prime
15. $3c^2 + 8c + 5$ $(3c+5)(c+1)$
16. $2p^2 - 9p + 4$ $(2p-1)(p-4)$
17. $2p^2 + 7p - 14$ Prime
18. $x^2 - 6x + 9$ $(x-3)^2$
19. $y^2 - 10y + 25$ $(y-5)^2$
20. $3x^2 - 13x - 20$ Prime
21. $2y^2 + 5y + 1$ Prime
22. $4r^2 - 4r + 1$ $(2r-1)^2$
23. $x^2 + x + 1$ Prime
24. $b^2 + 4b - 60$ $(b+10)(b-6)$
25. $7x^2 + 9x + 2$ $(7x+2)(x+1)$
26. $2r^2 + r - 15$ $(2r-5)(r+3)$
27. $8c^2 - 26c - 7$ $(4c+1)(2c-7)$
28. $x^2 + 8xy + 16y^2 = (?+4y)(?+4y)$ $(x+4y)(x+4y)$
29. $x^2 - xy - 12y^2 = (x+3y)(\ ?\ )$ $(x+3y)(x-4y)$
30. $3a^2 - 2ab - 5b^2 = (?-5b)(?+b)$ $(3a-5b)(a+b)$

43. $(2p-3q)(2p+q)$ 44. $(7c-3d)(3c-7d)$ 45. $(4R-3S)(3R+4S)$
46. $(a-8b)(a-b)$

ALGEBRA, BOOK ONE

$(x+2y)$ $(x+y)$ **31.** $x^2 + 3xy + 2y^2$

$(c-5d)$ $(c-d)$ **32.** $c^2 - 6cd + 5d^2$

$(x-6y)^2$ **33.** $x^2 - 12xy + 36y^2$

$(2m-3n)$ $(m+4n)$ **34.** $2m^2 + 5mn - 12n^2$

$(h-3k)$ $(h-6k)$ **35.** $h^2 - 9hk + 18k^2$

$(5m+n)$ $(3m-5n)$ **36.** $15m^2 - 22mn - 5n^2$

$(2x-y)$ $(x-y)$ **37.** $2x^2 - 3xy + y^2$

$(2y+7)$ $(y-3)$ **38.** $2y^2 + y - 21$

39. $(3a-4b)$ $(a+5b)$
40. Prime
41. $(h-5k)$ $(h+4k)$
42. $(3x-4y)$ $(2x-3y)$

39. $3a^2 + 11ab - 20b^2$

40. $3m^2 - 29mn + 20n^2$

41. $h^2 - hk - 20k^2$

42. $6x^2 - 17xy + 12y^2$

43. $4p^2 - 4pq - 3q^2$

44. $21c^2 - 58cd + 21d^2$

45. $12R^2 + 7RS - 12S^2$

46. $a^2 - 9ab + 8b^2$

[B]

47. $1 - 2x + x^2 = (1 - ?)(1 - ?)$ $(1-x)(1-x)$

48. $x^2 - 2x + 1 = (x - ?)(x - ?)$ $(x-1)(x-1)$

Compare the answers of exercises 47 and 48.

Factor when possible:

49. $13y + 10y^2 - 3 = 10y^2 + 13y - 3 = (\ ?\ )(\ ?\ )$

50. $-mn + m^2 - 42n^2 = m^2 - mn - 42n^2 = (\ ?\ )(\ ?\ )$

51. $5xy - 3y^2 + 2x^2 = 2x^2 + 5xy - 3y^2 = (\ ?\ )(\ ?\ )$

$(5y-1)$ $(2y+3)$ **52.** $7ab + 6a^2 - 3b^2$

$(m-7n)$ $(m+6n)$ **53.** $4b^2 + 4bc - 3c^2$

$(2x-y)$ $(x+3y)$ **54.** $8x^2 + 2xy - 3y^2$

$(2a+3b)$ $(3a-b)$ **55.** $3 - 10k - 8k^2$

$(2b+3c)$ $(2b-c)$ **56.** $2 - 11c + 12c^2$

$(4x+3y)$ $(2x-y)$ **57.** $3x^2 - 5xy - 12y^2$

$(3+2k)$ $(1-4k)$
$(2-3c)$ $(1-4c)$
$(3x+4y)$ $(x-3y)$

58. $-15 + r + 2r^2$ $(-5+2r)(3+r)$

59. $m^2 + 2mn - 8n^2$ $(m+4n)(m-2n)$

60. $x^2 + xy + y^2$ Prime

61. $10y^2 - 6 - 11y$

62. $2 + a^2 - 36a^4$

63. $2x^2 - 7x - 15$

61. $(5y+2)(2y-3)$

62. $(2+9a^2)(1-2a)(1+2a)$ [C]

63. $(x-5)(2x+3)$

Factor:

64. $x^4 + 2x^2 - 35 = (x^2\ ?\ ?)(x^2\ ?\ ?)$ $(x^2+7)(x^2-5)$

65. $a^2b^2 + ab - 6 = (ab\ ?\ ?)(ab\ ?\ ?)$ $(ab+3)(ab-2)$

66. $x^6 - x^3 - 20 = (x^3\ ?\ ?)(x^3\ ?\ ?)$ $(x^3-5)(x^3+4)$

(x^3-6) (x^3+3) **67.** $x^6 - 3x^3 - 18$

(y^2+5) (y^2-3) **68.** $y^4 + 2y^2 - 15$

(k^3-7) (k^3+2) **69.** $k^6 - 5k^3 - 14$

$(xy-6)$ $(xy+4)$ **70.** $x^2y^2 - 2xy - 24$

$(2x^2-3y^2)(x^2+4y^2)$ **71.** $2x^4 + 5x^2y^2 - 12y^4$

72. $A^2 + 4AB + 4B^2$

73. $1 - 7x^2 + 12x^4$

74. $10m^2 + 9m - 91$

75. $1 - 21x + 110x^2$

76. $8c^2 + 5c - 3$

334

72. $(A+2B)^2$
73. $(1-2x)(1+2x)(1-3x^2)$
74. $(2m+7)(5m-13)$

75. $(1-10x)(1-11x)$
76. $(8c-3)(c+1)$

77. $(a - b)^2 + 2(a - b) - 8 = (a - b + 4)(a - b - ?)$ *2*

78. $(x - y)^2 - 5(x - y) - 50 = (x - y ?)(?)$ *$-10)(x-y+5)$*

79. $x^4 - 10 x^2 + 25$ *$(x^2-5)^2$*   83. $x^4 + 5 x^2 - 36$ *$(x^2+9)(x-2)(x+2)$*

80. $a^6 - 13 a^3b + 32 b^2$ *Prime*   84. $x^4y^2 - x^2y - 30$ *$(x^2y-6)(x^2y+5)$*

81. $x^2y^2 - 2 xy - 48$ *$(xy-8)(xy+6)$*   85. $25 a^2 + 18 a - 12$ *Prime*

82. $r^2s^2 + rs - 12$ *$(rs+4)(rs-3)$*   86. $42 x^2 - 79 x + 35$ *$(7x-5)(6x-7)$*

87. The area of a rectangle is $2 x^2 + x - 190$. What may its base and altitude be? *$2x-19$ and $x+10$*

88. A dividend is $b^4 - 10 b^2 + 24$. Name a binomial divisor and the resulting quotient. *$b^2-4, b^2-6; b^2-6, b^2-4; b+2, b^3-2b^2-6b+12; b-2, b^3+2b^2-6b-12$*

Squaring Binomials [A]   See ① below.

You need to give particular attention to one special kind of multiplication—the squaring of a binomial. You know that $(x + y)^2$ means $(x + y)(x + y)$, and you know that the product is $x^2 + 2 xy + y^2$. Notice that in the product

1. The first term x^2 is the square of the first term x of the binomial.

2. The middle term $+ 2 xy$ of the product is found by adding $+ xy$ to $+ xy$. Since these two cross products are alike, it is only necessary to find one of them and double it.

$$\begin{array}{r} x + y \\ x + y \\ \hline x^2 + \quad xy \\ + \quad xy + y^2 \\ \hline x^2 + 2 xy + y^2 \end{array}$$

3. The last term $+ y^2$ of the product is the square of y, the last term of the binomial.

While you can always square a binomial by the usual multiplication procedure, you probably will find it simpler to use the outline just given. Real acquaintance with the steps of the outline will also help you in later work in equation solving. Make sure, therefore, that you understand the following examples.

Example 1. Square $(2 x + 3)$.

Solution. The first term of the product is the square of $2 x$, which is $4 x^2$. The middle term of the product is 2 times $2 x$ times 3, which is $12 x$. The last term of the product is the square of $+ 3$, which is 9.

Then $(2 x + 3)^2 = 4 x^2 + 12 x + 9$

① This is a very important special product. It must be thoroughly taught with meaning, and even then you will find students later carelessly saying $(a + b)^2 = a^2 + b^2$. Keep before them the fact that the middle term *must* be included.

ALGEBRA, BOOK ONE

Example 2. Find the value of $(3x - 5y)^2$.

Solution.
$$(3x)^2 = 9x^2$$
$$2 \text{ times } (3x) \text{ times } (-5y) = -30xy$$
$$(-5y)^2 = 25y^2$$
Then
$$(3x - 5y)^2 = 9x^2 - 30xy + 25y^2$$

Notice that if you square the *sum* of two numbers, as in Example 1 on page 335, the middle term of the product is *positive*, and that if you square the *difference* of two numbers, as in the example above, the middle term of the product is *negative*.

To Square a Binomial:

1. Square the first term.
2. Add twice the algebraic product of the two terms.
3. Add the square of the last term.

13. $x^2 - x + \frac{1}{4}$
14. $x^2 + \frac{2}{3}x + \frac{1}{9}$
15. $x^2 - x + .25$
16. $a^2 - \frac{2}{5}a + \frac{1}{25}$
17. $x^2 + .6x + .09$
18. $y^2 - 2.4y + 1.44$

[A]

EXERCISES

1. $(x + 2)^2$ $x^2 + 4x + 4$
2. $(a + 3)^2$ $a^2 + 6a + 9$
3. $(c - d)^2$ $c^2 - 2cd + d^2$
4. $(4 - c)^2$ $16 - 8c + c^2$
5. $(a + 7)^2$ $a^2 + 14a + 49$
6. $(m - 5)^2$ $m^2 - 10m + 25$

7. $(2x - 3)^2$ $4x^2 - 12x + 9$
8. $(x - 6)^2$ $x^2 - 12x + 36$
9. $(4x - 1)^2$ $16x^2 - 8x + 1$
10. $(x + 10)^2$ $x^2 + 20x + 100$
11. $(x - 9)^2$ $x^2 - 18x + 81$
12. $(4x - 7)^2$ $16x^2 - 56x + 49$

13. $(x - \frac{1}{2})^2$
14. $(x + \frac{1}{3})^2$
15. $(x - .5)^2$
16. $(a - \frac{1}{5})^2$
17. $(x + .3)^2$
18. $(y - 1.2)^2$

19. Find the missing parts of these statements:

The area of square I = __?__ a^2
The area of square IV = __?__ b^2
The area of rectangle II = __?__ ab
The area of rectangle III = __?__ ab
The sum of the areas of the four
figures = __?__. $a^2 + 2ab + b^2$
The length of each side of the
square = __?__. $a + b$
The area of the square = $(? + ?)^2$.
Therefore $(? + ?)^2 = ?^2 + ? ab + ?^2$
$$(a + b)^2 = a^2 + 2ab + b^2$$

$\rightarrow (a+b)^2$

	a	b
a	I	II
b	III	IV

336   It is possible to make a wood or plastic model for Ex. 19. This sometimes helps keep before the student that $(a + b)^2 \neq a^2 + b^2$.

SPECIAL PRODUCTS AND FACTORING

Finding the Square Roots of Trinomials [A]

In the last list of exercises you squared binomials and obtained square trinomials as results. You will now reverse this process. That is, you will find the square roots of perfect square trinomials and obtain binomial results.

Finding the square root of a number is done by factoring the number into two equal factors, either of which is the square root of the number.

A trinomial is a perfect square if, when it is arranged in either descending or ascending powers of one variable, the first and third terms are positive perfect squares and the middle term, disregarding its sign, is equal to twice the product of the square roots of the first and third terms.

Example 1. Find the positive square root of $x^2 + 8x + 16$.

Solution. The first term is the square of x and the third term is the square of 4. Also, $8x$ is 2 times x times 4. Therefore $x^2 + 8x + 16$ is a perfect square. Since the sign of the middle term is positive, the positive square root of $x^2 + 8x + 16$ is $x + 4$.

Then $\sqrt{x^2 + 8x + 16}$ equals $x + 4$.

Example 2. $\sqrt{x^2 - 10x + 25} = ?$

Solution. x^2 is the square of x, and 25 is the square of 5. Also $10x$ is twice x times 5. Therefore $x^2 - 10x + 25$ is a perfect square. The sign of $10x$ is negative. Then $\sqrt{x^2 - 10x + 25} = x - 5$.

[A]

EXERCISES

Tell which of the following trinomials are perfect squares, and give the positive square roots of the perfect squares.

1. $x^2 - 4x + 4$ *x - 2*
2. $m^2 - 6m + 9$ *m - 3*
3. $x^2 + x + 1$ *not perfect square*
4. $4x^2 - 4x + 1$ *2x - 1*
5. $9x^2 - 6x + 1$ *3x - 1*
6. $x^2 - 2x + 1$ *x - 1*
7. $y^2 + 12y + 36$ *y + 6*
8. $100y^2 + 10y + 1$ *not perfect square*
9. $x^2 - 14x + 49$ *x - 7*
10. $y^2 + 16y + 64$ *y + 8*
11. $a^2 + a + \frac{1}{4}$ *a + ½*
12. $2a^2 + 6ab + 9b^2$ *not perfect square*
13. $x^6 - 18x^3 + 81x^3$ *-9*
14. $c^2 + \frac{2}{3}c + \frac{1}{9}$ *c + ⅓*

337

ALGEBRA, BOOK ONE

Multiplying the Sum of Two Numbers by Their Difference [A]

A special product is obtained when the sum of two numbers is multiplied by their difference. Study the two multiplications below.

$$a + b$$
$$\underline{a - b}$$
$$a^2 + ab$$
$$\underline{\quad - ab - b^2}$$
$$a^2 \qquad - b^2$$

$$(a + b) \cdot (a - b) = a^2 - b^2$$
$$\lfloor + ab \rfloor$$
$$- ab$$

[A]

ORAL EXERCISES

The following exercises refer to the two multiplications above.

1. What words are omitted in the following?
a. $a + b$ is the __?__ of a and b. *sum*
b. $a - b$ is the __?__ of a and b. *difference*
c. $a^2 - b^2$ is the __?__ of $a + b$ and $a - b$. *product*
d. $a^2 - b^2$ is the difference of the __?__ of a and b. *squares*

2. Why is $+ ab$ called a cross product? *(See diagram of long method, page 327)*
3. What is the other cross product? *$- ab$*

4. Is the product of the two binomials a binomial or a trinomial? *Binomial*

Is the following rule clear to you?

> The product of the sum and difference of two numbers is equal to the square of the first number minus the square of the second number.

Example 1. $(x + 4)(x - 4) = ?$

Solution. The square of x is x^2 and the square of 4 is 16.

Then $\qquad\qquad (x + 4)(x - 4) = x^2 - 16$

Example 2. $(ab - 3)(ab + 3) = ?$

Solution. The square of ab is a^2b^2 and the square of 3 is 9.

Then $\qquad\qquad (ab - 3)(ab + 3) = a^2b^2 - 9$

338

[A]

EXERCISES

Multiply by inspection:

1. $(m+n)(m-n)$ m^2-n^2

2. $(c-d)(c+d)$ c^2-d^2

3. $(x+y)(x-y)$ x^2-y^2

4. $(c-3)(c+3)$ c^2-9

5. $(a+4)(a-4)$ a^2-16

6. $(x+7)(x-7)$ x^2-49

7. $(y-5)(y+5)$ y^2-25

8. $(k+h)(k-h)$ k^2-h^2

9. $(x^2-1)(x^2+1)$ x^4-1

10. $(3c-1)(3c+1)$ $9c^2-1$

11. $(5x-3)(5x+3)$ $25x^2-9$

12. $(2+k)(2-k)$ $4-k^2$

13. $(2x+n)(2x-n)$ $4x^2-n^2$

14. $(b-2a)(b+2a)$ b^2-4a^2

15. $(ab-1)(ab+1)$ a^2b^2-1

16. $(1-x)(1+x)$ $1-x^2$

17. $(3x^2-y)(3x^2+y)$ $9x^4-y^2$

18. $(10x+9)(10x-9)$ $100x^2-81$

19. $(4s+3t)(4s-3t)$ $16s^2-9t^2$

20. $(x+\frac{1}{2})(x-\frac{1}{2})$ $x^2-\frac{1}{4}$

21. $(0.5c-1)(0.5c+1)$ $0.25c^2-1$

22. $(\frac{3}{4}x-\frac{1}{2}y)(\frac{3}{4}x+\frac{1}{2}y)$ $\frac{9}{16}x^2-\frac{1}{4}y^2$

23. $(\frac{1}{7}x-\frac{1}{5}y)(\frac{1}{7}x+\frac{1}{5}y)$ $\frac{1}{49}x^2-\frac{1}{25}y^2$

24. $(0.3a-0.5b)(0.3a+0.5b)$ $0.09a^2-0.25b^2$

25. $(abc-\frac{1}{3})(abc+\frac{1}{3})$ $a^2b^2c^2-\frac{1}{9}$

26. $(0.1c+6)(0.1c-6)$ $0.01c^2-36$

Example 2. $(10+6)(10-6)=100-36=64.$

An interesting application to arithmetic.

[B]

Find the products:

27. $(8+3)(8-3)$ 55

28. $(11-4)(11+4)$ 105

29. $(1+10)(1-10)$ -99

30. $(50+1)(50-1)$ 2499

31. $(100-3)(100+3)$ 9991

32. $(70+2)(70-2)$ 4896

33. $19 \times 21 = (20-1)(20+1) = 400-1 = ?$ 399

34. $42 \times 38 = (40+2)(?) = ?$ $(40-2)=1596$

35. $37 \times 43 = (40-?)(40+?) = ?$ $3)(40+3)=1591$

36. 101×99 9999

37. 49×51 2499

38. 23×17 391

39. 25×15 375

40. 24×26 624

41. 52×48 2496

42. 18×22 396

43. 36×44 1584

44. 97×103 9991

45. 76×84 6384

46. 105×95 9975

47. 24×36 864

339

ALGEBRA, BOOK ONE

Factoring the Difference of Two Squares [A]

You have just learned how to multiply the sum of two numbers by their difference without using pencil and paper. You know that the product of the sum and difference of two numbers is equal to the difference of the squares of the numbers. Now we shall reverse the process by finding the two factors when their product, which is the difference of two squares, is given. Study the following examples until you understand the procedure.

Example 1.   Factor $x^2 - y^2$.

Solution. x^2 is the square of x and y^2 is the square of y. Then the square root of x^2 is x and the square root of y^2 is y. The sum of the square roots is $x + y$ and the difference of the square roots is $x - y$.

Then $$x^2 - y^2 = (x + y)(x - y)$$

Remember that the sum of the cross products of $(x + y)(x - y)$ is zero.

Example 2.   Factor $4\,c^4 - 25$.

Solution.   The square root of $4\,c^4$ is $2\,c^2$ and the square root of 25 is 5. One factor is $2\,c^2 + 5$ and the other is $2\,c^2 - 5$. Then $4\,c^4 - 25 = (2\,c^2 + 5)(2\,c^2 - 5)$.

Example 3.   Factor $1 - 81\,m^2$.

Solution. $\sqrt{1} = 1$ and $\sqrt{81\,m^2} = 9\,m$

Then $$1 - 81\,m^2 = (1 + 9\,m)(1 - 9\,m)$$

Example 4.   Factor $a^2 b^4 - .01$.

Solution. $a^2 b^4 - .01 = (ab^2 + .1)(ab^2 - .1)$

To Factor the Difference of Squares of Two Numbers:

1. Find the positive square root of each of the squares.
2. Write the sum of these square roots as one factor and the difference of the square roots (in the order given) as the other factor.

340

[A]

EXERCISES

Factor the following when possible:

1. $x^2 - m^2$ $(x-m)(x+m)$

2. $c^2 - b^2$ $(c-b)(c+b)$

3. $x^2 - 1$ $(x-1)(x+1)$

4. $c^2 - 4$ $(c-2)(c+2)$

5. $4 - c^2$ $(2-c)(2+c)$

6. $c^2 - d^2$ $(c-d)(c+d)$

7. $x^2 - 9$ $(x-3)(x+3)$

8. $y^2 - 16$ $(y-4)(y+4)$

9. $a^2 - 25$ $(a-5)(a+5)$

10. $m^2 - 36$ $(m-6)(m+6)$

11. $a^2 - 45$ Prime

12. $64 - x^2$ $(8-x)(8+x)$

13. $1 + c^2$ Prime

14. $4x^2 - 1$ $(2x-1)(2x+1)$

15. $9x^2 - 1$ $(3x-1)(3x+1)$

16. $1 - 9a^2$ $(1-3a)(1+3a)$

17. $c^2 - 9y^2$ $(c-3y)(c+3y)$

18. $x^2 - 25$ $(x-5)(x+5)$

19. $R^2 - r^2$ $(R-r)(R+r)$

20. $36h^2 - 25$ $(6h-5)(6h+5)$

21. $x^6 - y^6$ $(x^3-y^3)(x^3+y^3)$

22. $x^6 - 1$ $(x^3-1)(x^3+1)$

23. $9x^2 - 100$ $(3x-10)(3x+10)$

24. $49 - m^4$ $(7-m^2)(7+m^2)$

25. $64x^2 - 49y^2$ $(8x+7y)(8x-7y)$

26. $25r^2 - 1$ $(5r-1)(5r+1)$

27. $x^2 - \frac{1}{4}$ $\left(x-\frac{1}{2}\right)\left(x+\frac{1}{2}\right)$

28. $m^2 - \frac{1}{9}$ $\left(m-\frac{1}{3}\right)\left(m+\frac{1}{3}\right)$

29. $c^2 - \frac{1}{16}$ $\left(c-\frac{1}{4}\right)\left(c+\frac{1}{4}\right)$

30. $p^2 - \frac{1}{25}$ $\left(p-\frac{1}{5}\right)\left(p+\frac{1}{5}\right)$

31. $a^2b^2 - 4$ $(ab-2)(ab+2)$

32. $c^2d^2 - 9$ $(cd-3)(cd+3)$

33. $m^2n^2 - p^2$ $(mn-p)(mn+p)$

34. $c^2 - a^2b^2$ $(c-ab)(c+ab)$

35. $x^6 - y^2$ $(x^3-y)(x^3+y)$

36. $x^2 - y^4$ $(x-y^2)(x+y^2)$

37. $c^2d^2 - a^2b^2$ $(cd-ab)(cd+ab)$

38. $1 - a^2b^2c^2$ $(1-abc)(1+abc)$

39. $c^2d^2 + 16$ Prime

Types of Factoring

The following summary will help you to recognize the kinds of polynomials which you have learned to factor:

A Polynomial Can Be Factored

1. If it contains a monomial factor.
2. If it is a binomial that is the difference of two squares.
3. If it is a trinomial which is a perfect square
   or which can be factored by the "guess" method.

When factoring an expression, you should first determine whether it contains a monomial factor. If it does, be sure that you find the largest monomial factor. If there is no monomial factor, see if the expression is the difference of squares or a perfect square trinomial. If there is no monomial factor and the expression is a trinomial but not a perfect square, see if the "guess" method will factor it.

Now (or a bit later in the chapter) explain that expressions such as $x^2 - 7$ or $x - y$ can be factored if we expand our field of admissible factors. Show briefly that such factoring might involve radical signs or fractional exponents. Although the student at this time is not expected to do such factoring, he should not be under the impression that it does not exist.

[A]

EXERCISES

Some of the following polynomials have monomial factors, some are differences of squares, some are perfect square trinomials, some can be factored by the "guess" method, and some are prime, that is, they cannot be factored. Factor those which can be factored. *(ans. 13-33 at foot of pp. 342,343)*

$5(x+2)$ **1.** $5x + 10$ **12.** $2x^2 - 6x$ $2x(x-3)$ **23.** $c^2 - d^6$

$(x+1)$ $(x-1)$ **2.** $x^2 - 1$ **13.** $m^2 - 10m + 25$ **24.** $c^2 - 9c$

$(c+1)^2$ **3.** $c^2 + 2c + 1$ **14.** $1 - z^2$ **25.** $c^2 + 9c$

$3(x^2-6)$ **4.** $3x^2 - 18$ **15.** $a^2 - 11ac + 18c^2$ **26.** $c^2 - 9$

$(m-5)$ $(m+5)$ **5.** $m^2 - 25$ **16.** $r^2 - 7r - 60$ **27.** $6x^4 - 9x^2$

$(x+2)^2$ **6.** $x^2 + 4x + 4$ **17.** $b^2 - a^2$ **28.** $a^2b^2 - 2ab - 35$

Prime **7.** $x^2 + 4$ **18.** $\pi R + \pi r$ **29.** $100 - x^2$

$a(a-1)$ **8.** $a^2 - a$ **19.** $abx + a$ **30.** $9a^2 - 16b^2$

$(a-7)$ $(a+6)$ **9.** $a^2 - a - 42$ **20.** $12x^8 - 10x^6$ **31.** $a^2 + 4a + 4$

$(3a+1)$ $(2a-5)$ **10.** $6a^2 - 13a - 5$ **21.** $a^2 + 64$ **32.** $25x^2 - 36$

$(h-4)$ $(h-2)$ **11.** $h^2 - 6h + 8$ **22.** $c^2 - 29$ **33.** $x^3 - x^2 + x$

[A]

EXERCISES

Factor the polynomials which are not prime:

1. $p^2 - 6p + 9$
    $= (p - 3)(p - 3)$
    $= (?)^2$ $(p-3)^2$

2. $y^2 - 4y + 4$ $(y-2)^2$

3. $x^2 - 3x - 10$ $(x-5)(x+2)$

4. $c^2 - 6c - 9$ *Prime*

5. $6x^3y - 15x^2y - 3xy$
    $3xy(2x^2 - 5x - 1)$

6. $x^2 + 7x + 10$ $(x+2)(x+5)$

7. $p^2 - p - 56$ $(p-8)(p+7)$

8. $9 - 4x^2$ $(3-2x)(3+2x)$

9. $r^2 - 7r - 60$ $(r-12)(r+5)$

10. $-2a^3 + 4ab^2 - 6ac^2$
    $-2a(a^2 - 2b^2 + 3c^2)$

11. $a^2 - 64b^2$ $(a-8b)(a+8b)$

12. $m^2 - 14m + 49$ $(m-7)^2$

13. $-12 - x + x^2$ $(-4+x)(3+x)$

14. $2c^2 - 17c + 35$ $(c-5)(2c-7)$

15. $x^2 + 8x + 12$ $(x+6)(x+2)$

16. $12a^2 - 35ab$ $a(12a - 35b)$

17. $a^2 - 6ab^2 + 9b^4$ $(a-3b^2)^2$

18. $16x^2 + 8xy + y^2$ $(4x+y)^2$

19. $p^2 + p - 72$ $(p+9)(p-8)$

20. $1 + x^2$ *Prime*

21. $x^2 + 16xy - 16x^2$ $x(16y - 15x)$

22. $25x^2 - 1$ $(5x+1)(5x-1)$

23. $x^2 + 5xy - 36y^2$ $(x+9y)(x-4y)$

24. $c^2d^2 - 7cd - 35$ *Prime*

25. $2x^2 + 3x + 1$ $(x+1)(2x+1)$

26. $3x^2 - 14x + 8$ $(x-4)(3x-2)$

13. $(m-5)^2$ **16.** $(r-12)(r+5)$

14. $(1-z)(1+z)$ **17.** $(b-a)(b+a)$ **20.** $2x^6(6x^2-5)$

15. $(a-2c)(a-9c)$ **18.** $\pi(R+r)$ **21.** *Prime*

19. $a(bx+1)$ **22.** *Prime*

Some student will surely come up with apparently different answers. For example, he may factor $6 - 5x + x^2$ as $(3 - x)(2 - x)$ or $(x - 3)(x - 2)$. Explain that these answers are equivalent by multiplying one expression by $+1$ in the form of $(-1)(-1)$: $(-1)(3 - x)(-1)(2 - x) = (x - 3)(x - 2)$.

SPECIAL PRODUCTS AND FACTORING

27. $a^2b^2 - d^2$ *(ab +d)(ab -d)*

28. $6\,x^3y - 15\,x^2y - 24\,xy$ *3xy(2x²-5x-8)*

29. $y^2 - 20\,b + 100$ *Prime*

30. $a^2 - 4\,ab^2$ *a(a-4b²)*

31. $10\,x - 810$ *10(x-81)*

32. $4\,x^2 - 20\,x + 25$ *(2x-5)²*

33. $4\,x^5 - 3\,x^3$ *x³(4x²-3)*

34. $5\,x + 45$ *5(x+9)*

35. $a^2 - 1$ *(a+1)(a-1)*

36. $2\,a^2 + a - 10$ *(a-2)(2a+5)*

37. $x^2 - 5\,xy - 36\,y^2$ *(x-9y)(x+4y)*

38. $a^2b^2 - 16$ *(ab +4)(ab -4)*

39. $x^4 - 9\,x^2 + 8$ *(x²-8)(x-1)(x+1)*

40. $6\,y^2 - 8\,y - 14$ *2(3y-7)(y+1)*

41. $2\,c^2 + 5\,c + 2$ *(c+2)(2c+1)*

42. $12\,c^2 - 5\,c - 2$ *(4c+1)(3c-2)*

43. $k^{10} + 2\,k^5 + 1$ *(k⁵+1)²*

44. $2\,b^2 + 5\,b - 3$ *(2b-1)(b+3)*

45. $a^2b^2 - 6\,abc + 9\,c^2$ *(ab-3c)²*

46. $w^4x^4 - 81$ *(wx-3)(wx +3)(w²x²+9)*

Complete Factoring [A]

Often one or more factors of an algebraic expression can be factored. In factoring any expression, factoring should be continued until the factors are prime numbers (numbers that cannot be factored).

Example 1. Factor $5\,x^2 - 5\,x - 60$.

Solution. The *first* operation is to remove the largest monomial factor, if there is one. Then $5\,x^2 - 5\,x - 60 = 5(x^2 - x - 12)$. The factor $x^2 - x - 12$ is a trinomial. Using the "guess" method, $x^2 - x - 12 = (x - 4)(x + 3)$. The solution should be written:

$$5\,x^2 - 5\,x - 60 = 5(x^2 - x - 12)$$
$$= 5(x - 4)(x + 3)$$

Example 2. Factor $a^4 - 1$.

Solution. There is no monomial factor; $a^4 - 1$ is the difference of two squares.

Then $\qquad a^4 - 1 = (a^2 + 1)(a^2 - 1)$

$a^2 + 1$ cannot be factored. $a^2 - 1$ is the difference of two squares. Then $a^2 - 1 = (a + 1)(a - 1)$. The solution is written

$$a^4 - 1 = (a^2 + 1)(a^2 - 1)$$
$$= (a^2 + 1)(a + 1)(a - 1)$$

Directions for Complete Factoring:

1. Remove the largest monomial factor, if any.
2. Factor, if possible, any binomial or trinomial into prime factors.

From now on *factoring* means "factoring into prime factors."

exs. top p. 342

23. (c-d³)(c+d³)

24. c(c-9)

25. c(c+9)

26. (c-3)(c+3)

27. 3x²(2x²-3)

28. (ab -7)(ab +5)

29. (10-x)(10 +x)

30. (3a -4b)(3a+4b)

31. (a+2)² **343**

32. (5x-6)(5x+6)

33. x(x²-x + 1)

13. $c(3x+1)(x+2)$
14. $(a+5)(a-5)$
15. $a(a-25)$
16. $x(3x+y)(3x-y)$

17. $\pi(R-r)(R+r)$
18. $(w^2+1)(w+1)(w-1)$
19. $2\pi r(r+h)$
20. $(a^2+4)(a+2)(a-2)$ [A]

EXERCISES

Factor the following expressions. If any expression is prime, write "prime" after it on your paper.

$6(a+1)$ **1.** $6a+6$

$x(x-4)$ **2.** x^2-4x

$4(c-1)$ $(c+1)$ **3.** $4c^2-4$

$(x^2+a^2)(x-a)$ $(x+a)$ **4.** x^4-a^4

$x^2(x+3)$ $(x+4)$ **5.** $x^4+7x^3+12x^2$

$(2a-3)^2$ **6.** $4a^2-12a+9$

$4a(4a-b^2)$ **7.** $16a^2-4ab^2$

$5x(x+2y)$ $(x-2y)$ **8.** $5x^3-20xy^2$

$c(4c-9)$ **9.** $4c^2-9c$

$(m+4)^2$ **10.** $m^2+8m+16$

11. bx^2-9b $b(x-3)(x+3)$

12. x^2-16x $x(x-16)$

13. $3cx^2+7cx+2c$

14. a^2-25

15. a^2-25a

16. $9x^3-xy^2$

17. $\pi R^2-\pi r^2$

18. w^4-1

19. $2\pi r^2+2\pi rh$

20. a^4-16

see top of page

$a(a^3-16)$
21. a^4-16a

22. $3x^2-6$ $3(x^2-2)$

23. x^3-x $x(x+1)(x-1)$

24. x^3-x^2 $x^2(x-1)$

25. x^5-x^3 $x^3(x+1)(x-1)$

26. a^5-a^4 $a^4(a-1)$

27. a^4+1 Prime

28. a^4-16b^4 $(a+2b)(a-2b)(a^2+4b^2)$

29. ax^2-4ay^2 $a(x+2y)(x-2y)$

30. $5h^2+40h+60$ $5(h+2)(h+6)$

$(a^2-3)(a-1)$ $(a+1)$ **31.** a^4-4a^2+3

$3(t+2)$ $(t+8)$ **32.** $3t^2+30t+48$

$5(2x+1)$ $(x+3)$ **33.** $10x^2+35x+15$

$y^2(2a+3)$ $(3a-2)$ **34.** $6a^2y^2+5ay^2-6y^2$

$a(3a+5)$ $(a+1)$ **35.** $3a^3+8a^2+5a$

$2(2x-3)$ $(3x-1)$ **36.** $12x^2-22x+6$

37. $8a^2+16a+8$ $8(a+1)^2$

$8(x-3)$ $(x-7)$ **38.** $8x^2-80x+168$

$a(5c-1)$ $(2c+3)$ **39.** $10ac^2+13ac-3a$

$(m-5)$ $(m-7)$ **40.** $m^2-12m+35$

$x(ax-1)$ $(ax+1)$ **41.** x^3a^2-x

$(1-x)$ $(1+x)$ **42.** $1-x^2$

$(x+y)^2$ $(x-y)^2$ **43.** $x^4-2x^2y^2+y^4$

$6(c-7d)$ $(c-2d)$ **44.** $6c^2-54cd+84d^2$

$4(x+4)$ $(x-3)$ **45.** $4x^2+4x-48$

$\frac{1}{3}\pi h(R^2+r^2)$ **46.** $\frac{1}{3}\pi R^2h+\frac{1}{3}\pi r^2h$

$2\pi(R-r)$ **47.** $2\pi R-2\pi r$

see foot of pages 344, 345

48. $p+pqt$ $p(1+qt)$

49. $9x^3-81xy^2$

50. $4a^2-36a$

51. $6n^2-12np+6p^2$

52. x^4-9x^2+20

53. by^4-10by^2+9b

54. a^3-3a^2-4a

55. z^3-16z

56. $5d^2-10d+5$

57. $25-60a+36a^2$

58. $6k^2+15k+6$

59. abx^2-ab

60. $A^2B^2-5AB^3+6B^2$

61. $a^2b^2+a^2b-12a^2$

62. $x^2-22x+121$

63. $x^2+28xy+196y^2$

64. $9a^2b^2-16c^2$

49. $9x(x+3y)(x-3y)$
50. $4a(a-9)$
51. $6(n-p)^2$
52. $(x^2-5)(x-2)(x+2)$

53. $b(y-1)(y+1)(y-3)(y+3)$
54. $a(a-4)(a+1)$
55. $z(z+4)(z-4)$
56. $5(d-1)^2$

SPECIAL PRODUCTS AND FACTORING

Checking Your Understanding of Chapter 12

Before you leave Chapter 12, make sure that you can find mentally

	PAGE
1. The product of a monomial and a polynomial	321
2. The square of a binomial	335
3. The product of the sum and difference of two numbers	338
4. The product of any two binomials	326

Review if you should

Make sure that you can factor

1. A polynomial whose terms contain a common monomial factor	322
2. The difference of two squares	340
3. A trinomial of the form $ax^2 + bx + c$	330
4. A perfect square trinomial	337

Make sure that you know the meanings of, and can spell correctly, the following words and phrases:

	PAGE		PAGE
factoring	321	prime number	323
monomial	20	square	324
polynomial	20	square root	325
radical sign	325	trinomial	20

[A]

CHAPTER REVIEW

Multiply by inspection:

1. $\pi(a - b)$ $\pi a - \pi b$

2. $2\pi(m - n)$ $2\pi m - 2\pi n$

3. $3a(a^2 - 4a + 1)$ $3a^3 - 12a^2 + 3a$

4. $5c^2(c^2 - c + 3)$ $5c^4 - 5c^3 + 15c^2$

5. $ab(a^2 - ab + b^2)$ $a^3b - a^2b^2 + ab^3$

6. $-3(m^2 - n^2)$ $-3m^2 + 3n^2$

7. $2a^2(b^2 - 3b + 4)$ $2a^2b^2 - 6a^2b + 8a^2$

8. $(a - 1)(a + 1)$ $a^2 - 1$

9. $(a - 1)(a - 1)$ $a^2 - 2a + 1$

10. $(2x + 1)(x - 3)$ $2x^2 - 5x - 3$

11. $(3x - 4)(x + 2)$ $3x^2 + 2x - 8$

12. $(b - 4)^2$ $b^2 - 8b + 16$

13. $(x - 3y)(x - 3y)$ $x^2 - 6xy + 9y^2$

14. $(x - 3y)(x + 3y)$ $x^2 - 9y^2$

15. $(k - y)(k + 2y)$ $k^2 + ky - 2y^2$

16. $(2m - 1)(m + 5)$ $2m^2 + 9m - 5$

17. $(x^3 - 1)(x^3 + 2)$ $x^6 + x^3 - 2$

18. $(ab + 3)(ab - 2)$ $a^2b^2 + ab - 6$

19. $(3y + 5)(2y - 4)$ $6y^2 - 2y - 20$

20. $(pq - 5)(pq + 4)$ $p^2q^2 - pq - 20$

P. 344, Ex. 57. $(5 - 6a)^2$

58. $3(2k + 1)(k + 2)$

59. $ab(x + 1)(x - 1)$

60. $B^2(A^2 - 5AB + 6)$

61. $a^2(b + 4)(b - 3)$

62. $(x - 11)^2$

63. $(x + 14y)^2$

64. $(3ab - 4c)(3ab + 4c)$

345

Factor:

21. $6x - 6$ $6(x-1)$

22. $x^2 - 9$ $(x+3)(x-3)$

23. $a^2 - 36$ $(a+6)(a-6)$

24. $y^2 - 10y + 25$ $(y-5)^2$

25. $m^2 - 3m + 2$ $(m-1)(m-2)$

26. $2p^2 + p - 3$ $(2p+3)(p-1)$

27. $z^2 - z - 20$ $(z-5)(z+4)$

28. $25 - y^2$ $(5-y)(5+y)$

29. $bx^2 - dx^2$ $x^2(b-d)$

30. $10d^3 - 30cd$ $10d(d^2-3c)$

31. $a^2 + 4a + 4$ $(a+2)^2$

32. $a - a^3$ $a(1+a)(1-a)$

33. $1 - 6a + 9a^2$ $(1-3a)^2$

34. $9a^2y^2 - 16$ $(3ay-4)(3ay+4)$

35. $9a^2 - 9ay^2$ $9a(a-y^2)$

36. $x^3 - x^2 - 72x$ $x(x-9)(x+8)$

37. $6x^2 - 6a^2$ $6(x+a)(x-a)$

38. $x^4 - 6x^2 + 5$ $(x^2-5)(x-1)(x+1)$

39. $dm^2 - dn^2$ $d(m-n)(m+n)$

40. $bx - by$ $b(x-y)$

[A]

GENERAL REVIEW

What are the missing words and numbers in the following sentences?

1. The value of the variable in an equation is called the __?__ of the equation. *root*

2. The expression $3c^2 - 4c + 1$ has three __?__. *terms*

3. The result obtained by multiplying one number by another is their __?__. *product*

4. In the expression $4a^2b^5$ the number 5 is called the __?__ of b. *exponent*

5. In the expression $2x^3y^4$ the number 2 is the __?__ of x^3y^4. *coefficient*

6. 5 and 7 are the __?__ of 35. *factors*

7. The formula for the area of a circle is $A = \pi$ __?__. r^2

8. The equation $\dfrac{x}{3} = \dfrac{5}{6}$ is called a __?__. *proportion*

9. If 2 is subtracted from a certain number and the result multiplied by 4, the result equals the sum of twice the number and a number one less than the original. What is the number? *7*

10. Solve:

a. $3x - 4y = -17$ $x = -3,$
$2x - 5y = -16$ $y = 2$

b. $y = x + 2$ $x = 3,$
$3x - y = 4$ $y = 5$

346

11. Draw the graph for $y = x + 3$.

12. Draw the graph for $2x - y = 10$.

13. One factor of $x^2 - 8x + 12$ is $x - 6$. What is the other factor? $x - 2$

14. One factor of $x^3 - 3x^2 + 3x - 2$ is $x^2 - x + 1$. Find the other factor. $x - 2$

15. $l = a + (n - 1)d$. Find the value of n when $l = 47$, $a = 5$, and $d = 3$. 15

16. $x = 3y$. If y decreases, how does x change? decreases

17. At the grocery store, Mrs. Adams paid $2.83 for 3 loaves of bread and 2 dozen eggs. Mrs. Jones paid $2.97 for 2 loaves of bread and 3 dozen eggs. Both women paid the same price per loaf of bread and the same price per dozen eggs. What are those prices? bread, 51¢ ; eggs, 65¢

Solve for x:

18. $2x + 3 = 7x$ $\frac{3}{5}$

19. $6x - 9x = 0$ 0

20. $\frac{x}{2} - \frac{x}{3} = 1$ 6

21. $2x + 5 - 5(2 + x) = 3(x + 6)$ $-3\frac{5}{6}$

22. $4x - (x - 2) = 10 - x$ 2

23. $\dfrac{4x + 1}{2} - \dfrac{2x - 3}{3} = \dfrac{5x - 1}{4}$ -21

24. The larger of two numbers exceeds the smaller by 4. Five times the larger, decreased by 6 times the smaller, gives 8 as the result. What are the two numbers? $12, 16$

25. At one basketball game 1845 tickets were sold. Pupils paid 25 cents each for their tickets and outsiders paid 40 cents each. If the total receipts for the game were $553.35, how many tickets of each kind were sold? Outsiders, 614; pupils, 1231

26. The life span of an elephant is 9 years less than 3 times that of a grizzly bear. The sum of their average life spans is 115 years. What is the expected life span of the elephant? of the grizzly bear? bear, 31 yr. ; elephant, 84 yr.

27. From Earth to the star Antares is about 10.8 light years farther than one tenth the distance to the star Aldebaran. Their combined distance is 367.2 light years. How far is each from Earth? Aldebaran, 324 light yr. Antares, 43.2 light yr.

347

Write the indicated products: [Test A]

1. $3 a(a^2 + 2 a - 1)$ ~~$3a^3 + 6a^2 - 3a$~~

2. $(a + b)(a - b)$ ~~$a^2 - b^2$~~

3. $(x - 3)^2$ ~~$x^2 - 6x + 9$~~

4. $(x - 5)(x - 3)$ ~~$x^2 - 8x + 15$~~

5. $(2 x + 1)(3 x + 5)$ ~~$6x^2 + 13x + 5$~~

6. $(3 x + 7)^2$ ~~$9x^2 + 42x + 49$~~

Square as indicated:

7. $(5 a)^2$ ~~$25a^2$~~   8. $(- 3)^2$ ~~9~~   9. $(8 a^3)^2$ ~~$64a^6$~~   10. $(\frac{1}{2} gt)^2$ ~~$\frac{1}{4}g^2t^2$~~

Find the prime factors: *(ans. at foot of page)*

11. $4 a + 4 b$ 15. $x^2 - x - 2$ 19. $2 x^3 - 4 x^2 - 2 x$

12. $x^2 + 7 x + 12$ 16. $2 a^2 - 2 b^2$ 20. $1 - 25 a^2$

13. $c^2 - 5 c + 6$ 17. $5 y^2 + 17 y + 6$ 21. $3 y^2 - y - 4$

14. $x^2 - 9$ 18. $a^2 - 4 b^2$ 22. $3 x^2 - 21 x + 18$

Write the indicated roots:

23. $\sqrt{36}$ ~~6~~   24. $\sqrt{a^2b^2}$ ~~ab~~   25. $\sqrt{(x + y)^2}$ ~~$x+y$~~

Write the indicated products: [Test B]

1. $3 ab(a^2 + 5 a - 6)$ ~~$3a^3b + 15a^2b - 18ab$~~

2. $(2 x - 5 y)^2$ ~~$4x^2 - 20xy + 25y^2$~~

3. $(3 c + 1)(3 c - 1)$ ~~$9c^2 - 1$~~

4. $(5 x + 3 y)(3 x - 4 y)$ ~~$15x^2 - 11xy - 12y^2$~~

5. $(x - \frac{1}{2})^2$ ~~$x^2 - x + \frac{1}{4}$~~

6. $(6 ab + 3 c)(2 ab - 3 c)$ ~~$12 a^2b^2 - 12 abc - 9c^2$~~

Tell which of the following expressions are prime and which are not prime:

7. $x + 6$ ~~Prime~~   8. $x^2 - x - 12$ ~~Not prime~~   9. $x^2 + 9$ ~~Prime~~

Find the prime factors:

10. $2 a^4 - 4 a^3$ ~~$2a^2(a^2 - 2a - 2)$~~   18. $2 x^3 - 4 x^2 + 2 x$ ~~$2x(x-1)^2$~~

11. $x^2y^2 - 1$ ~~$(xy+1)(xy-1)$~~   19. $3 m^2 + 21 m - 3$ ~~$3(m^2 + 7m - 1)$~~

12. $x^2 - 6 x - 16$ ~~$(x-8)(x+2)$~~   20. $c^3 - c$ ~~$c(c+1)(c-1)$~~

13. $4 a^2 - \frac{1}{9}$ ~~$(2a+\frac{1}{3})(2a-\frac{1}{3})$~~   21. $x^3y^3 - 2 x^2y^2$ ~~$x^2y^2(xy-2)$~~

14. $12 x^2 + x - 8$ ~~Prime~~   22. $a^4 - 16$ ~~$(a^2+4)(a+2)(a-2)$~~

15. $2 \pi a^2 - 2 \pi b^2$ ~~$2\pi(a-b)(a+b)$~~   23. $a^4 - 5 a^2 + 4$ ~~$(a+1)(a-1)(a+2)(a-2)$~~

16. $3 - 19 c - 14 c^2$ ~~$(3+2c)(1-7c)$~~   24. $x^3 - 3 x^2 - 10 x$ ~~$x(x-5)(x+2)$~~

17. $ax^6 - ay^6$ ~~$a(x^3+y^3)(x-y)(x^2+y+y^2)$~~   25. $x^4 - 9 x^2 + 20$ ~~$(x^2-5)(x^2+2)(x^2-2)$~~

11. ~~$4(a+b)$~~
12. ~~$(x+3)(x+4)$~~
13. ~~$(c-3)(c-2)$~~
14. ~~$(x+3)(x-3)$~~

15. ~~$(x+1)(x-2)$~~
16. ~~$2(a+b)(a-b)$~~
17. ~~$(5y+2)(y+3)$~~
18. ~~$(a+2b)(a-2b)$~~

19. ~~$2x(x^2 - 2x - 1)$~~
20. ~~$(1-5a)(1+5a)$~~
21. ~~$(3y-4)(y+1)$~~
22. ~~$3(x-1)(x-6)$~~

Time, 40 Minutes

See how many of the following exercises you can do correctly in 40 minutes.

Factor: *(x+8)(x−5)*   *(x²−y)²*   *(3x+5)(3x−5)*

1. $x^2 + 3x - 40$ **3.** $x^4 - 2x^2y + y^2$ **5.** $9x^2 - 25$

2. $P + Prt$ *P(1+rt)*   **4.** $3r^2 - 3r$ *3r(r−1)*   **6.** $a^2 - 12a - 35$ *Prime*

7. How much less than zero is $x^2 - 4$? *4−x²*

8. Solve: $(2y - 1)^2 - 4(y^2 - 3y + 1) = 3y + 2$ *1*

9. Multiply: $(-6a^2)(4a)(-2a^3)$ *48a⁶*

10. If $a = 3$, $b = 2$, $c = -4$, find the value of $\dfrac{a^2 - 4b + c}{a}$. *−1*

11. Divide: $(3x^2 - x - 10)$ by $(x - 2)$ *3x+5*

Solve:

12. $2x + y = 17$ *x = 7,*
$x - 3y = -2$ *y = 3*

13. $.5x + .3y = 5.8$ *x = 8,*
$.4x - .2y = 2.0$ *y = 6*

14. Solve: $A = \frac{1}{2}lw$ for w *2A/l*

15. Solve: $\dfrac{6y - 5}{8} - \dfrac{4y - 1}{3} = \dfrac{1}{3} - y$ *1½*

Find the indicated square roots:

16. $\sqrt{64}$ *8*   **18.** $\sqrt{(a + b)^2}$ *a+b*   **20.** $\sqrt{.09}$ *0.3*

17. $\sqrt{121 a^8}$ *11a⁴*   **19.** $\sqrt{\dfrac{81 a^2}{25 b^2}}$ *9a/5b*   **21.** $\sqrt{36 a^2b^4}$ *6ab²*

22. Solve: $.3x + 1.4 = 1.1x - .2$ *2*

23. Multiply: $(a^2 - b^2)$ by $(a - b)$ *a³−a²b−ab²+b³*

24. Graph the equation: $x + 2y = 5$

25. Solve for y: $2ay - b^2 = 3b^2$ *2b²/a*

Nuclear-powered heart pacemaker.

National Institute of Health

The size of the electronic components of a nuclear-powered pacemaker are shown in relation to a dime.

NUMEC

Dear Don:

Thank you for your confidence in my opinion about your training for medical research. Of course you are right in saying that the best way to attack medical problems is through preventing them. Perhaps with medical people like you, there will be fewer patients for practicing physicians like me.

As you know we have already very nearly eradicated such diseases as cholera and yellow fever and such children's diseases as measles. We know how to control such diseases as typhoid fever by cleaning up the environment. There are many diseases caused by the lack of food, the wrong food, or too much food, but the prevention is pretty much out of the hands of doctors. The same can be said of diseases caused by toxic fumes such as those from cigarettes and automobile exhaust pipes.

There is, however, a rather long list of genetic diseases against which we are presently helpless. Perhaps you would be interested in trying to find a way to prevent PKU, a disease in which a single vital enzyme normally manufactured by the liver is missing. Sickle cell anemia, diabetes, muscular dystrophy, cystic fibrosis, hemophilia, and epilepsy are other genetic diseases on which we need help desperately.

Along an entirely different line, we need to learn how to prevent diseases that come from the stresses of life. Among these are atherosclerosis, stomach ulcers, and other gastro-intestinal disorders.

Any of these are worthy of your consideration. When you are at home during vacation, stop at my office and I will give you further information. You are wise to start planning even before you begin your medical training. In any endeavor it is wise to know where you are going.

Sincerely,

Joyce Weathers

Dr. Joyce Weathers

13

Using Special Products and Factoring in Solving Equations

Suggested Time Schedule
   Minimum   4 days
   Maximum   5 days

In this chapter you will find use
for the things
you have just been studying.

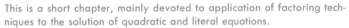

This is a short chapter, mainly devoted to application of factoring techniques to the solution of quadratic and literal equations.

   We hope you have been using in some way the articles which appear between the chapters and have found them inspiring and informative.

The Degree of an Equation [A].   (Review)

The degree of an equation in one variable is the same as the highest power of the variable in the equation after it has been cleared of fractions and parentheses. Since the graph of a first-degree equation is a straight line, it is often called a <u>linear equation</u>. Also a first-degree equation is sometimes called a <u>simple equation</u>. A <u>quadratic equation</u> is one of the second degree and a <u>cubic equation</u> is one of the third degree. Compare the three kinds of equations below:

SIMPLE EQUATIONS	QUADRATIC EQUATIONS	CUBIC EQUATIONS
$4x = 36$	$4x^2 = 36$	$x^3 = 8$
$7x + 2 = 23$	$x^2 - 6x + 18 = 0$	$x^3 - 4x^2 + 8 = 0$

Solving Equations by Factoring [A]

Any equation whose right member is zero and whose left member can be completely factored may be solved by the *factoring method*. Solving an equation by factoring depends upon the following principle:

> **If the product of two or more factors is zero, at least one of the factors is zero.**

[A]

ORAL EXERCISES

1. What is the value of 4×0? of $b \times 0$? of 0×0? *0; 0; 0*

2. If the product of two numbers is zero, are both numbers necessarily zero? Explain. *No. Because $a \cdot 0 = 0$; if either factor is zero the product is zero.*

3. What is the value of $(x - 1)(x + 2)$ if $x - 1 = 0$?   if $x + 2 = 0$? What is the value of x if $x - 1 = 0$? What is the value of x if $x + 2 = 0$? *0; 0; 1; −2*

4. If $x^2 - x - 6 = 0$, does $(x - 3)(x + 2) = 0$? If $x = 3$, does $x - 3 = 0$? If $x = 3$, does $(x - 3)(x + 2) = 0$? If $x = -2$, does $(x - 3)(x + 2) = 0$? What values of x make $x^2 - x - 6 = 0$? What are the roots of $x^2 - x - 6 = 0$? *Yes; yes; yes; yes; 3 and −2; 3 and −2*

Example 1. Solve $x^2 - 3x - 18 = 0$.

Solution. The right member is zero. We next factor the left member and have $(x - 6)(x + 3) = 0$. There are two ways of making this product equal zero. One way is setting $x - 6 = 0$ and the other way is setting $x + 3 = 0$. If $x - 6 = 0$, $x = 6$; and if $x + 3 = 0$, $x = -3$. The roots are 6 and -3.

---

① As usual we have supplied oral questions designed as preparation for the procedures to follow. Emphasize that a product is 0 if any one of its factors is 0.   **353**

To Solve an Equation by Factoring:

1. If necessary change the equation so that the right member is zero.
2. Factor the left member.
3. Set each factor containing the variable equal to zero.
4. Solve the resulting equations.
5. Prove each solution correct.

Example 2. Solve $4x^2 = 25$.

Solution. The equation must be written so that the right member is zero.

$$4x^2 = 25$$
$$4x^2 - 25 = 0$$

Factoring the left member $\quad (2x+5)(2x-5) = 0$

If $\quad 2x+5 = 0$	If $\quad 2x-5 = 0$
then $\quad 2x = -5$	then $\quad 2x = 5$
and $\quad x = -\frac{5}{2}$	and $\quad x = \frac{5}{2}$

PROOF. Does $4(-\frac{5}{2})^2 = 25$ and does $4(\frac{5}{2})^2 = 25$?
Does $\qquad 25 = 25$ and does $\qquad 25 = 25$? Yes.

Example 3. Solve $5x^2 = 2x$.

Solution.
$$5x^2 = 2x$$
$$5x^2 - 2x = 0$$
$$x(5x-2) = 0$$

$x = 0$	If $\quad 5x-2 = 0$
	then $\quad 5x = 2$
	and $\quad x = \frac{2}{5}$

PROOF. Does $5(0)^2 = 2(0)$ and does $5(\frac{2}{5})^2 = 2(\frac{2}{5})$?
Does $\qquad 0 = 0 \quad$ and does $\qquad \frac{4}{5} = \frac{4}{5}$? Yes.

EXERCISES

[A]

Solve by factoring: *answers at foot of page.*

1. $x^2 + 2x = 15$
2. $x^2 + 3x + 2 = 0$
3. $m^2 - 4 = 0$
4. $x^2 - 1 = 0$
5. $x^2 - 3x = 0$
6. $x^2 + 5x = 0$
7. $x^2 + 6x = -9$
8. $x^2 - 35 = 2x$
9. $x^2 - 4x + 4 = 0$
10. $x^2 = 9$
11. $x^2 - 6x = 0$
12. $x^2 - 2x = 24$

① In problems with identical factors, as in Ex. 9, some call 2 "the root," some say "2 is a multiple or double root."

354

1. -5, 3
2. -2, -1
3. -2, 2
4. -1, 1

5. 0, 3
6. 0, -5
7. -3, -3
8. 7, -5

9. 2, 2
10. -3, 3
11. 0, 6
12. 6, -4

13. $x^2 - 12x = -32$ $8, 4$

14. $5y^2 - 17y = 0$ $0, 3\frac{2}{5}$

15. $4n^2 = 4$ $-1, 1$

16. $y^2 - 4y = 21$ $7, -3$

17. $c^2 + 2 = 3c$ $2, 1$

18. $4x^2 + 16x - 20 = 0$ $-5, 1$

19. $4x^2 = 9$ $-\frac{3}{2}, \frac{3}{2}$

20. $y^2 - 8y = 0$ $0, 8$

21. $2y^2 = 9y - 9$ $1\frac{1}{2}, 3$

22. $\pi r^2 - 2\pi r = 0$ $0, 2$

23. $d^2 + 8d = 0$ $0, -8$

24. $y(y + 2) = 15$ $-5, 3$

25. $\frac{x^2}{6} + \frac{x}{3} = \frac{1}{2}$ $-3, 1$

26. $x^2 = \frac{5}{2} - \frac{3x}{2}$ $-2\frac{1}{2}, 1$

27. $6x^2 + \frac{13x}{2} = 7$ $-\frac{3}{4}, \frac{2}{3}$

28. $x^2 + 25 = 1 - 10x$ $-6, -4$

29. $\frac{x^2}{2} = 6x$ $0, 12$

30. $\frac{x^2}{12} + x + \frac{9}{4} = 0$ $-9, -3$

31. $\frac{y^2}{15} = \frac{y}{5} + \frac{2}{3}$ $5, -2$

32. $(y - 3)(y - 5) = y - 5$ $5, 4$

[B]

Solve for x:

33. $x^2 - a^2 = 0$ $-a, a$

34. $6x^2 + 7cx - 5c^2 = 0$ $-\frac{5c}{3}, \frac{c}{2}$

35. $\frac{x^2}{8} + yx = \frac{5y^2}{2}$ $-10y, 2y$

36. $\frac{x^2}{3} - \frac{c^2}{2} = \frac{cx}{6}$ $\frac{3c}{2}, -c$

37. $3x^2 - 10m^2 = \frac{7mx}{2}$ $-\frac{4m}{3}, \frac{5m}{2}$

38. $(x - 3)(x^2 - cx - 2c^2) = 0$ $3, 2c, -c$

Special Products in Equations [A]

The solutions of many equations which contain indicated multiplications are shortened when one can find the products mentally.

Example 1. Solve $(x - 6)^2 - (x + 3)(x - 1) = 11$.

Solution.
$$(x - 6)^2 - (x + 3)(x - 1) = 11$$
$$(x^2 - 12x + 36) - (x^2 + 2x - 3) = 11$$
$$x^2 - 12x + 36 - x^2 - 2x + 3 = 11$$
$$x^2 - 12x - x^2 - 2x = 11 - 36 - 3 \quad \text{①}$$
$$-14x = -28$$
$$x = 2$$

PROOF. Does $(2 - 6)^2 - (2 + 3)(2 - 1) = 11$?

Does $16 - 5 = 11$? Yes.

CAUTION. You should be sure to place the products of binomials in parentheses to avoid errors. This was done in the example above. In the exercises that follow find the products mentally.

① Students often make mistakes in signs or in omitting the middle term of a trinomial square. Each must decide for himself when he is capable of omitting some leading steps *without* making these errors.

355

[A]

Solve and prove:

3 **1.** $(x+1)^2 - x^2 = 7$ $\frac{1}{2}$ **3.** $(y-3)^2 = y^2 + 6$

2 **2.** $(x-5)^2 = x^2 + 5$ -1 **4.** $(m-1)(m+1) = (m+1)^2$

$-9, 2$ **5.** $(n+2)(2n+1) - (n-1)^2 = 19$

$-3, 3$ **6.** $(3x-1)(3x+1) - (2x-1)(2x+1) = 45$

1 **7.** $4y^2 + 7y = 10 + (2y-3)^2$

6 **8.** $4r^2 - 5(r-1) = (2r+5)(2r-5)$

4 **9.** $6x(3x-5) - 2x(9x+1) = -128$

2 **10.** $(5x+7)(6x-2) + 5(3x-9) = 30x^2 + 35$

$3\frac{3}{4}$ **11.** $(y-6)^2 - (y+4)^2 + 55 = 0$

[B]

Solve and prove:

2 **12.** $3(c-5)^2 + 2(c-4)^2 - 5c^2 - 15 = 0$

1 **13.** $(y+2)(4y-3) - 4(y+3)(y-3) = 35$

$\frac{1}{4}$ **14.** $(2-3x)^2 - (3x-1)(3x+1) = 2$

3 **15.** $x^2 + (x-1)^2 - (2x-1)(x-8) = 38$

$-2\frac{2}{3},$ 2 **16.** $(2x-1)(3x+4) - 3(x-1)(x+2) = 18$

Literal Equations [A]

A literal equation is one in which the unknown number and at least one of the known numbers are represented by letters. In solving some literal equations it is necessary to factor one or more expressions. The example illustrates the method of solving an equation of this kind.

Example. Solve $ax - a^2 = bx - b^2$ for x.

Solution. $ax - a^2 = bx - b^2$

$ax - bx = a^2 - b^2$

Factoring $x(a-b) = (a-b)(a+b)$

D_{a-b} $\dfrac{x(a-b)}{a-b} = \dfrac{(a-b)(a+b)}{a-b}$

or $x = a+b$

NOTE. You should be sure to transform the equation so that all terms containing the variable are in one member, and all other terms are in the other member.

Sometimes students become confused with so many letter symbols and fail to assemble *all* terms involving the variable together. Try underlining those terms containing the variable. Require checking.

USING SPECIAL PRODUCTS AND FACTORING

Solve for x:

1. $cx = d$ $\frac{d}{c}$

2. $mx - n = 0$ $\frac{n}{m}$

3. $(a - b)x = 2(a - b)$ 2

4. $ax - bx = 2a - 2b$ 2

5. $ax - 2a = bx - 2b$ 2

6. $(c + d)x = m(c + d)$ m

7. $(b - 3)x = b^2 - 6b + 9$ $b-3$

8. $ax - d = bx + c$ $\frac{c+d}{a-b}$

9. $ax + 9 = 3x + a^2$ $a+3$

10. $bx + 6b + b^2 = 0$ $-(6+b)$

11. $a - 2x = 3x - 4a$ a

12. $mx - m^2 = nx - mn$ m

13. $2b^2 - bx = 0$ $2b$

14. $mx - m^2 = x + m - 2$ $m+2$

15. $2bx + 4b = 2b + 4b^2 + x$ $2b$

16. $2bx = 9d - 5cx$ $\frac{9d}{2b+5c}$

17. $b - ax = a + ax$ $\frac{b-a}{2a}$

18. $a(bx + 2) = c$ $\frac{c-2a}{ab}$

19. $x - c^2 + c = -2 - cx$ $c-2$

20. $mx - 1 = nx$ $\frac{1}{m-n}$

21. Solve $A = P + Prt$ for P. $\frac{A}{1+rt}$

22. Solve $cst = r - s$ for s. $\frac{r}{ct+1}$

23. Solve $mf = mg - t$ for m. $\frac{-t}{f-g}$ or $\frac{t}{g-f}$

24. Solve $c = Ra + Rc$ for c. $\frac{Ra}{1-R}$

Solve for x:

25. $cx + 3b^2 = c^3 - 3bx$ $\frac{c^3-3b^2}{c+3b}$

26. $m^2x + n^2x = 2$ $\frac{2}{m^2+n^2}$

27. $d(a - x) = x(c - d)$ $\frac{ad}{c}$

28. $\frac{2\,acx}{3} = b$ $\frac{3b}{2ac}$

29. $5(x - b) = 4(x - a)$ $5b-4a$

30. $r(x - s) - r^2 = 2sr$ $r+3s$

31. $2m^2x + 2m^2 = 2m^4 + 2mx$ $m(m+1)$

32. $bcx + 5c = c^2 + 5bx$ $\frac{c}{b}$

33. $cx + c = 3x + c^2 - 6$ $c+2$

34. $adx + bd = cd + bcx + c^2$ $\frac{c^2+cd-bd}{ad-bc}$

35. $acdx - bcdk = bc^2x - bdhx$ $\binom{\text{see}}{\text{below}}$

36. $\frac{a + b}{2} = \frac{x}{3}$ $\frac{3(a+b)}{2}$

37. $a^2x - a^2 - ax = 6x - 2a - 3$ $\frac{a+1}{a+2}$

38. $a(x - 1) = x + 2a^2 - 3$ $2a+3$

39. $c - \frac{x}{2} - \frac{x}{3} = \frac{c}{6}(c - x) + \frac{x}{6}$ c

40. $a(3x + b) + b(x + b) = 6a^2$ $\frac{2a-b}{}$

41. Solve $C(R + nr) = en$ for n. $\frac{CR}{e-Cr}$

42. Solve $A = \pi r^2 + 2\pi rh$ for h. $\frac{A-\pi r^2}{2\pi r}$

Any verbal problem you have had so far could be solved by a first-degree equation having one variable or by a pair of first-degree equations. From now on some of the problems lead to quadratic equa-

35. $\dfrac{bcdk}{acd - bc^2 + bdh}$

tions, or equations of the second degree. In this course use only one variable in solving problems whose equations are quadratics.

Each number to be found in a problem whose equation is a quadratic has two values. Thus if you are asked in the problem to find two numbers, you are required to find four answers, two for each of the two numbers.

Example. The difference of two numbers is 3 and the sum of their squares is 29. Find the numbers.

Solution. Let $\quad\quad\quad\quad\quad x =$ the smaller number
Then $\quad\quad\quad\quad\quad\quad x + 3 =$ the larger number
$$(x + 3)^2 + x^2 = 29$$
$$(x^2 + 6x + 9) + x^2 = 29$$
$$x^2 + 6x + 9 + x^2 = 29$$
$$x^2 + x^2 + 6x + 9 - 29 = 0$$
$$2x^2 + 6x - 20 = 0$$
$$2(x^2 + 3x - 10) = 0$$
$$2(x + 5)(x - 2) = 0$$

If $x + 5 = 0$, | If $x - 2 = 0$,
then $x = -5$, the smaller no. | then $x = 2$, the smaller no.
$x + 3 = -2$, the larger no. | $x + 3 = 5$, the larger no.

Notice that the pair of numbers may be -5 and -2, or $+2$ and $+5$.

PROOF. $\quad (-2) - (-5) = 3 \quad\quad\quad\quad 5 - 2 = 3$
$\quad\quad (-2)^2 + (-5)^2 = 29 \quad\quad\quad 5^2 + 2^2 = 29$

PROBLEMS

[A]

1. The difference of the squares of two consecutive integers is 21. What are the integers? (Let $x =$ the smaller integer. Then $x + 1 =$ the larger integer.) *10, 11*

2. The difference of two numbers is 4 and the difference of their squares is 40. Find the numbers. *3, 7*

3. The area of a rectangle is 176 square inches. What are its dimensions if the length exceeds the width by 5 inches? *11 in. x 16 in.*

4. The square of a certain number is 56 more than the number itself. What is the number? (Two answers) *8, -7*

5. What is the number whose square exceeds 10 times itself by 96? *16, -6*

358

The interpretation of answers is the stumbling block here. For example, a student may say, "-5 and 2 are the answers" because the values of x have been so found. Also the student will need guidance in interpreting a negative number obtained as an answer. Point out that, while these numbers are legitimate solutions of the equations, as applied to an age or the length of a line they can have no meaning. Hence they may not be considered solutions of word problems unless they make sense as well as check.

6. Jessica uses a protractor to measure the complementary angles of a right triangle. One of the two angles is the square of the other. How many degrees are in each angle? *9°, 81°*

7. The sum of two numbers is 21 and their product is 104. What are the numbers? *8, 13*

8. What are the two consecutive odd integers the sum of whose squares is 202? *9, 11 or -9, -11*

9. Three times a number increased by twice the square of the number equals 44. Find the number. *4 or -5½*

10. Mary said to Priscilla, "If six times my age in ten years is subtracted from the square of my present age, the result is 52 years." How old is Mary? *14 yr.*

[B]

11. A city lot is 40 feet wide and 140 feet long. How wide a strip must be cut off one end and one side to make the area of the lot 4725 square feet? *5 ft.*

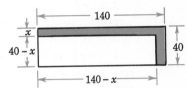

12. A rectangular flower bed is 10 feet wide and 25 feet long. If the length is increased by x feet and the width is decreased by x feet, the area is 216 square feet. Find x. *2*

13. The perimeter of a rectangle is 80 feet and its area is 384 square feet. Find the length and width. *24 ft. × 16 ft.*

14. A farmer wishes to build a granary for wheat that will hold 400 cubic feet. The bin is to be 8 feet high and twice as long as it is wide. Find its length and width. *10 ft. × 5 ft.*

15. A farmer planted 360 cherry trees, having 9 more trees in a row than the number of rows. How many rows did he have? *15*

[C]

16. A rectangular plot of ground is 20 feet long and 15 feet wide. The plot is surrounded by a walk whose area is two thirds the area of the plot. What is the width of the walk? *2½ ft.*

17. One number exceeds another by d and the sum of the numbers is s. What are the numbers? $\dfrac{s+d}{2}, \dfrac{s-d}{2}$

359

18. width, $\dfrac{p-2d}{4}$; length, $\dfrac{p+2d}{4}$

18. The perimeter of a rectangle is p and the length exceeds the width by d. Find the dimensions of the rectangle.

19. Is \$2 worth only \$1? Dick said it is and proved it as follows:

Ex. 19 is, of course, one of the most famous of fallacies— proving that $2 = 1$ by using the inadmissible operation of dividing by 0 in the form of $b - a$.

Let	$a = b$
M_b	$ab = b^2$
S_{a^2}	$ab - a^2 = b^2 - a^2$
Factor	$a(b - a) = (b - a)(b + a)$
D_{b-a}	$a = b + a$
	$a = 2a$
D_a	*No* $\quad 1 = 2$

Is his proof correct? Give a reason for your answer.

Division by $(b-a)$, which equals zero, is not permissible.

Digit Problems [B]

The word *digit* comes from the Latin word for finger. Since early peoples counted with their fingers, the figures 1, 2, 3, 4, 5, 6, 7, 8, 9, and 0, which stand for numbers, are also called <u>digits</u>.

In our way of writing numbers each digit has a place value. Thus in the number 358, the digit 3 tells the number of hundreds, the digit 5 tells the number of tens, and the digit 8 tells the number of units. In solving a problem dealing with the digits of a number you should remember that a number such as 358 means 3 hundreds $+$ 5 tens $+$ 8.

Example. In a number of two digits the tens' digit is four times the units' digit. If the digits of the number are interchanged, the resulting number is 54 less than the original number. What is the number?

Solution 1	Solution 2
Let $\quad x =$ the units' digit	Let $\quad t =$ the tens' digit
Then $\quad 4x =$ the tens' digit	and $\quad u =$ the units' digit
$40x + x =$ the number	$10t + u =$ the number
$10x + 4x =$ the new number	$10u + t =$ the new number
$10x + 4x = 40x + x - 54$	$\begin{cases} t = 4u \\ 10u + t = 10t + u - 54 \end{cases}$
$10x + 4x - 40x - x = -54$	Solve this set of equations and
$-27x = -54$	complete the solution.
$x = 2$, the units' digit	
$4x = 8$, the tens' digit	
The number is 82.	

The value of digit problems lies in the deeper understanding of our decimal number system. You may need to review it. Now is a good time to discuss numbers with other bases, particularly the binary system as either a new topic or a review if students have studied this in arithmetic. As time goes on, you will find more and more students coming to you with a better knowledge of the number system.

USING SPECIAL PRODUCTS AND FACTORING

[B] DIGIT PROBLEMS

1. The sum of the two digits of a number is 11. If the tens' digit is 3 more than the units' digit, what is the number? *74*

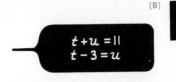

$$t + u = 11$$
$$t - 3 = u$$

2. In a two-digit number the sum of the digits is 8. If 18 is added to the number,

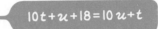

$$10t + u + 18 = 10u + t$$

the resulting number has the same digits as the original number. What is the original number? *35*

3. The value of a two-digit number is 3 more than 4 times the sum of its digits. If the sum of its digits is 8, what is the number? *35*

4. The sum of the two digits of a number is 9. If the number formed by interchanging the digits is subtracted from the number, the result is 27. Find the number. *63*

5. The difference of the two digits of a number is 5. If the value of the number is equal to three times the sum of the digits and the units' digit is the larger, find the number. *27*

6. Two numbers, each having two digits, differ by 27. The same digits are found in each number. If the smaller number is increased by its tens' digit and the larger number is increased by its units' digit, the smaller number is half the larger number. What are the two numbers? *25, 52*

Checking Your Understanding of Chapter 13

Before you begin the Chapter Review, be sure that you know

These pages will help you to review.

	PAGE
1. How to solve equations by factoring	353
2. How to solve more difficult literal equations	356
3. How to solve digit problems	360
4. How to spell and use correctly the following words:	

	PAGE		PAGE
cubic equation	353	origin	274
digit	360	proportion	232
linear equation	353	simultaneous	302
literal equation	356	vary	283

[A]

1. Give the degree of each of the following equations:

1st. **a.** $2x - 1 = 11$ *3d* **c.** $2x^3 = 54$ *1st.* **e.** $3x - 1 = x + 2$

2d **b.** $y^2 - 3y = 10$ *2d* **d.** $2x^2 - 5x = 0$ *3d* **f.** $4x^3 + 5x = 9$

2. Why is a first-degree equation called a linear equation?

Graph is straight line.

3. Complete: If the product of two numbers is zero, either __?__ or __?__ of the numbers __?__ zero. *one, both, is*

Solve the following quadratic equations:

4. $x^2 - 6x + 5 = 0$ *5, 1*   **8.** $y^2 + 3y = 40$ *-8, 5*

5. $x^2 - x - 30 = 0$ *6, -5*   **9.** $2x^2 - 5x = 3$ *-½, 3*

6. $x^2 = 10x$ *0, 10*   **10.** $x^2 - 64 = 0$ *-8, 8*

7. $x^2 = 36$ *-6, 6*   **11.** $2x^2 + 3x = 0$ *0, -3/2*

Solve the following literal equations for x:

12. $abx = c$ *c/ab*   **15.** $c^2(x - 1) = cx - 1$ *c+1/c*

13. $dx + e = 0$ *-e/d*   **16.** $2mx + 6n^2 = 3nx + 4mn$ *2n*

14. $mx - m^2 = nx - n^2$ *m+n*   **17.** $a(x - 1) = a^2 + 3(x - 4)$ *a+4*

Solve:

18. $(y + 5)^2 - y(y - 2) + 11 = 0$ *-3*

19. $(x - 3)(3x + 1) - (2x - 3)(2x + 3) = 18$ *-6, -2*

20. The length of a room is 3 feet more than the width. If the length and width are each increased by 2 feet, the area is increased by 58 square feet. Find the original dimensions of the room. *12 ft. x 15 ft.*

21. The area of a triangular pennant is 90 square inches. If the altitude is 3 inches more than the base, what are the lengths of the base and altitude? *12 in., 15 in.*

22. The square of a certain number is 40 more than 6 times the number. What is the number? *10 or -4*

23. The sum of the square of a certain number and 5 times the number is 24. Find the number. *-8 or 3*

24. Separate 18 into two parts such that the sum of their squares is 170. *7, 11*

25. Twice the square of a number exceeds eight times the number by 42. Find the number. *7 or -3*

1. Combine: $2x^3 - 3x^2 - 8x - 6 + x^2 + 2x - 1$ *2x³-2x²-6x-7*

2. From $5a^2 - 3a - 4$ take $a^3 - a^2 + 6$. *-a³+6a²-3a-10*

3. Multiply $2x^2 - 3xy + y^2$ by $x - 3y$. *2x³-9x²y+10xy²-3y³*

4. Divide $x^3 - 4x^2 - 7x + 6$ by $x + 2$. *x²-6x+5, Rem. -4*

5. Factor:

a. $x^2 - x - 12$ *(x-4)(x+3)*   **e.** $pq + q$ *q(p+1)*

b. $c^2 - 11c + 18$ *(c-9)(c-2)*   **f.** $x^4 - 14x^2 + 49$ *(x²-7)²*

c. $6x^2 - xy - y^2$ *(3x+y)(2x-y)*   **g.** $m^2n^2 - 4m^2n$ *m²n(n-4)*

d. $4x^2 - 25$ *(2x+5)(2x-5)*   **h.** $2x^2 - 2x$ *2x(x-1)*

Solve:

6. $8(y - 1) = 17 - (27 - 18y)$ *1*

7. $\dfrac{p}{4} = \dfrac{3}{8} - \dfrac{3p-1}{2}$ *½*

8. $16x^2 - 81 = 0$ *2¼, -2¼*

9. $b^2 + 12b + 27 = 0$ *-9, -3*

10. $(x - 1)^2 + 3 = 3x$ *4, 1*

11. $6x^2 + 15x + 6 = 0$ *-½, -2*

12. $\dfrac{x^2}{2} - \dfrac{x^2}{3} = \dfrac{3}{2}$ *-3, 3*

13. $3x = 5x^2$ *0, ⅗*

Solve the following sets of equations:

14. $2x + 3y = 9$
$5x = -3y$ *x = -3, y = 5*

15. $x - \dfrac{y}{3} = \dfrac{1}{6}$
$2x + \dfrac{y}{4} = \dfrac{5}{4}$ *x=½, y=1*

16. $x + y = 6$
$3x - 2y = 23$ *x= 7, y=-1*

17. $2\tfrac{1}{3}x - \tfrac{1}{2}y = 0$
$\dfrac{x+y}{5} = 2$ *x=1 13/17, y=8 4/17*

18. Find the value of $3x^2 + 2$ when x is 6 less than $3a$. *27a²-108a+110*

19. Solve, using one variable and also using two variables. The difference of two numbers is 5. Find the numbers if 3 times the smaller is 2 more than twice the larger. *12, 17*

20. Separate 44 into two parts such that if twice the smaller is subtracted from the larger, the remainder is 5. *13, 31*

21. If the area of a rectangle is $a^3 - b^3$ and the length is $a^2 + ab + b^2$, what is the width? *a-b*

22. Elsie is 4 years older than Sylvester. In 15 years one fifth of Elsie's age added to one seventh of Sylvester's age will equal 8 years. How old is each? *Sylvester, 6 yr.; Elsie, 10 yr.*

33. $4(2+3m)(2-3m)$ 35. $(a^2+1)(a+1)(a-1)$ 37. $(y^3-12)(y^3-3)$
34. $16(a+1)(a-1)$ 36. $(x+3)(x-3)(x+2)(x-2)$ 38. $5x^2(x-6)(x+5)$

ALGEBRA, BOOK ONE

23. At what price must a real-estate dealer purchase a lot in order that he may sell it for $1312.50 and make a 5% profit on the cost? $1250

Draw a graph for each equation:

24. $y = 2x - 3$ **26.** $5x = 15$ **28.** $y - 6x = 0$

25. $x = \frac{1}{2}y$ **27.** $3y = -12$ **29.** $2y + 5x = -10$

[B]

30. Solve $x(x-4) = (x-2)(x+2) - 4.$ 2

31. Solve $(x^2-1)(x^2+1) - (x^2+2)(x^2-3) - (x+7) = 0.$

32. Solve for x: $5x^2 + 4ax = a^2$ $\frac{a}{5}, -a$ 2, -1

Factor: (ans. at top of page)

33. $16 - 36 m^2$ **36.** $x^4 - 13x^2 + 36$

34. $16a^2 - 16$ **37.** $y^6 - 15y^3 + 36$

35. $a^4 - 1$ **38.** $5x^4 - 5x^3 - 150x^2$

39. Divide $x^5 + x^4 - x^3 - x^2$ by $x + 1.$ $x^4 - x^2$

[C]

40. Give the slopes and y-intercepts of the graphs of:

$\frac{1}{3}; 6$ **a.** $y = \frac{1}{3}x + 6$ $5; 0$ **c.** $y = 5x$ $\frac{1}{2}; -2\frac{1}{2}$ **e.** $2y = x - 5$

$-4; 4$ **b.** $y = 4 - 4x$ $1; -3$ **d.** $x - 3 = y$ $-\frac{4}{3}; -1\frac{2}{3}$ **f.** $3y = -4x - 5$

[Test A]

CHAPTER TESTS

Solve the following quadratic equations:

1. $x^2 - 9x + 20 = 0$ 5, 4   **4.** $2x^2 + x - 1 = 0$ $\frac{1}{2}, -1$

2. $x^2 = 6x$ 0, 6   **5.** $6x^2 - 19x = -10$ $\frac{2}{3}, 2\frac{1}{2}$

3. $\frac{x^2}{4} = 4$ $-4, 4$ **6.** $\frac{x^2}{3} - 2x + \frac{9}{4} = 0$ $\frac{9}{2}, \frac{3}{2}$

Solve the following literal equations for x:

7. $ax = b$ $\frac{b}{a}$.   **10.** $bx - 2b = 2c - cx$ 2

8. $x + a = b$ $b - a$ **11.** $mx - m^2 = 2x - m - 2$ $m+1$

9. $cx - 2c^2 = 0$ $2c$ **12.** $cxt = a - x$ $\frac{a}{ct+1}$

Solve:

13. $x(x+3) = x - 1$ -1 is double root

14. $(x+2)(2x+3) = (x-1)^2 - 9$ $-7, -2$

15. Three times a certain number increased by twice the square of the number equals 65. Find two numbers satisfying this condition. 5, $-6\frac{1}{2}$

USING SPECIAL PRODUCTS AND FACTORING

Solve the following literal equations for x:

1. $x^2 = b^2$ $b, -b$

4. $a(x - b) = a(a - 2b)$ $a - b$

2. $x^2 + 3c^2 = 4cx$ $3c, c$

5. $c(1 + x) = bx$ $\dfrac{c}{b-c}$

3. $\dfrac{x^2}{6} + \dfrac{a^2}{3} = \dfrac{ax}{2}$ $2a, a$

6. $\dfrac{a-b}{3} = \dfrac{x}{6} + \dfrac{x}{2}$ $\dfrac{a-b}{2}$

Solve:

7. $\dfrac{x^2}{2} = 3x$ $0, 6$

8. $\dfrac{x^2}{3} - \dfrac{1}{2} = \dfrac{23x}{12}$ $-\dfrac{1}{4}, 6$

9. $3(x - 3)^2 + 2(x + 4)(x - 4) = 3$ $-\dfrac{2}{5}, 4$

10. $(y + 2)(4y - 3) - 4(y + 2)(y - 2) = 21$ $2\dfrac{1}{5}$

11. The sum of the squares of two consecutive integers is 85. Find the integers. $-7, -6;$ or $6, 7$

12. A rectangular garden is 12 feet wide and 30 feet long. If the length is decreased by x feet and the width is increased by x feet, the area is 416 square feet. Find x. $4 ft.$ or $14 ft.$

Dear Dee,

Did you hear the reporter on T.V. talking about the new woman pilot? Later I read about her in the paper. Her name is Emily Howell.

What a fantastic job that is. Imagine flying a plane all over! I know the training must be stiff — what with learning to manage the plane and all of those dials and aerial maps. And think of all of the responsibility! But, just the same, I want to be a pilot, too.

Why don't you join me? We could take our training together. Wouldn't that be great! After all, we both like to study radio, navigation, and engines. There doesn't seem to be any reason why we couldn't qualify to become pilots. I'd love to try it. How about joining me?

Sincerely,
Josie

Frontier Airlines

14

Fractions

Suggested Time Schedule
Minimum   13 days
Maximum   15 days

*In this chapter you will learn
how to handle fractions with skill.* ▶

You will find this chapter one of the most difficult to teach. Many students have not understood arithmetic fractions and this lack is bound to hamper their progress here. They are inclined to perform oper,ations mechanically, depend on arbitrary rules, and not to see the *why* of procedures. For this reason we introduced fractions early in the text, developing them spirally and naturally to this point where the subject is thoroughly expanded.

Throughout the chapter, make frequent analogies between arithmetic and algebra. Practice as much as time permits in class with board and seat work. Make "lock-step" assignments, that is, save some exercises from the long sets and incorporate them into the lessons that follow. Do not let students forget while advancing.

Algebraic Fractions [A]

Fractions such as $\frac{1}{2}$, $\frac{1}{3}$, $\frac{3}{4}$, and $\frac{7}{5}$ are arithmetic (ăr'-ĭth-mĕt'-ĭk) fractions while fractions such as

$$\frac{a}{b}, \quad \frac{4}{c}, \quad \text{and} \quad \frac{x+3}{5}$$

are algebraic fractions. In this chapter you will add, subtract, divide, and multiply fractions which, in the main, are algebraic. This work is important because equations often contain complicated fractions.

The fraction $\frac{a}{b}$ is read "a divided by b." As in arithmetic, a is the numerator and b is the denominator. The numerator and denominator are the *terms* of the fraction. Recall that $b \neq 0$.

We define the multiplication of fractions as follows:

If a, b, c, and d, are real numbers and no denominator is zero, then

$$\frac{a}{b} \cdot \frac{c}{d} = \frac{ac}{bd}.$$

Changing the Denominator of a Fraction [A]

You know that $\frac{1}{2}$, $\frac{2}{4}$, and $\frac{3}{6}$ are equal, or equivalent, fractions. By the multiplicative property of 1, we know that if a is a real number, $a(1) = a$. This property is very useful in changing a fraction into an equal fraction with another denominator. For example, to find a fraction equal to $\frac{2}{5}$ but having the denominator 15, we may write:

$$\frac{2}{5} = \frac{2}{5}(1) \qquad \text{Why?}$$

But $1 = \frac{3}{3}$. (We choose $\frac{3}{3}$ because $3(5) = 15$.)
Substituting $\frac{3}{3}$ for 1 in the first statement gives

$$\frac{2}{5} = \frac{2}{5}\left(\frac{3}{3}\right)$$

By the principle in the preceding section, $\frac{2}{5}\left(\frac{3}{3}\right) = \frac{6}{15}$.

Consequently, $\frac{2}{5} = \frac{6}{15}$.

ORAL
EXERCISES

Tell how the second fraction is obtained from the first:

1. $\dfrac{2}{3} = \dfrac{4}{6}$

2. $\dfrac{1}{2} = \dfrac{5}{10}$

3. $\dfrac{m}{n} = \dfrac{am}{an}$

4. $\dfrac{x}{y} = \dfrac{3x}{3y}$

5. $\dfrac{12}{42} = \dfrac{2}{7}$

6. $\dfrac{24}{36} = \dfrac{2}{3}$

① *Equivalent fractions.* This important application of the multiplicative property of 1 is used throughout the work with fractions. To tie all together, use some concise phrase which can be frequently repeated such as "Multiply by 1 in the form of a/a" or "Change the *form*, but not the *value*, of the fraction."

369

7. $\dfrac{x^2}{xy} = \dfrac{x}{y}$

10. $\dfrac{4a - 4b}{8} = \dfrac{a - b}{2}$

8. $\dfrac{ab}{c} = \dfrac{abd}{cd}$

11. $\dfrac{(x+y)(x-y)}{x+y} = \dfrac{x-y}{1}$

9. $\dfrac{-3}{-4} = \dfrac{3}{4}$

12. $\dfrac{a^2 - b^2}{a+b} = \dfrac{a-b}{1}$

Find the missing numerator or denominator:

13. $\dfrac{5}{8} = \dfrac{15}{?24}$

16. $\dfrac{5}{3} = \dfrac{?20}{12}$

19. $\dfrac{?15}{12x} = \dfrac{5}{4x}$

14. $\dfrac{8}{3} = \dfrac{?16}{6}$

17. $\dfrac{4}{6a} = \dfrac{8}{?12a}$

20. $\dfrac{bc}{c^2} = \dfrac{b}{?c}$

15. $\dfrac{?2}{9} = \dfrac{4}{18}$

18. $\dfrac{3a}{?36} = \dfrac{a}{b}$

21. $\dfrac{a}{x} = \dfrac{?axy}{x^2y}$

22. $\dfrac{8bc}{24b^2} = \dfrac{c}{?3b}$

25. $\dfrac{x+4}{x-1} = \dfrac{?(x+4)(x+2)}{(x-1)(x+2)}$

23. $\dfrac{7}{x+y} = \dfrac{?14}{2x+2y}$

26. $\dfrac{2c+1}{c-3} = \dfrac{?c(2c+1)}{c^2 - 3c}$

24. $\dfrac{3m}{m+n} = \dfrac{?15m}{5(m+n)}$

27. $\dfrac{3b+5}{b-4} = \dfrac{?}{b^2 - 7b + 12}$
$(3b+5)(b-3)$

Reducing Fractions to Lowest Terms [A]

A fraction is in its simplest form when the numerator and denominator have no common integer factor except 1. Changing a fraction to its simplest form is called *reducing the fraction to lowest terms*. The multiplicative property of 1 is useful in reducing a fraction to its lowest terms. The following example shows how this is done.

Example 1. Reduce $\dfrac{14\,ax}{21\,a^3}$ to lowest terms.

Solution. $\dfrac{14\,ax}{21\,a^3} = \dfrac{2\,x(7\,a)}{3\,a^2(7\,a)}$

$\dfrac{14\,ax}{21\,a^3} = \dfrac{2\,x}{3\,a^2}\left(\dfrac{7\,a}{7\,a}\right)$

$\dfrac{14\,ax}{21\,a^3} = \dfrac{2\,x}{3\,a^2}\,(1)$, or $\dfrac{14\,ax}{21\,a^3} = \dfrac{2\,x}{3\,a^2}$

FRACTIONS

[A]

EXERCISES

Reduce each fraction to lowest terms:

1. $\dfrac{6}{18}$ $\frac{1}{3}$ 7. $\dfrac{x}{x^2}$ $\frac{1}{x}$ 13. $\dfrac{b^2c}{bc^2}$ $\frac{b}{c}$ 19. $\dfrac{a^7}{a^3}$ a^4

2. $\dfrac{5}{20}$ $\frac{1}{4}$ 8. $\dfrac{ax}{x^3}$ $\frac{a}{x^2}$ 14. $\dfrac{mn}{m^2n^2}$ $\frac{1}{mn}$ 20. $\dfrac{a^9}{a^7}$ a^2

3. $\dfrac{10}{25}$ $\frac{2}{5}$ 9. $\dfrac{3a}{6a^2}$ $\frac{1}{2a}$ 15. $\dfrac{r^3s^3}{rs}$ r^2s^2 21. $\dfrac{26\,x^4y^6}{39\,x^3y}$ $\frac{2xy^5}{3}$

4. $\dfrac{14}{35}$ $\frac{2}{5}$ 10. $\dfrac{9\,m}{12\,m}$ $\frac{3}{4}$ 16. $\dfrac{6\,ac}{15\,c^3}$ $\frac{2a}{5c^2}$ 22. $-\dfrac{90\,b^2c^3}{36\,a^3b^2}$ $\frac{5c^3}{2a^3}$

5. $\dfrac{15}{18}$ $\frac{5}{6}$ 11. $\dfrac{4\,x}{3\,x}$ $\frac{4}{3}$ 17. $\dfrac{xy}{x^2y^3}$ $\frac{1}{xy^2}$ 23. $\dfrac{-\,rst^4}{r^2st^4}$ $\frac{-1}{r}$

6. $\dfrac{12}{20}$ $\frac{3}{5}$ 12. $\dfrac{2\,a^3}{7\,a}$ $\frac{2a^2}{7}$ 18. $\dfrac{11\,a^2b}{33\,ac}$ $\frac{ab}{3c}$ 24. $\dfrac{180\,a}{100\,a}$ $\frac{9}{5}$

Example 2. Reduce $\dfrac{a^2 - 2\,a - 24}{5\,a - 30}$ to lowest terms.

Solution. $\dfrac{a^2 - 2\,a - 24}{5\,a - 30} = \dfrac{(a+4)(a-6)}{5(a-6)}$

$$\dfrac{a^2 - 2\,a - 24}{5\,a - 30} = \dfrac{a+4}{5}\left(\dfrac{a-6}{a-6}\right)$$

$$\dfrac{a^2 - 2\,a - 24}{5\,a - 30} = \dfrac{a+4}{5}\ (1)$$

$$\dfrac{a^2 - 2\,a - 24}{5\,a - 30} = \dfrac{a+4}{5}$$

Sometimes we shorten the process of writing long solutions as follows:

See ① below.
$$\dfrac{a^2 - 2\,a - 24}{5\,a - 30} = \dfrac{\overset{1}{\cancel{(a-6)}}(a+4)}{5\underset{1}{\cancel{(a-6)}}} = \dfrac{a+4}{5}$$

Observe that in this case $\dfrac{a-6}{a-6}$ has been written as $\frac{1}{1}$. Since $\frac{1}{1} = 1$, we are still using the multiplicative property of 1.

[A]

EXERCISES

1. Add 2 to each term of the fraction $\frac{8}{10}$. Reduce the resulting fraction to lowest terms. Does it equal $\frac{8}{10}$? Can one add a number to each term of a fraction without changing the value of the fraction? *No. In general, no.*

① Text explanations are necessarily written in detail. The student should use the shortened process indicated here. Urge that he arrange his work vertically. Then the eye follows a column of equivalent fractions. Errors are minimized.

2. Subtract some number from each term of the fraction $\frac{8}{10}$. Does the resulting fraction equal $\frac{8}{10}$? *no* Can one subtract the same number from each term of a fraction without changing the value of the fraction? *In general, no.*

3. Reduce each of the following to lowest terms:

a. $\dfrac{(x+1)(x-1)}{x-1}$ *x+1*

b. $\dfrac{(x+1)(x-1)}{3x-3}$ *x+1 / 3*

c. $\dfrac{(x+1)(3x-4+x)}{3x-3}$ *4(x+1) / 3*

d. $\dfrac{(3x+3)(2x-2)}{6x-6}$ *x+1*

Simplify each of the following fractions:

4. $\dfrac{5x+5}{6x+6}$ *5/6*

5. $\dfrac{4x-28}{6x-42}$ *2/3*

6. $\dfrac{7x-21}{8x-24}$ *7/8*

7. $\dfrac{5b^2+15b}{b^2+3b}$ *5*

8. $\dfrac{m}{m^2+m}$ *1/(m+1)*

9. $\dfrac{c^2-2c-15}{c^2-c-20}$ *c+3 / c+4*

10. $\dfrac{2m^3-6m^2+2m}{m^2-3m+1}$ *2m*

11. $\dfrac{x^2-1}{x^2-2x+1}$ *x+1 / x-1*

12. $\dfrac{6x^2+11x+4}{2x^2-9x-5}$ *3x+4 / x-5*

13. $\dfrac{a^2-6ab+9b^2}{a-3b}$ *a-3b*

14. $\dfrac{R^2-r^2}{Rr+R^2}$ *R-r / R*

15. $\dfrac{m^2-mn}{m^2+mn}$ *m-n / m+n*

Simplify:

16. $\dfrac{4ab^3c}{4ab+4bc}$ *ab²c / a+c*

17. $\dfrac{2x^2+xy-3y^2}{6x^2+5xy-6y^2}$ *x-y / 3x-2y*

18. $\dfrac{12x^2+2x-24}{12x^2-31x+20}$ *2(2x+3) / 4x-5*

19. $\dfrac{xy^2-13xy+22x}{y^2-9y-22}$ *x(y-2) / y+2*

20. $\dfrac{(a+b)^2(a-b)}{a^2-b^2}$ *a+b*

[B]

21. $\dfrac{3x^3+3x^2y-6xy^2}{x^3-3x^2y+2xy^2}$ *3(x+2y) / x-2y*

22. $\dfrac{k^4-8k^3+12k^2}{k^3-4k}$ *k²(k-6) / k+2*

23. $\dfrac{5xyz+15z}{x^2y^2-xy-12}$ *5z / xy-4*

24. $\dfrac{2a^2-10a+12}{a^3-3a^2+2a}$ *2(a-3) / a(a-1)*

372 *Important.* The beginning teacher will be surprised at the frequent error of canceling terms, $\dfrac{d+b}{d}$. Here are some ways which may help correct this error, each way designed to emphasize *meaning:* Avoid the use of the word "cancel," which seems to students to mean "wipe out any two things that look alike." Keep repeating the underlying property of 1. Say, "The numerator and denominator of a fraction may be divided by the same num-

Multiplication of Fractions [A]

As we said on page 369, in algebra, as in arithmetic, the product of two or more fractions is equal to the product of the numerators divided by the product of the denominators. The resulting fraction should be reduced to lowest terms.

Example 1. $\frac{3}{4} \times \frac{4}{9} = \frac{12}{36} = \frac{1}{3}$. A shorter method: $\dfrac{\overset{1}{\cancel{3}}}{\underset{1}{\cancel{4}}} \times \dfrac{\overset{1}{\cancel{4}}}{\underset{3}{\cancel{9}}} = \frac{1}{3}$.

Example 2. Multiply 12 by $1\frac{1}{3}$.

Solution. The denominator of 12 is 1 and $1\frac{1}{3} = \frac{4}{3}$.

Then $\qquad \dfrac{\overset{4}{\cancel{12}}}{1} \times \dfrac{4}{\underset{1}{\cancel{3}}} = \dfrac{16}{1}$ or 16

Example 3. Multiply $\dfrac{7\,ab^2}{3}$ by $\dfrac{15}{14\,a^2}$.

Solution. $\qquad \dfrac{\overset{b^2}{\cancel{7\,ab^2}}}{\underset{1}{\cancel{3}}} \times \dfrac{\overset{5}{\cancel{15}}}{\underset{2\,a}{\cancel{14\,a^2}}} = \dfrac{5\,b^2}{2\,a}$

[A]

EXERCISES

Multiply:

1. $\dfrac{2}{3} \times \dfrac{1}{2}$ $\quad \frac{1}{3}$

2. $\dfrac{3}{5} \times \dfrac{5}{9}$ $\quad \frac{1}{3}$

3. $\dfrac{a}{b} \times \dfrac{b}{a}$ $\quad 1$

4. $\dfrac{1}{5}$ of 20 $\quad 4$

5. $15 \times \dfrac{2}{3}$ $\quad 10$

6. $3\frac{1}{3} \times \dfrac{3}{10}$ $\quad 1$

7. $\dfrac{2}{3} \times 4$ $\quad \frac{8}{3}$

8. $\dfrac{7}{8} \times \dfrac{7}{8}$ $\quad \frac{49}{64}$

9. $\dfrac{8}{9} \times \dfrac{9}{8}$ $\quad 1$

10. $\dfrac{4\,b}{7} \times \dfrac{1}{2\,b^2}$ $\quad \frac{2}{7b}$

11. $\dfrac{c^2}{d} \times \dfrac{1}{c}$ $\quad \frac{c}{d}$

12. $\dfrac{3\,ab}{4} \times \dfrac{12}{b^4}$ $\quad \frac{9a}{b^3}$

13. $\dfrac{4}{x} \cdot 3$ $\quad \frac{12}{x}$

14. $\left(\dfrac{a}{b}\right) b^2$ $\quad ab$

15. $x^3 \cdot \dfrac{1}{x^4}$ $\quad \frac{1}{x}$

16. $\dfrac{\pi r}{1} \cdot \dfrac{1}{R^2}$ $\quad \frac{\pi r}{R^2}$

17. $\dfrac{a}{3} \cdot \dfrac{b}{2}$ $\quad \frac{ab}{6}$

18. $\dfrac{3\,c}{2\,ab} \cdot \dfrac{5\,a}{6\,c}$ $\quad \frac{5}{4b}$

19. $\dfrac{6\,m}{15\,mn^2} \cdot \dfrac{n}{8\,m^2}$ $\quad \frac{1}{20m^2n}$

20. $\dfrac{a}{b} \cdot 20$ $\quad \frac{20a}{b}$

21. $\dfrac{3}{4}\,(12\,a^2c)$ $\quad 9a^2c$

ber (except 0) . . . ." Keep illustrating that an expression may be divided without remainder only by one of its factors. Use arithmetic. Say: " $\dfrac{6+5}{2} = \dfrac{11}{2} = 5\frac{1}{2}$. Can this be shortened as follows:

$\dfrac{\overset{3}{\cancel{6}}+5}{\underset{?}{\cancel{2}}} = 8?$ " You will find other explanations successful, as the chapter unfolds.

$\dfrac{ab^7}{4}$ **22.** $\dfrac{a}{6} \cdot \dfrac{3\,b^7}{2}$ $\dfrac{1}{3}$ **25.** $\left(\dfrac{2\,c}{7}\right)\left(\dfrac{7}{6\,c}\right)$ $\dfrac{4c^4}{15d^5}$ **28.** $\dfrac{2\,c^3}{15\,d^6} \cdot 2\,cd$

$\dfrac{40a^2}{3b}$ **23.** $\dfrac{20\,a^2}{15\,b^3} \cdot 10\,b^2$ $\dfrac{1}{ace}$ **26.** $\dfrac{1}{a} \cdot \dfrac{1}{c} \cdot \dfrac{1}{e}$ $\dfrac{1}{2}$ **29.** $\dfrac{2\,c^5}{5\,b^4} \cdot \dfrac{10\,b^4}{8\,c^5}$

$\dfrac{y^2}{m^2 nx}$ **24.** $\dfrac{x^2 y^2}{m^3 n} \cdot \dfrac{m}{x^3}$ $\dfrac{a^3}{b^3}$ **27.** $\dfrac{a^2}{b^3} \cdot \dfrac{a^2}{b} \cdot \dfrac{b}{a}$ $\dfrac{r}{st}$ **30.** $\dfrac{r^2}{c} \cdot \dfrac{c}{rst}$

Example 4. $\quad \dfrac{4\,x^2 - 25\,y^2}{3\,x - 2\,y} \cdot \dfrac{9\,x^2 - 12\,xy + 4\,y^2}{2\,x^2 - 5\,xy}$

Solution. Factoring the numerators and denominators,

$$\dfrac{\overset{1}{\cancel{(2\,x - 5\,y)}}(2\,x + 5\,y)}{\cancel{3\,x - 2\,y}} \cdot \dfrac{\overset{1}{\cancel{(3\,x - 2\,y)}}(3\,x - 2\,y)}{x\cancel{(2\,x - 5\,y)}}$$

$$= \dfrac{(2\,x + 5\,y)(3\,x - 2\,y)}{x}$$

[A]

EXERCISES   Multiply as indicated:

$\dfrac{5}{4(x-y)}$

1. $\dfrac{x + y}{8} \cdot \dfrac{10}{x^2 - y^2}$ **9.** $\dfrac{a^2 - 6\,a + 5}{a + 1} \cdot \dfrac{a + 1}{a - 5}$ $a - 1$

$\dfrac{2}{3}$ **2.** $\dfrac{a + 3}{a - 5} \cdot \dfrac{2\,a - 10}{3\,a + 9}$ **10.** $\dfrac{m^2 - 64}{8} \cdot \dfrac{24}{m^2 - 15\,m + 56}$ $\dfrac{3(m+8)}{m-7}$

$\dfrac{1}{3}$ **3.** $\dfrac{2\,a}{3\,b} \cdot \dfrac{b^2 - b}{2\,ab - 2\,a}$ **11.** $\dfrac{1 - c^2}{b^3} \cdot \dfrac{b^2}{1 - 2\,c + c^2}$ $\dfrac{1+c}{b(1-c)}$

$\dfrac{3(x-1)}{4x}$ **4.** $\dfrac{x^2 - 1}{x^2 - 2\,x} \cdot \dfrac{3\,x - 6}{4\,x + 4}$ **12.** $\dfrac{b^2 + 6\,b + 9}{3} \cdot \dfrac{4\,b + 8}{b^2 + 7\,b + 12}$

$\dfrac{3}{2(x-b)}$ **5.** $\dfrac{3\,x + 3\,b}{4\,x^2} \cdot \dfrac{2\,x^2}{x^2 - b^2}$ **13.** $\left(\dfrac{2\,m^2 + 6}{15\,y^2}\right)\left(\dfrac{21\,y^4}{3\,m^2 + 9}\right)$ $\dfrac{14y^2}{15}$

$\dfrac{7}{3}$ **6.** $\dfrac{x^2 - 4}{(x - 2)^2} \cdot \dfrac{7\,x - 14}{3\,x + 6}$ **14.** $\dfrac{2\,r^2 - 7\,r - 15}{r^2 - 10\,r + 25} \cdot \dfrac{r^2 - 25}{2\,r^2 + 13\,r + 15}$ 1

$\dfrac{2}{x-y}$ **7.** $\dfrac{(x - y)^2}{3} \cdot \dfrac{6}{(x - y)^3}$ **15.** $\dfrac{x^2 + 4}{x^2 - 4} \cdot \dfrac{(x^2 - 4)^2}{x^4 - 16}$ 1

$\dfrac{3}{4}$ **8.** $\dfrac{3\,x - 12}{4\,x + 20} \cdot \dfrac{x^2 + 5\,x}{x^2 - 4\,x}$ **16.** $\dfrac{1}{3\,x + 2}\,(6\,x^2 - 11\,x - 10)$ $2x-5$

$\rightarrow$ 12. $\dfrac{4(b+2)(b+3)}{3(b+4)}$

374

[B]

Multiply:

17. $\dfrac{m-5}{2m-1} \cdot \dfrac{2m-1}{2m+1} \cdot \dfrac{4m^2-9}{2m^2-13m+15}$ *$\dfrac{2m+3}{2m+1}$*

18. $\dfrac{3a^2-27a+60}{2a^2-72} \cdot \dfrac{3a^2-17a-6}{a^3-25a}$ *$\dfrac{3(a-4)(3a+1)}{2a(a+6)(a+5)}$*

19. $\dfrac{2b^2+bx-3x^2}{b^2-3bx-18x^2} \cdot \dfrac{2bx^2+6x^3}{3b^2-2bx-x^2}$ *$\dfrac{2x^2(2b+3x)}{(b-6x)(3b+x)}$*

20. $\dfrac{3a^2-2ax-x^2}{4a^2-5ax-x^2} \cdot \dfrac{4a^2+11ax-3x^2}{3a^2+10ax+3x^2}$ *$\dfrac{(a-x)(4a-x)}{4a^2-5ax-x^2}$*

Division of Fractions [A]

We define the division of fractions as follows:

If *a*, *b*, *c*, and *d* are real numbers and no denominator is zero, then

$$\dfrac{a}{b} \div \dfrac{c}{d} = \dfrac{a}{b} \cdot \dfrac{d}{c}.$$

We say that $\dfrac{c}{d}$ and $\dfrac{d}{c}$ are reciprocals, that is, numbers whose product is 1. $\frac{1}{7}$ is the reciprocal of 7 because $\frac{1}{7} \cdot 7 = 1$. $\frac{3}{2}$ and $\frac{2}{3}$ are reciprocals.

Example. Divide $\dfrac{b^2-c^2}{c^2-3c-4}$ by $\dfrac{b-c}{c^2+c}$.

Solution.

$$\dfrac{b^2-c^2}{c^2-3c-4} \div \dfrac{b-c}{c^2+c} = \dfrac{\overset{1}{\cancel{(b-c)}}(b+c)}{(c-4)\cancel{(c+1)}} \cdot \dfrac{\overset{1}{\cancel{c(c+1)}}}{\underset{1}{\cancel{b-c}}} = \dfrac{c(b+c)}{c-4}$$

[A]

EXERCISES

Perform the indicated divisions:

1. $\dfrac{7}{8} \div \dfrac{1}{2}$ *$\dfrac{7}{4}$*

2. $\dfrac{6}{9} \div 3$ *$\dfrac{2}{9}$*

3. $\dfrac{2}{3} \div \dfrac{5}{6}$ *$\dfrac{4}{5}$*

4. $1 \div \dfrac{b}{c}$ *$\dfrac{c}{b}$*

5. $\dfrac{a}{b} \div c$ *$\dfrac{a}{bc}$*

6. $\dfrac{m^2}{n^2} \div \dfrac{2mn}{n^2}$ *$\dfrac{m}{2n}$*

7. $\dfrac{2a}{3b} \div \dfrac{6a^2}{b^2}$ *$\dfrac{b}{9a}$*

8. $3\frac{1}{3} \div \dfrac{2a}{3}$ *$\dfrac{5}{a}$*

9. $\dfrac{a}{b} \div (2c)$ *$\dfrac{a}{2bc}$*

375

$$21. \frac{4(x-2)}{x(x-4)}$$

$$24. \frac{4x(x-2)}{3(x+3)}$$

X 10. $\dfrac{1}{x^2} \div \dfrac{1}{x^3}$

$9(x-2)$ 11. $\dfrac{3x-6}{8} \div \dfrac{1}{24}$

$\dfrac{3(a-4)^2}{50}$ 12. $\dfrac{a-4}{5} \div \dfrac{10}{3a-12}$

$\dfrac{m-1}{4}$ 13. $\dfrac{(m-1)^2}{4} \div (m-1)$

$\dfrac{ab}{a-b}$ 14. $\dfrac{ab}{(a-b)^2} \div \dfrac{1}{a-b}$

$\dfrac{3+y}{3}$ 15. $\dfrac{9-y^2}{15} \div \dfrac{3-y}{5}$

$\dfrac{4}{c}$ 16. $\dfrac{c^2-9}{c^2+3c} \div \dfrac{c-3}{4}$

$\dfrac{x}{a+x}$ 17. $\dfrac{a-x}{y} \div \dfrac{a^2-x^2}{xy}$

18. $1 \div \dfrac{x-y}{x+y}$ $\dfrac{x+y}{x-y}$

19. $\dfrac{(a-3b)^2}{a^2-9b^2} \div \dfrac{a-3b}{a+3b}$ 1

20. $\dfrac{x^2+7x+6}{x^2+6x+5} \div \dfrac{x^3+6x^2}{x^2+5x}$ $\dfrac{1}{x}$

21. $\dfrac{x^2-7x+10}{x^2+3x} \div \dfrac{x^2-9x+20}{4x+12}$

22. $\dfrac{m^2-6m+5}{m-1} \div \dfrac{m-5}{m-1}$ $m-1$

23. $\dfrac{x^2+2xy+y^2}{x^2-2xy-3y^2} \div \dfrac{x+y}{x-3y}$ 1

24. $\dfrac{r^2-9r+14}{r^2+7r+12} \div \dfrac{3r^2-21r}{4r^3+16r^2}$

25. $\dfrac{3(a+b)}{4c^2} \div \dfrac{6(a^2-b^2)}{cd}$ $\dfrac{d}{8c(a-b)}$

[B]

Divide:

$2(x^2+1)$

26. $\dfrac{x^4-1}{3} \div \dfrac{x^2-1}{6}$

$4(x^2+y^2)$

27. $\dfrac{x^4-y^4}{x+y} \div \dfrac{x^2-y^2}{4x+4y}$

$\dfrac{x^2-3xy-2y^2}{(x-2y)(x-y)}$

28. $\dfrac{bx+by}{x-2y} \div \dfrac{bx^2-by^2}{x^2-3xy-2y^2}$

$\dfrac{(x-2)(x+1)}{x(x+2)(x-1)}$

29. $\dfrac{2x^3-2x^2-4x}{3x^2-3x-18} \div \dfrac{4x^3-4x^2}{6x-18}$

$\dfrac{(x-2)^2}{5(x+2)}$

30. $\dfrac{x^3+4x-4x^2}{x^3-2x^2} \div \dfrac{5x^2+20x+20}{x^3-4x}$

$\dfrac{a-2b}{a-b}$

31. $\dfrac{a+b}{a-b} \cdot \dfrac{a-2b}{a+2b} \div \dfrac{a+b}{a+2b}$

$\dfrac{3(a+2b)^2}{4(a-b)(a-2b)}$

32. $\dfrac{a+b}{a-b} \div \dfrac{a-2b}{a+2b} \cdot \dfrac{3a+6b}{4a+4b}$

NOTE. Be sure to use the reciprocal of the divisor.

Addition and Subtraction of Fractions [A]

In adding fractions we must remember that only fractions with like denominators can be added. This is true in algebra as in arithmetic.

Study each example, writing the steps as you go.

Example 1. Add: $\frac{1}{2} + \frac{2}{3}$

Solution. We see that the denominators 2 and 3 are both factors of 6. Consequently we change both $\frac{1}{2}$ and $\frac{2}{3}$ to fractions with the denominator 6.

$$\frac{1}{2} = \frac{1}{2}(1)$$
$$\frac{1}{2} = \frac{1}{2}(\frac{3}{3})$$
$$\frac{1}{2} = \frac{3}{6}$$

Similarly,
$$\frac{2}{3} = \frac{2}{3}(1)$$
$$\frac{2}{3} = \frac{2}{3}(\frac{2}{2})$$
$$\frac{2}{3} = \frac{4}{6}$$

Consequently, $\frac{1}{2} + \frac{2}{3} = \frac{3}{6} + \frac{4}{6} = \frac{7}{6}$

1. To add (or subtract) fractions, change them, if necessary, to equal fractions having the same denominator.
2. Then place the sum (or difference) of the numerators over the common denominator.
3. Reduce the result to lowest terms.

Example 2. Combine: $\frac{3}{5} + \frac{7}{5}$

Solution. The fractions have the same denominator. Then
$$\frac{3}{5} + \frac{7}{5} = \frac{10}{5} \text{ or } 2.$$

Example 3. Simplify $\dfrac{a}{3b} - \dfrac{4a}{3b}$.

Solution. $\dfrac{a}{3b} - \dfrac{4a}{3b} = \dfrac{-3a}{3b} = -\dfrac{a}{b}$

Example 4. $\dfrac{4}{b} + \dfrac{3}{b} = \dfrac{7}{b}$.

Suitable for oral work. Watch for reduction of fractions in final answers. Note the analogy between arithmetic and algebra.

ALGEBRA, BOOK ONE

EXERCISES

[A]

Add or subtract as indicated. Be sure your answer is in its simplest form.

2

1. $\dfrac{2}{3}+\dfrac{4}{3}$ $\dfrac{7}{a}$ **6.** $\dfrac{2}{a}+\dfrac{5}{a}$ $\dfrac{1}{x+1}$ **11.** $\dfrac{3}{x+1}-\dfrac{2}{x+1}$

1

2. $\dfrac{2}{15}+\dfrac{13}{15}$ $\dfrac{2}{x}$ **7.** $\dfrac{5}{x}-\dfrac{3}{x}$ $\dfrac{4}{x-y}$ **12.** $\dfrac{7}{x-y}-\dfrac{3}{x-y}$

$\dfrac{2}{3}$

3. $\dfrac{7}{12}+\dfrac{1}{12}$ $\dfrac{3}{a}$ **8.** $\dfrac{1}{2a}+\dfrac{5}{2a}$ 1   **13.** $\dfrac{a}{a+b}+\dfrac{b}{a+b}$

2

4. $\dfrac{14}{15}+\dfrac{16}{15}$ $\dfrac{a+b}{c}$ **9.** $\dfrac{a}{c}+\dfrac{b}{c}$ 2   **14.** $\dfrac{2x}{x-1}-\dfrac{2}{x-1}$

$\dfrac{2}{3}$

5. $\dfrac{7}{9}-\dfrac{1}{9}$ $\dfrac{-4}{5y}$ **10.** $\dfrac{2}{5y}-\dfrac{6}{5y}$ $2x+1$ **15.** $\dfrac{4x^2}{2x-1}-\dfrac{1}{2x-1}$

Example 5. Simplify $\dfrac{x}{6}+\dfrac{2x}{9}$

Solution. Before these two fractions can be added, they must be changed to equal fractions which have the same denominator. It saves time to change them to equal fractions which have the *lowest* common denominator. The smallest number that can be exactly divided by 6 and 9 is 18. Since the denominator 6 must be multiplied by 3 to give 18, the fraction $\dfrac{x}{6}$ should be multiplied by $\dfrac{3}{3}$. Then $\dfrac{x}{6}=\dfrac{3x}{18}$. Since the denominator 9 must be multiplied by 2 to give 18, the fraction $\dfrac{2x}{9}$ should be multiplied by $\dfrac{2}{2}$. Then $\dfrac{2x}{9}=\dfrac{4x}{18}$. The solution is written as follows:

$$\frac{x}{6}+\frac{2x}{9}=\frac{3x}{18}+\frac{4x}{18}=\frac{7x}{18}$$

Example 6. Simplify $4+\dfrac{a}{b}$.

Solution. The denominator of 4 is 1. The L.C.D. is b. Then

$$\frac{4}{1}+\frac{a}{b}=\frac{4b}{b}+\frac{a}{b}=\frac{4b+a}{b}$$

378 Students should write all steps as in Example 6 until confident and accurate enough to take short cuts.

Simplify:

1. $1 + \dfrac{c}{d}$ $\dfrac{c+d}{d}$

2. $\dfrac{1}{2} + \dfrac{5}{6}$ $\dfrac{4}{3}$

3. $8 + \dfrac{1}{3}$ $\dfrac{25}{3}$

4. $\dfrac{1}{a} + \dfrac{1}{b}$ $\dfrac{a+b}{ab}$

5. $\dfrac{1}{x} + 6$ $\dfrac{1+6x}{x}$

6. $\dfrac{m}{n} + \dfrac{1}{n}$ $\dfrac{m+1}{n}$

7. $\dfrac{a}{b} + 1$ $\dfrac{a+b}{b}$

8. $m + \dfrac{1}{n}$ $\dfrac{mn+1}{n}$

9. $\dfrac{2a}{3} - \dfrac{a}{5}$ $\dfrac{7a}{15}$

10. $\dfrac{3x}{4} - \dfrac{5x}{6}$ $\dfrac{-x}{12}$

11. $\dfrac{x}{y} + \dfrac{y}{x}$ $\dfrac{x^2+y^2}{xy}$

12. $\dfrac{x}{2y} - \dfrac{4}{y^2}$ $\dfrac{xy-8}{2y^2}$

13. $\dfrac{2a}{3} - \dfrac{a}{2} + \dfrac{a}{4}$ $\dfrac{5a}{12}$

14. $\dfrac{5m}{6} - \dfrac{5m}{12} - \dfrac{m}{3}$ $\dfrac{m}{12}$

15. $\dfrac{1}{m} + \dfrac{1}{n} + \dfrac{1}{p}$ $\dfrac{np+mp+mn}{mnp}$

16. $\dfrac{4}{a^2} + \dfrac{3}{a} + \dfrac{5}{a^3}$ $\dfrac{4a+3a^2+5}{a^3}$

Example 7. Combine: $\dfrac{a-3}{4} + \dfrac{2a-1}{5} - \dfrac{2a+15}{3}$

Solution. The L.C.D. $= 4 \times 5 \times 3 = 60$. When the denominators have no common factor, the L.C.D. is their product.

$$\dfrac{a-3}{4} + \dfrac{2a-1}{5} - \dfrac{2a+15}{3}$$

$$= \dfrac{15(a-3)}{60} + \dfrac{12(2a-1)}{60} - \dfrac{20(2a+15)}{60}$$

$$= \dfrac{15(a-3) + 12(2a-1) - 20(2a+15)}{60}$$

$$= \dfrac{15a - 45 + 24a - 12 - 40a - 300}{60}$$

$$= \dfrac{-a - 357}{60} \text{ or } -\dfrac{a+357}{60}$$

Example 7 serves as a guide for form of work. Point out that a good check in step 1 is to reduce mentally the derived fractions to test their equivalence to the originals.

Your best students may be able to omit some of these steps soon.

ALGEBRA, BOOK ONE *(answers at left margin)*

[A]

Left margin answers:

$\dfrac{4a+1}{6}$

$\dfrac{4a+30}{15}$

$\dfrac{9x+20y}{30}$

$\dfrac{6x+1}{36}$

$\dfrac{5x+y}{6}$

$\dfrac{-3a+11b}{20}$

$\dfrac{x^2+11xy}{60}$

$\dfrac{-b+12c}{36}$

$\dfrac{8x-16}{3x}$

10. $\dfrac{a^2-2b^2}{ab^2}$

11. $\dfrac{3b-3}{2a}$

12. $\dfrac{x^2-8x+1}{6x^2}$

13. $\dfrac{23a^2-20a-5}{14a^2}$

14. $\dfrac{5p^2+86p+4}{30p^2}$

15. $\dfrac{-20x^2+21x+2}{10x^2}$

16. $\dfrac{7a-8b}{12}$

17. $\dfrac{5m^2-2mn+2m-1}{m^2n}$

18. $\dfrac{r+s}{rs}$

19. $\dfrac{ab-a}{b^2}$

EXERCISES

Combine:

1. $\dfrac{a-1}{3}+\dfrac{2a+3}{6}$

2. $\dfrac{3a+5}{5}-\dfrac{a-3}{3}$

3. $\dfrac{5x+2y}{10}-\dfrac{3x-7y}{15}$

4. $\dfrac{4x-5}{12}-\dfrac{3x-8}{18}$

5. $\dfrac{x+y}{2}+\dfrac{x-y}{3}$

6. $\dfrac{a+3b}{4}-\dfrac{2a+b}{5}$

7. $\dfrac{x^2+xy}{10}-\dfrac{x^2-xy}{12}$

8. $\dfrac{2b+3c}{18}-\dfrac{5b-6c}{36}$

9. $\dfrac{2x-1}{3x}+\dfrac{4x-10}{2x}$

The L.C.D. is $6x$.

10. $\dfrac{3a-2b}{ab}-\dfrac{3b-a}{b^2}$

11. $\dfrac{a+b-1}{a}-\dfrac{2a-b+1}{2a}$

12. $\dfrac{3x^2-4x+1}{6x^2}-\dfrac{x+2}{3x}$

13. $\dfrac{2a-5}{14a^2}-\dfrac{4-a}{7a}+\dfrac{3a-2}{2a}$

14. $\dfrac{2p+1}{3p}-\dfrac{p-5}{2p}+\dfrac{p+4}{30p^2}$

15. $\dfrac{3x+1}{5x^2}-\dfrac{4x-3}{2x}$

16. $\dfrac{3a-2b}{4}-\dfrac{a+b}{6}$

17. $\dfrac{5m-2n}{mn}-\dfrac{1-2m}{m^2n}$

18. $\dfrac{1-r}{r}+\dfrac{1+s}{s}$

19. $\dfrac{a-b}{b}+\dfrac{b^2-a}{b^2}$

Example 8. Combine: $\dfrac{3}{a-b}+\dfrac{4}{a+2b}$

Solution. Since $a-b$ and $a+2b$ have no common factor, the L.C.D. is $(a-b)(a+2b)$.

$$\dfrac{3}{a-b}+\dfrac{4}{a+2b}$$

$$=\dfrac{3(a+2b)}{(a-b)(a+2b)}+\dfrac{4(a-b)}{(a-b)(a+2b)}$$

$$=\dfrac{3(a+2b)+4(a-b)}{(a-b)(a+2b)}$$

$$=\dfrac{3a+6b+4a-4b}{(a-b)(a+2b)}$$

$$=\dfrac{7a+2b}{(a-b)(a+2b)}$$

380

[A]

Combine:

1. $\dfrac{a+3}{a+2}+\dfrac{2a-1}{a+4}$ $\dfrac{3a^2+10a+10}{(a+2)(a+4)}$

5. $\dfrac{2}{x-1}-\dfrac{3}{x+1}$ $\dfrac{-x+5}{(x+1)(x-1)}$

2. $\dfrac{x-2}{3}+\dfrac{3}{x-2}$ $\dfrac{x^2-4x+13}{3(x-2)}$

6. $\dfrac{a}{a+2b}-\dfrac{3a}{a-b}$ $\dfrac{-2a^2-7ab}{(a-b)(a+2b)}$

3. $\dfrac{1}{x+2}-\dfrac{2}{x-3}$ $\dfrac{-x-7}{(x+2)(x-3)}$

7. $\dfrac{x}{x-5}+\dfrac{2x}{x+5}$ $\dfrac{3x^2-5x}{(x-5)(x+5)}$

4. $\dfrac{b}{a+b}-\dfrac{a}{a-b}$ $\dfrac{-a^2-b^2}{(a+b)(a-b)}$

8. $\dfrac{c}{c-6}-\dfrac{c}{c+6}$ $\dfrac{12c}{(c-6)(c+6)}$

Example 9. Combine: $\dfrac{1}{3a-6}+\dfrac{1}{6a}-\dfrac{1}{2a+4}$

Solution.

$\dfrac{1}{3a-6}+\dfrac{1}{6a}-\dfrac{1}{2a+4}$

$=\dfrac{1}{3(a-2)}+\dfrac{1}{6a}-\dfrac{1}{2(a+2)}$ The L.C.D. is $6\,a(a-2)(a+2)$.

$=\dfrac{(2\,a)(a+2)1}{6\,a(a-2)(a+2)}+\dfrac{(a-2)(a+2)1}{6\,a(a-2)(a+2)}-\dfrac{3\,a(a-2)1}{6\,a(a-2)(a+2)}$

$=\dfrac{2\,a(a+2)+(a-2)(a+2)-3\,a(a-2)}{6\,a(a-2)(a+2)}$

$=\dfrac{2\,a^2+4\,a+a^2-4-3\,a^2+6\,a}{6\,a(a-2)(a+2)}$

$=\dfrac{10\,a-4}{6\,a(a-2)(a+2)}=\dfrac{\overset{1}{\cancel{2}}(5\,a-2)}{\underset{1}{\cancel{2}}(3\,a)(a-2)(a+2)}$

$=\dfrac{5\,a-2}{3\,a(a-2)(a+2)}$

[B]

Combine:

1. $\dfrac{a}{a+1}+\dfrac{a^2}{a^2-1}$ $\dfrac{2a^2-a}{(a+1)(a-1)}$

4. $\dfrac{1}{6a-12}-\dfrac{4}{a-2}$ $\dfrac{-23}{6(a-2)}$

2. $\dfrac{3a}{a^2-4}+\dfrac{4}{a-2}$ $\dfrac{7a+8}{(a+2)(a-2)}$

5. $\dfrac{5}{a^2-1}+\dfrac{a+2}{3}$ $\dfrac{a^3+2a^2-a+13}{3(a^2-1)}$

3. $\dfrac{4x}{x+1}-\dfrac{3x^2}{x^2-1}$ $\dfrac{x^2-4x}{(x+1)(x-1)}$

6. $\dfrac{2h}{h^2-3h-4}+\dfrac{1}{h-4}$ $\dfrac{3h+1}{(h+1)(h-4)}$

Sections B and C are difficult and could be assigned to better students instead of some exercises in the "A" sections.

381

$\dfrac{4a^2-8a-5}{(a+3)(a-4)}$

$\dfrac{-4y+32}{(y+9)(y-6)}$

$\dfrac{-11m-8}{18m(m-1)}$

$\dfrac{7x-9}{(x+1)(x-1)}$

9. $\dfrac{2a^2+2ab+2b^2}{(a+b)(a-b)}$

10. $\dfrac{5c+7}{(c+6)(c-3)}$

7. $\dfrac{3a}{a+3}+\dfrac{a^2+4a-5}{a^2-a-12}$

8. $\dfrac{y+2}{y^2+3y-54}-\dfrac{5}{y+9}$

9. $\dfrac{a+b}{a-b}+\dfrac{a^2+b^2}{a^2-b^2}$

10. $\dfrac{3c-5}{c^2+3c-18}+\dfrac{2}{c-3}$

Combine:

$\dfrac{6x}{(x-4)(x-2)(x+4)}$ [C]

11. $\dfrac{2m-4}{9m^2-9m}-\dfrac{5}{6m-6}$

12. $\dfrac{5x}{x^2+x}+\dfrac{2x-4}{x^2-1}$

13. $\dfrac{x}{x^2-6x+8}-\dfrac{x}{x^2-16}$

14. $\dfrac{4}{x^2-16}-\dfrac{2}{x^2-8x+16}$

$\dfrac{2x-24}{(x+4)(x-4)^2}$

15. $\dfrac{y}{x^2+xy}-\dfrac{x}{xy+y^2}$ $\quad \dfrac{y-x}{xy}$

16. $\dfrac{a-4b}{a^2-7ab+12b^2}-\dfrac{a-3b}{a^2-ab-12b^2}$ $\quad \dfrac{5ab-21b^2}{(a-3b)(a-4b)(a+3b)}$

17. $\dfrac{a-1}{a+1}+\dfrac{a+1}{a-1}-\dfrac{2a^2+2}{a^2-1}$ $\quad 0$

18. $\dfrac{4}{x-2}+\dfrac{5}{x-3}-\dfrac{7}{x^2-5x+6}$ $\quad \dfrac{9x-29}{(x-3)(x-2)}$

19. $\dfrac{a}{a-b}+\dfrac{b}{a+b}+\dfrac{b^2-2ab}{a^2-b^2}$ $\quad \dfrac{a^2}{(a-b)(a+b)}$

20. $\dfrac{x-1}{x+2}-\dfrac{x+1}{x-2}+\dfrac{6x}{x^2-4}$ $\quad 0$

ADDITIONAL DRILL ①

Simplify: (ans. 10-15 at foot of page) [A]

$\dfrac{17x}{20}$ **1.** $\dfrac{3x}{5}+\dfrac{x}{4}$ **6.** $\dfrac{3c}{10}-\dfrac{4c}{12}$ $\dfrac{-c}{30}$ **11.** $\dfrac{3x-1}{3}-\dfrac{x}{4}$

$\dfrac{2y}{7}$ **2.** $\dfrac{3y}{7}-\dfrac{y}{7}$ **7.** $\dfrac{4x}{7}-\dfrac{9x}{10}$ $\dfrac{-23x}{70}$ **12.** $\dfrac{3c+2}{9}-\dfrac{c-5}{6}$

$\dfrac{7x}{10}$ **3.** $\dfrac{4x}{5}-\dfrac{x}{10}$ **8.** $\dfrac{2n}{5}-\dfrac{3n}{20}$ $\dfrac{n}{4}$ **13.** $\dfrac{3x-1}{4x^2}+\dfrac{2}{5x}$

$\dfrac{7y}{24}$ **4.** $\dfrac{3y}{8}-\dfrac{y}{12}$ **9.** $\dfrac{x}{4}-\dfrac{x}{3}$ $\dfrac{-x}{12}$ **14.** $\dfrac{a}{c}-\dfrac{a+n}{c+n}$

$\dfrac{a+2b}{6}$ **5.** $\dfrac{a}{6}+\dfrac{b}{3}$ **10.** $\dfrac{2a-1}{4}+\dfrac{3a+2}{6}$ **15.** $\dfrac{c^2}{c+3}-\dfrac{3c}{c-3}$

10. $\dfrac{12a+1}{12}$ 12. $\dfrac{3c+19}{18}$ 14. $\dfrac{an-cn}{c(c+n)}$

11. $\dfrac{9x-4}{12}$ 13. $\dfrac{23x-5}{20x^2}$ 15. $\dfrac{c^3-6c^2-9c}{(c+3)(c-3)}$

16. $\dfrac{3a^2 - 7ab + b^2}{(a+b)(a-b)}$

17. $\dfrac{-3x+1}{(x+2)(x-3)}$

Simplify: (ans. above)

16. $\dfrac{a^2 + b^2}{a^2 - b^2} + \dfrac{2a}{a+b}$

17. $\dfrac{x^2 + 3}{x^2 - x - 6} - \dfrac{x+1}{x-3}$

18. $\dfrac{c^2}{c^2 - 3c - 18} + \dfrac{6}{c-6}$

18. $\dfrac{c^2 + 6c + 18}{(c-6)(c+3)}$

19. $\dfrac{2x^2}{(1-x)(1+x)}$

19. $\dfrac{x}{1-x} - \dfrac{x}{1+x}$

20. $\dfrac{m}{3m+2} - \dfrac{m+1}{6m^2 + 13m + 6}$

20. $\dfrac{2m^2 + 2m - 1}{(3m+2)(2m+3)}$

FRACTIONS

[B]

21. $\dfrac{c^2 + 6c - 31}{30(c-1)(c+3)}$

21. $\dfrac{c-2}{5c-5} - \dfrac{c+1}{6c+18}$

[C]

Simplify:

22. $\dfrac{5}{2a-4} - \dfrac{3}{6a-12} - \dfrac{2}{3a+6}$ $\dfrac{4a+16}{3(a-2)(a+2)}$

23. $\dfrac{a+b}{a-b} - \dfrac{a-b}{a+b} - \dfrac{4ab}{a^2 - b^2}$ 0

24. $\dfrac{m+3}{2m^2 + 5m - 3} + \dfrac{m-2}{4m^2 - 1}$ $\dfrac{3m-1}{(2m-1)(2m+1)}$

25. $\dfrac{c}{c^2 + 2c - 3} - \dfrac{5c-1}{5c^2 + 17c + 6}$ $\dfrac{8c-1}{(c-1)(c+3)(5c+2)}$

Changing Common Fractions to Decimal Fractions [A]

We often find it necessary to change common fractions to decimal fractions.

Example. Change $\frac{3}{8}$ to a decimal fraction.

Solution. The fraction $\frac{3}{8}$ means that 3 is to be divided by 8. So we divide 3 by 8 and get 0.375.

$$\begin{array}{r} 0.375 \\ 8\overline{)3.000} \end{array}$$

[A]

Change the following to decimal fractions:

EXERCISES

1. $\frac{3}{5}$ 0.6
2. $\frac{3}{4}$ 0.75
3. $\frac{5}{4}$ 1.25

4. $\frac{13}{4}$ 3.25
5. $\frac{9}{100}$ 0.09
6. $\frac{32}{10}$ 3.2

7. $\frac{9}{50}$ 0.18
8. $\frac{5}{8}$ 0.625
9. $\frac{7}{32}$ 0.21875

10. $\frac{9}{64}$ 0.140625
11. $1\frac{5}{8}$ 1.625
12. $1\frac{7}{8}$ 1.875 (1)

Changing Decimal Fractions to Common Fractions and Mixed Numbers [A]

Example. Change 3.625 to a mixed number.

Solution. $3.625 = 3 + \frac{625}{1000} = 3 + \frac{5}{8} = 3\frac{5}{8}$

(1) Review for those weak in arithmetic. Use as class work, preferably.

383

[A]

EXERCISES Change to common fractions or mixed numbers:

$\frac{1}{2}$ **1.** 0.5 $\frac{4}{5}$ **4.** 0.8 $\frac{1}{8}$ **7.** .125 $\frac{17}{40}$ **10.** .425

$\frac{3}{4}$ **2.** 0.75 $\frac{3}{25}$ **5.** 0.12 $1\frac{1}{4}$ **8.** 1.25 $\frac{5}{16}$ **11.** 3125

$\frac{9}{20}$ **3.** 0.45 $\frac{3}{8}$ **6.** .375 $\frac{5}{8}$ **9.** .625 $1\frac{4}{13}$ **12.** 1.33$\frac{1}{3}$

The Three Signs of a Fraction [B]

Every fraction has three signs associated with it: the sign of the numerator, the sign of the denominator, and the sign of the fraction proper. When these signs are omitted, they are understood to be plus. Thus the fraction $\frac{3}{4}$ means $+\frac{+3}{+4}$. Consider the four fractions below.

$$+\frac{+8}{+2} = +(+4) = 4 \qquad\qquad -\frac{-8}{+2} = -(-4) = 4$$

$$+\frac{-8}{-2} = +(+4) = 4 \qquad\qquad -\frac{+8}{-2} = -(-4) = 4$$

The value of each fraction is 4. Each of the four fractions may be obtained from any one of the others by changing two of the three signs. These fractions illustrate the following rule:

The value of a fraction is not changed

1. If the sign of the numerator and the sign of the denominator are changed (if both terms are multiplied by -1). (Why?)
Or,
2. If the sign of the fraction and the sign of either the numerator or the denominator are changed.

Briefly, this rule may be stated as follows:

Any two of the three signs of a fraction may be changed without changing the value of the fraction.

[B]

EXERCISES ORAL Tell whether each statement is true or false:

True **1.** $+\frac{-8}{2} = -\frac{+8}{+2}$ *False* **3.** $-\frac{-a}{-b} = \frac{-a}{-b}$

True **2.** $\frac{-a}{-b} = \frac{a}{b}$ *False* **4.** $-\frac{m}{-n} = \frac{-m}{n}$

Note that pages 384–387 are designated B and C. This work will be needed by all who take second-year algebra. Although helpful this year, it can be omitted in classes who are having a hard time with fractions, or it can be studied independently by the few best students, while others are reviewing.

5. $\dfrac{c}{d} = -\dfrac{-c}{d}$ *True*

7. $\dfrac{-3}{4} = \dfrac{3}{4}$ *False*

6. $\dfrac{5}{-6} = \dfrac{-5}{6}$ *True*

8. $\dfrac{6}{-7} = -\dfrac{-6}{7}$ *False*

Example 1. Change $\dfrac{a-b}{c-d}$ to an equal fraction whose denominator is $d - c$.

  Solution. The denominator $c - d$ is to have the signs of its terms changed, or to be multiplied by -1. In this way we change the sign of the denominator. Then either the numerator or the fraction must have its sign changed. If we change the sign of the numerator, we must change the signs of all its terms.

Then $\qquad \dfrac{a-b}{c-d} = +\dfrac{b-a}{d-c},$ or $-\dfrac{a-b}{d-c}$

  Notice that the terms were rearranged after their signs were changed.

If either the numerator or the denominator of a fraction is a polynomial, you should remember that the sign of a polynomial is changed by changing all its signs, or by multiplying it by -1.

[B]

EXERCISES

Find the missing terms:

1. $\dfrac{a-3}{b-2} = +\dfrac{?}{2-b}$ *3- a*

5. $\dfrac{x-y}{b} = -\dfrac{?}{b}$ *y -x*

2. $\dfrac{c-d}{x-y} = -\dfrac{c-d}{?}$ *y-x*

6. $\dfrac{6}{2-y} = \dfrac{?}{y-2}$ *- 6*

3. $\dfrac{4-a}{x-y} = +\dfrac{?}{y-x}$ *a-4*

7. $-\dfrac{a^2-2b}{a^2-b^2} = +\dfrac{?}{a^2-b^2}$ *2b -a²*

4. $\dfrac{4}{a-b} = +\dfrac{?}{b-a}$ *- 4*

8. $\dfrac{a^2+b^2}{a^2-4} = -\dfrac{?}{4-a^2}$ *a² +b²*

It is often convenient to arrange the numerator and denominator of a fraction in descending (or ascending) powers of one letter or to make the first terms of the numerator and denominator positive.

Example 2. Reduce $\dfrac{x^2-6x}{24+2x-x^2}$ to lowest terms.

  Solution. We shall arrange the denominator in descending powers of x to agree with the numerator.

385

Then
$$\frac{x^2-6x}{24+2x-x^2}=\frac{x^2-6x}{-x^2+2x+24}$$

To make the solution easier we should have the first term of the denominator positive. Then, changing the sign of the denominator by multiplying each of its terms by -1, the denominator becomes $x^2-2x-24$. We do not wish to change the sign of the numerator, so we shall change the sign of the fraction proper. Then

$$\frac{x^2-6x}{24+2x-x^2}=-\frac{x^2-6x}{x^2-2x-24}=-\frac{x\overset{1}{\cancel{(x-6)}}}{\underset{1}{\cancel{(x-6)}}(x+4)}=-\frac{x}{x+4}$$

[B]

EXERCISES

Following the plan in Example 2, simplify these fractions: ①

1. $\dfrac{a^2-4a+3}{3-a}$ $-(a-1),$ or $1-a$

2. $\dfrac{x^2+x-12}{4-47x-12x^2}$ $\dfrac{3-x}{12x-1}$

3. $\dfrac{1-x^2}{3x^2-6x+3}$ $\dfrac{x+1}{3(1-x)}$

4. $\dfrac{(n-m)^2}{m^2+2mn-3n^2}$ $\dfrac{m-n}{m+3n}$

5. $\dfrac{4a-4b}{b^2-a^2}$ $-\dfrac{4}{a+b}$

6. $\dfrac{x^2-6x+9}{9-x^2}$ $\dfrac{3-x}{x+3}$

Example 3. Combine: $\dfrac{x+3}{x+1}+\dfrac{x+2}{1-x}+\dfrac{x^2+3}{x^2-1}$

Solution. The denominator of the second fraction should be rearranged.

$$\frac{x+2}{1-x}=\frac{x+2}{-x+1}=-\frac{x+2}{x-1}$$

Then
$$\frac{x+3}{x+1}-\frac{x+2}{x-1}+\frac{x^2+3}{(x+1)(x-1)}$$

$$=\frac{(x+3)(x-1)}{(x+1)(x-1)}-\frac{(x+1)(x+2)}{(x+1)(x-1)}+\frac{x^2+3}{(x+1)(x-1)}$$

$$=\frac{(x+3)(x-1)-(x+1)(x+2)+(x^2+3)}{(x+1)(x-1)}$$

$$=\frac{(x^2+2x-3)-(x^2+3x+2)+(x^2+3)}{(x+1)(x-1)}$$

$$=\frac{x^2+2x-3-x^2-3x-2+x^2+3}{(x+1)(x-1)}$$

$$=\frac{x^2-x-2}{(x+1)(x-1)}=\frac{(x-2)\overset{1}{\cancel{(x+1)}}}{\cancel{(x+1)}(x-1)}=\frac{x-2}{x-1}$$

① Discuss method if factored first, thus: $\dfrac{x(x-6)}{(4+x)(6-x)}$.

386 Since $\dfrac{x-6}{6-x}=-1$, we have $\dfrac{x}{4+x}(-1)$, or $-\dfrac{x}{4+x}$.

Also, as taught in the factoring section (see notes there), $(x-2)(x-3)=(2-x)(3-x)=$ $-(2-x)(x-3)=-(x-2)(3-x)$. Discuss how the value of an expression is affected by changing the signs of an even number of factors; of an odd number.

1. $\dfrac{2x^2 + 2xy + 2y^2 + x - y}{(x+y)(x-y)}$

$\dfrac{-2a-11}{(a-5)(a+4)}$ ← 2.

3. $\dfrac{9a^2 + 13a + 24}{4(a-1)(a+1)}$

4. $\dfrac{4x-48}{(x+5)(x-5)}$

[C]

FRACTIONS

EXERCISES

Combine: *(ans. above)*

1. $\dfrac{x+y}{x-y} + \dfrac{1}{x+y} - \dfrac{x^2+y^2}{y^2-x^2}$

2. $\dfrac{a^2+5a+1}{a^2-a-20} + \dfrac{a+3}{5-a}$

3. $\dfrac{4a}{a-1} + \dfrac{3a}{4-4a} - \dfrac{a^2-6}{a^2-1}$

4. $\dfrac{x-3}{x^2-25} + \dfrac{6}{x+5} + \dfrac{3}{5-x}$

Simplify:

5. $\dfrac{x^2-2x-8}{x^2-x^4} \times \dfrac{x^2-4x+4}{5x^2-30x+40}$ $-\dfrac{(x+2)(x-2)}{5x^2(x+1)(x-1)}$

6. $\dfrac{abx^2-aby^2}{x^2+2xy+y^2} \div \dfrac{x^2-2xy+y^2}{y^2-xy}$ $-\dfrac{aby}{x+y}$

See how many of these twenty exercises you can do correctly in 35 minutes:

PRACTICE TEST

1. $(-5a)(-3a^4) = ?$ $15a^5$
2. $(-2x)^3 = ?$ $-8x^3$
3. $(5x-1)(x^2+3x-3) = ?$
    $5x^3+14x^2-18x+3$

Factor:
4. $x^2 - 7xy + 12y^2$ $(x-4y)(x-3y)$
5. $8x^2 - 2x - 15$ $(4x+5)(2x-3)$
6. $8a^2 - 12ab$ $4a(2a-3b)$
7. $25c^2 - d^2$ $(5c+d)(5c-d)$
8. $2ay^2 + 14ay + 24a$
    $2a(y+4)(y+3)$

9. Solve $\frac{3}{5}c - \frac{1}{4}c = 1$. $2\frac{6}{7}$
10. $F = \frac{9}{5}C + 32$. Find F when $C = -40$. -40

Simplify:

11. $4a(a-b) - a^2$ $3a^2-4ab$
12. $2a - 3(a+1) - a$ -3
13. $\dfrac{4a}{8a^3}$ $\dfrac{1}{2a^2}$
14. $\dfrac{3x^2-3x}{x^2-1}$ $\dfrac{3x}{x+1}$
15. $\dfrac{c^2+c-2}{c^2+2c} \cdot \dfrac{c^2}{c-1}$ c
16. $\dfrac{y^2-5y+6}{y+4} \div (y-3)$ $\dfrac{y-2}{y+4}$
17. $\dfrac{2a+3b}{4b} - \dfrac{a+5b}{6b}$ $\dfrac{4a-b}{12b}$
18. $\dfrac{7x}{9} - \dfrac{5x-2}{6}$ $\dfrac{-x+6}{18}$
19. $\dfrac{y+2}{2y-18} - \dfrac{3y-1}{y-9}$ $\dfrac{-5y+4}{2(y-9)}$
20. $\dfrac{x+2}{x-2} + \dfrac{x-2}{x+2} - \dfrac{2x^2+2y^2}{x^2-4}$ $\dfrac{8-2y}{(x+2)(x-2)}$

① A good review exercise to check before proceeding.

① Remind students that in arithmetic we abbreviate $4 + \frac{3}{4}$ as $4\frac{3}{4}$, saying but not writing the "and."
Ask why this is impossible in algebraic fractions. Some may have said "4 × 5 + 3 over 5" for
so long that they have forgotten the meaning. Remind them that "4" means "4/1."

ALGEBRA, BOOK ONE

Changing Mixed Numbers to Fractions[A]

A mixed number consists of a whole number and a fraction. For example, $3\frac{2}{5}$, $1\frac{2}{3}$, and $a + \frac{1}{b}$ are mixed numbers. Notice that the plus sign is omitted in the arithmetic mixed numbers, but is not omitted in the algebraic mixed number. A mixed number is changed into a simple fraction by adding the whole number and the fraction.

Example 1. $4\frac{3}{5} = 4 + \frac{3}{5} = \frac{4}{1} + \frac{3}{5} = \frac{20}{5} + \frac{3}{5} = \frac{23}{5}$

Example 2. $a + \frac{b}{c} = \frac{a}{1} + \frac{b}{c} = \frac{ac}{c} + \frac{b}{c} = \frac{ac+b}{c}$

Example 3.

$$x + 3 - \frac{2x}{x-1} = \frac{x+3}{1} - \frac{2x}{x-1} = \frac{(x+3)(x-1)}{x-1} - \frac{2x}{x-1}$$

$$= \frac{(x+3)(x-1) - 2x}{x-1} = \frac{x^2 + 2x - 3 - 2x}{x-1}$$

$$= \frac{x^2 - 3}{x-1}$$

Some of the steps in the examples above can be done mentally.

EXERCISES

[A]

Change the following mixed expressions into common fractions: *(Ans. 10–15 at foot of page)*

$\frac{71}{10}$ **1.** $7 + \frac{1}{10}$ $\quad \frac{c-d}{d}$ **4.** $\frac{c}{d} - 1$ $\quad \frac{2a^2 - 3a + 3}{a}$ **7.** $2a - 3 + \frac{3}{a}$

$\frac{35}{4}$ **2.** $8\frac{3}{4}$ $\quad \frac{4x^2 - 5}{x}$ **5.** $4x - \frac{5}{x}$ $\quad \frac{c^3 + c^2 - 1}{c^2}$ **8.** $c + 1 - \frac{1}{c^2}$

$\frac{a+b}{b}$ **3.** $\frac{a}{b} + 1$ $\quad \frac{2x^2 - 3x + 1}{x}$ **6.** $2x - 3 + \frac{1}{x}$ $\quad \frac{6p^2 + 12p - 1}{3p}$ **9.** $2p + 4 - \frac{1}{3p}$

10. $h^2 + h + \frac{1}{h}$ $\qquad$ **13.** $y^2 + y - 3 + \frac{3}{4y}$

11. $4m^2 - 2m + 3 + \frac{1}{3m}$ $\qquad$ **14.** $x^2 - xy + y^2 + \frac{2}{xy}$

12. $7x^2 + 3x + 4 - \frac{1}{2x}$ $\qquad$ **15.** $c + d + e - \frac{1}{cd}$

388

10. $\frac{h^3 + h^2 + 1}{h}$

11. $\frac{12m^3 - 6m^2 + 9m + 1}{3m}$

12. $\frac{14x^3 + 6x^2 + 8x - 1}{2x}$

13. $\frac{4y^3 + 4y^2 - 12y + 3}{4y}$

14. $\frac{x^3y - x^2y^2 + xy^3 + 2}{xy}$

15. $\frac{c^2d + cd^2 + cde - 1}{cd}$

18. $\dfrac{4a^3+5a^2-a}{2a-1}$

16. $a - b + \dfrac{b^2}{a+b}$ $\quad \dfrac{a^2}{a+b}$

19. $x^2 + xy + y^2 + \dfrac{y^3}{2x-y}$ $\quad$ [B] $\dfrac{2x^3+x^2y+xy^2}{2x-y}$

17. $2x - y - \dfrac{-y^2}{x+y}$ $\quad \dfrac{2x^2+xy}{x+y}$

20. $a^2 - ab + b^2 - \dfrac{b^3}{a+b}$ $\quad \dfrac{a^3}{a+b}$

18. $2a^2 + 3a + 1 + \dfrac{a^2+1}{2a-1}$

21. $x^2 + xy - y^2 - \dfrac{x^3+2y^3}{x-2y}$ $\quad \dfrac{-x^2y-3xy^2}{x-2y}$

Changing Fractions into Mixed Expressions [A]

The fraction $\frac{14}{3}$ can be changed into the mixed number $4\frac{2}{3}$ by dividing the numerator 14 by the denominator 3. The fraction $\dfrac{12x^2 - 8x + 3}{4x}$ can be changed into the mixed expression

$3x - 2 + \dfrac{3}{4x}$ by dividing $12x^2 - 8x + 3$ by $4x$.

Example 1. Change $\dfrac{9y^2 + 6y - 2}{3y}$ into a mixed expression.

Solution. $\dfrac{9y^2 + 6y - 2}{3y} = 3y + 2 - \dfrac{2}{3y}$

[A] **EXERCISES**

Change into mixed expressions:

1. $\dfrac{x^3 + x^2 + 1}{x}$ $\quad x^2+x+\frac{1}{x}$

5. $\dfrac{4x^2y^2 - 6xy - 5}{2xy}$ $\quad 2xy-3-\frac{5}{2xy}$

2. $\dfrac{15x^2 - 20x + 2}{5x}$ $\quad 3x-4+\frac{2}{5x}$

6. $\dfrac{7a^3b - 8a^2b + 7}{a^2b}$ $\quad 7a-8+\frac{7}{a^2b}$

3. $\dfrac{12c^2 - 8c - 3}{2}$ $\quad 6c^2-4c-\frac{3}{2}$

7. $\dfrac{10y^4 - 8y^3 + 6}{2y^3}$ $\quad 5y-4+\frac{3}{y^3}$

4. $\dfrac{m^2n^2 + 6mn + 4}{mn}$ $\quad mn+6+\frac{4}{mn}$

8. $\dfrac{24x^3 - 16x^2 + 8}{8x}$ $\quad 3x^2-2x+\frac{1}{x}$

Example 2. Change $\dfrac{2x^2 + 2x - 7}{2x - 4}$ into a mixed expression.

Solution.

$$
\begin{array}{r}
x + 3 \\
2x - 4\overline{\smash{)}2x^2 + 2x - 7} \\
\underline{2x^2 - 4x} \\
6x - 7 \\
\underline{6x - 12} \\
5
\end{array}
$$

$$\dfrac{2x^2 + 2x - 7}{2x - 4} = x + 3 + \dfrac{5}{2x - 4}$$

① Watch for errors in signs. **389**
② The reverse process of page 388. This should help emphasize why one can't "cancel" 3y and one of the numerator terms.

[A]

Change into mixed or integral expressions:

1. $\dfrac{9\,y^4 + 15\,y^3 + y^2}{3\,y^2}$ $3y^2 + 5y + \frac{1}{3}$

2. $\dfrac{2\,x^2 + 3\,x + 2}{x + 2}$ $2x - 1 + \frac{4}{x+2}$

3. $\dfrac{5\,a^2 - 7\,a + 1}{a - 1}$ $5a - 2 - \frac{1}{a-1}$

4. $\dfrac{x^3 + 1}{x - 1}$ $x^2 + x + 1 + \frac{2}{x-1}$

5. $\dfrac{x^3 - 1}{x - 1}$ $x^2 + x + 1$

6. $\dfrac{3\,x^2 + 4\,xy - 4\,y^2 + 2}{x + 2\,y}$

$3x - 2y + \frac{2}{x+2y}$

Complex Fractions [B]

A <u>complex fraction</u> is one which has one or more fractions in its numerator, in its denominator, or in both its numerator and denominator. Examples of complex fractions are

$$\frac{\frac{1}{2}}{\frac{3}{4}}, \quad \frac{\dfrac{a+b}{3}}{7}, \quad \text{and} \quad \frac{1+\dfrac{1}{x}}{1-\dfrac{1}{x}}$$

There are two methods used in changing complex fractions to simple fractions: *Method 1.* Multiply both numerator and denominator of the fraction by the lowest common denominator of all fractions appearing in the numerator and denominator. This multiplies the fraction by 1. Why?

Method 2. Divide the numerator by the denominator. If this method is used, the numerator and denominator must be simple fractions.

Example. Simplify: $\dfrac{\dfrac{a^2 - b^2}{6}}{\dfrac{a + b}{3}}$

Solution 1. The L.C.D. is 6.

$$\frac{6\left(\dfrac{a^2 - b^2}{6}\right)}{6\left(\dfrac{a + b}{3}\right)} = \frac{a^2 - b^2}{2(a + b)} = \frac{\overset{1}{\cancel{(a + b)}}(a - b)}{2\underset{1}{\cancel{(a + b)}}} = \frac{a - b}{2}$$

Solution 2.

$$\frac{\dfrac{a^2 - b^2}{6}}{\dfrac{a + b}{3}} = \frac{a^2 - b^2}{6} \div \frac{a + b}{3} = \frac{\overset{1}{\cancel{(a + b)}}(a - b)}{\underset{1}{\cancel{3}}(2)} \times \frac{\overset{1}{\cancel{3}}}{\underset{1}{\cancel{a + b}}} = \frac{a - b}{2}$$

① Although marked B, it is suggested that you do some of these exercises in all classes. Solution 1 is a useful way to divide fractions, and we have found that students appreciate being taught it. It is the best method to use in checking fractional equations in the next chapter. Also, it is essential to use if the student continues with mathematics and science. Solution 2, although less meaningful, is sometimes easier.

Change to simple fractions:

1. $\dfrac{2\frac{2}{3}}{\frac{4}{5}}$ *10⁄3*

2. $\dfrac{3}{3\frac{1}{3}}$ *9⁄10*

3. $\dfrac{6 - \frac{4}{5}}{1 + \frac{3}{10}}$ *4*

4. $\dfrac{10 - \frac{1}{2}}{1 + \frac{1}{5}}$ *95⁄12*

5. $\dfrac{\frac{a}{b} + 1}{\frac{a}{b} - 1}$ *a+b⁄a-b*

6. $\dfrac{\frac{x}{y} - 1}{\frac{x}{y} + 1}$ *x-y⁄x+y*

7. $\dfrac{a}{1 - \frac{1}{a}}$ *a²⁄a-1*

8. $\dfrac{\frac{1}{x + y}}{\frac{x}{y}}$ *y⁄x(x+y)*

9. $\dfrac{1 - \frac{x}{y}}{1 - \frac{x^2}{y^2}}$ *y⁄y+x*

10. $\dfrac{\frac{x^2 - y^2}{3}}{\frac{x + y}{5}}$ *5(x-y)⁄3*

11. $\dfrac{4}{\frac{a + b}{a - b}}$ *4a-4b⁄a+b*

12. $\dfrac{m + \frac{m}{n}}{\frac{1}{n} + \frac{1}{n^2}}$ *mn*

13. $\dfrac{\frac{a + b}{a - b}}{\frac{a - b}{a + b}}$ *(a+b)²⁄(a-b)²*

14. $\dfrac{\frac{x^2}{3} - 3}{\frac{x}{6} - \frac{1}{2}}$ *2x+6*

15. $\dfrac{a - \frac{25}{a}}{a + 5}$ *a-5⁄a*

16. $\dfrac{a - 2 + \frac{3}{a}}{1 + \frac{1}{a}}$ *a²-2a+3⁄a+1*

17. $\dfrac{1 - \frac{2}{c} - \frac{3}{c^2}}{1 + \frac{1}{c}}$ *c-3⁄c*

18. $\dfrac{\frac{2x}{a - 3b}}{\frac{2xy}{2a - 6b}}$ *2⁄y*

19. $\dfrac{\frac{1}{x} + 1}{\frac{1}{x^2} - 1}$ *x⁄1-x*

Checking Your Understanding of Chapter 14

Now is the time to determine whether you have mastered
Chapter 14. Be sure that you know   PAGE

1. How to reduce fractions to lowest terms.   370
2. How to multiply and divide fractions.   373, 375
3. How to find the lowest common denominator of
fractions   378
4. How to combine fractions.   377

Do you
need
to review?

11. How to spell and use the following words:

PAGE	PAGE
complex 390	reciprocal 375

[A]

CHAPTER REVIEW

1. *Complete:* A fraction is unchanged if we multiply it by _?_.

2. Why do we factor the denominators when combining fractions? *To make it easier to find the L.C.D.*

Reduce to lowest terms:

$\frac{2bc}{3}$ **3.** $\frac{4\,abc}{6\,a}$ $\frac{n}{m}$ **6.** $\frac{mn}{m^2}$ $\frac{2x-5}{3x-1}$ **9.** $\frac{2\,x^2 + x - 15}{3\,x^2 + 8\,x - 3}$

$\frac{4}{a+b}$ **4.** $\frac{4\,a - 4\,b}{a^2 - b^2}$ $\frac{x}{x+5}$ **7.** $\frac{x^2 - 5\,x}{x^2 - 25}$ $\frac{a-1}{2b(2a+5)}$ **10.** $\frac{3\,a^2b - 3\,ab}{12\,a^2b^2 + 30\,ab^2}$

$\frac{2x}{3y^2}$ **5.** $\frac{8\,x^2y^3}{12\,xy^5}$ $\frac{3a^2}{5b}$ **8.** $\frac{12\,a^3b}{20\,ab^2}$ $\frac{4}{5a}$ **11.** $\frac{4\,ay - 4\,cd}{5\,a^2y - 5\,acd}$

Do as indicated:

12. $\frac{2\,a}{3} + \frac{5\,b}{6}$ $\frac{4a+5b}{6}$ **16.** $\frac{c^2}{c^2 - d^2} \div \frac{c}{c - d}$ $\frac{c}{c+d}$

13. $1 + \frac{a}{c}$ $\frac{a+c}{c}$ **17.** $\frac{x}{x + 1} \div \frac{x^2}{x^2 - 1}$ $\frac{x-1}{x}$

$\frac{3a^2 + 6a + 57}{(a-2)(a+7)}$ **14.** $\frac{a + 7}{a - 2} + \frac{2\,a - 4}{a + 7}$ **18.** $\frac{2\,x}{2\,x + x^2} \times \frac{x^2 - 4}{x^2}$ $\frac{2(x-2)}{x^2}$

15. $\frac{x + y}{x^2 - y^2} - \frac{2\,x - y}{x^2 - y^2}$ $\frac{2y-x}{x^2-y^2}$ **19.** $\frac{a}{b} \div \frac{2\,a^2}{b^2}$ $\frac{b}{2a}$

20. $\frac{b^2 - 2\,b - 24}{5} \div \frac{b^2 + 8\,b + 16}{10}$ $\frac{2(b-6)}{b+4}$

  Now is the test of your skill in teaching this chapter. We hope your students are at ease with fractions. However, do not expect that this will be the case with all.

Change to simple fractions:

21. $3\frac{2}{5}$ $\frac{17}{5}$

23. $x - 1 + \frac{x}{2}$ $\frac{3x-2}{2}$

25. $c + d - \frac{3}{c}$ $\frac{c^2+cd-3}{c}$

22. $a - \frac{1}{a}$ $\frac{a^2-1}{a}$

24. $x - 1 - \frac{1}{x}$ $\frac{x^2-x-1}{x}$

26. $a - 3 + \frac{1}{3}$ $\frac{3a-8}{3}$

Change into integral expressions:

27. $\frac{3125}{5}$ 625

29. $\frac{256}{2}$ 128

31. $\frac{a^2 - ab - 2\,b^2}{a - 2\,b}$ $a+b$

28. $\frac{100}{20}$ 5

30. $\frac{x^2 + x}{x}$ $x+1$

32. $\frac{x^2 + xy}{x + y}$ x

Change into mixed expressions:

33. $\frac{10\,x^2 - 15\,x + 3}{5}$ $2x^2-3x+\frac{3}{5}$

35. $\frac{x^2 + 7\,x + 1}{x + 1}$ $x+6 - \frac{5}{x+1}$

34. $\frac{3\,ab - 3\,c + 1}{3}$ $ab - c + \frac{1}{3}$

36. $\frac{y^2 - 3\,y + 4}{y - 2}$ $y-1+\frac{2}{y-2}$

[B]

Reduce to lowest terms:

37. $\frac{2\,c^2 - cd - d^2}{3\,cd - 5\,c^2 + 2\,d^2}$ $\frac{2c+d}{5c+2d}$

39. $\frac{2\,a^2 - 2\,b^2}{a^2 + ab - 2\,b^2}$ $\frac{2(a+b)}{a+2b}$

38. $\frac{x^4 - 1}{5\,x^2 - 5}$ $\frac{x^2+1}{5}$

40. $\frac{3\,xy - 3\,xy^2}{3\,x - 6\,xy - 9\,xy^2}$ $\frac{y(1-y)}{(1+y)(1-3y)}$

41. Combine: $\frac{x - 4}{x + 4} + \frac{x + 4}{x - 4} - \frac{2\,x^2}{x^2 - 16}$ $\frac{32}{(x+4)(x-4)}$

42. Simplify: $\dfrac{a + 1 - \dfrac{a}{6}}{a - 1 - \dfrac{a}{2}}$ $\frac{5a+6}{3a-6}$

43. Divide: $\frac{y^2 - y}{x^4 - x^2} \div \frac{y^3 + 3\,y^2 - 4\,y}{2\,x^2 - x - 1}$ $\frac{2x+1}{x^2(x+1)(y+4)}$

[A]

1. Simplify: $2\,ab + 3\,cd + 4\,ab - c^2 - 4\,cd$ $6ab - cd - c^2$

If $r = 2$, $s = 3$, and $t = -5$, find the value of

2. $\frac{r^2 + s^2 + t}{2\,r}$ 2

4. $\frac{t^3 + r^3 - 3}{t}$ 24

6. $(rst)^3$ $27,000$

3. $\frac{3\,r + 6\,r^2}{5}$ 6

5. $\frac{2\,r^2 + s^2}{s + t}$ $-8\frac{1}{2}$

7. $st + tr$ -25

Solve:

8. $x - 3 = 2$ *5*

9. $x + 6 = 0$ *−6*

10. $7x - 1.1 = .3$ *0.2*

11. $40x - 5 = 0$ *⅛*

12. $8c - 3 = 5c + 9$ *4*

13. $5(x + 2) = 37 - 4x$ *3*

14. $\frac{x}{20} + \frac{x}{3} - \frac{x}{6} = 13$ *60*

15. $30(m - 2) + \frac{m}{3} = \frac{5m + 481}{16}$ *3*

16. $.5y + 8 = 20.5$ *25*

17. $\frac{1}{4}(12x - 16) - \frac{1}{2}(8x - 4) = 0$ *−2*

18. $\frac{2(7x - 1)}{7} - \frac{3(3x + 5)}{14} = 0$ *1*

Solve for x:

19. $ax - b = 0$ *$\frac{b}{a}$*

20. $ax - b = c$ *$\frac{b+c}{a}$*

21. $a + bx = c$ *$\frac{c-a}{b}$*

22. $\pi rx = 16$ *$\frac{16}{\pi r}$*

23. $a(7 - x) = 5$ *$\frac{7a-5}{a}$*

24. $5cx - 3 = 7 - 5cx$ *$\frac{1}{c}$*

Solve by factoring:

25. $x^2 = x + 6$ *3, −2*

26. $x^2 = -4x$ *0, −4*

27. $4x^2 - 12x + 9 = 0$ *½, ½*

28. $b^2 - 10b = 56$ *14, −4*

29. Copy and complete the following table for $x - 3y = 6$:

x	− 8	− 6	− 4	− 2	0	2	4	6
y	?	?	?	?	?	?	?	?

−4⅔ −4 −3⅓ −2⅔ −2 −1⅓ −⅔ 0

30. Find the following products mentally: *(see foot of page)*

a. $(a - b)(a + b)$

b. $(a + 3)(a + 3)$

c. $2c^2(c^2 - c + 1)$

d. $(2x - 5)(3x - 4)$

e. $(x - 3y)^2$

f. $2\pi r(r + h)$

31. Solve for x and y: $3x - 4y = 11$ *$x = 1$,*
  $2x + 5y = -8$ *$y = -2$*

32. How many ounces of 30-cent tea must be mixed with 30 ounces of 40-cent tea to make a mixture of 33-cent tea?

33. An agent sells hose at \$1.08 a pair, making a profit of *70 oz.* 20% based on the cost. If there is no overhead, what is the per cent of profit based on the selling price? *16⅔ %*

394

30. *a. $a^2 - b^2$*
b. $a^2 + 6a + 9$
c. $2c^4 - 2c^3 + 2c^2$
d. $6x^2 - 23x + 20$
e. $x^2 - 6xy + 9y^2$
f. $2\pi r^2 + 2\pi rh$

34. If school paper costs x dollars per thousand sheets, how many dollars do y sheets cost? $\frac{xy}{1000}$

35. Factor into prime factors:

a. $x^3 - x$ $x(x-1)(x+1)$ **c.** $4 p^2 - 16 p + 12$ $4(p-1)(p-3)$

b. $3 x^2 - 3 x - 60$ $3(x-5)(x+4)$ **d.** $x^4 - y^4$ $(x^2+y^2)(x-y)(x+y)$

36. Solve for x: $2 bmx + 1 = x + 4 b^2 m^2$ $2bm+1$

37. Solve for x: $(x - a)(x - b) + a = x^2$ $\dfrac{a(1+b)}{a+b}$

38. Solve for y: $y^2 - 3 ay + 2 a^2 = 0$ $a, 2a$

39. Solve for m: $2 m^2 + 5 cm = 12 c^2$ $\frac{3c}{2}, -4c$

40. Solve for m and n: $\dfrac{m}{4} - \dfrac{n}{6} = \dfrac{1}{2}$ $m=6,$

$\dfrac{m}{3} - \dfrac{n}{2} = -1$ $n=6$

41. The perimeter of a rectangle is 204 feet, and the length is 22 feet more than the width. What are the dimensions of the rectangle? $40\,ft. \times 62\,ft.$

42. $i = prt$. What principal in $2\frac{1}{2}$ years at 5% will produce $\$52.50$ simple interest? $\$\,420$

43. A man invested $\$3000$, part at 6% and the remainder at 5%. The annual income from the 6% investment was $\$48$ greater than the income from the 5% investment. How much was invested at each rate? $6\%, \$1800; 5\%, \$1200$

[B]

44. Solve: $\dfrac{x + y}{2} - \dfrac{x - 3 y}{3} = 10$ $x=-3, y=7$

$\dfrac{x - y}{5} + \dfrac{y - 3 x}{2} = 6$

45. Solve: $x - \dfrac{x - 2}{3} = 6$ 8

46. Divide: $\dfrac{2 b^2 - 8}{4 b^2} \div \dfrac{3 b + 6}{2 b}$ $\dfrac{b-2}{3b}$

47. Combine: $\dfrac{1}{y - 7} - \dfrac{y + 2}{y^2 + 2 y - 35}$ $\dfrac{7y-21}{(y-7)(y+7)(y-5)}$

395

ALGEBRA, BOOK ONE

48. Divide: $12\,y^3 + 2\,y - 30\,y^2 - 5$ by $2\,y - 5$ $6y^2+1$

49. A customer bought a table for $22.05 at a 10% discount sale. What was the original price of the table? 24.50

50. Solve $S = \dfrac{a+l}{2}$ for l. $2S-a$

51. If you should make 12 hits in 42 times at bat, what batting average would you have? 0.286

52. Solve $x(x-3)+1-x(x-5)=0$. $-\frac{1}{2}$

CHAPTER
TESTS

[Test A]

Reduce to lowest terms:

$\frac{a^2}{2}$ **1.** $\dfrac{2\,a^3}{4\,a}$ $\frac{1}{3}$ **3.** $\dfrac{6(a-b)}{18(a-b)}$ $\frac{7}{8}$ **5.** $\dfrac{7\,x-21}{8\,x-24}$

$\frac{1}{y}$ **2.** $\dfrac{x}{xy}$ $\frac{2}{m+1}$ **4.** $\dfrac{2\,m}{m(m+1)}$ $\frac{a-b}{a+b}$ **6.** $\dfrac{a^2-2\,ab+b^2}{a^2-b^2}$

Multiply or divide as indicated:

$\frac{b}{2}$ **7.** $\dfrac{a}{8} \div \dfrac{a}{4\,b}$ $\frac{x+1}{y(x-1)}$ **10.** $\dfrac{x^2-1}{y^3} \cdot \dfrac{y^2}{x^2-2\,x+1}$

$\frac{y}{3}$ **8.** $\dfrac{x}{y} \cdot \dfrac{y^2}{3\,x}$ $\frac{x(x-3)(x-2)}{(x+2)(x+3)}$ **11.** $\dfrac{x^2-5\,x+6}{x^2+8\,x+12} \cdot \dfrac{x^3+6\,x^2}{x^2+3\,x}$

$\frac{1}{5}$ **9.** $\dfrac{2\,a}{5\,b} \cdot \dfrac{b^2-b}{2\,ab-2\,a}$ $\frac{m+3}{m}$ **12.** $\dfrac{m^2-6\,m+5}{m^2-1} \div \dfrac{m^2-5\,m}{m^2+4\,m+3}$

Combine:

$\frac{5}{a}$ **13.** $\dfrac{2}{a}+\dfrac{3}{a}$ $\frac{2x+y}{12}$ **17.** $\dfrac{x+y}{3}+\dfrac{x-y}{4}$

$\frac{a+b}{c}$ **14.** $\dfrac{a}{c}+\dfrac{b}{c}$ $\frac{x^2+1}{8x^2}$ **18.** $\dfrac{3\,x^2-6\,x+1}{8\,x^2}-\dfrac{x-3}{4\,x}$

$\frac{x+y}{y}$ **15.** $\dfrac{x}{y}+1$ $\frac{8a+4}{(a+2)(a-2)}$ **19.** $\dfrac{3}{a+2}+\dfrac{5}{a-2}$

$\frac{a}{2}$ **16.** $\dfrac{2\,a}{3}-\dfrac{a}{6}$ $\frac{5b}{(b-3)(b+2)}$ **20.** $\dfrac{b}{b-3}-\dfrac{b}{b+2}$

396

Reduce to lowest terms: *(ans. 1–15 at foot of page)*

1. $\dfrac{3\,x^2y^3}{21\,y^3z^2}$ **2.** $\dfrac{6\,abc}{4\,ab + 4\,bc}$ **3.** $\dfrac{1 - x^2}{4\,x^2 + x - 3}$

Change to mixed numbers or integral expressions:

4. $\dfrac{x^3 + 2\,x^2 + 1}{x}$ **5.** $\dfrac{a^3 + 1}{a + 1}$ **6.** $\dfrac{5\,a^2 - 7\,a + 1}{a - 2}$

Change to simple fractions:

7. $c + 1 - \dfrac{1}{c}$ **8.** $x - y + \dfrac{y^2}{x + y}$ **9.** $\dfrac{1 - \dfrac{y}{x}}{1 + \dfrac{y}{x}}$

Multiply or divide as indicated:

10. $3\,a \cdot \dfrac{a + 2}{6\,a^2 + 12\,a}$ **11.** $\dfrac{ax + ay}{x - 3\,y} \div \dfrac{ax^2 - ay^2}{x^2 - 4\,xy + 3\,y^2}$

Combine:

12. $\dfrac{x}{y^2} - \dfrac{y}{x^2}$ **14.** $\dfrac{3}{x + 4} - \dfrac{x - 3}{2\,x^2 + 7\,x - 4}$

13. $\dfrac{x + 1}{1 - x} + \dfrac{x - 1}{1 + x}$ **15.** $\dfrac{4}{a - 2} - \dfrac{3\,a + 2}{a^2 - 4}$

1. $\dfrac{x^2}{7z^2}$ *9.* $\dfrac{x - y}{x + y}$

2. $\dfrac{3ac}{2\,(a + c)}$ *10.* $\tfrac{1}{2}$

3. $\dfrac{1 - x}{4x - 3}$ *11.* 1

4. $x^2 + 2x + \tfrac{1}{x}$ *12.* $\dfrac{x^3 - y^3}{x^2 y^2}$

5. $a^2 - a + 1$ *13.* $\dfrac{4x}{(1 - x)(1 + x)}$

6. $5a + 3 + \dfrac{7}{a - 2}$ *14.* $\dfrac{5x}{(x + 4)(2x - 1)}$

7. $\dfrac{c^2 + c - 1}{c}$ *15.* $\dfrac{a + 6}{(a + 2)(a - 2)}$

8. $\dfrac{x^2}{x + y}$

397

When we think of insurance, we generally think of protection against sudden or unexpected losses, such as those caused by fire, storm, or accident, or against unforeseen expenses such as might arise in the event of sickness or death. This protection is furnished by an insurance company in return for payment of a relatively small amount of money, called a premium. Each premium is much smaller than the amount of protection which the person who pays it receives. However, a fire-insurance company, for example, knows that only a very few of the people who pay premiums to it will suffer loss from fire. The company will collect a great many small premiums during the year, but will be called upon to pay only a small number of claims. The number of dollars paid by a company in a year to persons who have lost property by fire should approximately balance the number of dollars paid to it in premiums, with due allowance for overhead and profit.

Insurance companies make extensive use of mathematics. They must determine the amount of premium which must be charged for insurance protection. These premiums are based upon the past experience of a great many companies, or upon government statistics of the number of fires, accidents, or deaths in relation to the total amount of property, or the total number of automobiles or people in the area which the company serves. In addition to the protection they afford, most life-insurance policies have cash and loan values, as well as options by which the policy may be discontinued and its cash value used to purchase a smaller paid-up policy or to extend the original policy for a certain period of time without further payment. Many policy owners also receive yearly dividends.

Tables of these premiums, values, and dividends are compiled by expert mathematicians called actuaries, of whom each insurance company has one or more. However, not all of the mathematical work in an insurance company is done by actuaries. A great deal of it is done by clerks who, working from the actuaries' tables, determine rates, values, and dividends for the thousands (in some large companies, millions) of individual policies. These clerks must be accurate with figures, and have a good working knowledge of high-school mathematics.

15

Fractional Equations

Suggested Time Schedule
Minimum   9 days
Maximum   11 days

*In this chapter you will learn
to solve some complicated equations.* ▶

FRACTIONAL EQUATIONS

How to Solve Fractional Equations [A]

Not all equations containing fractions are fractional equations. In a fractional equation the variable appears in a denominator. The equation $\frac{x}{2} - \frac{x}{4} = 1$ is an equation containing fractions, but is not a fractional equation. The equation $\frac{2x - 3}{x} + 1 = 2$ is a fractional equation.

A fractional equation is solved as any other equation containing fractions. Compare the solutions below:

$$\frac{x}{8} = 2 \qquad\qquad\qquad \frac{8}{x} = 2$$

$$\overset{1}{\cancel{8}}\left(\frac{x}{\cancel{8}}\right) = 8(2) \qquad\qquad \overset{1}{\cancel{x}}\left(\frac{8}{\cancel{x}}\right) = x(2)$$

$$x = 16 \qquad\qquad\qquad 4 = x$$

You should keep in mind the following steps for solving an equation containing one variable:

Solution of Equations in One Variable

1. If the equation contains fractions,
clear it of fractions by multiplying both members by the L.C.D.

2. Remove parentheses.

Note. *In some cases it is advisable to remove parentheses before clearing of fractions. This is often the case in decimal equations.*

If it is a first-degree equation,	If it is a second-degree equation,
3. Transform it so that all terms containing the variable are in the left member and all other terms are in the right member.	**3.** Transform it so that all terms are in the left member and simplify.
4. Simplify each member.	**4.** Factor the left member.
5. Divide each member of the equation by the coefficient of the variable.	**5.** Set each factor containing the variable equal to zero and solve the resulting equation.
6. Prove by substituting in the original equation.	**6.** Prove both roots correct by substituting in the original equation.

401

The following is an equation containing fractions, but it is not a fractional equation.

Example. Solve $\dfrac{x}{3} + \dfrac{2x-3}{5} = 6$

Solution. The L.C.D. is 15.

$$\frac{x}{3} + \frac{2x-3}{5} = 6$$

$$15\left(\frac{x}{3}\right) + 15\left(\frac{2x-3}{5}\right) = 15(6)$$

$$5x + 6x - 9 = 90$$

$$5x + 6x = 90 + 9$$

$$11x = 99$$

$$x = 9$$

PROOF. Does $\qquad \dfrac{9}{3} + \dfrac{18-3}{5} = 6?$

Does $\qquad\qquad 3 + 3 = 6?$ Yes.

[A]

REVIEW EXERCISES

Solve, and prove as directed by your teacher:

9 **1.** $\dfrac{2x}{3} = 6$ *25* **4.** $\dfrac{2x-5}{3} = 15$ *11⅓* **7.** $\dfrac{3x+1}{5} = 7$

18 2/7 **2.** $\dfrac{7x}{8} = 16$ *5* **5.** $\dfrac{3x-3}{4} = 3$ *9/14* **8.** $\dfrac{4x}{9} = \dfrac{2}{7}$

16 2/3 **3.** $\dfrac{3}{5}x = 10$ *1/5* **6.** $\dfrac{1}{3}x = \dfrac{2}{5}$ *16/21* **9.** $\dfrac{6x}{8} = \dfrac{4}{7}$

30 **10.** $\dfrac{x}{2} - \dfrac{x}{3} = 5$ *14* **16.** $\dfrac{3x-2}{10} + \dfrac{1}{5} = \dfrac{2x-7}{5}$

5 5/11 **11.** $\dfrac{2x}{3} = 5 - \dfrac{x}{4}$ *-4* **17.** $\dfrac{m+6}{9} - 7\dfrac{2}{9} = \dfrac{5m-1}{3}$

5/6 **12.** $\dfrac{2y-1}{2} = \dfrac{4y-1}{7}$ *2* **18.** $\dfrac{x+5}{4} - \dfrac{2x-1}{5} = \dfrac{23}{20}$

-14/5 **13.** $\dfrac{x-7}{2} + \dfrac{3x-5}{4} = -7$ *66* **19.** $\dfrac{y-1}{6} + \dfrac{2}{3} = 11\dfrac{1}{2}$

-10 **14.** $\dfrac{x-7}{2} - \dfrac{x-15}{3} + \dfrac{1}{6} = 0$ *5* **20.** $\dfrac{c-6}{2} - \dfrac{2(6-c)}{3} = \dfrac{-7}{6}$

-9 **15.** $\dfrac{x-3}{3} + 3 = \dfrac{x+4}{5}$ *1/2* **21.** $\dfrac{8b-1}{3} = 3 - \dfrac{10b+7}{6}$

Be sure to use this review. You may wish to write the first step of the Example as follows: $15\left(\dfrac{x}{3} + \dfrac{2x-3}{5}\right) = 15(6)$. Then use the distributive law to remove parentheses. This helps emphasize that the two members of the equation are treated alike, that is, multiplied by the L.C.D.

In the following decimal equations remember that $.2 = \frac{2}{10}$, $.25 = \frac{25}{100}$, and $.004 = \frac{4}{1000}$.

22. $.25 x = 12$ $\quad 48$

23. $.04 m = 8$ $\quad 200$

24. $.5 y + .2 y = 1.4$ $\quad 2$

25. $.03 x - .05 = .1$ $\quad 5$

26. $.05 m - .14 = .02$ $\quad 3.20$

27. $4 + .02 p = .25 p - .6$ $\quad 20$

28. $.1 n - .04 = .004 - .3 n$ $\quad 0.11$

29. $3(2 x - 3) + 8.1 = 0$ $\quad 0.15$

30. $.05(700 - 3 y) = 34.25$ $\quad 5$ $\longrightarrow$ Watch for the error

31. $.2(6 x + 7) - 4.5 = .1(2 x - 1)$ $\quad 3$ $\qquad 5(70000 - 300y) = 3425.$

32. $8(1.5 c - 3) - .4(c + 3) = - 4$ $\quad 1.827^+$

33. $.07(x - 6) + .3(2 x + 9) = 4.96$ $\quad 4$

Fractional Equations Having Monomial Denominators [A]

Example. Solve $\dfrac{21}{2y} - 4 = \dfrac{9}{y}$.

Solution. The L.C.D. is $2 y$.

$$\frac{21}{2 y} - 4 = \frac{9}{y}$$

$$2 y\left(\frac{21}{2 y}\right) - 2 y(4) = 2 y\left(\frac{9}{y}\right)$$

$$21 - 8 y = 18$$
$$- 8 y = 18 - 21$$
$$- 8 y = - 3$$
$$y = \tfrac{3}{8}$$

PROOF. Does $\dfrac{21}{2(\frac{3}{8})} - 4 = \dfrac{9}{\frac{3}{8}}$? Yes.

Solve and prove:

[A]

EXERCISES

1. $\dfrac{2}{x} + \dfrac{3}{x} = 5$ $\quad 1$

2. $\dfrac{7}{x} - \dfrac{5}{x} = 1$ $\quad 2$

3. $1 = \dfrac{2}{y}$ $\quad 2$

4. $\dfrac{5}{c} = 3$ $\quad 1\frac{2}{3}$

5. $\dfrac{3}{h} = - 1$ $\quad -3$

6. $4 - \dfrac{1}{y} = 0$ $\quad \frac{1}{4}$

7. $\dfrac{1}{y} + 6 = - 2$ $\quad -\frac{1}{8}$

8. $\dfrac{1}{x} - 9 = 0$ $\quad \frac{1}{9}$

9. $\dfrac{1}{3 x} - 7 = 4$ $\quad \frac{1}{33}$

10. $\dfrac{3}{p} + \dfrac{1}{5} = 5$ $\quad \frac{5}{8}$

11. $\dfrac{2}{b} + \dfrac{4}{b} - 3 = 0$ $\quad 2$

12. $\dfrac{4}{x} - \dfrac{2}{x} = \dfrac{2}{3} - \dfrac{3}{x}$ $\quad 7\frac{1}{2}$

13. $\dfrac{3}{2 x} - 1 = - \dfrac{7}{2 x} - \dfrac{3}{8}$ $\quad \frac{3}{8}$

Need for Proof [A]

When we solve an equation, we usually change it into one or more other equations. Usually the original equation and the equations derived from it have the same root or roots. Equations having the same root or roots are equivalent.

For example, the derived equations (2) and (3) and the original equation (1) are equivalent because 5 is *a root and the only root* of each of them.

$$3x + 1 = x + 11 \quad (1)$$
$$2x + 1 = 11 \quad (2)$$
$$2x = 10 \quad (3)$$
$$x = 5$$

When the same number is added to or subtracted from both members of an equation, the derived equation is equivalent to the original one; and when both members of an equation are multiplied or divided by any constant (zero excluded), the derived equation and the original one are equivalent. But when we multiply both members by an expression containing the variable, we may obtain a derived equation which has a root that is not a root of the original equation.

For example, consider the equation $x - 1 = 2$. Its only root is 3. Let us multiply both of its members by $x + 2$. When we solve the resulting equation $(x + 2)(x - 1) = 2(x + 2)$, we obtain the roots 3 and -2. Checking shows that 3 is a root of each of the five equations and that -2 is a root of each of the derived equations but not of the original. When we multiplied both members of $x - 1 = 2$ by $x + 2$, we multiplied by zero ($-2 + 2$) and introduced the root -2.

$$x - 1 = 2 \quad (1)$$
$$(x + 2)(x - 1) = 2(x + 2) \quad (2)$$
$$x^2 + x - 2 = 2x + 4 \quad (3)$$
$$x^2 - x - 6 = 0 \quad (4)$$
$$(x - 3)(x + 2) = 0 \quad (5)$$
$$x = 3 \text{ or } -2$$

Now let us try to solve $\dfrac{1}{x - 1} + \dfrac{1}{x} = \dfrac{1}{x(x - 1)}$. In (2), below, both members of (1) were multiplied by $x(x - 1)$, the L.C.D. Then $x = 1$. 1 is not a root because $1 \div 0$, in the Proof, has no meaning. The apparent root 1 was introduced by multiplying by zero. What can you say about the given equation?

$$\frac{1}{x - 1} + \frac{1}{x} = \frac{1}{x(x - 1)} \quad (1)$$
$$x + x - 1 = 1 \quad (2)$$
$$x = 1 \quad (3)$$

PROOF. Does $\dfrac{1}{1 - 1} + \dfrac{1}{1} = \dfrac{1}{1(0)}$? No.

Apparent roots may be introduced when we clear an equation of fractions or change an equation containing radicals into one without radicals. Do you see why it is important to prove that all solutions of a derived equation are solutions of the original equation?

An important page which needs careful study. Turn to page 406 and ask, "Suppose you obtain $x = 2$ when you solve Ex. 11. What would you conclude? Without doing the exercise or completely checking, state a value which could not be a root for the equation in Ex. 14, Ex. 19, etc."

Fractional Equations Having Polynomial Denominators [A]

Example 1. Solve $\dfrac{x+3}{x-1} - \dfrac{3}{x} = 1$.

Solution. The L.C.D. is $x(x-1)$.

$$\frac{x+3}{x-1} - \frac{3}{x} = 1$$

$$x(x-1)\frac{x+3}{x-1} - x(x-1)\frac{3}{x} = x(x-1)1$$

$$x^2 + 3x - 3x + 3 = x^2 - x$$

$$x^2 - x^2 + 3x - 3x + x = -3$$

$$x = -3$$

PROOF. Does $\dfrac{-3+3}{-3-1} - \dfrac{3}{-3} = 1?$

Does $0 + 1 = 1?$ Yes.

Example 2. Solve $\dfrac{4}{y+2} + \dfrac{7}{y+3} = \dfrac{y^2+44}{y^2+5y+6}$.

Solution. All denominators should be factored.

$$\frac{4}{y+2} + \frac{7}{y+3} = \frac{y^2+44}{y^2+5y+6}$$

$$\frac{4}{y+2} + \frac{7}{y+3} = \frac{y^2+44}{(y+2)(y+3)}$$

The L.C.D. must contain all the factors found in the denominators in order to be exactly divisible by each denominator. Then the L.C.D. is $(y+2)(y+3)$.

$$M_{(y+2)(y+3)}, \quad (y+2)(y+3)\frac{4}{y+2} + (y+2)(y+3)\frac{7}{y+3}$$

$$= (y+2)(y+3)\frac{y^2+44}{(y+2)(y+3)}$$

$$4y + 12 + 7y + 14 = y^2 + 44$$

$$-y^2 + 11y - 18 = 0$$

D_{-1}

Factoring

$$y^2 - 11y + 18 = 0$$

$$(y-2)(y-9) = 0$$

If $\quad y - 2 = 0 \qquad\qquad$ If $\quad y - 9 = 0$

$\qquad\qquad y = 2 \qquad\qquad\qquad\qquad\qquad y = 9$

PROOF. Does $1 + \dfrac{7}{5} = \dfrac{12}{5}?$ Yes.

Does $\dfrac{4}{11} + \dfrac{7}{12} = \dfrac{125}{132}?$ Yes.

405

[A]

EXERCISES Solve and prove:

1 **1.** $\dfrac{6}{y+1} = 3$

$4, -1\frac{1}{9}$ **11.** $\dfrac{14}{x-2} + \dfrac{12}{x+2} = 9$

-4 **2.** $\dfrac{12x}{x+3} = 48$

$0, 15$ **12.** $\dfrac{4}{x-3} + \dfrac{6}{x+3} = \dfrac{2}{3}$

$6, -5$ **3.** $x - 1 = \dfrac{30}{x}$

3 **13.** $\dfrac{3}{x+1} - \dfrac{x}{x-1} = \dfrac{3-x^2}{x^2-1}$

$3\frac{1}{2}, -2$ **4.** $y - \dfrac{3}{2} = \dfrac{7}{y}$

$-\frac{3}{5}$ **14.** $\dfrac{y+1}{y+3} - \dfrac{y-2}{y-3} = \dfrac{2}{y-3}$

$2, -3\frac{2}{3}$ **5.** $\dfrac{x-7}{x+1} + \dfrac{3x-1}{3} = 0$

14 **15.** $\dfrac{4}{y} + \dfrac{2}{y^2+3y} = \dfrac{5}{y+3}$

5 **6.** $\dfrac{x+1}{x-3} = 3$

$4\frac{8}{13}$ **16.** $\dfrac{x}{x-4} - \dfrac{5x}{3x-12} + 5 = 0$

-2 **7.** $\dfrac{3x-2}{5(x-2)} = \dfrac{2}{5}$

2 **17.** $\dfrac{2}{x-1} + \dfrac{2}{x+1} = \dfrac{8}{x^2-1}$

$1\frac{1}{2}$ **8.** $\dfrac{y-5}{y-3} - 1 = \dfrac{2}{y}$

$\frac{1}{2}$ **18.** $\dfrac{6}{y+1} + \dfrac{4}{y-1} = \dfrac{3}{y^2-1}$

$-\frac{4}{8}$ **9.** $\dfrac{c+2}{c-1} = \dfrac{c-3}{c+2}$

$2, -3\frac{1}{2}$ **19.** $\dfrac{x+6}{x+4} + \dfrac{2}{x+1} = \dfrac{3x}{x+1}$

$1\frac{1}{3}, 3$ **10.** $\dfrac{3}{x} = \dfrac{2}{x-4} + 3$

$2, 10$ **20.** $\dfrac{4x-1}{x+3} = \dfrac{2}{x+3} + \dfrac{x^2+11}{3x+9}$

$4, -1$ **21.** $\dfrac{2x+1}{x-1} - \dfrac{3x}{x+2} = \dfrac{5x-2}{x^2+x-2}$

[B]

Equations 22–26 reduce to linear equations and equations 27–30 reduce to quadratic equations. Solve:

6 **22.** $\dfrac{2x}{x+3} - \dfrac{3x-4}{2x+6} = \dfrac{5}{x+3}$

*23.** $\dfrac{3x}{x^2} - \dfrac{5}{x+6} - \dfrac{1}{x^2+6x} = 0$ $8\frac{1}{2}$

18 **24.** $\dfrac{4x}{x^2+5x} - \dfrac{3}{x^2+5x} = \dfrac{3}{x}$

No solution **25.** $\dfrac{y+2}{y-3} + \dfrac{y+3}{y+2} = \dfrac{2y^2+7}{y^2-y-6}$

$4\frac{1}{2}$ **26.** $\dfrac{6x^2-2x+5}{3x^2-2} = 2$

*All fractions in equations should be reduced to lowest terms before clearing equations of fractions.

406 Restate often the meaning of the process used. Students often confuse fractional equations with adding and subtracting fractions. Later, when the two are mixed (see particularly page 411), you will find some who say, "When do we drop the denominators?" Such a question indicates they have been accepting the ways to work such problems without real understanding. Emphasize that, in fractional equations, we multiply each

27. $\dfrac{4}{x-3} - \dfrac{4}{x} = \dfrac{1}{15}$ $\quad 15, -12$

28. $\dfrac{5}{x} - \dfrac{5}{x+2} = \dfrac{1}{12}$ $\quad 10, -12$

29. $\dfrac{7}{x+5} + \dfrac{4}{x} - \dfrac{3}{2} = 0$ $\quad -2\frac{2}{3}, 5$

30. $\dfrac{60}{x+3} - \dfrac{60}{x} + 1 = 0$ $\quad -15, 12$

[C]

Solve:

31. $\dfrac{3}{x} + \dfrac{5}{2x} = \dfrac{x+27}{x+2}$ $\quad \frac{1}{2}, -22$

32. $\dfrac{3}{3x-1} + \dfrac{6}{4x-3} = \dfrac{5}{2x+1}$ $\quad \frac{6}{13}$

33. $\dfrac{x}{x+1} - \dfrac{3x}{1-x} = \dfrac{55}{12}$ $\quad -1\frac{4}{7}, 5$

34. $\dfrac{2x-5}{x^2+3x+2} + \dfrac{x-6}{x^2-4} = \dfrac{3x+1}{x^2-x-2}$ $\quad \frac{2}{21}$

Literal Equations Containing Fractions [A]

A literal equation has at least one known number represented by a variable.

Example. Solve for y: $\dfrac{y}{a} - \dfrac{3}{b} = 5.$

Solution. $\qquad \dfrac{y}{a} - \dfrac{3}{b} = 5$

$M_{ab} \qquad ab\left(\dfrac{y}{a}\right) - ab\left(\dfrac{3}{b}\right) = 5\,ab$

$\qquad\qquad by - 3\,a = 5\,ab$

$D_b \qquad\qquad\quad by = 3\,a + 5\,ab$

$\qquad\qquad\qquad y = \dfrac{3\,a + 5\,ab}{b}$

PROOF. Does $\dfrac{3\,a + 5\,ab}{b} \div a - \dfrac{3}{b} = 5?$

Does $\qquad \dfrac{3}{b} + 5 - \dfrac{3}{b} = 5?$ Yes.

[A]

EXERCISES

Solve the following equations for x or y:

1. $\dfrac{a}{x} + b = 0$ $\quad -\dfrac{a}{b}$

2. $\dfrac{1}{x} + \dfrac{2}{x} = \dfrac{1}{a}$ $\quad 3a$

3. $\dfrac{ax}{c} + \dfrac{bx}{c} = 1$ $\quad \dfrac{c}{a+b}$

4. $\dfrac{x}{m} - \dfrac{x}{n} = 1$ $\quad \dfrac{mn}{n-m}$

407

member by the L.C.D. in order to clear the equation of fractions, whereas in adding and subtracting we change the form of the fractions in order to express them with a common denominator.

ALGEBRA, BOOK ONE

$a+4$ **5.** $x - 1 = a + \dfrac{3x - 12}{a}$ $\dfrac{a-b}{cd}$ **8.** $\dfrac{a - b}{cx} = d$

$\dfrac{3m+2}{3}$ **6.** $\dfrac{m}{2}(x - m) = \dfrac{m}{3}$ $2(a+b)$ **9.** $\dfrac{a^2 - b^2}{x} = \dfrac{1}{2}(a - b)$

$\dfrac{5a}{6}$ **7.** $\dfrac{2y + a}{2y - a} = 4$ $(c-1)$ **10.** $\dfrac{3}{y} = \dfrac{2y + 2}{cy} + \dfrac{c - y}{y}$

[B]

Solve for x:

$\dfrac{m}{n}$ **11.** $\dfrac{x - 1}{x + 1} = \dfrac{m - n}{m + n}$ $\dfrac{abc}{bc+ac+ab}$ **15.** $\dfrac{1}{a} + \dfrac{1}{b} + \dfrac{1}{c} = \dfrac{1}{x}$

$\dfrac{2c^2-2cd}{5d-2c}$ **12.** $\dfrac{3x}{c - d} - 2 = \dfrac{5x}{c}$ $c-2b$ **16.** $\dfrac{c}{b} - \dfrac{c^2}{bx} = \dfrac{2b - 3c}{x} + 1$

$\dfrac{9c-4d}{5}$ **13.** $\dfrac{1}{5(x - c)} = \dfrac{1}{4(c - d)}$ $a+b$ **17.** $\dfrac{x}{b} + \dfrac{b}{a} = \dfrac{a}{b} + \dfrac{x}{a}$

$2a$ **14.** $\dfrac{2a}{x} + \dfrac{1}{2x} = \dfrac{4a + 1}{4a}$ $\dfrac{(a-1)b}{a-2}$ **18.** $\dfrac{2}{a} - \dfrac{b}{ax} = \dfrac{x - b}{x}$

Pairs of Equations [A]

In solving pairs of equations, clear the equations of fractions and write them in standard form before trying to eliminate any variable. If you have forgotten how to solve them, review the directions on page 306.

[A]

EXERCISES   Solve:

$x=3,$ **1.** $\dfrac{x}{3} + \dfrac{y}{2} = 3$ $x=4000,$ **4.** $x + y = 7000$
$y=4$ $4x + 3y = 24$ $y=3000$ $.04x + .05y = 310$

$x=4,$ **2.** $\dfrac{3x}{8} + \dfrac{2y}{5} = \dfrac{7}{2}$ $x=3500,$ **5.** $x + y = 6000$
$y=5$ $\dfrac{x}{8} - \dfrac{y}{5} + \dfrac{1}{2} = 0$ $y=2500$ $.04x + .03y = 215$

$m=14,$ **3.** $\dfrac{m}{2} + \dfrac{n}{7} = 9$ $x=1,$ **6.** $\dfrac{1}{x} - \dfrac{1}{y} = \dfrac{2}{xy}$
$n=14$ $\dfrac{m}{7} + 5 = \dfrac{n}{2}$ $y=3$ $\dfrac{x}{y} = \dfrac{1}{3}$

408

Exercises in B and C groups are not needed in the average class. They are quite difficult.

FRACTIONAL EQUATIONS

[B]

Solve:

7. $\dfrac{a+1}{b-1}=\dfrac{4}{3}$ $a=4\frac{3}{5},$
$b=5\frac{1}{5}$

$\dfrac{2a-3}{b+1}=1$

8. $\dfrac{x+1}{y+5}=\dfrac{6}{5}$ $x=119,$

$\dfrac{x+1}{y+1}=\dfrac{5}{4}$ $y=95$

9. $\dfrac{4a-7}{5}-\dfrac{5b+3}{7}+7=0$

$a+3=4-\dfrac{5b-4}{7}$ $a=-2,$
$b=5$

10. $\dfrac{x-1}{y}=\dfrac{4}{5}$

$\dfrac{1}{x+y}+\dfrac{1}{x-y}=\dfrac{x+y+8}{x^2-y^2}$
$x=-27, y=-35$

[C]

Solve:

11. $\dfrac{2x}{3}+\dfrac{y}{3}=2a$ $x=-13a,$

$\dfrac{3x}{4}+\dfrac{2y}{5}=\dfrac{61a}{20}$ $y=32a$

12. $\dfrac{3x}{b}-\dfrac{y}{2b}=5$ $x=2\frac{7}{58}b,$

$\dfrac{7x}{2b}-\dfrac{3y}{b}=-\dfrac{3}{4}$ $y=2\frac{21}{29}b$

13. $\dfrac{1}{x}+\dfrac{1}{y}=\dfrac{2m}{xy}$ $x=\dfrac{4m-3n}{5}$

$\dfrac{2}{x}-\dfrac{3}{y}=\dfrac{3n}{xy}$ $y=\dfrac{6m+3n}{5}$

14. $\dfrac{b}{a+y}-\dfrac{a}{b-x}=0$ $x=b-a$

$\dfrac{a}{b-y}-\dfrac{b}{a+x}=0$ $y=b-a$

Solve for x and y:

15. $ax=by$ $x=\dfrac{a+b}{a},$
$abx+aby=(a+b)^2$ $y=\dfrac{a+b}{b}$

16. $mx-ny=0$ $x=n,$
$mx+ny=2mn$ $y=m$

17. $5x+3y=8a+b$ $x=\dfrac{16at+5b+24}{16},$
$3x+5y=8a-8$ $y=\dfrac{16a-3b-40}{16}$

18. $mx+ny=2m^2$ $x=\dfrac{2(m^2+mn+n^2)}{m+n},$
$nx+my=2n^2$ $y=-\dfrac{2mn}{m+n}$

Solving Formulas [A]

A formula is a literal equation which tells how the value of one variable may be found by performing certain operations upon the variables whose values are known.

The formula $V=lwh$ states that the volume of a rectangular solid is found by multiplying its length, width, and height together. Let us solve this formula for l.

$$V=lwh$$
$$lwh=V$$
D_{wh} $$l=\dfrac{V}{wh}$$

Following our scheme of developing important topics spirally, more difficult formulas are given here Most will be unknown to the class, since they come from such fields as physics and electronics. Ex plain that when students solve a formula for a differen letter, they are not really making a new formula, but jus changing the *subject* of the given one.

ALGEBRA, BOOK ONE

This last equation is a formula for finding the length of a rectangular solid when its volume, width, and height are known. The two
formulas $V = lwh$ and $l = \dfrac{V}{wh}$ express the same relationship of the
length, width, height, and volume of the rectangular solid, although
given in different form.

Example. Solve $v = \dfrac{b - u}{k}$ for b.

Solution.
$$v = \frac{b - u}{k}$$

M_k
$$k(v) = k\left(\frac{b - u}{k}\right)$$

or
$$kv = b - u$$
$$-b = -kv - u$$

D_{-1}
$$b = kv + u$$

This formula tells how to find b when k, v, and u are known.

What does $v = \dfrac{b - u}{k}$ tell?

We have changed the subject from v to b.

[A]

EXERCISES

1. Solve $V = lwh$ for h and express the resulting formula
as a rule. (*See ans. below*)

2. Solve $\pi = \dfrac{c}{2r}$ for r and make a rule for finding the radius of a circle when the circumference is given. (*See ans. below*)

3. Solve $v = \dfrac{b - u}{k}$ for u. $b - kv$

4. Solve $d = \dfrac{n + 2}{p}$ for p; for n. $p = \dfrac{n+2}{d}$; $n = dp - 2$

5. Solve $F = \dfrac{W}{R + 1}$ for W; for R. $W = FR + F$; $R = \dfrac{W - F}{F}$

6. Solve $M = \dfrac{t}{g - f}$ for t; for f. $t = Mg - Mf$; $f = \dfrac{Mg - t}{M}$

7. Solve $T = \dfrac{1}{a} + t$ for t; for a. $t = \dfrac{aT - 1}{a}$; $a = \dfrac{1}{T - t}$

[B]

8. Solve $g = \dfrac{T + Mf}{M}$ for M. $\dfrac{T}{g - f}$

410 1. $h = \dfrac{V}{lw}$. The height of a rectangular solid is equal to the volume divided by the product of the length and width. 2. $r = \dfrac{c}{2\pi}$. The radius of a circle is equal to the circumference divided by twice π.

9. Solve $A = 2\pi r(r + h)$ for h. $\dfrac{A - 2\pi r^2}{2\pi r}$

10. Solve $W = \dfrac{E^2 t}{R}$ for R. $\dfrac{E^2 t}{W}$

11. Solve $S = \dfrac{c - b}{b - a}$ for b. $\dfrac{aS + c}{S + 1}$

12. Solve $K = \dfrac{Wv^2}{2g}$ for v^2. $\dfrac{2gK}{W}$

13. Solve $W = T_1 V - T_2 V$ for V.   (T_1 and T_2 are different variables. T_1 is read "T sub one" and T_2 is read "T sub 2.")

14. Solve $n = \dfrac{s}{w} - 1$ for s. $w(n + 1)$ $\dfrac{W}{T_1 - T_2}$

15. Solve $F = .327\, vd^2$ for v. $\dfrac{F}{0.327\, d^2}$

[C]

16. Solve $c = \dfrac{1}{c_1} + \dfrac{1}{c_2} + \dfrac{1}{c_3}$ for c_1. $\dfrac{c_2 c_3}{c c_2 c_3 - c_3 - c_2}$

17. Solve $Ft = \dfrac{Wat}{g}$ for a. Solve it for F. Can you solve it for t? $a = \dfrac{Fg}{W}$; $F = \dfrac{Wa}{g}$; t may have any numerical value.

18. Solve $Ft = \dfrac{Wv^2}{gr}$ for r. $\dfrac{Wv^2}{Fgt}$

19. Solve $W = P\dfrac{2R}{R - r}$ for R. $\dfrac{Wr}{W - 2P}$

20. Solve $A = 2\pi r^2 + 2\pi rh$ for π. $\dfrac{A}{2r^2 + 2rh}$

21. Solve $h = \dfrac{2A}{b + b'}$ for A and express the resulting formula as a rule. $A = \dfrac{h(b + b')}{2}$ The area of a trapezoid is equal to ½ the product of the altitude and the sum of the 2 bases.

[A]

In adding fractions and in solving equations containing fractions, we first find the L.C.D. Some pupils become confused when adding fractions and solving equations containing fractions. Work and study carefully the following exercises.

REVIEW EXERCISES

1. Combine: $\dfrac{2a}{3} + \dfrac{5a}{6}$ $\dfrac{3a}{2}$ **2.** Solve: $\dfrac{2a}{3} + \dfrac{5a}{6} = 1$ $\dfrac{2}{3}$ ①

3. In Exercise 1 above did you change the value of $\dfrac{2a}{3} + \dfrac{5a}{6}$? Did you change the value of $\dfrac{2a}{3} + \dfrac{5a}{6}$ in Exercise 2?   no; yes

4. Why did you multiply 1 by 6 in Exercise 2? Because the left member of the equation was multiplied by 6.

411

ALGEBRA, BOOK ONE

5. Combine: $\dfrac{6x+7}{5} - \dfrac{9}{2} - \dfrac{2x-1}{10}$ x-3

6. Solve: $\dfrac{6x+7}{5} - \dfrac{9}{2} - \dfrac{2x-1}{10} = 0$ 3

7. Combine: $\dfrac{x-4}{9} - \dfrac{x+2}{6} - \dfrac{x}{3}$ $\dfrac{-7(x+2)}{18}$

8. Solve: $\dfrac{x-4}{9} - \dfrac{x+2}{6} = \dfrac{x}{3}$ -2

9. What is a ratio? a proportion? *(ans. at top of page)*

10. How many terms are there in a ratio? in a proportion?   *Two; four*

11. If $\dfrac{a}{b} = \dfrac{c}{d}$, show that $ad = bc$. Complete: In a proportion the product of the means is __?__. *equal to the product of the extremes.*

12. Use Exercise 11 to solve $\dfrac{2x-1}{3x+5} = \dfrac{2x+1}{3x-4}$. $-\dfrac{1}{24}$

Problems Whose Equations Contain Fractions [A]

Sometimes a problem in which you are to find two or more quantities may be solved by using a single variable. For example, in Ex. 8, p. 413, you may express both numbers in terms of the single variable x. However, this same problem may also be solved by using one variable to express the smaller number and another variable to express the larger number. If a problem requires a second degree equation, try to express all the quantities sought in terms of a single ① variable. (You have not yet studied the solving of two quadratic equations in two variables.)

[A]

PROBLEMS

1. A number increased by its square is 30. What is the number?   — 6, or 5

$-1\frac{1}{2}$, or 4   **2.** Twice the square of a certain number, decreased by five times the number, gives 12 as a result. Find the number.

3. The sum of a number and its reciprocal is $3\frac{1}{3}$. What is the number? (The reciprocal of 7 is $\frac{1}{7}$, and the reciprocal of $\frac{2}{3}$ is $\frac{3}{2}$.) $\frac{1}{3}$, or 3

4. A number exceeds its reciprocal by $3\frac{3}{4}$. What is the number? $-\frac{1}{4}$, or 4

Students have solved problems of the same general type before. The new difficulty is that the equations themselves are fractional. Perhaps your more independent thinkers will be challenged to discover a way to solve two equations with two variables when one is quadratic.

5. A number increased by three times its reciprocal is $9\frac{1}{3}$. Find the number. *$\frac{1}{3}$, or 9*

6. The sum of two numbers is 8. If 3 is added to four times the smaller and the result is divided by the larger, the quotient is 3. What are the numbers? *3 and 5*

7. A man lost $\frac{3}{4}$ of his money and then lost $500 more. He then had $\frac{3}{16}$ of what he had at first. How much had he at first? *$8000*

8. The difference of two numbers is 5. If three times the smaller is divided by the larger, the quotient is 1 and the remainder is 9. What are the numbers? *7 and 12*

Let $\qquad x =$ the smaller number
Then $\qquad x + 5 =$ the larger number

$$\frac{3x}{x+5} = 1 + \frac{9}{x+5}, \quad \text{or} \quad \frac{3x-9}{x+5} = 1$$

Complete the solution.

9. The numerator of a certain fraction exceeds the denominator by 3, and the value of the fraction is $\frac{4}{3}$. Find the fraction. (First find the numerator and denominator and then write the fraction.) *$\frac{12}{9}$*

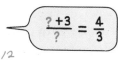

$$\frac{?+3}{?} = \frac{4}{3}$$

10. The denominator of a certain fraction is 2 greater than the numerator, and the value of the fraction is $\frac{4}{5}$. Find the fraction. *$\frac{8}{10}$*

11. The numerator of a certain fraction is 4 less than its denominator. If each term of the fraction is increased by 1, the value of the fraction is $\frac{2}{3}$. Find the fraction. *$\frac{7}{11}$*

12. The denominator of a certain fraction exceeds the numerator by 9. If the numerator is increased by 4, the value of the resulting fraction is $\frac{2}{3}$. What is the fraction? *$\frac{6}{15}$*

13. Two numbers have a difference of 6. What are the numbers if the smaller is $\frac{3}{4}$ of the larger? *18 and 24*

14. Mr. Jones has $2.90, consisting of nickels and dimes. If he has 36 coins in all, how many of each kind has he? *14 nickels, 22 dimes*

15. A boy has 10 coins, consisting of nickels and dimes. If the value of the nickels in cents is divided by the number of dimes, the quotient is $7\frac{1}{2}$. How many coins of each kind has he? *6 nickels, 4 dimes*

413

16. The width of a rectangle is $\frac{3}{4}$ of its length, and its perimeter is 126 feet. Find its dimensions. *27 ft. x 36 ft.*

17. The base of a rectangle is 4 feet longer than the altitude. Find the dimensions of the rectangle if its area is 45 square feet. *Base, 9 ft.; altitude, 5 ft.*

18. What are the dimensions of a rectangular flower bed containing 40 square feet if it takes 26 feet of fence to surround it? *5 ft. x 8 ft.*

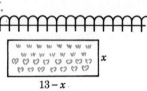

19. Dick is half as old as Bill. Four years ago twice Dick's age added to Bill's age was 32 years. How old is each? *Dick, 11 yr.; Bill, 22 yr.*

20. One half of Henry's age added to one third of Robert's age equals 11 years. In 6 years one third of Henry's age added to one seventh of Robert's age will equal 9 years. What are their present ages? *Henry, 12 yr.; Robert, 15 yr.*

21. Frank can mow a yard in 2 hours less time than Herman. Together they can mow the lawn in $1\frac{7}{8}$ hours. How many hours does it take each working alone to mow the lawn? *Frank, 3 hr.; Herman, 5 hr.*

22. Two men working together can paint a house in 6 days. If one man working alone can paint the house in 10 days, how long will it take the other man working alone to paint it? *15 da.*

23. What number increased by 20% of itself equals 74? *61⅔*

24. What number decreased by 25% of itself equals 69? *92*

25. A merchant sold a knife costing $7.25 for $9.95. What was his per cent of gain based upon the cost? What was his per cent of gain based upon the selling price? *37.24%; 27.14%*

26. In running a race, one sprinter, who runs $8\frac{1}{3}$ yards a second, requires two more seconds than another sprinter, who runs 10 yards a second. What is the distance of the race? *100 yds.*

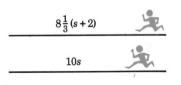

$$\frac{8\frac{1}{3}(s+2)}{10s}$$

27. A train runs between two cities 240 miles apart. If the train were to increase its speed 12 miles an hour, its running time would be lessened by one hour. What is its usual rate? *48 m.p.h.* [B]

28. The sum of two fractions is $\frac{7}{10}$ and the smaller is $\frac{4}{5}$ of the larger. What are the fractions? $\frac{7}{18}$, $\frac{14}{45}$

29. If each side of a square is decreased by 5 inches, the area of the square thus formed is 165 square inches less than that of the original square. Find the side and area of the original square. *19 in.; 361 sq. in.*

30. The denominator of a certain fraction exceeds the numerator by 1. The reciprocal of the fraction exceeds the fraction by $\frac{7}{12}$. Find the original fraction. $-\frac{4}{7}/\frac{3}{7}$, *or* $\frac{3}{4}$

31. The sum of the numerator and the denominator of a fraction is 8. If the numerator is doubled and the denominator is increased by 1, the value of the resulting fraction is 1. Find the fraction. $\frac{3}{5}$

32. Two pipes together can fill a swimming pool in 4 hours 48 minutes. How long will it take each pipe alone to fill the pool if the difference of their times is 4 hours? *8 hr., 12 hr.*

33. A bus driver because of snow was forced to drive at 10 miles an hour less than his usual speed, and he arrived 2 hours late at his destination 315 miles away. Find his usual rate. *45 m.p.h.*

34. A man made a trip of 170 miles, going the first half of the distance at 35 miles an hour and the second half of the distance at 50 miles an hour. How long did it take him to make the trip? *About 4 hr. 8 min.*

35. If the man in Example 34 had made the trip by going half the time at 35 miles an hour and the rest of the trip at 50 miles an hour, how long would it have taken him to make the trip? *4 hr.*

36. In a number of two digits, the tens' digit is four times the units' digit. If the difference of the digits is 6, what is the number? *82*

415

37. The sum of the two digits of a certain number is 16. If the digits are interchanged, the number is decreased by 18. What is the number? *97*

38. The sum of the two digits of a certain number is 6. If the number is divided by the number formed by interchanging the digits, the quotient is $\frac{5}{17}$. Find the original number. *15*

$$\frac{10t+u}{10u+t} = \frac{5}{17}$$

[C]

39. Robert walked 6 miles into the country and ran back 2 miles an hour faster than he went out, making the round trip in $2\frac{1}{2}$ hours. What were his rates going and coming? *Going, 4 m.p.h.; coming, 6 m.p.h.*

40. The tens' digit in a number of two digits exceeds the units' digit by 5. Find the number if it exceeds 10 times the tens' digit by 3. *83*

41. One excavating machine can dig a basement in five days and a second machine can do the same work in six days. The excavation was started by the first machine, but the machine broke down after 3 days. How many days are needed by the second machine to complete the work? *2 ⅖ days*

42. A tank can be filled by one pipe in 8 hours and emptied by another in 12 hours. If both pipes are turned on when the tank is half full, how many hours will it take to fill the tank? *12*

43. An iron bar of uniform cross section weighed 480 pounds. When the bar was made 4 feet longer by rolling it in a bar mill, it weighed 6 pounds less per linear foot. What was the original length of the bar? *16 ft.*

Wind and River Problems [B]   See ① below.

Most of you know how difficult it is to swim or to row a boat up a swiftly moving stream, and how easy it is to swim or to row a boat downstream. When you are swimming downstream, your distance from the starting point is equal to the distance you actually swim plus the distance that you are carried by the current. When you are swimming upstream, your distance from the starting point is equal to the distance you actually swim less the distance you are carried back by the current.

416 ① A new type of problem, involving opposing forces. It should not cause difficulty if illustrated vividly.

1. If a motorboat can go 10 miles an hour on a calm lake, how fast can it go downstream on a river flowing 2 miles an hour? How fast can it go upstream on the river? *12 m.p.h.; 8 m.p.h.*

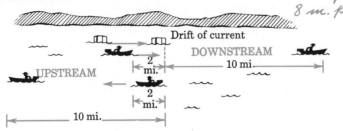

Drift of current

DOWNSTREAM

UPSTREAM

2 mi.

10 mi.

2 mi.

10 mi.

2. How fast can an airplane with a speed of 450 miles an hour go with the wind, when the wind is blowing 30 miles an hour? How fast can it go against the wind? *480 m.p.h. 420 m.p.h.*

3. A motorboat can go x miles an hour in still water. How fast can it go downstream on a river flowing 3 miles an hour? How fast can it go up the river? *(x+3) m.p.h.; (x-3) m.p.h.*

4. Suppose that you are in a railway coach that is going south at 60 m.p.h. What is your velocity with reference to the ground if you walk south in the car at 3 miles an hour? *63 m.p.h.*

Example. A river's current is 4 miles an hour. What speed must a motorboat have in order to go 24 miles down the river and back in $2\frac{1}{2}$ hours? *20 m.p.h.*

Solution.

Let $\quad x =$ the rate of the boat in miles an hour in still water

Then $x + 4 =$ the rate in miles an hour downstream
and $x - 4 =$ the rate in miles an hour upstream

Many pupils find it helpful to make a table when solving motion problems.

	TIME	RATE	DISTANCE
Downstream	$\dfrac{24}{x+4}$	$x + 4$	24
Upstream	$\dfrac{24}{x-4}$	$x - 4$	24

The student should complete the solution.

① It is possible to use two variables, the second representing time. If so used, two equations are needed and can be found by applying the formula $d = rt$ to the table.

EXERCISES

[B]

1. A man can row a boat 3 miles an hour in still water. How far down a river flowing 2 miles an hour can he go and return in his boat in 12 hours? *10 mi.*

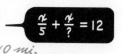

$$\frac{x}{5} + \frac{x}{?} = 12$$

2. An aviator flies 240 miles with the wind in 2 hours. He returns flying against the wind in 3 hours. Find the rate of the airplane and of the wind. *Plane, 100 m.p.h. wind, 20 m.p.h.*

3. An airplane whose rate in still air is 420 miles an hour can go 600 miles with the wind in the same time that it can go 520 miles against the wind. What is the speed of the wind? *30 m.p.h.*

4. An airplane can go 100 miles with the wind in 20 minutes, but the return trip against the wind requires 25 minutes. Find the rate of the wind and of the airplane in still air. *wind, 30 m.p.h.; plane, 270 m.p.h.*

5. A motorboat can go 24 miles upstream in $1\frac{1}{2}$ hours and return in 1 hour. Find the speed of the boat in still water. *20 m.p.h.*

6. An airplane flew from one city to another in forty minutes with the wind, and returned in fifty minutes against the same wind. If the rate of the wind was 12 miles an hour, how far apart were the cities? *80 mi.*

7. With the wind an airplane can go 200 miles in 1 hour and 20 minutes. Against the wind it can go 135 miles in $1\frac{1}{2}$ hours. Find the speed of the plane and the speed of the wind. *Plane, 120 m.p.h. Wind, 30 m.p.h.*

Checking Your Understanding of Chapter 15

If you have mastered this chapter, you know:

PAGE

1. The difference between a fractional equation and an equation containing fractions   401
2. How to solve fractional equations   401   **Do you need**
3. How to solve literal fractional equations   407   **to review?**
4. How to solve wind and river problems   417
5. How to spell and use the following words:

	PAGE		PAGE
abscissa	274	literal equation	356
coordinates	274	ratio	231
digit	360		

418

Solve:

1. $\dfrac{y}{5} = \dfrac{2y-9}{3} - 11$ *30*

2. $\dfrac{5y}{6} + y = \dfrac{y-6}{3}$ *-1⅓*

3. $x + \dfrac{1}{x} = 2$ *1, 1*

4. $\dfrac{3}{x} + \dfrac{x}{3} = 2\frac{1}{2}$ *1½, 6*

5. $\dfrac{7-4n}{6} - \dfrac{23-8n}{12} = \dfrac{2-n}{n}$ *8*

6. $\dfrac{5x-7}{3} + \dfrac{x-11}{x-5} = 4$ *2, 6⅕*

7. $\dfrac{y-1}{y+1} - \dfrac{y-2}{y-1} + \dfrac{1}{12} = 0$ *5, 7*

8. $\dfrac{x+4}{x+3} - \dfrac{x-1}{x} = \dfrac{7}{2x+6}$ *2*

9. $\dfrac{1}{y} - \dfrac{2}{y-1} = \dfrac{6}{2y^2+y}$ *½, -5*

10. $.3y - .02y = 7$ *25*

11. $3.2y + .4 = .8y + 10$ *4*

Solve for x:

12. $\dfrac{x-b}{x} = \dfrac{x}{x+a}$ *ab/(a-b)*

13. $a - \dfrac{a}{2x} = \dfrac{b}{x}$ *(a+2b)/2a*

14. Solve $b = \dfrac{m}{n-p}$ for p. *(bn-m)/b*

15. Solve $U = \dfrac{MV}{M+N}$ for M. *NU/(V-U)*

16. A rectangle is 3 rods longer than it is wide. If the width is divided by the length, the quotient is $\frac{4}{5}$. Find the dimensions of the rectangle. *12 rd. x 15 rd.*

17. One number is $\frac{1}{9}$ as large as another. If 3 is added to each number, then one of the numbers will be $\frac{1}{5}$ as large as the other. Find the numbers. *3, 27*

18. John has 27 coins in nickels and quarters. If their value is $4.95, how many are there of each? *18 quarters, 9 nickels*

19. An airplane travels five times as fast as an automobile. The airplane requires one hour longer to go 1000 miles than the automobile takes to go 160 miles. Find the rate of each. *auto, 40 m. p. h.; plane, 200 m. p. h.*

20. In 8 years Mary Jane will be $\frac{7}{12}$ as old as Betty, but 2 years ago she was $\frac{2}{7}$ as old as Betty. How old is each girl now? *Mary Jane, 6 yr.; Betty, 16 yr.*

21. If the fraction $\dfrac{x}{x+1}$ is subtracted from its reciprocal, the difference is $\frac{11}{30}$. Find the fraction. *⅚, or -⁶⁄₅*

22. A boy can row 5 miles upstream in $2\frac{1}{2}$ hours and return in $1\frac{1}{4}$ hours. How fast can he row in still water? *3 m. p. h.*

419

[A]

Solve:

4 **1.** $5(x + 4) + 9 = 49$ *3, 5*   **4.** $y(y - 6) = 2y - 15$

6, -4 **2.** $y(y - 2) = 24$ *$-2\frac{1}{2}$*   **5.** $3(y + 11) - 7(y - 2) = 57$

$\frac{1}{2}, -3$ **3.** $x(2x - 1) + 6x = 3$ *6*   **6.** $11c - (12 - 8c) = 2(7c + 9)$

7. Solve the following set of equations:

$$3a - 4b = 9 \quad a = 2,$$
$$3a + 8b = 0 \quad b = -\tfrac{3}{4}$$

8. Find the volume of a pyramid whose base is a square 3 feet on a side and whose height is 5 feet. $\left(\text{Use } V = \dfrac{s^2 h}{3}.\right)$
15 cu. ft.

9. Find the approximate horsepower of a six-cylinder engine on a tractor if the diameter of each piston is 4 inches. The formula is $P = \dfrac{nd^2}{2.5}$, in which n is the number of cylinders and d is the diameter of each piston. *38.4 H.P.*

10. Using the formula $c = 2\pi r$, copy and complete the following table. Use 3.14 for the value of π.

r	0	3.5	7	10.5	14	17.5
c	?	?	?	?	?	?

0   22.0   44.0   65.9   87.9   109.9

Graph the formula $c = 2\pi r$.

11. Factor:

a. $\pi R - \pi\pi$ *$(R-1)$*

b. $4x^2 - 8$ *$4(x^2-2)$*

c. $4x^2 + 8x$ *$4x(x+2)$*

d. $6s^2 + 12s$ *$6s(s+2)$*

e. $e^2 - e - 20$ *$(e-5)(e+4)$*

f. $e^3 - e^2 - e$ *$e(e^2-e-1)$*

g. $4x^2 - 324$ *$4(x+9)(x-9)$*

h. $3x^2 + 13xy - 10y^2$
$(3x-2y)(x+5y)$

12. Solve $A = hb$ for h; for b. *$h = \frac{A}{b}$; $b = \frac{A}{h}$*

13. Solve $P = 2l + 2w$ for l. *$\dfrac{P - 2w}{2}$*

14. Reduce $\dfrac{x^2 + x - 6}{2x^2 - x - 21}$ to lowest terms. *$\dfrac{x-2}{2x-7}$*

This is a good general review to maintain skills and tie together previously learned techniques. Important now that the end of the year is in sight. It is hoped that your schedule permits you to take time for it.

Do as indicated:

15. $\dfrac{x^2 - 6x}{4} \cdot \dfrac{x}{x-6}$ $\dfrac{x^2}{4}$

16. $\dfrac{x^2 + 4x}{2x + 1} \div \dfrac{x^2 - 16}{4x^2 - 1}$ $\dfrac{x(2x-1)}{x-4}$

17. $\dfrac{a}{b} + 1$ $\dfrac{a+b}{b}$

18. $\dfrac{y}{y^2 - 3y - 4} + \dfrac{1}{y - 4}$ $\dfrac{2y+1}{(y-4)(y+1)}$

19. $\dfrac{1}{a} + \dfrac{1}{b} + \dfrac{1}{c}$ $\dfrac{bc + ac + ab}{abc}$

20. $\dfrac{2y}{y^2 + y} - \dfrac{4y + 3}{y^2 - 1}$ $\dfrac{-2y-5}{(y+1)(y-1)}$

21. What is the haul of each of two trucks if 4 trips of the smaller and 3 trips of the larger make a total haul of 23 tons, whereas 5 trips of the smaller and one trip of the larger make a total haul of 15 tons? *Smaller, 2 T.; larger, 5 T.*

22. The seats in Yankee Stadium and $\frac{1}{2}$ those in Tiger Stadium total 86,725. The seats in Tiger Stadium and $\frac{1}{2}$ those in Yankee Stadium total 92,120. How many seats are in each? *Yankee Stadium, 54,220; Tiger Stadium, 65,010*

23. Solve graphically: $y - 3x = 9$
$$x + 2y = 4$$ *$x = -2, y = 3$*

If $a = 3$, $b = -1$, and $c = 0$, find the value of

24. $\dfrac{a^3b - bc}{9b}$ *3*

25. $(a - b)^3 + 4ab$ *52*

26. $abc - 4a^2$ *−36*

27. $\dfrac{15 + a^2b^3}{-6}$ *−1*

28. $a^2b^2 - 25$ *−16*

29. $4a^2b^3 + (ab)^3$ *−63*

Copy and complete the following sentences:

30. A quadratic equation is an equation of the __?__ degree. *second*

31. A trinomial has __?__ terms. *three*

32. In the division of fractions, the divisor is __?__. *inverted*

33. Before fractions can be combined they must have the same __?__. *denominator*

34. The numerator of the fraction $\dfrac{a}{b}$ is __?__ and the denominator is __?__. *a, b*

[B]

35. Solve $S = \frac{1}{2}gt^2$ for g. $\dfrac{2S}{t^2}$

36. Solve $\dfrac{1}{f} = \dfrac{1}{d_1} + \dfrac{1}{d_2}$ for d_1. $\dfrac{d_2 f}{d_2 - f}$

421

37. a. $(x^2+9)(x-3)(x+3)$
b. $a(a+1)(a-1)$
c. $5(x^2-2x+5)$
d. $6(x+4)(x-3)$
e. $5(a+b)(a-b)$
f. $2bx(1-3b+4x)$
g. $a^2(y-3)(y-2)$
h. $xy(3x-4y)(5x-6y)$

37. Factor: *(See ans. above)*

a. $x^4 - 81$

b. $a^3 - a$

c. $5x^2 - 10x + 25$

d. $6x^2 + 6x - 72$

e. $5a^2 - 5b^2$

f. $2bx - 6b^2x + 8bx^2$

g. $a^2y^2 - 5a^2y + 6a^2$

h. $15x^3y - 38x^2y^2 + 24xy^3$

38. Simplify: $\dfrac{3x^3 - 6x^2 - 24x}{2x^4 + 3x^3 - 2x^2}$ $\dfrac{3(x-4)}{x(2x-1)}$

39. Combine: $\dfrac{x+y}{x-y} - \dfrac{x-y}{x+y} - \dfrac{4xy}{x^2-y^2}$ 0

40. Multiply: $\dfrac{2ax^2 - 2ay^2}{x^2 - 3xy + 2y^2} \cdot \dfrac{4x - 8y}{ax + ay}$ 8

41. Divide $\dfrac{2a^3 + 2a^2b - 24ab^2}{5a^2 - 80b^2}$ by $\dfrac{4ab - 12b^2}{a^2 - 4ab}$ $\dfrac{a^2}{10b}$

Solve:

42. $\dfrac{2c}{2c-3} - \dfrac{3c}{2c+3} = \dfrac{15 - 2c^2}{4c^2 - 9}$ 1

43. $\dfrac{8}{n^2-1} = \dfrac{n}{n-1} + \dfrac{n}{n+1}$ $2, -2$

44. One number is two fifths as large as another. When 40 is subtracted from each of the numbers, one result is 10 times the other. What are the numbers? 48 and 120

45. A lawn can be mowed by one mower in 3 hours and by another in 2 hours. If both mowers are used, how many hours are required? $1\,\frac{1}{5}$ hr.

46. Jane can wash the dishes in 30 minutes and Harriet can wash them in 25 minutes. After Jane has been working for 10 minutes, Harriet begins to help her. How long will it take both girls to finish the dishes? $9\frac{1}{11}$ min.

Can you solve the following problem? If you can, you are one in a hundred.

47. After traveling an hour at constant speed a freight train is delayed 30 minutes to cool a hot box. It then proceeds at $\frac{6}{5}$ of its former rate and arrives 10 minutes late. If the detention had occurred 12 miles farther on, the train would have arrived 4 minutes later than it did. Find the whole distance traveled and the rate before the detention. (Use two letters.)
whole distance, 90 mi.; rate, 30 m.p.h.

Solve:

1. $\dfrac{3}{5}x = 10$ $16\frac{2}{3}$ **3.** $\dfrac{2x-3}{5} = 15$ 39 **5.** $\dfrac{2}{3}x - \dfrac{3}{5} = 0$ $\dfrac{9}{10}$

2. $\dfrac{3}{y} = 2$ $1\frac{1}{2}$ **4.** $\dfrac{3}{4x-1} = 1$ 1 **6.** $\dfrac{2}{y} + \dfrac{4}{y} = 4$ $1\frac{1}{2}$

7. $\dfrac{x-7}{x+3} - \dfrac{3x-10}{3x} = 0$ $1\frac{1}{2}$ **8.** $\dfrac{x}{x-6} - \dfrac{2x}{3x-18} + \dfrac{4}{3} = 0$ $4\frac{4}{5}$

9. Solve for x: $\dfrac{x}{a} + \dfrac{x}{b} = a + b$ ab

10. The square of a certain number, decreased by $\frac{1}{3}$ of the number, gives 34 as a result. Find two numbers satisfying this condition. $6, -5\frac{2}{3}$

11. The sum of two numbers is 12. If 5 times the larger is added to $\frac{1}{4}$ the smaller, the result is 41. Find the numbers. 4 and 8

Solve:

1. $\dfrac{4}{y} - \dfrac{3}{y-4} = \dfrac{7}{2}$ $2, 2\frac{2}{7}$ **2.** $\dfrac{x+4}{x-2} = \dfrac{48}{x^2-4}$ $4, -10$

3. $\dfrac{y+6}{y-5} + \dfrac{y+2}{y-2} = \dfrac{y^2+20}{y^2-7y+10}$ $6, -7$

4. $\dfrac{x+y}{2} + 2 = 0$ $x = -3,$ $y = -1$

$\dfrac{8}{x+y} - \dfrac{8}{x-y} = \dfrac{x+y+20}{x^2-y^2}$

5. Solve for b: $m = \dfrac{a-b}{b-c}$ $\dfrac{a+cm}{m+1}$

6. Solve for y: $\dfrac{2b}{y} + \dfrac{1}{2y} = \dfrac{4b+1}{4b}$ $2b$

7. The denominator of a certain fraction is 7 more than the numerator. If the numerator is increased by 8 and the denominator is decreased by 10, the result is 6 times the original fraction. What is the original fraction? $\dfrac{8}{15}$, or $\dfrac{-\frac{7}{5}}{\frac{28}{5}}$

TUNNELS

Lincoln Tunnel, showing rock excavation

Tunnels, like bridges, are constructed to improve transportation. They are made through mountains in order to level roadways and to shorten distances. They are constructed under bodies of water to do the work of bridges and ferries.

One of the longest vehicular tunnels in the world is the Holland Tunnel, which passes under the Hudson River, connecting New York City with Jersey City. This tunnel, consisting of two tubes, is more than one and a half miles long, and accommodates two lines of traffic each way. More than twenty million cars pass through it each year.

The Lincoln Tunnel, lying between the Holland Tunnel and the George Washington Bridge, is the newest Hudson River crossing. Its construction was started at each of the two entrances. Here the laborers (sand hogs), working in large machines called shields, began the construction of the large cast iron shell for the outer wall of the tunnel. The shields were pushed forward by large jacks. The work was strenuous, but each crew averaged about forty feet a day. The engineering on this work was so exact that when the first tube of the tunnel was "holed through," the shields met within a quarter of an inch. This tunnel consists of three 2-lane tubes, one 7482 feet long, a second 8216 feet long, and a third 8013 feet long.

The ventilating systems of the two tunnels are alike in most respects. The Holland Tunnel has a maximum ventilation of 3,760,000 cubic feet of fresh air per minute, and the Lincoln Tunnel has a maximum ventilation of 1,913,000 cubic feet per minute.

The planning and construction of tunnels such as these are testimonials to the practical value of mathematics. The mathematics involved in each project was immense, ranging from simple arithmetic to the mathematics taught in college.

Interior View of the Lincoln Tunnel

16

Powers, Roots, and Radicals

Suggested Time Schedule
Minimum   8 days
Maximum   12 days

*In this chapter you will learn
more about ways of writing
and finding repeated factors.*

Squaring Numbers [A]

In this chapter you will learn more about powers and roots of numbers. When a number is used two or more times as a factor, the product is called a power of that number.

Since $5^2 = 5 \times 5 = 25$, then 25 is the second power, or the square, of 5. Likewise x^8 is the square of x^4.

Example 1. $(4\,x^3)^2 = (4\,x^3)(4\,x^3) = 16\,x^6$

Example 2. $(-7\,a^5)^2 = (-7\,a^5)(-7\,a^5) = 49\,a^{10}$

Example 3. $\left(\frac{3}{4}\right)^2 = \frac{3}{4} \times \frac{3}{4} = \frac{9}{16}$

Example 4. $\left(\frac{2\,a}{3\,b^2}\right)^2 = \frac{2\,a}{3\,b^2} \times \frac{2\,a}{3\,b^2} = \frac{4\,a^2}{9\,b^4}$

ORAL EXERCISES

[A]

Study the four examples above and then supply the missing words:

1. The sign of the square of a positive number is __?__ *(positive)*, and the sign of the square of a negative number is __?__ *(positive)*.

2. The numerical coefficient of the square of a monomial is found by __?__ *(squaring)* the numerical coefficient of the monomial.

3. The exponent of each letter in the square of a monomial is found by multiplying the exponent of that letter in the monomial by __?__ *(two)*.

4. To square a fraction, we place the __?__ *(square)* of the numerator of the fraction over the square of the __?__ *(denominator)* of the fraction.

Find the indicated squares:

5. 3^2 *9*

6. $(-5)^2$ *25*

7. $(-6)^2$ *36*

8. 9^2 *81*

9. 10^2 *100*

10. $(-12)^2$ *144*

11. $(-4\,a)^2$ *$16\,a^2$*

12. $(7\,b)^2$ *$49\,b^2$*

13. $(2\,a^2)^2$ *$4a^4$*

14. $(xy)^2$ *$x^2 y^2$*

15. $(-abc^2)^2$ *$a^2 b^2 c^4$*

16. $(6\,x^2 y^3)^2$ *$36 x^4 y^6$*

17. $(0.1)^2$ *0.01*

18. $(-1.3\,r^2 s^3)^2$ *$1.69 r^4 s^6$*

19. $(0.1\,m^3 n)^2$ *$0.01 m^6 n^2$*

20. $(0.3\,a^2 b^3)^2$ *$0.09 a^4 b^6$*

21. $\left(\frac{2\,a^2 c}{5\,m}\right)^2$ *$\frac{4a^4 c^2}{25 m^2}$*

22. $\left(\frac{7\,a^5 b^6}{8\,y^3}\right)^2$ *$\frac{49 a^{10} b^{12}}{64 y^6}$*

23. $\left(\frac{2\,ab}{c^3}\right)^2$ *$\frac{4a^2 b^2}{c^6}$*

24. $\left(\frac{5\,x^3 y^5}{7\,mn}\right)^2$ *$\frac{25 x^6 y^{10}}{49 m^2 n^2}$*

25. $\left(\frac{rs^2 t^3}{a^2 b^3}\right)^2$ *$\frac{r^2 s^4 t^6}{a^4 b^6}$*

26. $\left(\frac{-4\,mn^2}{5\,s^4 t^5}\right)^2$ *$\frac{16 m^2 n^4}{25 s^8 t^{10}}$*

---

① Bring out the distinction between the exponent and the power. Do not let a student say "2 is the power of 5" for 5^2. The exponent merely indicates the power.

Zero as an exponent is a new idea. It may trigger the question, "What about $x^6 \div x^8$?" Explain that this can be written x^{-2}, which is the same as $1/x^2$. Negative exponents will be studied in second-year algebra.

ALGEBRA, BOOK ONE

The Zero Power of a Number [B]

So far we have been using exponents that are counting numbers. Let us now see what a zero exponent means. By the law of exponents for division,

$$x^6 \div x^6 = x^{6-6} = x^0.$$

You know that

$$x^6 \div x^6 = 1.$$

From these results we define x^0 as 1, where x may have any value except zero. Thus $8^0 = 1$, $100^0 = 1$, and $852^0 = 1$.

The Square Roots of Numbers [A]

When a number has two factors with the same absolute value, either factor is a square root of the original number. Since $9 = 3 \times 3$, a square root of 9 is 3. But 9 also equals $(-3)(-3)$. Therefore -3 is a square root of 9. Every positive number except zero has two square roots. They have the same absolute value, but are opposite in sign. The two square roots of $4\,x^6$ are $2\,x^3$ and $-2\,x^3$.

To indicate that the square root of a number is to be found, the sign $\sqrt{}$ combined with the bar is written over the number thus: $\sqrt{9}$. The sign $\sqrt{}$ is called the radical sign and the number under it the radicand. Taken together they are called a radical expression, or simply, a radical.

When the positive square root of a number is to be taken, the plus sign, or no sign at all, is written before the radical. When the negative square root of a number is to be taken, the minus sign is written before the radical. Thus $+\sqrt{25}$, or $\sqrt{25}$, means $+5$, and $-\sqrt{25}$ means -5. When both square roots of a number are to be taken, both the plus sign and the minus sign are written before the radical. Thus $\pm\sqrt{25}$ means $+5$ and -5. The positive square root of a number is called the principal square root of the number.

When a number has three equal factors, any one of the factors is called a cube root. To indicate that a cube root is to be found, a small 3 is written above the radical sign. Thus $\sqrt[3]{8} = 2$. The 3 is called the index. In square root the index is 2, but we seldom write the 2.

The degree or order of a radical is the same as the index of the root.

428   Clarify use of signs. Emphasize that although 9 has two square roots, it is *not* correct to write $\sqrt{9} = \pm 3$.

[A]

Find the indicated roots:

1. $\sqrt{9}$ $\quad$ *3*
2. $\sqrt{16}$ $\quad$ *4*
3. $\sqrt{25}$ $\quad$ *5*
4. $\sqrt[3]{27}$ $\quad$ *3*
5. $\sqrt{81}$ $\quad$ *9*
6. $\sqrt{121}$ $\quad$ *11*
7. $\sqrt{144}$ $\quad$ *12*
8. $\sqrt{x^2}$ $\quad$ *x*
9. $\sqrt{y^6}$ $\quad$ *y³*
10. $\sqrt[3]{125}$ $\quad$ *5*
11. $-\sqrt{25}$ $\quad$ *-5*
12. $-\sqrt{64}$ $\quad$ *-8*

13. $-\sqrt{y^6}$ $\quad$ *-y³*
14. $\pm\sqrt{36}$ $\quad$ *±6*
15. $\pm\sqrt{49}$ $\quad$ *±7*
16. $\pm\sqrt{121}$ $\quad$ *±11*
17. $\pm\sqrt{400}$ $\quad$ *±20*
18. $-\sqrt{900}$ $\quad$ *-30*
19. $-\sqrt{a^4}$ $\quad$ *-a²*
20. $\sqrt[3]{c^6}$ $\quad$ *c²*
21. $\sqrt{4\,a^{10}}$ $\quad$ *2a⁵*
22. $-\sqrt{16\,x^4}$ $\quad$ *-4x²*
23. $\sqrt{a^8 b^{10}}$ $\quad$ *a⁴b⁵*
24. $\sqrt{25\,c^6}$ $\quad$ *5c³*

25. $-\sqrt{81\,c^6}$ $\quad$ *-9c³*
26. $\sqrt{a^6 b^2 c^{12}}$ $\quad$ *a³bc⁶*
27. $\sqrt{100\,x^6 y^8}$ $\quad$ *10x³y⁴*
28. $\sqrt{36\,x^2 y^4}$ $\quad$ *6xy²*
29. $\sqrt{m^{10} y^{12}}$ $\quad$ *m⁵y⁶*
30. $\sqrt{49\,y^8}$ $\quad$ *7y⁴*
31. $\sqrt{.36}$ $\quad$ *0.6*
32. $\sqrt{.49\,m^4}$ $\quad$ *0.7m²*
33. $\sqrt{169\,a^4}$ $\quad$ *13a²*
34. $-\sqrt{1.44\,a^{10}}$ $\quad$ *-1.2a⁵*
35. $\sqrt{100\,m^4}$ $\quad$ *10m²*
36. $-\sqrt{81\,p^{12}}$ $\quad$ *-9p⁶*

Approximate Square Roots[A]

Many numbers do not have exact square roots. For example, there are no two factors which are alike and which multiplied give the product 8. We say that 8 is not a perfect square.

Although 8 has no exact square root, it is possible to find a number which multiplied by itself gives almost 8. The number 2.828 does that. We say that 2.828 is the *approximate square root* of 8. The numbers 2.8 and 2.83 are also approximate square roots of 8, but are not quite as accurate as 2.828. Obviously, when you are asked to find the square root of a number which is not a perfect square, it is intended that you find the approximate square root to a sensible number of decimal places. Those in the table on page 431 are given to three decimal places; that is, they are rounded off to three decimal places. Three decimal places are enough to use in the computations of this book; in fact, for most ordinary computations, one or two decimal places are sufficient.

When a table of square roots is not available, approximate square roots can be found by the method shown in the example on page 434.

Work with approximate numbers may or may not be new to your students, depending on previous training. If a new idea, they will need some extra explanation. Better still, study pages 513–518 at this time.

429

ALGEBRA, BOOK ONE

Using Tables to Find Squares and Square Roots of Numbers [A]

Using a table of squares and square roots is the easiest and shortest way to find the square root of a number.

[A]

EXERCISES

1. For what does "No." in the table on page 431 stand? For what does "Sq." stand? For what does "Sq. Root" stand? This table also gives the cubes and cube roots of numbers. *number; square of number; square root of number.*

2. Using this table, find the squares of

a. 18 *324*   **c.** 36 *1296*   **e.** 92 *8464*   **g.** 78 *6084*

b. 23 *529*   **d.** 49 *2401*   **f.** 99 *9801*   **h.** 53 *2809*

3. From the table find the positive square roots of

4.123 **a.** 17   *1.414* **c.** 2   *9.592* **e.** 92   *8.832* **g.** 78

5.00 **b.** 25   *1.732* **d.** 3   *9.950* **f.** 99   *7.280* **h.** 53

4. For which of the numbers in Exercise 3 were the square roots exact? For which were they approximate? *Exact for 25; approximate for all others.*

5. Using the table find the squares of

2 **a.** 1.414   *48* **c.** 6.928   *99* **e.** 9.950   *3* **g.** 1.732

10 **b.** 3.162   *30* **d.** 5.477   *83* **f.** 9.110   *6* **h.** 2.449

6. From the table find the positive square roots of

17 **a.** 289   *15* **c.** 225   *45* **e.** 2025   *73* **g.** 5329

14 **b.** 196   *26* **d.** 676   *99* **f.** 9801   *80* **h.** 6400

HINT: If you look for these numbers in the "Sq." column, in which column will you find the square roots?

7. In $c = \sqrt{a^2 + b^2}$ find c when $a = 5$ and $b = 8$. *9.434*

8. In $v = \sqrt{2\,gd}$ find v when $g = 32$ and $d = 1.5$. *9.798*

9. In $s = 16\,t^2$ find s when $t = 17$. *4624*

10. Find the side of a square whose area is 45 square inches. *6.708 in.*

11. Find the area of a circle whose radius is 27 inches. Use $A = 3.14\,r^2$. *2289.06 sq. in.*

12. The area of an equilateral triangle can be found by the formula $A = \frac{1}{4}\,s^2\sqrt{3}$. Use the formula to find A when $s = 5$. *10.825*

13. A square whose sides are 1 foot long has a diagonal $\sqrt{2}$ feet long. Find $\sqrt{2}$. *1.414*

430

Table of Powers and Roots

NO.	SQ.	SQ. ROOT	CUBE	CUBE ROOT	NO.	SQ.	SQ. ROOT	CUBE	CUBE ROOT
1	1	1.000	1	1.000	51	2,601	7.141	132,651	3.708
2	4	1.414	8	1.260	52	2,704	7.211	140,608	3.733
3	9	1.732	27	1.442	53	2,809	7.280	148,877	3.756
4	16	2.000	64	1.587	54	2,916	7.348	157,464	3.780
5	25	2.236	125	1.710	55	3,025	7.416	166,375	3.803
6	36	2.449	216	1.817	56	3,136	7.483	175,616	3.826
7	49	2.646	343	1.913	57	3,249	7.550	185,193	3.848
8	64	2.828	512	2.000	58	3,364	7.616	195,112	3.871
9	81	3.000	729	2.080	59	3,481	7.681	205,379	3.893
10	100	3.162	1,000	2.154	60	3,600	7.746	216,000	3.915
11	121	3.317	1,331	2.224	61	3,721	7.810	226,981	3.936
12	144	3.464	1,728	2.289	62	3,844	7.874	238,328	3.958
13	169	3.606	2,197	2.351	63	3,969	7.937	250,047	3.979
14	196	3.742	2,744	2.410	64	4,096	8.000	262,144	4.000
15	225	3.873	3,375	2.466	65	4,225	8.062	274,625	4.021
16	256	4.000	4,096	2.520	66	4,356	8.124	287,496	4.041
17	289	4.123	4,913	2.571	67	4,489	8.185	300,763	4.062
18	324	4.243	5,832	2.621	68	4,624	8.246	314,432	4.082
19	361	4.359	6,859	2.668	69	4,761	8.307	328,509	4.102
20	400	4.472	8,000	2.714	70	4,900	8.367	343,000	4.121
21	441	4.583	9,261	2.759	71	5,041	8.426	357,911	4.141
22	484	4.690	10,648	2.802	72	5,184	8.485	373,248	4.160
23	529	4.796	12,167	2.844	73	5,329	8.544	389,017	4.179
24	576	4.899	13,824	2.884	74	5,476	8.602	405,224	4.198
25	625	5.000	15,625	2.924	75	5,625	8.660	421,875	4.217
26	676	5.099	17,576	2.962	76	5,776	8.718	438,976	4.236
27	729	5.196	19,683	3.000	77	5,929	8.775	456,533	4.254
28	784	5.292	21,952	3.037	78	6,084	8.832	474,552	4.273
29	841	5.385	24,389	3.072	79	6,241	8.888	493,039	4.291
30	900	5.477	27,000	3.107	80	6,400	8.944	512,000	4.309
31	961	5.568	29,791	3.141	81	6,561	9.000	531,441	4.327
32	1,024	5.657	32,768	3.175	82	6,724	9.055	551,368	4.344
33	1,089	5.745	35,937	3.208	83	6,889	9.110	571,787	4.362
34	1,156	5.831	39,304	3.240	84	7,056	9.165	592,704	4.380
35	1,225	5.916	42,875	3.271	85	7,225	9.220	614,125	4.397
36	1,296	6.000	46,656	3.302	86	7,396	9.274	636,056	4.414
37	1,369	6.083	50,653	3.332	87	7,569	9.327	658,503	4.431
38	1,444	6.164	54,872	3.362	88	7,744	9.381	681,472	4.448
39	1,521	6.245	59,319	3.391	89	7,921	9.434	704,969	4.465
40	1,600	6.325	64,000	3.420	90	8,100	9.487	729,000	4.481
41	1,681	6.403	68,921	3.448	91	8,281	9.539	753,571	4.498
42	1,764	6.481	74,088	3.476	92	8,464	9.592	778,688	4.514
43	1,849	6.557	79,507	3.503	93	8,649	9.644	804,357	4.531
44	1,936	6.633	85,184	3.530	94	8,836	9.695	830,584	4.547
45	2,025	6.708	91,125	3.557	95	9,025	9.747	857,375	4.563
46	2,116	6.782	97,336	3.583	96	9,216	9.798	884,736	4.579
47	2,209	6.856	103,823	3.609	97	9,409	9.849	912,673	4.595
48	2,634	6.928	110,592	3.634	98	9,604	9.899	941,192	4.610
49	2,401	7.000	117,649	3.659	99	9,801	9.950	970,299	4.626
50	2,500	7.071	125,000	3.684	100	10,000	10.000	1,000,000	4.642

ALGEBRA, BOOK ONE

How to Find the Square Root of a Number [A]

The method of finding the square root of arithmetic numbers is based on algebra. First we shall find the square root of an algebraic expression. We know that $(a + b)^2 = a^2 + 2\,ab + b^2$. Then the square root of $a^2 + 2\,ab + b^2$ is $a + b$. The process is as follows:

$$
\begin{array}{r|l}
 & a + b \text{ the square root} \\
a & a^2 + 2\,ab + b^2 \\
 & \underline{a^2} \\
2\,a + b & +2\,ab + b^2 \\
 & \underline{+2\,ab + b^2} \\
 & \quad 0 \qquad 0
\end{array}
$$

The square root of a^2 is a, the first term of the root.

Subtracting a^2 leaves $2\,ab + b^2$. We know that b is the other term of the root. To get b we must divide $2\,ab$ by $2\,a$, which is twice the term already found.

Adding b to $2\,a$, we get $2\,a + b$ for the divisor.

Multiplying $2\,a + b$ by b, the last term of the root, we obtain $2\,ab + b^2$, which, when subtracted, leaves no remainder.

If in the identity $(a + b)^2 = a^2 + 2\,ab + b^2$, we let $a = 40$ and $b = 6$, we have, $(40 + 6)^2 = 1600 + 480 + 36$. Then we find the square root of $1600 + 480 + 36$ as follows:

The square root of 1600 is 40, the first term of the root.

Subtracting $\overline{40}^2$, or 1600, leaves 480 + 36.

Multiplying the part of the root already found by 2, we have

$$
\begin{array}{r|l}
 & 40 + 6 \text{ the square root} \\
40 & 1600 + 480 + 36 \\
 & \underline{1600} \\
80 + 6 & +480 + 36 \\
 & \underline{+480 + 36}
\end{array}
$$

$$2 \times 40 = 80$$
$$480 \div 80 = 6$$

Adding 6 to 80 we have $80 + 6$ as the divisor, and 6 is the next term in the root.

Multiplying $(80 + 6)$ by 6, we obtain $480 + 36$, which, when subtracted, leaves no remainder.

Then $40 + 6$ or 46 is the positive square root of $1600 + 480 + 36$, or 2116.

The method of finding the square roots of arithmetic numbers based on the above solutions is given in the following examples. Study carefully the different steps in Examples 1 and 2. It would be well to use pencil and paper to follow the solutions.

432

POWERS, ROOTS, AND RADICALS

Example 1. Find the positive square root of 2116.

Solution.   1. Separate the number into groups of two figures each, beginning to group at the *decimal point*. A bar can be placed over each group.

2. The first divisor is also the first figure of the quotient, or root. The divisor is 4, because 21 lies between 4 × 4 and 5 × 5.

3. Place the 16 under the 21 and subtract, getting 5 as the remainder. Bring down the 16. The new dividend is 516.

4. We are now ready for another division. To get the new divisor, we multiply the 4, the first figure in the root, by 2 (we always multiply by 2), and get 8 as the first figure of the second divisor.

5. There is one more figure in the divisor, and it is the next figure of the root. As in long division, this is the largest figure possible. By trial we find this figure to be 6. Then 86 is the complete divisor and 6 is the next figure in the quotient (root). Multiply 86 by 6, obtaining 516. Place the 516 under the 516 and subtract. Since there is no remainder, the positive square root of 2116 is 46.

PROOF.
$46^2 = 46 \times 46 = 2116.$

Example 2. Find the positive square root of 44,436.64.

Solution. Beginning at the decimal point, separate the number into groups of two figures each. The first divisor is 2, which is the first figure of the root, 2 × 2 = 4. Subtract 4 from 4. The remainder is zero. Bring down 44 as the next dividend.

Double the 2 in the divisor, obtaining 4 as the first figure of the second divisor. By trial the next figure of the divisor is 1, which is the second figure of the root. Multiply the divisor 41 by 1 and place the product under 44. Subtract, getting 3. Bring down the group 36. The third dividend is 336. (*Cont. on page* 434)

433

Multiply 21, the part of the root already found, by 2, obtaining 42, which is the first part of the third divisor. The last figure of the divisor and the third figure of the root is 0. Multiply 420 by 0, obtaining 0. Subtract, getting 336 as the first part of the fourth dividend.

Double 210, the part of the root already found, getting 420 as the first part of the fourth divisor. The last figure of the divisor and the fourth figure of the root is 8. Multiply 4208 by 8, getting 33,664. Subtract. There is no remainder.

Place the decimal point of the root above the decimal point of the original number. Then 210.8 is the required root. Note that each group of the number has a figure of the root above it.

PROOF. $210.8^2 = 44,436.64$

[A]

EXERCISES

Find the positive square roots of

27 **1.** 729	9.4 **7.** 88.36	2.66 **13.** 7.0756	902 **19.** 813604
34 **2.** 1156	1.46 **8.** 2.1316	21.1 **14.** 445.21	17.8 **20.** 316.84
53 **3.** 2809	10.7 **9.** 114.49	104 **15.** 10816	1100 **21.** 1210000
68 **4.** 4624	145 **10.** 21025	372 **16.** 138384	9.32 **22.** 86.8624
73 **5.** 5329	1.17 **11.** 1.3689	18.9 **17.** 357.21	22.03 **23.** 485.3209
7.8 **6.** 60.84	32.5 **12.** 1056.25	0.428 **18.** 0.183184	0.175 **24.** 0.030625

Computing Approximate Square Roots [A]

As has been explained previously, most numbers are not perfect squares. The number 7 is not a perfect square, since there is no whole number or fraction whose square is 7. Since we cannot find the exact square roots of such numbers, we find their approximate square roots · by computing their square roots to one or more decimal places. In most cases it is sufficient to find the roots to two or three decimal places.

Example. Find the approximate positive square root of 5 to the nearest hundredth.

Solution. Since the square root is to be found to the nearest hundredth, the root should be computed to three decimal places. Three groups of zeros must be added to give three decimal places in the root. The square root of 5 to three decimal places is 2.236. The square root of 5 to the nearest hundredth is 2.24, since 6 is more than 5.

```
         2. 2  3   6
      2 | 5.00 00 00
        | 4
     42 | 1 00
        |   84
    443 | 16 00
        | 13 29
   4466 | 2 71 00
        | 2 67 96
```

Emphasize that in working with approximate numbers one should always carry computation to one more place than finally desired, in order to round off correctly.

[A]

EXERCISES

Find the approximate positive square root of each number to the nearest hundredth:

1. 2 *1.41*   **4.** 11 *3.32*   **7.** 33.33 *5.77*   **10.** 32.4 *5.69*

2. 3 *1.73*   **5.** 20 *4.47*   **8.** 1.82 *1.35*   **11.** 42.17 *6.49*

3. 6 *2.45*   **6.** 28 *5.29*   **9.** .032 *0.18*   **12.** 99 *9.95*

If $A = \sqrt{b^2 - 4ac}$, find A when

13. $a = 1, b = 8, c = 9$ *5.29*   **16.** $a = 7, b = -49, c = 0$ *49*

14. $a = 1, b = 22, c = 2$ *21.82*   **17.** $a = -5, b = 14, c = -8$ *6*

15. $a = 2, b = -7, c = 3$ *5*   **18.** $a = 1, b = -1, c = -1$ *2.24*

Find the values of:

19. $\sqrt{a} + \sqrt{b}$ when $a = 25$ and $b = 64$. *13*

20. $\sqrt{a^2 + b^2}$ when $a = 5$ and $b = 12$. *13*

21. $\sqrt{a^2 + b^2}$ if $a = 16$ and $b = 30$. *34*

22. $2\sqrt{m} - 3\sqrt{n}$ when $m = 31,625$ and $n = 256$. *307.67*

Rational and Irrational Numbers [A]

You should recall from Chapter 1 that a rational number is a number that can be expressed by a fraction whose numerator is an integer and whose denominator is a non-zero integer. For example, $7, -6, \frac{1}{2}, \sqrt{25}, \sqrt{0.25}$ are rational numbers.

You should also recall that numbers such as $\sqrt{2}, \sqrt{15}$, and π are irrational because they cannot be expressed as the ratio of two integers. Only an approximation of irrational numbers can be found. The value of π has been computed to more than 700 decimal places, but no decimal can express its true value.

Two Important Principles of Radicals [A]

In simplifying, adding, multiplying, and dividing radicals, two important principles are used:

Principle 1. The square root of a product is equal to the product of the square roots of its factors; and conversely, the product of two square roots is equal to the square root of the product of the radicands.

$$\sqrt{ab} = \sqrt{a}\sqrt{b} \qquad \sqrt{a}\sqrt{b} = \sqrt{ab}.$$

Principles 1 and 2 are very useful and should be taught with meaning and practiced thoroughly.

Examples.

$$\sqrt{36} = \sqrt{4}\sqrt{9} \qquad\qquad \sqrt{9}\sqrt{36} = \sqrt{324}$$
$$\sqrt{100} = \sqrt{4}\sqrt{25} \qquad\qquad \sqrt{49}\sqrt{2} = \sqrt{98}$$
$$\sqrt{8} = \sqrt{4}\sqrt{2} \qquad\qquad \sqrt{5}\sqrt{2} = \sqrt{10}$$

Principle 2. The square root of a fraction is equal to the square root of the numerator divided by the square root of the denominator; and conversely, the quotient of two square roots is equal to the square root of the quotient of the radicands.

$$\sqrt{\frac{a}{b}} = \frac{\sqrt{a}}{\sqrt{b}} \qquad\qquad \frac{\sqrt{a}}{\sqrt{b}} = \sqrt{\frac{a}{b}}$$

Examples.

$$\sqrt{\frac{4}{9}} = \frac{\sqrt{4}}{\sqrt{9}} = \frac{2}{3} \qquad \sqrt{\frac{9}{25}} = \frac{\sqrt{9}}{\sqrt{25}} = \frac{3}{5} \qquad \sqrt{\frac{7}{8}} = \frac{\sqrt{7}}{\sqrt{8}}$$

$$\frac{\sqrt{2}}{\sqrt{3}} = \sqrt{\frac{2}{3}} \qquad \frac{\sqrt{16}}{\sqrt{25}} = \sqrt{\frac{16}{25}} = \frac{4}{5}$$

EXERCISES

[A]

1. Is $\sqrt{4}$ a radical? *yes* Is $\sqrt{4}$ a rational number? *yes*

2. State which of the following numbers are rational: ⟨3;⟩ −8; ¼; $\sqrt{20}$; ⟨$\sqrt{16}$;⟩ $\sqrt{40}$.

Multiply or divide, using Principles 1 and 2:

3. $\sqrt{4}\sqrt{25}$ $\sqrt{100}$ 7. $\sqrt{15} \div \sqrt{3}$ $\sqrt{5}$ 11. $\sqrt{10} \div \sqrt{5}$ $\sqrt{2}$

4. $\sqrt{2}\sqrt{3}$ $\sqrt{6}$ 8. $\sqrt{27} \div \sqrt{9}$ $\sqrt{3}$ 12. $\sqrt{18} \div \sqrt{2}$ $\sqrt{9}$

5. $\sqrt{9}\sqrt{3}$ $\sqrt{27}$ 9. $\sqrt{64} \div \sqrt{4}$ $\sqrt{16}$ 13. $\sqrt{3} \div \sqrt{1}$ $\sqrt{3}$

6. $\sqrt{12} \div \sqrt{3}$ $\sqrt{4}$ 10. $\sqrt{8} \div \sqrt{2}$ $\sqrt{4}$ 14. $\sqrt{6} \times \sqrt{2}$ $\sqrt{12}$

Complete:

15. $\sqrt{20} = \sqrt{?}\sqrt{5} = ?\sqrt{5}$ 4 2   18. $\sqrt{24} = \sqrt{?}\sqrt{6} = ?\sqrt{6}$ 4 2

16. $\sqrt{8} = \sqrt{?}\sqrt{2} = ?\sqrt{2}$ 4 2   19. $\sqrt{80} = \sqrt{?}\sqrt{5} = ?\sqrt{5}$ 16 4

17. $\sqrt{98} = \sqrt{?}\sqrt{2} = ?\sqrt{2}$ 49 7   20. $\sqrt{18} = \sqrt{?}\sqrt{2} = ?\sqrt{2}$ 9 3

436

Simplifying Radicals [A]

A radical can be simplified if

1. The indicated root can be found exactly.
2. The radicand contains a factor of which the indicated root can be taken.
3. The radicand is a fraction.

You should remember that a radical is in its simplest form when the radicand is a whole number and is as small as possible.

Example 1. Simplify $\sqrt{25}$.

Solution. $\sqrt{25} = 5$

Example 2. Simplify $3\sqrt{32}$.

Solution. The radicand 32 contains the perfect square factors 4 and 16. We must use the factor 16. Can you tell why?

$$3\sqrt{32} = 3\sqrt{16}\sqrt{2} = 3 \times 4\sqrt{2} = 12\sqrt{2}$$

Simplify the following radicals:

[A] **EXERCISES**

1. $\sqrt{9x^2}$ $3x$
2. $\sqrt{8}$ $2\sqrt{2}$
3. $\sqrt{12}$ $2\sqrt{3}$
4. $\sqrt{49}$ 7
5. $\sqrt{98}$ $7\sqrt{2}$
6. $\sqrt{20}$ $2\sqrt{5}$

7. $\sqrt{24}$ $2\sqrt{6}$
8. $\sqrt{40}$ $2\sqrt{10}$
9. $\sqrt{\frac{1}{16}}$ $\frac{1}{4}$
10. $\sqrt{50}$ $5\sqrt{2}$
11. $\sqrt{60}$ $2\sqrt{15}$
12. $\sqrt{100}$ 10

13. $\sqrt{80}$ $4\sqrt{5}$
14. $\sqrt{27}$ $3\sqrt{3}$
15. $\sqrt{18}$ $3\sqrt{2}$
16. $\sqrt{64}$ 8
17. $\sqrt{128}$ $8\sqrt{2}$
18. $\sqrt{16}$ 4

19. $\sqrt{48}$ $4\sqrt{3}$
20. $\sqrt{c^2d^4}$ cd^2
21. $3\sqrt{64}$ 24
22. $4\sqrt{27}$ $12\sqrt{3}$
23. $\sqrt{36x^{10}}$ $6x^5$
24. $5\sqrt{28}$ $10\sqrt{7}$

Example 3. Simplify $\sqrt{\frac{2}{3}}$.

Solution. This radical can be simplified because its radicand is a fraction. To make the denominator a perfect square we multiply it by 3. Then the numerator must be multiplied by 3.

Then $\qquad \sqrt{\frac{2}{3}} = \sqrt{\frac{6}{9}} = \frac{\sqrt{6}}{\sqrt{9}} = \frac{\sqrt{6}}{3}$, or $\frac{1}{3}\sqrt{6}$

Example 4. Simplify $\sqrt{\frac{4}{5}}$.

Solution.

$$\sqrt{\frac{4}{5}} = \sqrt{\frac{20}{25}} = \frac{\sqrt{20}}{\sqrt{25}} = \frac{2\sqrt{5}}{5}, \text{ or } \frac{2}{5}\sqrt{5}$$

ALGEBRA, BOOK ONE

EXERCISES

Transform the following radicals into their simplest forms:

1. $\sqrt{\frac{1}{2}}$ $\frac{1}{2}\sqrt{2}$

2. $\sqrt{\frac{1}{3}}$ $\frac{1}{3}\sqrt{3}$

3. $\sqrt{\frac{2}{5}}$ $\frac{1}{5}\sqrt{10}$

4. $\sqrt{\frac{a^2}{b^2}}$ $\frac{a}{b}$

5. $\sqrt{\frac{1}{6}}$ $\frac{1}{6}\sqrt{6}$

6. $4\sqrt{\frac{1}{7}}$ $\frac{4}{7}\sqrt{7}$

7. $3\sqrt{\frac{1}{3}}$ $\sqrt{3}$

8. $\sqrt{\frac{1}{8}}$ $\frac{1}{4}\sqrt{2}$

9. $\sqrt{\frac{1}{12}}$ $\frac{1}{6}\sqrt{3}$

10. $\sqrt{\frac{1}{20}}$ $\frac{1}{10}\sqrt{5}$

11. $\sqrt{\frac{4}{7}}$ $\frac{2}{7}\sqrt{7}$

12. $\sqrt{\frac{9}{5}}$ $\frac{3}{5}\sqrt{5}$

13. $\sqrt{\frac{2}{9}}$ $\frac{1}{3}\sqrt{2}$

14. $\frac{1}{3}\sqrt{\frac{1}{2}}$ $\frac{1}{6}\sqrt{2}$

15. $\frac{1}{2}\sqrt{\frac{3}{8}}$ $\frac{1}{8}\sqrt{6}$

Example 5. Simplify $\sqrt{\frac{1}{a^5}}$.

Solution. If a^5 is multiplied by a, the product is a perfect square.

Then $\qquad \sqrt{\frac{1}{a^5}} = \sqrt{\frac{a}{a^6}} = \frac{\sqrt{a}}{\sqrt{a^6}} = \frac{\sqrt{a}}{a^3}$, or $\frac{1}{a^3}\sqrt{a}$

EXERCISES

Simplify the following radicals:

1. $\sqrt{x^3}$ $x\sqrt{x}$

2. $\sqrt{x^5}$ $x^2\sqrt{x}$

3. $\sqrt{4a}$ $2\sqrt{a}$

4. $\sqrt{7x^2}$ $x\sqrt{7}$

5. $\sqrt{32a^3}$ $4a\sqrt{2a}$

6. $\sqrt{8y^2}$ $2y\sqrt{2}$

7. $\sqrt{m^3n^2}$ $mn\sqrt{m}$

8. $\sqrt{a^3b}$ $a\sqrt{ab}$

9. $\sqrt{ab^4}$ $b^2\sqrt{a}$

10. $\sqrt{8x^3}$ $2x\sqrt{2x}$

11. $\sqrt{\frac{1}{a}}$ $\frac{1}{a}\sqrt{a}$

12. $\sqrt{\frac{1}{a^2}}$ $\frac{1}{a}$

13. $\sqrt{\frac{2}{x^5}}$ $\frac{1}{x^3}\sqrt{2x}$

14. $\sqrt{\frac{4}{ab}}$ $\frac{2}{ab}\sqrt{ab}$

Square Roots of Fractions [A]

The square root of a fraction may be found by dividing the square root of the numerator by the square root of the denominator.

Example 1. $\sqrt{\frac{4}{25}} = \frac{2}{5}$

Example 2. $\sqrt{\frac{16\,a^4}{49\,b^6}} = \frac{4\,a^2}{7\,b^3}$

When the terms of a fraction are not perfect squares, the approximate square root may be found in three ways. These ways will be illustrated in finding the square root of the fraction $\frac{2}{3}$.

438

Example 3. Find the approximate square root of $\frac{2}{3}$.

Solution 1. Using the method of Examples 1 and 2,

$$\sqrt{\frac{2}{3}} = \frac{\sqrt{2}}{\sqrt{3}} = \frac{1.414}{1.732} = .816$$

Solution 2. Changing $\frac{2}{3}$ to a decimal, we have

$$\sqrt{\tfrac{2}{3}} = \sqrt{.666666} = .816$$

Solution 3. In this solution the denominator is made a perfect square by multiplying it by 3. Then the numerator must be multiplied by 3. The solution follows:

$$\sqrt{\frac{2}{3}} = \sqrt{\frac{6}{9}} = \frac{\sqrt{6}}{\sqrt{9}} = \frac{2.449}{3} = .816$$

In most cases the third method is used, since it is usually the shortest.

[A]

EXERCISES

Find the indicated roots:

1. $\sqrt{\dfrac{1}{4}}$ *½*   3. $\sqrt{\dfrac{x^2}{4y^2}}$ *x/2y*   5. $\sqrt{\dfrac{25\,c^2}{36\,d^2}}$ *5c/6d*   7. $\sqrt{\dfrac{m^{10}}{64\,x^6}}$ *m⁵/8x³*

2. $\sqrt{\dfrac{9}{25}}$ *3/5*   4. $\sqrt{\dfrac{y^6}{16\,m^2}}$ *y³/4m*   6. $\sqrt{\dfrac{9\,m^8}{49}}$ *3m⁴/7*   8. $\sqrt{\dfrac{16\,a^4}{121\,b^4}}$ *4a²/11b²*

Find the approximate square roots of the following fractions:

9. $\frac{3}{4}$ *0.866*   11. $\frac{2}{5}$ *0.6324*   13. $\frac{4}{7}$ *0.756*   15. $\frac{2}{9}$ *0.4713⁺*

10. $\frac{3}{8}$ *0.6122⁺*   12. $\frac{1}{3}$ *0.5773⁺*   14. $\frac{1}{2}$ *0.707*   16. $\frac{5}{8}$ *0.7905*

Combining Radicals [A]

Similar radicals are radicals having the same index and the same radicand. Thus $2\sqrt{5}$, $6\sqrt{5}$, and $\frac{1}{2}\sqrt{5}$ are similar radicals. Similar radicals can be added or combined by adding their coefficients.   ①

Example 1. Combine: $6\sqrt{2} + 3\sqrt{2} - 7\sqrt{2}$

Solution. $6\sqrt{2} + 3\sqrt{2} - 7\sqrt{2} = (6 + 3 - 7)\sqrt{2} = 2\sqrt{2}$

Example 2. Combine similar radicals:

$$2\sqrt{3} + 4\sqrt{5} + 6\sqrt{3} - 6\sqrt{5}$$

Solution. $2\sqrt{3} + 4\sqrt{5} + 6\sqrt{3} - 6\sqrt{5} =$
$2\sqrt{3} + 6\sqrt{3} + 4\sqrt{5} - 6\sqrt{5} =$
$(2 + 3)\sqrt{3} + (4 - 6)\sqrt{5} = 8\sqrt{3} - 2\sqrt{5}$

① Show that, in Example 1, a replacement for a in $6a + 3a - 7a = 2a$ is involved. The equivalence holds for all such replacements, including the current one of $a = \sqrt{2}$.

[A]

EXERCISES

Simplify by combining like terms:

1. $4\sqrt{3} + 2\sqrt{3} + 5\sqrt{3}$ $11\sqrt{3}$

2. $\sqrt{2} + \sqrt{2} + \sqrt{5}$ $2\sqrt{2}+\sqrt{5}$

3. $\sqrt{5} - \sqrt{5}$ 0

4. $3\sqrt{6} - 4\sqrt{6} - \sqrt{6}$ $-2\sqrt{6}$

5. $3\sqrt{3} + 9\sqrt{3} - 2\sqrt{3}$ $10\sqrt{3}$

6. $\sqrt{7} + \sqrt{7} + \sqrt{7}$ $3\sqrt{7}$

7. $5\sqrt{5} - 4\sqrt{5} - \sqrt{5}$ 0

8. $\sqrt{2} + 6\sqrt{2} - 6$ $7\sqrt{2}-6$

9. $10 - \sqrt{3} - 2\sqrt{3}$ $10-3\sqrt{3}$

10. $4\sqrt{5} - \sqrt{6} - \sqrt{5}$ $3\sqrt{5}-\sqrt{6}$

11. $10 - 2\sqrt{2} + 2\sqrt{2}$ 10

12. $7 + 5 - \sqrt{5}$ $12-\sqrt{5}$

13. $6 + \sqrt{6} - 10\sqrt{6}$ $6-9\sqrt{6}$

14. $\sqrt{a} - 7\sqrt{a} + 3$ $3-6\sqrt{a}$

15. $\sqrt{a} + \sqrt{ab} + 2\sqrt{a}$ $3\sqrt{a}+\sqrt{ab}$

16. $\sqrt{x} + \sqrt{y} + 9\sqrt{x}$ $10\sqrt{x}+\sqrt{y}$

Example 3. Simplify the radicals and combine:

$$3\sqrt{8} - \sqrt{50} + 6\sqrt{32}$$

Solution. $3\sqrt{8} - \sqrt{50} + 6\sqrt{32}$
$$= 3\sqrt{4}\sqrt{2} - \sqrt{25}\sqrt{2} + 6\sqrt{16}\sqrt{2}$$
$$= 6\sqrt{2} - 5\sqrt{2} + 24\sqrt{2} = 25\sqrt{2}$$

Example 4. Simplify the radicals and combine:

$$\sqrt{18} + \sqrt{20} - \sqrt{\tfrac{1}{2}} + \sqrt{125}$$

Solution. $\sqrt{18} + \sqrt{20} - \sqrt{\tfrac{1}{2}} + \sqrt{125}$
$$= \sqrt{9}\sqrt{2} + \sqrt{4}\sqrt{5} - \sqrt{\tfrac{2}{4}} + \sqrt{25}\sqrt{5}$$
$$= 3\sqrt{2} + 2\sqrt{5} - \tfrac{1}{2}\sqrt{2} + 5\sqrt{5} = \tfrac{5}{2}\sqrt{2} + 7\sqrt{5}$$

[B]

EXERCISES

1. $\sqrt{48} - \sqrt{75} + \sqrt{12}$

2. $\sqrt{8} - \sqrt{48} + \sqrt{50}$

3. $\sqrt{5} + \sqrt{20} + \sqrt{7}$

4. $3\sqrt{6} - \sqrt{24} + \sqrt{54}$

5. $4\sqrt{7} - \sqrt{28} - \sqrt{63}$

6. $\sqrt{75} + 4\sqrt{3} + \sqrt{18}$

7. $\sqrt{25} + \sqrt{125} - \sqrt{20}$

8. $\sqrt{\tfrac{1}{2}} + \sqrt{8} - \sqrt{98}$

9. $2\sqrt{18} + 3\sqrt{12} - \sqrt{\tfrac{1}{2}} - 6\sqrt{\tfrac{1}{3}}$

10. $4\sqrt{y} - \sqrt{x} + 9\sqrt{y} - \sqrt{9x}$

11. $2\sqrt{12} - \sqrt{75} + \sqrt{3} - \sqrt{\tfrac{1}{3}}$

12. $6\sqrt{a} + \sqrt{25a} - \sqrt{b} + \sqrt{a}$

13. $\sqrt{25a} + \sqrt{4a} - \sqrt{9a} + \sqrt{16a}$

14. $\sqrt{2} + 3\sqrt{27} + 2\sqrt{50} - \tfrac{1}{3}\sqrt{3}$

440

1. $\sqrt{3}$
2. $7\sqrt{2}-4\sqrt{3}$
3. $3\sqrt{5}+\sqrt{7}$
4. $4\sqrt{6}$
5. $-\sqrt{7}$

6. $9\sqrt{3}+3\sqrt{2}$
7. $5+3\sqrt{5}$
8. $-\tfrac{9}{2}\sqrt{2}$
9. $\tfrac{11}{2}\sqrt{2}+4\sqrt{3}$
10. $13\sqrt{y}-4\sqrt{x}$

11. $-\tfrac{1}{3}\sqrt{3}$
12. $12\sqrt{a}-\sqrt{b}$
13. $8\sqrt{a}$
14. $11\sqrt{2}+\tfrac{26}{3}\sqrt{3}$

Multiplying Monomials Containing Radicals [A]

Radicals having the same index can be multiplied. The product of the square roots of two or more numbers is equal to the square root of their product.

Example 1. $\sqrt{6} \times \sqrt{5} = \sqrt{30}$

Example 2. $3\sqrt{2} \times 4\sqrt{6} = 12\sqrt{12} = 12\sqrt{4}\sqrt{3} = 24\sqrt{3}$

[A] **EXERCISES**

Multiply:

1. $\sqrt{7}\sqrt{5}$ $\sqrt{35}$
2. $\sqrt{3}\sqrt{2}$ $\sqrt{6}$
3. $\sqrt{7}\sqrt{9}$ $3\sqrt{7}$
4. $\sqrt{6}\sqrt{2}$ $2\sqrt{3}$
5. $\sqrt{2}\sqrt{18}$ 6
6. $3\sqrt{6} \cdot 4\sqrt{5}$ $12\sqrt{30}$
7. $\sqrt{3} \cdot \sqrt{6}$ $3\sqrt{2}$
8. $2\sqrt{2} \cdot \sqrt{8}$ 8
9. $3\sqrt{2} \cdot 5\sqrt{8}$ 60
10. $\sqrt{3} \cdot \sqrt{15}$ $3\sqrt{5}$

11. $\sqrt{5}\sqrt{12}$ $2\sqrt{15}$
12. $5\sqrt{2} \cdot \sqrt{2}$ 10
13. $\sqrt{\frac{2}{3}} \times \sqrt{\frac{3}{2}}$ 1
14. $\sqrt{\frac{5}{9}} \cdot \sqrt{\frac{2}{3}}$ $\frac{1}{9}\sqrt{30}$
15. $\sqrt{5} \cdot \sqrt{5}$ 5
16. $\sqrt{\frac{1}{2}}\sqrt{2}$ 1
17. $\sqrt{\frac{1}{3}}\sqrt{6}$ $\sqrt{2}$
18. $\sqrt{\frac{1}{2}}\sqrt{8}$ 2
19. $2\sqrt{5} \cdot 3\sqrt{5}$ 30
20. $(\sqrt{2})^2$ 2

21. $\sqrt{5}\sqrt{125}$ 25
22. $3\sqrt{6} \cdot 2\sqrt{3}$ $18\sqrt{2}$
23. $5\sqrt{2} \cdot 6\sqrt{2}$ 60
24. $3\sqrt{6} \cdot 5\sqrt{3}$ $45\sqrt{2}$
25. $4\sqrt{3} \cdot \sqrt{3}$ 12
26. $\sqrt{11}\sqrt{11}$ 11
27. $\sqrt{12} \cdot \sqrt{3}$ 6
28. $7\sqrt{8} \cdot \frac{1}{2}\sqrt{2}$ 14
29. $3\sqrt{5}(-4\sqrt{5})$ -60
30. $(2\sqrt{3})^2$ 12

①

Multiplying Polynomials [C]

Study the following examples which show how polynomials containing radicals with index 2 are multiplied.

Example 1. $\sqrt{2}(4 - \sqrt{2}) = 4\sqrt{2} - \sqrt{4} = 4\sqrt{2} - 2.$

Example 2. Multiply $3 + \sqrt{2}$ by $1 - \sqrt{2}$.

Solution. $(3 + \sqrt{2})(1 - \sqrt{2}) = 3 - 3\sqrt{2} + \sqrt{2} - \sqrt{4}$
$$= 3 - 3\sqrt{2} + \sqrt{2} - 2$$
$$= 1 - 2\sqrt{2}$$

EXERCISES

Multiply as indicated and simplify each product. [C]

$2\sqrt{3}-2\sqrt{5}$

$24-4\sqrt{3}$

$3-\sqrt{6}$

$4\sqrt{5}-5$

$4\sqrt{3}-6\sqrt{2}$

$15\sqrt{2}-20\sqrt{3}$

1. $2(\sqrt{3}-\sqrt{5})$

2. $4(6-\sqrt{3})$

3. $\sqrt{3}(\sqrt{3}-\sqrt{2})$

4. $\sqrt{5}(4-\sqrt{5})$

5. $2\sqrt{3}(2-\sqrt{6})$

6. $5\sqrt{2}(3-2\sqrt{6})$

7. $(\sqrt{3}-\sqrt{2})(\sqrt{3}+\sqrt{2})$ 1

8. $(\sqrt{3}+\sqrt{2})^2$ $5+2\sqrt{6}$

9. $(\sqrt{5}+\sqrt{2})(\sqrt{5}+\sqrt{2})$ $7+2\sqrt{10}$

10. $(2\sqrt{7}-1)^2$ $29-4\sqrt{7}$

11. $(\sqrt{x+1}+3)^2$ $x+10+6\sqrt{x+1}$

12. $(\sqrt{a}+\sqrt{b})^2$ $a+b+2\sqrt{ab}$

Rationalizing Denominators [B]

You have already learned that a radical is not in its simplest form. if its radicand is a fraction. We also say that a fraction is not in its simplest form if it has a radical in its denominator. The process of transforming a fraction with an irrational denominator to one with a rational denominator is called *rationalizing the denominator*.

Example 1. Rationalize the denominator of $\dfrac{2}{\sqrt{3}}$.

Solution. $\dfrac{2}{\sqrt{3}}\times\dfrac{\sqrt{3}}{\sqrt{3}}=\dfrac{2\sqrt{3}}{\sqrt{9}}=\dfrac{2\sqrt{3}}{3}$, or $\dfrac{2}{3}\sqrt{3}$

EXERCISES

[B]

Rationalize the denominators of the following fractions:

1. $\dfrac{1}{\sqrt{2}}$ $\frac{1}{2}\sqrt{2}$

2. $\dfrac{1}{\sqrt{3}}$ $\frac{1}{3}\sqrt{3}$

3. $\dfrac{1}{\sqrt{5}}$ $\frac{1}{5}\sqrt{5}$

4. $\dfrac{1}{\sqrt{7}}$ $\frac{1}{7}\sqrt{7}$

5. $\sqrt{\dfrac{1}{a}}$ $\frac{1}{a}\sqrt{a}$

6. $\sqrt{\dfrac{1}{b}}$ $\frac{1}{b}\sqrt{b}$

7. $\dfrac{4}{\sqrt{6}}$ $\frac{2}{3}\sqrt{6}$

8. $\dfrac{2}{3\sqrt{2}}$ $\frac{1}{3}\sqrt{2}$

9. $\dfrac{a}{\sqrt{c}}$ $\frac{a}{c}\sqrt{c}$

10. $\dfrac{2\sqrt{3}}{\sqrt{5}}$ $\frac{2}{5}\sqrt{15}$

11. $\dfrac{5}{\sqrt{8}}$ $\frac{5}{4}\sqrt{2}$

12. $\dfrac{4\sqrt{5}}{\sqrt{6}}$ $\frac{2}{3}\sqrt{30}$

[C]

Example 2. Rationalize the denominator of $\dfrac{4-\sqrt{2}}{2+\sqrt{2}}$.

Solution. If we multiply $2+\sqrt{2}$ by $2-\sqrt{2}$, we obtain a rational product.

$$\frac{4-\sqrt{2}}{2+\sqrt{2}}\times\frac{2-\sqrt{2}}{2-\sqrt{2}}=\frac{8-4\sqrt{2}-2\sqrt{2}+\sqrt{4}}{2^2-(\sqrt{2})^2}$$

$$=\frac{10-6\sqrt{2}}{4-2}=5-3\sqrt{2}$$

442

Point out that in rationalizing the denominator of a fraction, as explained above, we are again using the multiplicative property of 1 to change the form but not the value of the fraction.

① In Ex. 21, show that $\sqrt{a} - \sqrt{b}$ and $\sqrt{a} + \sqrt{b}$ are factors of $a - b$. Mention that now students have extended their field of factoring as mentioned in Chapter 12 (page 341).

POWERS, ROOTS, AND RADICALS

Rationalize the denominators of:

13. $\dfrac{3}{\sqrt{2}-1}$ $3\sqrt{2}+3$

14. $\dfrac{2}{\sqrt{2}+3}$ $\dfrac{6-2\sqrt{2}}{7}$

15. $\dfrac{\sqrt{3}-\sqrt{2}}{\sqrt{3}+\sqrt{2}}$ $5-2\sqrt{6}$

16. $\dfrac{2+\sqrt{5}}{2-\sqrt{5}}$ $-9-4\sqrt{5}$

17. $\dfrac{\sqrt{5}-4}{2\sqrt{5}-2}$ $\dfrac{1-3\sqrt{5}}{8}$

18. $\dfrac{1-\sqrt{3}}{2+\sqrt{3}}$ $5-3\sqrt{3}$

19. $\dfrac{2\sqrt{5}-3}{\sqrt{5}-1}$ $\dfrac{7-\sqrt{5}}{4}$

20. $\dfrac{5\sqrt{2}-3}{2\sqrt{2}-4}$ $-\dfrac{4+7\sqrt{2}}{4}$

21. $\dfrac{\sqrt{a}+\sqrt{b}}{\sqrt{a}-\sqrt{b}}$ $\dfrac{a+b+2\sqrt{ab}}{a-b}$ ①

22. $\dfrac{3\sqrt{x}-1}{\sqrt{x}+1}$ $\dfrac{3x+1-4\sqrt{x}}{x-1}$

[A]

1. Complete: The square of either a positive or a negative number is __?__. *positive*

2. Find the following indicated powers:

a. $(-2a)^2$ $4a^2$ c. $(mn)^2$ m^2n^2 e. $(-5x)^2$ $25x^2$

b. $(3ac)^2$ $9a^2c^2$ d. $(-4x^2)^2$ $16x^4$ f. $(x^2y)^2$ x^4y^2

3. Find the two square roots of 184.96. ± 13.6

4. Square the following:

a. $\sqrt{3}$ 3 b. $\sqrt{4}$ 4 c. $\sqrt{\frac{1}{3}}$ $\frac{1}{3}$ d. $\sqrt{5}$ 5 e. $\sqrt{100}$ 100 f. $\sqrt{141}$ 141

5. The formula for finding the area of a triangle when the lengths of its three sides are known is $A = \sqrt{s(s-a)(s-b)(s-c)}$. In this formula a, b, and c are the lengths of the sides, and $s = \frac{1}{2}(a+b+c)$. Find A when $a = 10$, $b = 24$, and $c = 26$. 120

Equations Containing Radicals [C] See ② below.

A radical equation is one in which the variable is contained in the radicand. Thus $\sqrt{x} = 3$ and $\sqrt{2x-1} = 5$ are radical equations. The equation $2x - \sqrt{5} = 0$ is not a radical equation, since x is not in the radicand. The solution of a radical equation makes use of another axiom:

If a and b are real numbers such that $a = b$, and if n is any integer, then $a^n = b^n$.

② Note this is a C topic. If studied, be sure checking is emphasized. Reiterate often that squaring both members of the equation may introduce apparent roots, since the new equations are not equivalent to the original.

443

Example. Solve $2 + \sqrt{x} = 4$.

Solution.
$$2 + \sqrt{x} = 4$$
$$\sqrt{x} = 2$$
*P_2 $\qquad\qquad\qquad\qquad x = 4$

PROOF. Does $\qquad 2 + \sqrt{4} = 4?$
Does $\qquad\quad 2 + 2 = 4?$ Yes.

NOTE. Since the radical always means the positive square root, equations such as $\sqrt{x} = -5$ and $\sqrt{x} + 1 = 0$ are not solvable.

Directions for Solving an Equation Containing One Radical

1. Transform so that one member of the equation contains only the radical term.

2. Square both members of the equation and complete the solution.

3. Prove by substituting each root in the original equation.

Note. *These directions are for equations whose radicals have the index 2.*

EXERCISES

[C]

Solve and prove:

9 **1.** $\sqrt{x} = 3$

1 **2.** $\sqrt{x} = 1$

1 **3.** $\sqrt{3x + 1} = 2$

5 **4.** $\sqrt{x - 1} = 2$

5 **5.** $\sqrt{x + 4} = 3$

25 **6.** $\sqrt{2y - 1} = 7$

7 **7.** $2\sqrt{c + 2} = 6$

6 **8.** $5 = \sqrt{4b + 1}$

$6\frac{1}{9}$ **9.** $3\sqrt{x + 1} = 8$

26.01 **10.** $\sqrt{x} = 5.1$

$\frac{1}{4}$ **11.** $2\sqrt{x} - 1 = 0$

9 **12.** $3 + \sqrt{x} = 6$

$\frac{1}{16}$ **13.** $2 + 4\sqrt{y} = 3$

23 **14.** $\sqrt{2x - 10} - 6 = 0$

8 **15.** $3 - \sqrt{2c - 7} = 0$

16 **16.** $\sqrt{2c - 7} - 5 = 0$

14 **17.** $\sqrt{k - 5} - 3 = 0$

164 **18.** $\sqrt{x + 5} - 5 = 8$

49 **19.** $2\sqrt{x} - 14 = 0$

2500 **20.** $\sqrt{y} - 48 = 2$

$\frac{4h\sqrt{3}}{3}$ **21.** Solve $h = \frac{s}{4}\sqrt{3}$ for s.

$11r^2$ **22.** Solve $r = \sqrt{\dfrac{y}{11}}$ for y.

*P_2 means that both members of the equation are squared, or raised to the second power.

Checking Your Understanding of Chapter 16

Before you leave Chapter 16 make sure that you can   PAGE
1. Compute the square roots of an arithmetic number   432
2. Use a table of squares and square roots   430
3. Combine similar radicals   439

Do you need to review?

4. Multiply monomials containing radicals having the same index   441
5. Simplify radicals   437
6. Spell and use correctly the following words and phrases:

If you expect to do better than average work in the remainder of your study of mathematics, you will also want to make sure that you understand   PAGE
1. The meaning of a zero exponent   428
2. How to rationalize a denominator containing a radical   442
3. How to solve radical equations   443

[A]

CHAPTER REVIEW

1. When you square a positive number, what is the sign of the result? *Plus*

2. When you square a negative number, what is the sign of the result? *Plus*

3. How many square roots does any positive number have? *Two*

4. Simplify:

a. $(-9)^2$ *81*   **c.** $(\sqrt{x})^2$ *x*   **e.** $(\sqrt{7})^2$ *7*
b. $(\sqrt{9})^2$ *9*   **d.** $(\sqrt{a^3})^2$ *a^3*   **f.** $\sqrt{(1087)^2}$ *1087*

5. In the expression $4\sqrt[3]{5}$ what is the 3 called? the 5? *index, radicand*

6. $c = \sqrt{a^2 + b^2}$. Find c if $a = 36$ and $b = 15$. *39*

7. $c = \sqrt{a^2} + \sqrt{b^2}$. Find c when $a = 36$ and $b = 15$. *51*

445

8. $b = \sqrt{c^2 - a^2}$. Find b if $c = 35$ and $a = 21$. *28*

9. Find the value of $10 + 7\sqrt{81}$. *73*

10. Find the value of $\dfrac{\sqrt{x} + \sqrt{y}}{y - x}$ if $x = 225$ and $y = 361$. *$\frac{1}{4}$*

Find the positive square roots of:

204 **11.** 41616   *0.214* **13.** .045796   *2.14* **15.** 4.5796

29.2 **12.** 852.64   *0.52* **14.** .2704   *105.4* **16.** 11109.16

17. Find the positive square root of 17 to the nearest thousandth. *4.1231*

18. Find the positive square root of $\frac{5}{9}$ to the nearest hundredth. *0.745 +*

Transform the following radicals into their simplest forms:

$2\sqrt{5}$ **19.** $\sqrt{20}$ *$5\sqrt{5}$* **22.** $\sqrt{125}$ *$6\sqrt{3}$* **25.** $\sqrt{108}$

4 **20.** $\sqrt{16}$ *$\frac{1}{2}\sqrt{2}$* **23.** $\sqrt{\frac{1}{2}}$ *$9\sqrt{2}$* **26.** $3\sqrt{18}$

$2\sqrt{6}$ **21.** $\sqrt{24}$ *$\frac{1}{3}\sqrt{3}$* **24.** $\sqrt{\frac{1}{3}}$ *$15\sqrt{5}$* **27.** $5\sqrt{45}$

Simplify:

$\sqrt{15}$ **28.** $\sqrt{3}\sqrt{5}$ *$2\sqrt{3}$* **31.** $\sqrt{2}\sqrt{6}$ *3* **34.** $\sqrt{3}\sqrt{3}$

4 **29.** $\sqrt{5}\sqrt{3\frac{1}{5}}$ *1* **32.** $\sqrt{\frac{1}{2}}\sqrt{2}$ *5* **35.** $\sqrt{2}\sqrt{12.5}$

6 **30.** $\sqrt{12}\sqrt{3}$ *$4\sqrt{3}$* **33.** $\sqrt{3}\sqrt{16}$ *$5\sqrt{7}$* **36.** $\sqrt{5}\sqrt{35}$

Simplify the radicals and combine similar radicals. *(See foot of page)* [B]

37. $\sqrt{12} - \sqrt{80} - \sqrt{108} - \sqrt{5}$ **40.** $\sqrt{75} - 2\sqrt{5} + \sqrt{108}$

38. $\sqrt{28} - \sqrt{6} + \sqrt{63} - \sqrt{24}$ **41.** $6\sqrt{\frac{1}{3}} + 5\sqrt{\frac{1}{5}} + \sqrt{3}$

39. $\sqrt{18} - \sqrt{5} + \sqrt{20} - \sqrt{50}$ **42.** $2\sqrt{\frac{1}{2}} + 3\sqrt{\frac{1}{5}} + \sqrt{50}$

43. Simplify:

$\frac{1}{5}\sqrt{10}$ **a.** $\sqrt{\frac{2}{5}}$ *$\sqrt{3}$* **b.** $3\sqrt{\frac{1}{3}}$ *$2\sqrt{6}$* **c.** $6\sqrt{\frac{2}{3}}$ *$2\sqrt{2}$* **d.** $8\sqrt{\frac{1}{8}}$

44. Find the value of $\dfrac{2 + \sqrt{34}}{5}$ to the nearest hundredth. *1.57*

45. Find the value of $\dfrac{7 - \sqrt{15}}{2}$ to the nearest hundredth. *1.56*

37. $-4\sqrt{3} - 5\sqrt{5}$ *40.* $11\sqrt{3} - 2\sqrt{5}$

38. $5\sqrt{7} - 3\sqrt{6}$ *41.* $3\sqrt{3} + \sqrt{5}$

39. $\sqrt{5} - 2\sqrt{2}$ *42.* $6\sqrt{2} + \frac{3}{5}\sqrt{5}$

POWERS, ROOTS, AND RADICALS

[A]

GENERAL REVIEW

1. Find the number of gallons in a cylindrical jar whose height is 10 inches and whose base has a diameter of 10 inches. ($V = \pi r^2 h$, and 1 gal. = 231 cu. in.) *3. 4 gal.*

2. If $a = -4$, $b = 2$, and $c = 0$, find the value of

a. $\dfrac{3a+2}{bc-6}$ *$1\frac{2}{3}$*   **b.** $10 - 3ab$ *34*   **c.** $\dfrac{(ab)^3 + 300}{100 + b - a}$ *-2*

3. $V = \frac{4}{3}\pi r^3$. Find V when $r = 2.1$ and $\pi = 3.14$. *38.77*

4. $A = p + prt$. Find p when $A = \$836.20$, $r = 4\%$, $t = \frac{3}{4}$ *746.61*

5. One of the roots of the equation $x^4 - 3x^3 + 6x^2 - 8x = 30$ is among the following numbers: 1, 2, ③, 4, -1, -2. Find the root by substitution.

6. Multiply:

a. $(-3ab)(4c)(b^2)$ *$-12ab^3c$*   **c.** $(a - b + 1)(a - b - 1)$ *$a^2 - 2ab + b^2 - 1$*

b. $(-m^2n)(mn^3)$ *$-m^3n^4$*   **d.** $(x^2 - 3x + 4)(2x - 1)$ *$2x^3 - 7x^2 + 11x - 4$*

7. Divide:

a. $(-24a^3) \div (-4a)$ *$6a^2$*   **b.** $(x^2 - 6x + 9) \div (x + 1)$ *$x - 7$, rem. 16*

c. $(17y^2 - 20y + 12y^3 - 20) \div (3y + 5)$ *$4y^2 - y - 5$, rem. 5*

8. Combine:

a. $\dfrac{1}{3x} - \dfrac{1}{2x}$ *$-\frac{1}{6x}$*   **c.** $\dfrac{a-b}{2} + \dfrac{a-3b}{3}$ *$\frac{5a-9b}{6}$*

b. $\dfrac{m}{n} - c$ *$\frac{m-cn}{n}$*   **d.** $\dfrac{x-2y}{x+y} - \dfrac{x+y}{x-y}$ *$\frac{-5xy+y^2}{(x+y)(x-y)}$*

9. Solve:

a. $5x - 2 + 2(x + 2) = 6$ *$\frac{4}{7}$*   **c.** $2x - (x - 2) = -6$ *-8*

b. $6.7 - 3(x + .2) = 7x + 1.1$ *$\frac{1}{2}$*   **d.** $\dfrac{2+5x}{3} = \dfrac{x^2-x+4}{x}$ *-4, $1\frac{1}{2}$*

10. Solve:

a. $a + 2b = 8$ *$a=2$,*
    $3a - b = 3$ *$b=3$*

b. $\dfrac{3x}{8} + \dfrac{2y}{5} = \dfrac{7}{2}$ *$x=4$,*
    $\dfrac{y}{5} - \dfrac{x}{8} = \dfrac{1}{2}$ *$y=5$*

11. Divide: $\dfrac{x^2 - y^2}{x^2 - 3x - 4} \div \dfrac{x-y}{x^2+x}$ *$\frac{x(x+y)}{x-4}$*

12. Find the positive square root of 19.5364. *4.42*

447

13. Find to the nearest thousandth the positive square root of 19. *4.359*

[B]

14. Solve $\dfrac{x}{5} + \dfrac{y}{4} = 0$ *x=15,*

$\dfrac{x}{3} - \dfrac{y}{6} = 7$ *y = -12*

15. Simplify $\sqrt{18} - \sqrt{72} - \sqrt{98}$. *$-10\sqrt{2}$*

16. Simplify $\sqrt{50} - \sqrt{\tfrac{1}{2}} + \sqrt{54} + \sqrt{96}$. *$\tfrac{9}{2}\sqrt{2} + 7\sqrt{6}$*

17. Find the roots:

a. $\sqrt{64\,a^2}$ *8a*   **c.** $\sqrt{81\,m^4}$ *$9m^2$*   **e.** $\sqrt{.49\,c^6}$ *$0.7c^3$*

b. $\sqrt{\dfrac{1}{9}\,x^6}$ *$\tfrac{1}{3}x^3$*   **d.** $\sqrt{\dfrac{a^2}{b^4}}$ *$\tfrac{a}{b^2}$*   **f.** $\sqrt{.01\,x^4}$ *$0.1x^2$*

18. Separate 290 into two parts such that when the greater is divided by the smaller, the quotient is 6 and the remainder is 10. *40 and 250*

19. Solve by substitution: $3\,x - 2\,y = 0$ *x=2,*

$5\,x + 9\,y = 37$ *y = 3*

20. Solve $a^2 = b^2 + c^2 + 2\,cn$ for n.   *$\dfrac{a^2 - b^2 - c^2}{2c}$*

21. State the degree of each equation and solve it:

a. $3\,x = 10 + x$ *1st, x=5*   **c.** $4\,x^2 - 25 = 0$ *2d, $x = \pm\tfrac{5}{2}$*

b. $x^2 - x = 0$ *2d, x=0, 1*   **d.** $y^3 - 4\,y = 0$ *3d, y = 0, ± 2*

$x^2 + 2 + \dfrac{1}{x-1}$ ←

22. Change $\dfrac{x^3 - x^2 + 2\,x - 1}{x - 1}$ into a mixed number.

23. Multiply: $\dfrac{x^2 - 2\,x - 24}{x^2 + x} \cdot \dfrac{x^2 + 2\,x + 1}{x^2 - 6\,x}$ *$\dfrac{(x+4)(x+1)}{x^2}$*

24. A boy and a girl balance on a teeterboard. The boy is 6 feet from the fulcrum and the girl is 8 feet from it. Find their weights if the boy weighs 24 pounds more than the girl.

25. Rationalize the denominators: *girl, 72 lb.; boy, 96 lb.*

$\tfrac{1}{6}\sqrt{6}$ **a.** $\dfrac{1}{\sqrt{6}}$ *$\sqrt{3}$* **b.** $\dfrac{3}{\sqrt{3}}$ *$\tfrac{2}{5}\sqrt{10}$* **c.** $\dfrac{2\sqrt{2}}{\sqrt{5}}$ *$3\sqrt{2}$* **d.** $\dfrac{3\sqrt{10}}{\sqrt{5}}$

26. Find the value of

1 **a.** 10^0 *3* **b.** $\dfrac{3}{6^0}$ *8* **c.** $\sqrt{8^2}$ *8* **d.** $\sqrt{4^3}$

448

1. a. $16a^2$ b. $25a^6$
2. a. 9 b. $-6a$

[Test A]

1. Find the indicated squares: **a.** $(4\,a)^2$ **b.** $(-5\,a^3)^2$

2. Find the indicated square roots: **a.** $\sqrt{81}$ **b.** $-\sqrt{36\,a^2}$

3. Find the two square roots of 6084. ± 78

4. Find the square root of 132 to the nearest tenth. 11.5

5. Simplify: **a.** $\sqrt{12}$ $2\sqrt{3}$ **b.** $\sqrt{45}$ $3\sqrt{5}$

6. Simplify: **a.** $\sqrt{64}$ 8 **b.** $\sqrt{75}$ $5\sqrt{3}$

7. Simplify: **a.** $\sqrt{\frac{2}{5}}$ $\frac{1}{5}\sqrt{10}$ **b.** $\sqrt{\frac{1}{3}}$ $\frac{1}{3}\sqrt{3}$

8. Simplify: **a.** $\sqrt{\frac{4}{9}}$ $\frac{2}{3}$ **b.** $\sqrt{\frac{1}{20}}$ $\frac{1}{10}\sqrt{5}$

9. Simplify: **a.** $\sqrt{3}+5\sqrt{3}-2\sqrt{3}$ $4\sqrt{3}$

   b. $\sqrt{5}+\sqrt{5}-3$ $2\sqrt{5}-3$

10. Simplify: **a.** $\sqrt{2}\sqrt{18}$ 6 **b.** $\sqrt{3}\sqrt{6}$ $3\sqrt{2}$

[Test B]

1. Find the two square roots of 7089 to the nearest tenth. ± 84.2

2. Find the positive square root of 42436. 206

3. Find the positive square root of 172.4 to the nearest tenth. 13.1

4. Simplify: **a.** $5\sqrt{28}$ $10\sqrt{7}$ **b.** $\sqrt{24\,a^3}$ $2a\sqrt{6a}$

5. Simplify: **a.** $\sqrt{\frac{1}{12}}$ $\frac{1}{6}\sqrt{3}$ **b.** $\sqrt{\frac{4}{5}}$ $\frac{2}{5}\sqrt{5}$

6. Simplify: **a.** $\sqrt{\dfrac{1}{a^3}}$ $\frac{1}{a^2}\sqrt{a}$ **b.** $\sqrt{\dfrac{9}{ab}}$ $\frac{3}{ab}\sqrt{ab}$

7. Simplify: **a.** $\sqrt{\frac{1}{2}}-\sqrt{8}+\sqrt{128}$ $\frac{13}{2}\sqrt{2}$

   b. $2\sqrt{12}+\sqrt{3}-\sqrt{75}$ 0

8. Multiply: **a.** $3\sqrt{2}\cdot\sqrt{8}$ 12 **b.** $\sqrt{5}\cdot\sqrt{12}$ $2\sqrt{15}$

9. Rationalize the denominator: **a.** $\dfrac{3}{\sqrt{6}}$ $\frac{1}{2}\sqrt{6}$ **b.** $\dfrac{5}{3\sqrt{2}}$ $\frac{5}{6}\sqrt{2}$

10. Find the value of $\dfrac{3\sqrt{x}-\sqrt{y}}{2\,y-x}$ if $x=100$ and $y=64.$ $\frac{11}{14}$

449

Time was when the adventurers of a nation were knights in armor or men who sailed the seven seas. You will never set forth over uncharted oceans in search of new lands or gold and you will probably never so much as own a piece of armor. Neither will you load your family into a prairie schooner for a long trip to greater opportunities in the West. No, your adventures will be of a different sort.

The great things you do may be done at your desk or in a laboratory, as you go about your daily work. They will call not so much for physical endurance as for hardiness of mind and spirit. But the op-

portunities are still present—opportunities beyond even the imagining of the young people of other ages—the most exciting and the most challenging adventures the world has ever known.

We are on the verge of great discoveries. Notice these headlines. Dozens more can be found in recent newspapers and magazines.

One of these articles announces the finding of an atomic particle, apparently from outer space—a particle which moves at the almost unbelievable speed and energy of ten million billion volts and which changes matter into energy, after which the energy changes back into matter of a different form. And consider: Even the most powerful atom-smashing machine we have today produces particles with en-

ergies of only about six billion volts. Ten million billion to six billion! That tiny particle may revolutionize our world.

The other article mentions the recent designing of a rocket plane capable of traveling 10,000 miles per hour—a plane which it is believed can carry another plane (passenger) to a height of 30 miles in three or four minutes and then release it so that it can glide to its destination.

The world is indeed on the verge of great discoveries, but those discoveries will not be made by men and women unprepared in mathematics and science. If you are ambitious, be ready. Store in your mind every bit of mathematics you can find. The road to great discoveries is not an easy one, but it is an interesting one, and a glorious one.

17

Quadratic Equations

Suggested Time Schedule
Maximum   10 days
(Not in minimum course)

In this chapter you will discover new methods of solving equations. ▶

Kinds of Quadratic Equations [A]

A quadratic equation is one of the second degree. A quadratic equation in one variable contains the second power of the variable but no higher power.

If a quadratic equation contains the first power of the variable, as $3x^2 + x - 2 = 0$, it is called a <u>complete quadratic</u> equation. If it does not contain the first power of the variable, as $3x^2 - 27 = 0$, it is called an <u>incomplete</u>, or pure, quadratic equation.

In Chapter 13 you solved both complete and incomplete quadratic equations by the factoring method. In this chapter other methods of solving them will be studied.

How to Solve an Incomplete Quadratic Equation [A]

In the solution of incomplete quadratic equations use is made of another general principle or axiom:

If a and b are real numbers such that $a^n = b^n$, then $a = b$.

Example 1. Solve $x^2 - 18 = 0$.

Solution.
$$x^2 - 18 = 0$$
$$x^2 = 18$$

*R_2
$$x = \pm\sqrt{18}$$
$$x = \pm 3\sqrt{2}, \quad \text{or} \quad \pm 4.2426$$

PROOF. Does $(+3\sqrt{2})^2 - 18 = 0$? Yes.
Does $(-3\sqrt{2})^2 - 18 = 0$? Yes.

Although the square roots of x^2 are $\pm x$, we write only the positive x.

Example 2. Solve $x^2 - 9 = 0$.

Solution. First solve $x^2 - 9 = 0$ for x^2
$$x^2 = 9$$
R_2
$$x = \pm 3$$

PROOF. Does $(+3)^2 - 9 = 0$? Yes.
Does $(-3)^2 - 9 = 0$? Yes.

*R_2 means that the square roots of both members are taken.

① This could be explained by showing all possible combinations of signs: $+x = +3$, $+x = -3$, $-x = +3$, and $-x = -3$. These four are equivalent finally to just $x = \pm 3$. Refer to this again on page 461, where the method of completing the square is used.

Example 3. Solve $3x(x-4) - x(x+3) = 3(6-5x)$.

Solution.
$$3x(x-4) - x(x+3) = 3(6-5x)$$
$$3x^2 - 12x - x^2 - 3x = 18 - 15x$$
$$3x^2 - x^2 - 12x - 3x + 15x = 18$$
$$2x^2 = 18$$
$$x^2 = 9$$
R_2 $\qquad x = \pm 3$

Note that the equation was first solved for x^2.

To Solve an Incomplete Quadratic Equation,

1. Solve the equation for x^2.
2. Find the square roots of both members.
3. Prove each root correct by substituting in the original equation.

[A]

EQUATIONS

Solve the following quadratic equations. If any root is irrational, express it both as a radical in its simplest form and as a decimal.

±4 **1.** $x^2 = 16$ ±1 **7.** $4x^2 = 4$ ±15 **13.** $225 - y^2 = 0$

±6 **2.** $y^2 = 36$ ±5 **8.** $5c^2 = 125$ ±29 **14.** $2n^2 - 1682 = 0$

±9 **3.** $m^2 = 81$ ±8 **9.** $x^2 - 64 = 0$ ±1 **15.** $\dfrac{1}{x^2} - 1 = 0$

±10 **4.** $h^2 = 100$ ±1 **10.** $y^2 - 1 = 0$ ±4 **16.** $\dfrac{x^2 - 4}{4} = 3$

±10 **5.** $2x^2 = 200$ ±7 **11.** $2a^2 - 98 = 0$

±3 **6.** $3y^2 = 27$ ±6 **12.** $4p^2 - 144 = 0$ **17.** $\dfrac{3x^2}{4} - 3 = 6$ $\pm 2\sqrt{3}, (\pm 3.46)$

±5 **18.** $x(2x+3) = 3x + 50$ ±7 **22.** $4x^2 - 150 = x^2 - 3$

±2√3 **19.** $(x-2)^2 = 16 - 4x$ (± 3.46) ±½ **23.** $(2x+5)^2 = 20x + 26$

±√3 **20.** $\dfrac{x^2-1}{2} = 1$ (± 1.73) ±3 **24.** $\dfrac{x^2-3}{2} = \dfrac{2x^2}{9} + 1$

±2 **21.** $(y-1)(y+1) = 3$ ±½√30 **25.** $\dfrac{2x+5}{2} - x = \dfrac{x^2}{3}$ (± 2.74)

Solve for x:

±3 **26.** $mx^2 = 9m$ ±2b **28.** $4x^2 = 16b^2$ ±4/b **30.** $b^2x^2 - 16 = 0$

±2a **27.** $x^2 - a^2 = 3a^2$ ±a **29.** $ax^2 - a^3 = 0$ **31.** $x^2 - a = b$ $\pm\sqrt{a+b}$

[B]

Solve for x:

$\pm \frac{\sqrt{3}}{3}\sqrt{3(a-b)}$

32. $ax^2 = b$ $\pm\frac{1}{a}\sqrt{ab}$ **34.** $mx^2 = 1$ $\pm\frac{1}{m}\sqrt{m}$ **36.** $3x^2 = a - b$

33. $cx^2 = 2c$ $\pm\sqrt{2}$ **35.** $\pi x^2 - A = 0$ $\pm\frac{1}{\pi}\sqrt{\pi A}$ **37.** $x(x + a) = ax + c$ $\pm\sqrt{c}$

38. $\dfrac{2x}{3p} = \dfrac{x}{6p} + \dfrac{5}{x}$ $\pm\sqrt{10p}$ **40.** $2ax^2 - ab = 3ax^2$ $\pm\sqrt{-b}$

39. $8x - \dfrac{2}{3} = \dfrac{x(24 - x)}{3}$ $\pm\sqrt{2}$ **41.** $\dfrac{x^2 - a}{b} = \dfrac{x^2 - b}{a}$ $\pm\sqrt{a+b}$

(± 1.41)

42. $x(4x + 3) - 2x = 3 - (1 - x)$ $\pm\frac{1}{2}\sqrt{2}$ (± 0.71)

43. $(2x - 1)^2 - (x + 2)^2 = -4(2x - 3)$ $\pm\sqrt{5}$ (± 2.24)

[B]

SOLVING FORMULAS

Example. Solve the formula $s = \frac{1}{2}gt^2$ for t and find the positive value of t when $s = 100$ and $g = 32$.

Solution. $s = \frac{1}{2}gt^2$

M_2 $2s = gt^2$

$\qquad gt^2 = 2s$

$D_g \qquad t^2 = \dfrac{2s}{g}$

$R_2 \qquad t = \pm\sqrt{\dfrac{2s}{g}} = \pm\sqrt{\dfrac{2s}{g} \times \dfrac{g}{g}} = \pm\sqrt{\dfrac{2gs}{g^2}} = \pm\dfrac{1}{g}\sqrt{2gs}$

Substituting 32 for g and 100 for s,

$$t = \pm\dfrac{\sqrt{2 \times 32 \times 100}}{32} = \pm\dfrac{\sqrt{6400}}{32} = \pm 2.5$$

Since positive time was requested, $t = 2.5$.

1. Solve $E = \frac{1}{2}mv^2$ for the positive value of v and find v when $m = 4$ and $E = 20$. 3.162

2. Solve $A = \pi r^2$ for r and find the value of r when $A = 154$ and $\pi = 3\frac{1}{7}$. Assume r is a positive number. 7

3. Solve $\dfrac{a}{x} = \dfrac{x}{b}$ for positive x and find x when $a = 64$ and $b = 225$. ± 120

4. Solve $F = \dfrac{v^2 s}{8\pi d^2}$ for d and find d when $v = 16$, $s = 32$, $\pi = 3\frac{1}{7}$, and $F = 160$. $\pm\frac{4}{55}\sqrt{385}$, or ± 1.43

455

The Pythagorean Theorem [A]

As you know, a right triangle is a triangle having one of its angles a right angle. Right triangles were known and studied thousands of years ago. In the diagram a rope is stretched around stakes so that the sides of the triangle will be 3, 4, and 5 units in length. The right angle is opposite the side 5 units long. It is thought that this fact was known by the Babylonians. Does $5^2 = 4^2 + 3^2$?

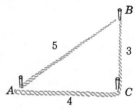

Years later a very important theorem (a statement to be proved) dealing with all right triangles was discovered and proved. It is believed that this theorem was first proved by Pythagoras, a very able Greek scholar. For this reason it is called the Pythagorean Theorem. It is stated as follows:

> In any right triangle the square of the hypotenuse
> is equal to the sum of the squares of the other two sides.

The hypotenuse of a right triangle is the side opposite the right angle. In the figure the side c is the hypotenuse. By the Pythagorean Theorem, $c^2 = a^2 + b^2$.

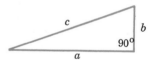

If $a = 9$ and $b = 12$, then $c^2 = ?$
If $a = 6$ and $b = 7$, then $c^2 = ?$

EXERCISES

[A]

It has been proved that if the sum of the squares of two sides of a triangle is equal to the square of the third side, the triangle is a right triangle.

Tell which of the following triangles are right triangles:

1 and 3 are right triangles

1. 2. 3. 4. 5.

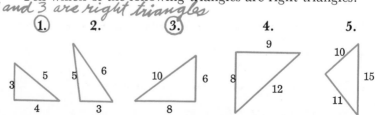

① An interesting and practical principle of geometry. Use visual aids, since proof is impossible here. One graphic method is to draw a 3-4-5 triangle on the graph blackboard, draw the three squares, and count the unit squares in their areas. See any geometry text for further discussion.

The following figures are right triangles or contain right triangles. Apply the Pythagorean Theorem and find the values of x.

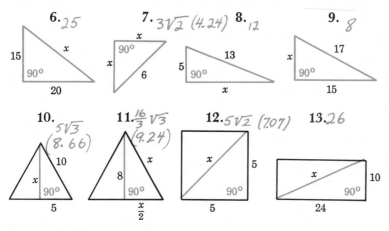

6. 25

7. $3\sqrt{2}$ (4.24)   **8.** 12   **9.** 8

15 | x | 90° | 20

x | 90° | x | 6

5 | 13 | 90° | x

x | 17 | 90° | 15

10.   **11.** $\frac{16}{3}\sqrt{3}$ **12.** $5\sqrt{2}$ (7.07)   **13.** 26

$5\sqrt{3}$ (8.66)

(9.24)

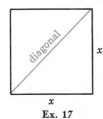

10 | x | 90° | 5

8 | x | 90° | $\frac{x}{2}$

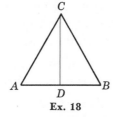

x | 5 | 90° | 5

x | 10 | 90° | 24

14. The hypotenuse of a right triangle is 25 feet and one side is 15 feet. How long is the other side? 20 ft.

15. Find the hypotenuse of a right triangle whose other two sides are 16 feet and 30 feet. 34 ft.

16. The hypotenuse of a right triangle is 30 feet and the other two sides are equal. How long is each? $15\sqrt{2}$ ft. (21.21)

17. Find the side of a square whose diagonal is $12\sqrt{2}$ feet. 12 ft.

diagonal | x | x

Ex. 17

C | A | D | B

Ex. 18

18. ABC is an equilateral triangle. Its altitude CD is perpendicular to AB and <u>bisects</u> (divides into two equal parts) AB. If each side of the triangle is 10 inches long, how long is the altitude CD? $5\sqrt{3}$ in. (8.66)

19. The length of a rectangle is three times its width. If the diagonal of the rectangle is 15 feet, what are its length and width? Length, $\frac{9}{2}\sqrt{10}$ or 14.299 ft.; width, $\frac{3}{2}\sqrt{10}$ or 4.743 ft.

457

20. Find the altitude of an equilateral triangle each of whose sides is 8 inches. *4√3 in. (6.93)*

[B]

21. ABC is an equilateral triangle whose side is s and whose altitude is a. Show that the altitude a of an equilateral triangle is given by the formula $a = \frac{s}{2}\sqrt{3}$.

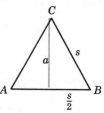

Using the formula $a = \frac{s}{2}\sqrt{3}$, find the altitudes of the equilateral triangles having the following sides:

22. 6 inches *(5.20 in.)* **23.** 16 feet *(13.86 ft.)* **24.** 5√3 feet **25.** 25√3 rods

3√3 in. *8√3 ft.* *7.5 ft.* *37.5 rd.*

26. What is the base of the equilateral triangle at the right? What is its altitude in terms of s? Show that the area of an equilateral triangle whose side is s and whose area is A is given by the formula $A = \frac{s^2}{4}\sqrt{3}$.

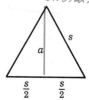

(1) 1; (2) ½√3

Using the formula $A = \frac{s^2}{4}\sqrt{3}$, find the areas of the equilateral triangles which have the following sides:

27. 6 inches *(15.59)* **28.** 16 feet *(110.85)* **29.** 8√3 inches *(85.14)* **30.** 20√3 feet *(519.6)*

9√3 sq. in. *64√3 sq. ft.* *48√3 sq. in.* *300√3 sq. ft.*

If the acute angles of a right triangle contain 30° and 60° respectively, the triangle is known as a 30–60° right triangle. In such a triangle the shortest side is half the hypotenuse. In the diagram, $a = \frac{1}{2} c$.

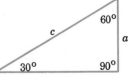

31. The hypotenuse of a 30–60° right triangle is 8 feet. How long are the other sides? *4 ft., 6.93 ft.*

32. The shortest side of a 30–60° right triangle is 6 inches. Find the lengths of the other two sides. *12 in., 10.39 in.*

33. Find the lengths of the hypotenuse and the shortest side of a 30–60° right triangle when the third side is 9√3 inches. *18 in., 9 in.*

34. Find the longest and shortest sides of a 30–60° right triangle if the third side is 4√3. *4 and 8*

35. The shortest side of a 30–60° right triangle is √6. Find the other two sides. *2√6 and 3√2 or 4.90 and 4.242*

458

Complete Quadratic Equations [A]*

As you have already learned, a complete quadratic equation contains both the second and first powers of the variable. The equations $2x^2 + 5x - 3 = 0$, $x^2 - 3x = -2$, and $x^2 + x = 0$ are complete quadratics.

There are four methods of solving complete quadratic equations. You know the factoring method. We shall now learn how to solve a complete quadratic by completing the square. Before you can use this method you must know how to square binomials quickly, find the square roots of perfect square trinomials, and form a perfect square trinomial when two of its terms are given.

Let us review Squaring Binomials, page 335, and Finding the Square Roots of Trinomials, page 337.

[A]

REVIEW EXERCISES

Square the following binomials as indicated:

1. $(x + 1)^2$ $x^2 + 2x + 1$ **5.** $(x - 7)^2$ $x^2 - 14x + 49$ **9.** $(m - \frac{1}{2})^2$ $m^2 - m + \frac{1}{4}$

2. $(x + 3)^2$ $x^2 + 6x + 9$ **6.** $(y + 4)^2$ $y^2 + 8y + 16$ **10.** $(y + \frac{1}{3})^2$ $y^2 + \frac{2}{3}y + \frac{1}{9}$

3. $(x - 1)^2$ $x^2 - 2x + 1$ **7.** $(c + 10)^2$ $c^2 + 20c + 100$ **11.** $(x + .02)^2$ $x^2 + .04x + .0004$

4. $(y + 2)^2$ $y^2 + 4y + 4$ **8.** $(h - 5)^2$ $h^2 - 10h + 25$ **12.** $(y + 1.3)^2$ $y^2 + 2.6y + 1.69$

Some of the following trinomials are perfect squares and some are not perfect squares. Find the square roots of the perfect squares: *14, 16, 17, 18 are not perfect squares. Other answers in right margin.*

13. $m^2 - 4m + 4$ **16.** $x^2 + 4x + 8$ **19.** $x^2 + .2x + 0.01$

14. $h^2 + h + 1$ **17.** $y^2 + 6y + 64$ **20.** $y^2 - 5y + 6\frac{1}{4}$

15. $y^2 + 6y + 9$ **18.** $x^2 + \frac{2}{3}x + 9$ **21.** $x^6 - 12x^3 + 36$

13. $\pm(m - 2)$
15. $\pm(y + 3)$
19. $\pm(x + 0.1)$
20. $\pm(y - \frac{5}{2})$
21. $\pm(x^3 - 6)$

Making a Perfect Square Trinomial [A]

In solving a complete quadratic equation by completing the square, it is necessary to make one member of the equation a perfect square trinomial.

*In most classes time will not be available to have all the pupils solve complete quadratic equations by completing the square and by formula. Either method may be omitted. Pages 460–464 show how to use the method of completing the square, and pages 464–466 give the formula method. The solution by completing the square has the advantage of being understood by the pupils, and of giving practice in adding fractions and simplifying fractional radicands. The formula method requires less time to teach if the derivation of the formula is omitted.

459

Example. Make a perfect square by adding a term to $x^2 + 8x$.

Solution. The square root of x^2 is x. Then x is the first term of the square root of this trinomial. Then we can write $x^2 + 8x + ? = (x + ?)^2$. Now $8x$ is twice the product of x and the missing term of the binomial. Then the missing term of the binomial is one half of 8 or 4. Now we can write $x^2 + 8x + ? = (x + 4)^2$. Then the missing term of the trinomial is 4^2 or 16. The trinomial is $x^2 + 8x + 16$.

[A]

EXERCISES

Find the missing terms in the following to make them perfect square trinomials:

9 **1.** $x^2 + 6x + ?$ $\frac{25}{4}$ **11.** $x^2 + 5x + ?$ $\frac{1}{9}$ **21.** $y^2 - \frac{2}{3}y + ?$

1 **2.** $x^2 + 2x + ?$ $\frac{49}{4}$ **12.** $x^2 - 7x + ?$ 0.01 **22.** $m^2 - .2m + ?$

9 **3.** $c^2 - 6c + ?$ $\frac{9}{4}$ **13.** $c^2 - 3c + ?$ 0.04 **23.** $r^2 + .4r + ?$

16 **4.** $m^2 - 8m + ?$ $\frac{81}{4}$ **14.** $y^2 - 9y + ?$ $\frac{1}{49}$ **24.** $c^2 - \frac{2}{7}c + ?$

25 **5.** $r^2 + 10r + ?$ $\frac{121}{4}$ **15.** $p^2 + 11p + ?$ $\frac{25}{36}$ **25.** $x^2 + \frac{5}{3}x + ?$

36 **6.** $x^2 - 12x + ?$ $\frac{225}{4}$ **16.** $x^2 - 15x + ?$ $\frac{1}{25}$ **26.** $h^2 + \frac{2}{5}h + ?$

4 **7.** $y^2 - 4y + ?$ $\frac{169}{4}$ **17.** $y^2 + 13y + ?$ $\frac{1}{100}$ **27.** $k^2 - \frac{1}{5}k + ?$

1 **8.** $r^2 - 2r + ?$ $\frac{1}{4}$ **18.** $x^2 + x + ?$ $4n^2$ **28.** $m^2 - 4mn + ?$

64 **9.** $a^2 - 16a + ?$ $\frac{1}{16}$ **19.** $x^2 - \frac{1}{2}x + ?$ b^2 **29.** $a^2 + 2ab + ?$

100 **10.** $x^2 + 20x + ?$ $\frac{1}{36}$ **20.** $y^2 + \frac{1}{3}y + ?$ 25 **30.** $x^4 - 10x^2 + ?$

Solving Quadratics by Completing the Square [A]

When solving a quadratic equation by completing the square, the left member is made a perfect square so that its square root can be taken. Example 1 illustrates the different steps in a solution.

Example 1. Solve $x^2 - 6x + 8 = 0$.

Solution. We first transform the equation so that the constant term is in the right member. We then have $x^2 - 6x = -8$. We next add $+9$ to the left member to make it a perfect square. Since we are adding $+9$ to the left member of the equation, we must also add $+9$ to the right member. Then $x^2 - 6x + 9 = 1$. We next find the square roots of both members, getting $x - 3 = \pm 1$. Then $x = 3 \pm 1$ and $x = 4$ or 2.

PROOF. Does $(4)^2 - 6(4) + 8 = 0$ and does $(2)^2 - 6(2) + 8 = 0$? Does $16 - 24 + 8 = 0$ and does $4 - 12 + 8 = 0$? Yes.

① **Directions for Solving a Quadratic Equation by Completing the Square**

1. Write the equation in the form $x^2 + bx = c$.
2. Add to each member the square of half of b.
3. Find the square root of each member,
  placing the $\pm$ sign before the square root of the right member.
4. Solve the two resulting equations.
5. Prove both roots by substituting them in the original equation.

Example 2. Solve $x^2 - 11 = 10\,x$.

Solution.
$$x^2 - 11 = 10\,x$$
$$x^2 - 10\,x = 11$$
A_{25} $\qquad x^2 - 10\,x + 25 = 36$
R_2 $\qquad\qquad\quad x - 5 = \pm 6$
$$x = 5 \pm 6; \qquad x = 11 \quad\text{or}\quad -1 \qquad ②$$

PROOF. Does $\quad (11)^2 - 11 = 10(11)?$ Yes.
  Does $\quad (-1)^2 - 11 = 10(-1)?$ Yes.

[A]

EXERCISES

Solve the following equations by completing the square:

1. $x^2 - 6\,x = 7$ *7, -1*
2. $y^2 - 4\,y = 5$ *5, -1*
3. $m^2 + 2\,m = 24$ *4, -6*
4. $h^2 - 10\,h = -24$ *6, 4*
5. $c^2 - 12\,c = 13$ *13, -1*
6. $x^2 - 16\,x = 17$ *17, -1*
7. $x^2 - 12\,x + 11 = 0$ *11, 1*
8. $x^2 + 18\,x + 17 = 0$ *-1, -17*

9. $x^2 + 4\,x = 117$ *9, -13*
10. $x^2 + 6\,x - 135 = 0$ *9, -15*
11. $x^2 - 6\,x - 91 = 0$ *13, -7*
12. $b^2 - 20\,b = 96$ *24, -4*
13. $x^2 + 20\,x + 75 = 0$ *-5, -15*
14. $h^2 - 10\,h = 336$ *24, -14*
15. $p^2 - 28\,p + 180 = 0$ *10, 18*
16. $x^2 + 20\,x = 1500$ *30, -50*

Example 3. Solve $x^2 - 3\,x - 18 = 0$.

Solution. $x^2 - 3\,x - 18 = 0$
$$x^2 - 3\,x = 18$$
$A_{\frac{9}{4}}$ $\qquad x^2 - 3\,x + \frac{9}{4} = \frac{81}{4}$
R_2 $\qquad\qquad\quad x - \frac{3}{2} = \pm\,\frac{9}{2}$
$$x = \frac{3}{2} \pm \frac{9}{2}$$
$$x = 6 \quad\text{or}\quad -3$$

$\left[\begin{array}{l}\frac{1}{2}\text{ of }3 = \frac{3}{2} \quad\text{and}\quad (\frac{3}{2})^2 = \frac{9}{4} \\ (\frac{18}{1} + \frac{9}{4} =) \frac{72}{4} + \frac{9}{4} = \frac{81}{4}\end{array}\right]$

Notice that we write $\frac{1}{2}$ of 3 in the form $\frac{3}{2}$, and not in the form $1\frac{1}{2}$.

① Do not spend too much time on this work. Consult your time schedule. Most classes will have time to just skim the material, possibly learning just enough about solution of equations to try a few of the word problems on page 469.
② See note on page 453.

461

EXERCISES

Solve:

-1,-4 1. $x^2 + 5x = -4$

4, 5 2. $y^2 - 9y = -20$

5,-2 3. $x^2 - 3x = 10$

4, 7 4. $x^2 - 11x = -28$

8, -5 5. $x^2 - 3x - 40 = 0$

1, 6 6. $x^2 - 7x + 6 = 0$

8, -7 7. $c^2 - c - 56 = 0$

8, -9 8. $x^2 + x = 72$

6, -5 9. $m^2 - m - 30 = 0$

11,-10 10. $h^2 - h = 110$

-15,-30 11. $y^2 + 45y + 450 = 0$

30,-25 12. $m^2 - 5m - 750 = 0$

30, -26 13. $x^2 - 4x = 780$

20,-27 14. $r^2 + 7r = 540$

Express the roots of the following equations in simplest radical form:

3±√17 15. $x^2 - 6x = 8$

2±2√3 16. $y^2 - 4y = 8$

-5±5√2 17. $x^2 + 10x = 25$

-1±2√2 18. $y^2 + 2y = 7$

4±3√2 19. $x^2 = 8x + 2$

5±√30 20. $y^2 = 10y + 5$

3±3√2 21. $x^2 - 9 = 6x$

3±2√3 22. $h^2 = 3 + 6h$

5±5√3 23. $x^2 = 10x + 50$

-7±4√3 24. $m^2 + 14m + 1 = 0$

Example 4. Solve $3x^2 + 7x + 3 = 0$.

Solution. $3x^2 + 7x + 3 = 0$

$3x^2 + 7x = -3$; this equation should be divided by 3 to get *one* x^2 as the first term.

D_3 $x^2 + \frac{7}{3}x = -1$ $\left[\frac{1}{2} \text{ of } \frac{7}{3} = \frac{7}{6} \text{ and } \left(\frac{7}{6}\right)^2 = \frac{49}{36}\right.$

$A_{\frac{49}{36}}$ $x^2 + \frac{7}{3}x + \frac{49}{36} = \frac{13}{36}$ $\left. \frac{49}{36} - 1 = \frac{49}{36} - \frac{36}{36} = \frac{13}{36}\right]$

R_2 $x + \frac{7}{6} = \pm \frac{\sqrt{13}}{6}$

$$x = -\frac{7}{6} \pm \frac{\sqrt{13}}{6}$$

$$x = \frac{-7 \pm \sqrt{13}}{6}$$

In decimal form, $x = -.566$, or -1.768.

The solution may be checked by substituting the decimal-form roots in the given equation. The roots will not check exactly. Why?

Be sure to learn and use all the different steps in the solution of a quadratic equation. The omission of steps usually results in errors.

4. $\dfrac{-4\pm\sqrt{11}}{5}$; or $-0.137, -1.463$

9. $\dfrac{-11\pm\sqrt{1781}}{10}$; or $3.12, -5.32$

8. $\dfrac{1\pm\sqrt5}{2}$; or $1.618, -0.618$

QUADRATIC EQUATIONS

10. $\dfrac{3\pm\sqrt{17}}{4}$; or $1.781, -0.281$

[A] **EXERCISES**

The roots of some of the following equations contain radicals. Express these roots in their simplest radical form and also in decimal form as shown in Example 4.

1. $2x^2 + 7x = 15\frac{3}{2}, -5$

2. $2x^2 - 3x + 1 = 0\frac{1}{2}, 1$

3. $6x^2 + x = 2\frac{1}{2}, -\frac{2}{3}$ *See top of page*

4. $5x^2 + 8x + 1 = 0$ *page* $\quad -0.809$

5. $2x^2 - 7x = 15\,5, -\frac{3}{2}$

6. $4x^2 + 1 = 5x\frac{1}{4}, 1$

7. $6x^2 + 13x = 8\frac{1}{2}, -\frac{8}{3}$

8. $x^2 - x - 1 = 0$ *See top of page*

9. $5y^2 + 11y - 83 = 0$

10. $2y^2 = 3y + 1$

11. $6x^2 = 1 - 5x\frac{1}{6}, -1$

12. $8c^2 + 6c + 1 = 0 -\frac{1}{4}, -\frac{1}{2}$

13. $4x^2 + 2x = 1 \dfrac{-1\pm\sqrt5}{4}$; or 0.309 $\quad -0.809$

14. $4x^2 - 1 = 3x\,1, -\frac{1}{4}$

15. $2x^2 - 10x = 95 \dfrac{5\pm\sqrt{43}}{2}$; or $5.7785,$ $\quad -0.7785$

16. $2x^2 - 6x + 2 = 0 \dfrac{3\pm\sqrt5}{2}$; or $2.618,$ $\quad 0.382$

17. $3m^2 - 11 = m\dfrac{1\pm\sqrt{133}}{6}$; or $2.088^+,$ $\quad -1.7555$

18. $3x^2 - 3x = 36\,4, -3$

19. $3k^2 + 8k + 5 = 0 -1, -\frac{5}{3}$

20. $3y^2 - 2 + 5y = 0\frac{1}{3}, -2$

Example 5. Solve $\dfrac{x-2}{x+2} - \dfrac{x+2}{x-1} = \dfrac{x^2-32}{x^2+x-2}.$

Solution.

$$\dfrac{x-2}{x+2} - \dfrac{x+2}{x-1} = \dfrac{x^2-32}{x^2+x-2}$$

$$\dfrac{x-2}{x+2} - \dfrac{x+2}{x-1} = \dfrac{x^2-32}{(x+2)(x-1)}$$

$M_{(x+2)(x-1)},$

$$(x+2)(x-1)\dfrac{x-2}{x+2} - (x+2)(x-1)\dfrac{x+2}{x-1}$$

$$= (x+2)(x-1)\dfrac{x^2-32}{(x+2)(x-1)}$$

$$(x-1)(x-2) - (x+2)^2 = x^2 - 32$$

$$(x^2 - 3x + 2) - (x^2 + 4x + 4) = x^2 - 32$$

$$x^2 - 3x + 2 - x^2 - 4x - 4 = x^2 - 32$$

$$x^2 - x^2 - x^2 - 3x - 4x = -2 + 4 - 32$$

$$-x^2 - 7x = -30$$

D_{-1} $\qquad x^2 + 7x = 30$

$A_{\frac{49}{4}}$ $\qquad x^2 + 7x + \frac{49}{4} = \frac{169}{4}$

R_2 $\qquad x + \frac{7}{2} = \pm\frac{13}{2}$

$$x = -\frac{7}{2} \pm \frac{13}{2}$$

$$x = 3 \quad \text{or} \quad -10$$

PROOF. Left to the student.

463

1. $(x + 4)^2 = 9 x^2$ $2, -1$

2. $(x + 1)(x - 4) = 50$ $9, -6$

3. $\dfrac{x}{x - 3} + \dfrac{8}{x + 2} = 3$ $6, \tfrac{1}{2}$

7. $\dfrac{x - 4}{x + 2} + \dfrac{x + 3}{x - 2} = \dfrac{9 x + 2}{x^2 - 4}$ 3

4. $4 x^2 = \dfrac{2 x}{3} + \dfrac{1}{2}$ $\dfrac{1 \pm \sqrt{19}}{12}$; or   [B] $0.45, -0.28$

5. $(2 x - 1)(3 x + 2) = 55$ $3, -3\tfrac{1}{6}$

6. $\dfrac{1}{y} + \dfrac{1}{2} = \dfrac{1}{y - 2}$ $1 \pm \sqrt{5}$; or $3.24, -1.24$

Solving Quadratic Equations by the Formula [A or B]

Any quadratic equation can be written in the general form $ax^2 + bx + c = 0$. In this equation a, b, and c represent known numbers and x stands for the unknown number. We shall now solve $ax^2 + bx + c = 0$ for x and obtain a formula for solving any quadratic equation.

$$ax^2 + bx + c = 0$$
$$ax^2 + bx = -c$$

D_a $x^2 + \dfrac{b}{a} x = -\dfrac{c}{a}$

$\left[\dfrac{1}{2} \text{ of } \dfrac{b}{a} = \dfrac{b}{2a} \text{ and } \left(\dfrac{b}{2a}\right)^2 = \dfrac{b^2}{4 a^2} \right.$

$\left. \dfrac{b^2}{4 a^2} - \dfrac{c}{a} = \dfrac{b^2}{4 a^2} - \dfrac{4 ac}{4 a^2} = \dfrac{b^2 - 4 ac}{4 a^2} \right]$

$A_{\frac{b^2}{4 a^2}}$ $x^2 + \dfrac{b}{a} x + \dfrac{b^2}{4 a^2} = \dfrac{b^2 - 4 ac}{4 a^2}$

R_2 $x + \dfrac{b}{2 a} = \dfrac{\pm \sqrt{b^2 - 4 ac}}{2 a}$

$$x = -\dfrac{b}{2 a} \pm \dfrac{\sqrt{b^2 - 4 ac}}{2 a}$$

$$x = \dfrac{-b \pm \sqrt{b^2 - 4 ac}}{2 a}$$

Now if $\dfrac{-b + \sqrt{b^2 - 4 ac}}{2 a}$ and $\dfrac{-b - \sqrt{b^2 - 4 ac}}{2 a}$ are each substituted for x in the original equation, they are found to be solutions. Thus, the following statement is true.

If	$ax^2 + bx + c = 0,$
then	$x = \dfrac{-b \pm \sqrt{b^2 - 4 ac}}{2 a}$

464

As suggested on page 461, the class may work only a few exercises by completing the square, develop the formula by this method, and then use the formula. This might give students a better over-all view of a subject to be thoroughly studied in second-year algebra. Here, call attention to the general form of the quadratic equation.

To determine the values of a, b, and c in the equation $4\,x^2 = 7 - x$, it must be written in the general form $4\,x^2 + x - 7 = 0$.

Example 1. Solve: $3\,x^2 - 5\,x = 2$

Solution. The right member must be zero; $3\,x^2 - 5\,x - 2 = 0$.
Comparing this equation with $ax^2 + bx + c = 0$, we see that $a = 3$, $b = -5$, and $c = -2$. Write the formula,

$$x = \frac{-b \pm \sqrt{b^2 - 4\,ac}}{2\,a}$$

Substituting $+3$ for a, -5 for b, and -2 for c in this formula, we get

$$x = \frac{+5 \pm \sqrt{25 - 4(+3)(-2)}}{6}$$

Simplifying $\quad x = \dfrac{5 \pm \sqrt{49}}{6}$

$$x = \frac{5 \pm 7}{6}$$

$$x = 2 \text{ or } -\tfrac{1}{3}$$

The proof is left to the student.

Example 2. Solve: $9\,x^2 + 12\,x = 1$

Solution. $\qquad\qquad\qquad 9\,x^2 + 12\,x = 1$

$$9\,x^2 + 12\,x - 1 = 0$$

Write the formula $\quad x = \dfrac{-b \pm \sqrt{b^2 - 4\,ac}}{2\,a}$

Substituting in the formula $a = +9$, $b = +12$, $c = -1$, we get

$$x = \frac{-12 \pm \sqrt{144 - 4(+9)(-1)}}{18}$$

Simplifying $\qquad\qquad x = \dfrac{-12 \pm \sqrt{180}}{18}$

$$x = \frac{-12 \pm 6\sqrt{5}}{18}$$

Reducing the fraction $\quad x = \dfrac{-2 \pm \sqrt{5}}{3}$

PROOF. Does $9\left(\dfrac{-2 + \sqrt{5}}{3}\right)^2 + 12\left(\dfrac{-2 + \sqrt{5}}{3}\right) = 1$?

Does $9 - 4\sqrt{5} - 8 + 4\sqrt{5} = 1$? Yes.

Similarly, we can show that $\dfrac{-2 - \sqrt{5}}{3}$ is a solution.

465

17. $\dfrac{3\pm\sqrt{29}}{2}$; or 4.192, -1.192

19. $3\pm2\sqrt{5}$; or 7.472, -1.472
20. $\dfrac{3\pm\sqrt{2}}{2}$; or 2.207, 0.793
21. $\dfrac{-2\pm\sqrt{5}}{3}$; or 0.079, -1.412

If you expect to continue the study of mathematics, review the quadratic formula each day until you can remember it.

[A or B]

EXERCISES

Solve by the quadratic formula and prove as indicated by your teacher: *(ans. 17, 19-21 at top of page)*

$\dfrac{3\pm\sqrt{13}}{2}$; or 3.303,

-0.303 **1.** $x^2 - 3x - 1 = 0$

$3, -4$ **2.** $x^2 + x = 12$

$\frac{3}{2}, -1$ **3.** $2x^2 - x - 3 = 0$

$-1\pm\sqrt{6}$; or 1.449, -3.449 **4.** $x^2 + 2x - 5 = 0$

$3\pm\sqrt{7}$; or 5.646, 0.354 **5.** $x^2 - 6x + 2 = 0$

$\frac{1}{3}, -2$ **6.** $3x^2 + 5x = 2$

$\frac{1}{5}, -2$ **7.** $5x^2 + 9x - 2 = 0$

$2, 1$ **8.** $x^2 - 3x + 2 = 0$

$4, -5$ **9.** $x^2 + x = 20$

$\dfrac{1\pm\sqrt{5}}{2}$; or 1.618, -0.618 **10.** $x^2 - x = 1$

$1, -2$ **11.** $x^2 + x = 2$

$7, -1$ **12.** $-x^2 + 6x + 7 = 0$

$\dfrac{4\pm\sqrt{6}}{}$; or 6.449, 1.551 **13.** $y^2 - 8y + 10 = 0$, y in this equation corresponds to x in the formula.

$9, 6$ **14.** $x^2 + 54 = 15x$

$\frac{4}{3}, -1$ **15.** $3y^2 = y + 4$

$\frac{1}{2}, -\frac{1}{3}$ **16.** $y + 1 = 6y^2$

17. $m^2 - 3m = 5$

$-\frac{5}{3}, 1$ **18.** $3m^2 + 2m = 5$

19. $x^2 - 6x = 11$

20. $4y^2 + 7 = 12y$

21. $18x^2 = 2 - 24x$

$1, -\frac{5}{3}$ **22.** $3x^2 + 2x = 5$

±1 **23.** $-x^2 + 1 = 0$

[A]

EXERCISES

Solve the following equations by factoring and then by completing the square or by formula:

$3, -2$ **1.** $x^2 - x - 6 = 0$

$6, -4$ **2.** $x^2 - 2x = 24$

$\frac{1}{2}, -2$ **3.** $2x^2 + 3x - 2 = 0$

$-\frac{1}{3}, -4$ **4.** $3x^2 + 13x + 4 = 0$

$-9, 4$ **5.** $x^2 + 5x = 36$

$1\frac{1}{4}, -1$ **6.** $4x^2 - x - 5 = 0$

$\frac{1}{3}, 1\frac{1}{3}$ **7.** $9x^2 + 4 = 15x$

$\frac{1}{2}, -4$ **8.** $4x^2 + 14x = 8$

$-8, 2$ **9.** $y^2 + 6y = 16$

$-15, 3$ **10.** $y^2 + 12y = 45$

[B]

Simplify the following equations and solve them by the method indicated by your teacher:

$3\frac{1}{2}, -5$ **11.** $x(2x + 3) = 35$

$5, 2$ **12.** $(x - 3)^2 = x - 1$

$-2, 4$ **13.** $(x + 2)(x - 4) = 0$

14. $x + \dfrac{1}{x} = \dfrac{3}{x} + 3$

$\dfrac{3\pm\sqrt{17}}{2}$; or 3.562, -0.562

$-9, 4$ **15.** $(x + 2)(x + 3) = 42$

$3, -1$ **16.** $x^2 + (x - 2)^2 = 10$

$\pm\frac{2}{5}\sqrt{-15}$ **17.** $\dfrac{3y}{2} + \dfrac{2}{y} - \dfrac{2y}{3} = 0$

$2, 1$ **18.** $(1 - x)^2 + (2 - x)^2 = 1$

466

19. $(1 + x)^2 + (2x + 1)^2 = 34$ *-3⅕,2*

20. $x(x - 2) + (2x - 3) + 2 = 0$ *±1*

21. $\dfrac{8}{x + 2} + \dfrac{x}{x - 3} = 3\tfrac{1}{2}$ *, 6*

22. $2x(x + 6) - 3x = 5$

23. $\dfrac{3}{x - 5} = 5 - \dfrac{2x}{x - 3}$ *½, -5 7, 4*

24. $1 + \dfrac{3}{x} = \dfrac{70}{x^2}$ *-10, 7*

[C]

Solve: *-48±√1506 ; or -1.52,*
            57   -0.16

25. $\dfrac{2}{3x} + 4 = \dfrac{5x}{6x + 7}$

26. $\dfrac{x - 3}{x + 1} - \dfrac{x + 2}{2x - 2} = -\dfrac{12}{x^2 - 1}$ *7, 4*

27. $\dfrac{2}{x - 1} - \dfrac{3}{8} = \dfrac{1}{x + 3}$ *-4⅓, 5*

28. $\dfrac{8}{x} - \dfrac{2 - 3x}{4x^2} = 15\tfrac{1}{2}$ *2/31, ½*

29. $\dfrac{3}{2y + 1} + \dfrac{2}{3} = \dfrac{5}{4y^2 - 1}$ *-3¼, 1*

30. $\dfrac{2x}{x - 1} + \dfrac{x}{x + 1} = \dfrac{4}{x^2 - 1}$ *-1⅓*

31. $\dfrac{7x + 4}{x^2 + 2x} = \dfrac{14}{x + 4}$ *1.824, -1.253*

32. $\dfrac{1}{x - 1} + \dfrac{1}{x - 2} = \dfrac{1}{x - 3}$ *3±√2; 4.414, 1.586*

33. $\dfrac{8}{x - 1} - \dfrac{4}{x + 3} = 1\tfrac{1}{2}$ *-4⅓, 5*

34. $\dfrac{x}{x + 3} + \dfrac{5}{x} = \dfrac{3}{2}$ *6, -5*

35. $\dfrac{2}{x - 1} - \dfrac{1}{3x + 1} = \dfrac{1}{4}$ *11±4√10 ; or 7.883, 3   -0.549*

36. $\dfrac{3}{x^2 - x} - \dfrac{5}{2x - 2} = \dfrac{1}{2}$ *-2±√10; or 1.162, -5.162*

37. $\dfrac{x}{2x - 2} = \dfrac{4}{x^2 - 1} + \dfrac{5}{x + 1}$ *9±√73; or 8.772, 2   0.228*

38. $\dfrac{2y + 3}{y^2 + y} - \dfrac{y + 5}{y^2 - y} = \dfrac{21}{8y^2 - 8}$ *61±3√641 ; or 8.56, 16   -0.94*

39. $\dfrac{x + 5}{x^2 + 7x + 12} = \dfrac{x - 1}{2x^2 + 5x - 3}$ *-3±√10; 0.162, -6.162*

40. $\dfrac{x}{x - 3} + \dfrac{x}{x + 3} = \dfrac{3 + x}{3x + 9}$ *±⅗√-5*

How to Solve Quadratic Equations Graphically [C]

A quadratic equation whose roots are real numbers can be solved very easily by the graphic method. Study the following example.

Example. Solve $x^2 - 3x = 4$ graphically.

Solution. The equation should be written as $x^2 - 3x - 4 = 0$. When different values are assigned to x, the expression $x^2 - 3x - 4$ takes on different values. Now suppose we let y represent this expression. That is, $x^2 - 3x - 4 = y$. In this case, when different values are assigned to x, y takes on different values.

467

We next prepare a table for the equation $f(x) = x^2 - 3x - 4$.

If $x =$	5	4	3	2	1	0	-1	-2
Then $f(x)$ or $x^2 - 3x - 4 =$	6	0	-4	-6	-6	-4	0	6

The points whose coordinates are these pairs of values are plotted on graph paper as shown at the right. Then a smooth curve is drawn through the points in order. This curve is the graph of $f(x) = x^2 - 3x - 4$. Solving the equation $x^2 - 3x - 4 = 0$ consists in finding the values of x which make $x^2 - 3x - 4$, or $f(x)$, equal to zero. The curve crosses

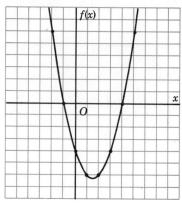

the x-axis at $x = 4$ and at $x = -1$. At these two points the value of $x^2 - 3x - 4$, or $f(x)$, is zero. Then $x = 4$ and $x = -1$ are solutions of $x^2 - 3x - 4 = 0$.

The curve which is the graph of $f(x) = x^2 - 3x - 4$ is a parabola. The parabola has many important applications in engineering and science. The path of a projectile fired from a gun would be a parabola if there were no air resistance. Lon-

gitudinal sections of automobile headlights are modified parabolas. The strongest simple arch is parabolic in shape.

[C]

EXERCISES Solve the following equations graphically:

3, −2 **1.** $x^2 - x - 6 = 0$ 3, −3 **7.** $x^2 - 9 = 0$

4, −2 **2.** $x^2 - 2x = 8$ 2, −2 **8.** $x^2 - 4 = 0$

5, −1 **3.** $x^2 - 4x - 5 = 0$ $\frac{1}{2}$, −3 **9.** $2x^2 + 5x - 3 = 0$

2, 3 **4.** $x^2 - 5x = -6$ $1\frac{1}{2}$, 3 **10.** $2x^2 - 9x + 9 = 0$

0, 2 **5.** $x^2 - 2x = 0$ 4, −3 **11.** $x^2 - x = 12$

0, −3 **6.** $x^2 + 3x = 0$ 3, 3 **12.** $x^2 - 6x + 9 = 0$

468

13. $3x^2 + 5x = 2$ $\frac{1}{3}, -2$ **15.** $2x^2 + x - 15 = 0$ $2\frac{1}{2}, -3$

14. $2x^2 - 5x = 18$ $4\frac{1}{2}, -2$ **16.** $x^2 - 8x + 16 = 0$ $4, 4$

Solve graphically, estimating each root to the nearest tenth:

17. $x^2 - 3x - 2 = 0$ $3.6, -0.6$ **20.** $10x^2 - 7x + 1 = 0$ $0.2, 0.5$

18. $x^2 - 5x - 1 = 0$ $5.2, -0.2$**21.** $x^2 + 4x - 1 = 0$ $0.2, -4.2$

19. $6x^2 - 7x + 2 = 0$ $0.5, 0.7$**22.** $6x^2 - 13x + 2 = 0$ $0.2, 2.0$

Solving Cubic Equations Graphically [C]

A cubic equation such as $x^3 - x^2 - 6x = 0$ can be solved graphically by drawing the graph of $f(x) = x^3 - x^2 - 6x$ and finding the values of x where the curve crosses the x-axis. The graph of this equation crosses the x-axis at $x = -2$, $x = 0$, and $x = 3$. Then -2, 0, and 3 are the roots of the equation. Notice that the curve has two turning points. A straight line cannot cut this curve in more than three points.

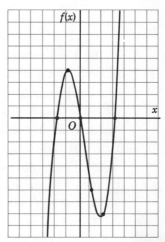

[C]

EXERCISES

Graph the following equations and find their roots:

1. $x^3 - 4x^2 + 4x = 0$ $0, 2, 2$ **3.** $x^3 + 3x^2 - 4x - 12 = 0$
                                                          $2, -2, -3$
2. $x^3 - x^2 - 4x + 4 = 0$ **4.** $x^3 - 16x = 0$ $0, 4, -4$
                  $1, 2, -2$

[A]

PROBLEMS

The following problems lead to quadratic equations. Remember that each number sought will have two values.

1. The square of a certain number is 30 more than the number. What is the number? $6 \text{ or } -5$

2. Twice the square of a certain number equals 40 increased by twice the number. Find the number. $5 \text{ or } -4$

3. A certain number added to its square equals twelve. What is the number? $-4 \text{ or } 3$

4. Twice the square of a certain number decreased by 6 times the number is 80. Find the number. $8 \text{ or } -5$

You will need to review the interpretation of negative numbers obtained as solutions.

5. The sum of two numbers is 14 and their product is 48. What are the numbers? *$x (14-x)$ =?* *6 and 8*

6. The difference of two numbers is 2 and the sum of their squares is 52. Find the numbers. *-6, -4; or 4, 6*

7. The sum of two numbers is 10 and the sum of their squares is 58. What are the numbers? *3 and 7*

8. The area of a rectangle is 192 square feet and the length is 4 feet more than the width. Find the length and width. *width, 12 ft.; length, 16 ft.*

9. The length of a rectangle exceeds twice its width by 6 feet. Find its length and width if its area is 176 square feet. *width, 8 ft.; length, 22 ft.*

10. The perimeter of a rectangle is 56 feet. Find the length of each side if its area is 195 square feet. *13 ft., 15 ft.*

11. The perimeter of a rectangle is 80 inches and its area is 396 square inches. Find its length and width. *18 in. wide, 22 in. long*

12. Find the value of x and $x + 4$ in the figure at the right. *12 and 16*

13. The hypotenuse of a right triangle is 85 inches long. Find the lengths of the two other sides if one exceeds the other by 35 inches. *40 in., 75 in.*

14. The diagonal of a square is 50 feet. How long is each of its sides? *35.35 ft.*

15. The diagonal of a square is 3 inches longer than one of its sides. Find the length of each of its sides. *7.24 in.*

16. Find the number of degrees in the angle which is 15° less than twice the square of its complement. *83°*

[B]

17. Find the legs of a right triangle if their difference is 7 and the hypotenuse is 13. *5 and 12*

18. One leg of a right triangle is 10 inches. Find the length of the hypotenuse if it is 2 inches longer than the other leg. *26 in.*

19. Find the bases and altitude of a trapezoid whose area is 126 square inches if the altitude is one third of the lower base and the lower base is 6 inches longer than the upper base. *Upper, 15 in.; lower, 21 in.; altitude, 7 in.*

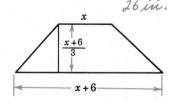

470

20. A man can do a piece of work in 2 days less than his son. If working together they can do the work in $4\frac{4}{9}$ days, how long will it take each working alone to do the work? *Man, 8 da.; son, 10 da.*

21. A fish pond can be filled in 4 hours by two pipes when both are used at the same time. How many hours are needed for each pipe to fill the pond if the smaller requires 3 more hours than the larger? *Larger, 6.77 hr.; smaller, 9.77 hr.*

22. A man made a round trip of 36 miles in 54 minutes. If his speed returning was 9 miles an hour faster than his speed going, what was his rate each way? *Going, 36 m.p.h.; returning, 45 m.p.h.*

23. A man makes a daily automobile trip of 80 miles at a certain rate. If he were to increase his rate 8 miles an hour he would make the trip in 30 minutes less time. What is his usual rate? *32 m.p.h.*

24. The difference between a side and the altitude of an equilateral triangle is 2. Find the altitude. *$6 + 4\sqrt{3}$, or 12.928*

Historical Note. The name of the person who first solved a quadratic equation is unknown. It is known, however, that Diophantus, who lived at Alexandria about 300 A.D., solved them by a method similar to our "completing the square" method.

During the next thousand years most of the work with quadratic equations was done by the Hindus. The most noted of the Hindu mathematicians were Brahmagupta (born about 598 A.D.), and Bhāskara (born about 1114 A.D.). The Hindu method of solving a quadratic equation follows:

$$2x^2 + 5x - 3 = 0$$
$$2x^2 + 5x = 3$$

*M_8 $\qquad\qquad$ $16x^2 + 40x = 24$

A_{25} $\qquad$ $16x^2 + 40x + 25 = 49$

R_2 $\qquad\qquad\qquad$ $4x + 5 = 7$

$$4x = 2$$
$$x = \tfrac{1}{2}$$

The early Hindus used only the positive square root in the solution. It was not until the time of Gauss (1777–1855), the great German mathematician, that the two roots of quadratic equations were understood.

*In the Hindu method both members of the equation are multiplied by 4 times the coefficient of x^2. Here $4 \times 2 = 8$.

Ask students the advantage of this version of completing the square.

471

Checking Your Understanding of Chapter 17

Before you begin the Chapter Review, be sure that you know

Do you need help?

PAGE

1. The difference between a complete quadratic equation and an incomplete quadratic equation   453
2. How to solve an incomplete quadratic equation
   by the square-root method   453
   and by the factoring method   353
3. How to solve a complete quadratic equation
   a. by factoring   353
   b. by completing the square   460
      or by the formula   464
4. How to spell and use the following words:

	PAGE		PAGE
hypotenuse	456	Pythagoras	456
pure quadratic	453	right triangle	456

[A]

CHAPTER REVIEW

Solve:

± 4 **1.** $x^2 = 16$

± 3 **2.** $3 x^2 = 27$

$\pm 4\sqrt{2}$ **3.** $4 m^2 = 128$

$\pm \frac{1}{2}$ **4.** $4 x^2 - 1 = 0$

$\pm \frac{2}{3}$ **5.** $9 x^2 - 4 = 0$

$\pm 2\sqrt{5}$ **6.** $x^2 - 5 = 15$

$\pm 5a$ **7.** $x^2 = 25 a^2$

$3, 1$ **8.** $m^2 - 4 m = -3$

$-2, -\frac{1}{2}$ **9.** $2 x^2 + 5 x + 2 = 0$

$\pm \frac{3}{2}$ **10.** $(2 x - 3)^2 = 6(3 - 2 x)$

$-2, -1$ **11.** $4 x^2 + 12 x + 8 = 0$

$-1 \pm \sqrt{6}$ **12.** $\dfrac{2}{x} - 1 = \dfrac{5}{x^2} - 2$

13. $x - 3\frac{1}{2} = \dfrac{3}{x + 1}$ $\dfrac{5 \pm \sqrt{129}}{4}$

14. $2 x + \dfrac{23}{x} = 8 x - \dfrac{21}{x}$ $\pm \frac{1}{3}\sqrt{66}$

15. $\dfrac{1}{x - 1} + \dfrac{1}{x + 1} = \dfrac{1 - x^2}{x^2 - 1}$ $-1 \pm \sqrt{2}$

16. Solve $K = \frac{1}{2} m v^2$ for v and find v to the nearest tenth when $K = 80$ and $m = 5$. $\pm \frac{1}{m}\sqrt{2Km}$; 5.7

17. Solve $s = \frac{1}{2} g t^2$ for t and find t to the nearest tenth when $s = 120$ and $g = 32$. $\pm \frac{1}{g}\sqrt{2gs}$; 2.7

18. Solve $A = \pi r^2$ for r and find r to the nearest tenth when $A = 55.23$ and $\pi = 3.14$. $\pm \frac{1}{\pi}\sqrt{\pi A}$; 4.2

19. State the Pythagorean Theorem. *(See page 456)*

20. Find the value x in the following right triangles:

a. 10

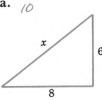

b. $\sqrt{145}$, or 12.04

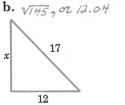

c. $8\sqrt{2}$, or 11.312

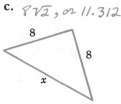

d. $\sqrt{514}$, or 22.7   **e.** 8

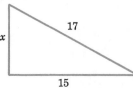

f. $5\sqrt{2}$, or 7.07

21. The two legs of a right triangle are equal. Find their lengths if the hypotenuse is 16 inches: 11.312 in.

22. Find the height of an equilateral triangle each of whose sides is 12 inches. 10.392 in.

23. The diagonal of a square is $12\sqrt{3}$. How long is each of its sides? 14.694

24. A rectangular field is 80 rods long and 30 rods wide. How long is each of its diagonals? 85.44 rd.

[A]

GENERAL REVIEW

1. From the sum of $4\,a^3 - 6\,a + 7\,a^2 - 6$ and $3\,a^3 - a - 5\,a^2$ take $7\,a^3 - 4\,a + 3\,a^2 - a + 1$. $-a^2 - 2a - 7$

2. Find the products:

a. $(-3\,x)(4\,x^2)$ $-12x^3$ **c.** $(-2\,ab)^3$ $-8a^3b^3$ **e.** $(x^2 - x + 1)(x - 3)$ $x^3 - 4x^2 + 4x - 3$

b. $(xy^2)(xy^3)$ x^2y^5 **d.** $\dfrac{2\,a}{3} \times \dfrac{9\,a}{10}$ $\dfrac{3a^2}{5}$ **f.** $\dfrac{a^2 - a - 6}{a + 1} \cdot \dfrac{5\,a + 5}{a^2 - 3\,a}$ $\dfrac{5(a+2)}{a}$

3. Multiply $x^2 - x - 12$ by $3\,x + 5$ and divide the product by $x + 3$. $3x^2 - 7x - 20$

4. Divide $18\,x^2y^3 - 12\,x^3y^2 - 6\,x^4y - 2\,xy$ by $2\,xy$. $9xy^2 - 6x^2y - 3x^3 - 1$

5. If $x = -4$ and $y = 3$, find the value of:

a. $x^3 + y^3$ -37 **c.** $3\,y^2 - 4\,x^2$ -37 **e.** $3\,x^2 - 5\,xy$ 108

b. $10 + xy$ -2 **d.** $(xy)^3 + 728$ -1000 **f.** $100 + 5\,xy$ 40

6. $\sqrt{x^6}$ $\overset{x^3}{}$; $\sqrt{75}$ $\overset{5\sqrt{3}}{}$; $\sqrt{\frac{1}{2}}$ $\overset{\frac{1}{2}\sqrt{2}}{}$; $\sqrt{\frac{1}{\pi^2}}$ $\overset{\frac{1}{\pi}}{}$; $\sqrt{\frac{25\,x^4}{9}}$ $\overset{\frac{5x^2}{3}}{}$.

7. Multiply $\sqrt{8}\cdot\sqrt{45}$; $\sqrt{20}\cdot\sqrt{72}$. *6√10; 12√10*

8. Multiply $\sqrt{50}\cdot\sqrt{\frac{1}{2}}\cdot\sqrt{18}$. *15√2*

9. Find the principal square root of 191406.25. *437.5*

Combine:

10. $\frac{5\,a}{6}-\frac{3\,a}{4}$ $\overset{\frac{a}{12}}{}$ **12.** $\frac{m}{n}-1$ $\overset{m-n}{n}$ **14.** $\frac{x-1}{3}-\frac{2\,x+1}{4}$ $\overset{-2x-7}{12}$

11. $\frac{a}{b}+1$ $\overset{a+b}{b}$ **13.** $\frac{a}{b}-\frac{b}{a}$ $\overset{a^2-b^2}{ab}$ **15.** $\frac{x+1}{8\,x}-\frac{x+5}{6\,x^2}$ $\overset{3x^2-x-20}{24x^2}$

16. Divide $\frac{a^2+4\,a}{2\,a+1}$ by $\frac{a^2-16}{4\,a^2-1}$. $\frac{a(2a-1)}{a-4}$

Solve:

17. $2(x-3)-4(x+2)=0$ *-7*   **19.** $c(c-3)-(c-5)=4$ $\overset{2\pm\sqrt{3}}{}$

18. $x(x-3)+3\,x=81$ *±9*   **20.** $50.5\,r=49+15.5\,r$ *1.4*

$\frac{1\pm\sqrt{5}}{2}$; or 1.618, -0.618

Solve:

[B]

$\frac{-1\pm\sqrt{73}}{4}$; or 1.886, -2.386

21. $\frac{x-1}{x^2-2}=\frac{x+3}{x^2+2}$ **22.** $\frac{1}{x}+\frac{2\,x}{x-1}=\frac{8}{x^2-x}$

23. $S=vt+\frac{1}{2}gt^2$. Find S when $v=8$, $t=6$, and $g=32.2$. *627.6*

24. $c=\frac{En}{R+rn}$. Find c when $n=8$, $E=30$, $R=8$, and $r=6$. $4\frac{2}{7}$

25. Solve graphically: $x+y=3$ *X=3½,*
$3\,x-y=11$ *y = -½*

26. Reduce $\frac{2\,a^2-5\,a-3}{8\,a^2+4\,a}$ to lowest terms. $\frac{a-3}{4a}$

27. Multiply $\frac{x^2-xy}{4\,x^2-6\,xy}$ by $\frac{4\,x^2-9\,y^2}{x^2-2\,xy+y^2}$. $\frac{2x+3y}{2(x-y)}$

28. Tell which of the following are irrational: $\sqrt{4}$; $\sqrt{5}$; $\sqrt[3]{8}$; $\sqrt[3]{125}$; $\sqrt{\frac{1}{3}}$. *√5 and √⅓*

29. How do you find the square root of a product? of a fraction? *(1) Find the square root of each factor and multiply these roots together. (2) Divide the square root of the numerator by the square root of the denominator.*

30. The number of seconds, t, for a pendulum to move from A to B, or from B to A is given by the formula $t = \pi \sqrt{\dfrac{\ell}{g}}$.

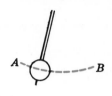

In this formula ℓ is the length of the pendulum in feet and g is the amount of acceleration in feet due to gravity. The clock ticks when the pendulum is at A or at B.

a. How many seconds are there between successive ticks of a clock whose pendulum is 2 feet long? Use 32.2 for g. *0.782⁺*

b. Find the length of the pendulum of a clock which ticks twice a second. Use 32.2 for g. *0.815⁺ ft.*

c. The value of g is less on a high mountain than at sea level. Will a clock run faster or more slowly on a mountain than at sea level? Should the pendulum be shortened or lengthened to make the clock run faster? *more slowly; shortened*

31. Combine: $\dfrac{2a+1}{2a-1} + \dfrac{2a-1}{2a+1} + \dfrac{6}{4a^2-1}$ *$\dfrac{8a^2+8}{(2a+1)(2a-1)}$*

32. Combine: $\dfrac{a-3b}{a^2-ab-12b^2} - \dfrac{a+3b}{a^2-7ab+12b^2}$

$\dfrac{-12ab}{(a-4b)(a+3b)(a-3b)}$

Solve for x and y:

33. $\dfrac{x+2y}{x-2} = 5$ *x = 3*

$\dfrac{2x-3y}{2x+3} = \dfrac{1}{3}$ *y = 1*

34. $\dfrac{x+2y}{x-y} = -\dfrac{1}{5}$

$\dfrac{x-y}{x+y} = 5$ *The equations are identical*

35. In a two-digit number the units' digit exceeds the tens' digit by 3. If the digits are interchanged, a number is formed which when added to the original number gives a sum of 77. Find the original number. *25*

36. Simplify $\sqrt{12} - \sqrt{50} - 2\sqrt{48} + 2\sqrt{18}$ *$\sqrt{2} - 6\sqrt{3}$*

37. There are three consecutive even integers such that if three fourths of the smallest is added to the sum of the other two the result is 39. What are the integers? *12, 14, 16*

CHAPTER
TESTS

Solve:

1. $x^2 = 64$ ± 8 **2.** $(x - 3)^2 = 2(17 - 3x)$ ± 5

Solve by completing the square:

3. $x^2 - 7 = 6x$ $7, -1$ **4.** $x^2 + 14x = 15$ $1, -15$ **5.** $4x^2 + 3 = 8x$ $\frac{3}{2}, \frac{1}{2}$

$\frac{1 \pm \sqrt{133}}{6}$; **6.** $3y^2 - 11 = y$ or $2.09, -1.76$ **7.** $(x - 1)^2 + (x - 2)^2 - 1 = 0$ $2, 1$

8. The hypotenuse of a right triangle is 17 and one side is 8. Find the remaining side.

9. Find the length of the diagonal of a rectangle which is 40 feet long and 9 feet wide. 41 ft.

10. The sum of two numbers is 15 and the sum of their squares is 117. What are the numbers? $6, 9$

[Test B]

Solve for x:

1. $bx^2 = 9b.$ ± 3 **2.** $ax^2 = 4.$ $\pm \frac{2}{a}\sqrt{a}$ **3.** $\pi x^2 - c = 0.$ $\pm \frac{1}{\pi}\sqrt{c\pi}$

4. Solve $E = \frac{1}{2}mv^2$ for v and find v when $m = 2$ and $E = 16.$

5. Find the altitude of an equilateral triangle each of whose sides is 10. $5\sqrt{3}$ $v = \pm \frac{1}{m}\sqrt{2Em}; 4$

Solve by completing the square or by formula:

6. $x^2 - x + 1 = 0$ $\frac{1 \pm \sqrt{-3}}{2}$ **7.** $3x + 1 = 4x^2$ $1, -\frac{1}{4}$

8. $\dfrac{x - 2}{x - 4} + \dfrac{x + 2}{x + 4} = \dfrac{8(x + 1)}{x^2 - 16}$ $6, -2$

9. The area of a rectangle is 216 square feet and the length is 6 feet more than the width. What is the length of the rectangle? 18 ft.

10. The hypotenuse of a right triangle is 30 feet. If one leg of the right triangle is 6 feet more than the other leg, find the length of the shorter leg. 18 ft.

Nature of the Roots of a Quadratic Equation [Optional]

The work on page 464 shows that for the equation $ax^2 + bx + c = 0.$

$$x = \frac{-b + \sqrt{b^2 - 4ac}}{2a} \quad \text{or} \quad x = \frac{-b - \sqrt{b^2 - 4ac}}{2a}.$$ Note that

when $b^2 - 4ac$ is a positive number, these two values for x are different numbers, and the equation has two different roots. The graph of such an equation intersects the x-axis in two different points. For example, consider the equation $x^2 + 4x + 3 = 0.$ Here

$a = 1$, $b = 4$, and $c = 3$. Thus $b^2 - 4\,ac$ equals $4^2 - 4(1)(3)$ or 4. Then

$$x = \frac{-b + \sqrt{b^2 - 4\,ac}}{2\,a} = \frac{-4 + \sqrt{4}}{2} = -1.$$

Also

$$x = \frac{-b - \sqrt{b^2 - 4\,ac}}{2\,a} = \frac{-4 - \sqrt{4}}{2} = -3.$$

A

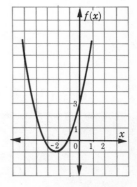

The graph of the equation is shown in drawing **A** at the right. Note that the graph intersects the x-axis at the points whose x-coordinates are -1 and -3.

If, for equation $ax^2 + bx + c = 0$, you find that $b^2 - 4\,ac = 0$, then

$$x = \frac{-b + \sqrt{b^2 - 4\,ac}}{2\,a} = \frac{-b + \sqrt{0}}{2\,a}$$

and

$$x = \frac{-b - \sqrt{b^2 - 4\,ac}}{2\,a} = \frac{-b - \sqrt{0}}{2\,a}.$$

Since $\dfrac{-b + \sqrt{0}}{2\,a} = \dfrac{-b - \sqrt{0}}{2\,a}$, the equation

B

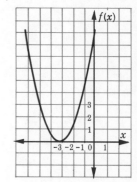

has two equal roots and its graph intersects the x-axis at just one point.

· For the equation $x^2 + 6x + 9 = 0$, $a = 1$, $b = 6$, and $c = 9$. Thus $b^2 - 4\,ac = 6^2 - 4(1)(9) = 0$. The two roots are therefore $\dfrac{-6 + \sqrt{0}}{2}$ and $\dfrac{-6 - \sqrt{0}}{2}$. Since each of these has the value -3, both roots are -3. The graph is shown in drawing **B**.

C

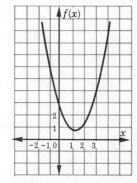

When $b^2 - 4\,ac$ is a negative number, then $\sqrt{b^2 - 4\,ac}$ is not a real number and is not considered in this text. The graph of such an equation can be drawn, but it does not intersect the x-axis. $x^2 - 3x + 3 = 0$ is such an equation. For it, $b^2 - 4\,ac = (-3)^2 - 4(1)(3) = -3$. Since $\sqrt{-3}$ is not a real number, $x^2 - 3x + 3$ has no real number roots. The graph is shown in drawing **C**.

477

Mathematics *IN BRIDGE BUILDING*

Golden Gate Bridge, San Francisco

A good bridge should have utility, strength, and beauty. To be beautiful a bridge should have simplicity, harmony of color, graceful lines, and good proportions.

Years ago small streams were crossed by fording or by using wooden bridges, and larger bodies of water were crossed by ferries. Today very few bridges are made of wood. The smaller bridges are made of steel or reinforced concrete, and the largest bridges are made wholly of steel.

Movable bridges are used to span rivers and bodies of water where stationary bridges interfere with boat traffic. There are various types of movable bridges. Some are lifted vertically, some open like double garage doors, and some are hinged at both ends and rotate upwards.

The arch bridge and the suspension bridge are the two main types of the large steel bridges.

The Rainbow Bridge at Niagara Falls is a good example of the steel arch bridge. It was completed in 1941 at a cost of about $3,000,000. It has the longest hingeless arch span in the world. It has a span of 960 feet and the rise of its arch is 150 feet. The deck of the bridge is of reinforced concrete and is 60 feet wide, providing for two lanes of vehicular traffic and one 10-foot sidewalk.

This bridge was built on the cantilever plan from each abutment, the two crews of workmen erecting the bridge from the abutments to meet at the middle.

The Golden Gate Bridge at San Francisco is an excellent example of the suspension bridge. It was completed in 1937. It has the longest clear span in the world, being 4200 feet long. Each of the two side spans is 1125 feet long, making the total length of the bridge 6450 feet. The total length of the bridge plus its approaches is about 7 miles. The steel towers which support the cables rise 746 feet above the low-water level. The cables contain 80,000 miles of steel wire and have a sag of 470 feet. The bridge is 90 feet wide and has six vehicular traffic lanes and two walks for pedestrians.

In a suspension bridge the weight is borne by heavy cables, which consist of a large number of strands of wire bound together. The cables of a suspension bridge form curves called parabolas. (If the cables supported only their own weight, the curves would be catenaries.)

The mathematics needed in the designing and construction of a large suspension bridge can be acquired in a college of engineering. The bridge engineer knows trigonometry, analytic geometry, calculus, mechanics, and differential equations.

18

Proportion and Variation

Suggested Time Schedule
Maximum   7 days
(Not in minimum schedule)

*You will learn in this chapter
how to express
certain number relationships
by proportion.*

This chapter deals with changes and comparisons among numbers. Ratio, proportion, and variation are new ideas to beginning pupils, and time is needed for students to understand them.   If time is short, it is better to omit the chapter than to take it haphazardly.   All the concepts will be carefully taught and used in demonstrative geometry and inter-mediate algebra.   Your remaining time this year could in most cases be more profitably spent in reviewing the basic principles taught to date. There are ample general reviews suitable for this purpose.   Have much board work in class and suitable written assignments, with frequent short tests.

Proportion [A]

In this chapter you will continue the study of proportion, begin the study of variation, and learn how proportion and variation are related.

You know that the ratio of one number to another is found by dividing the first number by the second. For example, the ratio of 2 to 3 is $\frac{2}{3}$. You know that an equation which says that two ratios are equal is called a proportion. Thus $\frac{1}{2} = \frac{3}{6}$ and $\frac{a}{b} = \frac{c}{d}$ are proportions.

Proportions are sometimes written in one line by using a colon (:) to indicate division. Thus $\frac{a}{b} = \frac{c}{d}$ can be written $a : b = c : d$. We say that a is the first *term* of the proportion, b the second, c the third, and d the fourth. The middle terms, b and c, are called the means and the outside terms, a and d, the extremes. In the proportion $\frac{1}{2} = \frac{3}{6}$, 2 and 3 are the *means*, and 1 and 6 the *extremes*.

The Test of a Proportion [A]

If both terms of the proportion $\frac{a}{b} = \frac{c}{d}$ are multiplied by bd, we have

$$\cancel{b}d\left(\frac{a}{\cancel{b}}\right) = \left(\frac{c}{\cancel{d}}\right)b\cancel{d}$$

or $ad = bc$

Notice that ad is the product of the extremes and bc the product of the means. We therefore know that the statement below is true.

> *In a proportion*
> *the product of the means is equal to the product of the extremes.*

It can be shown that if the product of two numbers is not equal to the product of two other numbers, the four numbers cannot form a proportion.

Example 1. Clear the proportion $\frac{2x}{3} = \frac{4}{7}$ of fractions.

Solution. Since $\frac{2x}{3} = \frac{4}{7}$ is a proportion, we know that

$$(3)(4) = (2x)(7), \text{ or } 12 = 14x.$$

① A ratio is a *quotient*. Remind students that any whole number can be written as an indicated quotient; e.g., $3 = 3/1$.

② Allow students to use the short cut stated here, but frown on the use of the term "cross multiply."

481

Example 2. Is $\frac{3}{4} = \frac{9}{16}$ a proportion?

Solution. Since 3×16 does not equal 4×9, we know that it was incorrect to place an equals sign between the two fractions. We know that the statement is not a proportion.

$\frac{4}{6} \text{ or } \frac{2}{3} \qquad \frac{x}{y} \qquad \frac{5}{2}$ [A]

EXERCISES

1. What is the ratio of 4 to 6? of x to y? of 5 to 2?

Which of the following are proportions? 3, 4, 6

2. $\frac{3}{7} = \frac{15}{36}$

4. $\frac{18}{27} = \frac{10}{15}$

6. $\frac{6a}{9b} = \frac{10a}{15b}$

3. $\frac{8}{7} = \frac{16}{14}$

5. $\frac{25}{36} = \frac{36}{52}$

7. $8 : 12 = 12 : 16$

Solve for x in each proportion:

$2\frac{1}{2}$ **8.** $\frac{x}{3} = \frac{5}{6}$

$\frac{bc}{a}$ **10.** $\frac{a}{b} = \frac{c}{x}$

± 4 **12.** $\frac{x-2}{3} = \frac{4}{x+2}$

± 8 **9.** $\frac{4}{x} = \frac{x}{16}$

156.25 **11.** $\frac{x}{5} = \frac{125}{4}$

$\frac{1}{3}$ **13.** $\frac{x-3}{x+3} = \frac{x+5}{x-7}$

14. State the principle of proportion that enables one to clear an equation such as $\frac{2x}{x+3} = \frac{x}{2}$ of fractions. *In a proportion the product of the means equals the product of the extremes.*

Solve for y:

15. $\frac{y-6}{3} = \frac{1}{4}$ $6\frac{3}{4}$

16. $\frac{3}{7} = \frac{1}{y}$ $2\frac{1}{3}$

Using Proportions to Solve Problems [A]

The principle of proportion provides an easy way to solve many problems. Consider the question: If 2 squares of chocolate are needed in making 25 cookies, how many squares are needed for 50 cookies?

The answer is found quickly if we think: "50 cookies are twice 25 cookies; therefore the chocolate needed must be twice 2 squares, or 4 squares."

If we set down the information about the chocolate and the cookies in a table, we can easily see the proportion.

Number of Squares of Chocolate	Number of Cookies to Be Made
2	25
4	50

PROPORTION AND VARIATION

If the numbers 2 and 4 of the left-hand column are written as $\frac{2}{4}$, they give the ratio of the smaller amount of chocolate to the larger amount. If the numbers 25 and 50 of the right-hand column are written as $\frac{25}{50}$, they give the ratio of the smaller number of cookies to the larger number. Since the fractions are equal, we have the proportion $\frac{2}{4} = \frac{25}{50}$. It says that the amount of chocolate is proportional to the number of cookies.

The following problem has been solved by using a proportion.

Example. The Smith family finds that it uses 5 loaves of bread in 2 weeks. At that rate, how many loaves will it use in a year (52 weeks)?

Solution. Let x equal the number of loaves used in 52 weeks.

If we set down the information in a table, we have:

Number of Loaves	Number of Weeks
5	2
x	52

The information in the table gives the proportion

$$\frac{5}{x} = \frac{2}{52}$$

Solving the proportion,

$$2x = 260$$
$$x = 130, \text{ number of loaves used in a year}$$

PROOF. $5 \div 2 = 2\frac{1}{2}$, the number of loaves used per week
$130 \div 52 = 2\frac{1}{2}$, the number of loaves used per week
Both sets of information give the same number of loaves per week.

[A]   EXERCISES

1. If the Brown family uses 2 pounds of butter in 3 weeks, how much will it use in 52 weeks? $34\frac{2}{3}$ *lb.*

No. of lb. of butter	No. of weeks
?	?
?	?

2. Last week Sam's car used 8 gallons of gasoline for a trip of 132 miles. At that rate, how much gasoline will be needed for a trip of 500 miles? 30.3 *gal.*

483

3. If $1\frac{1}{2}$ inches on a map represents 60 miles, how many miles does 4 inches represent? *160 mi.*

4. If Sue spent 37 minutes in typing 3 pages of a report, how long will it take her to complete the work if 10 pages remain and she types these at the same rate? *123⅓ min.*

5. The Smiths are estimating the cost of a brick wall at the back of their lot. If 617 bricks are needed for 100 square feet of the type of wall they plan to build, how many bricks will they need for 270 square feet? *1666*

6. If 2 bricks weigh 9 pounds, how much will 500 bricks weigh? *2250 lb.*

7. If a recipe for $2\frac{1}{2}$ dozen cookies calls for $\frac{1}{3}$ cup of butter, how much butter will be needed for $7\frac{1}{2}$ dozen cookies? *1 cup*

Similar Polygons[A]

Similar polygons are polygons which have the same shape. They are polygons whose corresponding angles are equal and whose corresponding sides are in proportion.

These two triangles (polygons with three sides) are similar ($\sim$). Notice that $\angle A = \angle D$, $\angle B = \angle E$, and $\angle C = \angle F$. The sides are proportional, since $\frac{6}{9} = \frac{8}{12}$, $\frac{6}{9} = \frac{10}{15}$, and $\frac{8}{12} = \frac{10}{15}$.

These two rectangles are not similar. Their corresponding angles are equal but their corresponding sides are not proportional. Is $\frac{4}{4} = \frac{8}{6}$?

These two polygons are not similar. Since $\frac{4}{2} = \frac{6}{3}$, their corresponding sides are proportional; but the corresponding angles are not equal.

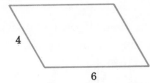

4

6

2

3

The study of similarity is interesting and useful. The architect, draftsman, and surveyor use similarity in preparing their sketches and drawings. So do the dressmaker, photographer, and carpenter.

[A]

EXERCISES

1. Are these rectangles similar? Why? *Yes. Corresponding angles equal, and corresponding sides in proportion.*

9

12

15

20

2. Are these figures similar? Why? *No. Do not have same number of sides, so do not contain corresponding sides or corresponding angles.*

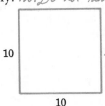

8   8

8

10

10

3. Are these rectangles similar? Why? *No. Corresponding sides not in proportion.*

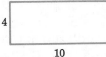

4

10

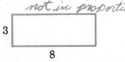

3

8

4. The sides of one triangle are 8 inches, 12 inches, and 15 inches. The shortest side of a similar triangle is 6 inches. Find the other two sides. $\left(\dfrac{x}{15} = \dfrac{6}{8} \text{ and } \dfrac{y}{12} = \dfrac{6}{8} \right)$ *$11\frac{1}{4}$ in., 9 in.*

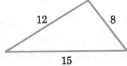

12   8

15

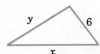

y   6

x

485

5. The sides of one triangle are 5, 12, and 13 inches. Find the shortest side of a similar triangle if its longest side is 91 inches. 35 in.

6. A building casts a shadow 110 feet long when a 6-foot post casts a shadow 3 feet long. How high is the building?

220 ft.

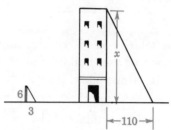

7. When a flagpole 80 feet high casts a shadow 55 feet long, what is the length of the shadow cast by a telephone pole 25 feet high? 17.187⁺ ft.

[B]

8. Some boys wishing to find the height of a flagpole *EF* placed pins at *A* and *B* in a cardboard so that *A*, *B*, and *F* were in a straight line. From the pin at *B* they suspended a plumb

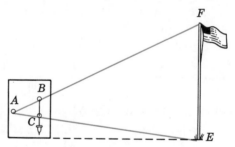

bob. Then they placed a pin in the cardboard at *C* where the plumb line crossed the line drawn from *A* to *E*. By measuring they found the following measurements: $AE = 66$ feet, $AC = 6$ inches, and $BC = 5\frac{1}{5}$ inches. What was the height of the pole? 57.2 ft.

Inversely Proportional Quantities [A]

Have you ever tried cutting a cake, or a pan of fudge, into equal pieces? If you have, you know that the more pieces you make, the smaller each piece must be. You know, for example, that if you were

486

to cut a cake having 216 square inches of top surface area into 18 equal pieces, each piece would have a top area of 216 ÷ 18, or 12

square inches, but if you were to cut the cake into 24 equal pieces, each piece would have a top area of 216 ÷ 24, or 9 square inches.

We can set down this information in a table, thus:

Square Inches of Top Surface per Piece	Number of Pieces
9	24
12	18

Study of the table shows that while the ratio of the size of the pieces ($\frac{9}{12}$) is not equal to the ratio of the number of pieces ($\frac{24}{18}$), the ratios are equal when one of them is inverted. If we invert $\frac{24}{18}$, we have the proportion $\frac{9}{12} = \frac{18}{24}$. The numbers 9 and 12 are inversely proportional to the numbers 24 and 18.

When four numbers are so related that the ratio of the first two (taken in order) is equal to the inverse (inverted form) of the ratio of the other two (taken in order), we say that the numbers are inversely proportional.

Inversely proportional quantities are all about us and affecting us every day of our lives. The greater the speed at which we travel, the shorter is the time which it takes us to make a specific trip; the higher we fly, the less dense (the thinner) the air around us; the greater the cost of one pencil, the smaller the number of pencils we can buy for a dollar; the more pressure we exert on the snowball we make, the smaller the ball becomes. If we hope to understand the world in which we live, we must learn to understand the mathematics of inversely proportional relationships. Study the following example carefully, then try the Exercises on pages 488–489.

Example. If 10 carpenters can build a house in 30 days, how long will it take 12 carpenters to do the same work, provided it can be done as efficiently by 12 as by 10?

Solution. If we let x represent the number of days needed by 12 carpenters, and set down the information in a table, we have

Number of Carpenters	Number of Days
10	30
12	x

Reasoning tells us that as the number of men doing a job increases, the time needed for completing the job decreases. It tells us that the number of carpenters is inversely proportional to the number of days. We must, therefore, invert one of the ratios. We write

$$\frac{10}{12} = \frac{x}{30}$$
$$12\,x = 300$$
$$x = 25$$

Twelve carpenters can do the work in 25 days.

PROOF. If 12 carpenters work 25 days they will produce 25×12, or 300, days of work.

If 10 carpenters work 30 days they will produce 30×10, or 300, days of work.

The work produced in either case is the same as the work produced in the other.

[A]

EXERCISES

1. If 2 men can paint a house in 8 days, how long will it take 3 men to do the work? $5\frac{1}{3}\,da.$

No. of men	No. of days
?	?
?	x

2. If 6 people share the expense of renting a cottage at the lake for a week, it costs each one $5.00. How much will it

cost each person if 4 people share the rent on the same cottage for a week? $7.50

3. If a bowl of punch will make 36 servings of 1 cup each, how many servings will it make if the cups are filled only $\frac{2}{3}$ full? 54

4. A factory employing 200 men can complete a certain number of television sets when the men work 40 hours per week. If the number of hours is cut to 35 per week, how many men will be required to do the same amount of work? 229

5. If a motorist, driving 40 miles an hour, can make a certain trip in 6 hours, how long will it take him if he averages only 30 miles an hour? 8 hr.

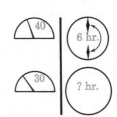

6. An army camp, expecting 300 men, has enough food to last them 14 days. If 350 men are sent to the camp, for how many days will the food last? 12 da.

7. At 40 miles per hour a man can drive from Centerville to Middletown in 4 hours. At what rate must he drive to make the trip in $3\frac{1}{2}$ hours? 45 $\frac{5}{7}$ m.p.h.

8. If 2 girls can complete a certain mimeographing job in 7 hours, in how many hours can the job be completed if 3 girls are put to work on it? It is assumed that 3 can work as efficiently as 2. 4 $\frac{2}{3}$ hr.

Variables and Constants [A] See ① below.

One formula for finding the area of a circle is $A = \pi r^2$. You know that this formula can be used for finding the area of any circle, whatever the value of r. For each value of r there is a value of A. When r changes, so does A. Although r and A change in value, the value of π is always the same. The numbers A and r are called <u>variables</u> and the number π is called a <u>constant</u>. The area A is said to be a <u>function</u> of the radius r, since it has one value for each value of r. Also, the expression πr^2, which equals A, is a function of r. In the formula $A = \pi r^2$, r is the <u>independent variable</u> and A is the <u>dependent variable</u>.

① If there is not enough time for adequate explanation of the material dealing with variation, it had better be omitted.

489

[A]

1. The formula for finding the perimeter of this triangle is $p = 3s$. Copy and complete the table below it:

If $s =$	1	2	3	4	5	6	7	8	9	10	30
Then $p =$	? 3	? 6	? 9	? 12	? 15	? 18	? 21	? 24	? 27	? 30	? 90

When s increases, how does p change? Why is s called the independent variable? *p increases; values of s are given and they determine p.*

2. When one constant is multiplied by another, is the product a constant or a variable? *Constant*

3. When a variable is multiplied by a constant, is the product a constant or a variable? *Variable*

4. Tell which is the dependent variable in each formula:

a. $F = \frac{9}{5} C + 32$ *F*   **c.** $s = 16 t^2$ *s*
b. $C = \frac{5}{9}(F - 32)$ *C*   **d.** $V = \frac{1}{6} \pi D^3$ *V*

5. The formula for finding the area of a rectangle is $A = bh$. In this formula b and h are independent variables.

a. What kind of variable is A? *Dependent*

b. What happens to A when h remains unchanged and b is doubled? *Doubled*

c. How does A change when both b and h are doubled?

d. How is A affected when h is halved and b is doubled? *multiplied by 4.*

e. How does A change when both b and h are trebled? *unchanged.*

multiplied by 9.

Example. $f(x) = x^2 - 3x$. Find $f(2)$.

Solution. The letter f stands for *function*; $f(x) = x^2 - 3x$ means that the function of x is $x^2 - 3x$. In $f(2)$ the (2) means that the value of x in the function is 2.

$$f(x) = x^2 - 3x$$
$$f(2) = 4 - 6$$
$$f(2) = -2$$

490

1. $f(x) = x^2 + 4x + 1$. Find $f(3)$; $f(-3)$. $22; -2$

2. $f(y) = 3y^2 - 4y + 1$. Find $f(4)$; $f(1)$; $f(0)$. $33; 0; 1$

3. $f(x) = x^3 - 1$. Find $f(2)$; $f(-2)$. $7; -9$

4. $f(t) = 100t - 16t^2$. Find $f(4)$; $f(6)$. $144; 24$

5. $f(x) = x^2 - 4x + 7$. Find $f(4)$. 7

Direct Variation [A]

The cost of n articles at 10 cents each is given by the formula $c = 10n$. The following table and graph are based on this formula.

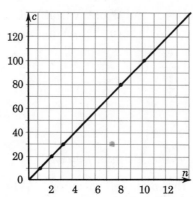

c	n
0	0
10	1
20	2
30	3
80	8
100	10

For each positive value of n there is a value of c. From the table you can see that any value of c (zero excepted) divided by its correspond-ing value of n gives 10, and that any value of n divided by its corre-sponding value of c gives $\frac{1}{10}$. For this reason any number of propor-tions can be formed from these sets of values. Two examples are $\frac{3}{30} = \frac{8}{80}$ and $\frac{20}{2} = \frac{30}{3}$.

If we divide both members of $c = 10n$ by n, we get $\frac{c}{n} = 10$. This again shows that the ratio of c to n is always equal to 10. From this discussion you should be able to understand this:

> If two variables change so that one divided by the other equals a con-stant, the numbers *vary directly*.

When two quantities vary directly, either *varies directly* as the other and is *directly proportional* to the other.

The subject of variation is particularly important in science. However, any stu-dent concentrating on science usually plans to take two more years of mathe-matics, and can study this topic in detail later. Point out the interesting variety of ways to express variation—verbally, as a formula, in table form, and graphically.

It should be noted that in this section we are speaking of the ratio of *c* to *n* or *n* to *c*, whereas in earlier sections of this chapter we were speaking of the ratio of one value of *c* to another value of *c* and the ratio of one value of *n* to another value of *n*.

EXERCISES

1. In the table at the right, state the ratio of *a* to *b* for each pair of values shown. Is the ratio constant for the whole table? *5: 1; yes*

Write the formula which shows the relation of *a* to *b*. *a = 5b*

[A]

b	a
1	5
2	10
3	15
4	20
5	25

In exercises 2 and 3 one variable is directly proportional to the other. What are the missing numbers?

2.

y	x
16	2
40?	5
32	? 4
56?	7
72	? 9

3.

p	n
25 ?	30
15	? 18
30	36
75 ?	90
40?	48

4. Change the formula $c = \pi d$ into a rule. What does $\frac{c}{d}$ equal? Is this a direct variation? What is the constant in $c = \pi d$? *(See bottom of page)*

5. In $c = 2\pi r$, which is the dependent variable? What does $\frac{c}{r}$ equal? How does *c* vary? *c; 2π; directly as r.*

6. $i = 0.04\,p$. What is the constant in this formula? What does $\frac{i}{p}$ equal? *0.04; 0.04*

Inverse Variation [A]

In direct variation the quotient of the two variables is constant and either variable increases when the other increases.

Now let us examine the table at the right. You will observe that the product of any set of values of *x* and *y* is 20. The equation which shows the relation of *x* and *y* is $xy = 20$. Here *x varies inversely as y* and *y varies inversely as x*. The graph for this equation, using only the positive values of *x* and *y*, follows.

y	x
20	1
10	2
5	4
4	5
2½	8
1	20

4. (1) The circumference of a circle is equal to the product of π and the diameter. (2) π (3) yes (4) π

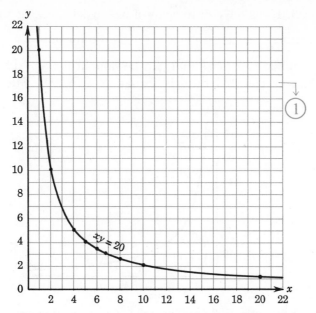

$xy = 20$

What do you know of the graph of an equation in which the variables vary directly? vary inversely? In the equation $xy = 20$, how does y change when x increases? Learn the following definition regarding inverse variation.

> If two variables change so that their product is constant, they vary inversely.

[A]

EXERCISES

1. Find the product pv for each pair of values in the following table. Is the value constant throughout the table? *yes*

Product is 80 for each pair.

v	p
16	5
20	4
1	80
$\frac{1}{2}$	160
$\frac{4}{3}$	60
120	$\frac{2}{3}$

Write the formula for the table above. $pv = 80$

2. $xy = 48$. Copy and complete the following table for x and y when their product is 48.

y	x
48	1
16	3
4	?12
8	6
12	?4
1	?48

How do x and y vary above? *Inversely*

① Tell students that this graph is one branch of a hyperbola. If you have models of conic sections for other classes, you might use them at this time to show a physical hyperbola. In fact, some students might like to do some research for a class report, especially since the hyperbola is mentioned in space travel. (See especially books and articles by Wernher von Braun and Willy Ley.)

3. If c is the cost in cents of one article and n is the number of these articles, then $n = \dfrac{300}{c}$ is the formula for finding the number of articles that can be bought for $3. This formula can be changed into the equation $nc = 300$. The graph for

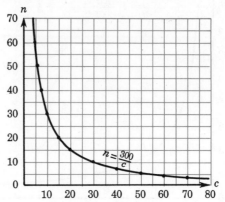

this formula is shown above. How does this graph compare with the graph of an equation expressing direct variation?

This is not a straight-line graph as is that in the case of direct variation.

Direct and Inverse Variation [A]

The three equivalent equations which show that x and y vary directly are $\dfrac{x}{y} = k$; $x = ky$; and $y = \dfrac{x}{k}$. In each of these equations k is a constant. The three equivalent equations which show that x and y vary inversely are $xy = k$; $x = \dfrac{k}{y}$; and $y = \dfrac{k}{x}$.

ORAL EXERCISES

D = directly, I = inversely [A]

Tell how the variables vary in the following equations:

1. $x = 3y$ *D*
2. $xy = 10$ *I*
3. $x = \dfrac{7}{y}$ *I*
4. $y = \dfrac{6}{x}$ *I*
5. $h = \tfrac{1}{3}k$ *D*

6. $c = 2\pi r$ *D*
7. $m = \dfrac{1}{3n}$ *I*
8. $z = 5y$ *D*
9. $\dfrac{m}{n} = 30$ *D*
10. $pv = 40$ *I*

11. $h = 100s$ *D*
12. $S = \tfrac{1}{2}p$ *D*
13. $c = \pi d$ *D*
14. $nm = 45$ *I*
15. $s = 16t$ *D*

[A]

1. Write the formula for the perimeter p of the polygon at the right. Then copy and complete the table. *$p = 5a$*

Do p and s vary directly or inversely? Is p a function of s? How does p change when s increases? What is the ratio of p to s? of s to p? *Directly; yes; increases; $p:a = 5:1; a:p = 1:5$*

p	s
5 *?*	1
10 ?	2
15 ?	3
20 ?	4
30 ?	6
50 ?	10

2. Copy and complete the following table, based upon the formula $p = s + 6$. Note that the table could be written vertically as in Exercise 1.

s	1	2	3	4	6	8	10	20
p	*? 7*	*? 8*	*? 9*	*? 10*	*? 12*	*? 14*	*? 16*	*? 26*

Do p and s vary directly? Do they vary inversely? *No; no.*

3. Here is a diagram of a bicycle pump filled with 20 cubic inches of air. The air pressure is 14.6 pounds per square inch. The pressure and the volume of the air inside the pump obey the law expressed by the formula $pv = 292$ when no air is allowed to escape. Using this formula, copy and complete the following table. Tell whether p and v vary directly or inversely.

v	1	2	4	8	10	16	50	100
p	*2? 92*	*1? 46*	*? 73*	*36.5*	*29.2*	*18?.25*	*5?.84*	*2?.92*

inversely

4. Draw the graph of $xy = 32$.

5. Draw the graph of $\dfrac{x}{y} = 32$.

6. Copy and complete this table, based upon the equation $y = 4x^2$. Does y vary directly as x? as x^2? Draw the graph

x	-6	-5	-4	-3	-2	-1	0	1	2	3	4	5	6
y	*1?44*	*1?00*	*?64*	*?36*	*?16*	*?4*	*?0*	*?4*	*?16*	*?36*	*?64*	*100*	*1?44*

of the formula $y = 4x^2$. (It is not necessary to plot the points whose abscissas are -6, -5, -4, 4, 5, and 6.) *No.*

495

7. Let $a = 6$ in the formula $A = ab$. How does A vary? If b is doubled, how does A change? *Directly as b; doubled.*

8. In the formula $A = ab$, A varies jointly with a and b. If a is doubled and b is trebled, how is A changed? *Multiplied by 6*

9. $A = \pi r^2$. Does A vary directly or inversely as r? Does A vary directly as r^2? *Neither; Yes.*

10. *(1) Directly as v^2 (2) directly   (3) Multiplied by 4.*   [B] ①

10. $E = \dfrac{Wv^2}{32\,r}$, where W and v are variables. How does E change with respect to v? with respect to W? How does E change when W is unchanged and v is doubled?

11. The kinetic energy of a football player in motion can be expressed by the formula $E = \dfrac{Ws^2}{64}$. In this formula W is the weight in pounds of the player, s is his speed in feet per second, and E is the number of foot-pounds of energy.

Copy and complete the following table to show how hard each of four boys can hit the line of scrimmage:

PLAYERS	WEIGHT IN POUNDS	SPEED IN FEET PER SECOND	KINETIC ENERGY IN FT.-LB.
Earl White	160	20	? *1000*
Bryant Foster	192	? *16*	768
Chester Frank	? *144*	18	729
Tony Pinelli	128	24	? *1152*

Which of these boys seems to be the best prospect for a fullback? for a guard? *Probably Pinelli, White*

12. $i = prt$ is the simple-interest formula. Which numbers are variables? If p and r are constant, how does i vary? If i and t are constant, how does p vary? *All four; directly as t; Inversely as r.*

13. The formula $d = 0.07\,v^2$ gives the stopping distance of a car when the brakes are applied. How does d change when v is doubled? *Multiplied by 4*

14. The volume of a sphere can be found by the formula $V = \frac{4}{3}\pi r^3$. How does V vary with respect to r? How does V change when r is doubled? How does V change when r is trebled? *Directly as cube of r; multiplied by 8; multiplied by 27.*

496

① In exercises such as 9, ask "If r is doubled, how is A changed?" Do not be surprised when many say "doubled." The result of such changes can be effectively demonstrated by drawings on the graph chalkboard. Cubic blocks make a good visual aid for volume situations as in Ex. 14. Also ask such questions as "If a balloon is blown up to twice its original diameter, how much more air does it hold than originally?"

How to Express Variations by Proportions [C]

We have learned that if two variables change so that one divided by the other equals a constant, they vary directly. We have also learned that if two variables change so that their product is constant, they vary inversely.

If x and y are two variables which vary directly, $\frac{x}{y} = k$ and $x = ky$. Let x_1 and x_2 represent two different values of x, and let y_1 and y_2 represent the corresponding values of y. Then $x_1 = ky_1$ and $x_2 = ky_2$. If we divide the members of the first equation by the members of the second, we get $\frac{x_1}{x_2} = \frac{ky_1}{ky_2}$ which can be simplified as $\frac{x_1}{x_2} = \frac{y_1}{y_2}$.

This proportion is another way of expressing the fact that x varies directly as y. Can you remember how it is written? Notice that if the information is set down in a table, the table is the same as the tables you used in solving proportions.

x	y
x_1	y_1
x_2	y_2

If the variables x and y vary inversely, $xy = k$. If x_1 and x_2 are two different values of x, and y_1 and y_2 the corresponding values of y, then $x_1y_1 = k$ and $x_2y_2 = k$. Since quantities which are equal to the same quantity are equal to each other, $x_1y_1 = x_2y_2$. This is the same relationship as the one expressed by the proportion $\frac{x_1}{x_2} = \frac{y_2}{y_1}$.

This proportion is another way of expressing the fact that x varies inversely as y. Notice that if the values of x and y are set down in a table

x	y
x_1	y_1
x_2	y_2

the proportion can be obtained by setting the values of x in the left-hand column equal to the inverse (inverted form) of the ratio of the values in the right-hand column.

Pages 497–501 provide interesting advanced work for your very best students who have time to investigate it. Meanings and applications should be stressed.

[C]

1. How do a and b vary in the proportion $\frac{a_1}{a_2} = \frac{b_1}{b_2}$? in the proportion $\frac{a_1}{a_2} = \frac{b_2}{b_1}$? *Directly; inversely*

2. How do x and y vary in the proportion $\frac{x_1}{x_2} = \frac{y_2}{y_1}$? in the proportion $\frac{y_2}{y_1} = \frac{x_1}{x_2}$? *Inversely; inversely*

3. Express the variation $c = 2\pi r$ by a proportion. $\frac{c_1}{c_2} = \frac{r_1}{r_2}$

4. How does A vary in $\frac{A_1}{A_2} = \frac{r_1^2}{r_2^2}$? *Directly as square of r.*

5. How does A vary in the formula $A = s^2$? Express this variation by a proportion. *Directly as square of s;* $\frac{A_1}{A_2} = \frac{s_1^2}{s_2^2}$

6. Using the constant k, change the proportion $\frac{c_1}{c_2} = \frac{n_1}{n_2}$ to a variation. $c = kn$

Example 1. x varies directly as y, and x is 60 when y is 52. Find x when y is 78.

Solution 1. Since x varies directly as y, $x = ky$, k being a constant.
Then
$$60 = 52\,k$$
$$52\,k = 60$$
$$k = \tfrac{15}{13}$$
Then
$$x = \tfrac{15}{13}\,y$$
When $y = 78$
$$x = \tfrac{15}{13}(78) = 90$$

Solution 2.
$$\frac{x_1}{x_2} = \frac{y_1}{y_2}$$

$x_1 = 60$, $y_1 = 52$, and $y_2 = 78$. Let $x = x_2$.
Then
$$\frac{60}{x} = \frac{52}{78}$$
$$52\,x = 60 \times 78$$
$$x = 90$$

Solution 3.

x	y
60	52
x	78

Since this is a proportion,
$$\frac{60}{x} = \frac{52}{78}$$
$$52\,x = 60 \times 78$$
$$x = 90$$

498

Some Everyday Instances of Variation

Direct Variations.

1. The total cost or selling price of like objects varies directly as the number of objects.

2. The amount of work done varies directly as the number of men (or machines) and as the time.

$$\left(\frac{W_1}{W_2} = \frac{n_1 t_1}{n_2 t_2}\right)$$

Inverse Variations.

1. The time required to go a given distance varies inversely as the speed.

2. The time required to do a given amount of work varies inversely as the number of persons doing the work.

3. If two pulleys are connected by a belt, their diameters vary inversely as the number of their revolutions.

4. The number of persons required to do a piece of work varies directly as the amount of work and inversely as the time for doing it.

$$\left(\frac{n_1}{n_2} = \frac{W_1 t_2}{W_2 t_1}\right)$$

[C]

WRITTEN EXERCISES

1. x varies directly as y and $x = 20$ when $y = 15$. Find x when $y = 27.$ *36*

2. x varies directly as y. If $x = 51$ when $y = 3$, find x when $y = 5.$ *85*

3. m varies inversely as n. If $m = 54$ when $n = 60$, find m when $n = 72$. $\left(\dfrac{m_1}{m_2} = \dfrac{n_2}{n_1}\right)$ *45*

4. p and v vary inversely. If $p = 55$ when $v = 28$, find v when $p = 22$. *70*

5. x varies directly as y. If $x = 30$ when $y = 18$, find x when $y = 27$. *45*

6. s varies directly as the square of r. If $s = 5026.56$ when $r = 20$, find s when $r = 25.$ *7854*

7. A varies directly as the square of t. If $A = 2304$ when $t = 12$, find A when $t = 10$. *1600*

499

8. x varies inversely as y. If $x = 24$ when $y = 8$, find x when $y = 6$. *32*

9. x varies inversely as y. If $x = 66$ when $y = 2$, find x when $y = 12$. *11*

10. m varies inversely as y. If $m = 6.5$ when $y = 5$, find m when $y = 17.5$. *1$\frac{6}{7}$*

11. Two numbers vary inversely. If the first is 10 when the second is 45, find the second when the first is 15. *30*

12. A certain amount of air occupies 1500 cubic feet when its pressure is 30 pounds. How many cubic feet will it occupy when its pressure is increased to 70 pounds? *642$\frac{6}{7}$*

13. If 60 men can do a piece of work in 42 days, how long will it take 45 men to do the same work? *56 da.*

14. If 20,000 copies of a book sell for $18,800, what is the selling price of 15,500 of them? *$14,570*

15. If 10 six-inch pipes can fill a pool in 24 hours, how long will it take 8 of these pipes to fill the pool? *30 hr.*

Example 2. If 12 men require 4 days to lay 40 rods of water pipe, how many men are needed to lay 160 rods of the same kind of pipe in 6 days?

Solution.
$$\frac{n_1}{n_2} = \frac{W_1 t_2}{W_2 t_1}$$

Then
$$\frac{12}{n_2} = \frac{40 \times 6}{160 \times 4} = \frac{3}{8}$$
$$3\,n_2 = 96$$
$$n_2 = 32, \text{ the number of men}$$

[C]

EXERCISES

1. If 18 men in 10 hours can pick 1080 bushels of tomatoes, how long will it take 24 men to pick 1152 bushels of tomatoes? *8 hr.*

2. If a crew of 75 men can construct 4 miles of road in 18 days, how much road can 45 men complete in 32 days? *4$\frac{4}{15}$ mi.*

3. The area of a triangle is expressed by the formula $A = \frac{1}{2}\,bh$. Express this fact by a proportion. *$\frac{A_1}{A_2} = \frac{b_1\,h_1}{b_2\,h_2}$*

4. A motor with a speed of 1700 r.p.m. and a belt wheel $2\frac{7}{8}''$ in diameter is used to drive an air compressor in an electric refrigerator. How large should the drive wheel of the compressor be so that its speed is 650 r.p.m.? *7$\frac{1}{2}$ in., approx.*

5. $I = \dfrac{E}{R}$ is a formula for finding I, the amount of current, when the number of volts, E, and the resistance, R, are known.

a. How does I vary with respect to E? to R? *Directly; inversely*

b. Solve this formula for E; for R. $E = IR;\ R = \dfrac{E}{I}$

c. If an electric heater uses 22 amperes of electricity when the voltage is 110 volts, how much current will it use when the voltage drops to 100 volts? (In this problem R is constant.) *20 amp.*

6. $d = .137\sqrt{h}$ is a formula for finding the distance, d, in miles one can see from a height h feet above the earth's surface.

a. How does d vary? **b.** How far can one see on the ocean from a point 100 feet above the surface? *Directly as square root of h; 1.37 mi.*

Musical Ratios [C]

When the string of a musical instrument is plucked or struck it vibrates back and forth causing waves in the air which eventually reach our ears and produce sound. The number of waves produced in one second is known as the frequency of vibration. In singing, our vocal chords are the strings which vibrate to produce sound.

When two or more tones of a piano, or two or more voices, blend in harmony, the tones have vibrations whose frequencies are proportional to any of the simple numbers 1, 2, 3, 4, 5, and 6. For

STOCK, BOSTON, Daniel S. Brody

example, Judith's tone of G with a frequency of 392 vibrations per second is in harmony with Skippy's tone of E having a frequency of 330 vibrations per second because the ratio of their frequencies is approximately 6:5.

The *major scale* consists of eight tones whose frequencies are proportional to the numbers 24, 27, 30, 32, 36, 40, 45, and 48. The names of these tones are in order *do, re, mi, fa, sol, la, ti,* and *do.* The first note is called the keynote. These eight tones are selected to form the scale because they have a large number of harmonious combinations. For example, *mi* and *do* sound well together because the ratio of their frequencies is $\frac{30}{24}$ or $\frac{5}{4}$, the numbers 5 and 4 being numbers of the series 1, 2, 3, 4, 5, 6 previously mentioned. The major scale may start with any frequency. For example, the keynote *do* may start with C, which has a frequency of 264, or with A, which has a frequency of 440. The *interval* between two tones is the ratio of their frequencies.

The *tempered scale* is a modified major scale. The octave in this scale is divided into twelve equal intervals, called half-steps. These half-steps separate twelve tones which are produced on the piano by seven white and five black keys. The tempered scale makes it possible to play the piano in any key.

The following table gives the frequencies of the two scales in the key of C, the A tone in each scale having a frequency of 440.

NOTES	C	D	E	F	G	A	B	C'
TONES	do	re	mi	fa	sol	la	ti	do
MAJOR SCALE	264	297	330	352	396	440	495	528
TEMPERED SCALE	261.6	293.7	329.6	349.2	392	440	493.8	523.2

[C]

EXERCISES

1. Find the interval between C and D in the major scale; in the tempered scale. $\frac{8}{9}$; $\frac{872}{979}$

2. Find the interval of the octave in each scale, that is, the interval between C' and C. $2 : 1$

3. The *perfect fifth* is the interval between two tones whose frequencies have the ratio 3:2. Name a perfect fifth. G to C,

4. The *major third* interval has the ratio 5:4. Name a major third. A to F, E to C, B to G

5. When the picture on page 501 was taken Judith's note was G and Skippy's note was E in the first measure of the following music. What was the interval between their tones? 6:5

6. What are the intervals between their tones in the next measure? 6:5, 5:4, 5:4, 6:5

502

PROPORTION AND VARIATION

Before you leave Chapter 18 make sure that you

PAGE

1. Can recognize a proportion when you see one 481
2. Can use the principle of proportion to solve problems 482
3. Know the meaning of *inversely proportional* and can use the principle to solve problems 486
4. Can recognize direct variation and inverse variation when the variations are expressed in tables and simple equations 494
5. Can spell and use correctly the following words and phrases:

	PAGE		PAGE
constant	489	inversely proportional	486
dependent variable	489	means	481
direct variation	491	proportion	481
extremes	481	ratio	481
function	489	similar polygons	484
independent variable	489	variable	489
inverse variation	492		

If you aim for better than average mathematical understanding, you will also want to be able to

PAGE

1. Express variations by proportions 497
2. Solve problems involving variation 497

[A]

CHAPTER REVIEW.

1. Solve for y the proportion $y : 6 = 7 : 3$. *14*

2. Name the means and extremes of $x : y = 7 : 8$. *means, y and 7; extremes, x and 8.*

3. Complete: In a proportion the product . . . *of the means is equal to the product of the extremes.*

4. How high is a telegraph pole which casts a shadow of 36 feet when a flagpole 120 feet high casts a shadow of 92 feet? *$46\frac{22}{23}$ ft.*

5. What is the ratio of 6 to 8? of $7x$ to $21x^2$? *$\frac{3}{4}$; $\frac{1}{3x}$*

6. Solve for m: $\dfrac{2m-3}{6} = \dfrac{7}{m+1}$ *5, $-4\frac{1}{2}$*

7. Form a proportion from $hk = mn$. *$\frac{h}{m} = \frac{n}{k}$, $\frac{h}{n} = \frac{m}{k}$, $\frac{m}{h} = \frac{k}{n}$, $\frac{n}{h} = \frac{k}{m}$.*

503

8. The sides of one triangle are 7 inches, 10 inches, and 13 inches. If the longest side of a similar triangle is 19.5 inches, find the length of the shortest side of it. *10.5 in.*

9. Suppose y varies directly as x.

a. Write this relation using c as the constant. $y = cx,$ or $\frac{y}{x} = c$

b. Express this relation by a proportion. $\frac{y_1}{y_2} = \frac{x_1}{x_2}$

10. Suppose m varies inversely as n. Write this relation using k as the constant. $mn = k,$ or $m = \frac{k}{n}$

11. If y varies directly as x and $y = 14$ when $x = 3.5$, find the constant. *4*

12. Copy and complete: $x^2 - 4x + 5$ is a __?__ of x. *function*

13. $y = 2x^2 - x + 3$. Find y when $x = -3$. *24*

14. How does x vary with respect to y in the following equations? *D = directly, I = inversely*

a. $7x = 8y$ *D*

c. $y = \dfrac{4}{x}$ *I*

e. $\dfrac{2}{x} = \dfrac{y}{10}$ *I*

b. $3xy = 7$ *I*

d. $y = 3x$ *D*

f. $cx = dy$ *D*

15. Copy and complete: In direct variation the __?__ increase together and __?__ together *variables, decrease*

[A]

GENERAL REVIEW

1. Take $\frac{1}{2}x - \frac{1}{3}y + \frac{1}{4}$ from $\frac{1}{3}x - \frac{2}{3}y - \frac{1}{5}$.

2. Multiply $4a^3 - 3a^2b - 9ab^2 + 6b^3$ by $-4a^2b$.

3. Divide $21a^4 - 27a^3 - 12a^2 + 3a$ by $-3a$.

4. Simplify $4(x - a) - (5x + 3a) + (x - a)$.

5. Multiply $a^2 - 5ab - 2b^2$ by $2a - b$.

6. Divide $x^3 - 3x^2y + 3xy^2 + y^3$ by $x - y$.

7. Reduce $\dfrac{x^2 + 5x}{2x^2 - 50}$ to lowest terms. $\dfrac{x}{2(x-5)}$

8. Multiply $\dfrac{a^2 + ab - 2b^2}{3a^2 - 3ab}$ by $\dfrac{a^2 - ab}{a^2 + 4ab + 4b^2}$. $\dfrac{a-b}{3(a+2b)}$

9. Combine: $\dfrac{1}{x} + \dfrac{1}{y} - \dfrac{1}{z}$ $\dfrac{yz + xz - xy}{xyz}$

10. Solve: $3x - 4y = 7$ $x = 2\frac{3}{5}, y = \frac{1}{5}$
$x + 2y = 3$

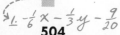

1. $-\frac{1}{6}x - \frac{1}{3}y - \frac{9}{20}$

504

2. $-16a^5b + 12a^4b^2 + 36a^3b^3 - 24a^2b^4$
3. $-7a^3 + 9a^2 + 4a - 1$

4. $-8a$
5. $2a^3 - 11a^2b + ab^2 + 2b^3$
6. $x^2 - 2xy + y^2$, Rem. $2y^3$

7 *12.* $\dfrac{3 \pm \sqrt{73}}{8}$; *or 1.443, -0.693*

Solve:

11. $x + .01\,x = 1.515$ *1.5*   **14.** $x^2 - 2\,x = 3$ *3, 1*

12. $4\,x^2 - 3\,x - 4 = 0$ **15.** $3\,x(x+2) - 5(x+2) = 14$ $\frac{8}{3}$, -3

13. $\dfrac{2\,x}{3} + \dfrac{6}{x} = 5$ *1½, 6*   **16.** $\dfrac{2\,x - 7}{x - 6} = \dfrac{6\,x + 1}{3\,x + 7}$ *1 15/28*

17. Tell which of the following statements concerning this triangle are true and which are false: $T = true$, $F = false$

a. $a^2 + b^2 = c^2$ T

b. $a + b = c$ F

c. $c^2 - a^2 = b^2$ T

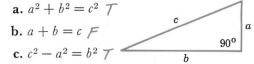

d. $c = \sqrt{a^2 + b^2}$ T

e. $c - b = a$ F

f. $a^2 = \sqrt{c^2 - b^2}$ F

18. Factor:

a. $a^2 - 1$ *(a+1)(a-1)*   **c.** $bx - b$ *b(x-1)*   **e.** $5\,x^2 - 30\,x + 45$ *5(x-3)²*

b. $x^2 - 5\,x + 6$ **d.** $2\,x^2 + x - 15$ **f.** $3\,x^2 + 8\,x - 3$

(x-2)(x-3)   *(2x-5)(x+3)*   *(3x-1)(x+3)*

19. Simplify $\sqrt{8}$; $\sqrt{50}$; $\sqrt{\frac{1}{2}}$. *2√2 ; 5√2 ; ½√2*

20. Solve $6 : 10 = 16 : x$ for x. *26 ⅔*

21. Find $12\frac{1}{2}\%$ of 224. *28*

22. Find what per cent 12 is of 72. *16⅔ %*

23. An electric refrigerator sold for $159 after a 40% discount was allowed. What was the original price? *$265*

24. Find the hypotenuse of a right triangle if its legs are 18 feet and 20 feet long. *26.90 ft.*

25. Find the side of a square whose diagonal is 30 feet. *21.21 ft.*

[B]

Solve:

26. $(3\,x + 5)^2 - 30\,x = 43$ **27.** $\dfrac{x}{x + 3} - \dfrac{x}{x - 3} = \dfrac{x^2 + 8}{x^2 - 9}$ *-2, -4*

±√2, or ±1.414

28. Which of the four values of x, $x = 1, 2, 3,$ or 4, will give the fraction $\dfrac{3}{x + 1}$ the greatest value? *x = 1*

29. How much smaller than $-3\,x$ is $9\,x$ when $x = -2$? *24*

30. For what value of x does $\dfrac{3\,x}{4} = x + 6$? *-24*

Solve for x:

31. $bx - a = cx + d$ $\dfrac{a+d}{b-c}$

32. $\dfrac{x}{3} - \dfrac{a}{2} = \dfrac{b}{5}$ $\dfrac{15a+6b}{10}$

33. $a(x - a) = b(x + a - 3b)$ $\dfrac{a^2+ab-3b^2}{a-b}$

34. $\dfrac{x}{x - n} = \dfrac{x + m}{x}$ $\dfrac{mn}{m-n}$

35. Two quarts of gasoline are mixed with five quarts of kerosene. How many quarts of kerosene must be added to the mixture to make it five-sixths kerosene? 5

[C]

Solve:

36. $\dfrac{10}{x} = \dfrac{x}{10 - x}$ $-5 \pm 5\sqrt{5}$; or $6.18, -16.18$

37. $x^2 = 9(9 - x)$ $\dfrac{-9 \pm 9\sqrt{5}}{2}$; or $5.562, -14.562$

38. Combine: $\dfrac{a - b}{a + b} + \dfrac{2a + b}{b - a} - \dfrac{a^2 - 3b^2}{a^2 - b^2}$ $\dfrac{-2a^2-5ab+3b^2}{(a+b)(a-b)}$

39. Factor:

a. $\frac{1}{2} x^2 - \frac{1}{2} y^2$ $\frac{1}{2}(x+y)(x-y)$

b. $6 p^2 - 5 p - 1$ $(6p+1)(p-1)$

c. $5 ay^2 - 25 ay + 30 a$ $5a(y-3)(y-2)$

d. $x^4 - 256$ $(x^2+16)(x+4)(x-4)$

40. A man invested part of $15,000 at 7% and the remainder at 5%. If the income from the 7% investment was $750 more than the income from the 5% investment, how much was invested at each rate? $7\%, \$12,500; 5\%, \$2500$

41. A train makes a run of 120 miles in a given time. If it were to make the run 3 miles an hour faster, its time for the run would be 10 minutes less. Find its usual rate. $45\,m.p.h.$

42. Show that the altitude of an equilateral triangle with each side equal to $2\sqrt{2}$ is $\sqrt{6}$.

43. Solve $x^2 + 3 x - 40 = 0$ by graphing. $x = -8, 5$

44. Which is larger, and by how much, $5\sqrt{2}$ or $2\sqrt{5}$? $5\sqrt{2}$ is larger by 2.598

45. Simplify:

a. $\sqrt[3]{\dfrac{m^2}{m^3}}$ $\frac{1}{m}\sqrt[3]{m^2}$

b. $2 x\sqrt{x^5}$ $2x^3\sqrt{x}$

c. $3\sqrt{\dfrac{1}{3}}$ $\sqrt{3}$

d. $\sqrt{3}\sqrt{6}$ $3\sqrt{2}$

e. $x\sqrt{\dfrac{1}{xy}}$ $\frac{1}{y}\sqrt{xy}$

f. $\sqrt{xy}\sqrt{x}$ $x\sqrt{y}$

Solve for x in each proportion:

1. $\dfrac{x}{5} = \dfrac{3}{10}$ *1.5*

2. $\dfrac{2}{x} = \dfrac{x}{8}$ *±4*

3. $\dfrac{a}{b} = \dfrac{c}{x}$ *$\dfrac{bc}{a}$*

4. The sides of a triangle are 6, 8, and 12 inches respectively. The longest side of a similar triangle is 21 inches. Find the lengths of the other two sides. *$10\frac{1}{2}$ in., 14 in.*

5. In the formula $P = 4\,s$, when s increases how does P change? *increases*

6. In the formula $A = \pi r^2$, is π a variable or a constant?

7. In the formula $c = 2\,\pi r$, do c and r vary directly or *constant* inversely? *Directly*

8. Tell how the two variables vary in each of the following equations: *D = directly, I = inversely*

a. $xy = 4$ *I*   **b.** $p = \dfrac{40}{v}$ *I*   **c.** $S = \dfrac{b}{2}$ *D*   **d.** $s = 16\,t$ *D*

9. In the formula $A = bh$, if both b and h are doubled, how is A changed? *Multiplied by 4.*

10. In the equation $y = \dfrac{2}{x}$, if the value of x is multiplied by 4, how is y changed? *Divided by 4.*

Solve for x in each proportion:

1. $\dfrac{a}{x} = \dfrac{x}{b}$ *$\pm\sqrt{ab}$*

2. $\dfrac{x-4}{3} = \dfrac{x-2}{5}$ *7*

3. The length and width of one rectangle are 36 and 10 respectively. The length and width of a second rectangle are 54 and 15 respectively. Are the two rectangles similar? *yes*

4. The sides of one triangle are 5, 6, and 7 inches respectively. The shortest side of a similar triangle is 12. Find the two remaining sides. *$14\frac{2}{5}$ in., $16\frac{4}{5}$ in.*

5. The hypotenuse of a right triangle is 16 feet and its base is 10 feet. Find the hypotenuse of a similar right triangle if its base is 25 feet. *40 ft.*

6. Which is the dependent variable in the formula $F = \frac{9}{5}C + 32$? *F*

7. If $f(x) = x^2 - 2\,x + 3$, find $f(3)$. *6*

8. In the equation $mn = 15$, how do m and n vary? *Inversely*

507

ALGEBRA, BOOK ONE

9. In the formula $s = 16\,t^2$, how does s vary with reference to t? *Directly as square of t.*

10. In the formula $E = \dfrac{Wv^2}{32\,r}$, how does E vary with respect to W? with respect to r? *Directly; inversely*

CUMULATIVE
TEST
(Chapters
10–18)

Time 35 Minutes

On your paper write the word or number for each blank to make the following statements true:

1. A set of linear equations is __?__ when the graphs of the equations cross each other. *Consistent and independent*

2. A set of linear equations is __?__ when the graphs of the equations are parallel. *Inconsistent*

3. If the edge e in the formula $V = e^3$ is multiplied by 5, the volume is multiplied by __?__. *125*

4. A right angle contains __?__ degrees. *90*

5. If A in the formula $A = 4\,\pi r^2$ is divided by 9, then r is __?__ by __?__. *divided, $\sqrt{9}$ (or 3)*

6. Solve for x and y: $\quad x + 5\,y = 19 \quad X=4,$
$\qquad\qquad\qquad 6\,x - 7\,y = 3 \quad y=3$

7. Factor:
a. $6\,m - 6\,x$ *6(m−x)* **b.** $a^3 - a$ *a(a+1)(a−1)* **c.** $4\,a^2 - 64$ *4(a+4)(a−4)*

8. Solve for x: $\quad ax - bx = 2\,bx - a \quad \dfrac{-a}{a-3b}$

9. Solve by factoring: $y^2 - 56 + y = 0$ *7,−8*

10. Find and express in its simplest form the ratio of 28 to 63. $\dfrac{4}{9}$

11. Solve by completing the square: $3\,x^2 + 5\,x + 2 = 0$ $-\dfrac{2}{3},-1$

12. Combine: $1 + \dfrac{c}{d}$ $\dfrac{d+c}{d}$

13. If 20 gallons of paint will cover 6600 square feet, how many gallons of paint will be needed to cover 2310 square feet? Solve by variation or proportion. *7*

14. Simplify: **a.** $\sqrt{27}$ *3√3* **b.** $\sqrt{\tfrac{2}{5}}$ $\tfrac{1}{5}\sqrt{10}$

15. Divide $\dfrac{10\,n - 5}{3\,n^2}$ by $\dfrac{2\,n - 1}{15\,n}$. $\dfrac{25}{n}$

508

16. How long will it take $9500 to earn $3135 when it is invested at 6% simple interest? *$5\frac{1}{2}$ yr.*

17. Expand: $(x - 6y)^3$ *$x^3 - 18x^2y + 108xy^2 - 216y^3$*

18. A man has 25 coins in quarters and dimes. The value of the coins is $4.00. Find the number of coins of each kind he has. Solve, using two letters. *10 quarters, 15 dimes*

19. The length of a rectangular flower bed is 50% greater than the width. Find the dimensions of the bed if its perimeter is 130 feet. *26 ft. × 39 ft.*

20. The distance d in feet that a ball will roll down an inclined plane in t seconds is given by the formula $d = kt^2$, k being a constant. By trial it was found that the ball rolled 27.9 feet in 3 seconds. How far will the ball go in 5 seconds? *77.5 ft.*

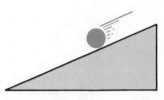

509

H. Armstrong Roberts

There are many kinds of engineering. Among these are electrical engineering, mechanical engineering, civil engineering, hydraulic engineering, mining engineering, powerhouse engineering, and steam engineering.

Civil engineering is the science that relates to the building of highways and railroads, the construction of tunnels and canals, and the surveying of lands.

In civil engineering, distances are measured by the steel tape, and angles are measured by the transit. Indirect measurements are made by the use of trigonometry.

Sometimes civil engineers specialize in city or county engineering. A city or county engineer measures lands, locates boundary lines, makes plans for sewers and levees, looks after the grades of streets, curbs, and sidewalks, and supervises the construction of public buildings. Today there is much interest in community planning. Whole communities —streets, homes, shopping centers, and so on—are planned for beauty, convenience, and safety. Such planning increases the demand for civil engineers.

Most civil engineers are graduates of engineering schools. Pupils who look forward to entering an engineering school should be proficient in mathematics in high school. They should take all the mathematics offered in high school—at least two years of algebra, plane and solid geometry, and trigonometry. They must be interested in new and better ways of doing things. They must have imagination.

At present there is a big demand for engineers of all kinds, and strangely enough, the greatest shortages exist in the top positions. If you are hoping to become a civil engineer, why not try to do the kind of school work which will fit you for one of these? It means that you will have to do your very best, but it pays.

19

Numerical Trigonometry

Suggested Time Schedule
Maximum, 9 days
(Not in minimum course)

*In this chapter
you will be introduced to a new subject
and learn how it is used
to find distances to inaccessible points.*

This chapter could be studied at any time during the second semester. The modern trend is to include numerical trigonometry in the algebra and geometry courses, thus saving time for other topics during the senior year.

You may have already taught the topic of approximate measurement on pages 513–518. It should be studied at some time during the year even if you do not have time for the trigonometry. The meaning of approximate measurement, and computation with such numbers, should be part of each student's mathematical knowledge. It may be that your students have been well grounded in this subject in previous arithmetic courses, but to many it is a new idea.

The Two Kinds of Measurement [A]

There are two kinds of measurement, direct and indirect. A <u>direct measurement</u> is made by applying a ruler, yardstick, tape measure, protractor, or other measuring instrument to the object to be measured and noting how many times the dimension, or the angle, contains the unit of measure. An <u>indirect measurement</u> is made when it is *computed* from measurements already known. These two methods of measurement will be illustrated by two examples.

Suppose a man wishes to find the diagonal AC of room $ABCD$.

He can measure AC directly by stretching a tape from A to C and reading the measurement on the tape. If he has no tape, he can use a yardstick or a foot rule and apply it end to end along line AC. The man may measure AC indirectly in many ways. For

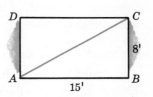

example, he can measure AB and BC directly and compute AC by the Pythagorean Theorem. Thus $AC = \sqrt{\overline{AB}^2 + \overline{BC}^2} = \sqrt{15^2 + 8^2} = 17$, the number of feet.

Suppose a farmer wishes to know how many bushels of wheat there are in a granary. He can measure the wheat directly by placing it in bushel baskets or by weighing it. He can measure the wheat indirectly by finding the length, width, and height of the granary by direct measurements and dividing the number of cubic inches in its volume by 2150.4, the number of cubic inches in a bushel.

Measurements Are Approximate [A]

<u>Any measurement is only approximate.</u> For example, if a boy is measuring the length of a room, he may use a yardstick on which the scale is not accurate, he may make an error in reading the numbers on the yardstick, he may not lay the stick exactly along the line of measurement, or he may make errors in placing the stick end to end.

If a boy using a yardstick measures the width of a desk, he may say the width is 24 inches because the width is nearer 24 inches than 23 inches or 25 inches. The boy then is measuring the width to the *nearest inch*. In this measurement the figure 2 is exact and the figure 4 is approximate. If another boy using a ruler marked off in tenths of an inch measures the width, he may say that the width is 24.7 inches because the width is nearer 24.7 inches than 24.6 inches or 24.8 inches.

This boy is measuring the width to the *nearest tenth* of an inch. The figures 2 and 4 are exact and the figure 7 is approximate. A skilled mechanic using a more delicate instrument may record the width as 24.73 inches. He would be measuring to the *nearest hundredth* of an inch.

The size of the unit chosen for a measurement determines the precision of the measurement. For example, a measurement to a thousandth of an inch is said to be more precise than one made to a tenth of an inch. Some measurements need to be more precise than others. In rough timber work the carpenter needs only to measure to the nearest fourth of an inch, while the machinist frequently makes measurements to the nearest thousandth of an inch.

How Numbers Are Rounded Off [A]   See ① below.

No doubt you have heard a statement such as the following: "In round numbers Columbus, Ohio, is 300 miles from Chicago." The distance between Columbus and Chicago is approximately 314 miles. There may be some mistake in this measurement. Suppose we are not sure that the figures 1 and 4 in 314 are correct. Then we would say, "In round numbers the distance is 300 miles." In this case the number 314 has been rounded off to the nearest hundred. If we are sure of the 3 and 1 but not of the 4 in 314, we round off the number to the nearest ten and obtain 310.

When a measurement such as 7.23 is expressed correct to the nearest tenth as 7.2, the number 7.23 is said to be rounded off to the nearest tenth. When rounded off to the nearest tenth, the numbers 7.20, 7.21, 7.22, 7.23, and 7.24 become 7.2. When 7.26, 7.27, 7.28, and 7.29 are rounded off to the nearest tenth, they become 7.3. Since 7.25 is just as near 7.2 as 7.3, either 7.2 or 7.3 may be called the rounded off number. It is common practice in such a case to make the last retained figure *even*. According to this practice 7.25 rounded off to the nearest tenth becomes 7.2 and 7.15 rounded off to the nearest tenth becomes 7.2.

The number 134.589 rounded off to the nearest hundredth is 134.59; to the nearest tenth is 134.6; to the nearest unit is 135; to the nearest ten is 130; and to the nearest hundred is 100.

[A]

EXERCISES   Round off the following numbers to the nearest tenth:

7.3 **1.** 7.32   17.3 **3.** 17.31   2.3 **5.** 2.31   4.4 **7.** 4.35

4.3 **2.** 4.26   18.8 **4.** 18.78   4.4 **6.** 4.45   .8 **8.** .8453

① Students are probably familiar with this topic. Note the method of rounding when the dropped digit is 5. This is in accordance with the most common practice. The other method is to round *up* when 5 is a final digit.

Round off the following numbers to the nearest hundredth:

9. 9.215 *9.22*   **11.** 7.545 *7.54*   **13.** 2.630 *2.63*

10. 6.346 *6.35*   **12.** 10.575 *10.58*   **14.** 3.1652 *3.17*

Significant Figures [A]

Instead of saying that 4.3 is the result of rounding off 4.32 to the nearest tenth, we sometimes say that 4.3 is the result of rounding off 4.32 to two *significant figures*. Likewise, we can say that 1.73, 2.03, and .254 each contain three significant figures.

When a measurement is made, it should be recorded so as to show the accuracy of the measurement. Thus a length recorded as 52 feet means that the measurement has been made to the nearest foot; a length recorded as 52.3 feet means that the measurement has been made to the nearest tenth of a foot; and a length recorded as 52.36 feet means that the measurement has been made to the nearest hundredth of a foot. In each of these measurements all the figures except the last are exact and the error in the last figure is not greater than one half unit; that is, 52.3 feet means that the measurement is between 52.25 and 52.35 feet. The figures in each of these measurements are *significant* for they all have a real meaning, each one except the last being exactly correct, and the last having an error not greater than one half unit.

In general, all the figures of a number are significant. The only exception is in the case where zero is used merely as a place holder following a decimal point. The zeros in the numbers 20.5, 106.7, and 409.05 are significant, while the zeros in the numbers .025 and .0036 are not significant. The zero in the measurement 4.0 feet is significant, since it shows that the measurement has been made to the nearest tenth. Likewise, if the two zeros in the number 23.00 inches are used to show that the measurement is made to the nearest hundredth of an inch, they are significant.

The position of the decimal point in a number has no bearing on the number of significant figures in it. Thus each of the numbers 2.35, .0678, and 344 has three significant figures.

In a number such as 5200 we cannot be sure of the number of significant figures from the number itself. More information is necessary. If 5200 miles is measured to the nearest mile, it has 4 significant figures. If it is measured to the nearest 10 miles it has 3 significant

ALGEBRA, BOOK ONE

figures, and if it is measured to the nearest 100 miles it has two significant figures.

[A]

ORAL EXERCISES

Round off the following numbers to three significant figures:

1. 7843 *7840*   **3.** .0946 *0946*   **5.** 192.5 */92*   **7.** 86260 *86300*

2. 2.6185 *2.62*   **4.** 278.0 *278*   **6.** 18.35 */8.4*   **8.** 12143 *12100*

State the degree of precision to which the following recorded measurements have been made: *to the nearest*

.1 ft. **9.** 7.3 ft.   *.001 in.* **11.** 18.803 in.   *1 yd.* **13.** 6 yd.

.01 in. **10.** 1.29 in.   *.01 in.* **12.** 12.00 in.   *.1 ft.* **14.** 70.0 ft.

Computations with Approximate Numbers[A]

When we compute with exact numbers, we can point to a specific number and say, "This is the sum," or "difference," or "product," or "quotient." When we compute with approximate numbers, we can only say, "The sum (or difference, or product, or quotient) is approximately this number." If, for example, we attempt to find the perimeter of a triangle whose sides have been measured and found to be 2.9 feet, 3.7 feet, and 5.3 feet, we add 2.9, 3.7, and 5.3, obtaining 11.9. We cannot, however, say that the perimeter is exactly 11.9 feet. We can only say that the perimeter is approximately 11.9 feet.

The reason is apparent when we consider what we mean when we give the result of a measurement. When we say that one side of the triangle has been measured and found to be 2.9 feet long, we do not mean that the length is exactly 2.9 feet; we only mean that the length is closer to 2.9 than to either 2.8 or 3.0. In other words, we mean that the true length is between 2.85 and 2.95 (2.85 and 2.95 included). When we say that measurement shows a second side to be 3.7 feet, we mean that its true length ranges from 3.65 to 3.75. When we say that measurement shows the third side to be 5.3 feet, we mean that the true length ranges from 5.25 to 5.35. From the additions below we see that the true perimeter is not less than 11.75 and not more than 12.05.

2.85	2.9	2.95
3.65	3.7	3.75
5.25	5.3	5.35
11.75	11.9	12.05

516 Emphasize that sums and differences of approximate numbers depend on the precision, while products and quotients depend upon the number of significant figures. The explanations in this section are designed to convince students of the desirability of not retaining an unreasonable number of figures in an answer. You will still find some students who think that the more places in an answer, the better.

The sum or difference of two approximate numbers can be no more precise than the less precise of the two. Therefore, in making measurements which are to be added or subtracted, we ordinarily use the same unit of measure throughout our work. If, for example, we wish to find the perimeter of a triangle by measuring the lengths of the three sides, it would be foolish to measure two sides to the nearest thousandth of a foot if the third side had been measured only to the nearest tenth of a foot—the sum will not be more precise than the nearest tenth of a foot. If it is desired to have the sum or difference correct to the nearest thousandth of a foot, all the measurements should be made to the nearest thousandth of a foot. This is a good working rule.

In situations where we must add or subtract approximate numbers having different degrees of precision, we round off all the numbers to the precision of the least precise before we perform the computation. If, for example, we wish to add three lengths which have been measured and found to be 8.16 feet, 10.3 feet, and 11.437 feet, we round off the numbers to 8.2, 10.3, and 11.4. Since 8.2 + 10.3 + 11.4 = 29.9, we say that the sum is approximately 29.9 feet.

To add or subtract approximate numbers,
  round off the numbers
  so that they have the same degree of precision
  as the least precise.
The result will have the same degree of precision as the numbers.

Let us now consider a problem involving multiplication of approximate numbers. Suppose that we wish to find the area of a rectangle whose length is 7.3 inches and whose width is 4.6 inches. If 7.3 and 4.6 are the exact dimensions of the rectangle, its area is exactly 33.58 square inches.

7.25	7.3	7.35
4.55	4.6	4.65
3625	4 38	3675
3 625	29 2	4 410
29 00	33.58	29 40
32.9875		34.1775

If 7.3 and 4.6 are found by measurement, 7.3 is some number between 7.25 and 7.35, and 4.6 is some number from 4.55 to 4.65. Then the true area is more than 32.9875 and less than 34.1775. It is the practice of computers to round off the product 33.58 and say that the area is 34 square inches. This example illustrates the following rule for multiplying approximate numbers:

> The product of two approximate numbers should not contain more significant figures than either the multiplier or the multiplicand.

Example. Multiply 7.312 by 4.3.

Solution. $7.312 \times 4.3 = 31.4416$

The number 7.312 has *four* significant figures and 4.3 has *two* significant figures. Then the product should have only two significant figures. Therefore $7.312 \times 4.3 = 31$.

The following rule applies to division of approximate numbers.

> The quotient of two approximate numbers should not contain more significant figures than either the divisor or dividend.

Example. Divide 1825.2 by 1.754.

Solution. $1825.2 \div 1.754 = 1040.5+$

Since 1.754 contains only four significant figures, the quotient 1040.5+ must be rounded off to contain only four significant figures. Therefore, $1825.2 \div 1.754 = 1041$.

EXERCISES

[A]

Exercises 1–6 deal with approximate numbers. Perform the indicated operations:

1. $1.6 + 3.15 + .068$ *4.9* 3. $17.2 + .12$ *17.3* 5. 23.52×1.654 *38.90*

2. $172.3 - 42.55$ *129.7* 4. $21.36 \div 5.6$ *3.8* 6. $140.0 \div 2$ *70*

Numerical Trigonometry [A]

The word *trigonometry* means "triangle measurement." In the pages which follow you will be studying triangle measurement. However, the usefulness of trigonometry is not confined to the solution of tri-

NUMERICAL TRIGONOMETRY

angles alone. Without trigonometry one could not go very far into the study of radio, light, heat, electricity, navigation, astronomy, or any field of engineering. More advanced work in trigonometry is required for work in these fields.

Facts about Angles [A]

For your work in trigonometry you need to recall:

1. An angle, abbreviated ∠, is the figure formed by two lines meeting at a point.
2. A right angle contains 90°.
3. An acute angle is less than a right angle.
4. An obtuse angle contains more than 90° and less than 180°.
5. Two lines are perpendicular (⊥) when they form a right angle.
6. An angle may be named in three ways: by a capital letter at its vertex, as ∠ A; by a small letter within the angle, as ∠ m; and by three capital letters, as ∠ BAC. In reading an 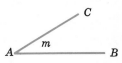 angle by three letters, the letter at the vertex is the middle letter.

Facts about Triangles [A]

The following facts are needed in the study of trigonometry:

1. The symbol for triangle is △.
2. A right triangle has one right angle.
3. The sum of the angles of a triangle is 180°.
4. Any triangle has two acute angles.
5. Two triangles which have the same size and shape are congruent (≅). Either will fit exactly upon the other.
6. Two triangles which have exactly the same shape are similar (∼).
7. Two triangles are similar when their corresponding angles are equal and their corresponding sides are proportional.
8. The hypotenuse of a right triangle is the side opposite the right angle. In the figure the side AC opposite right angle B is the hypotenuse. The side BC is *opposite* ∠ A and the side AB is *opposite* ∠ C. The side AB is *adjacent* to ∠ A and the side BC is *adjacent* to ∠ C.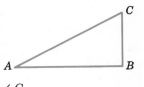
9. The legs of a right triangle are the sides which form the right angle. The legs of △ ABC are AB and BC.

519

[A]

1. What angle of △ *DEF* is a right angle? *∠E*

2. Which angles of △ *DEF* are acute? *∠s F and D*

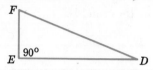

3. Using three letters, name ∠ *E*; ∠ *D*; ∠ *F*. *∠DEF; ∠EOF;*
∠EFD

4. What is the name of side *DF*? *Hypotenuse*

5. Which two sides of △ *DEF* are perpendicular? *EF and ED*

6. How many degrees are there in the sum of ∠ *D* and ∠ *F*?
90°

△ *HKS* and △ *PTW* are similar, *HS* corresponding to *PW*
and *HK* corresponding to *PT*.

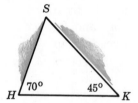
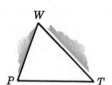

7. How many degrees are there in ∠ *S*? in ∠ *P*? in ∠*T*?
in ∠ *W*? *65°; 70°; 45°; 65°*

8. $\dfrac{HS}{PW} = \dfrac{SK}{WT}.$ Why?   **9.** Does $\dfrac{HS}{SK} = \dfrac{PW}{WT}?$ *yes*

Corresponding sides ~△
are proportional

Surveyors' Instruments [A]

For making direct measurements out of doors the surveyor uses the
steel tape and *leveling rod* for measuring linear distances and the *transit*
for measuring angles. The steel tape is 100 feet long and graduated
into tenths of a foot. The transit is made to measure both vertical
and horizontal angles.

The picture on the following page shows a transit and the upper
part of its tripod. Essentially a transit consists of a telescope with
cross hairs and two circular protractors. To measure angles in a vertical plane the telescope is revolved about a horizontal axis, and to
measure angles in a horizontal plane it is revolved about a vertical
axis.

See ① below.

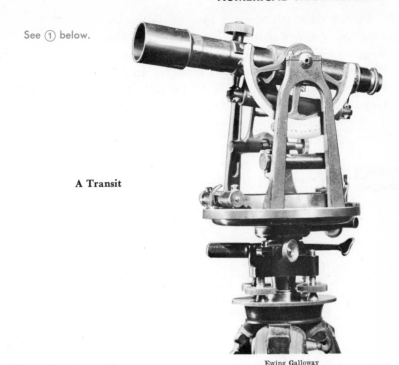

A Transit

Ewing Galloway

The Tangent of an Angle [A]

An algebra teacher asked each member of the class to draw a right triangle having an acute angle of 30°. Then the teacher asked the pupils to measure the sides of their triangles and find to the nearest tenth the ratio of the side opposite the 30° angle to the leg adjacent to the 30° angle.

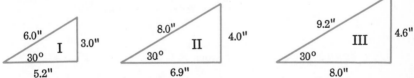

The pupil having triangle I divided 3 by 5.2, the pupil having triangle II divided 4 by 6.9, and the pupil having triangle III divided 4.6 by 8.0. All three of these pupils found the ratio to be about 0.58. If all the pupils in the class had drawn their triangles correctly, the corresponding sides of their triangles would have been proportional, and all pupils would have found the ratio to be 0.58. We call this kind of ratio the <u>tangent</u> of the angle. Thus tangent 30° = 0.58.

① Most schools do not have a transit available. If a surveyor or engineer lives in your town, he might be willing to demonstrate with his instrument. Barring this, you might make a demonstration model. (See Shuster and Bedford, *Field Work in Mathematics.* Yoder Instruments, East Palestine, Ohio.) As a simpler device, a protractor can be mounted on a revolving disc to illustrate the principle.

In any right triangle the tangent (abbreviated *tan*) of either acute angle is the ratio of the length of the leg opposite the angle to the length of the leg adjacent to the angle. In this figure the tangent of $\angle A$ is $\frac{8}{15}$, or .53. This is written $\tan A = \frac{8}{15}$. For any angle x, $\tan x$ = $\frac{\text{leg opposite } \angle x}{\text{leg adjacent to } \angle x}$.

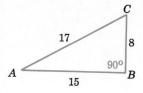

EXERCISES

1. What is the value of tan $\overset{2}{A}$? of tan $\overset{1}{D}$? of tan $\overset{1/2}{C}$? of tan $\overset{1}{F}$? [A] of tan K? of tan L? of tan P? of tan R?

4/5   5/4   5/12   12/5

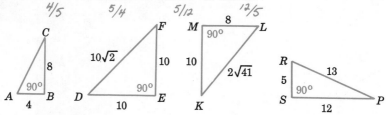

2. Below are three right triangles having $\angle A = \angle D = \angle R$. Find the value of tan A; of tan D; of tan R. Does the value of the tangent of an angle depend upon the size of the triangle?

¾ ; ¾ ; ¾ ; no

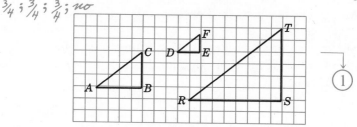

3. In the figure above does $\angle C = \angle F = \angle T$? *Yes*

4. What is the value of tan C? of tan F? 4/3 ; 4/3

5. Draw a right triangle PQR having $PQ = 3$ inches, $QR = 6$ inches, and $\angle Q$ a right angle. Write the tangent of $\angle P$. Write the tangent of $\angle R$. 2 ; ½

6. Draw a square having each side 2 inches long. Letter the vertices A, B, C, and D. Draw a diagonal line joining A and C. Write the tangent of $\angle BAC$.

522 ① This graphical method of showing the constant nature of the tangent function of any particular angle is effective. The diagram can also be made by making one basic triangle on graph paper, and then extending the sides of $\angle A$, drawing appropriate vertical lines. Students can learn a great deal about the tables of functions by actually computing a short table by such measurements and comparing with the table on page 524. This can be repeated for the sine and cosine later.

7. In the figure below $\angle AOB$ contains $10°$, $AO = 10$ units, and $AB = 1.8$ units. Then $\tan AOB = \dfrac{1.8}{10} = .18$. Using your protractor and ruler, complete the table in like manner.

Does the value of the tangent increase or decrease as the size of the angle increases? Give the reason why the tangent of an angle is a function of the angle. *increases; value of tangent depends on size of angle.*

$\angle$	DEGREE	TAN
AOB	10°	.18
AOC	? 20°	? .36
AOD	? 30°	? .58
AOE	? 40°	? .84
AOF	? 50°	1.19
AOG	? 60°	1.73

Table of Tangents [A]

In the last exercise you learned how to make a small table of tangents. These results by careful measurements may be made correct to two significant figures. By using methods of higher mathematics it is possible to make tables in which the values of the tangents are correct to four or more decimal places. On page 524 is a table of sines, cosines, and tangents given correct to four decimal places. This table gives the tangents of angles from $1°$ to $89°$. To find $\tan 62°$ from this table, first look in the column headed "ANGLE" for the angle $62°$. Then in the column headed "TAN," in the same horizontal line as $62°$, find the number 1.8807. Then $\tan 62° = 1.8807$ to the nearest ten-thousandth.

[A] **ORAL EXERCISES**

Using the table on page 524, find the following:

1. $\tan 32°$. 6249
2. $\tan 45°$ 1.0000
3. $\tan 16°$ .2867
4. $\tan 20°$ .3640
5. $\tan 10°$ .1763
6. $\tan 34°$. 6745
7. $\tan 19°$ .3443
8. $\tan 1°$ .0175
9. $\tan 89°$ 57.2900
10. $\tan 80°$ 5.6713
11. $\tan 71°$ 2.9042
12. $\tan 65°$ 2.1445
13. $\tan 60°$ 1.7321
14. $\tan 30°$ .5774
15. $\tan 15°$ .2679

523

Table of Natural Functions

ANGLE	SIN	COS	TAN	ANGLE	SIN	COS	TAN
				45°	.7071	.7071	1.0000
1°	.0175	.9998	.0175	46°	.7193	.6947	1.0355
2°	.0349	.9994	.0349	47°	.7314	.6820	1.0724
3°	.0523	.9986	.0524	48°	.7431	.6691	1.1106
4°	.0698	.9976	.0699	49°	.7547	.6561	1.1504
5°	.0872	.9962	.0875	50°	.7660	.6428	1.1918
6°	.1045	.9945	.1051	51°	.7771	.6293	1.2349
7°	.1219	.9925	.1228	52°	.7880	.6157	1.2799
8°	.1392	.9903	.1405	53°	.7986	.6018	1.3270
9°	.1564	.9877	.1584	54°	.8090	.5878	1.3764
10°	.1736	.9848	.1763	55°	.8192	.5736	1.4281
11°	.1908	.9816	.1944	56°	.8290	.5592	1.4826
12°	.2079	.9781	.2126	57°	.8387	.5446	1.5399
13°	.2250	.9744	.2309	58°	.8480	.5299	1.6003
14°	.2419	.9703	.2493	59°	.8572	.5150	1.6643
15°	.2588	.9659	.2679	60°	.8660	.5000	1.7321
16°	.2756	.9613	.2867	61°	.8746	.4848	1.8040
17°	.2924	.9563	.3057	62°	.8829	.4695	1.8807
18°	.3090	.9511	.3249	63°	.8910	.4540	1.9626
19°	.3256	.9455	.3443	64°	.8988	.4384	2.0503
20°	.3420	.9397	.3640	65°	.9063	.4226	2.1445
21°	.3584	.9336	.3839	66°	.9135	.4067	2.2460
22°	.3746	.9272	.4040	67°	.9205	.3907	2.3559
23°	.3907	.9205	.4245	68°	.9272	.3746	2.4751
24°	.4067	.9135	.4452	69°	.9336	.3584	2.6051
25°	.4226	.9063	.4663	70°	.9397	.3420	2.7475
26°	.4384	.8988	.4877	71°	.9455	.3256	2.9042
27°	.4540	.8910	.5095	72°	.9511	.3090	3.0777
28°	.4695	.8829	.5317	73°	.9563	.2924	3.2709
29°	.4848	.8746	.5543	74°	.9613	.2756	3.4874
30°	.5000	.8660	.5774	75°	.9659	.2588	3.7321
31°	.5150	.8572	.6009	76°	.9703	.2419	4.0108
32°	.5299	.8480	.6249	77°	.9744	.2250	4.3315
33°	.5446	.8387	.6494	78°	.9781	.2079	4.7046
34°	.5592	.8290	.6745	79°	.9816	.1908	5.1446
35°	.5736	.8192	.7002	80°	.9848	.1736	5.6713
36°	.5878	.8090	.7265	81°	.9877	.1564	6.3138
37°	.6018	.7986	.7536	82°	.9903	.1392	7.1154
38°	.6157	.7880	.7813	83°	.9925	.1219	8.1443
39°	.6293	.7771	.8098	84°	.9945	.1045	9.5144
40°	.6428	.7660	.8391	85°	.9962	.0872	11.4301
41°	.6561	.7547	.8693	86°	.9976	.0698	14.3007
42°	.6691	.7431	.9004	87°	.9986	.0523	19.0811
43°	.6820	.7314	.9325	88°	.9994	.0349	28.6363
44°	.6947	.7193	.9657	89°	.9998	.0175	57.2900

Find the angles whose tangents are

16. .5317 28°   **21.** .0175 1°   **26.** .3249 18°

17. .6745 34°   **22.** .1051 6°   **27.** .7002 35°

18. 8.1443 83°   **23.** 7.1154 82°   **28.** .2126 12°

19. 1.7321 60°   **24.** .9325 43°   **29.** .4245 23°

20. 1.3270 53°   **25.** 19.0811 87°   **30.** 2.0503 64°

Angles of Elevation and Depression [A]

In this sketch point A is in a valley and point B is on a hill. Lines AC and BD are horizontal lines in the same plane. If you have a transit at A pointing along the horizontal line AC and wish to focus it on point B, you must turn the telescope through angle x. In

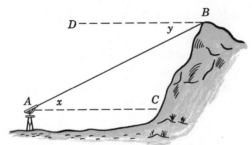

the process the line of sight has been elevated from the horizontal line AC. We say "x is the <u>angle of elevation</u> of B from A." Now suppose the transit is placed at B and focused on A. In this case the line of sight is lowered from the horizontal line BD. We say "y is the <u>angle of depression</u> of A from B." Notice that the angle of elevation is above the horizontal, and that the angle of depression is below the horizontal. If you measure angles x and y you will find that the angle of elevation of B from A is equal to the angle of depression of A from B.

Line of Sight [A]

When the observer at A uses the transit to sight an object at B, we say that the line AB is the <u>line of sight</u>. Thus the line of sight is the line drawn from the observer's eye to the object. If the line of sight is above the horizontal line, the angle between the lines is the angle of elevation. If the line of sight is below the horizontal line, the angle is the angle of depression.

---

① Make this topic realistic by actual demonstration if possible. A device to illustrate the raising or lowering of the line of sight from the horizontal can be made from two strips of wood or cardboard hinged at one end so that angles of different sizes can be formed.

Using the Tangent to Solve Problems[A]

The following examples illustrate how the tangent is used in problems of indirect measurement:

Example 1. At a point 60 feet from the foot of a flagpole the angle of elevation of its top is 67°. How high is the pole?

Solution. $\angle B = 90°$

$$\frac{x}{60} = \tan 67°$$

$$x = 60 \tan 67°$$

From the table $\tan 67° = 2.3559$

Then $x = 60(2.3559)$

$x = 141.354$

Rounding off the result, $BC = 141.4$ feet.

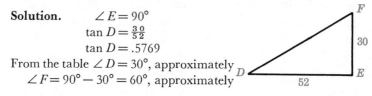

If 60 feet is found by measurement, 141.4 feet should be rounded off to 140 feet. In this example no allowance is made for the height of the transit. What is the height of the flagpole in this example if the telescope is 4.5 feet above the ground?

Example 2. One side of a right triangle is 52 feet and the other side is 30 feet. Find the size of each acute angle.

Solution. $\angle E = 90°$

$\tan D = \frac{30}{52}$

$\tan D = .5769$

From the table $\angle D = 30°$, approximately

$\angle F = 90° - 30° = 60°$, approximately

[A]

EXERCISES

1. The angle of elevation of the sun is 42°. How high is a chimney which casts a shadow 240 feet long? *216.096 ft., (220 ft.)*

2. From an observation point the angle of elevation of an airplane was 82°. How high was the plane above the ground if the point directly beneath it was on the same level as, and 1500 feet from, the point of observation? *10,673.1 ft., (11,000 ft.)*

3. Two Girl Scouts standing 300 yards from the foot of a cliff and on a level with it found the angle of elevation of its top to be 34°. How high was the cliff? *202.35 yd., (200 yd.)*

526

These problems should interest students—they can measure the height of a tree without climbing it! A word about the answers. They are given first to four significant digits corresponding to the four-place table (p. 524) in order to check computation. Then each answer is rounded to conform to the given data, using this scheme: linear measurements to four significant figures correspond to angular measurements to the nearest minute, linear measurements to three significant figures correspond to angular measurements to the

4. *ABCD* is a rectangle with diagonal *BD*, ∠ *ABD* = 40°, and *AB* = 34 inches. Find the area of the rectangle. *970.02 sq. in., (970 sq. in.)*

5. Two boys wish to find the distance from point *A* to point *C* across a river. They set a stake at *C* making ∠ *BCA* = 90°. They find that ∠ *B* = 66° and *BC* = 160 feet. How long is *AC*? *359.36 ft., (360 ft.)*

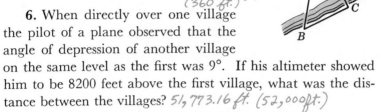

6. When directly over one village the pilot of a plane observed that the angle of depression of another village on the same level as the first was 9°. If his altimeter showed him to be 8200 feet above the first village, what was the distance between the villages? *51,773.16 ft. (52,000 ft.)*

7. From the top of Jefferson High School the angle of depression of a point *P*, 1850 feet away, is 2°. How high is the building if *P* is on the same level as its base? *64.565 ft.(65 ft.)*

8. The sketch at the right shows a simple leveling instrument for measuring horizontal angles. *M* is a smooth, 1-inch board about a foot square. *A*, *B*, and *C* are small round sticks which fit into holes in *M*. *E* is a cardboard protractor circle glued to *M*. A pointer is fastened to *M* with a nail or screw. The board *M* can be leveled with a small spirit level by sliding the board on the sticks. Make an instrument of this kind.

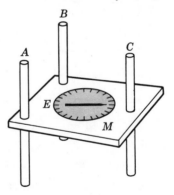

9. A flagpole casts a shadow 45 feet long when the sun's rays form an angle of 24° with the ground. Find the height of the flagpole. *20.03 ft. (20 ft.)*

10. Find the length of the shadow cast by a 90-foot tower when the sun's rays make an angle of 40° with the ground. *107.26 ft. (110 ft.)*

11. Find the angle of elevation of the sun when a 25-foot pole casts a 40-foot shadow. *32°, to nearest degree*

nearest ten minutes, and linear measurements to two significant figures correspond to angular measurements to the nearest degree.

ALGEBRA, BOOK ONE

The Sine of an Angle [A]

The sine of an angle is another important ratio. In any right triangle the <u>sine</u> (abbreviated *sin*) of either acute angle is the ratio of the leg opposite the angle to the hypotenuse. Thus in triangle *ABC*,

$$\text{the sine of } \angle A = \frac{BC}{AB},$$

or,

$$\sin A = \frac{BC}{AB}$$

Also,

$$\sin B = \frac{AC}{AB}.$$

In general,

$$\sin x = \frac{\text{leg opposite } x}{\text{hypotenuse}}.$$

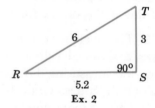

[A]

ORAL EXERCISES

1. *ABCD* is a rectangle. Find the tangent of ∠ *BAC*; of ∠ *BCA*. Find the sine of ∠ *BAC*; of ∠ *BCA*; of ∠ *DAC*; of ∠ *DCA*. $\frac{3}{4}$; $\frac{4}{3}$; $\frac{3}{5}$; $\frac{4}{5}$; $\frac{4}{5}$; $\frac{3}{5}$

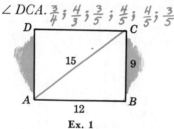

Ex. 1   Ex. 2

2. Using △ *RST*, find tan *T*; sin *R*; sin *T*. *1.73; $\frac{1}{2}$; 0.87*

Using the table on page 524, find the following:

.4067 **3.** sin 24°   *.0872* **6.** sin 5°   *.2588* **9.** sin 15°

.8910 **4.** sin 63°   *.9962* **7.** sin 85°   *.5878* **10.** sin 36°

.9877 **5.** sin 81°   *.1392* **8.** sin 8°   *.3090* **11.** sin 18°

From the same table find the angles whose sines are

59° **12.** .8572   *16°* **15.** .2756   *86°* **18.** .9976

48° **13.** .7431   *70°* **16.** .9397   *1°* **19.** .0175

4° **14.** .0698   *80°* **17.** .9848   *47°* **20.** .7314

21. As an angle increases in size, how does the value of its sine change? *Increases*

22. Can the sine of an angle be as small as zero? *Yes*

23. Can the sine of an angle be as large as one? *yes*

528

Using the Sine to Solve Problems

Study the example carefully.

Example. How high is a kite if it is at the end of a string 600 feet long which makes an angle of 48° with the ground?

Solution.

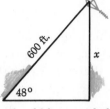

$$\frac{x}{600} = \sin 48°$$

$$x = 600 \sin 48°$$

From the table $\quad \sin 48° = .7431$

Then $\qquad\qquad x = 600(.7431)$

$$x = 445.86$$

To four significant figures, $x = 445.9$ feet

If 600 feet is found by measurement, 445.9 feet should be rounded off to 446 feet.

[A]

EXERCISES

1. A railroad track has an angle of elevation of 1°. What is the difference in altitude of two points on the track a mile apart? *92.40 ft., (92 ft.)*

2. *CD* is the altitude of equilateral triangle *ABC*. How large is ∠ *B*? ∠ *BCD*? Using the sine of ∠ *B*, find *CD* if *BC* = 10 inches. Using the sine of ∠ *BCD*, find *BD*. *60°; 30°; 8.660 in.; 5 in.*

3. A 24-foot pole leaning against the side of a house makes an angle of 20° with the house. How far from the house is the foot of the pole? *8.208 ft. (8.2 ft.)*

4. The side of a square is 14 feet. Find the diagonal, using the sine function. Check your answer, using the Pythagorean Theorem. *19.799⁺ ft. (20 ft.)*

5. A smokestack is 170 feet high. Find the length of a guy wire which is fastened to the stack 20 feet from the top and makes an angle of 40° with the ground. *233.35 ft. (230 ft.)*

6. Points *A* and *B* are on the opposite sides of a lake. A boy knows that line *AB* runs north and south. Then he places a stake at *C* directly east of *AB*. He then measures *AC* and ∠ *BCA*. If *AC* = 1960 feet and ∠ *BCA* = 42°, what is the length of *AB*? *1311.436 ft. (1300 ft.)*

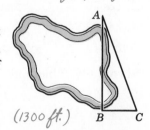

The meaning of sine and cosine functions and application to simple problems can be taught in the same way as was the tangent ratio. This section should cause no difficulty.

[C]

7. *ABC* is a triangle with $CD \perp AB$.

a. Show that $CD = AC \sin A$.

b. Show that the area of
$\triangle ABC = \frac{1}{2} AC \cdot AB \sin A$.

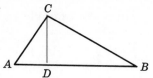

The Cosine of an Angle [A]

The third important ratio that depends upon the size of an angle is the <u>cosine</u> (pronounced kō'sīn and abbreviated cos). In any right triangle the cosine of either acute angle is the ratio of the leg adjacent to the angle to the hypotenuse. Thus in $\triangle ABC$,

$$\cos A = \frac{AC}{AB}.$$

In general,

$$\cos x = \frac{\text{leg adjacent to } x}{\text{hypotenuse}}.$$

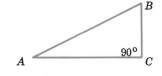

[A]

ORAL EXERCISES

1. *DEF* is a right triangle with $\angle E = 90°$. Find $\tan D$; $\tan F$; $\sin D$; $\sin F$; $\cos D$; $\cos F$. How does $\sin D$ compare with $\cos F$? How does $\cos D$ compare with $\sin F$? $\frac{5}{12}$; $\frac{12}{5}$; $\frac{5}{13}$; $\frac{12}{13}$; $\frac{12}{13}$; $\frac{5}{13}$; $\sin D = \cos F$; $\cos D = \sin F$.

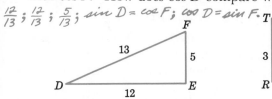
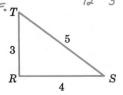

2. *RST* is a right triangle with $\angle R = 90°$. Find $\tan S$; $\tan T$; $\sin S$; $\sin T$; $\cos S$; $\cos T$. How does $\cos S$ compare with $\sin T$? $\frac{3}{4}$; $\frac{4}{3}$; $\frac{3}{5}$; $\frac{4}{5}$; $\frac{4}{5}$; $\frac{3}{5}$; $\cos S = \sin T$

Using the table on page 524, find the following:

.2419 **3.** cos 76°   .8829 **6.** cos 28°   .0175 **9.** cos 89°

.8480 **4.** cos 32°   .8660 **7.** cos 30°   .7547 **10.** cos 41°

.9511 **5.** cos 18°   .5000 **8.** cos 60°   .9205 **11.** cos 23°

From this table find the angles whose cosines are

47° **12.** .6820   1° **14.** .9998   17° **16.** .9563

63° **13.** .4540   45° **15.** .7071   40° **17.** .7660

530

Using the Cosine of an Angle [A]

The following problem illustrates the use of the cosine.

Example. A guy wire attached to the top of a telephone pole reaches a stake in the ground 30 feet from the foot of the pole, and makes an angle of 56° with the line drawn from the stake to the foot of the pole. How long is the wire?

Solution. $\dfrac{30}{x} = \cos 56°$

Then $\dfrac{30}{x} = .5592$

$M_x \qquad 30 = .5592\,x$

$\qquad\qquad x = 53.6$, the number of feet in the length of the wire.

If 30 feet is found by measurement, 53.6 should be rounded off to 54.

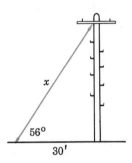

[A]

EXERCISES

1. A guy wire of a pole meets the ground 42 feet from the foot of the pole, and makes an angle of 45° with the ground. How long is the guy wire? *59.397⁺ft. (60ft.)*

2. A machinist wishes to drill 5 holes in a circular plate. These holes a.e to be equally distant from each other and 8 inches from the center of the plate. How far apart shall the centers of the holes be placed? *9.4048 in. (9.4 in.)*

Ex. 2

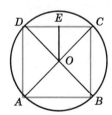 Ex. 3

3. *ABCD* is a square inscribed in a circle with a 12-inch diameter.

a. How long is *AO*? *DO*? *6 in.; 6 in.*

b. *OE ⊥ DC*. How large is ∠ *DOC*? ∠ *DOE*? ∠ *ODE*? *90°; 45°; 45°*

c. Find the length of *EO* using the sine ratio. *4.2426 in. (4.2 in.)*

d. Find the length of *EO* using the Pythagorean Theorem. *4.242 in.*

[C]

4. *ABC* is a right triangle with hypotenuse *AB* and *CD* ⊥ *AB*.

a. Show that *AD* = *AC* cos *A*.

b. Show that *DB* = *BC* cos *B*.

c. Show that $AB = \dfrac{AC}{\sin B}$.

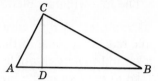

5. The radius of the circle below is 16 inches. The line-segment *AB* is 7 inches, *AC* = *CB*, and *OC* ⊥ *AB*.

a. Find *AC*. *3.5 in.*   **c.** Find ∠ *OAC*.   *77°*

b. Find ∠ *AOC*. *13°* **d.** Find the area of △ *AOC*; of △ *AOB*.

e. Find the area of sector *AOB*. (A sector is a figure formed by two radii and an arc of a circle.) *58.1 sq. in. (58 sq. in.)*

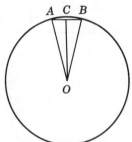

*5.d. 27.3 sq. in. (27 sq. in.);
54.6 sq. in. (55 sq. in.)*

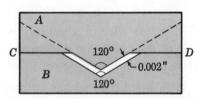

6. The two metal plates *A* and *B* are placed together along line *CD* as shown in the figure. The angle parts fail to close by .002 of an inch. The plates are so made that they will fit exactly when a uniform width is ground off plate *A* along the straight part of *CD*. What is this width? (Draw a right triangle showing the width to be found.) *.0023096 in. (.0023 in.)*

Interpolation [C]

When a right angle is divided into 90 equal parts, each part is called a degree. If an angle of one degree is divided into 60 equal parts, each part is called a minute (abbreviated ′). Then 1° = 60′.

Suppose we wish to find the sine of an angle of 32° 30′. The table on page 524 does not give the sine of 32° 30′, but it does give the sines of 32 and 33 degrees and from these two sines we can find the approximate value of 32° 30′.

From the table   sin 33° = .5446
and   sin 32° = .5299

There is no need to teach interpolation in first-year algebra. The topic has been included in the text for those who wish to have some challenging material for a few students or to answer the question "What do you do when the numbers cannot be found in the table?"

Since 32° 30′ is halfway between 32° and 33°, its sine is about halfway between .5299 and .5446. To find the number halfway between .5299 and .5446, we first find the difference of these two numbers, which is .0147. Then we take half of this difference, which is .0073½. Then add .0073½ to the smaller number, .5299, and obtain .5372. Then sin 32° 30′ = .5372.

This method of estimating a value that is not given in the table is called <u>interpolation</u>. Study the form and method of interpolation as given in the following examples:

Example 1. Find sin 18° 12′.

Solution. 12′ is $\frac{1}{5}$ of a degree. Since 18° 12′ is $\frac{1}{5}$ the way from 18° to 19°, its sine is about $\frac{1}{5}$ the way from .3090 to .3256.

$$\begin{array}{rl} \sin 19° = & .3256 \\ \sin 18° = & \underline{.3090} \\ \text{difference} = & .0166 \\ \tfrac{1}{5} \text{ of difference} = & .0033 \\ .3090 + .0033 = & .3123 \end{array}$$

Then $\qquad\qquad \sin 18° 12′ = .3123$

Why is .0033 added to .3090?

Example 2. Find tan 72° 45′.

Solution. 45′ is $\frac{3}{4}$ of a degree. Then tan 72° 45′ is about $\frac{3}{4}$ the way from 3.0777 to 3.2709.

$$\begin{array}{rl} \tan 73° = & 3.2709 \\ \tan 72° = & \underline{3.0777} \\ \text{difference} = & .1932 \\ \tfrac{3}{4} \text{ of difference} = & .1449 \\ 3.0777 + .1449 = & 3.2226 \end{array}$$

Then $\qquad\qquad \tan 72° 45′ = 3.2226$

[C]

EXERCISES

Find the value of

1. sin 8° 30′ .1478
2. tan 24° 15′ .4505
3. sin 76° 30′ .9723
4. tan 20° 30′ .3740
5. sin 42° 6′ .6704

6. tan 24° 24′ .4536
7. sin 65° 40′ .9111
8. tan 47° 36′ 1.0953
9. sin 18° 12′ .3123
10. tan 77° 6′ 4.3688

11. sin 15° 10′ .2616
12. tan 53° 20′ 1.3435
13. sin 85° 50′ .9974
14. tan 4° 40′ .0816
15. sin 5° 48′ .1010

533

Example 3. Find cos 18° 15′.

Solution. 15′ is $\frac{1}{4}$ of one degree. The cosine becomes smaller as the angle increases. Then .0014 must be subtracted from cos 18°.

$$\cos 18° = .9511$$
$$\cos 19° = .9455$$
$$\text{difference} = .0056$$
$$\tfrac{1}{4} \text{ of difference} = .0014$$
$$.9511 - .0014 = .9497$$

Then
$$\cos 18° 15′ = .9497$$

EXERCISES

[C]

Find the value of

.7038 **1.** cos 25° 20′	.4173 **6.** cos 65° 20′	.9443 **11.** cos 19° 12′
.8280 **2.** cos 34° 6′	.9753 **7.** cos 12° 45′	.7343 **12.** cos 42° 45′
.9772 **3.** cos 12° 15′	.6734 **8.** cos 47° 40′	.0941 **13.** cos 84° 36′
.1722 **4.** cos 80° 5′	.4736 **9.** sin 28° 16′	.8807 **14.** cos 28° 16′
.9970 **5.** cos 4° 25′	.5377 **10.** tan 28° 16′	6.7146 **15.** tan 81° 30′

Example 4. Find $\angle A$ if its sine = .3867.

Solution. In the table no angle is given whose sine is .3867. We can see that the angle is between 22° and 23°. We must find what part of the way .3867 is from .3746 to .3907.

$$\sin 23° = .3907$$
$$\sin 22° = .3746$$
$$\text{difference} = .0161$$

The difference between .3867 and .3746 is .0121. Then .3867 is $\frac{.0121}{.0161}$ of the way from .3746 to .3907. Then $\angle A$ is about $\frac{.0121}{.0161}$ of one degree more than 22°, or $\frac{121}{161}$ of 60′ more than 22°.

$$\tfrac{121}{161} \times 60′ = 45′$$

Then,
$$\angle A = 22° 45′$$

Example 5. Find $\angle A$ if cos A = .4279.

Solution. From the table we see that $\angle A$ is greater than 64° and less than 65°. We must find how many minutes must be added to 64° to make $\angle A$.

$$\cos 64° = .4384$$
$$\cos 65° = .4226$$
$$\text{difference} = .0158$$

$.4384 - .4279 = .0105$. Then $\angle A$ is $\frac{.0105}{.0158}$ of the way from 64° to 65°. $\frac{.0105}{.0158} \times 60′ = 40′$. Then $\angle A = 64° 40′$.

534

Find ∠ A when *(ans. 1-12 at bottom of page)*

1. sin A = .2784   **5.** sin A = .2504   **9.** tan A = 1.6386

2. cos A = .9088   **6.** tan A = .3574   **10.** cos A = .2798

3. tan A = .1435   **7.** cos A = .9503   **11.** tan A = 2.1159

4. cos A = .9805   **8.** sin A = .3969   **12.** sin A = .7960

Exercises 13–17 apply to △ ABC in which ∠ B is the right angle.

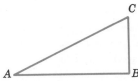

13. Find AC when BC = 2000 feet and ∠ A = 21° 10′. *5538.6⁺ ft. (5540 ft.)*

14. Find BC when AB = 265.2 feet and ∠ C = 54° 15′. *190.88⁺ ft. (190.9 ft.)*

15. Find ∠ A when BC = 195.3 feet and AC = 200.0 feet. *77°34′*

16. Find ∠ C when BC = 1000 and AC = 1600. *51°19′*

17. Find the area of △ ABC when ∠ A = 18° 30′ and AC = 500.0. *37,604.06 sq. units (37,600 sq. units)*

18. If a hill has a slope of 8°, how far up the hill will a dam 62 feet high raise the water? *445.40⁺ ft. (450 ft.)*

19. The Washington Monument is 555 feet high. What is the angle of elevation of its top when viewed from a point a mile away and on a level with the base of the monument? *6°, approx.*

20. △ ABC is isosceles. Find the area of the triangle if AC and BC are 24 inches each and ∠ B = 35°. *270.7182 sq. in. (270 sq. in.)*

21. Find the angles of an isosceles triangle if the base is 20 inches and each of the other sides is 18 inches. *∠A=∠B=56°15′, ∠C=67°30′ (∠A=∠B=56°, ∠C=68°)*

Historical Note. Trigonometry had its beginnings in Egypt and Babylonia four thousand years ago, when heights and distances were found by indirect measurement. Thales, the founder of geom-

1. 16°10′   *5. 14°30′*   *9. 58°36′*
2. 24°39′   *6. 19°40′*   *10. 73°45′*
3. 8°10′   *7. 18° 9′*   *11. 64°42′*
4. 11°19′   *8. 23°23′*   *12. 52°45′*

etry, calculated the heights of the great pyramids of Egypt by indirect measurement about 550 B.C.

Hipparchus (180–125 B.C.), the greatest of the Greek astronomers, could rightly be called the father of trigonometry, for he was the first to study the subject on a scientific basis. He developed trigonometry to solve his astronomy problems. The accuracy of his observations and computations may be judged by the fact that he determined the length of the year to within six minutes of its real value.

The next contribution to trigonometry was made by the Hindus and the Arabs. They introduced the trigonometric functions we now have, and prepared tables of natural functions.

It was not until the fourteenth century that the trigonometry of the Arabs was introduced into Europe. Additions to the subject were made by Regiomontanus (1464), a German; by Vieta (1580), a Frenchman; by Napier (1614), a Scotsman; and by Sir Isaac Newton (1729), an Englishman.

Checking Your Understanding of Chapter 19

Before you leave Chapter 19 make sure that you know

Should you review?

8. The meaning and spelling of each of the following
words or phrases:

	PAGE		PAGE
adjacent	519	opposite	519
angle of depression	525	precision of a measurement	514
angle of elevation	525	significant figures	515
approximate numbers	513	sine	528
cosine	530	tangent	521
hypotenuse	519	trigonometry	518

If you wish to be a better than average mathematics student,
you will also want to be able to use interpolation for estimating values not given in the table of trigonometric functions.

[A]

GENERAL
REVIEW

Solve:

1. $\dfrac{3x}{5} - \dfrac{x}{4} = 1$ *2 6/7*

2. $\dfrac{x}{2} - \dfrac{x}{6} = 10$ *30*

3. $\dfrac{y-3}{3} + 3 = \dfrac{y+4}{5}$ *-9*

4. $\dfrac{x-3}{5} + \dfrac{2x-1}{3} = 6$ *8*

5. $\dfrac{2}{5} - \dfrac{1+2x}{5x} = \dfrac{7}{10}$ *-2/7*

6. $\dfrac{4x-1}{2x+2} = \dfrac{2x-3}{x-1}$ *2 1/3*

Solve by completing the square:

7. $x^2 + 6x = 16$ *2, -8*

8. $x^2 - 4x = 96$ *12, -8*

9. $x^2 - 8x = 273$ *21, -13*

10. $x^2 - 10x = 299$ *23, -13*

11. $2x^2 - 5x - 3 = 0$ *3, -1/2*

12. $3x^2 + 19x = -6$ *-1/3, -6*

13. $7x^2 - 20x - 3 = 0$ *3, -1/7*

14. $3x^2 + x - 1 = 0$
$\dfrac{-1 \pm \sqrt{13}}{6}$, or .434, -.768

15. Reduce $\dfrac{m^2 - 25}{2m^2 - 13m + 15}$ to lowest terms. *$\dfrac{m+5}{2m-3}$*

16. The denominator of a fraction is 3 greater than the numerator. Find the fraction if its value is $\frac{4}{5}$. *12/15*

17. Find the number of degrees in each of two complementary angles if 5 times the larger exceeds 4 times the smaller
by 270°. *70°, 20°*

18. How many pounds of 90-cent candy and how many
pounds of candy at $1.20 per pound should be used to make a
mixture of 60 pounds worth $1.00 a pound? *90¢, 40 lb.;
$1.20, 20 lb.*

537

19. A number increased by 15% of itself equals 94.3. What is the number? *82*

20. Solve for x and y: $5x - 3y = 46$ *x = 8,*
$$2x + 5y = 6 \quad y = -2$$

21. Five times the square of a number is 79,380. Find the number. *± 126*

22. Find the square root of 6.6049. *± 2.57*

23. Complete $\sqrt{a}\sqrt{b} = \sqrt{?}$. *√ab*

24. Solve $7c(2c - 1) + 2c(5 - 7c) - 18 = 0$. *6*

25. Divide $x^3 - 3x^2 + 3x - 2$ by $x - 1$. *$x^2 - 2x + 1$, Rem. −1*

26. Separate 165 into two parts whose ratio is 4 : 7. *60, 105*

$14\frac{2}{9}$,
$17\frac{7}{9}$ **27.** The sides of one triangle are 16, 20, and 27. The longest side of a similar triangle is 24. Find the other two sides.

28. A kite string 465 feet long makes an angle of 42° with the ground. Assuming that the string is straight, find the height of the kite. *311.1315 ft. (310 ft.)*

29. What is the angle of elevation of an inclined plane that rises 1 inch in 10 feet? *28°, approx.*

30. Tell whether all rectangles are similar, and give the reason for your answer. *(See top of page)*

31. Are all squares similar? Why? *(See top of page)*

32. Add: $\dfrac{2c - 4}{3} - \dfrac{6 - 5c}{4}$ *$\dfrac{23c - 34}{12}$*

33. Solve the equation $4x^2 + 7x = 2$ by all the methods that you know. *$\frac{1}{4}$, −2*

34. What are the three ways of finding the square root of $\frac{1}{3}$? *(See bottom of page)*

[C]

35. What is the slope of the graph of $2x - 3y = 12$? *⅔*

36. Using the slope and y-intercept, graph the equation $5x + 2y = 8$.

37. Find the angles of an isosceles triangle if the base is 8.0 inches and each of the equal sides is 10.0 inches. *66° 25′,*
66° 25′; 47° 10′ (or 66°, 66°, 47°) **38.** Solve by formula: $3x^2 - 9x - 4 = 0$. *$\frac{9 \pm \sqrt{129}}{6} = 3.392^+,$*
$-.392^+$

39. Solve $\sqrt{5x + 1} - 6 = 0$. *7*

40. Show that 5 is not a root of $\sqrt{x + 7} + 4 = 0$.

---

538 *34. (1) Change $\frac{1}{3}$ to decimal 0.333… and extract its square root. (2) Divide square root of numerator by square root of denominator. (3) Change $\frac{1}{3}$ to $\frac{3}{9}$, take the square root of both terms of $\frac{3}{9}$, and divide square root of numerator by square root of denominator.*

[Test A]

1. Round off the following numbers to the nearest tenth:

a. 7.86 *7.9*   **b.** 26.34 *26.3*   **c.** .09 *0.1*   **d.** 321.12 *321.1*

2. Round off the following numbers to three significant figures: **a.** 2148 *2150*   62.17 *62.2*   **c.** .0324 *0.0324*   **d.** 1.617 *1.62*

3.

Find x. *7.5228*   Find y. *12.435*   Find z. *5.8176*

4.

5.

6. An 18-foot ladder leaning against a house makes an angle of 55° with the level ground. How far from the house is the foot of the ladder? *10.3248, or 10 ft.*

7. When the angle of elevation of the sun is 27°, a telephone pole casts a shadow 36 feet long. How high is the telephone pole? *18.342, or 18 ft.*

8. Find ∠ x in the diagram to the nearest degree. *14° approx.*

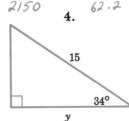

42.4

x

41.2

Time, 40 Minutes

See how many of these 35 problems you can do in 40 minutes. If you can do 10 problems correctly, you are just passing; if you can do 20 correctly, you are doing good work; if you can do 25 or more correctly, you are doing excellent work.

In Exercises 1–5 write + for your answer if the statement is true and − for your answer if the statement is false.

1. If the numerator and denominator of a fraction are equal, the value of the fraction is zero. −

2. One of the values of x that satisfies the equation $x^2 + 5x + 4 = 0$ is − 4. +

3. The product of any two numbers with like signs is a number having the same sign. −

4. $A = \frac{1}{2} ab$, when a and b are both doubled, A is doubled. −

5. $x^2 + y^2 = (x + y)^2$ −

539

Copy and complete statements 6–10, using in each case one of the following words: constant, greater, exponent, function, coefficient, variable, less, ratio.

6. If x is a negative number, then $x^2 - 2x$ is __?__ than $x^2 + 2x$. *greater*

7. In the expression $6 x^3$, 6 is the __?__ of x^3. *coefficient*

8. A variable that depends for its value upon the value of some other variable is a __?__ of the other variable. *function*

9. In the formula $p = 4s$, p and s are variables and 4 is a __?__. *constant*

10. $\frac{2}{3}$ is the __?__ of 12 to 18. *ratio*

Factor:

11. $a^4 - 1$ $(a^2+1)(a+1)(a-1)$

13. $4 c^2 - 28 c + 49$ $(2c-7)^2$

12. $3 a^2 - 2 ay - 8 a$ $a(3a-2y-8)$

14. $m^2 - 2m - 24$ $(m-6)(m+4)$

15. Solve: $5 a - a^2 = 7 - (a + a^2)$ $1\frac{1}{6}$

16. Find the value of $15 a^3 - 8 a^2 + 2$ when $a = 2$. *90*

17. If 10 is 4 more than $2 a$, what is the value of $3 a - 5$? *4*

18. Simplify: $10 - 2(3 a - 1)$ $12 - 6a$

19. Find the value of $\frac{1}{x} + 3$ when $x = \frac{1}{3}$. *6*

20. $f(x) = x^2 - 4x - 6$. Find $f(3)$. *-9*

21. A board is x feet long. When a piece a feet long is cut off one end and a piece b feet long is cut off the other end, how many inches long is the piece remaining? $12(x-a-b)$ in.

22. $i = prt$. How long must \$3000 be invested at 5% simple interest to produce \$450 interest? *3 yr.*

23. Each end of a rectangle is $3 y - 1$. Find the top and bottom of the rectangle if its perimeter is $10 y + 4$. $2y + 3$

24. A merchant sold an automobile for \$1575 at a margin of 25% of the cost. Find the cost. *\$1260*

25. Solve $3(x + 4)(x - 4) - x(3 x - 5) = 12$. *12*

26. Solve $x^2 - 20x = -91$. *7, 13*

27. Solve $x^2 + 6x = 11$. *$-3 \pm 2\sqrt{5}$, or 1.472, -7.472*

28. A room is 14 feet long and 12 feet wide. Find its diagonal. *$2\sqrt{85}$ or 18.44 ft.*

29. Solve $\dfrac{x}{4} - \dfrac{y}{6} = \dfrac{1}{2}$ *$x = 6$,*

$\dfrac{x}{3} - \dfrac{y}{2} = -1$ *$y = 6$*

30. A tower casts a shadow of 20 feet when a man 6 feet tall casts a shadow of $1\frac{1}{2}$ feet. How high is the tower? *80 ft.*

31. If 10 men can build a shed in 4 days, how many men are needed to build the shed in 8 days? *5*

32. Multiply: $3\sqrt{6}\sqrt{\frac{2}{3}}$. *6*

33. Simplify the radicals and combine:

$$\sqrt{12} - \sqrt{18} + \sqrt{50} - \sqrt{27}.$$ *$2\sqrt{2} - \sqrt{3}$*

34. For what values of x does $\sqrt{x^2 - 6x + 9} = x - 3$? *3 or greater*

35. In a $\triangle ABC$, $AB = 6$, $BC = 8$, and $\angle B = 90°$. What is the value of sin A? *0.8000*

20

Review by Topics

*Exercises for reviewing
the year's work* ▶

Chapter 20 offers you a set of exercises arranged topic by topic, suitable
for extra work, review, or class practice at any time of the year.

COMBINING TERMS

Simplify by combining like terms:

1. $3a + 4b - 5a + 4c - 6b$ $\quad -2a - 2b + 4c$
2. $x - y + z - 4x - 4y - 3z$ $\quad -3x - 5y - 2z$
3. $3m - 4n + 4p - 6m - 8n - 4p$ $\quad -3m - 12n$
4. $3h - 4 + 7h - 5h - 2 - h$ $\quad 4h - 6$
5. $2abc - 3b + 2c - 5a - abc - 2a - 2c$ $\quad abc - 7a - 3b$
6. $2.3a + 1.7b - 4.5 - 4.4a - 5.2b$ $\quad -2.1a - 3.5b - 4.5$
7. $\frac{1}{2}x - \frac{1}{3}y + \frac{1}{6}x - \frac{1}{2}y$ $\quad \frac{2}{3}x - \frac{5}{6}y$
8. $2.3c + 4.1d + 5.2c - 8.6d + c$ $\quad 8.5c - 4.5d$
9. $10x^3 + 5x^2 - 2x + 1 - x^3 - 10x^2 - 2x - 1$ $\quad 9x^3 - 5x^2 - 4x$
10. $\frac{7}{9}c + \frac{1}{3}c + .4b - .15b$ $\quad \frac{10}{9}c + 0.25b$

ADDING POLYNOMIALS

Add:

1. $2x - 3y + 4z$, $5x - y - z$, and $-x - y + z$ $\quad 6x - 5y + 4z$
2. $3x^2 - 2x + 1$, $4x^2 - x - 9$, and $-6x^2 + 7x + 1$ $\quad x^2 + 4x - 7$
3. $4a + 3b - c$, $5a - c + b$, and $4b - 6a$ $\quad 3a + 8b - 2c$
4. $2x - 1$, $-3x + 2$, $4x - 5$, and $10x - 11$ $\quad 13x - 15$
5. $3ab - 4bc + 5cd$, $-bc + ab$, and $8ab - cd$ $\quad 12ab - 5bc + 4cd$
6. $x^3 - 2x^2y - xy^2 + 2y^3$ and $-x^3 - x^2y + 5xy^2 + y^3$ $\quad -3x^2y + 4xy^2 + 3y^3$
7. $ab^2 - a^2b + ab$ and $-ab^2 - 3a^2b + 4ab$ $\quad -4a^2b + 5ab$
8. $st + st^2 - t^3$, and $3st^2 - ts - 3t^3$ $\quad 4st^2 - 4t^3$
9. $.3x - 4.5y + 3.1z$ and $-.8x - 2.5y - .6z$ $\quad 0.5x - 7y + 2.5z$
10. $\frac{1}{2}x - \frac{1}{3}y + \frac{1}{5}z$ and $\frac{1}{3}x - \frac{1}{4}y - \frac{2}{3}z$ $\quad \frac{5}{6}x - \frac{7}{12}y - \frac{7}{15}z$

SUBTRACTING POLYNOMIALS

1. From $5x - 3y + 2z$ take $x + y + z$. $\quad 4x - 4y + z$
2. From $5a - 4b + 6c$ take $6a - 7b - 3c$. $\quad -a + 3b + 9c$
3. Take $2a + 3b - 7c$ from $-3a + 9b - 6c$. $\quad -5a + 6b + c$
4. Take $3x^3 - 2x^2 + 7$ from $5x^2 - 2x - 9$. $\quad -3x^3 + 7x^2 - 2x - 16$
5. Find the remainder when the subtrahend is $3x^2 - xy - y^2$ and the minuend is $x^2 - 4xy + y^2$. $\quad -2x^2 - 3xy + 2y^2$

ALGEBRA, BOOK ONE

6. The remainder is $x - 5$ and the subtrahend is $x^2 + 2x + 1$. Find the minuend. $x^2 + 3x - 4$

7. Subtract $ab - ac + 5\,ad$ from 0. $-ab + ac - 5\,ad$

8. How much smaller is $x^2 - 3$ than $2x + 1$? $-x^2 + 2x + 4$

9. How much larger than $8a - 5b$ is $-3a + 5b$? $-11a + 10b$

10. By how much does $4x - 5y + 1$ exceed $3y - x + 2$?
$5x - 8y - 1$

━━━━━━━━ **REMOVING PARENTHESES** ━━━━━━━━

Simplify:

1. $(3x - 4y + z) + (2x - y - z)$ $5x - 5y$

2. $(4a - 2b + c) - (3a - 4b - c)$ $a + 2b + 2c$

3. $4 + (x - 1) - (3x + 1)$ $-2x + 2$

4. $2k + (3k - 1) - [4k + 6]$ $k - 7$

5. $(2x^3 - 3x^2 + x) - (x^2 - 1) + 4x^2$ $2x^3 + x + 1$

6. $1 - x + (6x - 3) - (8 - 2x)$ $7x - 10$

7. $1 + 3(c - 1) - 4(2c - 4)$ $-5c + 14$

8. $1 + 3(x - 4) - 5(2x - 5)$ $-7x + 14$

9. $(3x - 1)4 - 5(6x + 7) + 3(x + 2)$ $-15x - 33$

10. $x(x - 3) - (x^2 - 6) - [x^2 - 2x + 9]$ $-x^2 - x - 3$

━━━━━━━━ **MULTIPLYING POLYNOMIALS** ━━━━━━━━

Multiply as indicated:

$a^2 + a - 6$ **1.** $(a + 3)(a - 2)$ $6x^2 - xy + 15y^2$ **6.** $(3x - 5y)(2x + 3y)$

$c^2 + 2c - 15$ **2.** $(c - 3)(c + 5)$ $x^3 - 3x^2 + 3x - 1$ **7.** $(x^2 - 2x + 1)(x - 1)$

$x^2 - y^2$ **3.** $(x - y)(x + y)$ $x^2 - y^2 + 2y - 1$ **8.** $(x - y + 1)(x + y - 1)$

$x^2 - 4y^2$ **4.** $(x - 2y)(x + 2y)$ $c^3 + c^2 + c + 6$ **9.** $(c^2 - c + 3)(c + 2)$

$c^2d^2 - 2cd - 3$ **5.** $(cd + 1)(cd - 3)$ $x^3 + y^3$ **10.** $(x^2 - xy + y^2)(x + y)$

━━━━━━━━ **DIVIDING POLYNOMIALS** ━━━━━━━━

Divide:

$m^2 - 2$ **1.** $4m^3 - 8m$ by $4m$ **5.** $6x^3 - 12x^2 - 30x$ by $-3x$

$-4x + 6$ **2.** $8x^2 - 12x$ by $-2x$ $-2x^2 + 4x + 10$ **6.** $8x^3y^2 - 16x^2y^4$ by $4x^2y^2$

$-c^2 + c$ **3.** $c^2 - c$ by -1 $2x - 4y^2$ **7.** $10x^3y - 15x^2y^2$ by $5x^2y$

$-c + 1$ **4.** $c^2 - c$ by $-c$ $2x - 3y$ **8.** $8x^4 - 4x^2 - 4x$ by $-4x$ $-2x^3 + x + 1$

544

9. $(x^2 + 8x + 12) \div (x + 2)$ $x+6$

10. $(a^2 - 13a + 12) \div (a - 1)$ $a-12$

11. $(x^2 - 2x - 35) \div (x + 5)$ $x-7$

12. $(4a^2 + 7ab - 2b^2) \div (4a - b)$ $a+2b$

13. $(x^3 - 3x^2 + 3x - 1) \div (x - 1)$ x^2-2x+1

14. $(12a^3 + 34a^2 - 30) \div (3a + 4)$ $4a^2+6a-8,$ Rem. 2

15. $(2c^3 - 5c + 6 - 3c^2) \div (c^2 + 2 - 3c)$ $2c+3$

16. $(8x^3 - y^3) \div (2x - y)$ $4x^2+2xy+y^2$

EVALUATION

If $a = 6$, $b = 3$, and $c = 2$, find the value of

1. a^2 36   **5.** abc 36   **9.** $a^2 - bc$ 30

2. b^3 27   **6.** $4abc$ 144   **10.** $ab - 8bc + 2ac$ -6

3. c^4 16   **7.** $a^2 - b^2$ 27   **11.** $a^3 + b^3 + c^3$ 251

4. $3a^2$ 108   **8.** $bc - 6$ 0   **12.** $5b - 4a + 3c$ -3

If $x = 4$, $y = -2$, and $z = -1$, find the value of

13. $2x - 3y + 1$ 15   **17.** $y^2 + 10z + z^2$ -5

14. $x^2 - 4x + y$ -2   **18.** $-4x - 3y + 5z$ -15

15. $xy + 8z - x$ -20   **19.** $xyz - y^2$ 4

16. $2xy - xy - y^2$ -12   **20.** $xy + 3yz$ -2

If $a = 6$, $b = -5$, and $c = 0$, find the value of

21. $a^2 + b^2 + c^2$ 61

22. $4abc - 10$ -10

23. $bc + a^3$ 216

24. $\dfrac{ab}{a + b}$ -30

25. $\dfrac{1}{a} + \dfrac{1}{b} + \dfrac{c}{1}$ $-\dfrac{1}{30}$

26. $\dfrac{5a^2 + 30ab}{ab}$ 24

27. $d = 2r$. Find d when $r = 15.1$. 30.2

28. $V = \pi r^2 h$. Find V when $\pi = 3.14$, $r = 20$, and $h = 30$. 37,680

29. $S = 180(n - 2)$. Find S when $n = 11$. 1620

30. $A = \dfrac{h}{2}(b + b')$. Find A when $b = 8$, $b' = 14$, and $h = 1$. 11

31. $S = \frac{1}{2}gt^2$. Find S when $t = 5$ and $g = 32.16$. 402

32. $C = \dfrac{V}{R}$. Find C when $V = 832$ and $R = 40$. 20.8

ALGEBRA, BOOK ONE

SPECIAL PRODUCTS AND FACTORING

Write the products:

$xa+xb$ **1.** $x(a+b)$ $12x^2+5x-25$ **9.** $(3x+5)(4x-5)$

$3am-3bm+3cm$ **2.** $3m(a-b+c)$ $x^2+4xy+4y^2$ **10.** $(x+2y)^2$

x^2+6x+9 **3.** $(x+3)^2$ $3a^4x+3a^3x^2+3a^2x^3$ **11.** $3a^2x(a^2+ax+x^2)$

$4x^2-4x+1$ **4.** $(2x-1)^2$ $14x^2+5xy-y^2$ **12.** $(7x-y)(2x+y)$

x^2-16 **5.** $(x+4)(x-4)$ $9x^2-12xy+4y^2$ **13.** $(3x-2y)^2$

$3ab-a^2b^2$ **6.** $ab(3-ab)$ $-5a^3+5ab^2$ **14.** $-5a(a^2-b^2)$

$9x^2+30x+25$ **7.** $(3x+5)^2$ $1-a^2$ **15.** $(1-a)(1+a)$

$a^2-12a+35$ **8.** $(a-5)(a-7)$ a^4-9 **16.** $(a^2-3)(a^2+3)$

Find the prime factors: *(23-34 at bottom of page. 39-42 at top)*

$2(x-y)$ **17.** $2x-2y$ **23.** m^2-4n^2 **29.** $a^2+ab-20b^2$

$x(x^3-1)$ **18.** x^4-x **24.** $a^2+2ab+b^2$ **30.** $2x^2+x-6$

$4xy(1-2xy)$ **19.** $4xy-8x^2y^2$ **25.** $1+4b+4b^2$ **31.** $3a^2-4a-4$

$P(1+rt)$ **20.** $P+Prt$ **26.** $9-c^2$ **32.** $6x^3+x^2-5x$

$(a-b)(a+b)$ **21.** a^2-b^2 **27.** x^2+3x+2 **33.** a^3-a

$(x-4)(x+4)$ **22.** x^2-16 **28.** x^2-6x-7 **34.** $4a-4ab^2$

$x(x-2)(x+2)$ **35.** x^3-4x **39.** $4n^2-16n-20$

$2(b+3)^2$ **36.** $2b^2+12b+18$ **40.** $a^4+2a^3+a^2$

$2c(c-3)(c-2)$ **37.** $2c^3-10c^2+12c$ **41.** $20a-8ax-ax^2$

$3(x+9y)(x-5y)$ **38.** $3x^2+12xy-135y^2$ **42.** a^4-81

LINEAR EQUATIONS

Solve:

1. $3x-6=x+10$ 8 **9.** $7(m-4)-(m-4)=0$ 4

2. $x+6=-5x+12$ 1 **10.** $3(x-2)-3=0$ 3

3. $-2c+8=c-4$ 4 **11.** $2(y-6)=3(y-2)$ -6

4. $x-3=0$ 3 **12.** $x^2+3=(x+5)(x+9)$ -3

5. $8+x=-x+5$ $-1\frac{1}{2}$ **13.** $(x+1)^2-(x-2)^2=21$ 4

6. $10h+1=8h+2$ $\frac{1}{2}$ **14.** $4-(x-2)(x+7)=24-x^2$ $-1\frac{1}{5}$

7. $4r-10=7r+5$ -5

8. $x-3(x+4)=2$ -7 **15.** $\dfrac{x}{2}-\dfrac{x}{3}=2$ 12

546

23. $(m+2n)(m-2n)$ **27.** $(x+1)(x+2)$ **31.** $(a-2)(3a+2)$

24. $(a+b)^2$ **28.** $(x-7)(x+1)$ **32.** $x(x+1)(6x-5)$

25. $(1+2b)^2$ **29.** $(a+5b)(a-4b)$ **33.** $a(a+1)(a-1)$

26. $(3-c)(3+c)$ **30.** $(2x-3)(x+2)$ **34.** $4a(1+b)(1-b)$

16. $\frac{3n}{4} + \frac{2n}{5} = \frac{5n}{6} + \frac{19}{3}$ *20*

19. $3 - \frac{3x}{2} = \frac{8-4x}{7}$ *2*

17. $3(4-x) - 7(x-2) = 9x + 7$ *1*

20. $\frac{x-5}{2} + \frac{x+5}{2} = 0$ *0*

18. $\frac{5}{6}x + 21 = \frac{2}{3}x + 18$ *-18*

21. $\frac{4x+3}{7} - \frac{x+5}{3} = 4$ *22*

22. $\frac{c-12}{10} = \frac{3(2c+1)}{5} - \frac{3c-6}{2}$ *12*

23. $\frac{5}{x+4} = \frac{4}{x-4}$ *36*

29. $\frac{3}{x+4} + \frac{1}{x} = \frac{4}{x-2}$ *-2/5*

24. $\frac{c+5}{c-3} = \frac{1}{2}$ *-13*

30. $\frac{2}{m-3} + \frac{1}{m+1} = \frac{3}{m-4}$ *6/7*

25. $\frac{x}{x-3} + \frac{3}{x+2} = \frac{x^2}{x^2-x-6}$ *1 4/5*

31. $\frac{x+1}{x-1} - \frac{x-1}{x+1} = \frac{5x+2}{x^2-1}$ *-2*

26. $\frac{1}{x} + \frac{1}{x+3} = \frac{2}{x-3}$ *-1*

32. $\frac{4x+8}{2x-3} = \frac{2(x+3)}{x-1}$ *5*

27. $3(y+2) - 2(y-3\frac{1}{2}) = 15$ *2*

33. $\frac{4c}{2c-1} = \frac{2c}{2c+1} + 1$ *-1/6*

28. $\frac{2}{x} + \frac{3}{x-1} = \frac{5}{x+1}$ *1/4*

34. $\frac{2r-1}{r} - \frac{r}{r-1} = 1$ *1/2*

QUADRATIC EQUATIONS

Solve by factoring:

1. $x^2 - 4x = 0$ *0, 4*
5. $x^2 + x = 42$ *6, -7*
8. $4x^2 - 20x = 0$ *0, 5*

2. $x^2 - 36 = 0$ *±6*
6. $2x^2 + x = 28$ *3½, -4*
9. $x + 7 = \frac{18}{x}$ *2, -9*

3. $x^2 - 3x + 2 = 0$ *2, 1*
7. $\frac{x^2}{3} = 27$ *±9*

4. $x^2 - 4x = 96$ *12, -8*

Solve by completing the square or by formula:

10. $2x^2 - 3x + 1 = 0$ *1, 1/2*
15. $m^2 - 2m + 1 = 0$ *1, 1*

11. $y^2 - 6y = 1$ *3 ± √10; or 6.162, -0.162*
16. $y^2 + \frac{5}{2}y = 6$ *1/2, -4*

12. $x^2 - 7x + 2 = 0$

17. $3x^2 + 2x = 8$ *1/3, -2*

13. $y^2 - 3y - 10 = 0$ *5, -2*
18. $(x+1)^2 - 9 = 0$ *2, -4*

14. $2x^2 - 7x + 3 = 0$ *3, 1/2*
19. $3h^2 - 10h + 3 = 0$ *3, 1/3*

12. $\frac{7 ± \sqrt{41}}{2}$; or 6.702, 0.298

$\dfrac{9 \pm 7\sqrt{17}}{8}$, or

$4.733, -2.483$

20. $\dfrac{4(x^2 - 5)}{x^2 - 9} = \dfrac{9}{x - 3}$

22. $\dfrac{x - 3}{2x} + 5 = \dfrac{9x + 7}{3x - 5}$ $5, \frac{1}{5}$

24. $\dfrac{x + 5}{x^2 - 3x} = \dfrac{4x}{x - 3}$ $1\frac{1}{4}, -1$

23. $\dfrac{1}{x} + \dfrac{2}{x - 3} = \dfrac{5}{6}$ $6, \frac{3}{5}$

Solve for y:

24. $ay^2 + by + c = 0$ $\dfrac{-b \pm \sqrt{b^2 - 4ac}}{2a}$

25. $y^2 + 2(b - 1) + b^2 = 0$ $\pm \sqrt{2 - 2b - b^2}$

RADICAL EQUATIONS

Solve:

1. $2\sqrt{x} = 1$ $\frac{1}{4}$

2. $\sqrt{2x} - 6 = 0$ 18

3. $\sqrt{x} - 7 = 0$ 49

4. $\sqrt{x - 5} = 2$ 9

5. $2\sqrt{y + 2} = 6$ 7

6. $\sqrt{2x - 7} - 5 = 0$ 16

7. $x - 7 = \sqrt{x^2 - 7}$ no solution

8. $4 + \sqrt{x + 1} = x - 1$ 8

SETS OF EQUATIONS

Solve:

$x = 2, y = 1$ **1.** $2x + 3y = 7$
$\qquad 4x - 5y = 3$

$x = 4, y = -1$ **2.** $5x - 3y = 23$
$\qquad x + y = 3$

$x = 4, y = 5$ **7.** $\dfrac{x}{4} - \dfrac{y}{5} = 0$
$\qquad x - y = -1$

$x = 24, y = 15$ **8.** $\dfrac{x}{3} + \dfrac{y}{5} = 11$
$\qquad \dfrac{x}{2} - \dfrac{y}{3} = 7$

$x = 2, y = -2$ **3.** $3x + y = 4$
$\qquad x + 3y = -4$

4. $4m - 5n = 8$
$\qquad 2m + 3n = 10$ 12
$\qquad m = \frac{37}{11}, n = \frac{12}{11}$

9. $\dfrac{7y - 4}{5} + \dfrac{2x - 3}{2} = \dfrac{3}{2}$

$x = 1, y = 2$ $\dfrac{5x - 2}{3} + \dfrac{2y + 1}{5} = 2$

10. $\dfrac{2x - y}{2} + \dfrac{x + y}{4} = 8$

$x = 6, y = -2$ $3(x + y) - (x - y) = 4$

$x = -1, y = -5$ **5.** $3x = 5y + 22$
$\qquad 5x - y = 0$

6. $c = d + 3$
$\qquad 4d - c = 12$ $c = 8, d = 5$

FRACTIONS

Reduce to lowest terms:

$\dfrac{2}{3b}$ **1.** $\dfrac{4a}{6ab}$

$\dfrac{2}{3x}$ **2.** $\dfrac{6xy}{9x^2y}$

$\dfrac{1}{x - y}$ **3.** $\dfrac{x + y}{x^2 - y^2}$

$\dfrac{x - y}{x + 2y}$ **4.** $\dfrac{(x - y)^2}{x^2 + xy - 2y^2}$

$\dfrac{a}{a + 3}$ **5.** $\dfrac{a^2 - 4a}{a^2 - a - 12}$

$\dfrac{b}{x + b}$ **6.** $\dfrac{bx + b^2}{x^2 + 2bx + b^2}$

Multiply:

7. $\dfrac{15\,a^6}{8\,y^2}\cdot\dfrac{16\,y^3}{5\,a^4}$ $6a^2y$

9. $\dfrac{x^2+4x+4}{x^2-x-6}\cdot\dfrac{x^2-6x+9}{3x+6}$ $\dfrac{x-3}{3}$

8. $\dfrac{3\,y}{7\,x}\cdot\dfrac{21\,x}{9\,y^3}\cdot\dfrac{2\,y^2}{5\,x}$ $\dfrac{2}{5x}$

10. $\dfrac{7\,a-14}{1-x^2}\cdot\dfrac{2\,x+2}{5\,a-10}$ $\dfrac{14}{5-5x}$

Divide:

11. $\dfrac{4\,x^2}{3\,y}\div\dfrac{x}{9\,y}$ $12x$

14. $\dfrac{a^2-1}{a^2-4}\div\dfrac{3\,a-3}{5\,a+10}$ $\dfrac{5(a+1)}{3(a-2)}$

12. $\dfrac{4\,b}{5\,m}\div\dfrac{6\,abc}{m^3}$ $\dfrac{2m^2}{15ac}$

15. $\dfrac{a+4}{a^2+2\,a-3}\div\dfrac{3\,a+12}{a^2+3\,a}$ $\dfrac{a}{3(a-1)}$

13. $\dfrac{x^2-4}{x^2-1}\div\dfrac{x+2}{x-1}$ $\dfrac{x-2}{x+1}$

16. $\dfrac{x^2-25}{x^2+10x+25}\div\dfrac{x^2+5x}{x^2+2x-15}$ $\dfrac{(x-5)(x-3)}{x(x+5)}$

Combine:

17. $\dfrac{x}{3}-\dfrac{2\,x}{7}$ $\dfrac{x}{21}$

22. $\dfrac{a-1}{a+1}+\dfrac{a+1}{a-1}$ $\dfrac{2a^2+2}{(a+1)(a-1)}$

18. $\dfrac{a}{b}+1$ $\dfrac{a+b}{b}$

23. $\dfrac{4\,x}{x^2-9}+\dfrac{5}{x+3}$ $\dfrac{9x-15}{(x+3)(x-3)}$

19. $\dfrac{c}{d}+\dfrac{d}{c}$ $\dfrac{c^2+d^2}{cd}$

24. $\dfrac{x^2+2\,x}{x^2+7\,x+10}-\dfrac{x-3}{x+2}$ $\dfrac{15}{(x+2)(x+5)}$

20. $\dfrac{2}{a}+\dfrac{3}{b}-\dfrac{4}{c}$

25. $\dfrac{5\,x}{x-3}+\dfrac{x^2-2\,x}{x^2-5\,x+6}$ $\dfrac{6x}{x-3}$

21. $\dfrac{x-1}{2}-\dfrac{x+3}{3}$ $\dfrac{x-9}{6}$

26. $\dfrac{c-1}{c^2-3\,c}+\dfrac{1}{c}$ $\dfrac{2c-4}{c^2-3c}$

27. $\dfrac{a+2}{a+3}+\dfrac{a-3}{a+1}-\dfrac{a^2-6}{a^2+4\,a+3}$ $\dfrac{a^2+3a-1}{(a+3)(a+1)}$

28. $\dfrac{5\,b-1}{b^2+3\,b}+\dfrac{6\,b}{b^2+8\,b+15}-\dfrac{2\,b+1}{b^2+5\,b}$ $\dfrac{9b^2+17b-8}{b(b+3)(b+5)}$

Change to simple fractions:

29. $\dfrac{1+\dfrac{1}{a}}{a-\dfrac{1}{a}}$ $\dfrac{1}{a-1}$

31. $\dfrac{4\,a-\dfrac{1}{a}}{2+\dfrac{1}{a}}$ $2a-1$

30. $\dfrac{\dfrac{a^2-1}{a}}{\dfrac{a-1}{a^2}}$ $a(a+1)$

32. $\dfrac{a+b+\dfrac{b^2}{a}}{a+b+\dfrac{a^2}{b}}$ $\dfrac{b}{a}$

$\dfrac{2bc+3ac-4ab}{abc}$

549

POWERS AND ROOTS

Find the following powers:

81   **1.** 9^2 *$4a^2$*   **4.** $(-2a)^2$ *$0.01c^4$*   **7.** $(.1\,c^2)^2$

a^6   **2.** $(a^2)^3$ *$-64m^3$*   **5.** $(-4m)^3$ *$\frac{1}{8}a^3b^6$*   **8.** $(\frac{1}{2}ab^2)^3$

a^6   **3.** $(a^3)^2$ *x^6y^3*   **6.** $(x^2y)^3$ *$1.728x^6$*   **9.** $(1.2\,r^2)^3$

Find the indicated roots:

10b   **10.** $\sqrt{100\,b^2}$ *-4*   **14.** $-\sqrt{16}$ *$0.3h^3$*   **18.** $\sqrt[3]{.027\,h^9}$

$8a^3$ **11.** $\sqrt{64\,a^6}$ *$-5y^2$*   **15.** $\sqrt[3]{-125\,y^6}$ *$7y$*   **19.** $\sqrt{49\,y^2}$

$-2m$ **12.** $\sqrt[3]{-8\,m^3}$ *$4x^2y$*   **16.** $\sqrt{16\,x^4y^2}$ *$-a^5b^6$*   **20.** $-\sqrt{a^{10}b^{12}}$

x^3y^2   **13.** $\sqrt{x^6y^4}$ *$1.2c^4$*   **17.** $\sqrt{1.44\,c^8}$ *ab^2c^3*   **21.** $\sqrt{a^2b^4c^6}$

Find the positive square root of

33   **22.** 1089   *3.685*   **24.** 13.5776   *.287*   **26.** .082369

10.8   **23.** 116.64   *111.3*   **25.** 12387.69   *.0369*   **27.** .00136161

Simplify:

$4\sqrt{2}$ **28.** $\sqrt{32}$ *$9\sqrt{3}$*   **31.** $3\sqrt{27}$ *$10\sqrt{5}$*   **34.** $5\sqrt{20}$ *$\frac{1}{3}\sqrt{6}$*   **37.** $\sqrt{\frac{2}{3}}$

14   **29.** $\sqrt{196}$ *$a\sqrt{a}$*   **32.** $\sqrt{a^3}$ *$a^2\sqrt{b}$*   **35.** $\sqrt{a^4b}$ *$\frac{1}{2}\sqrt{2}$*   **38.** $\sqrt{\frac{1}{2}}$

$5\sqrt{2}$ **30.** $\sqrt{50}$ *$4\sqrt{6}$*   **33.** $2\sqrt{24}$ *$4\sqrt{3}$*   **36.** $2\sqrt{12}$ *$\frac{2}{5}\sqrt{5}$*   **39.** $\sqrt{\frac{4}{5}}$

$-\sqrt{3}$ **40.** $2\sqrt{3}-\sqrt{27}$ *$3\sqrt{3}$*   **44.** $\sqrt{48}+4\sqrt{3}-5\sqrt{3}$

$8\sqrt{2}$ **41.** $\sqrt{18}+\sqrt{50}$ *$6-2\sqrt{2}+2\sqrt{3}$*   **45.** $\sqrt{36}-\sqrt{8}+\sqrt{12}$

$\sqrt{5}$ **42.** $\sqrt{20}-\sqrt{5}$ *$2\sqrt{2}$*   **46.** $3\sqrt{8}+4\sqrt{\frac{1}{2}}-6\sqrt{2}$

$\frac{1}{3}\sqrt{3}$ **43.** $\sqrt{27}-8\sqrt{\frac{1}{3}}$ *$12\sqrt{3}$*   **47.** $5\sqrt{12}+2\sqrt{27}-4\sqrt{3}$

$-11\sqrt{2}-18\sqrt{5}$ **48.** $2\sqrt{50}-3\sqrt{98}+10\sqrt{\frac{1}{5}}-4\sqrt{125}$

Rationalize the denominators:

$\frac{4}{3}\sqrt{3}$ **49.** $\dfrac{4}{\sqrt{3}}$ *$\sqrt{7}$*   **52.** $\dfrac{7}{\sqrt{7}}$ *$\frac{2}{9}\sqrt{3}$*   **55.** $\dfrac{2}{3\sqrt{3}}$

$\frac{1}{2}\sqrt{2}$ **50.** $\dfrac{1}{\sqrt{2}}$ *$\frac{1}{2}\sqrt{6}$*   **53.** $\dfrac{\sqrt{3}}{\sqrt{2}}$ *$1+\frac{1}{2}\sqrt{6}$*   **56.** $\dfrac{\sqrt{2}+\sqrt{3}}{\sqrt{2}}$

$\frac{1}{3}\sqrt{15}$ **51.** $\dfrac{\sqrt{5}}{\sqrt{3}}$ *$\frac{3}{4}\sqrt{2}$*   **54.** $\dfrac{3}{\sqrt{8}}$ *$\frac{2}{3}\sqrt{15}$*   **57.** $\dfrac{2\sqrt{5}}{\sqrt{3}}$

1. Two boys received $1.60 for mowing a lawn. If the older boy did three times as much work as the younger, how much money should each boy receive? *Younger, 40¢; older, $1.20*

2. A rectangle is four times as long as it is wide, and the perimeter is 300 inches. Find the width and length of the rectangle. (Always make a drawing for a problem, if possible.) *l, 120 in.; w, 30 in.*

3. The number of boys in an algebra class is one less than three times the number of girls. If there are 39 pupils in the class, how many of them are girls? *10*

4. The sum of a certain number and 6 is 19. What is the number? *13*

5. 42 is equal to a certain number increased by 14. What is the number? *28*

6. Four times a certain number equals 96 increased by the number. What is the number? *32*

7. If 20 is added to three times a certain number, the sum is 101. Find the number. *27*

8. The sum of two numbers is 620 and the larger is 3 times the smaller. What are the numbers? *155, 465*

9. The sum of two numbers is 63 and one is 27 larger than the other. What are the numbers? *18, 45*

10. The sum of two numbers is 44 and one exceeds the other by 18. What are the numbers? *13, 31*

11. Four times a certain number, decreased by 5, equals 25 decreased by 6 times the number. What is the number? *3*

12. The number of B grades in a class was 4 times the number of A grades, the number of C grades was 6 times the number of A grades, the number of D grades equaled the number of B grades, and the number of E grades equaled the number of A grades. If there were 32 grades in all, how many of each kind were there? *A and E, 2 each; B and D, 8 each; C, 12*

13. One truck can carry 4 tons of freight at a time, and a larger truck can carry 6 tons at a time. How many trips must each truck make if they make a total haul of 58 tons and the smaller truck makes 2 more trips than the larger? *5, 7*

14. The difference of two numbers is 10. If twice the larger is subtracted from five times the smaller, the remainder is 22. What are the numbers? *14, 24*

15. The sum of two numbers is 62. Three times the smaller exceeds twice the larger by one. Find the numbers. *25, 37*

16. The sum of two numbers is 45. If 3 times the larger is increased by 4 times the smaller, the sum is 155. Find the numbers. *20, 25*

17. Separate 1200 into two parts so that one part shall be 800 less than three times the other. *500, 700*

18. A farmer sold 425 bushels of wheat and oats for $1268.25. How many bushels of each did he sell if he received $4.10 a bushel for the wheat and $1.39 for the oats? *250 wheat, 175 oats*

19. The sum of two numbers is 108. If twice their difference is subtracted from the smaller, the remainder is 9. What are the numbers? *63, 45*

20. The sum of two numbers is 40. The difference of five times the larger and four times the smaller exceeds seven times the smaller by 8. Find the numbers. *28, 12*

21. The perimeter of a rectangle is 156 inches. If the length is decreased by 13 inches and the width is increased by 13 inches, the figure becomes a square. What are the dimensions of the rectangle? *length, 52 in.; width, 26 in.*

22. John thought of a number and multiplied it by 5. He then subtracted 92 from the result and found that the difference thus obtained lacked 11 of being twice the number he first chose. What was the original number? *27*

23. A man gave to one son one third of his money, and to another son one fourth of his money. He had $10 left. How much had he at first? *$24*

24. If two pianos cost $600 more than four radios, and if five pianos cost $1350 more than 12 radios, find the cost of a piano and of a radio. *Piano, $450; radio, $75*

25. The sum of two numbers is 19, and the sum of their squares is 185. Find the numbers. *8, 11*

26. The difference of two numbers is 2 and the sum of the squares is 74. What are the numbers? *-7, -5; or 5, 7*

27. The denominator of a fraction exceeds its numerator by 3. If each term of the fraction is increased by 7, the value of the new fraction is $\frac{3}{4}$. What was the original fraction? $\frac{2}{5}$

28. The numerator of a certain fraction is 2 less than half the denominator, and the value of the fraction is $\frac{1}{3}$. What is the fraction? $\frac{4}{12}$

29. Twice the square of a number, decreased by 5 times the number, equals 3. Find the number. $-\frac{1}{2}$ or 3

30. If the square of a number is subtracted from 8 times the number, the remainder is 12. What is the number? 2 or 6

PERCENTAGE PROBLEMS

1. A man spends 18% of his monthly salary for rent. If his rent is $135 a month, what is his salary for a month? $750

2. How much money must a man invest at 4% to produce an annual income of $600? $15,000

3. A number decreased by 10% of itself equals 405. What is the number? 450

4. A number increased by 16% of itself equals 185.6. Find the number. 160

5. A merchant sold goods for $2592 and made a gain of 8% of the cost. Find the cost if there was no overhead. $2400

6. How cheaply can a grocer sell berries that cost 64 cents a quart if he must make a profit of 20% of the selling price? 80¢ a qt

7. 500% of a number is 75. Find the number. 15

8. A man sold an automobile for $1295, which was 30% less than it cost. What did the car cost? $1850

9. When wheat is ground into flour, 18% of the wheat is a by-product. How much wheat is needed to make 100 pounds of flour? 122.0 lb.

10. A dealer wishes to buy hats that can be retailed at $3.92. At what price must he buy them if the margin is 40% of the cost? $2.80

11. One of two complementary angles is 25% larger than the other. How large is each? 40°, 50°

12. The population of a certain city has increased 15% in the last 10 years. If the present population is 109,200, what was the population 10 years ago? *94,957 approx.*

13. A number less $12\frac{1}{2}$% of itself is 567. What is the number? *648*

14. A chair sold for $10.08 after discounts of 30% and 20% were made. What was the list price? *$18*

15. Dick's father sold his plane for $12,150. This was 10% less than the plane cost him. What was the cost of the plane? *$13,500*

16. A man bought a bicycle and sold it for $96, gaining as many per cent of the cost as the cost of the bicycle in dollars. Find the cost of the bicycle. *$60*

COIN PROBLEMS

1. A man has two more nickels than dimes, and has $1.15 in all. How many coins of each kind has he? *7 dimes, 9 nickels*

2. A boy has twice as many nickels as dimes, and 5 more half dollars than nickels. Find the number of each kind of coins if their total value is $6.10. *3 dimes, 6 nickels, 11 half-dollars*

3. A girl has two more nickels than dimes, and three more quarters than nickels, having in all $3.35. How many coins of each kind has she? *5 dimes, 7 nickels, 10 quarters.*

4. A purse contains 21 coins, consisting of nickels and dimes. How many coins of each kind does it contain if their total value is $1.65? *9 nickels, 12 dimes*

5. A safe contains 120 coins, the value of which is $10. If the coins consist of nickels and dimes, how many of each kind are in it? *40 nickels, 80 dimes*

6. A sum of $14 is made up of 92 coins, consisting of dimes and quarters. How many are there of each? *60 dimes, 32 quarters*

7. Dick gave the grocer $3.60, consisting of 20 half dollars, quarters, and nickels. If there were 3 times as many nickels as half dollars, how many coins of each kind were there? *12 nickels, 4 quarters, 4 half-dollars*

8. The value of some nickels and quarters is $1.60. If there are one third as many nickels as quarters, how many nickels are there? *2*

9. A boy's coins, consisting of nickels and dimes, amount to $2.15. If the number of dimes exceeds 3 times the number of nickels by 4, find the number of each kind of coin. *5 nickels, 19 dimes*

10. A newsboy had $2.65, consisting of nickels, dimes, and quarters. If the number of dimes exceeded the number of nickels by 1, and if the number of quarters was equal to the number of nickels decreased by 1, what was the number of each kind of coin? *7 nickels, 8 dimes, 6 quarters*

AGE PROBLEMS

1. Henry is 10 years older than John. In 8 years twice Henry's age will equal 3 times John's age. How old is each now? *John, 12 yr.; Henry, 22 yr.*

2. Roy is 5 years older than Bert. If the sum of their ages in six years will be 33 years, how old is each now? *Bert, 8 yr.; Roy, 13 yr.*

3. The sum of the ages of Mary and her mother is 60 years. In 20 years twice Mary's age, increased by her mother's age then, will equal 138 years. How old is each? *Mary, 18 yr.; mother, 42 yr.*

4. Robert is 14 years old and his father is 38 years old. How many years ago was the father 7 times as old as the boy? *10*

5. A man was 30 years old when his son was born. His age now exceeds 3 times his son's age by 6 years. How old is each? *Man, 42 yr.; son, 12 yr.*

6. Two years ago a man was 4 times as old as his son. In 3 years the father will be only 3 times as old as his son. How old is each? *Man, 42 yr.; son, 12 yr.*

7. Frank is 4 times as old as Karl. In 10 years he will be only twice as old as Karl. How old is each now? *Karl, 5 yr., Frank, 20 yr.*

8. The sum of the ages of a father and son is 49 years. Four years ago the father's age was one year more than 3 times the son's age. How old is each now? *Father, 35 yr.; son, 14 yr.*

9. John's age is 3 years more than twice Bill's age. Three years ago John was 4 times as old as Bill was then. How old is each now? *Bill, 6 yr.; John, 15 yr.*

10. Ann is 7 years older than Jane. One year ago she was twice as old as Jane. How old is each now? *Jane, 8 yr.; Ann, 15 yr.*

11. Frank is 5 times as old as Dick. Two years ago he was 7 times as old as Dick. How old is each now? *Dick, 6 yr.; Frank, 30 yr.*

12. Jim is 10 years old and his father is 3 times as old. In how many years will Jim be half as old as his father? *10*

GEOMETRY PROBLEMS

1. The perimeter of a rectangle is 170 feet. If the length exceeds 5 times the width by 1 foot, what is the area of the rectangle? *994 sq. ft.*

2. One angle of a triangle exceeds another by 12°, and the third angle exceeds twice the smallest by 48°. How large is each angle? *30°, 42°, 108°*

3. Five times one of two complementary angles equals four times the other. How large is each? *40°, 50°*

4. Two angles are supplementary. If 7 times the smaller is subtracted from 3 times the larger, the difference is 190°. How large is each? *35°, 145°*

5. Find the angle whose supplement is three times its complement. *45°*

6. One angle of a triangle is 115° larger than another. The third angle exceeds twice the smallest by 9 degrees. How large is each angle? *14°, 129°, 37°*

7. One angle of a triangle exceeds another by 2 degrees. The sum of these two angles exceeds the third angle by 28°. How large is each angle? *51°, 53°, 76°*

8. How large a rectangular field, whose length is to exceed twice its width by 10 rods, can be enclosed by a mile of fence? *50 rd. × 119 rd.*

9. Find the circumference of a circle whose radius is 30 inches. *188.4 in.*

10. Find the radius of a circle whose circumference is 148 inches. *23.57 in., approx.*

11. How large is each angle of a triangle in which the second angle is 10° more than the first and the third is 5° less than three times the first? *First, 35°; second; 45°; third, 100°*

12. What are the lengths of the sides of a triangle whose perimeter is 226 inches if the second side is three fourths as long as the first and the third side is 28 inches longer than the first? *First, 72 in.; second, 54 in.; third, 100 in.*

13. The length of a rectangle is 2 feet more than twice its width, and its perimeter is 40 feet. Find its area. *84 sq. ft.*

14. Find the angle whose supplement is 6 degrees larger than 8 times its complement. *78°*

15. The length of a rectangle exceeds twice its width by 4 feet. The area of the rectangle is 144 square feet more than twice that of a square whose side equals the width of the rectangle. What are the dimensions of the rectangle? *W., 36 ft.; L., 76 ft.*

16. One of two complementary angles exceeds the square of the other by 18°. How large are the two angles? *8°, 82°*

17. A tree 50 feet high casts a shadow 42 feet long at the same time that another tree casts a shadow 24 feet long. How high is the second tree? *28 4/7 ft.*

18. The hypotenuse of a right triangle is 117 feet. Find the other two sides if their sum is 153 feet. *45 ft., 108 ft.*

LEVER PROBLEMS

1. Jack, who sits 6 feet from the fulcrum, balances Carl who sits 8 feet from the fulcrum. If Jack weighs 70 pounds, how much does Carl weigh? *52 1/2 lb.*

2. Mary, who weighs 135 pounds and sits 4 feet from the fulcrum, balances Imogen who weighs 67.5 pounds. How far from the fulcrum is Imogen? *8 ft.*

3. A weight of 30 pounds balances a weight of 50 pounds on the other side of the fulcrum. If one weight is 2 feet farther from the fulcrum than the other, where is each weight located? *30-lb. weight 5 ft. from fulcrum; 50-lb. wt., 3 ft.*

4. The weight on the short arm of a lever is 27 pounds more than the weight on the other arm. If the arms are 6 feet and 8 feet, find each weight. *108 lb., 81 lb.*

5. Two weights whose sum is 128 pounds are placed at the ends of a balanced lever. If one arm is 7 feet long and the other arm is 9 feet long, find the two weights. *72 lb., 56 lb.*

6. Where is the fulcrum of a lever 93 inches long if a weight of 70 pounds at one end balances a weight of 54 pounds at the other? *40.5 in. from 70-lb weight.*

7. Charlene weighs 60 pounds and Jane 70 pounds. They have a ten-foot teeterboard. How far from Charlene must the fulcrum be placed in order that the two girls may balance each other?

8. Packages weighing 30 pounds and 35 pounds respectively are hung from the ends of a six-foot rod. How far from the 35-pound weight must the fulcrum be placed in order that the two packages may balance?

9. Robert and Arthur are playing seesaw. Their weights balance when Robert is 6 feet from the fulcrum and Arthur is 7 feet from the fulcrum. If Robert weighs 84 pounds, how much does Arthur weigh?

10. Tom and Dick balance on a teeterboard when they are 6 feet and 8 feet respectively from the point of support. If Dick is replaced by Harry, who weighs 5 pounds more, it is found that Tom must sit $6\frac{1}{2}$ feet from the fulcrum. What is the weight of each boy?

MOTION PROBLEMS

1. *A* goes 8 miles an hour and *B* goes 20 miles an hour in the opposite direction. How many hours has *B* been traveling when they are 180 miles apart, if *A* starts 2 hours before *B*?

2. *A* and *B*, who are 566 miles apart, start in automobiles to meet each other, *A* driving 40 miles an hour and *B* driving 36 miles an hour. How soon will they meet if *A* has an accident and is delayed for 2 hours?

3. A boat starts from Baltimore for Norfolk at 10 miles an hour. Two hours later another boat starts from Baltimore for Norfolk at 14 miles an hour. How long will it take the second boat to overtake the first?

4. Train *A* travels at the rate of 40 miles an hour and train *B* at the rate of 34 miles an hour. Train *A* leaves Philadelphia for Harrisburg at 8 o'clock. Train *B* leaves Harrisburg for Philadelphia at 9 o'clock. The distance between the two cities is 100 miles. How long will train *B* travel before meeting train *A*?

5. Two trains start at the same time from towns 385 miles apart and meet in 5 hours. If the rate of one train is 7 miles an hour less than the rate of the other, what is the rate of each?

6. Two automobiles started toward each other at the same time from points 300 miles apart and met in 5 hours. If one traveled twice as rapidly as the other, what were their rates? *20 m.p.h., 40 m.p.h.*

7. Two airplanes are traveling in opposite directions at the rate of 490 and 510 miles an hour, respectively. If they started at the same time from the same place, how soon after the start will they be 1500 miles apart? *In 1½ hr.*

8. An automobile makes a trip of 280 miles in 7 hours and 20 minutes. In making the trip it goes 28 miles through towns and the remainder of the distance on a national highway. If the speed through the towns is half of that on the highway, what is the speed through the towns? *21 m.p.h.*

9. An airplane can go 990 miles with the wind in the same time that it can go 930 miles against the wind. If the rate of the wind is 15 miles an hour, what is the rate of the airplane in still air? *480 m.p.h.*

10. A certain train makes a daily run of 260 miles. One day the train is one hour late in starting, and the engineer runs the train 13 miles an hour faster than usual to arrive on time. What is the usual rate of the train? *52 m.p.h.*

WORK PROBLEMS

1. *A* can do a piece of work in 10 days and *B* can do it in 8 days. If they work together, how many days are needed? *4 4/9 da*

2. One pipe can fill a cistern in 12 hours and a smaller pipe can fill the cistern in 15 hours. If both pipes are used, how many hours are needed? *6 2/3 hr.*

3. Frank can hoe the garden in 7 hours and Bill can hoe it in 9 hours. If both are at work how many hours are needed? *3 15/16 hr.*

4. *A* can do a piece of work in 15 days and *B* can do it in 20 days. If *A* works 5 days alone on the job and then *B* helps him to complete it, how long does *B* work? *5 5/7 da.*

5. One printing press can produce 4000 evening papers in an hour, and a second press can produce 3000 of the papers in an hour. After the first press has been printing for 1½ hours it must stop for repairs. How much time will be needed for the second press to run in order to complete the daily edition of 15,000 papers? *3 hr.*

6. Two backhoes working together can excavate for a building foundation in 80 hours. If one backhoe can do the work $\frac{2}{3}$ as fast as the other, how long would it take each backhoe to do the work alone? *slower shovel, 200 hr.; faster, 133⅓ hr.*

7. One section gang can lay a mile of oil pipe in 8 days. With the help of a second gang of men, the work can be done in 5 days. How long would it take the second gang to lay the oil pipe working alone? *13⅓ da.*

8. *A* can do a piece of work in 5 days, *B* can do it in 7 days, and *C* can do it in 10 days. How long will it take *A*, *B*, and *C* to do the work when working together? *2 8/31 da.*

=========== **MIXTURE PROBLEMS** ===========

1. A grocer has some tea worth $5.20 a pound and another brand of tea worth $4.00 a pound. How many pounds of each must he use to make a mixture of 100 pounds that can be sold for $4.72 a pound? *$5.20, 60 lb.; $4, 40 lb.*

2. How many pounds of candy worth 50 cents a pound and how many worth 90 cents a pound must be used to make a 75-pound mixture which is worth 76 cents a pound? *50¢, 26¼ lb.; 90¢, 48¾ lb.*

3. How many pounds of nuts worth $2.10 a pound must be mixed with 50 pounds of nuts worth $2.87 a pound to make a mixture worth $2.61 a pound? *25.5 lb., approx.*

4. How much milk testing 4% butterfat should be used with milk testing 25% butterfat to make 200 pounds of milk testing 12% butterfat? *123 17/21 lb.*

5. How much water must be added to a quart of 90% alcohol solution to make a mixture that contains 50% alcohol? *0.8 qt.*

6. How much water must be added to 3 quarts of acid 95% pure to make a mixture containing 25% acid? *8.4 qt.*

7. A radiator contains 2 gallons of a mixture of alcohol and water. If the mixture is 70% alcohol, how much pure alcohol must be added to make it 80% alcohol? *1 gal.*

8. A cereal maker mixed 10 bushels of wheat worth $4.00 a bushel with 30 bushels of oats worth $1.40 a bushel. He estimated the cost of the mixing to be $4.80. What was the value of the mixture per bushel? *$2.17*

560

INVESTMENT PROBLEMS

1. A farmer invested $30,000, part at 7% and the remainder at 6%. If his income on both investments was $2050, how much did he invest at each rate? *7%, $25,000 ; 6%, $5000*

2. $10,000 is invested, part at 6% and the remainder at 5%. The yearly income from both investments is $566. Find the amount of each investment. *6%, $6600; 5%, $3400*

3. Part of $7000 was invested at 6% and the other part at 5%. If the 6% investment yielded $90 more than the other, what was the amount of each investment? *6%, $4000; 5%, $3000*

4. A woman invested some money at 4%, and $500 more than this sum at 6%. If the total income from these investments was $580, find how much was invested at each rate. *4%, $5500; 6%, $6000*

5. How can $8000 be invested, part at 4% and the remainder at 6%, so that both investments produce the same income? *4%, $4800; 6%, $3200*

6. A man lends some money at 5% and an equal amount at 3%. If the income from the 5% loan is $80 more than the income from the 3% loan, how much is loaned at each rate? *$4000*

7. How can $6000 be divided so that one part can be loaned at 4% and the other at 7%, making an average of 6% on the $6000? *4%, $2000; 7%, $4000*

8. How much can a person afford to pay for eight $1000 7% bonds so as to make $6\frac{1}{2}$% on his investment? *$8615.38 approx.*

9. $2000 is invested at 4%, $3000 at 5%, and $1200 at 6%. What rate of interest is received on the three investments combined? *about 4.87%*

10. In how many years will the simple interest on a principal invested at 6% equal the principal itself? *$16\frac{2}{3}$ yr.*

11. A man has $4500 invested at 6% and a second sum invested at 7%. If the income from the second investment exceeds that from the first sum by $80, what is the second sum? *$5000*

12. A girl has one sum of money invested at 5%, and a second sum $1500 larger than the first, invested at 6%. Her total income from these sums is $200. How much has she invested at each rate? *5%, $1000; 6%, $2500*

VARIATION PROBLEMS

1. c varies directly as n, and $c = 45$ when $n = 25$. Find c when $n = 36$. *64.8*

2. A formula for the area of a sphere is $V = \frac{\pi}{6} d^3$. How does V vary with respect to d? *Directly as cube of d.*

3. $S = gt - \frac{1}{2} gt^2$. Does S vary directly as t? Does it vary directly as the square of t? *No; no.*

4. Write the formula for the following table: *x = 2y + 1*

x	1	5	9	13	17
y	0	2	4	6	8

5. How do c and d vary in $c = \pi d$? *Directly*

6. How do I and R vary in $I = \frac{E}{R}$? *Inversely*

7. How do E and R vary in $I = \frac{E}{R}$? *Directly*

8. If 5 men can do a piece of work in 12 days, how many men are needed to do the work in 20 days? *3*

9. If 24 yards of cloth cost $36.00, find the cost of 30 yards of the cloth. *$45*

10. If 40 men in 42 days can dig a trench 8 miles long, how many days will be needed for 10 men to dig a trench 12 miles long? *252*

Selected Answers
for Odd-Numbered Exercises
from Chapters 1–19

Chapter 1 **Pages 3–4** 1. $\{1, 2, 3, \cdots, 10\}$ 3. $\{21, 23, 25\}$ 5. $\{\frac{1}{1}, \frac{1}{2}, \frac{1}{3}, \frac{2}{1}, \frac{2}{2}, \frac{2}{3}, \frac{3}{1}, \frac{3}{2}, \frac{3}{3}\}$
7. $\{12, 24, 36, 48\}$ **Page 5** 1a. finite 1c. infinite 1e. infinite **Page 6** 1a.
$\{2, 4, 6, 8, 10\}$ 1c. $\{1, 2, 3, 4, 5, 6\}$ 1e. $\{1, 2, 3, \cdots, 10\}$ 1g. $\{4, 5, 6, 7\}$

Pages 10–11 1. $\{10, 15, 30\}$; 20¢; 60¢ 3. $\frac{n}{5}$ **Pages 11–12** 1. $\{9, 14, 19, 24\}$
3. $\{\frac{6}{5}, \frac{6}{4}, \frac{6}{3}, \frac{6}{2}\}$ 5. $\{\frac{1}{5}, \frac{2}{5}, \frac{3}{5}, \frac{4}{5}, 1, \cdots, 20\}$ 7a. 8 7c. 2 7e. 2 7g. 5 9a. 5
9c. $11\frac{1}{2}$ 9e. $7\frac{1}{2}$ 9g. 16 **Page 13 (middle)** 1. $4(5)$, or $4 \cdot 5$, or 20 3. $8 \cdot r$, or $8(r)$,
or $8r$ 5. $x(y)$, or xy, or $x \times y$ 7. $3 \cdot 6$, or $3 \cdot 6$, or 18 9. rs, or $r(s)$, or $r \times s$
Page 16 1. 13 3. 6 5. 1 7. 40 9. 16 11. 2 13. 8 15. 48 17. 5
19. 22 **Pages 18–19** 1a. $2 + 3$ 1c. $0 + 4$ 1e. $6 + 4a$ 3a. 10 3c. $\frac{13}{12}$, or $1\frac{1}{12}$
Pages 19–20 1a. $3 + 6$ 1c. $4 + 3$ 1e. $x^2 + 2x$ 1g. $6y + y^2$ 1i. $5m^2n + 15mn$
3. No. Distributive Property of Multiplication over Addition. 5a. $6(2 + 3) = 6(2) + 6(3)$
5c. $4(5) + 4(2) = 4(5 + 2)$ **Page 21** 1. $9h$ 3. $7k$ 5. $4c$ 7. $3xy + 16x^2$
9. $9b + 5p$ 11. $10b$ 13. $4 + 2m$ 15. 0 17. $13x^2 + 3xy + 4y^2$ 19. $\frac{1}{6}x + \frac{7}{6}y$
21. $15a^3 + 2a^2 + 10$ **Pages 22–23** 1. 4 3. 150 5. 400 7. 7 9. 14 11. 36
13. 29 15. 10 17. 27 19. 30 21. 18 23. $2\frac{1}{6}$ 25. 24 27. $\frac{1}{4}$ **Page 23** 1. 3
3. $4w$ 5. $6x$ 7. $y + 7$ 9. $5x$ **Pages 25–26** 1. $\{1, 2, 3, 4, \cdots, 9\}$ 7. $n + 1$
9. exponent 11. $3a; 3$ 13. 0 15a. $12x^2$ 15c. $3x^3 + 13x^2$ 17a. $a + b$
17c. $2a^2$ 17e. $h - 10$ 19a. 10 19c. 12 19e. $7\frac{1}{2}$

Chapter 2 **Page 31** 1. equation; true 3. inequality; true 5. equation; false
7. inequality; false 9. equation; true 11. equation; false **Page 32** 1. false 3. false
5. true 7. true 9. true **Page 33** 1. true 3. false 5. false 7. true 9. false
Pages 33–34 1. $\{2\}$ 3. $\{5\}$ 5. $\{0, 1, 2, 3\}$ 7. $\{3\}$ 9. $\emptyset$ 11. $\{0, 1\}$ **Page 36**
1. $x = 4$ 3. $y = 16\frac{2}{3}$ 5. $h = 5.5$ 7. $x = 160$ 9. $x = 72$ 11. $x = 1$ **Page 37**
1. $x = 13$ 3. $x = 10$ 5. $e = 13.6$ 7. $n = 8.2$ **Page 38** 1. $x = 4$ 3. $y = 8$
5. $y = 0$ 7. $h = 84$ 9. $y = 19$ 11. $h = \frac{3}{2}$ or $1\frac{1}{2}$ **Page 39** 1. $x = 24$ 3. $y = 70$
5. $p = 90$ 7. $x = \frac{1}{2}$ **Pages 39–40** 1. $x = 10$ 3. $x = 2$ 5. $x = 8$ 7. $x = 4$
9. $y = 11$ 11. $r = \frac{5}{4}$ or $1\frac{1}{4}$ 13. $x = 0$ 15. $m = 5$ 17. $x = 10.0$ 19. $t = 23$
21. $a = \frac{1}{2}$ 23. $x = 6$ **Page 40** 1. $x = 3$ 3. $x = 4$ 5. $m = 72$ 7. $r = 15$
9. $m = 1$ **Pages 41–42** 1. $x = 3$ 3. $x = 6$ 5. $x = 3$ 7. $c = 90$ 9. $c = 4$
11. $x = 4\frac{1}{2}$ 13. $y = 7$ 15. $m = 2$ 17. $x = 0.4$ 19. $y = 1200$ 21. $x = 6$
23. $m = 12$ 25. $y = \frac{1}{7}$ 27. $c = 3\frac{1}{2}$ 29. $m = 17\frac{1}{2}$ 31. $x = 1$ 33. $x = 2\frac{1}{2}$
35. $x = 1\frac{3}{4}$ 37. $x = 15$ 39. $y = 0$ 41. $k = 1$ 43. $x = 13$ 45. $h = 12$ 47. $x = 0$
49. $x = 3$ 51. $x = 1$ 53. $y = 3$ 55. $k = 6$ 57. $x = 12$ 59. $r = 2$
Pages 42–43 1. $5x = 80$ 3. $x + 5 = 34$ 5. $5x = 45$ 7. $5x - x = 60$
9. $6 = 2x - 10$ 11. $x - 7 = 13$ 13. $9x - 5 = 42 - 20$ 15. $\frac{2}{3}x = 8$ 17. $\frac{7}{100}x +$
$\frac{4}{100}x = 88$, or $0.07x + 0.04x = 88$ 19. $7x - 76 = 92$ **Pages 45–48** 1. 51 3. 127
5. 123 7. 45 and 9 9. 53 11. 14 13. 5 15. 14 years 17. 36 19. 7000
21. \$60,000 23. 184 and 92 25. 125, 375, and 500 27. Flo, \$2.20; Bernice, \$1.65
29. length, 20 feet; width, 10 feet 31. Patricia, 15 blocks; Jane, 3 blocks 33. Bill, 11 years;
Father, 44 years 35. 168 and 28 37. glycerine, $2\frac{2}{3}$ ounces; turpentine, $2\frac{2}{3}$ ounces; water,
$10\frac{2}{3}$ ounces 39. 15 inches **Pages 50–51** 3. a right angle 5. an obtuse angle
7. $\angle AOD$; $\angle AOC$, $\angle BOC$, and $\angle BOD$ 9a. complementary 9c. neither
9e. complementary **Pages 51–52** 1. $180°$ 3. $40°$ 5. $30°; 80°; 10°; (90 - x)°$
7. $60°$ **Pages 52–53** 1. $60°, 120°$ 3. $5°, 85°$ 5. $20°, 100°, 60°$ 7. $14°, 112°$
Page 53 1. $x = 4$ 3. $r = 2$ 5. $y = 2$ 7. $x = 2\frac{1}{9}$ 9. $x = 1$ **Pages 54–55**
1. $x > 6$ 3. $x > 4$ 5. $x > 11$ 7. $x < 11$ 9. $x < 5$ 11. John earned less than
\$65.00 13. any amount less than 3 gallons

Chapter 3 **Pages 64–70** 1. 256 ft. 3. 4.33 lb. per sq. in. 5. 8.660 lb. per sq. in.
7. 125 lb. 9. \$37.80 11. \$675 13. simple interest; $A = \$364$ 15. 1430 mi.

17. 5760 ft.　　**19.** $4\frac{1}{2}$ hr.　　**21.** 16, 64, 144, 256, 400, 576, 1024, 4096　　**21a.** it increases
21c. yes　**23.** *63 in.*: Normal, 126.5 lb.; overweight, 3.5 lb.; *72 in.*: Normal, 176 lb. (same　as
actual)　　**25.** more than 211.75 ft.　　**27.** 2.7　　**29.** 3,379,200 ft.-lb.　　**31.** $P = 4$　　**33.** $W =$
$13\frac{3}{4}$　**35.** $W = 128,000$　　**Pages 71–72**　**1.** 80 sq. in.　　**3.** $47\frac{1}{8}$ sq. ft.　　**5.** 332.64 sq. in.
7. $30\frac{1}{3}$ sq. yd.　　**9.** 354.0 ft.　　**11.** $P = 2m + 2n$, or $P = 2(m + n)$; $A = mn$　　**13.** $A = s^2$
15. $A_1 = b^2$;　$A_2 = a^2$; $A = b^2 - a^2$　　**17.** $A = 28$ sq. in.; $P = 32$ in.　　**Page 73**　　**1.** 110 sq. in.
3. 8 sq. in.　　**5.** $4\frac{1}{2}$　　**7.** 100.4　　**Pages 73–74**　**1.** 54　　**3.** 123.54　　**5.** 2115.00　　**7.** $4x$
9. 84 sq. in　　**Page 75**　**1.** 154 sq. in.; 44 in.　　**3.** $86\frac{5}{8}$ sq. in.; 33 in.　　**7.** A becomes 4 times
as great　　**9.** about $2\frac{1}{2}$ yd.　　**11.** about 720　　**Pages 76–77**　**1.** $V = 1280$　　**3.** $V = 902.7$
5. 8640 cu. in.　　**7.** 860 sq. ft.　　**9.** 25 sq. in.; 150 sq. in.; 125 cu. in.　　**11.** $179\frac{1}{5}$ bu.
13. the volume of the larger cube is 8 times that of the smaller.　　**15.** about 5024 cu. in.
17. about 1306 sq. in.　　**19.** V, about 4190 cu. ft.; S, about 1257 sq. ft.　　**21a.** V, about 905 cu.
in.; S, about 452 sq. in.　　**21c.** V, about 180 cu. in.; S, about 154 sq. in.　　**21e.** V, about 1064
cu. ft.; S, about 504 sq. ft.　　**21g.** V, about 18,480 cu. ft.; S, about 3380 sq. ft.　　**Pages 78–80**

1. $s = c + g + e$　　**3.** $F = \frac{9}{5}C + 32$　　**5.** $a = \dfrac{x + y}{2}$　　**7.** $P = 2w + 2l$ or $P = 2(w + l)$
9. $P = a + b + c$　　**11.** $A + B + C = 180°$　　**13.** $s = \frac{1}{2}c$　　**15.** $F = 15 + 5n$　　**17.** if hr.
$(h) \not> 20, c = (7h)$¢; if hr. $(h) > 20, c = (60 + 4h)$¢　　**19.** $i = 12f$　　**21.** $F = n + 37$
Pages 80–81　**1.** $c = 56n$; 280, 336, 392　　**3.** $y = 2x + 1$; 11, 13, 15, 17, 19　　**Page 81**
1. $P = 4x + 12$　　**3.** $P = 4x + 8$　　**5.** $P = 8x + 8$

Chapter 4　　**Page 92**　　**1.** -3　　**3.** $+7$ feet　　**5.** 60° east longitude　　**7.** 6 in. below
average　　**9.** 46 B.C.　　**Page 98**　　**1.** -2　　**3.** 7　　**5.** 6　　**7.** -9　　**Page 99**　　**1.** $\$7 +$
$\$6 = \$13$　　**3.** $30 - 50 = -20$ (ft.)　　**5.** $-6 + 10 = +4$ (steps)　　**7.** $\$80 - \$60 + \$20 =$
$+\$40$　　**9.** 1　　**11.** $+4$　　**13.** 11　　**15.** -11　　**17.** -15　　**19.** 1　　**21.** 8; 6; 10; 9
Page 100　　**1.** $-2x$　　**3.** b　　**5.** $3r$　　**7.** $6A$　　**9.** $11x$　　**11.** $-5a^2$　　**13.** $-2.5y$
15. $-4bc$　　**17.** $\frac{1}{3}x$　　**19.** $-\frac{13}{12}b$　　**Page 101**　　**1.** $2a - 2b$　　**3.** $7y$　　**5.** $1 - 9x$
7. $4mn + 2n^2$　　**9.** $a - b$　　**11.** $2x^2 + 5x$　　**13.** $x^2 + y^2$　　**15.** $4a - b + 5c$　　**17.** $2x^3$
$- 5x^2 - 4x$　　**19.** 6　　**21.** $2a + h$　　**23.** $3x$　　**Pages 102–103**　　**1a.** 15　　**1c.** -18
1e. -5　　**1g.** 4　　**3a.** 20　　**3c.** 50　　**3e.** -35　　**3g.** -9　　**5.** -15　　**7.** -9　　**9.** -80
11. 2　　**13.** -5　　**15.** 16　　**17.** 1　　**19.** -100　　**21.** 7, -3, 4, -6; same　　**23.** -12; $+12$
Page 104　　**1a.** 0　　**1c.** 0　　**1e.** 3　　**1g.** 3　　**1i.** 6　　**Pages 105–106**　　**3a.** -4
3c. -2　　**3e.** -6　　**3g.** -2　　**5a.** -0.4　　**5c.** 0.02　　**5e.** -10　　**5g.** -3　　**7.** -8
9. 5　　**11.** 900　　**13.** $\frac{1}{3}$　　**15.** $-2\frac{2}{5}$　　**17.** -20　　**19.** 8　　**21.** 2　　**23a.** -3　　**23c.** 6
23e. 8　　**23g.** -60　　**23i.** 144　　**23k.** -144　　**25a.** -24　　**25c.** -24　　**25e.** $5\frac{1}{3}$
25g. $-2\frac{2}{3}$　　**27.** 50; 14; -22　　**Page 108 (middle)**　　**1.** $-35x^2$　　**3.** $-12m^2$　　**5.** x^2
7. $-\frac{1}{6}k^2$　　**9.** $\frac{1}{5}h^2$　　**11.** x^2　　**13.** $0.1p^2$　　**15.** $0.5c^2$　　**Pages 108–109**　　**1.** $-28a^3$
3. $-80m$　　**5.** x^{10}　　**7.** $25a^2b^4$　　**9.** $-42b^7$　　**11.** $-10x^4$　　**13.** $9c^4dx$　　**15.** $0.8x^9$
17. 10^7　　**Page 110**　　**1.** $3a^2$　　**3.** $-2x$　　**5.** $-4ab$　　**7.** $2x$　　**9.** $-2x^3$　　**11.** $-2p^2$
13. 4　　**15.** $3m^4$　　**17.** $2m$　　**19.** 12　　**21.** $2a$　　**23.** $-b$　　**Page 111**　　**1.** 25
3. $-\frac{227}{144}$　　**5.** 24　　**7.** -44　　**9.** $3\frac{3}{5}$　　**11.** $+6$; -18; 18　　**13.** 0　　**15.** 9
Pages 112–113　　**1.** No; -2　　**3a.** -9　　**3c.** -13　　**3e.** 0　　**Pages 114–115**　　**1a.** 6
1c. 9　　**1e.** -2　　**1g.** 20　　**3a.** 1　　**3c.** 13　　**3e.** 1　　**3g.** 15　　**5a.** 6　　**5c.** -19
5e. -7　　**5g.** -28　　**9a.** $7x^2$　　**9c.** $5s^2$　　**9e.** 0　　**9g.** $6c$　　**11a.** $\frac{1}{2}x$　　**11c.** $\frac{2}{5}x$
11e. $-2p$　　**11g.** $-1\frac{1}{3}y$　　**13.** -2　　**15.** 18　　**17.** 2　　**19.** -12　　**21.** 2　　**23.** -14

25. 334 yr.　　**Page 117 (top)**　　**1.** $\frac{4}{7}$　　**3.** $\dfrac{21m}{5}$　　**5.** $\dfrac{-3c}{4d}$　　**7.** $\dfrac{4m}{5n}$　　**9.** 50　　**11.** $\dfrac{b^3}{a}$

13. $4x$　　**15.** $\frac{45}{2}$　　**17.** $\dfrac{6y}{x}$　　**19.** $\dfrac{5}{a}$　　**21.** $\dfrac{2a^2}{5}$　　**Page 117 (bottom)**　**1.** 1　　**3.** $\frac{4}{7}$　　**5.** 2

7. x　　**9.** $\dfrac{a + b}{c}$　　**11.** $\dfrac{2}{c}$　　**13.** $\dfrac{1}{xy}$　　**15.** x　　**Page 118**　　**1.** $1\frac{1}{2}$　　**3.** $\dfrac{3c}{8}$　　**5.** $\dfrac{2x}{9}$

7. $\dfrac{5m}{12}$　　**9.** $\dfrac{-x}{2}$　　**11.** $\dfrac{7m}{12}$　　**13.** $\dfrac{-a}{12}$　　**15.** $\dfrac{-1}{2a}$

Chapter 5　　**Pages 129–130**　　**1.** $x = -8$　　**3.** $x = 12$　　**5.** $x = 5$　　**7.** $c = -7$
9. $y = -3$　　**11.** $x = -8$　　**13.** $x = -4$　　**15.** $c = 4$　　**17.** $y = -\frac{1}{3}$　　**Pages 130–131**
1. $x = 13$　　**3.** $c = 7$　　**5.** $h = -7$　　**7.** $h = -2$　　**9.** $m = -5$　　**11.** $x = 7$　　**13.** $h =$

-2 **15.** $k = -4$ **17.** $x = -1$ **19.** $x = 9$ **21.** $c = 0.7$ **23.** $m = 0.7$ **25.** $n = 8.2$
27. $m = 1.35$ **29.** $x = -2$ **Pages 131–132**   **1.** $x = 2$ **3.** $x = 2$ **5.** $c = -15$
7. $h = -8$ **9.** $x = 2$ **11.** $y = -4$ **13.** $x = \frac{1}{2}$ **15.** $x = 7$ **Page 132**   **1.** $x = 15$
3. $x = 49$ **5.** $x = 35$ **7.** $x = 135$ **9.** $m = -49$ **11.** $k = 200$ **13.** $y = 12$
15. $x = 0$ **17.** $c = -3\frac{3}{4}$ **Page 133**   **1.** $x = 8$ **3.** $m = 7$ **5.** $c = 1$ **7.** $r = 5$
9. $x = -2$ **11.** $x = 11$ **13.** $y = 2$ **15.** $k = 1\frac{1}{2}$ **17.** $h = -1$ **19.** $y = 3\frac{1}{3}$
21. $x = 3$ **23.** $m = 1$ **25.** $x = 18$ **Pages 134–135**   **1.** $l = 20$ **3.** $l = 27$ **5.** $l = 36.3$
7. $w = 17$ **9.** $w = 4.7$ **11.** $A = 88$ **13.** $b = 26$ **15.** $b = 36$ **17.** $V = 864$
19. $l = 9$ **21.** $l = 6.2$ **Pages 135–136**   **1.** $0, 3, 6, 9, 12, -3, -6, -9, -12$ **3.** $2, 6,$
$10, 14, 18, 22, 26, 30$ **5a.** directly   **5c.** directly   **Pages 137–138**   **1.** $y = 2x$, or $x = \frac{1}{2}y$; $x = 5, 6, 7$ **3.** $m = n + 7$, or $n = m - 7$; $m = 12$; $n = 10$; $n = 14$ **5.** $x + 3y = 18,$
or $x = 18 - 3y$; $x = 3, 0, -3$ **7.** $s = 4t^2$, $s = 144, 196$ **9.** $c = 4d + 2$; $c = 42, 50, 82, 98$
Page 139   **1.** $x > 2$ **3.** $y < -2$ **5.** $x < 4$ **7.** $m > 9$ **Page 140**   **1.** true
3. true   **5.** false   **Pages 141–143**   **1.** $10 - x$ **3.** $4 + 6$; $x + y$; $r - s$ **5.** $9x$ cents;
$46x$ cents   **7.** 60; $12y$; $36c$ **9.** 4; $2x$; $6y$; xy **11.** $x + 1$ **13.** $3x + 6$ **15.** $0.80x,$
or $\frac{80}{100}x$, or $0.8x$, or $\frac{8}{10}x$, or $\frac{4x}{5}$; $\frac{25}{100}y$, or $0.25y$, or $\frac{1}{4}y$; $\frac{rs}{100}$, or $0.01\,rs$; $\frac{pm}{100}$, or $0.01\,pm$

17. $6x$ ft.; $2x^2$ sq. ft.   **19.** $(x + 6)$ ft.   **21.** 3 hr.; $16\frac{2}{3}$ hr.; $\frac{x}{30}$ hr.; $4x$ hr.   **23.** 16; 24; $2k$; $4c$

25. $5x$ **27.** $(y - 5)$ yr.; $(y - 8)$ yr.; $(y - x)$ yr.   **Pages 143–145**   **1.** 63 **3.** -12
5. 32 **7.** 42 **9.** $15, 45$ **11.** $13, 31$ **13.** $\$1895, \$2150$ **15.** 40 ft. × 140 ft.
17. $18, 19$ **19.** $-114, -115, -116$ **21.** $45, 47$ **23.** $18, 20, 22$ **Pages 147–149**
1a. $\$7.20$ **1c.** $\$63$ **1e.** 54 **1g.** 5 **1i.** 25 **3a.** 37.5 **3c.** 21 **3e.** 100 **5.** 46.5
7. 4 **9.** $22\frac{2}{9}\%$ **11.** 30 **13.** 25% **15.** $\$900$ **17.** 0.12 **19.** 4.5% **21.** $18\frac{2}{11}\%$
23. 310 **25.** 450 **27.** $15¢$ a quart   **29.** $\$130$

Chapter 6   **Pages 160–162**   **1.** 10 ft.   **3.** $8x - 2y - z$ **5.** $c + 6a$ **7.** $-2k^2 - 11k - 5$ **9.** $-9a - 13b$ **11.** $-11xy - 11y^2$ **13.** $3ax - 17$ **15.** $-2x^3 - 4x^2 - 11$
17. $5a - b$ **19.** $-2x - 3y - 6z$ **21.** $4ab + b^2$ **23.** $7a - b - 2c$ **25.** $8a - 10$
27. $6x - 8$ **29.** $6x - 3$ **31.** $3x^4 - 6x^3 + x^2 + 5x - 8$ **33.** $-15x^3 + 2x^2 - 3x$
35. $\frac{5}{6}x - \frac{1}{2}y + \frac{3}{5}z$ **37.** $a^2 - \frac{1}{2}a - \frac{7}{3}$ **39.** $0.6x - 1.2y + 15z$ **41.** $4x^2 - 10xy$
43. $8a + 8b - 4c$ **45.** 12 **Pages 164–165**   **1.** $2x + 7$ **3.** $2x + 4y + 4z$
5. $-3r - 5s + 2t$ **7.** $a - 8b + 6$ **9.** $-3x^2 - 2x - 3$ **11.** $2k - 3m + 6n + 6$
13. $-a + 4b + 4c$ **15.** $2a + 3b + 2c$ **17.** $-y + x$ **19.** $-a + 4b + 2$ **21.** $4x - 5$
23. $-\frac{1}{4}a - \frac{1}{12}b + \frac{1}{5}c$ **25.** $2a^2 + 3a - 6$ **27.** $-2a - 2b + c$ **29.** $-\frac{3}{10}a - \frac{9}{20}b - \frac{1}{6}c$ **31.** $13a^3 - 2a^2 + 5a - 11$ **33.** $P = 4x^2 - 30x + 40$ **Pages 166–167**   **1.** x^4
3. a^8 **5.** c^{12} **7.** x^9 **9.** x^{15} **11.** $9a^2$ **13.** $25a^6$ **15.** x^2y^2 **17.** x^5 **19.** a^7
21. a^7 **23.** $\frac{1}{4}x^2$ **25.** a^4b^6 **27.** $-m^6n^3$ **29.** $24a^2$ **31.** $-5bc^2$ **33.** $12cd$ **35.** a^4
Pages 168–169   **1.** $4a + 20$ **3.** $18b - 6c$ **5.** $4ax^2 - 5ay$ **7.** $-3a + 3b - 15c$
9. $-4c^2 + 16cd - 12$ **11.** $21m^3 - 3m^2 + 9m$ **13.** $6x^3 - 9x^2 - 3x$ **15.** $-30a - 5b + 35$ **17.** $7c^2 - 14c - 21$ **19.** $2x^3 + 2x^2 + 2x$ **21.** $-x^2 - 3x - 6$
23. $8a^2 - 12a$ **25.** $(14c^2 - 2cd)$ cents   **27.** $x^2 + 8x$ **29.** $5c^3d^2 - 5c^2d^3 + 15c^2d^2$
31. $28x^2y - 16xy^2 + 64y^3$ **33.** $5w - 5w^2 - 15w^3$ **Page 170**   **1.** $x = 18$ **3.** $x = \frac{7}{8}$
5. $x = 10$ **7.** $r = -\frac{1}{2}$ **9.** $x = 10$ **11.** $y = 12$ **13.** $x = 3\frac{5}{9}$ **15.** $y = 1.89$
Pages 171–172   **3.** $2x - 4$ **5.** $3r + s$ **7.** $-5m^2 + 3$ **9.** $b - c$ **11.** $n - m$
13. $8a^3 + 2a^2$ **15.** $-7c^2 + 14c + 1$ **17.** $3m^3 - 2m^2 - m$ **19.** $a^7 - a^6 + a^4$
21. $x - 1$ **23.** $-3x + 1$ **25.** $-\frac{3}{2}x - 3$ **27.** $r_1^2 - r_2^2$ **29.** $v - \frac{1}{2}gt$ **31.** $(2x - 3y)$ ft.   **33.** am days   **35.** $4x^3 - 5x^2 + 2x + 1$ **37.** $-x + x^2 - 2x^3 + 3x^4 - x^5$
39. $-x^3 + 8x^2 - 2x + 1$ **41.** $60b - 7a$ **Page 173 (top)**   **1.** $8x - 20$ **3.** $-2c + 2m$ **5.** $-12 + 6x$ **7.** $x^3 - x^2$ **9.** $-3 + 3x$ **11.** $4m - 28$ **13.** $4a^2 - 4x^2$
15. $p + prt$ **17.** $4a + 2b$ **19.** $4x - 60$ **21.** $x - 2$ **23.** $9x - 6y$ **Page 173**
(bottom)   **1.** $8p - 16$ **3.** $-6x - 1$ **5.** $16 - 12y$ **7.** $20 - 7c$ **9.** $3y - 20$
Page 174   **1.** $11x - 1$ **3.** $13 - 3x$ **5.** $17c + 3$ **7.** $-2b$ **9.** $b^2 - a$ **11.** $-2x$
13. $p^2 + p$ **Pages 175–176**   **1.** 1 **3.** $4a + 4$ **5.** $5 - y$ **7.** 6 **9.** $-2c - 3$
11. $2 + m$ **13.** $6 - x$ **15.** $6t - 35$ **17.** $7h - 1$ **19.** $5x + 1$ **21.** 10 **23.** $x - 2y$
25. $-x - 6$ **27.** $6x$ **29.** $2a^2 + ab + b^2$ **31.** $12b - a$ **33.** $-2a^3b - 4a^2b^2 + ab^3$
35. $-6p^2 + 6p - 6$ **Pages 176–177**   **1.** $(m^2 - 2mn + 3) - (4y^2 + 3y - 2)$ **3.** $+$

$(-4x^2 - 3x - 1) - (-h^2 - 5h + 8)$ **5.** $(3x^2 + bx + 2x) - (8y^2 - cy + 3y)$

Chapter 7   **Pages 185–186**   **1.** $x = 1$ **3.** $x = 3\frac{1}{3}$ **5.** $x = 29$ **7.** $x = 4\frac{5}{6}$
9. $c = -13$ **11.** $y = 2$ **13.** $x = 3$ **15.** $x = 1\frac{1}{2}$ **17.** $y = 7$ **19.** $r = -1$
21. $p = -8\frac{1}{2}$ **23.** $m = 4$ **25.** $x = \frac{1}{2}$ **27.** $c = 8\frac{1}{2}$ **29.** $x = 3\frac{1}{13}$ **31.** $h = \frac{1}{2}$
33. $x = -\frac{1}{2}$ **35.** $x = 10$ **37.** $x = 7$ **39.** $y = 24$ **41.** $x = -6$ **43.** $x = \frac{1}{2}$
45. $x = 4$ **Page 187**   **1.** conditional   **3.** identity   **5.** conditional   **7.** neither
9. neither   **Pages 188–189**   **1.** $x + 3$; $2x - 3$; $4m + (m + 4)$, or $5m + 4$ **3.** a^2; $2a^2$;
b^3; $(3c - 1)^2$ **5.** 16; xy; $7(y + 3)$ **7.** $(8x^2 + 4) \div 4 = 2x^2 + 1$ **9.** $4(x + 3) = 35$
11. $9 - x = 4x - 1$ **13.** $8(x - 6) = 16$ **15.** $5(x + 10) = 20$ **Pages 189–190**
1. 18, 22   **3.** large truck, 5; small truck, 7   **5.** 6500, 8100   **7.** 24, 37   **9.** 780 lb., 920 lb.
11. 50°, 48°, 82°   **Pages 191–192**   **1.** greater; $x + 6$ **3.** $8 - 6 = 2$, $8 = 6 + 2$, $8 - 2$
$= 6$ **5.** $x + 10$ **7.** $3x + 7$ **9.** $2x + 18$ **Page 192**   **1.** 162, 158   **3.** 26, 66
5. 30, 117   **7.** 10, 32   **Pages 194–195**   **1.** 20, 25   **3.** 114, 136   **5.** 500, 700   **7.** 18,
31, 42   **9.** 6, 13   **11.** 68, 72   **13.** 29, 47   **15.** $68\frac{5}{8}$, $87\frac{3}{8}$ **Pages 196–197** **1.** 9 nickels,
7 dimes   **3.** 3 dimes, 6 nickels, 11 half-dollars   **5.** 9 nickels, 12 dimes   **7.** 25 10-cent
stamps, 3 25-cent stamps   **9.** 14 nickels, 40 dimes, 24 quarters   **Pages 198–199** **1.** James,
12 yr.; Henry, 22 yr.   **3.** Mary, 18 yr.; mother, 42 yr.   **5.** son, 12 yr.; father, 42 yr.
7. Carl, 5 yr.; Frank, 20 yr.   **Pages 200–201**   **1.** $52\frac{1}{2}$ **3.** 30 lb., 5 ft. from fulcrum; 50 lb.,
3 ft.   **5.** 72 lb. on short arm; 56 lb. on long arm   **7.** 640 lb.   **9.** $13\frac{1}{3}$ ft. from $7\frac{1}{2}$ lb.
weight; $16\frac{2}{3}$ ft. from 6-lb. weight   **11.** about 8.79 ft.   **Pages 201–202**   **1.** 994 sq. ft.
3. 40°, 50°   **5.** 45°   **7.** 51°, 53°, 76°   **9.** 42°, 65°, 73°

Chapter 8   **Page 214**   **1.** $x = 1\frac{1}{3}$ **3.** $m = \frac{1}{10}$ **5.** $y = -11\frac{2}{3}$ **7.** $k = 96$ **9.** c
$= 72$ **11.** $x = 1\frac{5}{7}$ **13.** $x = -36$ **15.** $x = 3\frac{7}{11}$ **17.** $h = 1$ **19.** $y = 30$ **21.** $c =$
21   **Pages 215–216**   **1.** $x = 22$ **3.** $x = 1\frac{1}{19}$ **5.** $c = -3$ **7.** $y = 12$ **9.** $x = 7$
11. $c = -2$ **13.** $y = 9$ **15.** $k = 18$ **17.** $k = 10\frac{1}{7}$ **19.** $x = 6$ **21.** $x = -13$
23. $x = -28\frac{4}{11}$ **25.** $x = 50$ **Page 217**   **1.** $x = 40$ **3.** $p = 200$ **5.** $r = 20$
7. $b = 5$ **9.** $y = 150$ **11.** $y = 50$ **13.** $r = 80$ **15.** $x = 64$ **17.** $y = -0.5$
19. $y = -2\frac{2}{9}$ **21.** $x = 20.969^+$ **23.** $p = 250$ **25.** $x = 330$ **27.** $x = 4$ **29.** $x = 3$
31. $y = 7.843^+$ **Pages 218–219** **1.** $\frac{2}{3}m$, or $\frac{2m}{3}$ **3.** $\frac{1}{2}c$, or $\frac{c}{2}$ **5.** $\frac{4}{7}y$, or $\frac{4y}{7}$ **7.** $m - 5$
9. $\frac{4}{5}(2x - 3)$ **11.** the sum of $\frac{3}{4}x$ and 5   **15.** $\frac{5}{7}x - 14$ **17.** $\frac{1}{9}x + 4$ **19.** $20 - y$;
$\frac{3}{5}(20 - y)$ **21.** $20 - w$; $\frac{5}{6}w$; $\frac{7}{8}(20 - w)$ **23.** $\frac{2}{3}x = 60$ **25.** $\frac{7}{8}x + 6 = 20$ **27.** $\frac{1}{4}x - $
$\frac{1}{6}x = 1$ **Pages 219–221**   **1.** 30   **3.** 60 ft. × 45 ft.   **5.** 25, 35   **7.** 40°, 50°   **9.** 36°,
144°   **11.** 54°   **13.** $\frac{5}{8}$ **15.** 12 yr.   **17.** man, 42 yr.; brother, 36 yr.   **19.** 840   **21.** 12
23. 21 in., 14 in., 9 in.   **25.** 2 ft. from larger boy   **27.** 18, 30   **29.** $75   **31.** 24 yr.
Page 223   **1.** $273   **3.** $9   **5.** $19.03, or $19   **7.** $41.10   **9.** $10.20   **11.** $2500;
$2350; about 6.71%; about 6.27%   **Pages 224–225**   **1.** $600   **3.** $1500   **5.** $5\frac{1}{2}\%$
7. $4\frac{1}{2}\%$ **9.** $1.34   **11.** $37.54   **13.** 8%   **Pages 225–226**   **1.** $5440   **3.** 7%
5. $1432   **7.** $9520   **9.** 3 yr. 11 mo. 15 da.   **Page 226**   **1.** .337   **3.** 141   **5.** .300
Page 227   **1.** to construct school buildings; the people   **3.** $4\frac{1}{2}\%$; $4\frac{1}{20}\%$, or $4.05 a share
5. $(x + 800)$ dollars   **7.** $(3000 - x)$ dollars; $(.01x + 150)$ dollars   **Pages 228–229**
1. 8%, $4000; 5%, $4500   **3.** 8%, $12,000; 6%, $13,500   **5.** 5%, $2800; 4%, $1500
7. $5000   **9.** 6%, $6000; $5\frac{1}{2}\%$, $2500   **11.** $6181.82   **Pages 230–231**   **1.** $x = a - b$
3. $x = b + h$ **5.** $x = 2a$ **7.** $y = \frac{25c}{3}$ **9.** $y = \frac{3m}{2}$ **11.** $x = 6k$ **13.** $x = \frac{23b}{6}$
15. $y = 3a$ **17.** $x = \frac{a + b^2}{3b}$ **19.** $x = 1$ **21.** $l = \frac{A}{w}$ $w = \frac{A}{l}$ **23.** $l = \frac{2A}{w}$; $w = \frac{2A}{l}$
25. $n = \frac{S + 360}{180}$ **27.** $g = \frac{2S}{t^2}$ **29.** $a = l - dn + d$ **31.** $b = \frac{2A - hb'}{h}$
Pages 233–234   **1.** $ad = bc$; bc; ad; *Boxed rule:* means, product   **3a.** $y = 24$ **3c.** $y = 10$
3e. $y = 12$ **3g.** $y = 3m$ **5.** 4 ft., 8 ft.   **7.** 9 yd.   **9.** 6

Chapter 9   **Pages 245–246**   **1.** $x^2 + 2x + 1$ **3.** $a^2 + 5a + 6$ **5.** $g^2 + 13g + 42$
7. $x^2 - 8x + 16$ **9.** $x^2 - 49$ **11.** $r^2 + 2rs + s^2$ **13.** $a^2 - b^2$ **15.** $2x^2 - 5xy - 3y^2$

566

17. $6x^2 - 13xy + 6y^2$ **19.** $mx - nx + my - ny$ **21.** $x^3 + 2x^2 - 2x + 3$ **23.** $-x^3 +$ $14x + 15$ **25.** $x^3 - 4x^2 + 7x - 6$ **27.** $a^3 - 7a^2 + 15a - 9$ **29.** $16a^2 + 8a + 1$ **31.** $x^4 - 8x^3 + 28x^2 - 48x + 36$ **33.** $-3a^2 - a$ **35.** $4y^2 - 12y + 5$ **39.** $4x^2 -$ $12x + 9$ **41.** $(x^2 - 3x - 18)$ cents **43.** $x^4 - y^4$ **45.** $2x^2 - 14.6x - 3$ **47.** $x^4 + x^2$ $+ 1$ **49.** $2y^4 - 5y^3 + 5y - 2$ **51.** $a^2 - b^2 + 2bc - c^2$ **53.** $6x^4 + 3x^3 - 17x^2 - 12x$ **55.** $x^2 + 2xy + 2xz + y^2 + 2yz + z^2$ **57.** $a^3 - 3a^2b + 3ab^2 - b^3$ **Page 247** **1.** $-x^2 + 2x + 3$ **3.** $5c^2 - 22c - 15$ **Page 248** **1.** $x = 3$ **3.** $y = 1$ **5.** $c = 2$ **7.** $x = 4$ **9.** $x = 2$ **11.** $x = \frac{1}{3}$ **13.** $x = -2$ **15.** $x = 4$ **17.** $x = -1$ **19.** $x = -3$ **21.** $x = \frac{7}{11}$ **23.** $x = -1$ **25.** $x = 1$ **27.** $x = 7$ **29.** $x = 5$ **Pages 251–253** **1.** $6\frac{2}{7}$ hr. **3.** $1\frac{1}{2}$ hr. **5.** 27 m.p.h. **7.** in 5 hr. **9.** 420 m.p.h., 600 m.p.h. **11.** 24 min. **13.** 420 mi., one way **Page 254** **1.** $1\frac{1}{3}$ hr. **3.** $5\frac{1}{4}$ hr. **5.** 14.9 min. $3\frac{9}{11}$ hr. **Pages 255–258** **1.** 20 **3.** oats, 25 bu.; wheat, 75 bu. **5.** 12 lb., 34¢; 18 lb., 54¢ **7a.** 1 grapefruit, 2 pineapple, 3 orange **7b.** $45\frac{1}{2}$¢ **7c.** 33 cans **9.** 25 lb. **11.** 600 oz. **13.** 8%, 180 T.; 3%, 120 T. **15.** 30 lb. **Pages 261–262** **1.** $x - 3$ **3.** $c + 8$ **5.** $x - 5$ **7.** $x - 2$ **9.** $t + 4$ **11.** $2x + 9 + \dfrac{135}{x - 7}$ **13.** $3x + 7 + \dfrac{13}{x - 2}$ **15.** $x + 1$ **17.** $x - 2$ **19.** $x + y$ **21.** $3x + 4y$ **23.** $x^2 + 9$ **25.** $4x - 3$ **27.** $a^2 + a - 11$ **29.** $x^2 - 3x$ $+ 1$ **31.** $x^2 - 3x + 1$ **33.** $6x^2 + 6x - 12$ **35.** $a^2 - a + 1$ **37.** $a^2 + 2a + 4$ **39.** $x^2 - xy + y^2$ **41.** $x^2 - 4x + 16$ **43.** $x^3 + x^2 + x + 1$ **45.** $x^3 - x^2 + x - 1 + \dfrac{2}{x + 1}$ **47.** $a^2 + ab + b^2$ **49.** $x^4 - x^3 + x^2 - x + 1$ **51.** $a^2 - ab - ac + b^2 - bc + c^2 - \dfrac{2b^3}{a + b + c}$

Chapter 10 **Page 280** **1.** function **3.** not a function **Pages 285–286** **17.** the relation is defined by $y = x + 4$ **21.** $A = t^3$ **Page 288** **3.** b, m **Pages 289–290** **1a.** slope, 4; y-intercept, 1 **1c.** slope, $\frac{2}{5}$; y-intercept, 0 **1e.** slope, 1; y-intercept, 10 **3.** slope, -1; y-intercept, 1 **5.** slope, -1; y-intercept, 0 **7.** slope, $-\frac{5}{2}$; y-intercept, 3

Chapter 11 **Pages 304–305** **1.** consistent and independent, $x = 3, y = 2$ **3.** consistent and independent, $x = 2, y = 2$ **5.** consistent and independent, $x = 3, y = -2$ **7.** consistent and independent, $x = 4, y = 4$ **9.** inconsistent, no common solution **11.** consistent and independent, $x = -1$, $y = 2$ **13.** consistent and independent, $x = 3, y = -2$ **17.** consistent and independent, $s = -1, t = -3$ **19.** consistent and independent, $x = 3\frac{2}{7}$, $y = -7\frac{1}{7}$; or $x = 3.3, y = -7.1$, approx. **21.** consistent and independent, $x = \frac{1}{2}, y = 4$ **Page 307 (bottom)** **1.** $x = 6, y = 4$ **3.** $x = 9, y = 4$ **5.** $x = 7, y = -2$ **7.** $m = -2, n = 3$ **9.** $x = 2, y = 5$ **11.** $E = 11$, $F = 8$ **13.** $r = 20, s = 21$ **15.** $x = 16, y = 35$ **17.** equations inconsistent **19.** $h = -7, k = -8$ **21.** $x = 50, y = 8$ **Page 309** **1.** Ex. 2, 3, 4, 5, 7, 11 **3.** $x = -1, y = 1$ **5.** $a = 6, b = 3$ **7.** $x = -4, y = 5$ **9.** $x = 1, y = -2$ **11.** $m = 3, n = \frac{1}{3}$ **13.** $A = -6, B = -5$ **15.** $x = -5, y = 2$ **17.** $x = 3, y = -4$ **19.** $x = 3, y = 5$ **Pages 310–311** **1.** $x = \frac{1}{2}, y = 2$ **3.** $x = 8, y = 1$ **5.** $x = -1\frac{3}{5}, y = -4\frac{4}{5}$ **7.** $x = 5, y = -4$ **9.** $x = 8, y = 4$ **11.** $a = 4, b = -6$ **13.** $x = \frac{1}{5}, y = 4$ **15.** $x = -1, y = -3$ **17.** $x = 3000, y = 5000$ **19.** $a = 1, b = \frac{3}{4}$ **Pages 312–314** **1.** 21, 12 **3.** 18, 15 **5.** 18°, 72° **7.** 112°, 68° **9.** 112 in. × 312 in. **11.** 6%, $11,000; 8%, $4000 **13.** father, 36 yr., son, 8 yr. **15.** $3\frac{1}{2}$ T., $4\frac{1}{2}$ T. **17.** Charles, 10 yr.; Fred, 24 yr. **19.** 76°, 14° **21.** round steak, $1.55; rib steak, $2.50 **23.** 40 lb.

Chapter 12 **Page 321 (middle)** **1.** $3a + 6$ **3.** $ab - 4a$ **5.** $abc + 2ab$ **7.** $4(a - b)$ **9.** $2(a + 3)$ **Pages 323–324** **1.** $3(n + 1)$ **3.** $5(x - 5)$ **5.** $6(x - y)$ **7.** $3a(b + c)$ **9.** prime **11.** $c(c - 1)$ **13.** $a(x + 1)$ **15.** $\pi(R - r)$ **17.** $10(2c - 3d)$ **19.** $7y(x - 2)$ **21.** $P(1 + rt)$ **23.** $5(x^2 - x - 2)$ **25.** prime **27.** $x(x^2 - x - 42)$ **29.** $5k(k^2 + k - 12)$ **31.** $11(2m^2 - 3m + 6)$ **33.** $\frac{1}{2}(x + y - z)$ **35.** $\pi r(r + l)$ **37.** $x^2y^3(1 - x^2y^2)$ **39.** $\frac{1}{8}t$ $(x - 3y)$ **41.** $3y^4(y - 2z - 3yz)$ **43.** $bx(ac - abc + b)$ **45.** $8a^7(3b^2 + 5a^3b^5 - 6a^5)$ **47.** $\pi R^2; \pi r^2$ **49.** $S = \frac{1}{2}n(a + l)$ **Page 326** **5.** hk^2 **7.** $11p$ **9.** $15a^4$ **11.** $3mx^3$ **13.** $x - y$ **15.** 1.5 **17.** $5ab^2c^3$ **19.** the number you started with **21.** -1 **23.** 8

567

25. 3　　**Pages 328–330**　　**1.** $a^2 + 3a + 2$　　**3.** $c^2 + 7c + 12$　　**5.** $c^2 - c - 12$　　**7.** $a^2 - 4$　　**9.** $1 + 3x + 2x^2$　　**11.** $14 - 5x - x^2$　　**13.** $x^2 - 3x - 10$　　**15.** $a^2 - 21a + 20$　　**17.** $y^2 + 2y - 80$　　**19.** $49c^2 + 28c - 5$　　**21.** $20c^2 - 11c - 4$　　**23.** $x^4 - 7x^2 + 12$　　**25.** $x^2 + 4xy + 4y^2$　　**27.** $6 - 17y + 12y^2$　　**29.** $3a^4 - 13a^2 + 4$　　**31.** $a^4 - 5a^2 + 4$　　**33.** $11x^2 - 21x - 2$　　**35.** $m^2 - 64n^2$　　**37.** $x^2y^2 - 11xy - 12$　　**39.** $9a^2 - 16b^2$　　**41.** $x^4 + 3x^2y^2 + 2y^4$　　**43.** $x^2 + 0.7x + 0.12$　　**45.** $b^2 + \frac{1}{12}b - \frac{1}{12}$　　**47.** $x^4y^2 - 7x^2y + 12$　　**49.** $\frac{1}{6}x^2 + \frac{1}{6}px - p^2$　　**51.** $\frac{6}{5}c^2 + \frac{16}{5}abc + \frac{1}{2}a^2b^2$　　**53.** $\frac{5}{8}x^2 + x - 3\frac{1}{5}$　　**55.** $x^2 + 0.2x + 0.01$　　**57.** $x^2 + \frac{3}{4}x + \frac{1}{8}$　　**59.** $\frac{1}{4}x^2 - 2cx + 4c^2$　　**61.** $x^2 + \frac{1}{3}xy - \frac{2}{9}y^2$　　**63.** $c^4 - 1.1bc^2 + 0.24b^2$　　**65.** $c^2 + 2c - 3$　　**Page 331**　　**1.** $(a + 2)(a + 4)$　　**3.** $(m + 1)(m + 2)$　　**5.** $(a + 1)(a + 1)$　　**7.** $(y + 1)(y + 8)$　　**9.** $(x + 3)(x + 8)$　　**11.** $(x + 6)(x + 1)$　　**13.** $(k + 5)(k + 3)$　　**Pages 331–332**　　**1.** $(c - 2)(c + 1)$　　**3.** $(m - 6)(m + 5)$　　**5.** $(c + 5)(c - 4)$　　**7.** $(a + 7)(a - 6)$　　**9.** $(x - 1)(x + 3)$　　**11.** $(x - 9)(x + 2)$　　**13.** $(y - 10)(y + 4)$　　**Page 332**　　**1.** $(x - 4)(x - 1)$　　**3.** $(x - 3)(x - 1)$　　**5.** $(x - 2)(x - 9)$　　**7.** $(a - 5)(a - 4)$　　**Pages 333–335**　　**1.** $(3x + 1)(x - 5)$　　**3.** $(6x - 5)(x + 1)$　　**5.** $(3x + 2)(3x - 1)$　　**7.** $(x + 7)(x - 4)$　　**9.** $(3x + 2)(5x + 4)$　　**11.** $(3x - 1)^2$　　**13.** $(3c - 5)(c + 1)$　　**15.** $(3c + 5)(c + 1)$　　**17.** prime　　**19.** $(y - 5)^2$　　**21.** prime　　**23.** prime　　**25.** $(7x + 2)(x + 1)$　　**27.** $(4c + 1)(2c - 7)$　　**29.** $(x + 3y)(x - 4y)$　　**31.** $(x + 2y)(x + y)$　　**33.** $(x - 6y)^2$　　**35.** $(h - 3k)(h - 6k)$　　**37.** $(2x - y)(x - y)$　　**39.** $(3a - 4b)(a + 5b)$　　**41.** $(h - 5k)(h + 4k)$　　**43.** $(2p - 3q)(2p + q)$　　**45.** $(4R - 3S)(3R + 4S)$　　**47.** $(1 - x)^2$　　**49.** $(5y - 1)(2y + 3)$　　**51.** $(2x - y)(x + 3y)$　　**53.** $(2b - c)(2b + 3c)$　　**55.** $(3 + 2k)(1 - 4k)$　　**57.** $(3x + 4y)(x - 3y)$　　**59.** $(m + 4n)(m - 2n)$　　**61.** $(5y + 2)(2y - 3)$　　**63.** $(x - 5)(2x + 3)$　　**65.** $(ab + 3)(ab - 2)$　　**67.** $(x^3 - 6)(x^3 + 3)$　　**69.** $(k^3 - 7)(k^3 + 2)$　　**71.** $(2x^2 - 3y^2)(x^2 + 4y^2)$　　**73.** $(1 - 2x)(1 + 2x)(1 - 3x^2)$　　**75.** $(1 - 10x)(1 - 11x)$　　**77.** $(a - b + 4)(a - b - 2)$　　**79.** $(x^2 - 5)^2$　　**81.** $(xy - 8)(xy + 6)$　　**83.** $(x^2 + 9)(x - 2)(x + 2)$　　**85.** prime　　**87.** $2x - 19$ and $x + 10$　　**Page 336**　　**1.** $x^2 + 4x + 4$　　**3.** $c^2 - 2cd + d^2$　　**5.** $a^2 + 14a + 49$　　**7.** $4x^2 - 12x + 9$　　**9.** $16x^2 - 8x + 1$　　**11.** $x^2 - 18x + 81$　　**13.** $x^2 - x + \frac{1}{4}$　　**15.** $x^2 - x + 0.25$　　**17.** $x^2 + 0.6x + 0.09$　　**Page 337**　　**1.** $x - 2$　　**3.** not a perfect square　　**5.** $3x - 1$　　**7.** $y + 6$　　**9.** $x - 7$　　**11.** $a + \frac{1}{2}$　　**13.** $x^3 - 9$　　**Page 339**　　**1.** $m^2 - n^2$　　**3.** $x^2 - y^2$　　**5.** $a^2 - 16$　　**7.** $y^2 - 25$　　**9.** $x^4 - 1$　　**11.** $25x^2 - 9$　　**13.** $4x^2 - n^2$　　**15.** $a^2b^2 - 1$　　**17.** $9x^4 - y^2$　　**19.** $16s^2 - 9t^2$　　**21.** $0.25c^2 - 1$　　**23.** $\frac{1}{49}x^2 - \frac{1}{25}y^2$　　**25.** $a^2b^2c^2 - \frac{1}{9}$　　**27.** 55　　**29.** -99　　**31.** 9991　　**33.** 399　　**35.** 1591　　**37.** 2499　　**39.** 375　　**41.** 2496　　**43.** 1584　　**45.** 6384　　**47.** 864　　**Page 341**　　**1.** $(x - m)(x + m)$　　**3.** $(x - 1)(x + 1)$　　**5.** $(2 + c)(2 - c)$　　**7.** $(x - 3)(x + 3)$　　**9.** $(a + 5)(a - 5)$　　**11.** prime　　**13.** prime　　**15.** $(3x + 1)(3x - 1)$　　**17.** $(c - 3y)(c + 3y)$　　**19.** $(R + r)(R - r)$　　**21.** $(x - y)(x^2 + xy + y^2)(x + y)(x^2 - xy + y^2)$　　**23.** $(3x - 10)(3x + 10)$　　**25.** $(8x + 7y)(8x - 7y)$　　**27.** $(x - \frac{1}{2})(x + \frac{1}{2})$　　**29.** $(c + \frac{1}{4})(c - \frac{1}{4})$　　**31.** $(ab + 2)(ab - 2)$　　**33.** $(mn - p)(mn + p)$　　**35.** $(x^3 + y)(x^3 - y)$　　**37.** $(cd + ab)(cd - ab)$　　**39.** prime　　**Page 342**　　**1.** $5(x + 2)$　　**3.** $(c + 1)^2$　　**5.** $(m + 5)(m - 5)$　　**7.** prime　　**9.** $(a - 7)(a + 6)$　　**11.** $(h - 4)(h - 2)$　　**13.** $(m - 5)^2$　　**15.** $(a - 2c)(a - 9c)$　　**17.** $(b + a)(b - a)$　　**19.** $a(bx + 1)$　　**21.** prime　　**23.** $(c - d^3)(c + d^3)$　　**25.** $c(c + 9)$　　**27.** $3x^2(2x^2 - 3)$　　**29.** $(10 - x)(10 + x)$　　**31.** $(a + 2)^2$　　**33.** $x(x^2 - x + 1)$　　**Pages 342–343**　　**1.** $(p - 3)^2$　　**3.** $(x - 5)(x + 2)$　　**5.** $3xy(2x^2 - 5x - 1)$　　**7.** $(p - 8)(p + 7)$　　**9.** $(r - 12)(r + 5)$　　**11.** $(a - 8b)(a + 8b)$　　**13.** $(-4 + x)(3 + x)$　　**15.** $(x + 6)(x + 2)$　　**17.** $(a - 3b^2)^2$　　**19.** $(p + 9)(p - 8)$　　**21.** $x(16y - 15x)$　　**23.** $(x + 9y)(x - 4y)$　　**25.** $(x + 1)(2x + 1)$　　**27.** $(ab + d)(ab - d)$　　**29.** prime　　**31.** $10(x - 81)$　　**33.** $x^3(4x^2 - 3)$　　**35.** $(a + 1)(a - 1)$　　**37.** $(x - 9y)(x + 4y)$　　**39.** $(x^2 - 8)(x - 1)(x + 1)$　　**41.** $(c + 2)(2c + 1)$　　**43.** $[(k + 1)(k^4 - k^3 + k^2 - k + 1)]^2$　　**45.** $(ab - 3c)^2$　　**Page 344**　　**1.** $6(a + 1)$　　**3.** $4(c + 1)(c - 1)$　　**5.** $x^2(x + 3)(x + 4)$　　**7.** $4a(4a - b^2)$　　**9.** $c(4c - 9)$　　**11.** $b(x + 3)(x - 3)$　　**13.** $c(3x + 1)(x + 2)$　　**15.** $a(a - 25)$　　**17.** $\pi(R + r)(R - r)$　　**19.** $2\pi r(r + h)$　　**21.** $a(a^3 - 16)$　　**23.** $x(x + 1)(x - 1)$　　**25.** $x^3(x + 1)(x - 1)$　　**27.** prime　　**29.** $a(x + 2y)(x - 2y)$　　**31.** $(a - 1)(a + 1)(a^2 - 3)$　　**33.** $5(x + 3)(2x + 1)$　　**35.** $a(3a + 5)(a + 1)$　　**37.** $8(a + 1)^2$　　**39.** $a(5c - 1)(2c + 3)$　　**41.** $x(ax + 1)(ax - 1)$　　**43.** $(x + y)^2(x - y)^2$　　**45.** $4(x + 4)(x - 3)$　　**47.** $2\pi(R - r)$　　**49.** $9x(x + 3y)(x - 3y)$　　**51.** $6(n - p)^2$　　**53.** $b(y - 1)(y + 1)(y + 3)(y - 3)$　　**55.** $z(z + 4)(z - 4)$　　**57.** $(5 - 6a)^2$　　**59.** $ab(x + 1)(x - 1)$　　**61.** $a^2(b + 4)(b - 3)$　　**63.** $(x + 14y)^2$

Chapter 13   **Pages 354–355**   **1.** $-5, 3$ **3.** $-2, 2$ **5.** $0, 3$ **7.** $-3, -3$ **9.** $2, 2$
11. $0, 6$ **13.** $8, 4$ **15.** $-1, 1$ **17.** $2, 1$ **19.** $-\frac{3}{2}, \frac{3}{2}$ **21.** $1\frac{1}{2}, 3$ **23.** $0, -8$
25. $-3, 1$ **27.** $-1\frac{3}{4}, \frac{2}{3}$ **29.** $0, 12$ **31.** $5, -2$ **33.** $-a, a$ **35.** $-10\,y, 2\,y$
37. $-\dfrac{4\,m}{3}, \dfrac{5\,m}{2}$ **Page 356**   **1.** $x = 3$ **3.** $y = \frac{1}{2}$ **5.** $n = -9, n = 2$ **7.** $y = 1$ **9.** x

$= 4$ **11.** $y = 3\frac{3}{4}$ **13.** $y = 1$ **15.** $x = 3$ **Page 357**   **1.** $\dfrac{d}{c}$ **3.** 2 **5.** 2 **7.** b

$- 3$ **9.** $a + 3$ **11.** a **13.** $2\,b$ **15.** $2\,b$ **17.** $\dfrac{b - a}{2\,a}$ **19.** $c - 2$ **21.** $\dfrac{A}{1 + rt}$

23. $\dfrac{-t}{f - g}$, or $\dfrac{t}{g - f}$ **25.** $\dfrac{c^3 - 3\,b^2}{c + 3\,b}$ **27.** $\dfrac{ad}{c}$ **29.** $5\,b - 4\,a$ **31.** $m(m + 1)$ **33.** $c + 2$

35. $\dfrac{bcdk}{acd - bc^2 + bdh}$ **37.** $\dfrac{a + 1}{a + 2}$ **39.** c **41.** $n = \dfrac{CR}{e - Cr}$ **Pages 358–360**   **1.** $10, 11$

3. 11 in. $\times$ 16 in.   **5.** 16 or -6 **7.** $8, 13$ **9.** 4 or $-5\frac{1}{2}$ **11.** 5 ft.   **13.** 24 ft. $\times$ 16 ft.

15. 15 **17.** $\dfrac{s + d}{2}$; $\dfrac{s - d}{2}$

Chapter 14   **Page 371**   **1.** $\frac{1}{3}$ **3.** $\frac{2}{5}$ **5.** $\frac{5}{6}$ **7.** $\dfrac{1}{x}$ **9.** $\frac{1}{2}$ **11.** $\frac{4}{3}$ **13.** $\dfrac{b}{c}$

15. $r^2 s^2$ **17.** $\dfrac{1}{xy^2}$ **19.** a^4 **21.** $\dfrac{2\,xy^5}{3}$ **23.** $\dfrac{-1}{r}$ **Pages 371–372**   **3a.** $x + 1$

3c. $\dfrac{4(x + 1)}{3}$ **5.** $\frac{2}{3}$ **7.** 5 **9.** $\dfrac{c + 3}{c + 4}$ **11.** $\dfrac{x + 1}{x - 1}$ **13.** $a - 3\,b$ **15.** $\dfrac{m - n}{m + n}$

17. $\dfrac{x - y}{3\,x - 2\,y}$ **19.** $\dfrac{x(y - 2)}{y + 2}$ **21.** $\dfrac{3(x + 2\,y)}{x - 2\,y}$ **23.** $\dfrac{5\,z}{xy - 4}$ **Pages 373–374**   **1.** $\frac{1}{3}$

3. 1 **5.** 10 **7.** $\frac{8}{3}$ **9.** 1 **11.** $\dfrac{c}{d}$ **13.** $\dfrac{12}{x}$ **15.** $\dfrac{1}{x}$ **17.** $\dfrac{ab}{6}$ **19.** $\dfrac{1}{20\,m^2 n}$ **21.** $9\,a^2 c$

23. $\dfrac{40\,a^2}{3\,b}$ **25.** $\frac{1}{3}$ **27.** $\dfrac{a^3}{b^3}$ **29.** $\frac{1}{2}$ **Pages 374–375**   **1.** $\dfrac{5}{4(x - y)}$ **3.** $\frac{1}{3}$ **5.** $\dfrac{3}{2(x - b)}$

7. $\dfrac{2}{x - y}$ **9.** $a - 1$ **11.** $\dfrac{1 + c}{b(1 - c)}$ **13.** $\dfrac{14\,y^2}{15}$ **15.** 1 **17.** $\dfrac{2m + 3}{2m + 1}$ **19.** $\dfrac{2\,x^2(2\,b + 3\,x)}{(b - 6\,x)(3\,b + x)}$

Pages 375–376   **1.** $\frac{7}{4}$ **3.** $\frac{4}{5}$ **5.** $\dfrac{a}{bc}$ **7.** $\dfrac{b}{9\,a}$ **9.** $\dfrac{a}{2\,bc}$ **11.** $9(x - 2)$ **13.** $\dfrac{m - 1}{4}$

15. $\dfrac{3 + y}{3}$ **17.** $\dfrac{x}{a + x}$ **19.** 1 **21.** $\dfrac{4(x - 2)}{x(x - 4)}$ **23.** 1 **25.** $\dfrac{d}{8\,c(a - b)}$ **27.** $4(x^2 + y^2)$

29. $\dfrac{(x - 2)(x + 1)}{x(x + 2)(x - 1)}$ **31.** $\dfrac{a - 2\,b}{a - b}$ **Page 378**   **1.** 2 **3.** $\frac{2}{3}$ **5.** $\frac{2}{3}$ **7.** $\dfrac{2}{x}$ **9.** $\dfrac{a + b}{c}$

11. $\dfrac{1}{x + 1}$ **13.** 1 **15.** $2\,x + 1$ **Page 379**   **1.** $\dfrac{c + d}{d}$ **3.** $\frac{25}{3}$ **5.** $\dfrac{1 + 6\,x}{x}$

7. $\dfrac{a + b}{b}$ **9.** $\dfrac{7\,a}{15}$ **11.** $\dfrac{x^2 + y^2}{xy}$ **13.** $\dfrac{5\,a}{12}$ **15.** $\dfrac{np + mp + mn}{mnp}$ **Page 380**   **1.** $\dfrac{4\,a + 1}{6}$

3. $\dfrac{9\,x + 20\,y}{30}$ **5.** $\dfrac{5\,x + y}{6}$ **7.** $\dfrac{x^2 + 11\,xy}{60}$ **9.** $\dfrac{8\,x - 16}{3\,x}$ **11.** $\dfrac{3\,b - 3}{2\,a}$ **13.** $\dfrac{23\,a^2 - 20\,a - 5}{14\,a^2}$

15. $\dfrac{-20\,x^2 + 21\,x + 2}{10\,x^2}$ **17.** $\dfrac{5\,m^2 - 2\,mn + 2\,m - 1}{m^2 n}$ **19.** $\dfrac{ab - a}{b^2}$ **Page 381**

1. $\dfrac{3\,a^2 + 10\,a + 10}{(a + 2)(a + 4)}$ **3.** $\dfrac{-x - 7}{(x + 2)(x - 3)}$ **5.** $\dfrac{-x + 5}{(x + 1)(x - 1)}$ **7.** $\dfrac{3\,x^2 - 5\,x}{(x + 5)(x - 5)}$

Pages 381–382   **1.** $\dfrac{2\,a^2 - a}{(a + 1)(a - 1)}$ **3.** $\dfrac{x^2 - 4\,x}{(x + 1)(x - 1)}$ **5.** $\dfrac{a^3 + 2\,a^2 - a + 13}{3(a^2 - 1)}$

7. $\dfrac{4\,a^2 - 8\,a - 5}{(a + 3)(a - 4)}$ **9.** $\dfrac{2\,a^2 + 2\,ab + 2\,b^2}{(a + b)(a - b)}$ **11.** $\dfrac{-11\,m - 8}{18\,m(m - 1)}$ **13.** $\dfrac{6\,x}{(x - 4)(x - 2)(x + 4)}$

15. $\dfrac{y - x}{xy}$　17. 0　19. $\dfrac{a^2}{(a - b)(a + b)}$　**Page 383**　1. 0.6　3. 1.25　5. 0.09

7. 0.18　9. 0.21875　11. 1.625　**Page 384**　1. $\frac{1}{2}$　3. $\frac{9}{20}$　5. $\frac{3}{25}$　7. $\frac{1}{8}$　9. $\frac{5}{8}$

11. $\frac{5}{16}$　**Page 385**　1. $3 - a$　3. $a - 4$　5. $y - x$　7. $2b - a^2$　**Page 386**　1. $-(a - 1)$, or

$1 - a$　3. $\dfrac{x + 1}{3(1 - x)}$　5. $-\dfrac{4}{a + b}$, or $\dfrac{-4}{a + b}$　**Page 387 (top)**　1. $\dfrac{2x^2 + 2xy + 2y^2 + x - y}{(x + y)(x - y)}$

3. $\dfrac{9a^2 + 13a + 24}{4(a - 1)(a + 1)}$　**Pages 388–389**　1. $\frac{71}{10}$　3. $\dfrac{a + b}{b}$　5. $\dfrac{4x^2 - 5}{x}$　7. $\dfrac{2a^2 - 3a + 3}{a}$

9. $\dfrac{6p^2 + 12p - 1}{3p}$　11. $\dfrac{12m^3 - 6m^2 + 9m + 1}{3m}$　13. $\dfrac{4y^3 + 4y^2 - 12y + 3}{4y}$

15. $\dfrac{c^2d + cd^2 + cde - 1}{cd}$　17. $\dfrac{2x^2 + xy}{x + y}$　19. $\dfrac{2x^3 + x^2y + xy^2}{2x - y}$　**Page 389**　1. $x^2 + x + \dfrac{1}{x}$

3. $6c^2 - 4c - \frac{3}{2}$　5. $2xy - 3 - \dfrac{5}{2xy}$　7. $5y - 4 + \dfrac{3}{y^3}$　**Page 390**　1. $3y^2 + 5y + \frac{1}{3}$

3. $5a - 2 - \dfrac{1}{a - 1}$　5. $x^2 + x + 1$　**Page 391**　1. $\frac{10}{3}$　3. 4　5. $\dfrac{a + b}{a - b}$　7. $\dfrac{a^2}{a - 1}$

9. $\dfrac{y}{y + x}$　11. $\dfrac{4a - 4b}{a + b}$　13. $\dfrac{(a + b)^2}{(a - b)^2}$

Chapter 15　**Page 403**　1. $x = 1$　3. $y = 2$　5. $h = -3$　7. $y = -\frac{1}{8}$　9. $x = \frac{1}{33}$
11. $b = 2$　13. $x = 8$　**Pages 406–407**　1. $y = 1$　3. $x = 6, -5$　5. $x = 2, -3\frac{2}{3}$
7. $x = -2$　9. $c = -\frac{1}{8}$　11. $x = 4, -1\frac{1}{9}$　13. $x = 3$　15. $y = 14$　17. $x = 2$　19. $x = 2, -3\frac{1}{2}$　21. $x = 4, -1$　23. $x = 8\frac{1}{2}$　25. no solution　27. $x = 15, -12$　29. $x = -2\frac{2}{3}, 5$　31. $x = \frac{1}{2}, -22$　33. $x = -1\frac{4}{7}, 5$　**Pages 407–408**　1. $x = -\dfrac{a}{b}$　3. $x = \dfrac{c}{a + b}$

5. $x = a + 4$　7. $y = \dfrac{5a}{6}$　9. $x = 2(a + b)$　11. $x = \dfrac{m}{n}$　13. $x = \dfrac{9c - 4d}{5}$　15. $x =$

$\dfrac{abc}{bc + ac + ab}$　17. $x = a + b$　**Pages 408–409**　1. $x = 3, y = 4$　3. $m = 14, n = 14$
5. $x = 3500, y = 2500$　7. $a = 4\frac{3}{5}, b = 5\frac{1}{5}$　9. $a = -2, b = 5$　11. $x = -13a$,

$y = 32a$　13. $x = \dfrac{4m - 3n}{5}, y = \dfrac{6m + 3n}{5}$　15. $x = \dfrac{a + b}{a}, y = \dfrac{a + b}{b}$

17. $x = \dfrac{16a + 5b + 24}{16}, y = \dfrac{16a - 3b - 40}{16}$　**Pages 410–411**　3. $u = b - kv$　5. $W = FR +$

$F; R = \dfrac{W - F}{F}$　7. $t = \dfrac{aT - 1}{a}; a = \dfrac{1}{T - t}$　9. $h = \dfrac{A - 2\pi r^2}{2\pi r}$　11. $b = \dfrac{aS + c}{S + 1}$

13. $V = \dfrac{W}{T_1 - T_2}$　15. $v = \dfrac{F}{0.327d^2}$　**Pages 412–416**　1. -6, or 5　3. $\frac{1}{3}$, or 3　5. $\frac{1}{3}$,
or 9　7. \$8000　9. $\frac{12}{9}$　11. $\frac{7}{11}$　13. 18 and 24　15. 6 nickels, 4 dimes　17. base,
9 ft.; altitude, 5 ft.　19. Dick, 11 yr.; Bill, 22 yr.　21. Frank, 3 hr.; Herman, 5 hr.　23. $x = 61\frac{2}{3}$　25. 37.24%; 27.14%　27. 48 mph　29. 19 in.; 361 sq. in.　31. $\frac{3}{5}$　33. 45 mph
35. 4 hr.　37. 97　39. going, 4 mph; coming, 6 mph　41. $2\frac{2}{5}$ days　43. 16 ft.

Chapter 16　**Page 429**　1. 3　3. 5　5. 9　7. 12　9. y^3　11. -5　13. $-y^3$
15. ± 7　17. ± 20　19. $-a^2$　21. $2a^5$　23. a^4b^5　25. $-9c^3$　27. $10x^3y^4$　29. m^5y^6
31. 0.6　33. $13a^2$　35. $10m^2$　**Page 430**　3a. 4.123　3c. 1.414　3e. 9.592　3g.
8.832　5a. 2　5c. 48　5e. 99　5g. 3　7. 9.434　9. 4624　11. 2289.06 sq. in.
13. 1.414　**Page 434**　1. 27　3. 53　5. 73　7. 9.4　9. 10.7　11. 1.17　13. 2.66
15. 104　17. 18.9　19. 902　21. 1100　23. 22.03　**Page 435**　1. 1.41　3. 2.45
5. 4.47　7. 5.77　9. 0.18　11. 6.49　13. 5.29　15. 5　17. 6　19. 13　21. 34
Page 436　3. $\sqrt{100}$　5. $\sqrt{27}$　7. $\sqrt{5}$　9. $\sqrt{16}$　11. $\sqrt{2}$　13. $\sqrt{3}$　15. $2\sqrt{5}$
17. $7\sqrt{2}$　19. $4\sqrt{5}$　**Page 437**　1. $3x$　3. $2\sqrt{3}$　5. $7\sqrt{2}$　7. $2\sqrt{6}$　9. $\frac{1}{4}$
11. $2\sqrt{15}$　13. $4\sqrt{5}$　15. $3\sqrt{2}$　17. $8\sqrt{2}$　19. $4\sqrt{3}$　21. 24　23. $6x^5$　**Page 438**

(top) 1. $\frac{1}{2}\sqrt{2}$ 3. $\frac{1}{5}\sqrt{10}$ 5. $\frac{1}{6}\sqrt{6}$ 7. $\sqrt{3}$ 9. $\frac{1}{6}\sqrt{3}$ 11. $\frac{2}{7}\sqrt{7}$ 13. $\frac{1}{3}\sqrt{2}$
15. $\frac{1}{8}\sqrt{6}$ **Page 438 (middle)** 1. $x\sqrt{x}$ 3. $2\sqrt{a}$ 5. $4a\sqrt{2a}$ 7. $mn\sqrt{m}$ 9. $b^2\sqrt{a}$
11. $\frac{1}{a}\sqrt{a}$ 13. $\frac{1}{x^3}\sqrt{2x}$ **Page 439** 1. $\frac{1}{2}$ 3. $\frac{x}{2y}$ 5. $\frac{5c}{6d}$ 7. $\frac{m^5}{8x^3}$ 9. 0.866^+
11. 0.632^+ 13. 0.756^- 15. 0.471^+ **Page 440 (top)** 1. $11\sqrt{3}$ 3. 0 5. $10\sqrt{3}$
7. 0 9. $10-3\sqrt{3}$ 11. 10 13. $6-9\sqrt{6}$ 15. $3\sqrt{a}+\sqrt{ab}$ **Page 440 (bottom)**
1. $\sqrt{3}$ 3. $3\sqrt{5}+\sqrt{7}$ 5. $-\sqrt{7}$ 7. $5+3\sqrt{5}$ 9. $\frac{11}{2}\sqrt{2}+4\sqrt{3}$ 11. $-\frac{1}{3}\sqrt{3}$
13. $8\sqrt{a}$ **Page 441** 1. $\sqrt{35}$ 3. $3\sqrt{7}$ 5. 6 7. $3\sqrt{2}$ 9. 60 11. $2\sqrt{15}$ 13. 1
15. 5 17. $\sqrt{2}$ 19. 30 21. 25 23. 60 25. 12 27. 6 29. -60 **Page 442**
(top) 1. $2\sqrt{3}-2\sqrt{5}$ 3. $3-\sqrt{6}$ 5. $4\sqrt{3}-6\sqrt{2}$ 7. 1 9. $7+2\sqrt{10}$ 11. x
$+10+6\sqrt{x+1}$ **Pages 442–443** 1. $\frac{1}{2}\sqrt{2}$ 3. $\frac{1}{5}\sqrt{5}$ 5. $\frac{1}{a}\sqrt{a}$ 7. $\frac{2}{3}\sqrt{6}$ 9. $\frac{a}{c}\sqrt{c}$

11. $\frac{5}{4}\sqrt{2}$ 13. $3\sqrt{2}+3$ 15. $5-2\sqrt{6}$ 17. $\dfrac{1-3\sqrt{5}}{8}$ 19. $\dfrac{7-\sqrt{5}}{4}$

21. $\dfrac{a+b+2\sqrt{ab}}{a-b}$ **Page 444** 1. $x=9$ 3. $x=1$ 5. $x=5$ 7. $c=7$ 9. $x=$

$6\frac{1}{9}$ 11. $x=\frac{1}{4}$ 13. $y=\frac{1}{16}$ 15. $c=8$ 17. $k=14$ 19. $x=49$ 21. $s=\dfrac{4h\sqrt{3}}{3}$

Chapter 17 **Pages 454–455** 1. $x=\pm4$ 3. $m=\pm9$ 5. $x=\pm10$ 7. $x=\pm1$
9. $x=\pm8$ 11. $a=\pm7$ 13. $y=\pm15$ 15. $x=\pm1$ 17. $x=\pm2\sqrt{3}$, or ±3.46
19. $x=\pm2\sqrt{3}$, or ±3.46 21. $y=\pm2$ 23. $x=\pm\frac{1}{2}$ 25. $x=\pm\frac{1}{2}\sqrt{30}$, or ±2.74
27. $x=\pm2a$ 29. $x=\pm a$ 31. $x=\pm\sqrt{a+b}$ 33. $x=\pm\sqrt{2}$ 35. $x=\pm\dfrac{1}{\pi}\sqrt{\pi A}$
37. $x=\pm\sqrt{c}$ 39. $x=\pm\sqrt{2}$, or ±1.41 41. $x=\pm\sqrt{a+b}$ 43. $x=\pm\sqrt{5}$, or ±2.24
Page 455 1. ±3.162 3. $x=\pm120$ **Pages 456–458** 7. $x=3\sqrt{2}$ or 4.24 9. x
$=8$ 11. $x=\frac{16}{3}\sqrt{3}$, or 9.24 13. $x=26$ 15. 34 ft. 17. 12 ft. 23. $8\sqrt{3}$ or 13.86 ft.
25. 37.5 rd. 27. $9\sqrt{3}$ or 15.59 sq. in. 29. $48\sqrt{3}$ or 83.14 sq. in. 31. 4 ft. and 6.93 ft.
33. 18 in. and 9 in. 35. $2\sqrt{6}$ or 4.90, and $3\sqrt{2}$ or 4.242 **Page 459** 1. x^2+2x+1
3. x^2-2x+1 5. $x^2-14x+49$ 7. $c^2+20c+100$ 9. $m^2-m+\frac{1}{4}$ 11. x^2+
$0.04x+0.0004$ 13. $\pm(m-2)$ 15. $\pm(y+3)$ 17. not a perfect square 19. $\pm(x+$
$0.1)$ 21. $\pm(x^3-6)$ **Page 460** 1. 9 3. 9 5. 25 7. 4 9. 64 11. $\frac{25}{4}$
13. $\frac{9}{4}$ 15. $\frac{121}{4}$ 17. $\frac{169}{4}$ 19. $\frac{1}{16}$ 21. $\frac{1}{9}$ 23. 0.04 25. $\frac{25}{36}$ 27. $\frac{1}{100}$ 29. b^2
Page 461 1. $x=7,-1$ 3. $m=4,-6$ 5. $c=13,-1$ 7. $x=11,1$ 9. $x=9,$
-13 11. $x=13,-7$ 13. $x=-5,-15$ 15. $p=10,18$ **Page 462** 1. $x=-1,$
-4 3. $x=5,-2$ 5. $x=8,-5$ 7. $c=8,-7$ 9. $m=6,-5$ 11. $y=-15,-30$
13. $x=30,-26$ 15. $x=3\pm\sqrt{17}$ 17. $x=-5\pm5\sqrt{2}$ 19. $x=4\pm3\sqrt{2}$ 21. x
$=3\pm3\sqrt{2}$ 23. $x=5\pm5\sqrt{3}$ **Page 463** 1. $x=\frac{3}{2},-5$ 3. $x=\frac{1}{2},-\frac{2}{3}$ 5. x
$=5,-\frac{3}{2}$ 7. $x=\frac{1}{2},-\frac{8}{3}$ 9. $y=\dfrac{-11\pm\sqrt{1781}}{10}$ or $3.12,-5.32$ 11. $x=\frac{1}{6},-1$ 13. x
$=\dfrac{-1\pm2.236}{4}$ or $0.309,-0.809$ 15. $x=\dfrac{5\pm6.557}{2}$ or $5.7785,-0.7785$ 17. $m=$

$\dfrac{1\pm\sqrt{133}}{6}$ or $2.088^+,-1.7555$ 19. $k=-1,-\frac{5}{3}$ **Page 464** 1. $x=2,-1$ 3. $x=6,\frac{1}{2}$

5. $x=3,-3\frac{1}{2}$ 7. 3 **Page 466** 1. $x=\dfrac{3\pm\sqrt{13}}{2}$ or $3.303,-0.303$ 3. $x=\frac{3}{2},-1$

5. $x=3\pm\sqrt{7}$ or $5.646,0.354$ 7. $x=\frac{1}{5},-2$ 9. $x=4,-5$ 11. $x=1,-2$ 13. y

$=4\pm\sqrt{6}$; or $6.449,1.551$ 15. $y=\frac{4}{3},-1$ 17. $m=\dfrac{3\pm\sqrt{29}}{2}$ or $4.192,-1.192$ 19. $x=$

$3\pm2\sqrt{5}$ or $7.472,-1.472$ 21. $x=\dfrac{-2\pm\sqrt{5}}{3}$ or $0.079,-1.412$ 23. $x=\pm1$ **Pages**

466–467 **1.** $x = 3, -2$ **3.** $x = \frac{1}{2}, -2$ **5.** $x = -9, 4$ **7.** $x = \frac{1}{3}, 1\frac{1}{3}$ **9.** $y = -8, 2$ **11.** $x = 3\frac{1}{2}, -5$ **13.** $x = -2, 4$ **15.** $x = -9, 4$ **17.** $y = \pm\frac{2}{5}\sqrt{-15}$ **19.** $x = -3\frac{1}{5}, 2$ **21.** $x = \frac{1}{2}, 6$ **23.** $x = 7, 4$ **25.** $x = \dfrac{-48 \pm \sqrt{1506}}{57}$ or $-1.52, -0.16$ **27.** $x = -4\frac{1}{3}, 5$ **29.** $y = -3\frac{1}{4}, 1$ **31.** $x = \dfrac{2 \pm 2\sqrt{29}}{7}$ or $1.824, -1.253$ **33.** $x = -4\frac{1}{3}, 5$ **35.** $x = \dfrac{11 \pm 12.648}{3}$ or $7.883, -0.549$ **37.** $x = \dfrac{9 \pm \sqrt{73}}{2}$ or $8.772, 0.228$ **39.** $x = -3 \pm \sqrt{10}$ or $0.162, -6.162$ **Pages 468–469** **1.** $x = 3, -2$ **3.** $x = 5, -1$ **5.** $x = 0, 2$ **7.** $x = 3, -3$ **9.** $x = \frac{1}{2}, -3$ **11.** $x = 4, -3$ **13.** $x = \frac{1}{3}, -2$ **15.** $x = 2\frac{1}{2}, -3$ **17.** $x = 3.6, -0.6$ **19.** $x = 0.5, 0.7$ **21.** $x = 0.2, -4.2$ **Page 469** **1.** $x = 0, 2, 2$ **3.** $x = 2, -2, -3$ **Pages 469–471** **1.** 6 or -5 **3.** -4 or 3 **5.** 6 and 8 **7.** 3 and 7 **9.** width, 8 ft.; length, 22 ft. **11.** width, 18 in.; length, 22 in. **13.** 40 in. and 75 in. **15.** 7.24 in. **17.** 5 and 12 **23.** 32 mph

Chapter 18 **Page 482** **1.** $\frac{4}{6}$, or $\frac{2}{3}$; $\dfrac{x}{y}$; $\frac{5}{2}$ **3.** proportion **5.** not a proportion **7.** not a proportion **9.** $x = \pm 8$ **11.** $x = 156.25$ **13.** $x = \frac{1}{3}$ **15.** $y = 6\frac{3}{4}$ **Pages 483–484** **1.** $34\frac{2}{3}$ lb. **3.** 160 mi. **5.** 1666 bricks **7.** 1 cup **Pages 485–486** **1.** Yes **3.** No **5.** 35 in. **7.** 17.187^{+} ft. **Pages 488–489** **1.** $5\frac{1}{3}$ da. **3.** 54 servings **5.** 8 hours **7.** $45\frac{5}{7}$ mph **Page 490** **3.** a variable **5a.** a dependent variable **5c.** A is multiplied by 4. **5e.** A is multiplied by 9 **Page 491** **1.** $22; -2$ **3.** $7; -9$ **5.** 7 **Page 492** **1.** $5:1$; yes; $a = 5b$ **5.** $c; 2\pi$; directly as r **Pages 493–494** **1.** The product is 80 for each pair; yes; $pv = 80$ **3.** This is not a straight-line graph as is that in the case of direct variation **Pages 495–496** **7.** A varies directly as b; A is doubled **9.** A varies neither directly nor inversely as r; Yes **13.** d is multiplied by 4 **Pages 499–500** **1.** $x = 36$ **3.** $m = 45$ **5.** $x = 45$ **7.** $A = 1600$ **9.** $x = 11$ **11.** 30 **13.** 56 da. **15.** 30 hr.

Pages 500–501 **1.** 8 hr. **3.** $\dfrac{A_1}{A_2} = \dfrac{b_1 h_1}{b_2 h_2}$ **Page 502** **1.** $\frac{8}{9}$; $\frac{872}{979}$ **3.** G to C, B to E, and C' to F **5.** $6:5$

Chapter 19 **Pages 514–515** **1.** 7.3 **3.** 17.3 **5.** 2.3 **7.** 4.4 **9.** 9.22 **11.** 7.54 **13.** 2.63 **Page 518** **1.** 4.9 **3.** 17.3 **5.** 38.90 **Pages 522–523** **3.** Yes **5.** $\tan P = \frac{6}{3} = 2$; $\tan R = \frac{3}{6} = \frac{1}{2}$ **Pages 526–527** **1.** 216.096, or 216.1 ft. (or 220 ft.)* **3.** 202.35, or 202.4 yd. (or 200 yd.) **5.** 359.36, or 359.4 ft. (or 360 ft.) **7.** 64.565, or 64.56 ft. (or 65 ft.) **9.** 20.03 ft., (or 20 ft.) **11.** 32°, to the nearest degree **Pages 529–530** **1.** 92.40 ft. (or 92 ft.) **3.** 8.208 ft. (or 8.2 ft.) **5.** 233.35^{+} ft. (or 230 ft.) **Pages 531–532** **1.** 59.397^{+} ft. (or 60 ft.) **3a.** 6 in.; 6 in. **3c.** 4.2426 in. (or 4.2 in.) **5a.** 3.5 in. **5c.** 77°, to the nearest degree **5e.** 58.1 sq. in. (or 58 sq. in.) **Page 533** **1.** .1478 **3.** .9723 **5.** .6704 **7.** .9111 **9.** .3123 **11.** .2616 **13.** .9974 **15.** .1010 **Page 534** **1.** .9038 **3.** .9772 **5.** .9970 **7.** .9753 **9.** .4736 **11.** .9443 **13.** .0941 **15.** 6.7146 **Page 535** **1.** 16° 10′ **3.** 8° 10′ **5.** 14° 30′ **7.** 18° 9′ **9.** 58° 36′ **11.** 64° 42′ **13.** 5538.6^{+}, or 5539 ft. (or 5540 ft.) **15.** 77° 34′ **17.** 37,604.06 sq. units (or 37,600 sq. units) **19.** about 6°

* The correspondence between angular and linear measurements is: 2 significant digits in a linear measurement corresponds to 1° in angular measurement; 3 significant digits in a linear measurement corresponds to 10′ in angular measurement; 4 significant digits in a linear measurement corresponds to 1′ in angular measurement. The answer between parentheses is rounded off to agree with the angular measurement.

572

ABCDEFG 0798765

PRINTED IN THE UNITED STATES OF AMERICA